ROGET'S
21st CENTURY
THESAURUS

ROGET'S
21st CENTURY
THESAURUS

THOMAS NELSON PUBLISHERS
Nashville

Published in Nashville, Tennessee by Thomas Nelson, Publishers

Library of Congress Cataloging-in-Publication Data

Roget's 21st century thesaurus
    p. cm.
  ISBN 0-8407-6830-3 (PB)
  1. English language—Synonyms and antonyms. I. Thomas Nelson Publishers. II. Title: Roget's twenty-first century thesaurus.
PE1591.R716 1992
423′.1—dc20   92-6946
                                                    CIP

7 8 9 10 — 96 95 94

Publisher's Preface

Leap into the future with Thomas Nelson's Roget's 21st Century Thesaurus. Our concise, modern edition is an abridged version of Roget's original work published in 1852. With more than 1,000 entries, this powerful reference is an essential part of every school, home and office library. Included is a "plan of classification" (following Roget's original format) and a tabular synopsis of categories to aid you as you search for the perfect synonym. To assure clarity, all antiquated and duplicated entries have been removed.

The publishers are certain that you will find this resource both beneficial and enlightening as you use it to explore the depths of the English language.

How to Use Roget's Thesaurus

PETER MARK ROGET (1779—1869) was a British lexicographer and physician. *Roget's Thesaurus*, a standard reference work for over a century, represents his highly personal view of how the English language reflects the structure of the universe. In some ways, that view is dated today; but the complex structure and breadth of the thesaurus still prove surprisingly helpful to the modern user.

For most users, the key to the synonyms in the body of the book lies in the alphabetical listing in the index. The uniqueness of Roget's original plan of classification provides the user with access to related words and requires nothing more than a near-synonym to help locate the word sought. *Roget's Thesaurus* is more than simply a synonym dictionary—both in the lists following individual headwords and in the grouping of headwords under the various sections, it is a diverse collection of associated and related words and phrases.

For example, suppose you are looking for a synonym for *lull*: a check in the index yields the reference number, 403; turning to that entry provides the synonyms *silence, stillness, quiet, hush, peace*.

But, suppose you are trying to find a verb meaning 'to feel very dissatisfied' and the synonyms listed under *discontent* are not "strong" enough for your purpose. A brief check of the related, contiguous headwords will lead you to the entry for *regret* which provides the synonyms *lament, deplore, bemoan, bewail, rue*.

This edition of *Roget's Thesaurus* has a number of other special features. Dictionaries of synonyms, unless they are of considerable size, rarely provide alphabetical listings of all the words in the book. In this edition, you will find every word listed in the index.

Larger books may provide more synonyms, but the user of a thesaurus is rarely looking for a rare or unusual word: he wants an equivalent word that is part of everyday language. This edition is the only abridged *Roget's Thesaurus* available. While retaining the original structure and all the 1,000 headwords, all antiquated words and phrases have been removed. In addition, the book has been modernized to include the most current usage and the newest developments in language.

In this abridgment, many duplications have been omitted to save space. For maximum usefulness, the user should look through other associated parts of speech for the word he is seeking, for adjectives and verbs can yield nouns and adverbs, and vice versa. For example, adverbs can be formed by adding *-ly* to some adjectives and nouns by adding *-ness* to some adjectives.

The Publisher

Caution: If the word selected is not completely familiar, check its meaning and usage in this volume's dictionary before risking its use in an incorrect or unidiomatic context.

*The words shown in **boldface** in the index indicate they are the title or heading of a category.*

Plan of Classification
(following the original Roget plan)

Tabular Synopsis of Categories

Class I. ABSTRACT RELATIONS
I. EXISTENCE

1. existence
2. nonexistence
3. substantiality
4. unsubstantiality
5. intrinsicality
6. extrinsicality
7. state
8. circumstance

II. RELATION

9. relation
10. nonrelation
11. consanguinity
12. correlation
13. identity
14. contrariety
15. difference
16. uniformity
16a. lack of uniformity
17. similarity
18. dissimilarity
19. imitation
20. nonimitation
20a. variation
21. copy
22. prototype
23. agreement
24. disagreement

III. QUANTITY

25. quantity
26. degree
27. equality
28. inequality
29. mean
30. compensation
31. greatness
32. smallness
33. superiority
34. inferiority
35. increase
36. decrease
37. addiction
38. deduction
39. adjunct
40. remainder
40a. decrement
41. mixture
42. simpleness
43. junction
44. disjunction
45. link

VIII. CAUSATION

Class II. SPACE
I. SPACE IN GENERAL

180. space (indefinite)

180a. inextension
181. region (definite)
182. place

183. situation
184. location
186. presence
188. inhabitant
190. contents

185. displacement
187. absence
189. habitation
191. receptacle

II. DIMENSIONS

192. size
194. expansion
196. distance
198. interval
200. length
202. breadth, thickness
204. layer
206. height
208. depth
210. summit
212. verticality
214. suspension
216. parallelism
218. inversion
219. crossing
220. exteriority
222. centrality
223. covering
225. dress
227. environment
229. circumscription
230. outline
231. edge
232. enclosure
233. limit

193. littleness
195. contraction
197. nearness
199. contiguity
201. shortness
203. narrowness, thinness
205. filament
207. lowness
209. shallowness
211. base
213. horizontality
215. support
217. obliquity

221. interiority

224. lining
226. undress
228. interspersion

234. front
235. rear
236. side
237. opposition
238. right
239. left

III. FORM

240. form
241. formlessness
242. symmetry
243. distortion
244. angularity
245. curvature
246. straightness
247. circularity
248. convolution
249. rotundity
250. convexity
251. flatness
252. concavity
253. sharpness
254. bluntness
255. smoothness
256. roughness
257. notch
258. fold
259. furrow
260. opening
261. closure
262. perforator
263. stopper

IV. MOTION

264. motion
265. rest
266. journey
267. navigation
268. traveler
269. mariner, flier
270. transference
271. carrier
272. vehicle
273. ship
274. velocity
275. slowness
276. impulse
277. recoil
278. direction
279. deviation
280. precedence
281. sequence
282. progression
283. regression
284. propulsion
285. traction
286. approach
287. recession
288. attraction
289. repulsion
290. convergence
291. divergence

Class III. MATTER
I. MATTER IN GENERAL

316. materiality
318. world
319. gravity

317. immateriality

320. levity

II. INORGANIC MATTER

321. density
323. hardness
325. elasticity
327. tenacity
329. structure
330. granularity
331. friction
333. fluidity
335. liquefaction
337. water
339. moisture
341. ocean
343. gulf, lake
345. marsh
347. stream
348. river
350. conduit
352. semiliquidity
354. pulpiness

322. thinness
324. softness
326. inelasticity
328. brittleness

332. lubrication
334. gaseity
336. vaporization
338. air
340. dryness
342. land
344. plain
346. island

349. wind
351. air-pipe
353. bubble, cloud
355. unctuousness
356. oil
356a. resin

III. ORGANIC MATTER

357. animate matter
359. life

358. inanimate matter
360. death
361. killing
362. corpse
363. interment

364. animality

365. vegetation

366. animal
368. zoology
370. ranching
372. mankind
373. man
375. sensibility
377. pleasure
379. touch
380. sensations of touch
382. heat
384. calefaction
386. furnace
388. fuel
389. thermometer
390. taste
392. pungency
393. condiment
394. savoriness
396. sweetness
398. odor
400. fragrance
402. sound
404. loudness
406. snap
408. resonance

410. stridency
411. cry
413. melody, concord
415. music
416. musician
417. musical instruments
418. hearing
420. light

367. vegetable
369. botany
371. agriculture

374. woman
376. insensibility
378. pain

381. numbness
383. cold
385. refrigeration
387. refrigerator

391. tastelessness

395. unsavoriness
397. sourness
399. inodorousness
401. fetor
403. silence
405. faintness
407. roll
408a. nonresonance
409. sibilation

412. ululation
414. discord

419. deafness
421. darkness

422. dimness

423. luminary
425. transparency

424. shade
426. opacity

Class IV. INTELLECT
I. FORMATION OF IDEAS

559. artist
560. language
561. letter
562. word
563. neology
564. nomenclature
565. misnomer
566. phrase
567. grammar
568. solecism
569. style
570. perspicuity
571. obscurity
572. conciseness
573. diffuseness
574. vigor
575. feebleness
576. plainness
577. ornament
578. elegance
579. inelegance
580. voice
581. muteness
582. speech
583. inarticulateness
584. loquacity
585. taciturnity
586. public address
587. response
588. conversation
589. soliloquy
590. writing
591. printing
592. correspondence
593. book
594. description
595. dissertation
596. compendium
597. poetry
598. prose
599. the drama

Class V. VOLITION
I. INDIVIDUAL VOLITION

600. will
602. willingness
604. resolution
604. perseverance
606. obstinancy

609. choice

611. predetermination
613. habit
615. motive

617. plea
618. good
620. intention
622. pursuit

625. business
626. plan
627. method
628. mid-course
630. requirement
631. instrumentality
632. means
633. instrument
634. substitute
635. materials
636. store
637. provision

601. necessity
603. unwillingness
605. irresolution

607. recantation
608. caprice
609a. neutrality
610. rejection
612. impulse
614. disuse
615a. absence of motive
616. dissuasion

619. evil
621. chance
623. avoidance
624. relinquishment

629. circuit

638. waste
639. sufficiency

640. insufficiency
642. importance
644. utility
646. expedience
648. goodness

641. redundance
643. unimportance
645. inutility
647. inexpedience
649. badness

650. perfection	651 imperfection
652. cleanness	653. uncleanness
654. health	655. disease
656. salubrity	657. insalubrity
658. improvement	659. deterioration
660. restoration	661. relapse
662. remedy	663. bane
664. safety	665. danger
666. refuge	667. pitfall
668. warning	
669. alarm	
670. preservation	
671. escape	
672. deliverance	
673. preparation	674. nonpreparation
675. essay	
676. undertaking	
677. use	678. disuse
	679. misuse
680. action	681. inaction
682. activity	683. inactivity
684. haste	685. leisure
686. exertion	687. repose
688. fatigue	689. refreshment
690. agent	
691. workshop	
692. conduct	
693. direction	
694. director	
695. advice	
696. council	
697. precept	
698. skill	699. unskillfulness
700. expert	701. bungler
702. cunning	703. artlessness
704. difficulty	705. facility
706. hindrance	707. aid

708. opposition
709. cooperation
710. opponent
711. auxiliary
712. party
713. discord
714. concord
715. defiance
716. attack
717. defense
718. retaliation
719. resistance
720. contention
721. peace
722. warfare
723. pacification
724. mediation
725. submission
726. combatant
727. arms
728. arena
729. completion
730. noncompletion
731. success
732. failure
733. trophy
734. prosperity
735. adversity
736. mediocrity

II. INTERSOCIAL VOLITION

737. authority
738. laxity
739. severity
740. lenience
741. command
742. disobedience
743. obedience
744. compulsion
745. master
746. servant
747. scepter
748. freedom
749. subjection
750. liberation
751. restraint
752. prison
753. keeper
754. prisoner
755. commission
756. abrogation
757. resignation
758. consignee
759. deputy
760. permission
761. prohibition

762. consent
763. offer   764. refusal
765. request   766. deprecation
767. petitioner
768. promise
769. compact
770. conditions
771. security
772. observance   773. nonobservance
774. compromise

775. acquisition   776. loss
777. possession   777a. exemption
778. participation
779. possessor
780. property
781. retention   782. relinquishment
783. transfer
784. giving   785. receiving
786. apportionment
787. lending   788. borrowing
789. taking   790. restitution
791. stealing
792. thief
793. booty
794. barter
795. purchase   796. sale
797. merchant
798. merchandise
799. market
800. money
801. treasurer
802. treasury
803. wealth   804. poverty
805. credit   806. debt
807. payment   808. nonpayment
809. expenditure   810. receipt

Class VI. AFFECTIONS
I. AFFECTIONS IN GENERAL

II. PERSONAL AFFECTIONS

868. fastidiousness
869. satiety
870. wonder
871. expectance
872. prodigy
873. repute
874. disrepute
875. nobility
876. commonalty
877. title
878. pride
879. humility
880. vanity
881. modesty
882. ostentation
883. celebration
884. boasting
885. insolence
886. servility
887. blusterer

III. SYMPATHETIC AFFECTIONS

888. friendship
889. enmity
890. friend
891. enemy
892. sociality
893. seclusion, exclusion
894. courtesy
895. discourtesy
896. congratulations
897. love
898. hate
899. favorite

900. resentment
901. irascibility
901a. sullenness

902. endearment
903. marriage
904. celibacy
905. divorce
906. benevolence
907. malevolence
908. malediction
909. threat
910. philanthropy
911. misanthropy
912. benefactor
913. evildoer
914. pity
914a. pitilessness
915. condolence
916. gratitude
917. ingratitude

918. forgiveness

919. revenge
920. jealousy
921. envy

IV. MORAL AFFECTIONS

922. right
924. claim
926. duty

928. respect

931. approbation
933. flattery
935. flatterer
937. vindication
939. probity

942. disinterestedness
944. virtue
946. innocence
948. good man
950. penitence
952. atonement
953. temperance

955. asceticism
956. fasting
958. sobriety
960. purity

963. legality
965. jurisdiction
966. tribunal
967. judge
968. lawyer
969. lawsuit
970. acquittal

923. wrong
925. unrightfulness
927. dereliction of duty
927a. exemption

929. disrespect
930. contempt

932. disapprobation
934. detraction
936. detractor
938. accusation
940. improbity
941. knave

943. selfishness
945. vice
947. guilt
949. bad man
951. impenitence

954. intemperance
954a. sensualist

957. gluttony
959. drunkenness
961. impurity
962. libertine

964. illegality

971. condemnation

973. reward

972. punishment
974. penalty
975. scourge

V. RELIGIOUS AFFECTIONS

976. diety
977. angel
979. fabulous spirit
981. heaven
983. theology
983a. orthodoxy
985. revelation
987. piety

990. worship

978. devil
980. demon
982. hell

984. heterodoxy
986. religious writings
988. impiety
989. irreligion
991. idolatry
992. sorcery
993. spell
994. sorcerer

995. churchdom
996. clergy
998. rite
999. canonicals
1000. temple

997. laity

ROGET'S THESAURUS

Class I

Words Expressing Abstract Relations

I. Existence

1 existence *n* being, entity, subsistence, reality, actuality, presence, fact, matter of fact, truth, science of existence: ontology.

v exist, be, subsist, live, breathe; occur, happen, take place; consist in, lie in; endure, remain, abide, survive, last, stay, continue.

adj existent, extant; prevalent, current, afloat; real, actual, true, positive, absolute; substantial, substantive; well founded, well grounded.

adv actually, in fact, in reality.

2 nonexistence *n* inexistence; insubstantiality, nonentity; blank, *tabula rasa*, void, emptiness, nothingness; potential, possibility; annihilation, extinction, obliteration, total destruction.

v not exist; pass away, perish, die, die out, disappear, dissolve; annihilate, destroy, obliterate, wipe off the face of the earth; nullify, void; take away, remove.

adj nonexistent, inexistent; blank, void, empty; unreal, baseless, unsubstantial, intangible, ineffable, spiritual, spectral; unborn, uncreated, unbegotten, unconceived; potential, possible; exhausted, gone, lost, departed, extinct, defunct; fabulous, visionary, imaginative, ideal, conceptual, abstract.

3 substantiality *n* materiality, corporality, tangibility, material existence, bodiliness, matter, stuff; creature, being, person, body, flesh and blood, substance; thing, object, article.

adj substantive, substantial, corporeal, material, bodily, physical, concrete, tangible, palpable, corporal, materialistic.

4 unsubstantiality *n* nothingness; nothing, naught, nil, nullity, zero; shadow, phantom, apparition, dream, illusion; fallacy, inanity, frivolity; hollowness, blank, void; flimsiness, thinness, slightness.

v vanish, evaporate, fade, dissolve, melt away, disappear.

adj unsubstantial, baseless, groundless, ungrounded, without foundation, fallacious, erroneous, untenable; insignificant, slight, thin, trifling, frivolous; imaginary, visionary, dreamy, shadowy, ethereal, airy, immaterial, spectral, illusory, incorporeal, intangible, bodiless, abstract; vacant, vacuous, empty, blank, hollow.

5 intrinsicality *n* ego, essence, quintessence, gist, pith, marrow, sap, lifeblood, backbone, heart, soul, core; principle, nature, constitution, construction, character, type, quality; habit, temper, temperament, personality, spirit, humor, grain, moods, features, peculiarities, aspects, idiosyncrasies, tendencies, bents; inbeing, inherence, essentiality.

v be intrinsic, be inherent.

adj intrinsic, inherent, implanted, innate, inborn, inbred, ingrained; essential, fundamental, basic, normal; inherited, congenital, hereditary, indigenous, in the blood, in the genes; instinctive, instinctual, internal, personal, subjective; characteristic, peculiar, idiosyncratic; fixed, set in one's ways, invariable, unchangeable, incurable, ineradicable.

adv intrinsically, at bottom, in effect, practically, virtually, substantially.

6 extrinsicality *n* extraneousness, externals.

adj extrinsic, extraneous, external, adventitious; collateral, accidental, incidental, objective.

adv extrinsically.

7 state *n* condition, case, circumstances, situation, status, surroundings, pass, plight, pickle; mood, temper, frame;

constitution, structure, form, phase, frame, fabric, stamp, set, fit, mold; mode, style, fashion, light, complexion, character; tone, tenor, turn.

v be in a state.

8 circumstance *n* situation, phase, position, condition, posture, attitude, place, point; footing, standing, status; occasion, happening, event, juncture, conjunction; predicament, exigency, emergency, crisis, pinch, plight, pass; climax, apex, turning point.

adj circumstantial, conditional, provisional; contingent, incidental, adventitious; critical, climactic.

adv under the circumstances, under the conditions; thus, in such wise; accordingly, that being the case, since, seeing that, as matters stand; conditionally, provided, if, in case; if so, if it so happen, in the event of, provisionally, unless.

II. Absolute Relation

9 relation *n* connection, concern, bearing, reference; correlation, analogy; similarity, affinity, homogeneity, alliance, association, nearness; approximation, relationship; comparison, ratio, proportion; link, tie, bond.

v relate to, refer to; bear upon, regard, concern, touch, affect, have to do with, pertain to, appertain to, belong to; bring into relation with, associate, connect, parallel; link, bind, tie.

adj relative, relative to, relating to, referable to, with reference to; belonging to; related, connected, associated, affiliated, allied; in the same category, relevant.

adv as regards, about, concerning, with relation to, with reference to, with regard to, with respect to, in connection with, under the head of, in the matter of.

10 [absence of relation] **non-relation** *n* irrelation, dissociation, lack of connection; disconnection, disjunction; inconsequence, irreconcilability, disagreement, heterogeneity; independence.

v have no relation to, have no bearing upon, have nothing to do with, have no connection with.

adj unrelated, irrespective, unallied, unconnected, disconnected, heterogeneous, independent; adrift, insular, isolated; extraneous, strange, alien, foreign, outlandish, exotic; irrelevant, inapplicable, not pertinent, beside the mark, off base; remote, farfetched, out-of-the-way, forced, detached, distanced; incidental, parenthetical.

adv parenthetically, by the way, by the by; incidentally.

11 [relations of kindred] **consanguinity** *n* relationship, kindred, blood; parentage, paternity, maternity, lineage, heritage; filiation, affiliation, connection, alliance, tie; family, blood relation, ties of blood, kinsman, kinfolk, kith and kin, relation, relative, one's own, one's own flesh and blood; fraternity, sorority, brotherhood, sisterhood; race, stock, generation.

v be related to, claim relationship with.

adj related, akin, consanguineous, allied, affiliated, connected; kindred, familial.

12 [double or reciprocal relation] **correlation** *n* correspondence, reciprocity, reciprocation, interdependence, mutuality, interchange, exchange.

v reciprocate, alternate, interchange, interact, interdepend; interchange, exchange; correlate, correspond, relate.

adj reciprocal, mutual, correlative, corresponding, analogous, complementary; equivalent, interchangeable, alternate.

adv reciprocally.

13 identity *n* sameness, exactness, equality, correspondence, parallelism, unity, convertibility, resemblance, similarity; self, oneself, name, personality; facsimile, duplicate, replica, copy, reproduction.

v be identical, coincide, coalesce.

adj identical, self, the same, selfsame; coincident, coinciding, coalescent, indistinguishable; one, equal, equivalent.

adv identically.

14 contrariety *n* contrast, foil, antithesis, oppositeness, opposition, contradiction, antipathy, antagonism; the reverse, the inverse, the converse, inversion, subversion, reversal, the opposite, antipodes.

v be contrary, contrast with, differ from, oppose; invert, revert, turn upside down; contradict, contravene; antagonize.

adj contrary, opposite, counter, converse, reverse; opposed, antithetical, contrasted, antipodean, antagonistic, opposing; conflicting, inconsistent, contradictory; negative, hostile.

15 difference *n* discrepancy, disparity, dissimilarity, inconsistency, variance, variation, diversity, imbalance, disagreement, inequality, inequity, divergence, contrast, contrariety; discrimination, distinction, nice distinction, shade, nuance, subtlety.

v differ, vary; diversify, modify, change, alter; contrast, mismatch; discriminate, distinguish.

adj different, diverse, heterogeneous, unlike, divergent, altered, changed, deviant, deviating, variant, varied, modified; diversified, various, divers, miscellaneous, manifold; other, another, not the same, unequal, unmatched, wide apart; distinctive, characteristic, discriminative.

16 uniformity *n* homogeneity, permanence, continuity, consistency, stability, accordance, standardization, conformity, agreement; regularity, constancy, evenness, sameness; monotony, routine, invariability.

v be uniform, accord with; conform to, assimilate; level, smooth, even.

adj uniform, homogeneous, of a piece, consistent; consistent, regular, constant, even, level; invariable, unchanging, unvarying, unvaried, unchanged, constant, regular; undiversified, solid, plain, dreary, monotonous, routine.

adv uniformly; always, invariably, without exception; ever, forever.

16a lack of uniformity *n* diversity, irregularity, unevenness, inconsistency, nonconformity, heterogeneity.

adj diversified, varied, irregular, inconsistent, motley, patchwork, uneven, rough; multifarious, of various kinds.

17 similarity *n* resemblance, likeness, similitude, semblance, affinity, approximation, parallelism; agreement, correspondence, analogy; brotherhood, family likeness; repetition, sameness, uniformity, identity; the like, fellow, match, pair, mate, twin, double, counterpart; alter ego, chip off the old block, birds of a feather, like two peas in a pod; simile, parallel, type, image, representation.

v be similar, resemble, look like, bear a resemblance, take after, approximate, parallel, match, rhyme with.

adj similar, resembling, like, alike; twin; analogous, parallel, of a piece; allied to, akin to, corresponding; approximate, much the same, near, close, something like; imitative, mock, pseudo, simulating, representing, representative; exact, true, lifelike, faithful, true to life, identical.

adv as if, so to speak; as it were, as if it were; quasi, just as.

18 dissimilarity *n* dissimilitude, unlikeness, difference; diversity, disparity, divergence; novelty, originality, uniqueness.

v be unlike, differ from, bear no resemblance; vary, diversify, differentiate.

adj dissimilar, unlike, different, disparate; unique, new, novel, unprecedented, unmatched, unequaled; diversified.

19 imitation *n* copying; copy, duplication, reproduction, replica; mocking, mimicry, aping; simulation, impersonation, representation, semblance, approximation, paraphrase, parody; plagiarism, forgery.

v imitate, copy, mirror, reflect, impersonate, duplicate, reproduce, simulate, counterfeit; mock, take off, mimic, ape, personate, parody, caricature, travesty; follow, emulate, pattern after, model oneself on, parallel, follow, take after.

adj imitative, modeled after, modeled on, based on; fake, phony, counterfeit, false, imitation, mock; duplicate, second hand.

adv literally, word for word, to the letter.

20 nonimitation *n* originality, uniqueness.

adj unimitated, uncopied; unmatched, unparalleled; inimitable, original, unique, special, one of a kind, rare, exceptional.

20a variation *n* alteration, change, modification; divergency, deviation, aberration, innovation.

v vary, change; deviate, diverge, alternate, modify.

adj varied, modified, diversified, altered, changed.

21 [result of imitation] **copy** *n* facsimile, counterpart, effigy, form, likeness, similitude, semblance, cast, mold, model, representation, image, portrait; reflection, shadow, echo; transcript, transcription, reproduction, imitation, carbon, ditto, stencil, duplicate, reprint, transfer, replica; parody, caricature, burlesque, travesty, paraphrase; counterfeit, forgery, deception.

adj faithful, lifelike, exact, similar.

22 [thing copied] **prototype** *n* original, model, pattern, precedent, standard; type, archetype, exemplar, paradigm, module, example; text, copy, design; die, mold; matrix mint, seal, punch, intaglio, negative, plate, stamp.

v be an example, set an example.

23 agreement *n* unanimity, harmony, accord, accordance, concord, union, unity, understanding, settlement, treaty, pact; uniformity, conformity, consistency, congruity, logic, correspondence, parallelism, apposition; consent, assent, concurrence, cooperation.

v agree, accord, harmonize; correspond, tally, *(informal)* jibe; meet, suit, fit, befit, square with, dovetail, match; adapt, fit, accommodate, adjust.

adj agreeing, accordant, correspondent, congenial, harmonious; reconcilable, comfortable, compatible, congruous, consistent, logical, consonant, commensurate; in accordance with, in harmony with, in keeping with; apt, apposite, pat, pertinent; agreeable, happy, felicitous.

24 disagreement *n* discord, dissonance, dissidence, disunion, discrepancy, nonconformity, incongruity, dissension, conflict, opposition, antagonism, difference; disparity, disproportion, mismatch, variance, divergence, inequity, inequality.

v disagree, clash, jar, argue, quarrel, dispute.

adj disagreeing, discordant, dissonant, inharmonious; at variance, hostile, conflicting, antagonistic, clashing, disputing, factious, dissenting, irreconcilable, incompatible, inconsistent with; incongruous, disproportionate, disparate, divergent; disagreeable, uncongenial, mismatched; out of joint, out of step, out of tune.

III. Simple Quantity

25 [absolute quantity] **quantity** *n* size, mass, volume, amount, measure, measurement, substance, strength; mouthful, spoonful, handful; stock, batch, lot, dose.

adj quantitative, some, any, more or less.

26 [relative quantity] **degree** *n* grade, extent, measure, amount, ratio, standard, height, pitch; reach, range, scope, rate, caliber; gradation, shade, tint; tenor, tone, compass; sphere, station, rank, standing; point, mark, stage, level; intensity, strength.

adj comparative, gradual, shading off.

adv by degrees, gradually, step by step, bit by bit, little by little, inch by inch, drop by drop; in some degree, to some extent; up to a point.

27 [sameness of quantity or degree] **equality** *n* parity, symmetry, balance, counterbalance; evenness, monotony, level; equivalence, equipose, equilibrium; par, even keel, quits; identity, similarity; tie, dead heat, draw, drawn game, neck and neck race; match, peer, equal, mate, fellow, brother; equivalent.

v equal, match, reach, keep pace with, run abreast; come up to; balance, even the score; equalize, level, trim, adjust; strike a balance; restore equilibrium.

adj equal, even, level, monotonous, coequal, symmetrical, balanced; on a par with, on a level with, on an equal footing with, up to the mark; equivalent, tantamount, synonymous, quits, even, much the same, all one, one and the same; drawn, half and half, six of one and half a dozen of another.

adv equally, to all intents and purposes.

28 [difference of quantity or degree] **inequality** *n* disparity, dissimilarity, difference, odds; unevenness, imbalance; inferiority, shortcoming, deficiency, imperfection, inadequacy; mediocrity; superiority.

v be unequal, have the advantage, turn the scale, turn the tide; topple, overmatch; not come up to, fall short of, not come up to snuff.

adj unequal, uneven, imbalanced; disparate, partial, inferior, insufficient, deficient, inadequate, mediocre, short.

29 mean *n* medium, average, balance, middle, mid-point, center, median, golden mean; compromise, neutrality.

v split the difference, take the average, move to the center.

adj mean, intermediate, middle, average, standard, normal, neutral; mediocre, middle class, bourgeois, commonplace, run of the mill, egalitarian.

adv on the average, in the long run.

30 compensation *n* equation; indemnification, requital; compromise, measure for measure, tit for tat, eye for an eye, retaliation, equalization; setoff, off-set, counterpoise, ballast; indemnity, equivalent, *quid pro quo*, amends, reparation.

v compensate, indemnify, recompense, remunerate; counterbalance, counterpoise, countervail, offset, counteract, balance, balance out, make up for, square, even out, equalize; cover, neutralize, nullify; redeem, atone, make amends.

adj compensatory, compensating, equivalent, equal.

adv but, however, yet, still, notwithstanding, nevertheless, although, though, nonetheless; howbeit, albeit; at all events, at any rate, be that as may, even so, on the other hand, at the same time.

31 greatness *n* magnitude, size, bulk, dimensions, vastness; multitude; enormousness, immensity, might, strength, intensity, fullness; importance, distinction, eminence, renown; quantity, store, volume, mass, bulk, heap; abundance, sufficiency.

v be great, soar, tower, rise above, transcend; enlarge, increase, expand.

adj great, large, considerable, big, huge, mammoth, gigantic; ample, abundant, sufficient; full, intense, strong; widespread, extensive, wholesale; goodly, noble, precious, mighty; utter, uttermost, arch, profound, intense, consummate; extraordinary, important, unsurpassed, supreme; complete, total; vast, immense, enormous, extreme, inordinate, excessive, extravagant, exorbitant, outrageous, monstrous; towering, stupendous, prodigious, marvelous; unlimited, infinite; absolute, positive, stark, decided, unequivocal, essential, perfect; remarkable, notable, noteworthy.

adv [in a positive degree] truly; decidedly, unequivocally, absolutely, essentially, fundamentally, downright; [in a complete degree] entirely, completely, totally, wholly; abundantly, fully, amply, widely; [in a great or high degree] greatly, much, indeed, very, very much, most, pretty, pretty well, enough, in a great measure, to a large extent; richly, on a large scale, ever so much; mightily, powerfully; extremely, exceedingly, intensely, exquisitely, consummately, acutely, indefinitely, immeasurably, beyond compare, beyond measure, beyond all bounds, incalculably, infinitely; [in a supreme degree] pre-eminently, superlatively, supremely, incomparably; [in a too great degree] immoderately, inordinately, exorbitantly, excessively, enormously, preposterously, monstrously, out of all proportion, with a vengeance; [in a marked degree] particularly, remarkably, singularly, curiously, uncommonly, unusually, peculiarly, notably, signally, strikingly, pointedly, mainly, chiefly; famously, egregiously, prominently, glaringly, emphatically, strangely, wonderfully, amazingly, surprisingly, astonishingly, incredibly, marvelously, stupendously; [in a violent degree] violently, furiously, severely, desperately, tremendously, extravagantly; [in a painful degree] painfully, sadly, sorely, bitterly, piteously, grievously, miserably, cruelly, woefully, lamentably, shockingly, frightfully, fearfully, dreadfully, terribly, horribly.

32 smallness *n* littleness, tininess, diminutiveness; slenderness, thinness, paltriness, slightness; paucity, fewness, sparseness, scarcity; unimportance, triviality, inconsequentiality, pettiness, insignificance; meanness, sordidness, selfishness, narrow-mindedness; small quantity, modicum, atom, particle, molecule, point, speck, dot, dab, mote, jot, iota; minutiae, details, *soupçon,* scintilla, granule; drop, droplet, drizzle, sprinkling, dash, smack, tinge; dole, scrap, shred, splinter; mite, bit, morsel, crumb, seed; snippet, snatch, slip; chip, sliver; nutshell thimbleful, spoonful, handful, mouthful; fragment, fraction, drop in the ocean; trifle.

v be small.

adj small, little, tiny, diminutive, petite, miniature, minuscule, minute, microscopic, infinitesimal, fine; unimportant, trivial, minor, secondary, trifling, inconsequential, petty, paltry, insignificant; slender, thin, slight, scanty, scant, meager, insufficient; few, sparse, scarce; low, so-so, middling, tolerable, inconsiderable, inappreciable; mean, sordid, selfish, narrow, narrow-minded, illiberal, ungenerous; feeble, weak, faint.

adv [in a small degree] to a small extent; a wee bit; slightly, imperceptibly, faintly; miserably, wretchedly; insufficiently, imperfectly; passably, pretty well, well enough; [in a certain or limited degree] partially, in part, to a certain degree; some, rather, to some degree; simply, only, purely, merely, at the least; ever so little; almost, nearly, well nigh, short of, not quite, all but, near the mark; scarcely, hardly, barely, only just, no more than; [in an uncertain degree] about, thereabouts, somewhere about; [in no degree] noway, nowise, not at all, not in the least, not a bit, not a jot, not a whit, in no respect, by no means, on no account.

33 superiority *n* supremacy, pre-eminence, ascendancy, transcendence; excellence, greatness, nobility, eminence, worthiness, preponderance, predominance, prevalence, advantage; majority; quality, high caliber.

v be superior, exceed, excel, transcend, outdo, outweigh, outrival, outrank; pass, surpass; top, cap, outstrip, eclipse, predominate, prevail; take precedence, come first.

adj superior, greater, major, higher, exceeding; supreme, greatest, utmost, paramount, pre-eminent, foremost, crowning; first-rate, important, excellent, unrivaled, matchless, priceless, unparalleled, unequaled, unsurpassed, inimitable, incomparable, superlative, beyond, compare, transcendent.

adv beyond, more, over, over and above, at its height; [in a superior or supreme degree] eminently, pre-eminently, prominently, surpassingly, superlatively, supremely, above all, to crown all, *par excellence;* principally, especially, particularly, peculiarly.

34 inferiority *n* low quality, deficiency, imperfection, shortcoming, inadequacy; mediocrity, commonalty, commonness, poorness, meanness; minority, subordination, subjection.

v be inferior, fall short of, come short of, not come up to, not pass muster; want, lack.

adj inferior, minor, less, lesser, deficient; poor, indifferent, mean, base, bad, shabby, paltry, humble, imperfect, mediocre, common, commonplace, second-rate; poorer; secondary, minor, subordinate, lower; diminished, reduced, unimportant.

adv less, subpar; short of, under

35 increase *n* growth, augmentation, enlargement, extension, expansion, addition, increment, accretion, aggrandizement; development, rise, ascent.

v increase, grow, dilate, enlarge, expand, multiply; augment, add to, enlarge, greaten; extend, spread out, prolong; advance, rise, sprout, ascend; raise, exalt, deepen, heighten, intensify, magnify, redouble; aggrandize.

adj increasing, growing; additional, incremental; developmental.

36 decrease *n* diminution, abatement, decline, reduction, wane, falling-off, contraction, dwindling, shrinking, lessening, ebb, ebbing; subtraction, abridgment, shortening; depreciation, deterioration.

v decrease, lessen, abate, fall off, decline, contract, shrink, dwindle, wane, ebb, subside; diminish, deteriorate, depreciate, languish, decay; abridge, shorten, subtract.

adj decreased, decreasing, on the wane.

37 addition *n* increment, increase, enlargement, aggrandizement, accession; supplement, adjunct, attachment, addendum; annexation, interposition, insertion; uniting, joining.

v add, annex, affix, subjoin, tack on, append, attach, join, supplement, increase, augment, make an addition to; accrue, accumulate, pile up; total, sum, add up; reinforce.

adj additional, supplemental, supplementary; extra, accessory, auxiliary.

adv in addition, more, plus; and, also, likewise, too, further, furthermore, besides, to boot, etc., and so on, and so forth; over and above, moreover; with, as well as, together with, along with, in conjunction with.

38 deduction *n* subtraction, retrenchment, withdrawal, removal; mutilation, amputation, curtailment; shortening, abbreviation; decrease, cutback.

v deduct, subtract, retrench, withdraw, remove; take from, take away; shorten, abbreviate, cut back, pare down, reduce, decrease, diminish, curtail, eliminate, deprive of; mutilate, amputate, cut off, cut away, excise; pare, thin, thin out, prune, scrape, file.

adj subtracted, subtracting; removable, reducible; deductible.

adv less, short of; minus, without, excepting, except, with the exception of, save, exclusive of.

39 [thing added] **adjunct** *n* addition, affix, suffix, appendage, annex, augmentation, increment, reinforcement, accessory, accompaniment, sequel; addendum, complement, supplement, appendix, attachment; rider, offshoot, episode, corollary.

adj additional.

40 [thing remaining] **remainder** *n* residue, remains, remnant, leftover, excess, superfluity, balance, surplus, rest, relic; leavings, odds and ends, residuum, dregs, refuse, crumbs, stubble, ruins, skeleton, stump.

v remain, survive, be left; be left over.

adj remaining, left, left over, residual; over, odd, spare, unused; superfluous; surviving.

40a [thing deducted] **decrement** *n* discount, defect, loss, deduction.

41 mixture *n* admixture, mix, combination, mingling, amalgamation, junction; infusion, suffusion, transfusion; infiltration, interlarding, interpolation; adulteration, thing mixed: tinge, tincture, touch, dash, sprinkling, spice, seasoning, infusion, compounds: alloy, amalgam, mélange, pastiche, miscellany, medley, patchwork, hotchpotch, gallimaufry, conglomeration, jumble, potpourri, farrago; cross, hybrid, mongrel.

v mix, join; combine, blend, mingle, commingle, confuse, jumble, unite, compound, amalgamate, adulterate; interlard, interlace, intertwine, interweave, interpolate; conjoin, associate, consort; instill, imbue, infuse, suffuse, transfuse, infiltrate, dash, tinge, tincture, season, blend, cross.

adj mixed, composite, half-and-half, hybrid, cross, mongrel, heterogeneous; motley, variegated, miscellaneous, promiscuous, indiscriminate.

adv among, amongst, amid, amidst, with; in the midst of.

42 [freedom from mixture] **simpleness** *n* purity, homogeneity; elimination, sifting, purification.

v simplify; sift, winnow, eliminate, strain, clean, purify; disentangle.

adj simple, uniform, homogeneous, single, pure, clear; unmixed, unadulterated, elemental, elementary, basic.

43 junction *n* joining, union; connection, conjunction, annexation, attachment; coupling, marriage, wedlock; confluence, communication, concatenation; meeting, assemblage, assembly, reunion; joint, joining, juncture, pivot, hinge, articulation; seam, stitch, linkage, link.

v join, unite, connect, link up, link; associate; put together, piece together, bind together; attach, fix, affix, fasten, bind, secure, clinch, twist, tie, string, strap, sew, lace, stitch, hem, knit, button, buckle, hitch, lash, splice gird, tether, picket, moor, harness, leash; chain; fetter, lock, hook, couple, link, yoke, bracket; marry, wed, bridge over, span; pin, bolt, clasp, clamp, screw, rivet; solder, weld, fuse; entwine, interlace, intertwine, interweave; entangle.

adj joined, joint; corporate, compact; firm, fast, close, tight, taut, secure, set, inseparable, indissoluble.

adv jointly, in conjunction with; fast, firmly; intimately.

44 disjunction *n* disconnection, disunion, disengagement, dissociation, discontinuity; isolation, insularity, insulation, separateness; dispersion; separation, parting; detachment, segregation; divorce; division, subdivision, break, fracture, rupture; dismemberment, dislocation, severance; fissure, breach, rent, split, rift, crack, cut, slit, incision.

v disjoin, disconnect, disengage, disunite, dissociate, divorce, part, detach, separate, disentangle, cut off, rescind, discontinue; segregate, set apart, keep apart, isolate, insulate; cut adrift, loose, set free, liberate; divide, subdivide, sever, dissever, cut, saw, snip, chop, ax, cleave, rive, rend, slit, split, splinter, chip, crack, snap, break, tear, burst, rend; wrench, rupture, shatter; hack, hew, slash, slice, cut up, carve, dissect, tear to pieces; disband, disperse, dislocate, break up, apportion, divide; part, part company, separate, leave.

adj disjoined, discontinuous, disjunctive; isolated, insular; separate, apart, asunder, loose, adrift, free; unattached, unconnected.

adv separately, one by one, severally, apart, adrift, asunder.

45 link *n* connective, connection, vinculum, copula, tie, bond, bridge; junction, bracket.

v link, bond, join, connect, conjoin, fasten, pin, bind, tie; bridge, span.

46 coherence *n* cohesion, cohesiveness, adherence, adhesion, adhesiveness; connection, union, conglomeration, aggregation, consolidation; stickiness, inseparability.

v cohere, adhere, stick, cling, cleave, hold, take hold, clasp, hug; hang together, stay together; glue, cement,

paste, solder, weld; consolidate, solidify, agglomerate.

adj cohesive, adhesive, adhering, sticky; tenacious, tough; united, unified, inseparable, inextricable, *(informal)* together, *(informal)* tight.

47 incoherence *n* looseness, laxity, relaxation, nonadhesion; loosening, disjunction, disconnection; disagreement, inconsistency, incongruity.

v loosen, make loose, slacken, relax; detach, disjoin.

adj nonadhesive, noncohesive, detached, loose, slack, lax, relaxed, segregated, unconsolidated; inconsistent, incongruous, illogical, absurd, rambling.

48 combination *n* mixture; junction; union, unification, synthesis, incorporation, amalgamation, coalescence, fusion, blend, blending, mix, centralization; compound, alloy, amalgam, composition, composite.

v combine, unite, incorporate, amalgamate, absorb, blend, mix, merge, fuse, marry, consolidate, coalesce, centralize, cement, harden, solidify.

adj combined, unified.

49 decomposition *n* analysis, dissection, dissolution, breaking down; disjunction; corruption, decay, rot, putrefaction.

v decompose, analyze, dissolve; resolve into its elements, dissect, disperse, crumble; decay, rot, turn.

adj decomposed.

50 [principal part] whole *n* totality, entirety, total, sum, aggregate; unity, completeness, integrity, indivisibility; bulk, mass, lump; body, trunk.

v form a whole, integrate, embody, amass, aggregate, assemble; amount to, come to, add up to.

adj whole, total, full, entire, undiminished, undivided, integral, complete, unimpaired, unbroken, faultless, sound, intact; indivisible, indissoluble.

adv wholly, altogether; totally, completely, entirely, all, all in all, wholesale, in a body, collectively, in the main, on the whole.

51 part *n* division, portion, piece, fragment, fraction, lump, bit, component, constituent, ingredient, element, section, segment, subdivision; member, limb, branch, bough, off-shoot, ramification; compartment, department, class.

v part, divide, break, disjoin; partition, apportion, allot.

adj fractional, fragmentary, sectional; divided, split up.

adv partly, in part, partially; piecemeal, bit by bit, by installments, in dribs and drabs, in drips and snatches; in detail.

52 completeness *n* wholeness, entirety, totality, solidarity, fullness, intactness, unity, perfection; thoroughness.

v complete, accomplish, fulfill, finish; fill, charge, load, replenish; fill up, fill in; saturate.

adj complete, entire, whole, full, intact, undivided, one, perfect, fulfilled; full, good, absolute, thorough, solid; exhaustive, radical, sweeping, thoroughgoing; consummate, unmitigated, sheer, unqualified, unconditional; brimming, brimful, chock-full, saturated crammed, replete, fraught.

adv completely, altogether, outright, wholly, totally quite, utterly, fully, thoroughly, in all aspects, in every respect, out and out, to all intents and purposes; throughout, from first to last, from beginning to end, from top to bottom, from head to foot, every whit, every inch.

53 incompleteness *n* deficiency, shortcoming, insufficiency, imperfection; immaturity; noncompletion.

[part wanting] defect, deficit, omission, interval, break; discontinuity, missing link.

v be incomplete, fall short of; lack; neglect.

adj incomplete, imperfect, unfinished, uncompleted; defective, deficient, wanting, lacking, failing, short, short of; meager, lame, limp, perfunctory, sketchy, crude, immature; in progress, in preparation, going on, ongoing, proceeding.

adv incompletely.

54 composition *n* constitution, make-up, form; combination, compilation, incorporation, inclusion, synthesis.

v be composed of, be made up of, consist of; include, contain, hold, comprehend, take in, admit, embrace, embody; compose, constitute, form, make.

adj constituting.

55 exclusion *n* omission, exception, rejection, repudiation; exile, seclusion, segregation, separation, elimination, prohibition; restraint, keeping out.

v exclude, bar, leave out, shut out, keep out; reject, repudiate, blackball, throw out; lay aside, put aside, set aside; relegate, segregate, separate, seclude, banish, exile; pass over, omit, eliminate, weed out, winnow.

adj exclusive, not included in; inadmissible.

56 component *n* component part, integral part, element, constituent, ingredient; contents, feature, member, part; personnel.

v enter into, be part of, form part of; merge in, share in, participate; belong to, appertain to; form, make, constitute.

adj inclusive, comprehensive.

57 extraneousness *n* extrinsicality, externality; superfluousness; foreign body, foreign substance; intrusion.

v be extraneous, be unnecessary.

adj extraneous, foreign, alien, extrinsic, external; not germane, nonessential, superfluous; excluded.

IV. Order

58 order *n* regularity, uniformity, arrangement, harmony, symmetry; course, routine, method, methodology; disposition, array, arrangement, system, economy, discipline, orderliness; gradation, progression, series, sequence, continuity; rank, place, grade, class, degree.

v order, regulate, manage, adjust, arrange, systematize, standardize, rank.

adj orderly, regular, systematic, methodical; in order, neat, tidy, well-regulated, well-organized, organized, uniform, symmetrical, businesslike, shipshape.

adv in order, methodically, in turn, in its turn; step by step, at regular intervals, systematically.

59 disorder *n* derangement, disarray, untidiness, irregularity, anomaly; anarchy, anarchism, disunion, discord; confusion, jumble, mess, muddle, hash, hodgepodge, chaos; perplexity, labyrinth, wilderness, jungle; raveling, entanglement, complication, convolution; turmoil, ferment, agitation, trouble, row, disturbance, convulsion, tumult, uproar, riot, rumpus, ruckus, scramble, fracas, melee, pandemonium.

v disorder, put out of order, derange, ruffle, rumble; confuse, jumble, mess up.

adj disorderly, out of order, out of place, irregular, desultory; anomalous, disorganized, straggling, unsystematic, untidy, slovenly, messy; indiscriminate, chaotic, confused, deranged; anarchic, inverted, convoluted, topsy-turvy; complex, complicated, perplexed, involved, raveled, entangled, knotted, tangled; troublesome, problematical; riotous, violent, turbulent, tumultuous.

adv irregularly, helter skelter; at cross purposes, *(informal)*, after the flood.

60 [reduction to order] **arrangement** *n* plan, method, organization; preparation, groundwork, planning; sorting, disposal, disposition, distribution, assortment, allotment, apportionment, graduation, groupings; analysis, classification, division, ordering, systematization.

v arrange, dispose, place, form; set out, marshal, range, array, rank, group, parcel out, allot, apportion, assign, dole out, distribute; sort, sift, put into shape; plan, prepare, organize, lay the groundwork; classify, divide, file, register, catalog, record, tabulate, index, graduate, rank; regulate, systematize, coordinate, organize, settle, fix; unravel, disentangle, straighten out.

adj arranged, ordered; methodical, orderly, regular, systematic.

61 [subversion of order] **derangement** *n* disorder, mess, disarray, disorganization; discomposure, disturbance, dislocation, perturbation, interruption.

v derange, disarrange, discompose, displace, misplace; mislay, disorder, disorganize; embroil, disconcert, convulse, unsettle, disturb, confuse, trouble, perturb, jumble, muddle, fumble; unhinge, dislocate, throw out of gear, throw out of whack; invert, turn upside down, turn

topsy-turvy; complicate, confound, tangle, entangle; litter, scatter, mix.

62 precedence *n* coming before, the lead, superiority; precursor, antecedence; importance, consequence; priority, preference.

v precede, come before, forerun, come first; head, lead the way, usher in, introduce; set the fashion, influence, establish; have precedence, take precedence; place before, prefix, preface.

adj preceding, precedent, antecedent, anterior, prior, before; former, foregoing; preliminary, prefatory, introductory; preparatory.

adv before; in advance.

63 sequence *n* coming after, following, succession, order, series; posteriority; continuation; order of succession; outcome, consequence, result, sequel.

v succeed, come after, follow, ensure; replace.

adj succeeding, following; consequent, subsequent; proximate, next; sequential, consecutive.

adv after, subsequently; behind.

64 precursor *n* antecedent, precedent, predecessor, forerunner, pioneer, leader, bellwether; herald, harbinger; prelude, preamble, preface, prolog, proem, prefix, foreword, introduction; heading, frontispiece, groundwork; preparation.

adj prefatory, introductory, preliminary, precursory.

65 sequel *n* continuation, extension, supplement, outgrowth, offshoot, result, consequence, inference, deduction; result, consequence, aftermath, outcome, effect; conclusion, end, culmination, denouement, finale, finish; appendage, suffix, epilog, postscript, tag, train, trail, wake; afterthought, afterpiece, second thoughts.

66 beginning *n* commencement, opening, outset, start, initiation, inauguration; introduction, prelude; outbreak, onset, brunt; initiative, first move; origin, cause, source, bud, germ, genesis, birth, nativity, cradle; starting point, first step, square one; title page, head, heading; rudiments, basics, elements.

v begin, commence, open, start, initiate, inaugurate; conceive; set out, embark, depart; usher in, lead the way, take the lead, take the initiative, head, stand at the head, launch, set in motion, get going, take the first step, break ground; burst forth, break out; begin at the beginning, start again, start over, make a fresh start; originate, conceive, think up.

adj initial, introductory, inaugural; incipient; embryonic, rudimental, primal, essential, natal, nascent; first, foremost, leading; maiden, virgin.

adv first, in the first place, first and foremost; in the bud, in its infancy; from the beginning.

67 end *n* close, termination, conclusion, finale, finish, last word; consummation, climax, apex, dénouement; goal, destination; expiration, death, finality; limit, extreme, extremity; breakup, last stage, final stage, turning point, death blow.

v end, close, finish, terminate, conclude; expire, die, come to a close, draw to a close, run its course, run out, pass away; bring to an end, put an end to, make an end of, wrap up; get through, complete, consummate; stop, desist, call it quits.

adj final, terminal, concluding; conclusive, crowning, definitive, last, ultimate, consummate; ended, settled, decided, over, concluded, played out.

adv finally, at last, once and for all, over and done with.

68 middle *n* center, midpoint, midst; mean, midcourse, middle ground, compromise; core, kernel, heart, nucleus, nub; equidistance, bisection; equator, diaphragm, midriff.

adj middle, medial, mean, mid, median, midmost; intermediate, equidistant, central, halfway.

adv midway, halfway, in the middle.

69 [uninterrupted sequence **continuity** *n* continuousness, consecutiveness, progression, constant flow, succession, train, series, chain, string, scale, gradation; round, suite; procession, column, retinue; pedigree, genealogy, lineage; rank, file, line, row, range, tier.

v follow in a line; arrange in a series, string together, file, thread, graduate, tabulate.

adj continuous, progressive, successive, serial, consecutive, unbroken, un-

interrupted, gradual; linear, in a line; perennial, constant.

adv continuously, in succession, consecutively; gradually, step by step, in a column.

70 [interrupted sequence] **discontinuity** *n* disjunction, disconnectedness; interruption, break, fracture, fault, flaw, crack, cut; gap, interval, caesura, pause, *(informal)* breather, rest, intermission, parenthesis, episode.

v alternate; discontinue, break, interrupt, intervene; pause, rest, take a breather, stop; break in upon, interpose; disconnect.

adj discontinuous, disconnected, unconnected, broken, interrupted; fitful, spasmodic, desultory, intermittent, irregular; alternate, recurrent, periodic.

adv at intervals, in snatches, by fits and starts.

71 term *n* rank, station, stage, step, phase; scale, grade, degree, status, position, place, point, mark, period, limit; stand, standing, footing.

72 assemblage *n* collection, levee, gathering, ingathering, muster; concourse, conflux, congregation; meeting, reunion; assembly, congress, convention, conclave, council; miscellany, compilation, menagerie; crowd, throng, mob, flood, rush, rash, deluge, press, crush, horde, body, tribe, crew, gang, squad, band, party, swarm, flock, bevy; company, troop, regiment, squadron, army; host, multitude, populace, clan, brotherhood, sisterhood, association; group, cluster, clump, batch, pack, assortment; accumulation, heap, lump, pile, mass, conglomeration, conglomerate, aggregation, aggregate; quantity.

v assemble, come together, collect, gather, muster; meet, unite, join, rejoin; cluster, flock, swarm, surge, stream, herd, crowd, throng, associate; congregate, concentrate, huddle; bring together, draw together, place together, lump together; convene, invoke; compile, group, assemble, unite; amass, accumulate, store.

adj assembled; closely packed, dense, crowded, teeming, swarming, populous.

73 dispersion *n* divergence, spreading, radiation, dissemination, diffusion, dis-

74

sipation, distribution, apportionment, division.

v disperse, scatter, sow, disseminate, diffuse, shed, spread, dispense, disband, distribute, apportion, divide; break up, dispel, cast forth, strew, cast, sprinkle; issue, deal out, dole out.

adj dispersed, spread, scattered, strewn, diffuse, diffusive; sparse, widespread, broadcast; adrift, stray, disheveled.

74 [place of meeting] **focus** *n* center, gathering place, haunt, rendezvous, rallying point, headquarters, club, retreat.

v focus, bring to a point, bring to a focus; center on, bring out, clarify, elucidate.

75 class *n* division, subdivision, category, heading, order, section; department, province, domain; type, kind, sort, genus, species, variety, family, race, tribe, cast, clan, breed, sect.

76 inclusion *n* admission, acceptance into, incorporation, comprehension, reception.

v include, comprise, comprehend, contain, admit, embrace, receive, accept; inclose, circumscribe, encircle, encompass, embody, incorporate; number among, count among, fall under.

adj inclusive, comprehensive, extensive, all-embracing, compendious, sweeping; including, incorporating.

77 exclusion *n* (see 55).

78 generality *n* universality, catholicity, miscellany, miscellaneousness; generalization, simplification, oversimplification; prevalence, common run.

v be general, be universal, prevail, be true for everyone; render general, generalize, universalize; make a generalization, abstract, simplify.

adj general, universal, catholic, common, ecumenical, egalitarian, worldwide; prevalent, prevailing, rife, current; generic, collective, all-encompassing, comprehensive, all-inclusive, broad, widespread.

79 specialty *n* speciality, skill, ability, talent; individuality, singularity, distinctive feature, particularity, personality, characteristic, mannerism, idiosyncrasy, nonconformity; particulars, details, items; special feature.

v specify, particularize, individualize, specialize; designate, determine, single out, isolate, differentiate; be specific, come to the point, detail, get down to particulars.

adj special, particular, especial, individual, specific, proper, personal, original, private, respective, definite, certain, endemic, peculiar, characteristic, marked, appropriate, exclusive, singular, exceptional, idiomatic, unique.

adv specially, especially, in particular; each, apiece, severally, respectively, each to each, each to his own; in detail.

80 regulation *n* regularity, uniformity, constancy, clockwork, precision, exactness; routine, custom, formula, rule, form, procedure; standard, model, precedent, prototype; conformity, convention; nature, law, principle; normal state, ordinary condition, normalcy; hard and fast law.

adj regular, uniform, constant, steady; customary, conventional, formal, formulaic, procedural.

81 multiformity *n* variety, diversity.

adj multifold, multifarious, manifold, many-sided; heterogeneous, motley, mosaic; indiscriminate, irregular, diversified, diverse; of every description, all manner of kinds.

82 conformity *n* observance, compliance, assent; conventionality, customariness, agreement; example, instance, specimen, sample, illustration, exemplification, case in point.

v conform to, accommodate oneself to, adapt to; be regular, conform, follow the rules, obey the rules, go by the rules, comply, assent, agree, yield, give in, accept, harmonize; illustrate, stand as an example, embody.

adj conformable to rule, adaptable, agreeable, compliant, malleable; conventional, customary, standard, ordinary, common, habitual, usual, natural, normal, typical; formal, orthodox, strict, rigid, uncompromising; exemplary, illustrative.

adv by rule, in conformity with, in accordance with, in keeping with, consistent with; for the sake of conformity, as a matter of course, for form's sake; invariably, uniformly.

83 unconformity *n* nonconformity, unconventionality, nonobservance, informality; anomaly, variation, inconsistency, irregularity, incongruity, oddity, eccentricity, peculiarity, aberration, abnormality, exception; violation of custom, infraction, infringement; individuality, originality, mannerism, idiosyncrasy, quirk.

v be unconformable.

adj unconformable, unconventional; unnatural, odd, eccentric, peculiar, aberrant, abnormal, exceptional; anomalous, inconsistent, irregular, incongruous, arbitrary, whimsical, wanton; unusual, uncustomary, uncommon, rare, singular, unique, extraordinary; queer, quaint, strange; original, fantastic, newfangled, bizarre, outlandish, exotic, esoteric.

adv unless, except, save, beside.

V. Number

84 number *n* numeral, symbol, figure, cipher, digit, integer, round number, whole number, fraction; sum, total, product.

adj numeral; prime, fractional, decimal; positive, negative.

85 numeration *n* numbering; tallying, enumeration, reckoning, computation, calculation; arithmetic, calculus, algebra; statistics, poll, census, roll call; arithmetic operations.

v number, count, tell, tally, enumerate, add up, sum, reckon, compute, calculate, take account; muster, poll, recite; add, subtract, multiply, divide.

adj numeral, numerical; arithmetical, analytic, algebraic, statistical, numerable, computable, calculable.

86 list *n* catalog, index, listing, inventory, schedule, register, record, ledger, tally, file, table, calendar; directory, gazette, atlas, dictionary, thesaurus; roll, checklist.

87 unity *n* oneness, singleness, singularity, individuality; unification, unison, uniformity.

v unite, join, combine; isolate, insulate, seclude.

adj one, sole, single, solitary, lone; individual, apart, alone; unaccompanied, unattended, singlehanded, solo; singular, odd, unique; isolated, insular.

adv singly.

88 accompaniment *n* association, partnership, company; accessory, adjunct, concomitant, attachment, complement, attendant, fellow, associate, coexistence.

v accompany, join, escort, convoy, wait on; coexist with, consort with; associate with, couple with.

adj accompanying, fellow, twin, joint; associated with, coupled with; accessory, concomitant, attendant.

adv with, together with, along with, in company with, hand in hand, side by side; therewith, herewith.

89 duality *n* dualism, doubleness, polarity, biformity, duplexity; two, deuce, couple, brace, pair, twins.

v pair, mate, couple, bracket, pair off, yoke.

adj two, twain; dual, twin, two-sided, binary, binomial, duplex; coupled, both.

90 duplication *n* doubling, reduplication; iteration, repetition; renewal.

duplicate, double, copy, carbon, facsimile.

v double; redouble, reduplicate; repeat, renew; duplicate.

adj double; doubled, duplicated; twin, duplicate, second.

adv twice, once more, over again.

91 bisection *n* halving, bifurcation, twofold division, forking, dichotomy, *(informal)* fifty-fifty split.

v bisect, divide in two, halve, divide, split, cut in two, cleave, fork, bifurcate; split down the middle, *(informal)* go halves.

adj bisected, cloven, cleft, halved; bipartite; bifurcated; semi-, demi-, hemi-.

92 triality *n* trinity; three, triad, triplet, trio.

adj three, threefold, triform, tertiary.

93 triplication *n* tripling; triplicity.

v triple, treble, cube.

adj triple, treble; threefold, triplicate; third.

adv three times, thrice; in the third place, thirdly; triply, trebly.

94 trisection *n* tripartition, threefold division, third, third part.
 v trisect, divide into three parts.

95 quaternity *n* four, tetrad, quartet, quarter.
 v square, reduce to a square.
 adj four, fourfold, quadrilateral.

96 quadruplication *n* quadrupling, multiplying by four.
 v multiply by four, quadruplicate.
 adj four, fourfold, quadruple; fourth.
 adv four times, in the fourth place, fourthly.

97 quadrisection *n* quartering, quadripartition, fourfold division; fourth part, quarter.
 v quarter, divide into four parts.
 adj quartered, quadripartite.

98 five, etc. *n* five; six, half a dozen; seven; eight; nine; ten, decade; eleven; twelve, dozen; thirteen, baker's dozen, long dozen; twenty, score; twenty-five, quarter of a hundred; fifty, half a hundred; hundred, century, centenary; thousand.

99 quinquesection *n* fivefold division
 adj quinquepartite.

100 [more than one] **plurality** *n* two or more, couple, few, several; majority, multitude.
 adj plural, more than one, upwards of, some, several, many, numerous.

100a [less than one] **fraction** *n* fractional part, segment, subdivision, part, portion.

101 zero *n* nothing, naught, *(informal)* zip; none, shutout; nobody.

102 multitude *n* multitudinous, multiplicity, profusion, mass, quantity, volume, abundance, amplitude, enormity; numbers, array, scores, droves, host, throng, collection; mob, crowd, assemblage.
 v be numerous, swarm with, teem with, crowd, swarm, outnumber, multiply; people, populate.
 adj multitudinous, manifold, profuse, multiple, teeming, populous, crowded, thick; many, several, sundry, various, numerous; endless, infinite.

103 fewness *n* paucity, scarcity, sparseness, scantiness; small number, small quantity; infrequency.
 diminution of number: reduction, weeding, elimination.
 v render few, reduce, diminish, weed, thin, eliminate, eradicate.
 adj few, not many, scanty, scarce, sparse, rare, few and far between, limited, meager; sporadic, occasional, infrequent; reduced, diminished, pared back.

104 repetition *n* iteration, reiteration, recapitulation, restatement; sameness, monotony, harping, recurrence, tautology; redundance; rhythm, beat, echo, reverberation; reappearance, reproduction, duplication.
 v repeat, iterate, reiterate, recapitulate, restate, rehash, go over again, harp on, hammer; reproduce, duplicate, echo; recur, revert, return, reappear; resume, return to, go back to; rehearse, go over the same ground.
 adj repeated, repetitious, recurrent, recurring, frequent, incessant, neverending, unceasing; repetitive, redundant, tautological; rhythmic, reverberant, reverberating; monotonous, harping, iterative; habitual.
 adv repeatedly, often, again, anew, afresh, over again, once more; over and over, again and again, year after year; ditto, encore.

105 infinity *n* infinitude, infiniteness, perpetuity, endlessness, boundlessness, inexhaustibility, immeasurability, limitlessness, vastness, expanse.
 v be infinite, have no limits, know no bounds, go on forever.
 adj infinite, countless, numberless, limitless, boundless, measureless, unlimited, interminable, inexhaustible, incalculable; immense, vast, endless, perpetual; incomprehensible; eternal, perfect, omnipotent, absolute.
 adv infinitely, *ad infinitum*.

VI. Time

106 time *n* duration, extent; period, interval, spell, term, space, span, season, stage; course; interim, interlude; interregnum, intermission; respite, break, timeout; era, epoch, season, age, year, date.

v time, measure, pace; continue, last, endure, go on, remain, persist, stand; pass time, spend time, while away the time, waste time, kill time, fill up the time.

adj permanent, lasting, durable; timely.

adv while, whilst, during, in the course of, for the time being, in due time; meantime, meanwhile, in the meantime, in the interim; till, until, up to, yet; the whole time, all the time, throughout, for good *(informal)* for keeps.

107 absence of time *n* no time; outside time.

adv never, at no time; on no occasion, nevermore.

108 [definite duration or period of time] **period** *n* interval, age, era, eon, epoch, term, time; year, decade, century, millennium; lifetime, generation.

109 [indefinite duration] **course** *n* march of time, course of time, flux, passing time.

v elapse, lapse, flow, run, proceed, advance, pass, flit, fly, slip, slide, drag, creep, crawl; run its course; expire, go by, pass by.

adv in due time, in due course, in due season, in time.

110 [long duration] **durability** *n* permanence, persistence, continuance, lastingness, standing, stability; survival, longevity; protraction, prolongation.

v last, remain, stand, endure, abide, continue, persist; tarry, drag on, drag out, prolong, protract, eke out, draw out, lengthen; outlive, outlast, survive.

adj permanent, durable, lasting, long-standing, stable, immutable, invariable, constant; enduring, abiding, perpetual; lingering, protracted, prolonged, spun-out.

adv long, for a long time, ever so long; long ago; all day long, all the live-long day.

111 [short duration] **transience** *n* impermanence, evanescence, ephemerality, transitoriness, mortality; suddenness,

swiftness, changeableness, vicissitude, uncertainty.

v be transient, flit, pass away, fly, gallop, vanish, fade, evaporate, melt.

adj transient, transitory, evanescent, ephemeral, fleeting, flitting, flying, passing; impermanent, temporal, temporary, provisional, short-lived; perishable, precarious, vulnerable, mortal; brief, quick, brisk; sudden, momentary, instantaneous.

adv temporarily, for the moment, for a time; awhile, soon; briefly.

112 [endless duration] **perpetuity** *n* eternity, timelessness, everlastingness, endlessness, infinity; constancy, endurance, durability, ceaselessness.

v last forever, endure, go on forever; perpetuate, immortalize, eternalize.

adj perpetual, eternal, timeless, everlasting, endless; unceasing, ceaseless, interminable, neverending, continuous, incessant, uninterrupted; unfading, imperishable, unvulnerable, immortal.

adv perpetually, always, ever, evermore, forever; constantly, continuously.

113 [point of time] **instantaneousness** *n* suddenness, abruptness; moment, instant, second, twinkling, trice, flash, crack, burst.

v be instantaneous, twinkle, flash.

adj instantaneous, momentary, sudden, instant, abrupt.

adv instantaneously, in no time, *(informal)* in two shakes (of a lamb's tail), presto, suddenly, like a shot, in a moment, all of a sudden, in a jiffy; immediately, on the spur of the moment, on a moment's notice.

114 [estimation, measurement and record of time] **chronometry** *n* chronology, timetable; almanac, calendar, register, chronicle, log, annal(s), journal, diary; clock, watch, stopwatch, timepiece, chronometer.

v fix the time, mark the time; date, register, chronicle; measure time, mark time, beat time.

adj chronological.

115 [false estimate of time] **anachronism** *n* misdate, misplacement, chronological error; disregard of time.

v misdate, antedate, postdate, anticipate; take no note of time.

adj misdated; undated, overdue; anachronistic, out of place, misplaced.

116 antecedence *n* priority, anteriority, precedence, pre-existence; antecedent, predecessor, precursor, forerunner.

v precede, antedate, come before; go before, lead, forerun; dawn, presage, herald, break the ground.

adj antecedent, prior, previous, anterior, preceding, pre-existent; former, foregoing, aforementioned; precursory, introductory.

adv before, prior to; earlier, previously, ere, already, yet, beforehand.

117 posteriority *n* succession, sequence; subsequence, following, continuance; successor, sequel, follower; future, futurity.

v follow after, come after, go after, succeed, be subsequent to.

adj posterior, subsequent, following, after, later, succeeding, successive, ensuing, resulting; posthumous.

adv subsequently, after, afterwards, since, later; next, close upon, thereafter, thereupon; ultimately.

118 present time *n* the present juncture, the present day; the times, the time being, right now.

adj present, actual, instant, current, existing.

adv at this time, at this moment; at the present time, now, at present, nowadays.

119 different time *n* other time; another time.

adv at that time, at that instant; then, on that occasion; when, whenever, whensoever; at some other time, at a different time, at some time or other.

120 contemporaneousness *n* simultaneousness, synchronism, simultaneity, coincidence, concurrence, coexistence, concomitance.

v coexist, concur, accompany, go side by side, keep pace with; synchronize.

adj simultaneous, coincident, concurrent, concomitant, coexisting; contemporary, contemporaneous, coeval.

adv simultaneously, concurrently, together, at the same time.

121 the future *n* futurity, hereafter, time to come, tomorrow, morrow; millennium, doomsday, day of judgment, crack of doom, flood; advent, eventuality; destiny, fate; heritage, heirs, posterity; prospect, expectation, anticipation.

v look forward, anticipate, expect, foresee; approach, await, threaten, impend, come near, draw near, come on.

adj future, to come; coming, impending, near, close at hand, in prospect; eventual, ulterior.

adv prospectively, hereafter, in future, in course of time, tomorrow; eventually, ultimately, sooner or later; henceforth, from this time; soon, early, on the eve of, on the point of, on the brink of.

122 the past *n* past time, days of old, days of yore, days gone by, yesterday, yesteryear, former times, ancient times; retrospection, memory; antiquity, history, time immemorial, remote past; ancestry, lineage, forbears; heritage.

v run its course, pass away, pass, lapse, blow over.

adj past, gone, gone by, passed away, bygone, elapsed, lapsed, expired, extinct, forgotten, irrecoverable, obsolete; former, pristine, late; foregoing, last, latter, recent; looking back, retrospective; retroactive.

adv formerly, of old, of yore, ago, over; long ago, years ago, a long while back, some time ago; lately, of late; retrospectively, ere now, before now, hitherto, heretofore; already, yet, up to this time.

123 newness *n* novelty, recentness, freshness; immaturity, greenness, youth, juvenility, innovation, uniqueness, originality; renovation, restoration; modernity, modernism, stylishness, fashionableness, newfangledness, fashion, faddishness, the latest thing, futurism, trendiness.

v renew, renovate, restore; modernize.

adj new, novel, recent, fresh; green, immature, unripe, young, youthful, untried, untested, virgin, virginal; modern, late, new, newfangled, stylish, fashionable, faddish, trendy, brand-new, up-to-date; renovated restored, spick and span.

adv newly, afresh, anew, lately, just now, of late.

124 oldness n age, antiquity; maturity, ripeness; decline, decay, old age, senility, superannuation; archaism, antiquarianism, relic, thing of the past; tradition, custom, common law.

v be old, have had its day, have seen its day; become old, age, fade.

adj old, ancient, antique; time-honored, venerable, traditional, vintage, of long standing; elderly, aged, hoary, decayed, senile, decrepit; primeval, primitive, aboriginal, primordial, antediluvian, prehistoric, archaic; traditional, prescriptive, customary, immemorial, inveterate, rooted; antiquated, outdated, outmoded, of other times; out of date, obsolete, out-of-fashion, out-of-style, gone by, stale, old-fashioned, timeworn, crumbling, ramshackle, run-down, wasted.

125 morning. noon n morning, morn, dawn, daybreak, sunrise, sunup, forenoon, break of day, peep of day, prime of day, morningtide, matins, cockcrow, first blush, antemeridian, A.M.

noon, midday, noonday, noontide, meridian, prime, height, noontime.

spring, springtime; summer, summertime, midsummer.

126 evening. midnight n evening, eve, eventide, dusk, vespers, nightfall, sundown, sunset, twilight, curfew, bedtime; afternoon, post meridian, P.M.

midnight, end of the day, close of the day, witching hour, dead of night.

autumn, fall, harvest time; winter.

127 youth n juvenility, infancy childhood, boyhood, girlhood; minority, tender years, young years, formative years, never generation, tender age; cradle, nursery; puberty.

adj young, youthful, juvenile, green, callow, budding, immature, developing, underage, formative; younger, junior.

128 age n old age, advanced age, senility, years, gray hairs, declining years, golden years, mature years, decrepitude, anility, superannuation, longevity, ripe age, ripe old age; maturity, seniority, eldership.

adj aged, old, advanced, gray, elderly; senile, decline, failing, waning, ripe, overripe, mellow, venerable, wrinkled, wizened; older, elder, eldest.

129 infant n baby, babe, babe in arms, nursling, little one, tot, toddler, chick, kid, lamb, cherub; youth, youngster, child, minor; girl, lass, maiden, miss, schoolgirl; boy, lad, stripling, master, schoolboy.

adj infantile, infantlike, puerile, girlish, boyish, childish, babyish; newborn, young.

130 veteran n old man, old woman, patriarch, matriarch, grandmother, grandfather, grandsire, seer, graybeard, forefather, elder.

adj aged, old.

131 adolescence n majority, adulthood, manhood, womanhood, maturity, ripeness, fullness, puberty, pubescence; teenage years, prepubescence.

v come of age, grow up, attain majority.

adj adolescent, teenage, pubescent, of age, grown up, full grown, adult, womanly, manly, marriageable, nubile.

132 earliness n punctuality, promptitude, speediness, readiness, expedition, alacrity, quickness, haste; suddenness; prematurity, precocity, precipitation, anticipation.

v be early, be beforehand; anticipate, forestall, steal a march on, get a head start; bespeak, secure, engage, pre-engage; accelerate, expedite, quicken, hasten, make haste, make time, hurry.

adj early, timely, punctual, on time, prompt; premature, precipitate, precocious, anticipatory; sudden, instantaneous, immediate, expeditious; unexpected.

adv early, soon, anon, betimes, before long; punctually, to the minute, on time, on the dot; beforehand, prematurely, precipitately, too soon, hastily, in anticipation, unexpectedly; suddenly, instantaneously, at short notice, on the spur of the moment; at once, on the spot, on the instant, at sight, straight, offhand, straightway; forthwith, summarily, immediately, shortly, quickly, speedily; presently, by and by, directly.

133 lateness n tardiness, slowness, sloth, tarrying, dilly-dallying, loitering; delay, procrastination, postponement, adjournment, retardation, protraction, prolongation; respite, reprieve, suspension, moratorium, stop, stay.

v be late, tarry, wait, stay, bide, take time, linger, loiter, dawdle, shilly-shally, dilly-dally; put off, defer, delay, lay over, suspend; retard, postpone, adjourn; procrastinate, prolong, protract, drag out, draw out, lengthen, table, shelve, stall.

adj late, tardy, slow, dilatory, backward, unpunctual; delayed, overdue, belated.

adv late; backward, at the eleventh hour, at length, at last; ultimately, behind time; too late; slowly, leisurely, deliberately, at one's leisure, on one's own time.

134 opportuneness *n* timeliness, opportunity, occasion, suitable time, proper time, suitability, high time; crisis, turn, juncture; turning point, given time; nick of time, golden opportunity; clear stage, open field.

v be opportune, be suitable; seize the opportunity, seize the time, seize the day, *carpe diem,* use the occasion; suit the occasion, be expeditious, strike while the iron is hot.

adj opportune, timely, well-timed, seasonable, suitable, appropriate; providential, lucky, fortunate, happy, favorable, fortuitous, propitious, auspicious.

adv opportunely, in due time, in the nick of time, just in time, now or never; by the way, by the by, speaking of, while on the subject; on the spot, on the spur of the moment, since the occasion presents itself.

135 inopportuneness *n* untimeliness, unseasonableness, improper time, unsuitable time; *(informal)* bad timing; intrusion; anachronism.

v be ill timed, mistime, intrude, break in upon, *(informal)* butt in; lose an opportunity, waste an occasion, *(informal)* blow one's chance, let the opportunity slip by; waste time.

adj inopportune, untimely, unpropitious, unseasonable, unsuitable, inauspicious, unfavorable, unfortunate, unsuited, untoward, unlucky; ill-timed, mistimed, poorly timed; unpunctual; premature.

136 frequency *n* repetition, recurrence, iteration, reinteration.

v recur, repeat, reiterate; keep on, continue; attend regularly, visit often, patronize.

adj frequent, oft-repeated, recurring, incessant, constant, continual, perpetual; habitual, customary.

adv often, oft, oftentimes, frequently, repeatedly, day after day; daily, hourly, every day; perpetually, continually, constantly, incessantly, at all times; commonly, habitually, customarily; sometimes, occasionally, at times, now and then, every once in a while, from time to time.

137 infrequency *n* rarity, rare occurrence; long shot, surprise, *(informal)* mindblower.

v be rare, be infrequent.

adj infrequent, occasional, sporadic, rare, uncommon, unusual, unheard of, unprecedented; few, scant, scarce.

adv infrequently, rarely, seldom, scarcely, hardly; not often, hardly ever.

138 regularity [of recurrence] *n* periodicity, intermittence; beat, pulse, pulsation, rhythm; alternation, oscillation, vibration; bout, round, turn, revolution, rotation, rpm; cycle, period, routine; punctuality, regularity, steadiness.

v recur, revolve, return, come in its turn, come round again; beat, pulsate, alternate.

adj regular, periodic, periodical; serial, recurrent, cyclical, cyclic, recurring, rhythmical, rhythmic; intermittent, alternate, every other; regular, steady, punctual, continual, constant, regular as clockwork.

adv regularly, periodically, serially, cyclically; intermittently, alternately; by turns, in turn, in rotation, off and on, round and round.

139 irregularity [of recurrence] *n* uncertainty, unpredictability, haphazardness, fitfulness, capriciousness.

v be irregular, be haphazard.

adj irregular, uncertain, unpredictable, haphazard, fitful, capricious, flickering; spasmodic, sporadic.

adv irregularly, fitfully, capriciously, by fits and starts.

VII. Change

140 change *n* alteration, modulation, modification, variation, mutation, permutation, qualification, deviation, turn, shift, innovation; diversion, break; transformation, transfiguration, transmutation, metamorphosis; conversion, revolution, inversion, reversal; displacement, transference, transposition; changeableness.

v change, alter, vary, modulate, qualify, diversify, tamper with, play with, experiment with; turn, shift, veer, tack, swerve, warp, deviate, turn aside; turn, take a turn, *(informal)* hang a turn; modify, revamp, transform, transfigure, transmute, metamorphose, convert; innovate, restructure, give a new turn to, recast, redesign, remodel.

adj changed, newfangled; changeable, variable, transformable; innovative.

141 permanence *n* stability, invariability, unalterability, immutability, constancy; endurance, durability, persistence; maintenance, preservation, conservation; obstinacy, immovability, inflexibility, immobility, rigidity.

v endure, bide, abide, stay, remain, last, persist, stand, stand fast; maintain, keep, keep up, preserve; subsist, live, outlive, survive.

adj permanent, lasting, unchanged, unchanging, fixed, stable, invariable, constant; enduring, durable, abiding, everlasting; intact, inviolate; persistent.

adv permanently, for good, for good and all.

142 cessation *n* discontinuation, discontinuance, halt, stoppage, termination, suspension, interruption, stopping; pause, rest, lull, respite, truce, break; interregnum, abeyance; completion, end, finish; stop, death.

v cease, discontinue, terminate, desist, stay; break off, leave off, hold, stop, pull up, stop short, halt, pause, rest; suspend, interrupt, delay, cut short, arrest, bring to a standstill; complete; end, finish, close up shop; wear away, go out, die out, pass away, die.

143 continuance [in action] *n* continuation, continuity, protraction, prolongation, maintenance, perpetuation; persistence, perseverance, repetition.

v continue, persist, go on, keep on, hold on; abide, keep, pursue, stick to; maintain course, carry on, keep up; sustain, uphold, hold up, keep going, maintain, preserve, perpetuate, prolong.

adj continuing, uninterrupted, unvarying; continuous, persistent, perpetual.

144 conversion *n* transformation, transmutation, reduction, change, changeover, resolution, assimilation; passage, transit, transition, shifting, flux; growth, progress, development; chemistry, alchemy.

v be converted into, become, turn into, lapse, shift; pass into, grow into, ripen into, merge into; melt, grow, ripen, mature, mellow; convert into, resolve into; make, render; mold, form, model, remodel, remake, do over, reform, reorganize; assimilate, bring into, reduce to.

adj convertible, transmutable, changeable.

145 reversion *n* return, revulsion, reverting, returning; alternation, rotation; inversion; recoil, reaction, reflex, repercussion, rebound, boomerang, ricochet, backlash, repulse; retrospection, retrogression, retrogradation, falling back; restoration, going back; turning point, turn of the tide.

v revert, return, turn back, reverse; relapse, regress, fall back; recoil, rebound; retreat; restore; undo, unmake; turn the tide.

146 [sudden or violent change] **revolution** *n* revolt, rebellion, overthrow, overturn, coup, *coup d'état*, rising, uprising, mutiny, counterrevolution; breakup, destruction, subversion, clean sweep; spasm, convulsion, throe, revulsion.

v revolt, rebel, rise, rise up; revolutionize, remodel, recast, change.

adj revolutionary, rebellious; new.

147 substitution *n* replacement, supplanting, commutation, exchange, change, shift.

substitute, expedient, makeshift, stopgap, equivalent, double, alternative, representative.

v substitute, put in the place of, change, exchange, interchange; replace, supplant, supersede, take the place of, stand for, represent, pinch hit, substitute for, sub; redeem, commute, alternate.

adv instead, in place of, in lieu of.

148 [double or mutual change] **interchange** *n* exchange, commutation, permutation, transposition; reciprocation, reciprocity, intercourse; barter, swap, trade; interchangeability; retaliation, reprisal, requital, retort, crossfire.

v interchange, exchange, barter, trade, swap, bandy, transpose, commute, reciprocate; give and take, battle with words; retort, requite, retaliate.

adj interchangeable, all-purpose, multi-purpose; reciprocal; mutual.

adv in exchange, vice versa, turn and turn about.

149 changeableness *n* mutability, inconstancy, volatility, instability; malleability, adaptability, versatility, mobility; vacillation, irresolution, indecision, capriciousness, oscillation, alternation, fluctuation, vicissitude; restlessness, fidgetiness, disquiet, disquietude; unrest, agitation.

v fluctuate, oscillate, vary, waver, flounder, shuffle, hem and haw, vacillate, tremble, alternate.

adj changeable, mutable, variable, malleable, adaptable, adjustable, versatile, mobile, transformable, convertible; inconstant, unsteady, unstable, unreliable, vacillating, oscillating, fluctuating; volatile, fitful, fickle, capricious, mercurial, indecisive, irresolute, flighty, impulsive, fanciful, erratic, wayward, wanton; restless, fidgety, tremulous, agitated; unfixed, unsettled.

150 stability *n* immutability, unchangeableness, constancy; firmness, fixity, solidity, steadiness, soundness, balance, stabilization, equilibrium, quiescence; immobility, immovability, fixedness; steadfastness, reliability, resolution, determination, obstinacy, stubbornness, pertinacity, tenacity, doggedness, will, pluck, resoluteness; permanence, endurance, perseverance, durability; continuity, uniformity changelessness.

v be firm, stick fast, stand firm; settle, establish, fix, set, stabilize; retain, keep hold; make sure, fasten, make solid.

adj stable, fixed, rigid, firm, steady, established, strong, sturdy, immovable, invariable, unvarying, permanent, unchangeable, unchanging, unalterable, immutable; enduring, constant, durable, lasting, abiding, secure, fast, perpetual; unwavering, steadfast, staunch, reliable, steady, solid, sound, balanced; resolute, obstinate, dogged, willful, stubborn, pertinacious, tenacious.

151 present events *n* event, occurrence, incident, affair, eventuality, happening, proceeding, transaction, fact; phenomenon; circumstance, situation, particular; adventure, episode, thrill; crisis, pass, emergency, contingency, impasse; things, doings, affairs, matters, issues; the world, life, the times.

v happen, occur, take place, come to pass, take place, come about, come round; fall out, turn out, befall, chance, prove, eventuate; turn up, crop up, arise, arrive, issue, ensue, start, hold; take its course, pass off; experience, meet with, meet up with, fall to, be one's lot, be one's fortune, find, encounter, undergo, go through, live through, endure, put up with.

adj happening, going on, doing, current; eventful, stirring, bustling, busy, full of incident.

adv eventually, finally; as things go, in the course of things, as it happens.

152 future events *n* destiny, luck, lot, chance, fortune, karma, doom, end; future, futurity, next world, hereafter; prospects, expectations, tomorrow.

v impend, hang over, hover, threaten, loom, await, come on, approach; foreordain, preordain; destine, predestine, doom, have in store for.

adj impending, destined; coming, in store, to come, at hand, near, close by, imminent, brewing, forthcoming; in the wind, in the cards, in prospect, looming, on the horizon.

adv in time, in the long run, in good time, in its own sweet time, eventually.

VIII. Causation

153 cause *n* origin, source, principle, element; prime mover, first cause; author, producer, creator; mainspring, agent, catalyst; groundwork, foundation, support; spring, fountain, well, fount, font; genesis, descent, remote cause, influence; pivot, hinge, axis, turning point; egg, germ, embryo, root, nucleus, seed; causality, causation, origination, production.

v cause, originate, give rise to, occasion, sow the seeds of, kindle, bring to pass, bring about; produce, create, set up, develop; found, broach, institute; induce, evoke, elicit, draw, provoke; determine, decide; conduce to, contribute, have a hand in, influence, effect.

adj causal, generative, productive, formative, creative; primal, primary, original, embryonic.

adv because.

154 effect *n* consequence, issue, derivation, upshot, outgrowth, development, fruit, crop, harvest, product, outcome, end, conclusion; offspring, offshoot; complications, concomitants, side effects.

v be the effect of, be due to, be owing to; originate in, originate from, rise from, spring from, proceed from, emanate from, come from, grow from, issue from, flow from, result from; depend upon, hinge upon.

adj owing to, resulting from, due to, derivable from, caused by; derived from, evolved from; derivative, hereditary.

adv consequently, as a consequence, necessarily.

155 [assignment of cause] **attribution** *n* theory, ascription, assignment, rationale, reference to, accounting for; imputation, derivation; explanation, interpretation, reason why.

v attribute to, ascribe to, impute to, refer to, point to, trace to, assign to; account for, derive from; theorize, speculate.

adj attributed, attributable, referable, due to, owing to.

adv hence, thence, therefore, *ergo*, for, since, on account of, because; why? wherefore? whence? how come? how so?

156 [absence of assignable cause] **chance** *n* fortune, fate, accident, hap, hazard, luck, fluke, *(informal)* freak; gamble, lottery, tossup, fifty-fifty chance, throw of the dice, heads or tails; probability, possibility, contigency, odds; speculation, gaming, gambling.

v chance, hap, turn up; fall to one's lot; stumble on, light on; take one's chances.

adj chancy, causal, fortuitous, accidental, *(informal)* iffy, adventitious, haphazard, random, indeterminate, flukey, *(informal)* freaky.

adv by chance, by accident; at random; perchance, as chance will have it.

157 power *n* potency, strength, puissance, might, force, energy, vigor; control, command, dominion, authority, rule, sway, ascendancy, sovereignty, omnipotence; ability, capability, capacity, facility, competence, competency, efficacy; validity, cogency.

v be powerful, control, command, rule; confer power, empower, invest, endow; arm, strengthen, authorize; compel, force.

adj powerful, potent, strong, mighty, energetic; able, capable, competent, efficacious, equal to, up to, effective, efficient, adequate; omnipotent, almighty; influential, forceful.

adv powerfully.

prep by virtue of, by dint of.

158 impotence *n* inability, incapability, incapacity, infirmity, debility, disability; inefficacy, inefficiency, incompetence, ineptitude, feebleness, weakness, frailty, powerlessness; helplessness, prostration, paralysis, collapse, exhaustion; decrepitude, senility; sexual failure, barrenness.

v be impotent; collapse, faint, swoon, drop; render powerless, disable, disarm, incapacitate, disqualify, invalidate; cramp, tie the hands, paralyze, muzzle; cripple, maim, lame, hamstring, throttle, strangle, tie up in knots; unman, unnerve, enervate; shatter, exhaust, weaken; emasculate.

adj impotent, powerless, incapable, unable, incompetent, ineffective, inefficient, ineffectual, inept, unfit, unfitted, unqualified; disabled, incapacitated, crippled, paralyzed, paralytic; decrepit, senile, exhausted, worn out, used up, limp, spent; weak, frail, infirm, feeble, helpless; harmless; sterile, barren, frigid; emasculated, inadequate, inoperative; futile, fruitless, bootless, vain.

159 strength *n* power, force, might, vigor, health, stoutness, hardiness, lustihood, stamina, energy, potency, capacity; spring, bounce, tone, elasticity, tension; virility, vitality, nerve, verve; strengthening, invigoration, refreshment.

v strengthen, invigorate, brace, nerve, fortify, sustain, harden, steel; vivify, revivify, refresh, reinforce, restore.

adj strong, mighty, vigorous, forceful, hard, stout, robust, sturdy, hardy, powerful, potent, puissant; irresistible, invincible, indomitable, unconquerable, impregnable, inextinguishable, incontestable; able-bodied, athletic, muscular, sinewy, strapping, gigantic, Herculean.

adv strongly, by force.

160 weakness *n* debility, relaxation, languor, enervation; impotence, infirmity, fragility, flaccidity; frailty, delicacy, softness; senility, decrepitude.

v be weak, drop, crumble, give way, teeter, totter, tremble, shake, halt, limp, fade, languish, decline, flag, fail; weaken, enfeeble, cramp, debilitate, shake, enervate, unnerve; relax; dilute, water down.

adj weak, feeble, infirm, sickly; languid, faint, dull, slack, spent; limp, flaccid, powerless, impotent; relaxed, unstrung, unnerved; frail, fragile, delicate, flimsy; rickety, drooping, teetering, tottering, withered, shaky, shattered; palsied, decrepit, lame; decayed, rotten, worn, seedy, wasted, laid low.

161 production *n* creation, formation, fabrication, construction, manufacture; building, architecture, erection; organization, establishment; workmanship, craftsmanship, performance; achievement, product, end result; flowering, fructification, fruition, fulfillment; gestation, evolution, development, growth; gensis, generation, procreation; authorship, publication, works, *oeuvre*.

v produce, perform, operate, do, make, form, construct, fabricate, frame, contrive, manufacture; build, raise, rear, erect, put up; set up, establish, constitute, compose, organize, institute; achieve, accomplish, fulfill; bud, flower, blossom, bloom, bear fruit, bring forth; propagate, beget, generate, procreate, engender; breed, hatch, develop, bring up; induce, cause.

adj productive, constructive, formative, creative; generative; prolific, blooming.

162 [nonproduction] **destruction** *n* waste, dissolution, breaking up, disruption; consumption; fall, downfall, ruin, perdition; breakdown, wreck, wrack, havoc, mess, chaos, cataclysm; desolation, extinction, annihilation; demolition; overthrow, subversion, suppression; dilapidation, devastation, road to ruin.

v perish, fall, tumble, topple, fall to pieces, break up, crumble, go to the dogs, go to wrack and ruin; destroy, do away with, demolish, tear up, overturn, overthrow, wipe out, *(informal)* waste; upset, subvert, undo; waste, squander, dissipate, dispel, dissolve; smash, squash, squelch, shatter, crumble, batter, crush, pull to pieces; fell, sink, scuttle, wreck, swamp, ruin, raze, level, expunge, erase, sweep away; lay waste, ravage, gut; disorganize, dismantle, take apart; devour, devastate, desolate, sap, exterminate, extinguish, stamp out, trample out, crush out, eradicate.

adj destructive, subversive, ruinous, incendiary, deadly, lethal, fatal; destroyed, wiped out, extinct.

163 reproduction *n* renovation, restoration, renewal, revival, regeneration, revivification, resuscitation, reanimation, resurrection; reappearance; generation, childbirth.

v reproduce, renovate, restore, renew, revive, regenerate, revivify, resuscitate, breathe new life into, reanimate, refashion, resurrect, bring back to life; give birth to, multiply, people the world.

adj reproductive; regenerative, restorative; renascent, reappearing, resurgent.

164 producer *n* originator, inventor, author, founder, generator, mover, creator maker, architect; backer, angel.

165 destroyer *n* spoiler, waster, ravager, wrecker, killer, assassin, executioner;

cankerworm, bane; iconoclast, rebel, pessimist, cynic, nihilist, misanthrope.

166 parentage n family, ancestry, lineage, genealogy; procreator, progenitor.

paternity: fatherhood, fathership; father, dad, pop, sire, papa, *(informal)* old man; grandfather, grandsire.

maternity: motherhood; mother, mom, ma, mamma, mummy, mum, *(informal)* old lady; grandmother.

adj parental, familial, ancestral, lineal, paternal, maternal; patriarchal, matriarchal.

167 posterity n progeny, breed, issue, offspring, brood, litter, family, children, grandchildren, heirs; child, son, daughter; descendant, heir, scion, *(informal)* chip off the old block; heredity.

adj filial.

168 productiveness n fecundity, fertility, fruitfulness, productivity; multiplication, propagation, procreation; creativity, inventiveness, originality.

v make productive, fructify, fulfill; procreate, generate, conceive, impregnate, fertilize; teem, multiply, produce, reproduce.

adj productive, prolific, fruitful, copious; teeming, fertile, fecund; procreative, generative, life-giving.

169 unproductiveness n infertility, sterility, barrenness, unfruitfulness, impotence; unprofitableness, wastefulness.

v be unproductive, do nothing, produce nothing, come to nothing.

adj unproductive, unfruitful, infertile, barren, sterile, arid; unprofitable, useless.

170 agency n operation, force, working, function, office, maintenance, exercise, work, play; causation, instigation, instrumentality, influence.

v operate, work, do; act, perform, play, support, sustain, maintain, take effect, quicken, strike; come into play, have free play; bring to bear upon, influence.

adj operative, efficient, efficacious, effectual, practical; at work, on foot, in operation, in force, in play, in action.

adv through the agency of, by means of.

171 energy n force, power, strength, intensity, vigor, zeal, dynamism, pep, fire, spirit, ebullience, life; activity, agitation, exertion, effervescence, ferment, fermentation, ebullition, bustle.

v give energy, energize, stimulate kindle, excite, inflame, exert; strengthen, invigorate; sharpen, intensify.

adj energetic, strong, forcible, potent, forceful, active, powerful, intense, vigorous, zealous, dynamic, ebullient, spirited, animated, keen, vivid, sharp, acute, incisive trenchant, biting; invigorating, rousing, stimulating; energized.

172 inertness n inertia, inactivity, torpor, languor, dullness, immobility, passivity, passiveness, lifelessness; quiescence, latency; inexcitability, sloth, indolence, irresolution, indecisiveness, cowardice, spinelessness.

v be inert, be inactive.

adj inert, inactive, immobile, unmoving, motionless, lifeless, passive, dead; sluggish, dull, heavy, flat, slack, tame, slow, blunt, torpid, languid; latent, dormant, sleeping, smoldering, quiescent.

adv in suspense, in abeyance.

173 violence n vehemence, fury, ferocity, impetuosity, boisterousness, turbulence, ebullition, effervescence, intensity, severity, acuteness; energy, force, might; fit, paroxysm, orgasm, spasm, convulsion, throe; exacerbation, exasperation, hysterics, excitability, passion; outbreak, outburst, uproar, riot, explosion, blow-up, blast, eruption; turmoil, disorder, ferment, agitation, storm, tempest; destruction, brutality, fighting, combat, warfare, hostilities; injury, wrong, outrage, injustice.

v be violent, ferment, effervesce; romp, rampage, run wild, run riot, rush, tear, run headlong, run amuck, go wild, kick up a row, *(informal)* flip out, go beserk; bluster, rage, roar, riot, storm, boil, boil over, fume, foam; explode, go off, detonate, thunder, blow up, flare, burst; render violent, sharpen, stir up, quicken, excite, incite, urge, lash, whip up, stimulate; irritate, inflame, kindle, accelerate, aggravate, exasperate, exacerbate, convulse, infuriate, madden, fan the fire, whip into a frenzy.

adj violent, vehement, acute, sharp; rough, rude, bluff, boisterous, brusque, abrupt, wild, impetuous, rampant; disorderly, turbulent, blustering, raging, riotous, tumultuous, obstreperous; raving, frenzied, *(informal)* freaked, mad, unhinged, insane; desperate, furious, frantic, hysterical; savage, fierce, ferocious, physical, brutal, combative; uncontrollable, ungovernable, irrepressible, excited; spasmodic, convulsive, orgasmic; explosive, volcanic, stormy.

adv violently; by storm, by force.

174 moderation *n* temperateness, temperance, reasonableness, judiciousness, deliberateness, fairness; gentleness, mildness, calmness, peacefulness; quiet, calm, composure; lenity, lenience; relaxation, assuagement, tranquilization, pacification, mitigation; measure, middle ground, middle of the road.

v moderate, ally, meliorate, calm, pacify, assuage, lull, smooth, compose, still, calm, quiet, hush, sober, mitigate, soften, mollify, temper, qualify, alleviate, appease, lessen, abate, diminish; slake, curb, tame; arbitrate, referee, umpire, regulate.

adj moderate, temperate, reasonable, judicious, deliberate, fair, gentle, mild, calm, cool, sober, measured, unruffled, quiet, tranquil, still, peaceful, pacific; unexciting, even, smooth, bland, palliative; lenient, relaxed, easy going.

adv moderately, in moderation, within reason.

175 influence *n* importance, weight, pressure, preponderance, prevalence, sway; predominance, ascendancy; dominance, reign, rule, authority, power, control, capability; input, *(informal)* say, persuasion, play, leverage, vantage ground; patronage, protection, auspices.

v be influential, have a say, have input, carry weight, affect, sway, impress, bias, direct, control; move, activate, incite, impel, rouse, arouse, induce, persuade; dominate, predominate, outweigh, override, prevail.

adj influential, important, weighty; prevalent, rife, rampant, dominant, predominant; potent, powerful, effective, authoritative.

175a absence of influence *n* impotence, powerlessness; unimportance, irrelevancy.

adj uninfluential, unpersuasive, weak, impotent, *(informal)* wishy-washy.

176 tendency *n* aptness, aptitude, disposition, predisposition, proclivity, proneness, propensity, susceptibility, inclination, leaning, bias, drift, trend, bent, turn; quality, nature, temperament; idiosyncrasy, cast, vein, mood, humor.

v tend, contribute, conduce, lead, dispose, incline, verge, bend to, gravitate toward, lean, drift, tend, affect; promote, influence.

adj tending, leaning; conducive, working toward, in a fair way to; liable, likely; influential, instrumental, useful, subsidiary, subservient.

177 liability *n* susceptibility, penchant, vulnerability, predilection, propensity, tendency; drawback, hindrance, obstacle, difficulty, impediment; responsibility, obligation, debt, debit, indebtedness, pledge.

v be liable, incur, lay oneself open to, run the risk of, stand a chance, expose oneself to.

adj liable, subject, exposed, likely, open, in danger of; obliged, responsible, accountable, answerable; contingent, incidental, possible.

178 concurrence *n* accordance, accord, agreement, consent, assent; cooperation, collaboration, partnership, alliance, concert, union.

v concur, conduce, conspire, contribute; agree, unite, combine, hang together, pull together, cooperate, collaborate; keep pace with, run parallel, go hand in hand with.

adj concurrent, cooperative, collaborative, joint, allied with, of one mind, at one with, in concert with.

179 counteraction *n* opposition, antagonism, contrariety, polarity; clashing, collision, interference, resistance, friction; reaction, response, counterblast, counter maneuver; neutralization, check, curb, hindrance; repression, restraint.

v counteract, run counter to, clash, cross, interfere with, conflict with; jostle, run up against, oppose, antagonize, withstand, resist, hinder, impede, check, curb, repress, restrain; recoil, react; neutralize, nullify, cancel out, undercut, undermine, undo; counterpoise offset, balance out, compensate.

adj counteracting, antagonistic, conflicting, contrary, reactionary.

adv although.

prep in spite of, against.

Class II

Words Relating to Space

I. Space in General

180 [indefinite space] **space** *n* extension, extent, expanse, span, stretch, scope, range, latitude, spread, proportions, sweep, capacity, play, swing, expansion; elbowroom, room, breathing space, leeway; open space(s), free space, waste, desert, wild, wilderness; unlimited space, wide world, heavens, universe, solar system, outer space, abyss, the void, infinity.

adj spacious, roomy, extensive, expansive, capacious, ample; widespread, vast, worldwide, boundless, limitless, unlimited, infinite.

adv extensively, far and wide, right and left, from the four corners of the world, all over, from pole to pole, under the sun, on the face of the earth, from all points of the compass, to the four winds.

180a inextension *n* nonextension, point, atom.

181 [definite space] **region** *n* sphere, ground, soil, area, realm, quarter, orb, hemisphere, circuit, circle; domain, tract, territory, country, county, province; clime, climate, zone, meridian, latitude.

adj regional, provincial, territorial.

182 [limited space] **place** *n* spot, point; niche, nook, hole, pigeonhole; locality; locale, situation.

adv somewhere, in some place, here and there, in various places.

183 situation *n* position, locality, locale, latitude and longitude, location; footing, standing, standpoint; aspect, attitude, posture, perspective, pose; place, site, station, post, predicament, whereabouts; bearings, direction; topography, geography; map, chart.

v be situated, be located, lie, have its seat in; situate, locate.

adj situated, located; local, topical, topographical.

adv here and there, hereabouts, thereabouts, in such and such a place.

184 location *n* place, situation; establishment, settlement, installation; anchorage, mooring, encampment.

v locate, place, situate, put, lay, set, make a place for, seat; station, lodge, quarter, house, post, install; establish, fix, settle, root; graft, plant; inhabit, domesticate, colonize, take root, establish roots, come to rest, settle down, take up quarters, locate oneself, relocate; squat, perch, bivouac, burrow, get a footing, encamp.

adj located, placed, ensconced, rooted, settled, moored.

185 displacement *n* dislocation, misplacement, derangement, transposition; ejection, expulsion, banishment, removal, exile.

v displace, dislodge, disestablish; misplace, disturb, disorder, unsettle, derange, confuse; transpose, set aside, transfer, remove, unload, empty, eject, expel, banish, exile; vacate, depart, leave.

adj displaced; unplaced, unhoused, unsettled, unestablished; homeless, out of place, misplaced, out of its element.

186 presence *n* attendance, company; occupancy, occupation; ubiquity, omnipresence, permeation, pervasion, pervasiveness, diffusion, dispersion; nearness, vicinity, proximity, closeness.

v be present; look on, attend, stand by, remain, find oneself; occupy, inhabit, dwell, stay, sojourn, live, abide, lodge, nestle, roost, perch, tenant; fill, pervade, permeate, run through.

adj present, attending; occupying, inhabiting, resident, moored; ubiquitous, omnipresent, pervasive, diffused; near close, in proximity.

adv here, there, and everywhere; in presence of.

187 absence *n* nonappearance, nonattendance, absenteeism, nonresidence; emptiness, void, vacuum, vacancy, vacuity.

v be absent; keep away, play truant, absent oneself, stay away.

adj absent, not present, away, out, not here, not in, not present, off; wanting, lacking, missing, nonexistent; vacant, empty, void, vacuous, devoid.

adv without, minus, nowhere, *sans;* elsewhere.

188 inhabitant *n* resident, dweller, occupant; tenant, inmate, boarder, lodger; native, townsman, villager, citizen; population, community, society, state, people, race, nation.

v inhabit, live, reside, dwell.

adj indigenous, native, domestic.

189 habitation *n* abode, residence, domicile, lodging, dwelling, address, habitation, housing, quarters; home, homestead, motherland, fatherland, country; nest, lair, den, cave, hole, hiding place, cell, hive, haunt, habitat, perch, roost, retreat, *(informal)* pad, *(informal)* crashpad.

v inhabit, take up one's abode.

190 [things contained] **contents** *n* stuffing, cargo, lading, freight, shipment, haul, load, bale, burden.

v load, lade, ship, haul, charge, fill, stuff.

191 receptacle *n* container, holder, repository, vessel, receiver, depository, reservoir; storage areas; bulk containers; liquid containers; wrapping.

II. Dimensions

192 size *n* proportions, dimensions, magnitude, bulk, volume; largeness, greatness; expanse, amplitude, mass; capacity, tonnage; corpulence, obesity, plumpness; hugeness, enormousness, immensity; monstrosity, enormity; giant, monster, mammoth, behemoth, leviathan, elephant; lump, bulk, block, mass, clod, thumper, whopper, strapper, *(informal)* mother, mountain, mound, heap.

v be large; become large, expand.

adj sizable, large, big, great, considerable, bulky, voluminous, ample, massive, massy; capacious, comprehensive, spacious; mighty, towering, magnificent; corpulent; stout, fat, plump, obese, portly; full-grown, stalwart, brawny; hulky, unwieldy, bulky, lumpish, whopping, thundering, thumping; overgrown; huge, immense, enormous, mighty, vast, amplitudinous, stupendous; monstrous, gigantic, colossal.

193 littleness *n* smallness, diminutiveness, tininess; epitome; microcosm; vanishing point.

v be little; become little, decrease.

adj little, small, minute, diminutive, microscopic, submicroscopic; tiny, puny, wee, miniature, pigmy, dwarf, undersized, underdeveloped, dwarfish, stunted, dumpy, squat; imperceptible, invisible, infinitesimal.

194 expansion *n* increase, enlargement, extension, growth, development; augmentation, aggrandizement, increment, amplification; spreading, swelling, distention, puffiness, dropsy.

v expand, wide, enlarge, extend, grow, increase, swell, fill out; dilate, stretch, spread; bud, sprout, shoot, germinate, open, burst forth; outgrow, overrun; spread, extend, aggrandize; distend, develop, amplify, spread out, magnify; inflate, puff up, blow up, stuff, pad, cram, fatten; exaggerate.

adj expanded, larger; swollen, expansive, widespread, overgrown, exaggerated, bloated, fat, turgid, tumid, dropsical; pot-bellied, chubby, corpulent, obese, heavy; full-blown, full-grown.

195 contraction *n* reduction, diminution; decrease, lessening, shrinking; collapse, emancipation, attenuation, atrophy; condensation, compression, compactness, compendium, squeezing.

v contract, become small, lessen, decrease, dwindle, shrink, narrow, shrivel, collapse, wither, wizen, fall away, waste, wane, ebb, decay, deteriorate; diminish, contract, draw in, constrict, condense, compress, squeeze, crush, crumple up, pinch, squash, cramp; pare, reduce, attenuate, scrape, file, grind, chip, shave, shear, cut down; circumscribe, limit, restrain, confine.

adj contracting, astringent; shrunk, shrunken, contracted; wizened, stunted, waning; compact.

196 distance *n* remoteness, farness, background, offing, far cry to, horizon, elongation; interval, remove, gap, span, reach, range; outpost, outskirts, foreign parts.

v be distant; extend to, stretch to, reach to, spread to; range.

adj distant, far off, far away, remote, far, afar, outlying, removed, at a distance, away, younder, yon; inaccessible, out of the way, unapproachable.

adv far off, far away, afar, away, a long way off.

197 nearness *n* closeness, propinquity, proximity, proximation; vicinity, neighborhood, contiguity; short distance, earshot, close quarters, stone's throw, gunshot, hair's breadth; approach, access.

v be near, adjoin, neighbor, border upon, touch, stand next to; approximate, come close to, resemble; converge, crowd.

adj near, high, close, neighboring, adjoining, adjacent, bordering; proximate, approximate; at hand, handy; intimate.

adv near, nigh, hard by, close to, close upon, within reach, at one's fingertips.

198 interval *n* separation, space, break, gap, caesura, interspace, interstice, distance, hiatus, skip, division, opening; pause, recess, interim, respite, interlude, interregnum, interruption, term, spell, period; cleft, crevice, chink, cranny, crack, slit, fissure, rift, flaw, breach, rent, gash, cut, leak; ditch, dike, gorge, ravine, abyss, gulf.

v gape, open; intervene, interrupt.

199 continuity *n* contact, contiguousness, proximity, apposition, juxtaposition, touching, abutment, meeting.

v be contiguous, join, adjoin, abut on, border, touch, meet, graze, adhere; coincide, coexist.

adj contiguous, touching, in contact, end to end; close, near.

200 length *n* distance, extent, longitude, span, reach, range; lengthiness, elonga-

tion, size; duration, continuance, term, period.

v be long, stretch out, sprawl; extend to, reach to, stretch to; lengthen, stretch, elongate, extend; prolong, protract, draw out, spin out.

adj long, lengthy, extended, outstretched; lengthened, interminable; linear, lineal, longitudinal; tall, stringy, protracted, lanky.

adv lengthwise, at length, longitudinally.

201 shortness *n* brevity, littleness; shortening, abridgment, abbreviation, conciseness, condensation; retrenchment, curtailment, reduction.

v be short; shorten, abridge, abbreviate, condense, compact, compress, epitomize; retrench, cut short, reduce, pare down, clip back, cut back, prune, shear, shave, crop, chop up, hack up, truncate.

adj short, brief, curt; compendious, compact, compressed, condensed; stubby, stunted, stumpy, squat, dumpy; concise, pointed; curtailed, cut back, reduced, shortened, abbreviated, abridged.

202 breadth. thickness *n* breadth, width, latitude, amplitude, extent, diameter.

thickness, density, denseness, heaviness, bulk, body.

v be broad; expand, widen, be thick; thicken.

adj broad, wide, ample, extended, expansive, large; outspread, outstretched.

thick, dense, heavy, bulky, solid, compact; dumpy, squat, thickset.

203 narrowness. thinness *n* narrowness, slenderness, exiguity, closeness, straitness, scantiness, slightness, slimness.

thinness, slenderness, slimness, leanness, lankness, meagerness, skinniness.

v be narrow; narrow, taper, be thin; thin, slenderize, slim; dilute, water down.

adj narrow, close, slender, thin, fine, threadlike, slim, delicate; restricted, confined, limited; thin, emaciated, lean, skinny, meager, gaunt, spindly, lanky, scrawny, haggard, pinched, skeletal, wasted; frail, unsound, fragile; weak, shrill, faint, feeble; watery, waterish, diluted, unsubstantial.

204 layer *n* stratum, substratum, bed, zone, floor, stage, story, tier, slab, tablet,

board, sheet, platter; scale, coat, peel,
membrane, film, leaf, slice.

v slice, shave, pare, peel; plate, coat,
veneer; cover; layer

adj layered, stratified, tiered; scaly,
filmy, membranous, flaky.

205 filament *n* thread, fiber, strand, hair,
cilia, tendril, gossamer, wire, strand,
vein.

adj fibrous, threadlike, wiry, stringy,
ropy; capillary.

206 height *n* altitude, stature, elevation,
tallness; prominence, eminence, pre-
eminence, loftiness, sublimity; top,
peak, pinnacle, acme, summit, zenith,
culmination.

v tower, soar, hover, cap, command;
mount, bestride, surmount, overhang;
heighten, elevate, raise up, rise up.

adj high, tall, elevated, towering,
skyscraping, gigantic, huge, colossal;
distinguished, prominent, eminent, pre-
eminent, exalted, lofty, sublime; overhanging, overlying.

207 lowness *n* depression, debasement,
prostration; flatness, proneness; lowlands, flatlands.

v be low; lie low, lie flat, crouch,
slouch, wallow, grovel; underlie; lower,
depress.

adj low, flat, level, low-lying;
crouched, squat, prone, supine, prostrate, depressed; groveling, abject,
sordid, mean, base, lowly, degraded, de-
based, ignoble, vile.

adv under, beneath, underneath, below, down, downward; underfoot, underground; downstairs, belowstairs.

208 depth *n* deepness, profundity, obscurity; depression, bottom, unfathomable
space; pit, hollow, shaft, well, crater,
chasm, abyss, bottomless pit; central
part, midst, middle, bosom, womb,
base, heart, core; soundings, draft, submersion, dive.

v deepen, hollow, plunge, sink, dig,
excavate; sound, have the lead, take
soundings.

adj deep, deep-seated, profound,
mysterious, obscure, unfathomable;
sunk, buried, submerged; bottomless,
soundless, fathomless, unfathomed,
abysmal yawning, gaping.

adv beyond one's depth, out of one's
depth, over one's head.

209 shallowness *n* superficiality, banality,
triviality, frivolity, flimsiness, emptiness, vacancy; shallow, shoal, sand bar.

adj shallow, superficial, slight, cursory, trivial, banal, trashy, flimsy, substanceless, empty, vacuous, vacant;
skin-deep, ankle-deep, knee-deep.

210 summit *n* top, peak, apex, pinnacle,
vertex, acme, culmination, zenith;
height, pitch, maximum, climax; crowning point, turning point, watershed.

v culminate, climax, crown, top.

adj highest, top, topmost, uppermost,
tiptop; capital, head, polar; supreme,
supernal.

211 base *n* bottom, stand, rest, pedestal,
dado, understructure, substructure, foot,
basis, foundation, ground, groundwork;
principle, touchstone, fundamental part,
element, ingredient; bottom, nadir, foot,
sole, heel.

adj bottom, undermost, nethermost;
fundamental, basic, elemental; based
on, founded on, grounded on, built on;
base, vile, venal.

212 verticality *n* perpendicularity, erect-
ness; wall, precipice, cliff.

v be vertical, stand up straight, stand
upright, stand erect, stand straight and
tall.

adj vertical, upright, erect, perpendicular, straight, bolt upright, plumb.

adv vertically, on end, endwise.

213 horizontality *n* flatness; level, plane,
stratum; horizon; recumbency, lying
down, reclination, proneness, supination, prostration.

v be horizontal, lie, recline, lie down,
lie flat, sprawl; render horizontal, flatten, level, prostrate, knock down, floor,
fell.

adj horizontal, level, even, plane,
flat, smooth; prone, supine, prostrate.

adv horizontally, on one's back.

214 suspension *n* hanging down, free
swinging; pendant, tail, train, flap, pendulum.

v suspend, hang, swing, dangle; flap,
trail, flow; depend.

adj suspended, pendent, hanging,

swinging, dangling, pendulous; dependent.

215 support *n* foundation, base, basis, ground, footing, hold; supporter, prop, brace, stay, rib, truss, stalk, stilts, splint; bar, rod, boom, outrigger; staff, stick, crutch; bracket, ledge, shelf, trestle, buttress.

v support, bear, carry, hold, sustain, shoulder, bolster; shore up, hold up, prop up, brace; help, aid, maintain, sustain; base, found, ground.

adj supporting, supported; fundamental.

216 parallelism *n* coextension; comparison, affinity, correspondence, semblance, likeness, resemblance, analogy, equation.

v parallel, compare, relate, associate, connect, correspond to, equate.

adj parallel, coextensive, collateral, aligned, equal; like, similar, allied, corresponding, correlative, analogous, equivalent.

217 obliquity *n* incline, inclination, slope, slant, leaning, tilt, list, bend, curve; acclivity, rise, ascent, grade, rising ground, hill, bank; declivity, decline, downhill, dip, fall; steepness.

v be oblique, slope, slant, lean, incline, stoop, decline, descend; bend, careen, slouch, sidle; render oblique, sway, bias, slat, warp, incline, bend, crook, tilt, distort.

adj oblique, inclined; sloping, tilted; askew, asquint, awry, crooked; uphill, rising, ascending; downhill, falling, descending; declining, declivitous; steep, abrupt, sharp, precipitous; diagonal, transverse.

adv obliquely, on one side; askew, askance, edgewise, at an angle; sidelong, sideways, slantwise.

218 inversion *n* subversion, reversion, contraposition, transposition, transposal, conversion; contrariety, contradiction, opposition, polarity, antithesis; reversal, overturn, somersault, turn of the tide, revulsion, revolution.

v be inverted, turn about, wheel about, go about, turn over, go over, tilt over; invert, subvert, reverse, overturn, upturn, upset, turn topsy-turvy; transpose.

adj inverted, inside out, wrong side out, upside down, topsy-turvy; inverse, reverse, obverse, opposite.

adv inversely.

219 crossing *n* intersection, grade crossing, crossroad, interchange; network, reticulation; net, netting, network, web, mesh, wicker, lace; mat, matting, plait, trellis, lattice, grating, grille, gridiron, tracery, fretwork, filigree; knot, entanglement.

v cross, intersect, interlace, intertwine, interweave, interlink, crisscross, twine, intwine, weave, twist, wreathe; dovetail, splice, link, link up; mat, plait, plat, braid; tangle, entangle, ravel; net, knot, twist.

adj crossing; crossed, matted, transverse; weaved, woven, intertwined, interlaced.

220 exteriority *n* outside, exterior; surface, superficies; covering, skin, face, appearance, façade, aspect, facet.

v be exterior, lie around, encircle.

adj exterior, external, outer, outside, outward, superficial; outlying, extraneous, foreign, extrinsic.

adv externally, out, over, outwards.

221 interiority *n* interior, inside, inner part, center, interspace; subsoil, substratum, contents, substance, pith, marrow, backbone, heart, bowels, belly, guts, lap, womb; recesses, innermost recesses, hollows, nook, niche, cave.

v be interior, be inside; inclose, circumscribe; intern; embed, insert.

adj interior, internal, inside, inner, inward, inmost, innermost; deepseated, inlaid, embedded, ingrained, innate, inherent, intrinsic, inborn; private, secret, intimate, confidential; home, domestic.

adv internally; inward, within, indoors, withindoors.

222 centrality *n* center, middle, midst; core, kernel, nucleus, heart, pole, axis, pivot, navel, nub, hub; centralization; center of gravity.

v be central; centralize, concentrate; focus on, bring into focus, get to the heart of.

adj central, middle, pivotal, focal, concentric; middlemost.

adv centrally; middle, midst.

223 covering n cover; canopy, awning, tent, marquee; umbrella, parasol, sunshade; shade, screen, shield; roof, ceiling, thatch, shed; top, lid; bandage, wrappings; coverlet, blanket, sheet, quilt, tarpaulin; skin, fleece, fur, hide; clothing, mask; peel, crust, bark, rind; veneer, coating, facing, varnish.

v cover, superimpose, overlay, overspread; wrap, encase, face, case, veneer, paper; conceal, cover over.

adj covered. clothed, wrapped; protected.

224 lining n inner coating, coating; filling, stuffing, padding, wadding.

v line, stuff, wad, pad, fill; coat, incrust, face, cover.

adj lined.

225 dress n clothing, covering, raiment, drapery, costume, attire, garb, apparel, wardrobe, outfit, clothes; equipment, livery, gear, rigging, trappings, togs, accouterments; uniforms, regimentals, suit.

v dress, clothe, drape, robe, array, fit out, deck out, garb, rig out, apparel; equip, harness, outfit, uniform; cover, wrap, wrap up, sheathe, swathe, swaddle.

adj dressed, clothed, clad, invested.

226 undress n nudity, nakedness, bareness, dishabille.

v undress, uncover, divest, expose, disrobe, strip, bare, doff, peel, take off, put off, lay open.

adj undressed, nude, naked, bare, stark-naked, exposed, in the buff, *au naturel*, in the altogether, in one's birthday suit; undressed, unclad, undraped, disrobed.

227 environment n environs, surroundings, outskirts, suburbs, purlieus, precincts, neighborhood.

v environ, surround, encompass, compass, inclose, enclose, circle, encircle, gird, twine round, hem in.

adj surrounding, circumjacent.

adv around, about; without; on every side, on all sides, right and left, every which way.

228 interspersion n interjacence, interlocation, interpenetration, permeation; interjection, interpolation, interlineation, intercalation; intervention, interference, interposition, intrusion; insinuation; insertion.

v intervene, come between, get between, interpenetrate; intersperse, permeate, introduce, throw in, work in, interpose, interject, interpolate, insert; interfere, intrude, obtrude.

adj intervening, interjacent; parenthetical, episodic; intrusive.

adv between, betwixt, among, amid, amongst; in the thick of, betwixt and between; parenthetically.

229 circumscription n limitation, enclosure; confinement, restraint.

v circumscribe, limit, bound, confine, inclose; surround, hedge in, fence in, wall in; imprison, restrain; enfold, bury, incase.

adj circumscribed, confined, restrained, imprisoned; buried in, immersed in, embosomed, embedded.

230 outline n circumference, perimeter, periphery; circuit, lines, contour, profile, silhouette.

v outline, draw, sketch, trace, profile.

231 edge n frame, fringe, trimming, trim, edging, skirting, hem; verge, brink, brim, lip, margin, border, skirt, rim, mouth; threshold, door, porch, portal; coast, shore.

v edge, skirt, border; trim, hem.

232 enclosure n envelope, case, wrapper; girdle; pen, fence, fold, cote, corral, stockyard, paddock, yard, pound, compound; fence, pale, paling, balustrade, rail, railing; hedge; wall, barrier, barricade; gate, gateway, door, doorway; boundary, border.

v enclose, circumscribe.

233 limit n boundary, bounds, extent, confine, term, pale, verge; termination, terminus; frontier, marches, outer edges, unknown; boundary line, border, edge; turning point, flood gate.

v limit, restrain, restrict, confine, check, hinder, bound, circumscribe, define.

adj limited, definite; terminal.

adv thus far, only so far, thus far and no further.

234 front n forefront, foreground, lead; face, frontage, façade, frontispiece, proscenium; vanguard, front rank, first rank, head of the column, advanced guard.

v front, face, confront; be in front, stand in front; come to the front.

adj fore, foremost; front, frontal, anterior, forward.

adv before, in front, in advance; ahead, right ahead, in the foreground; in the lead.

235 rear *n* back, background, rearguard, rear rank; distance, hinterland; rump, buttocks, posterior, rear, backside, hindquarters; wake, train; reverse, other side of the coin, *(informal)* flipside.

v be behind, bring up the rear; rear, bring up, nurture, raise; elevate, lift, loft, lift up, hold up; build, put up, erect.

adj rear, back, hindmost; posterior.

adv behind, in the rear, in the background, at the heels; after, aft, rearward.

236 side *n* laterality, flank, quarter, lee, hand; cheek, jowl, shoulder; profile, lee side, broadside.

v be on the side; be side by side, be cheek to cheek; flank, skirt, outflank, sidle.

adj sidelong, lateral; flanking, skirting; flanked.

adv sideways, sidelong; broadside, on one side, abreast, alongside, beside, side by side, cheek by jowl; laterally.

237 opposition *n* opposite, contraposition, opposite side, opposite poles, polarity, antithesis, reverse, inverse; counterpart, companion piece, complement.

v be opposite; stand as opposites, oppose.

adj opposite, reverse, inverse, converse; antipodal, antithetical, countering, opposing; fronting, facing, diametrically opposite; complementary.

adv over, over the way, over against; poles apart; face to face.

238 right *n* right hand, right side; offside, starboard.

adj right-handed, dextral.

239 left *n* left had, left side; near side, port.

adj left-handed, sinistral.

III. Form

240 form *n* shape, outline, mold, appearance, cast, cut, configuration; make, formation, frame, construction, cut, set, build, trim; mold, model, pattern; posture, attitude, convention, rule, formality, formula, ceremony, conformity.

v form, shape, figure, fashion, carve, cut, chisel, hew, cast; shape, model, mold, fashion, cast, construct, build; stamp, cast, type.

adj formal, ceremonial, ceremonious, conventional; regular, set, fixed, stiff, rigid.

241 formlessness *n* shapelessness, amorphism, asymmetry; disorder, chaos; misproportion, deformity, disfigurement, defacement, mutilation, truncation.

v deface, disfigure, deform, mutilate, truncate.

adj formless, shapeless, amorphous, asymmetrical, unformed, unshaped, unfashioned, unshapely, misshapen, out of proportion, disordered, chaotic; rough, rude, coarse, barbarous, rugged.

242 [regularity of form] symmetry *n* shapeliness, finish, comeliness, gracefulness, grace, beauty; proportion, uniformity, parallelism; regularity, evenness, balance, order, harmony, agreement.

adj symmetrical, shapely, well set, finished; beautiful, lovely; classic, classical, formal, chaste, severe; regular, uniform, balanced, harmonious, ordered; even, parallel, equal.

243 [irregularity of form] distortion *n* contortion, warp, buckle, screw, twist, crookedness, obliquity; deformity, malformation, misproportion, disfigurement, monstrosity, ugliness; asymmetry.

v distort, contort, warp, buckle, screw, twist, wrest; writhe, grimace, make faces; deform, disfigure, misshape.

adj distorted, out of shape, irregular, unsymmetrical, awry, askew, crooked; not true, not straight, uneven; misshapen, ill-made, ill-fashioned, ill-proportioned, malformed, deformed.

244 angularity *n* bifurcation, bend, fork, crook, notch, angle; elbow, knee, knuckle, crotch; right angle, acute angle, obtuse angle; corner, nook, niche, recess.

v angle, tilt, bend, fork, bifurcate.

adj angular, bent, crooked, jagged, serrated; forked, bifurcate, cornered, V-shaped, hooked; akimbo.

245 curvature *n* curve, incurvature, bend; flexure, bending, crook, hook; deflection, turn, deviation, detour, sweep, curl, winding; curve, arc, arch, arcade, vault, bow, crescent, half-moon, horseshoe, loop; parabola, hyperbola.

v be curved, sweep, sag; deviate, turn; render curved, bend, curve, deflect, in flect, crook; turn, round, arch, arch over, bow, curl, coil, recurve.

adj curved, bowed, vaulted, hooked, arched, arced; circular, nonlinear, semicircular, rounded, crescent, crescent-shaped, lunar, demi-lune.

246 straightness *n* directness; inflexibility, stiffness; straight line, direct line, bee line.

v be straight, go straight; render straight, straighten, rectify, correct, right; put right, put straight, unbend, unfold, uncurl, unravel.

adj straight, even true, unbent, direct, rectilinear, linear, not curved, uncurved; square, erect, perpendicular, vertical, upright; candid, forthright, definite, reliable, plain, blunt, frank, sure, positive, irrefutable, certain, unequivocal, inescapable; honest, honorable, fair, just, equitable, impartial, aboveboard, reputable, scrupulous, worthy, lawful, licit, conscientious, decent, ethical; correct, sound, sane, accurate, true; sober, conventional, provincial, *(informal)* unhip, *(informal)* square, *(informal)* not with it.

247 [simple circularity] **circularity** *n* roundness, rotundity; circle, ring, hoop, areola; bracelet, armlet; eye, loop, wheel, cycle, orb, orbit; zone, belt, cord, band, sash, girdle, circuit; wreath, garland, crown, corona, coronet; necklace, collar; ellipse, oval.

v round; go around, encircle, circle.

adj round, rounded, circular, oval, elliptic, elliptical, egg-shaped.

248 [complex circularity] **convolution** *n* involution, winding, wave, undulation, sinuosity, meandering, twist, twirl; coil,

roll, curl, buckle, spiral, corkscrew, worm, tendril; serpent, snake, eel; maze, labyrinth.

v wind, twine, entwine, twirl, wave, undulate, meander, turn; twist, coil, roll; wrinkle, curl, frizz, frizzle; wring, contort.

adj convoluted, winding, twisted; wavy, undulating, circling, snaky, serpentine; involved, intricate, complex, complicated, labyrinthine, tortuous, mazy; spiral, coiled.

adv in and out, round and round.

249 rotundity *n* roundness, cylindricality, sphericity, globularity; cylinder, barrel, drum; roll, roller, rolling pin; sphere, globe, ball, spheroid, globule; bulb, pellet, pill, marble, pea, knob, pommel.

v sphere, form into a sphere, roll into a ball, round.

adj rotund, round, circular, ball-shaped; cylindrical, spherical, globular; egg-shaped, pear-shaped, ovoid.

250 convexity *n* prominence, projection, swelling, bulge, protuberance, protrusion; hump, hunch, bunch; knob, node, nodule, bump, clump; pimple, pustule, pock, growth, polyp, blister, boil; nipple, teat, pap, breast; nose, beak, snout, nozzle; peg, button, stud, ridge; cupola, dome, arch; relief, high relief, low relief; hill, mountain, cape, ness, promontory, headland; jetty, ledge, spur.

v project, bulge, protrude, jut out, stand out, stick out, stick up, start up, shoot up, swell up; raise; emboss.

adj convex, prominent, protuberant; bossed, nodular, bunchy, hummocky, bulbous, swollen, swelling, bloated, bowed, arched, bellied; salient, in relief, raised.

251 flatness *n* smoothness, evenness; plane, level; plate, platter, table, tablet, slab.

v flatten, level, even off.

adj flat, plane, even, smooth; level, smooth, horizontal; flat as a pancake.

252 concavity *n* depression, dip, hollow, indentation, dent, cavity, dint, dimple; excavation, pit, trough; cup, basin, crater; valley, vale, dale, dell, glade, grove, glen, cave, cavern.

v render concave, depress, hollow,

scoop, scoop out, gouge; dig, delve, excavate, mine, stave in, tunnel.

adj concave, hollow, hollowed out; indented, dented, sunken, cupped; cavernous. rounded inward, incurved.

253 sharpness *n* acuteness, pointedness; point, spike, spine, needle, pin, prick, prickle, spur, barb, thorn; knife edge, cutting edge, razor edge.

v be sharp, taper to a point; sharpen, point, whet, barb, strop, grind, whittle.

adj sharp, keen, acute, trenchant; pointed, peaked, conical, spiked, spiky, tapering; studded, prickly, barbed, spiny, thorny, bristling, thistly; craggy, snaggy; cutting, sharp edged, razor sharp.

254 bluntness *n* dullness; obtuseness, roughness.

v be blunt; render blunt, dull, take off the point, round the edge.

adj blunt, dull, obtuse, dimwitted; rough, gruff; rounded, round, unsharpened, unpointed.

255 smoothness *n* polish, gloss; lubrication, lubricity.

v smooth, plane, file, scrape, shave, sand, sandpaper; level, press, flatten, roll; iron, steam press; polish, burnish, rub, wax, sleek, buff, glaze; lubricate, oil, grease.

adj smooth, polished, glossy, shiny, sleek, silken, silky; even, level, sanded; soft, downy, velvety; slippery, glassy, oily.

256 roughness *n* asperity, irregularity, corrugation, nodulation; grain, texture, pile, nap.

v roughen, rough up, crinkle, ruffle, rumple, crumple.

adj rough, uneven, irregular, rugged, scabrous, knotted, craggy, gnarled; shaggy, coarse, hairy, bristly, hirsute; scraggly, prickly, bushy; unpolished, unsmooth, rough-hewn, textured; downy, velvety, fluffy, woolly.

adv against the grain.

257 notch *n* dent, nick, cut, scratch, indentation; saw, tooth, scallop.

v notch, nick, cut, scratch, indent, jag, scarify, scallop.

adj notched, toothed, serrated.

258 fold *n* plait, ply, crease, pleat, tuck; wrinkle, ripple, rimple, pucker, ruffle.

v fold, double, plait, crumple, crease, pleat, wrinkle, crinkle, ripple, curl, rumple, frizzle, rimple, ruffle, pucker, corrugate; tuck, hem, gather.

adj folded.

259 furrow *n* groove, rut, scratch, streak, cut, crack, score, incision, slit; channel, gutter, trench, gulley, ditch, dike, moat, trough; ravine, valley.

v furrow, dig, plow; channel, flute, groove, incise, cut, engrave, etch, seam, cleave, score; wrinkle, knit, pucker

adj furrowed, ribbed, striated, fluted.

260 opening *n* hole, gap, aperture, orifice, perforation, pinhole, peephole, keyhole; slot, slit, rift, breach, cleft, chasm, fissure, rent; outlet, inlet, vent; portal, porch, gate, hatch, door, doorway, gateway; way, path, channel, passage.

v open, ope, gape, yawn; perforate, pierce, tap, bore, drill; mine, tunnel, dig to daylight; impale, spike, spear, gore, spit, stab, puncture, lance, stick, prick, riddle; uncover, unclose, lay bare, expose, bare, reveal; lay open, cut open, rip open, throw open.

adj open, unclosed, uncovered, exposed; ajar, wide-open, gaping, yawning; perforated, porous, reticulated, permeable; accessible, available, public.

261 closure *n* blockade, shutting up, obstruction, stoppage, clogging, sealing, plugging; contraction; constipation; culmination; cessation, completion, termination, windup; lid, top, cap, stopper, plug, barrier.

v close, plug, block up, stop up, fill up, cork up, cork, button up, stuff up, shut up, dam up; blockade, obstruct, hinder; bar, bolt, stop, seal, choke, throttle, shut.

adj closed, shut, unopened; unpierced, impervious, impermeable; impenetrable, impassable, pathless; tight, snug, airtight, unventilated, watertight, hermetically sealed.

262 perforator *n* piercer, borer, auger, drill, awl, scoop, corkscrew, probe, lancet, scalpel, needle, pin, stiletto, puncher, hole puncher, gouge; knife, spear, bayonet.

263 stopper *n* lid, cap, cover; cork, spike, stopcock, pin, plug, tap, faucet, valve, spigot, rammer, ramrod; wadding, stuffing, padding, stopping, bandage, tourniquet.

IV. Motion

264 motion *n* movement, action, activity, move, going; progress, locomotion; mobilization, mobility, movableness, motive power; unrest, restlessness; stream, flow, flux, run, course, stir; rate, pace, step, tread, stride, gait; velocity, speed.

v move, go, hie, budge, stir, pass, flit; hover around, hover about; shift, slide, glide, roll, roll on, flow, drift, stream, run, sweep along; wander, meander, browse, stroll, walk, perambulate; dodge, keep on one's toes, keep moving, hit the road, *(informal)* truck; move, impel, propel; mobilize.

adj moving, in motion, traveling, on the road; transitional, shifting, mobile, movable; mercurial, restless, unquiet, nomadic, transient.

adv under way; on the move, on the go, on the march.

265 rest *n* quiescence, stillness, quietude, calm, calmness, tranquillity, repose, serenity, peace, silence; pause, lull, cessation; stagnation, immobility, fixity.

v rest, be still, stand still, lie still, stand immobile, keep quiet, repose; remain, stay, pause, wait, mark time, hold, halt, stop short, cease, desist, discontinue, stop; stagnate, be inactive, immobilize; dwell, settle, settle down, establish roots; alight, arrive; stand fast, stand firm, stick fast; quell, becalm, hush, stay, lull, lull to sleep, tranquilize.

adj restful, quiescent, still, calm, tranquil, peaceful, undisturbed, unruffled, serene, silent; motionless, fixed, stationary; unmoved, stable, at rest, at a standstill, stock-still, sleeping, dormant, inactive, stagnant.

266 [locomotion by land] **journey** *n* traveling, travel, excursion, tour, trip, expedition, jaunt, pilgrimage; wayfaring, roving, gadding about, *(informal)* bumming around, nomadism, vagabondism; migration, immigration, moving; walk, promenade, constitutional, stroll, pere-

grination, perambulation, march, stroll, saunter, jaunt outing, hike, airing; horsemanship, horseback riding; drive, driving, motoring, ride, spin; cycling, biking; procession, cavalcade, caravan, file, cortege, column.

v journey, travel, tour, take a trip; flit, take wing, *(informal)* hit the road, rove, ramble, roam, prowl, *(informal)* bum, *(informal)* bum around, range, traverse, scour the country, wander, meander, saunter, gad about; move, migrate, immigrate.

adj journeying, traveling, on the road; itinerant, peripatetic, rambling, roving, gadding, flitting, vagrant, nomadic, migratory, wayfaring.

267 [locomotion by water or air] **navigation** *n* voyage, sail, cruise, passage, boat ride; aquatics, boating, yachting, sailing, shipping.

flight, air travel, flying, gliding; aeronautics, aviation.

v navigate; sail, put to sea, embark, shove off, spread the sails, make sail, take oar; go boating, cruise, float, drift, coast; row, paddle, pull, scull, punt, steam; ride the waves.

fly, take off, take wing, take to the skies; aviate, soar, glide, fly over, plane, jet.

adj sailing, nautical, naval, maritime, seagoing, seafaring, ocean-going; afloat; navigable.

flying, jetting; aloft, in flight; aviational, aeronautical, aerial.

268 traveler *n* wayfarer, journeyer, rover, rambler, wanderer, free spirit, nomad, vagabond, bohemian, gypsy, itinerant, vagrant, tramp, hobo, straggler, waif; pilgrim, palmer, seeker, quester; voyager, passenger, tourist, sightseer, excursionist, vacationer, globe-trotter, jet-setter; immigrant, emigrant, refugee, fugitive; pedestrian, walker, cyclist, biker, rider, horsewoman, horseman, equestrian, driver.

269 mariner, flier *n* mariner, sailor, seaman, seafaring man, sea dog; pilot, skipper, captain, commander, helmsman, steersman; crew, hands, mates; navigator, flier, airman, aviator, aviatrix, pilot, skipper; astronaut, cosmonaut, spaceman.

270 transference *n* transfer, move, shift, transit, transition, passage, transmission, transport, transplantation, transposition; removal, relegation, deportation, extradition.

v transfer, transmit, transport, convey, carry, bear, pass; move, shift, conduct, convey, bring, fetch, reach; send, delegate, consign, turn over, hand over, deliver; transpose, transplant, displace, remove, relegate, deport, extradite; shovel, ladle.

adj transferable, transmittable, transmissible, transportable, movable, portable.

271 carrier *n* porter, bearer, messenger, runner, courier; postman, letter carrier; conductor, conveyor, transporter; freighter, ship, barge; train, locomotive; truck, vehicle, carriage; beast of burden.

272 vehicle *n* conveyance, carriage, transportation, rig; car, motorcar, automobile, *(informal)* wheels, truck; wagon, cart, coach, chaise, buggy; bicycle, bike, motorcycle, motorscooter; train, sleeping car, cattle car, boxcar.

273 ship *n* vessel, boat, liner, freighter, steamer, schooner, sailboat, motorboat, merchant ship, barge, tugboat, tanker, trawler, yacht, cruiser, yawl, ketch, brig, brigantine, square-rigger, sloop, cutter, launch; navy, fleet.

airplane, plane, jet, jumbo jet, aircraft, glider, helicopter, dirigible, blimp, balloon, spaceship, capsule, module, space station.

274 velocity *n* rapidity, quickness, swiftness, celerity, speed, alacrity; acceleration, pickup; spurt, rush, dash, race, flying, flight.

v move quickly, speed, hie, hasten, post, scamper, run, race, shoot, tear, whisk, sweep, rush, dash, dash off; bolt, bound, spring, dart, flit; hurry, hasten, haste, accelerate, *(informal)* turn on the juice, quicken, speed up, take off like a shot.

adj fast, speedy, swift, rapid, quick, brisk, fleet; nimble, agile, expeditious, light-footed, fast as a bullet, quick as lightning.

adv swiftly, apace, at full speed, at full gallop, posthaste.

275 slowness *n* languor, sluggishness, slackness, sloth, indolence; deliberateness, moderation, leisureliness; tardiness.

v move slowly, creep, crawl, lag, drawl, linger, loiter, saunter, trail, drag, dawdle; plod, trudge, lumber; grovel, sneak, steal, worm one's way, inch; waddle, wobble, shuffle, hobble, limp, shamble, amble, traipse, slouch, mince, mince steps, halt; flag, totter, teeter, stagger; retard, hinder, impede, obstruct; slacken, check, relax, moderate; brake, curb, slow, put on the brakes.

adj slow, slack, late, tardy; gentle, easy, unhurried, deliberate, gradual, moderate, leisurely; languid, sluggish, indolent, lazy; tedious, humdrum, dull, boring; dense, stupid.

adv slowly, leisurely; at half speed, at a snail's pace; gradually, little by little, step by step, inch by inch, bit by bit, one step at a time.

276 impulse *n* impetus, implosion, push, thrust, shove; propulsion; sudden impulse, yearning, craving; reaction, response, reflex; collision, clash, encounter, shock, bump, crash; impact; blow, stroke, knock, rap, tap, slap, smack, pat, dab; hit, whack, thwack, slam, punch, belt, kick, thump, cut, thrust, lunge.

v impel, push, urge, thrust, shove, heave, prod, shoulder, jostle, hustle, hurtle, jog, jolt; start, give a start to, set going, get going, drive; run against, bump against, butt against; collide with, run into, bang into, butt; strike, knock, bang, hit, thump, beat, slam, dash, punch, thwack, whack; batter, pelt, buffet, butt; hit, rap, slap, tap, pat, dab.

277 recoil *n* reflex, rebound, ricochet, boomerang, backfire, backlash; snap, elasticity; reverberation, resonance; reaction, response, rebuff, repulse, revulsion.

v recoil, rebound, richochet, boomerang, snap back, spring back, fly back; react, respond; reverberate, echo, quiver.

adj reactionary; elastic, backfiring.

278 direction *n* bearing, course, set, drift, tenor, trend, tendency, inclination;

tack, aim, determination, intention; points of the compass, cardinal points; line, path, road, range, line of march; alignment.

v direct, point, aim; tend toward, point toward, conduct to, go to; bend, tend, verge, incline, determine; steer for, make for, aim at, level at, set one's sights on, take aim, hold a course for, be bound for.

adj direct, straight; bound for; undeviating, unswerving.

adv toward, on the road to; hither, thither, whither; directly, straight, straightforward, point-blank, on a line with.

279 deviation *n* diversion, digression, departure from, aberration; divergence, zigzag, detour, circuit; warp, refraction; swerving.

v deviate, alter one's course, turn, bend, curve, swerve, heel, bear off; divert, deflect, shift, shunt, draw aside, crook, warp; stray, straggle, digress, ramble, rove, drift, go astray, go adrift; wander, wind, twist, meander; veer, turn aside, change direction, steer clear of, dodge.

adj deviating, errant, aberrant; discursive, desultory, loose, rambling, digressive, stray, erratic, undirected; circuitous, indirect, zigzag, roundabout, crooked.

adv astray, roundabout, wide of the mark; circuitously.

280 [going before] **precedence** *n* priority; leading, heading, the lead, van, vanguard; precursor, coming beforehand.

v precede, go before, forerun; usher in, introduce, herald; head, take the lead, lead the way; take precedence, have priority, come first, come before.

adv in advance, before, ahead, in the vanguard, in front.

281 [going after] **sequence** *n* coming after, following, sequel; shadow, dangler, train.

v follow, come in sequence, go after; attend, be attendant on, follow in the steps of, follow in the wake of, trail, shadow; pursue; lag, fall behind.

adj following; sequential.

adv behind, after; in the rear.

282 [motion forward] **progression** *n* progress, improvement proceeding, advance, advancement, headway; growth, rise, increase, development.

v proceed, advance, progress, get on, get along, gain ground, press onward, forge ahead, make headway, make progress, make strides, stride forward; grow, develop, increase, improve.

adj advancing; progressive, advanced.

adv forward, onward; forth, on, ahead.

283 [motion backward] **regression** *n* retrogression, retreat, recession, retirement, withdrawal; reflux, backwater, return, recoil; backsliding; deterioration, decrease, fall.

v regress, recede, return, revert, retreat, back out, back down, turn back, fall back, drop out, retire, withdraw; lose ground, drop off, fall behind; ebb, shrink, shy.

adj retrograde, retrogressive; regressive, refluent, reflex.

adv backwards; aboutface.

284 propulsion *n* propulsive force, impulse, push, projection, thrust, drive, impulsion, impetus; throw, fling, toss, shot, discharge.

v propel, project, throw, fling, cast, pitch, chuck, toss, heave, hurl; drive, sling, push, shove; send off, fire off, discharge, shoot, launch, let fly; put in motion, set in motion, start, get going, impel; expel.

adj propulsive.

285 traction *n* drawing, hauling, pulling, towing, towage; yank, tug, drag, jerk.

v draw, pull, haul, lug, drag, tug, tow, trail, train, take in tow; wrench, jerk, yank.

adj tractile; in tow.

286 [motion towards] **approach** *n* access, advent, advance; nearness, approximation.

v approach, near, draw near, move towards, get close to; gain on, get closer to; pursue, trail.

adj approaching; approximate; impending, imminent.

287 [motion from] **recession** *n* retirement, withdrawal; flight, removal, retreat; regression, return, falling back, regress; reaction, reversal, recoil; departure, leave-taking.

v recede, move back, go back, move away from, retire, withdraw; drift, abate, fade, wane, ebb, subside, drift away, fall back, shrink; react, revert, relapse, recoil, regress; run away, fly, avoid.

288 attraction *n* attractiveness, inclination, affinity; pull, magnetism, gravity.

v attract, draw, drag, pull, magnetize, exert force; interest, invite, engage, fascinate, lure, allure, charm, decoy, bait.

adj attractive, attracting, enticing, seductive, alluring; have pull, magnetic, gravitational.

289 repulsion *n* aversion, antipathy, dislike; repulse, rebuff.

v repel, push, back, drive away, chase away, rebuff, beat back; repulse, revolt, offend, sicken, disgust, displease, irritate.

adj repulsive, repellent, averse, repelling.

290 convergence *n* confluence, conflux, concurrence, concourse, congress, coming together, meeting, joining.

v converge, concur, come together, meet, join, unite; gather together, concentrate, center.

adj convergent, confluent, concurrent.

291 divergence *n* division, radiation, spread, severance, separation, refraction, deflection; ramification, furcation, branching, forking, detachment; deviation, aberration, disparity, difference, variance, heterogeneity.

v diverge, ramify, radiate, branch off, fork, spread, swerve, scatter, disperse; divide, separate, part, sever; vary, deviate, dissent, disagree.

adj divergent, radial, radiant, centrifugal.

292 arrival *n* advent, coming; reaching, attainment, landing, debarkation, disembarkation; reception, welcome, welcoming.

v arrive, get to, come to, reach a point, attain, complete; light, alight, dismount; land, disembark, debark, deplane, detrain.

293 departure *n* embarkation; outset, start, starting point, place of departure, point of departure; removal, exit; exodus, flight; leave-taking, valediction, *adieu*, farewell, goodbye.

v depart, go away, take one's leave, start, set out, leave, retire, quit, withdraw, absent, go, *(informal)* split, take off, *(informal)* cut out, move off, move out, ship out, pack it up; vacate, evacuate, abandon; sally, set forth, set forward, go forth; embark, set sail, put out to sea, shove off, get under way, enplane, entrain.

294 [motion into] **ingress** *n* entrance, entry; influx, intrusion, inroad, incursion, invasion, irruption, penetration, infiltration; insinuation, insertion.

v enter, come in, pour in, flow in; burst in, break in, invade, intrude; penetrate, infiltrate, insinuate oneself.

adj incoming, inbound.

295 [motion out of] **egress** *n* exit, issue; emergence, emanation; outbreak, outburst, eruption; evacuation, leakage, percolation, oozing, drainage, drain; outpouring, gush, effluence, effusion, discharge.

v emerge, emanate, issue; pass out of, come out of, pour out of, flow out of; exude, leak, ooze, drain, drip, trickle, dribble; gush, gush out, pour out, spout, flow out, discharge; escape, find vent.

adj outgoing, outward, outbound.

296 [motion into, actively] **reception** *n* admission, admittance, entry, entrée; importation, introduction, initiation, induction, absorption; ingestion, eating, drinking; suction, sucking; insertion, injection.

v give entrance to, admit, introduce, usher, initiate, induct; receive, import, bring in, ingest, absorb, imbibe.

297 [motion out of, actively] **ejection** *n* rejection, expulsion, eviction, dislodgment, banishment, exile; emission, effusion, discharge, evacuation, regurgitation, elimination.

v reject, eject, expel, evict, dislodge, banish, exile; push aside, push away, turn away, brush aside; empty, drain, clear out, clean out, purge, void, evacuate; vomit, spew, regurgitate, throw up, *(informal)* puke, retch, *(informal)* barf, belch out, burp out; discharge, eliminate, discard, get rid of, do away with, cast off, cut adrift, turn out, throw out, oust.

298 eating *n* dining, supping, taking nourishment; ingestion, chewing, mastication; imbibition, drinking, food, nourishment, nutrition, nutriment, sustenance, subsistence, provender, provisions, rations, keep, board, fare; drink, beverage, potion, draught.

v eat, feed, breakfast, lunch, dine, sup, break bread; taste, devour, wolf, swallow, gulp, bolt, gulp down, fall to, dig in; chew, masticate, bite, bite into, chomp, munch, crunch, gnaw, nibble, peck at; live on, live off, fatten, feast on.

drink, drink up, drink one's fill, quaff, *(informal)* down, chug, empty, sip.

adj eatable, edible, digestible; drinkable, potable; nutritious, nutritive.

299 excretion *n* discharge, emanation, exhalation, secretion, effusion, perspiration, sweat; evacuation, elimination, urination; hemorrhage, bleeding.

v excrete; emanate, exhale; secrete, perspire, seat; eliminate, evacuate; urinate.

300 [forcible ingress] **insertion** *n* implantation, injection, inoculation, infusion, importation, insinuation, interpolation; immersion, submersion, dip, plunge.

v insert, introduce, put in; inject, infuse, instill, inoculate, impregnate, imbue; graft, ingraft, implant, plant, bud; thrust in, stick in, shove in, ram in, stuff in, tuck in, press in, drive in; immerse, merge; dip, plunge.

301 [egress] **extraction** *n* removal, elimination, extrication, eradication, extirpation, extermination, ejection; wrench, squeezing, pulling.

v extract, draw, draw out, take out, pull out, tear out, rip out, pluck out; wring from, wrench, pull; root out, weed out, rake out, eradicate, uproot, pull up, extirpate; evolve, elicit, draw forth; extricate, remove, eliminate; squeeze out.

302 [motion through] **passage** *n* transmission; permeation, penetration, infiltration; ingress, egress; voyage, trip, tour, excursion, journey; way, route, channel,

avenue, road, path, way, thoroughfare, conduit.

v pass, pass through; penetrate, permeate, thread, go through, cut across; ford, traverse, cross; go, move, proceed; leave, go away, depart.

303 [motion beyond] **infringement** *n* transgression, trespass, encroachment, infraction.

v infringe, transgress, trespass, encroach; surpass, go beyond, shoot ahead of, overrun; overstep, overreach, overshoot; outstrip, outrun, outride, outdo; exceed, surmount, transcend, soar.

adv beyond the mark, ahead.

304 [motion short of] **shortcoming** *n* failure, falling short; default, defalcation; incompleteness, imperfection, deficiency, insufficiency, noncompletion.

v fall short, come up short, come short of, not reach; want, lack; fail, break down, collapse, come to nothing; fall through, cave in.

adj deficient, lacking, insufficient; incomplete, imperfect.

305 ascent *n* ascension; rising, rise, upgrowth; leap, jump; acclivity, hill, grade.

v ascend, rise, mount, climb upward, climb, arise; clamber, mount, scale, go up, get up; tower, soar, hover, surmount, scale the heights.

adj ascendant; rising, acclivitous.

306 descent *n* declension, inclination, declination, slope, declivity, grade, decline, drop, cliff, precipice, dip, hill; fall, falling, descending, sinking; downfall, tumble, slip, tilt, trip, lurch.

v descend, go down, drop down, come down, drop, fall, gravitate, slip, slide, settle; decline, set, sink, droop, wilt, slump; dismount, alight, get down; swoop down, stoop; tumble, trip, stumble, lurch, pitch, topple, tilt, sprawl.

adj declivitous, sloping, precipitous, steep; descending.

307 elevation *n* raising; erection, lift; upheaval; sublimation, exaltation; prominence, height.

v elevate, heighten, raise, lift, lift up, erect; set up, tilt up, rear, hoist, heave; uplift, upraise, uprear; exalt, enhance, advance; take up, drag up, fish up, drag, dredge.

adj elevated, stilted, rampant.

308 depression *n* lowering; dip, concavity; upset, overturn, overthrow; prostration, abasement, debasement, degradation; bow, curtsy, genuflection, kowtow, obeisance.

v depress, lower, let down, take down, cast down, let drop, let fall; sink, debase, bring low, abase, degrade, reduce; overthrow, overturn, upset, prostrate, level, fell; bow, curtsy, genuflect, kowtow, kneel, bend over, make obeisance.

adj depressed; at a low ebb; prostrate, horizontal.

309 leap *n* jump, hop, spring, bound, vault; dance, caper, frisk, buck.

v leap, jump, hop, spring, bound, vault, hurtle, hurdle; dance, caper, trip, skip, frisk, bob, flounce, start; trip the light fantastic toe, dance all night.

adj leaping; frisky, lively, springy.

310 plunge *n* dip, dash, rush, dive, leap; ducking, dunking, submersion, immersion.

v plunge, immerse, submerge, douse, souse, dunk, dip; dash, rush, hasten, hurry; dive, leap, jump; descend, drop, fall, hurtle over.

311 circular motion *n* circulation, circularity; turn, excursion; circumvention, circumnavigation, circling; turning; coil, corkscrew, spiral; full circle, full turn, turn, circuit, lap.

v turn, bend, wheel, turn a circle, turn around, make a U-turn, put about, make a complete circle; circle, go around, circuit, circumnavigate; whisk, twirl, twist.

adj circuitous, roundabout; circular.

312 rotation *n* revolution, gyration, circulation, roll; spinning, pirouette, convolution; whir, whirl, eddy, vortex, whirlpool, maelstrom; cyclone, tornado.

v rotate, turn, spin, revolve, wheel, whirl, twirl, spin around; pivot, swivel, circle around.

adj rotating, rotary, gyratory, revolving.

313 evolution *n* evolvement, unfolding, development.

v evolve, unfold, unfurl, unroll, unwind, develop.

adj evolutionary, evolutional.

314 [motion to and fro] **oscillation** *n* vibration, pulsation, undulation; pulse, beat, *(informal)* vibes, ripple, wave; alternation, coming and going, ebb and flow, ups and downs, flux and reflux; fluctuation, vacillation, irresolution.

v oscillate, vibrate, vacillate, swing, fluctuate, vary; undulate, wave; pulsate, beat, throb, ripple; reel, quake, quiver, quaver, shake; roll, toss, pitch; flounder, stagger, totter.

adj oscillating; undulatory; pulsating.

adv to and fro, up and down, back and forth, seesaw, zigzag, in and out, from side to side.

315 [irregular motion] **agitation** *n* stir, ripple, tremor, shake, jog, jolt, jar, jerk, shock, quiver, quaver, twitter, flicker, flutter; disquiet, perturbation, commotion, turbulence, turmoil, tumult; hubbub, bustle, fuss, ado, racket, fits; spasm, throe, throb, palpitation, convulsion, fit; disturbance, disorder, restlessness, hypertension; ferment, fermentation, ebullition, effervescence, hurly-burly; tempest, storm, groundswell, whirlpool, vortex; whirlwind, tornado, cyclone, twister.

v be agitated, shake, tremble, quiver, quaver, quake, shiver, twitter, writhe, toss, shuffle, tumble, stagger, bob, reel, sway; waggle, wriggle, dance, prance, stumble, shamble, flounder, totter, teeter, flounce, flop; throb, pulsate, beat, palpitate, go pit-a-pat; flutter, flicker, bicker, bustle; ferment, effervesce, foam, boil, bubble, simmer; agitate, shake, convulse, toss, tumble, bandy, flap, whisk, jerk, hitch, jolt, joggle, jostle, buffet, hustle, disturb, stir, shake up, churn, jounce, wallop, whip.

adj agitated, shaking, pulsating, tremulous, convulsive, jerky, shaky, throbbing.

adv by fits and starts; in convulsions, in fits.

Class III
Words Relating to Matter

I. Matter in General

316 materiality *n* corporeality, substantiality, flesh and blood, physicality; matter, body, substance, brute matter, physical elements, material; object, article, thing, materials.

science of matter; physics, natural philosophy, physical science, materialism. materialist, physicist.

v materialize, embody, body in.

adj material, bodily, corporeal, physical, somatic; sensible, tangible palpable, touchable, substantial, unspiritual, materialistic.

317 immateriality *n* incorporeality, insubstantiality, spirituality, ineffability.

adj immaterial, incorporeal, unsubstantial, intangible, ineffable, untouchable, bodiless, unreal, unearthly, spiritual, psychical, otherworldly.

318 world *n* creation, nature, universe, solar system, galaxy, globe, earth, wide world, sphere, macrocosm; heavens, firmament, vault, celestial spaces, space, sky; heavenly bodies, planets, asteroids, comets, meteors, constellations.

adj worldly, mundane, terrestrial, earthly, sublunary; cosmic, celestial, heavenly, astral, solar, lunar.

adv in all creation, on the face of the earth, under the sun, here below.

319 gravity *n* gravitation, weight, heaviness, pull, pressure, load, burden.

v gravitate, weigh, pull, press, encumber, load, be heavy.

adj weighty, heavy, heavy as lead, ponderous, lumpish, cumbersome, burdensome, cumbrous, massive, unwieldy, like a ton of bricks.

320 levity *n* lightness, buoyancy, volatility; ferment, leaven, yeast.

v be light, float, swim, waft; lighten, leaven.

adj light, subtle, airy, weightless, ethereal, volatile, buoyant, feathery.

II. Inorganic Matter

321 density *n* solidity, solidness, impenetrability, impermeability; condensation, solidification, consolidation, concretion, coagulation, petrification, hardening, crystallization, thickening; solid body, mass, block, knot, lump, conglomerate.

v be dense; solidify, condense, consolidate, coagulate, congeal, set, cohere, crystallize, petrify, harden; condense, compress, thicken.

adj dense, solid, compact, close, thick, substantial, massive; impenetrable, impermeable, coherent, cohesive, indivisible, indissoluble, insoluble.

322 thinness *n* rarity, tenuity; rarefaction, expansion, dilation, inflation.

v thin, rarefy, expand, dilate, inflate.

adj thin, rare, fine, tenuous, compressible, flimsy, slight, light; unsubstantial.

323 hardness *n* rigidity, firmness, inflexibility, temper; induration, petrification, ossification, crystallization.

v harden, stiffen, cement, petrify, temper, ossify.

adj hard, solid, firm, inflexible, rigid, resistant, adamantine, impenetrable, strong, hard as a rock, hard as nails, tough.

324 softness *n* pliability, flexibility, pliancy, malleability, ductility, tractility, plasticity, flaccidity, elasticity; mollification, softening.

v soften, mollify, mash, knead, temper, bend, yield, give, relent, relax.

adj soft, tender, supple, pliant, pliable, flexible, limber, plastic, ductile, tractile, tractable, plastic, malleable, moldable, impressible, elastic; flabby, limp, flimsy, flaccid, doughy, mushy, squishy, waxy, soft as butter.

325 elasticity *n* springiness, spring, resilience, resiliency, give.

v be elastic, spring, give, bend, stretch; spring back, recoil,

adj elastic, tensile, springy, resilient, buoyant, rubbery.

326 inelasticity *n* want of elasticity, flaccidity, limpness, softness, mushiness.

adj inelastic, flaccid, limp.

327 tenacity n toughness, strength, cohesiveness, cohesion; stubbornness, obstinacy, grit.

adj tenacious, cohesive, tough, strong, resistant, gristly, stringy, gummy, adhesive, sticky, viscous, glutinous; stubborn, obstinate.

328 brittleness n fragility, frailty, breakability.

v be brittle; break, crack, snap, split, shiver, splinter, crumble, burst, fly, fly to pieces, shatter, give way.

adj brittle, fragile, breakable, frangible, delicate, frail, splintery, crisp.

329 structure n organization, constitution, anatomy, frame, framework, mold, form, architecture, construction, texture: tissue, grain, web, surface; coarseness; fineness.

adj structural, organizational, anatomical, anatomic, architectural textural: fine, delicate, subtle, gossamery, filmy; coarse, homespun, rough, woolly.

330 granularity n pulverulence, sandiness, graininess, friability; powder, dust, sand, grit, grain, particle, crumb, fine powder.

reduction to powder; pulverization, granulation, disintegration, abrasion, attenuation, filing.

tools for pulverization: mill, grater, rasp, file, mortar and pestle, grinder, grindstone.

v grind, pulverize, granulate, grate, scrape, file, abrade, rasp, pound, beat, crush, crumble, disintegrate.

adj granular, powdery, mealy, floury, branny, dusty, sandy, arenose, gritty, crumbly.

331 friction n attrition, rubbing, abrasion, elbow-grease.

v rub, scratch, scrape, scrub, fray, rasp, curry, scour, polish, rub out, erase, grind.

332 [absence or prevention of friction] **lubrication** n anointment, oiling, greasing, coating, lathering.

v lubricate, oil, grease, lather; anoint.

333 fluidity n liquidity, liquefaction, solubility, fluency.

v be fluid, flow, run, pour, stream; liquefy.

adj fluid, liquid, watery, serous, sappy, juicy, soluble; fluent, unstable.

334 gaseity n gaseousness, vaporousness, volatility.

adj gaseous, vaporous, airy, etheric, voluble, evaporable; flatulent, windy.

335 liquefaction n liquefying, deliquescence, melting, thawing, solubleness, dissolution.

v liquefy, melt, thaw, dissolve.

adj deliquescent, soluble, dissolvable, solvent.

336 vaporization n atomization, steaming, boiling, distillation, gasification, evaporation.

v vaporize, atomize, distill, evaporate, gasify, boil, steam.

adj vapory, vaporous, volatile, evaporable, gaseous.

337 water n liquid, serum, lymph, fluid, aqua.

v add water, water, wet, moisten, dip, immerse, submerge, plunge, douse, dunk, drown, soak, steep, wash, sprinkle, splash, souse, drench; dilute; deluge, inundate.

adj watery, aqueous, liquid, fluid, wet, moist, humid, soggy, sodden, rheumy, hydrous, juicy, lush, succulent; waterish, adulterated, transparent, thin, weak, tasteless, insipid, vapid, flat, feeble, dull.

338 air n atmosphere, stratosphere, the open, open air, blue sky, sky; weather, climate, clime; ventilation, current, breath of air, wind, breeze.

v air, ventilate, fan, aerate, freshen, refresh, cool.

adj airy, open, exposed, breezy, windy; flatulent; effervescent; atmospheric, aerial, ethereal, aeriform.

adv in the open air, out in the open, out of doors, in the wide open spaces, under the stars.

339 moisture n dampness, humidity, dankness, dew, wetness, condensation; perspiration.

v moisten, sponge, damp, bedew, wet, soak, saturate, sodden, sop, drench; perspire.

adj moist, damp, watery, humid, dank, dewy, muggy, juicy, wet; soggy, mushy, marshy, muddy.

340 dryness *n* drought, aridity, dessication, drainage, evaporation.

v dry, dry up, soak up, sponge, swab, wipe; drain, parch, evaporate.

adj dry, arid, parched, juiceless, sapless, dry as a bone.

341 ocean *n* sea, main, deep, brine, salt water, waters, high seas, waves, billows, great waters, tides.

adj oceanic, marine, maritime, seagoing, oceanographic.

342 land *n* earth, ground, dry land, mother earth, *terra firma;* continent, inlands, interior, shore, coast, terrain, dirt, soil, rock, chalk; real estate, lands, grounds, acres, acreage.

v land, alight, arrive, disembark, come ashore, go ashore, tie up, set foot on dry land.

adj earthy, terrestrial, earthly, alluvial, landed, territorial, continental.

adv ashore, on land, on dry land.

343 gulf, lake *n* gulf, bay, inlet, estuary, bayou, arm, fjord, firth, lagoon, cove, mouth, natural harbor, sound, straits.

lake, loch, lough, mere, tarn, basin, reservoir, lagoon, pond, pool.

344 plain *n* plateau, champaign, grassland, pasture, pasturage, meadow, flat, moor, heath, tundra, prairie, lowland, steppe, field, desert, basin, fields, grounds.

345 marsh *n* swamp, morass, moss, fen, bog, quagmire, slough, wash, mud.

adj marshy, swampy, boggy, quaggy, soft, muddy, sloppy, squashy.

346 island *n* isle, islet, atoll, reef, ait, key, bar, holm, ridge, eyot, archipelago.

adj insular, sea-girt.

347 [fluid in motion] **stream** *n* stream, etc. (of water) **348;** (of air) **249.** *v* flow, etc., **348;** blow, etc., **349.**

348 [water in motion] **river** *n* running water, jet, spurt, squirt, spout, splash, rush, gush, torrent; fall, cascade, inundation, deluge; rain, rainfall, storm; trickle, drizzle, shower; stream, course, flux, flow, flowing, current, tide, race; spring, rill, rivulet, stream, river, tributary; rapids, flood, whirlpool, maelstrom, vortex, eddy; wave, billow, surge, swell, ripple, surf, breaker, white caps,

rough seas, rolling seas, choppy seas; irrigation, pump, hose.

v flow, run, gush, pour, spout, roll, jet, well issue; drop, drip, dribble, drizzle, trickle, stream, overflow, inundate, deluge, flow over, splash, swash; gurgle, murmur, babble, bubble, sputter, spurt, regurgitate; ooze, flow out, squeeze; rain, rain hard, rain cats and dogs, rain in torrents, rain in buckets; flow into, open into, drain into; pour, pour out, shower down, irrigate, drench, spill.

adj fluent, tidal, streamy, showery, rainy, trickly, drizzly, bubbly.

349 [air in motion] **wind** *n* draft, air, breath of air, puff, whiff, zephyr, drift, blow; fresh wind, stiff breeze, keen blast, trade wind, gust, blast, breeze, squall, gale, storm, tempest, hurricane, whirlwind, tornado, twister, cyclone, monsoon.

v blow, waft, blow hard, blow great guns, stream, gust, blast, storm; respire, breathe, pant, puff, gasp, wheeze, cough; fan, ventilate, inflate, pump, blow up.

adj windy, drafty, breezy, stormy, tempestuous, cyclonic.

350 [channel for the passage of water] **conduit** *n* channel, duct, aqueduct, canal, trough, gutter, dike, main, gully, moat, ditch, drain, sewer, culvert, sough, siphon, pipe, tube, hose, funnel, tunnel, artery, spout, floodgate, watergate, sluice, lock, valve.

351 [channel for the passage of air] **airpipe** *n* tube, shaft, flue, chimney, funnel, vent, hole, windpipe, duct.

352 semiliquidity *n* viscosity, adhesiveness, stickiness, glutinosity, pastiness.

v thicken, mash, squash, churn, beat up, blend.

adj semiliquid, semifluid; milky, muddy, creamy, slushy, starchy, gummy, gluey, sticky, slimy, oozy, thick, succulent, viscous, viscid, glutinous, adhesive, clammy.

353 [mixture of air and water] **bubble. cloud** *n* bubble, foam, froth, head, lather, suds, spray, surf, yeast; effervescence, fermentation, bubbling, boiling, gurgling, foaming.

cloud, vapor, fog, mist, haze, steam

nebula, nebulosity, cloudiness, opacity, dimness.

v bubble, boil, foam, froth, gurgle, lather, effervesce, ferment, fizzle.

cloud, fog, mist, steam, shadow, darken, cast over, steam up.

adj bubbly, foamy, frothy; effervescent.

cloudy, foggy, misty, hazy, steamy.

354 pulpiness *n* pulp, paste, dough, curd; fleshiness, fattiness, sponginess.

v pulp, mash, squeeze, juice, squash.
adj pulpy, pasty, doughy, fleshy, meaty, fatty.

355 unctuousness *n* unctuosity, oiliness, greasiness, lubricity; lubrication, ointment, grease, oil, anointment.

v oil, grease, lubricate.
adj unctuous, oily, greasy, oleaginous, slippery, slimy, slick.

356 oil *n* fat, butter, cream, grease, tallow, suet, lard, dripping, blubber; soap, wax; petroleum, gasoline, kerosene, propane, naphtha; vegetable oil, salad oil, olive oil, linseed oil; ointment, unguent, liniment, salve, balm.

356a resin *n* rosin, gum, wax, amber, ambergris, bitumen, pitch, tar, asphalt; varnish, lacquer, shellac, mastic, sealing wax, putty.

v resin, rosin; varnish, shellac, lacquer, overlay.
adj resinous, gummy, waxy.

III. Organic Matter

357 animate matter *n* nature, natural world, animated nature, living beings, organisms, organic remains, animal life, plant life, fauna, flora; protoplasm, cell.

science of living beings: biology, natural history, zoology, botany, anatomy, physiology, organic chemistry.

naturalist, biologist, zoologist, botanist.

adj animate, organic.

358 inanimate matter *n* mineral world, mineral kingdom, inorganic matter, brute matter.

science of the mineral kingdom: mineralogy, geology, metallurgy.

adj inanimate, inorganic, mineral.

359 life *n* existence, being; animation, vigor, vivacity, vitality, energy, vital spark, vital flame, lifeblood, spirit, soul; respiration, breath, breath of life; nourishment, nutriment, staff of life.

v be alive, live, breathe, respire, exist, subsist; be born, come into the world, see the light; quicken, revive, come to; give birth to, bring to life, vitalize; vivify, reanimate; keep alive, *(informal)* keep going, *(informal)* hang in there.

adj alive, live, vigorous, vivacious, vital, energetic, lively, alive and kicking, active.

360 death *n* decease, demise, expiration, passing, dissolution, departure, release, rest, quietus, fall; end, cessation, loss of life, extinction, dying, mortality, doom, finale, stop; last breath, final gasp, death rattle, death agonies, hand of death, dying day, *rigor mortis;* decay, fatality, natural causes, death blow.

v die, decease, pass away, pass on, perish, expire, depart, dissolve; cease, end, vanish, disappear; fail, subside, fade, sink, fall, decline, wither, decay; be taken, yield, give in, breathe one's last, end one's days, depart this life, be no more, drop off, pop off, drop dead, drop down dead, break one's neck, give up the ghost, shuffle off the mortal coil, go the way of all flesh, turn to dust, *(informal)* kick the bucket, *(informal)* go out like a light, *(informal)* croak.

adj dead, lifeless, extinct, defunct, late, gone, no more, dead and gone, dead as a door nail; deadly, fatal, lethal.

361 [destruction of life; violent death] **killing** *n* murder, homicide, assassination, slaughter, bloodshed, carnage, butchery, massacre, holocaust; suffocation, strangulation, garrote, hanging, electrocution, gassing, drawing and quartering; suicide, regicide, parricide, matricide, fratricide, infanticide; death blow, finishing stroke, *coup de grace,* execution; suicide; slaughtering, hunting, coursing, shooting, fishing; butcher, slayer, murderer, executioner, assassin, cutthroat, thug, guerilla, saboteur, garroter.

v kill, put to death, murder, slaughter, butcher, massacre, execute, behead, decapitate, guillotine, dispatch, *(informal)* waste; *(informal)* wipe out, strangle, garrote, hang, throttle, choke, stifle, suffocate, smother, asphyxiate, drown, gas, electrocute, stab, bayonet, cut, cut to pieces, cut to ribbons, mutilate, run through, put to the sword, shoot, gun down, do away with, *(informal)* blow away; hunt, spear; cut off, nip in the bud, cut down, give no quarter, decimate; commit suicide, destroy oneself, blow one's brains out, put an end to oneself.

adj murderous, homicidal, bloodthirsty, bloody, gory; mortal, fatal, lethal, deadly, deathly; suicidal.

362 corpse *n* body, remains, carcass, corse, cadaver, empty vessel, bones, skeleton, relics, mortal remains, mortal coil, clay, dust, ashes, earth, carrion, fodder, food for worms, shade, ghost.

adj corpselike, cadaverous.

363 interment *n* burial, sepulture, entombment, inhumation; cremation; funeral, funeral rites, obsequies, wake; knell, death bell, dirge, elegy; shroud, winding sheet, grave clothes; coffin, shell, sarcophagous, urn, pall, bier, catafalque, hearse; grave, pit, sepulchre, tomb, vault, crypt, catacomb, mausoleum, cemetery, burial ground, mortuary, graveyard, charnel house, morgue; monument, gravestone, tombstone, headstone, *memento mori;* exhumation, disinterment, autopsy, post mortem examination.

v inter, bury, lay in the grave, lay to rest, lay in the ground, consign to the grave, entomb; lay out, mummify, embalm; cremate; exhume, disinter, unearth.

adj burial, funeral, funeral, mortuary, sepulchral, cinerary.

364 animality *n* corporality, animal life, living being, flesh, flesh and blood; physique, strength, vigor, vitality.

adj animalistic, bodily, corporeal, fleshly.

365 vegetation *n* vegetable life, growth, plant life.

adj vegetative; rank, dense, lush, fecund.

366 animal *n* animal kingdom, brute creation, fauna; beast, brute, creature, living thing, creeping thing, dumb animal; mammal, quadruped, bird, reptile, fish, crustacean, shellfish, mollusk,

worm, insect; flocks and herds, wild animals, domestic animals, livestock, game, beasts of the field, fowls of the air.

adj animal, animalistic, zoological.

367 vegetable *n* vegetable kingdom, flora, plant life, flowerage, herbage, shrubbery, foliage, leafage, leaves, foliation, verdure, greens; tree, shrub, bush, creeper, herb, fruit, grass.

v vegetate, germinate, shoot, sprout, shoot up, grow, swell, spring up, develop, increase, flourish, blossom, bloom.

adj vegetable, vegetal, vegetative, leguminous, herbal, herbaceous, botanic, verdant.

368 [science of animals] **zoology** *n* morphology, zoography, embryology, anatomy; comparative anatomy, animal physiology, comparative physiology, anthropology, ornithology, icthyology, paleontology, entomology.

adj zoological.

369 [science of plants] **botany** *n* phytology, vegetable physiology, dendrology; flora, botanic garden.

adj botanical, herbal, horticultural.

370 [management of animals] **ranching** *n* breeding, raising; taming, domestication; veterinary science.

v ranch, raise, breed; tame, domesticate, train, housebreak; cage, bridle, restrain.

adj bred; tame, domestic, domesticated, housebroken.

371 [management of plants] **agriculture** *n* farming, cultivation, husbandry, tillage; agronomy, agrobiology, agrology, agronomics; gardening, horticulture, floriculture, landscaping, arboriculture; forestry.

v cultivate, till, till the soil, work the land, farm, garden, sow, seed, plant; reap, mow, cut; plow, plough, harrow, rake, weed, hoe, lop; garden, landscape.

adj agricultural, agrarian; arable, fertile.

372 mankind *n* human race, man, woman, humankind, human species, humanity, mortality, people, human being, person, personage, individual, creature, fellow creature, fellow man, mortal, body, soul, somebody, someone, one, party, head, hand, heart.

people, persons, folk, public, society, community, group, general public, society of men, civilization, commonwealth, commonweal, body politic, human community, population, millions, multitudes.

adj human, mortal, personal, individual; social, national, civic, public; cosmopolitan, humanitarian.

373 man *n* make, manhood, masculinity, he, him; gentleman, sir, mister, Mr., master, swain, fellow, chap, boy.

male animal: cock, drake, gander, dog, boar, stag, hart, buck, stallion, tomcat, billygoat, ram, bull, ox; gelding, steer.

adj male, masculine, manly.

374 woman *n* female; womanhood, femininity, she, her; lady, gentlewoman, madam, madame, miss, *(informal)* ma'am, Ms., Mrs., matron, girl.

female animal: hen, bitch, sow, doe, roe, mare, nannygoat, ewe, cow.

adj female, feminine, womanly.

375 sensibility *n* sensation, sensitiveness, feeling, responsiveness, impressibility; sensation, impression, touch; consciousness.

v be sensible, be sensitive to, feel, touch, perceive; render sensible, sharpen, cultivate, stir, excite, sensitize; cause sensation, impress, excite an impression, stir.

adj sensitive, sensible, sensuous; perceptive, sentient, responsive, susceptible, conscious, aware, alive, acute, sharp, keen, vivid, lively.

adv to the quick.

376 insensibility *n* lack of feeling, obtuseness, paralysis, numbness, anesthesia; insusceptibility, unresponsiveness, unconsciousness.

v be insensible; render insensible, blunt, pall, numb, benumb, paralyze, deaden, freeze, anesthetize; cloy, stuff, satiate, drown; stupefy, stun.

adj insensible, senseless, unsusceptible, unresponsive, insensitive, numb, hard, dead; dull, dense, thick, obtuse, unperceptive; anesthetic, paralytic.

377 pleasure *n* bodily pleasure, sensuality, sensuousness, physical gratification, sex, sexuality, sensual delight, ecstasy, orgasm, climax; titillation, teasing; comfort, ease, relish, delight, joy, luxury, luxuriousness, pleasure, lap of luxury.

v feel pleasure, receive pleasure, enjoy, relish, revel in, bask in, swim in, luxuriate, feast on, wallow in, gloat over, *(informal)* dig, *(informal)* get off on, *(informal)* be turned on, *(informal)* get into; give pleasure, *(informal)* turn on, thrill, excite.

adj pleasurable, sensual, sensuous, sexual, voluptuous, luxurious, ecstatic, orgasmic, climactic; agreeable, comfortable, cordial, delightful, joyful; palatable, sweet, tasty; fragrant; melodious, lovely.

adv in comfort, in ecstasy, on a bed of roses.

378 pain *n* suffering, dolor, ache, aching, smart, shoot, shooting, twinge, twitch, gripe, grip, hurt, cut, sore, soreness, tenderness, discomfort, malaise, disease; spasm, cramp, crick, stitch, convulsion, throe, throb, pang; torment, torture, rack, anguish, agony.

v feel pain, suffer, undergo pain, ache, smart, bleed, tingle, shoot, twinge, twitch, writhe, wince, hurt; inflict pain, hurt, chafe, sting, bite, gnaw, gripe, pinch, tweak, grate, gall, fret, prick, pierce, wring, convulse; torment, torture, wrack, agonize.

adj painful, dolorous, sore, tender, raw, uncomfortable; convulsive, torturous.

379 touch *n* contact, feeling, tactility, palpability, impact, feel, sensation; manipulation, handling, rubbing, massaging, fondling, fingering, kneading, stroking, brushing, grazing over.

v touch, feel, handle, finger, fondle, thumb, paw, grab, rub, massage, knead, stroke, brush, manipulate, run the fingers over, graze over.

adj tactual, tactile, palpable.

380 sensations of touch *n* itching, tickling, titillation, scratching, pricking, stinging.

v itch, tingle, creep, thrill, prick, scratch, sting.

adj itching; ticklish, scratchy, itchy.

381 numbness *n* physical insensibility, lack of feeling, deadness.

v benumb, anesthetize, deaden, dull, drug.

adj numb, dull, benumbed, insensible, unfeeling, frozen, drugged, dead, deadened, dulled.

382 heat *n* warmth, caloricity, caloric, temperature; glow, flush, warmth, intensity, ardor, passion, fever, fervor, zeal; fire, spark, flame, blaze.

v be hot, glow, flush, sweat, swelter, smoke, stew, simmer, seethe, boil, burn, broil, blaze, flame; smolder, parch, fume, pant; heat, warm, thaw, defrost; stimulate, stir, animate, arouse.

adj hot, warm, mild, genial, tepid, lukewarm, unfrozen; heated, torrid, sultry, burning, fiery; sunny, tropical, suffocating, stifling, sweltering, oppressive, reeking, baking; fiery, incandescent, ebullient, glowing, smoking, blazing, on fire, afire, in flames, aflame, ablaze; ardent, fervent, fervid, angry, furious, vehement, intense, excited, excitable, irascible, animated, violent, passionate.

383 cold *n* coldness, iciness, frigidity, chilliness, coolness.

v be cold, shiver, quake, shake, tremble, shudder, quiver; chill, freeze, refrigerate.

adj cold, chilly, chill, cool, frigid, gelid, frozen, freezing, bitter, bitter cold, numbing, nipping, cutting, shivering, bleak, raw, frost-bitten, icy, glacial, frosty, wintry, hibernal, arctic, polar; impassionate, unemotional, apathetic, unresponsive, unsympathetic, stoical, unfeeling, indifferent, coldblooded, heartless, imperturbable; polite, formal, reserved, hostile; deliberate, depressing, dispiriting, disheartening.

adj coldly, bitterly.

384 calefaction *n* heating, melting, fusion, liquefaction, combustion; cauterization; calcination; incineration, cremation; carbonization.

v heat, warm, chafe; fire, set fire to, set on fire, kindle, light, ignite, rekindle; melt, thaw, fuse, liquefy; burn, inflame, roast, broil, toast, cook, fry, grill, singe, parch, bake, scorch; brand, cauterize, sear, burn in; boil, digest, stew, sauté, cook, scald, parboil, simmer; take fire, catch fire.

adj heated, warmed, fired, burnt, scorched; molten; flammable, combustible, volcanic.

385 refrigeration *n* cooling, congelation, glaciation, icing; solidification, hardening.

v refrigerate, keep cold, chill, ice, congeal, freeze; cool, fan, refresh; benumb, starve, pinch, nip, cut, pierce, bite; quench, put out, stamp out, extinguish.

adj cooled, frozen, chilled; incombustible, inflammable, fireproof.

386 furnace *n* oven, stove, range; hearth, heater, kiln, oil burner, space heater, blast furnace, forge, fire place, fiery furnace.

387 refrigerator *n* ice box, fridge, ice chest, frigidaire, cold storage, freezer, ice house.

388 fuel *n* firing, combustible; coal, hard coal, anthracite, bituminous coal, soft coal, carbon, coke, charcoal; wood, firewood, kindling, brushwood, log, cinder, ember, ash; turf, peat, fuel, oil, fossil fuel, petroleum, gasoline, kerosene; gas, natural gas, propane; electricity; unclear power; solar energy; waterpower, windpower.

v fuel, feed, stoke, fire; power.

adj carbonaceous; combustible, flammable, burnable.

389 thermometer *n* thermometograph, thermoscope, thermostat, telethermometer, pyrometer, calorimeter, glass, mercury.

390 taste *n* flavor, savor, sensation, gusto, relish; smack, smatch, tang, aftertaste; morsel, bit, sip.

v taste, flavor, savor, smatch, smack; tickle the palate, tickle the tastebuds; smack the lips.

adj tasty, savory, flavory, flavorful, flavored; palatable, digestible, *(informal)* edible.

391 tastelessness *n* insipidity; blandness, flatness, unsavoriness.

v be tasteless.

adj tasteless, insipid, bland, flat,

weak, mild, vapid, wishy-washy, (informal) plastic, pasty.

392 pungency n piquancy, poignancy, tang, bite, nip, sharpness, acridity, bitterness, hotness, sourness, unsavoriness.

v be pungent; make pungent, season, spice, salt, pepper, pickle, brine, devil, smoke, curry.

adj pungent, strong, full-flavored, seasoned, highly seasoned, spiced; sharp, biting, nippy, acrid, bitter, sour, stinging, spicy, salty, peppery, piquant, hot; unsavory.

393 condiment n seasoning, flavoring, sauce, spice, relish; salt, pepper.

v season.

394 savoriness n flavor, flavorfulness, taste, tastiness, relish, piquancy, zest, tang, delectability, palatability.

v be savory, tickle the palate, taste good, taste great; savor, enjoy, appreciate, relish, like, taste.

adj savory, good, tasty, palatable, nice, dainty, delectable, flavorful, appetizing, delicate, delicious, exquisite, rich, luscious, full-flavored, pungent, ambrosial.

395 unsavoriness n tastelessness, flavorlessness, blandness; acridness, sourness.

v be unsavory, be unpalatable, taste bad, sicken, disgust, pall, nauseate, turn the stomach, make one sick.

adj unsavory, tasteless, flavorless, bland, flat; bad tasting, ill-flavored, acrid, bitter, sour, unpalatable, inedible, offensive, repulsive, nasty, vile, sickening, nauseous, loathsome, unpleasant, awful.

396 sweetness n sugariness, saccharinity, syrupiness, stickiness.

v sweeten, sugar, candy.

adj sweet, sugary, syrupy, honeyed, saccharine, candied, sticky gooey, luscious, lush, cloying; sweetened.

397 sourness n acridity, tartness, sharpness, vinegariness, acerbity, acidity.

v sour, acidify, acerbate, curdle, acidulate, ferment, spoil.

adj sour, acid, bitter, tart, sharp, vinegary, acidulous, astringent, acerbic, acrid; fermented, rancid, bad, spoiled, turned, curdled, gone bad; styptic, hard, rough.

398 odor n smell, scent; effluvium; exhalation, emanation; fume, essence, redolence.

v have an odor, smell, smell of, give out a smell; smell, scent, sniff, snuff, inhale.

adj odorous, odoriferous, smelly, strong smelling, redolent, pungent.

399 inodorousness n absence of smell, odorlessness.

v be inodorous, not smell, have no odor, be odorless.

adj odorless, scentless, unsmelling.

400 fragrance n aroma, redolence, perfume, sweet smell, sweet scent, smell.

v be fragrant, smell sweet, have a perfume, scent, perfume.

adj fragrant, aromatic, redolent, spicy, scented, perfumed, sweet scented, sweet smelling, odoriferous, odorific.

401 fetor n bad smell, bad odor; foul smell, offensive smell, stink, stench, fume, foulness, fetidness, rancidity, rankness, fustiness, mustiness.

v have a bad smell, smell bad, smell rotten, smell, stink, reek.

adj fetid, strong smelling, bad, strong, fulsome, offensive, rank, rancid, noisome, mephitic, miasmic, musty, fusty, foul, rotten, putrid, reeking, stinking, stinky, suffocating, nauseating, nauseous, (informal) gross.

402 sound n noise, tone, pitch, sound vibrations, strain, sonority, sonorousness, twang, intonation, cadence; audibility, resonance, voice.

science of sound: acoustics, phonology, phonetics, electronic sound, reproduction.

v sound, make a noise; give out sound, emit sound; resound, echo.

adj sounding, sonorous, resonant, audible, distinct.

403 silence n stillness, quiet, peace, hush, lull, quiescence, dead silence; muteness, speechlessness, taciturnity.

v silence, still, hush, stifle, muffle, stop, muzzle, gag; be silent, hold one's tongue, shut up, keep quiet, be still.

adj silent, quiet, still calm, noiseless, soundless, hushed, quiescent; mute, speechless, taciturn; solemn, soft, deathlike, awful, silent as the grave.

adv silently.

404 loudness *n* loud noise, power, resonance, thunderousness, roaring, vociferousness, clamorousness; din, clang, clangor, clamor, noise, roar, uproar, hubbub, boom, racket, outcry; blast, peal, swell, flourish of trumpets, boom; thunder, explosion.

v be loud, peal, swell, clang, boom, thunder, fulminate, roar, resound, bellow, scream, holler, shout; ring in the ears, pierce the ears, split the eardrums, stun, deafen; shake, awake.

adj loud, noisy, vociferous, resounding, clamorous, deafening, stentorian, boisterous, tumultuous, sonorous, deep, full, powerful, thundering, ear-splitting, piercing, uproarious, obstreperous, shrill, sharp.

adv loudly, noisily, at the top of one's voice, at the top of one's lungs, aloud.

405 faintness *n* faint sound, whisper, breath, undertone, murmur, hum; inaudibility; hoarseness.

v whisper, breathe, murmur, hum, mutter, speak softly, speak in low tones.

adj faint, whispered, indistinct, dim, inaudible, barely audible, low, stifled, muffled, murmured, muted; gentle, soft, languid, floating, flowing; hoarse, husky.

406 [sudden and violent sounds] **snap** *n* rap, thud, burst, explosion, detonation, discharge, firing, salvo, pop, bang, blast.

v rap, snap, tap, knock, click, clash, crack, crackle, crash, beat.

407 [repeated and protracted sounds] **roll** *n* drumming, tapping, rumbling, grumbling; dingdong, whirring, droning; rat-atat, rubadub, pitapat; quaver, quiver, clutter, racket; peal of bells; reverberation.

v roll, drum, rumble, grumble, rattle, clatter, patter, clack; hum, trill, shake; chime, peal, toll; tick, beat.

408 resonance *n* ring, ringing, chime, clang, clangor, boom, roll, roar, rumble, thunder, vibrato, timbre, twang, vibration, reverberation, tintinnabulation, booming, quaver, ding-dong, echoing, sonorousness.

v resound, reverberate, re-echo; ring, jingle, chink, clink; gurgle, echo, ring in the ear.

adj resonant, resounding, reverberant, reverberating; deep-toned, deep-sounding.

408a nonresonance *n* dead sound, thud, thump, muffled, drums, cracked bell; damper, mute, muffler.

v sound dead, thud, thump; muffle, dampen, mute.

adj nonresonant, dampened, muted, muffled, deadened; dead.

409 [hissing sounds] **sibilation** *n* hissing, wheezing, buzzing, zipping, whooshing; high note.

v hiss, buzz, whiz, wheeze, whoosh, zip, rustle, whistle, fizzle; squash, sneeze.

adj sibilant; hissing, wheezy.

410 [harsh sounds] **stridency** *n* discord, dissonance, harshness, raucousness, atonality, clashing, grinding, grating, rasping, sharpness, creaking, shrillness.

v creak, grate, jar, jangle, clank, clink, grid, grate; scream, yelp.

adj strident, sharp, high, acute, shrill, atonal, unharmonious, unmusical, dissonant, discordant, cacophonous; piercing, ear-piercing, cracked; creaking, harsh, coarse, hoarse, rough, gruff, grating, jarring, guttural, squawking, acute, scratching, croaking, rasping, sour, clashing.

411 cry *n* shout, scream, yell, shriek, roar, howl, wail; exclamation, outcry, clamor, vociferation; hubbub, hullabaloo, chorus, hue and cry; entreaty, appeal, solicitation, plea, plaint, prayer, crying, weeping, wailing, sobbing, lament, whimper, whimpering, tears, moaning.

v cry, roar, shout, bawl, brawl, hoop, whoop, yell, bellow, howl, scream, screech, shriek, squeak, squeal, whine, whimper, wail, weep, sob, moan, lament; cheer, hoot; grumble, groan, complain; vociferate, raise one's voice, sing out, cry out, yell out, exclaim, holler, shout at the top of one's lungs.

adj crying, clamorous; vociferous; solicitous; stentorian.

412 [animal sounds] **ululation** *n* howling, crying, belling, screeching, singing, growling, purring.

v cry, roar, bellow, bark, yelp, yap, growl, snarl, howl, bay, grunt, snort, neigh, bray, mew, purr, caterwaul, bleat, low, moo, squeak, oink, baa, crow, croak, screech, caw, coo, gobble, quack, cackle, gaggle, chuck, cluck, clack, chirp, chirrup, twitter, cuckoo, hum, buzz, hiss, blatter.

413 melody. concord *n* melodiousness, tunefulness, sweet sounds, mellifluence, musicalness, euphony; timbre, tone color, pitch; tune song, aria, theme, measure, plainsong, canticle, strain, lay.

harmony, harmoniousness; rhythm, meter; symphony, euphony, consonance, attunement, modulation, syncopation; counterpoint, polyphony; concordance, pleasing combination.

v harmonize, chime, symphonize, blend; tune, accord.

adj melodious, musical, tuneful, melodic, lyrical, euphonious, singing, ringing, sweet-sounding, euphonic, mellifluous, dulcet, mellow, clear, sweet, rich, soft, silvery, agreeable, pleasing.

concordant, harmonious, agreeing, symphonious, suiting, congenial, blending, synchronized, consistent, in rapport, in unison, confluent, conjoined, symmetrical, proportionate, consonant, compatible.

414 discord *n* dissonance, atonality; harshness; racket, noise, inharmoniousness.

v be discordant; jar, grate.

adj discordant, dissonant, atonal, harsh; out of tune, tuneless, unmelodious, inharmonious, unmusical; jarring, grating, cacophonous, screeching.

415 music *n* sweet sounds, pleasing sounds, harmonious sounds, melody, song, tune, strain, air, harmony; classical music, popular music, folk music, jazz, electronic music; orchestral music, instrumental music, symphonic music, chamber music; ragtime, reggae, swing, bebop, bop, barrelhouse, rock; pop music, vocal music, choral music, solo, duet, duo, sonata, trio, quartet, quintet, sextet, septet, octet.

v make music, perform; compose.

adj musical, lyrical; instrumental, orchestral, symphonic, vocal, choral, operatic.

416 musician [performance of music] *n* artist, performer, concert artist, player, soloist, instrumentalist, vocalist, accompanist, singer, minstrel; symphony orchestra, orchestra, chamber orchestra, band, rock and roll band, group, combo, ensemble, chamber group, quartet, trio; chorus, choir, vocal group.

v make music, play, perform, strike up, concertize, execute, accompany, present the music, solo, improvise, play the notes; sing, croon, warble, vocalize, spin a melody.

adj musical, instrumental, vocal, choral, operatic; lyrical, harmonious, brilliant, sharp, incisive.

417 musical instruments *n* orchestra, band, brass band, marching band, military band, ensemble, group; strings, plucked instruments, bowed instruments, hammered instruments; woodwinds, winds, tubed instruments, reed instruments, brass instruments; percussion; synthesizer.

418 hearing *n* audition, auscultation, listening, perception, audibility, ear; regarding, attending, heeding.

hearer, auditor, listener; eavesdropper.

v hear, listen, attend, lend an ear, bend an ear, *(informal)* tune in, give a hearing to, give audience to, prick up one's ears, be all ears; overhear, eavesdrop; heed, regard.

adj hearing, auditory, auricular.

419 deafness *n* hardness of hearing, inaudibility.

v be deaf, not hear; turn a deaf ear to, plug up one's ears; deafen, stun, split the eardrums.

adj deaf, stone-deaf, hard of hearing; deafened, stunned; unheeding, inattentive.

420 light *n* ray, beam, stream, gleam, streak; sunbeam, moonbeam, aurora, dawn, sunrise, day-break, day, daylight, light of day, sunshine, broad daylight, glow, glint, glimmering; sun, moon; flush, halo, glory, aureole; spark, scintilla, scintillation, flash, blaze, coruscation; flame, lightening, flare; luster, sheen, shimmer, reflection, refraction; brightness, brilliancy, splendor, effulgence, radiance, illumination, radiation, luminosity, lucidity.

science of light: optics, photography, radioactivity.

v shine, glow, glitter, glisten, gleam, beam, flare, flare up, glare, flash, glimmer, shimmer, flicker, sparkle, scintillate, coruscate, flash, blaze; light, reflect, dazzle, bedazzle, daze, radiate; lighten, enlighten, light, irradiate, shed light upon, cast light upon, illuminate, illumine, kindle, fire.

adj luminous, lucent; light, bright, vivid, splendid, resplendent, lustrous, shiny, radiant; sheeny, glossy, glassy, sunny, burnished; cloudless, clear, unclouded; effulgent, blazing, ablaze, phosphorescent, aglow; iridescent.

421 darkness *n* blackness; obscurity, doom, murkiness, murk; duskiness, dusk, dimness; night, midnight, dead of night; shade, shadow, umbra, penumbra; obscuration, adumbration, extinction, eclipse, total eclipse.

v be dark; darken, obscure, shade, dim, shadow, overcast, cloud, becloud; extinguish, put out, blow out, snuff out.

adj dark, obscure, black, pitch black, nocturnal, overcast, cloudy, darkened; dingy, lurid, murky, gloomy, oppressive; shadowy, shady, umbrageous.

422 dimness *n* duskiness, shadowiness, gloominess, cloudiness, mist, mistiness, haze, haziness, fogginess, paleness, shade, nebulosity, gray, grayness.

v be dim, grow dim, darken, obscure, adumbrate, becloud, cloud, shadow, shade, eclipse, cloud over; blur, dull, fade, pale; glimmer, twinkle, flutter, flicker, waver.

adj dim, dull, dingy, lackluster, darkish, darkened, gray, dark, faint, pale, cloudy, misty, murky, overcast, nebulous, shadowy, umbrageous, blurry, hazy, opaque, foggy, bleary, gloomy, lurid, leaden.

423 [source of light] **luminary** *n* natural light, sun, moon, stars, flame, fire, spark, phosphorescence; artificial light, lamp, gas lamp, oil lamp, kerosene lamp, electric light, lantern, torch, candle, taper, light bulb.

v light, illuminate.

adj self-luminous; phosphorescent, radiant.

424 shade *n* cover, awning, umbrella, parasol, sunshade; screen, curtain, shutter, blind, gauze, veil, mantle, mask, sunglasses, *(informal)* shades; cloud, mist, fog, shadow.

v shade, veil, cover, screen, curtain, veil, draw a curtain, pull the shade, cast a shadow.

adj shady, shadowy, cloudy.

425 transparency *n* transparence, translucence, diaphanousness, clearness, lucidity, limpidity, thinness, sheerness, gauziness, flimsiness.

v be transparent, transmit light.

adj transparent, pellucid, lucid, diaphanous, translucent limpid, clear, crystalline, see-through, sheer, gauzy, flimsy.

426 opacity *n* opaqueness, darkness, cloudiness, filminess, haziness, mistiness, nontransparency.

v be opaque, obstruct the passage of light.

adj opaque, impervious to light, impenetrable to light, dim, filmy, thick, smoky, misty, smoggy, shady, murky, cloudy, hazy, obscure, clouded, foggy, unclear, frosted, nontransparent, nontranslucent.

427 semitransparency *n* opalescence, milkiness, pearliness; film, mist.

v let in partial light.

adj semitransparent, semipellucid, semiopaque, opalescent, pearly, nacreous, milky.

428 color *n* hue, tint, tinge, dye, complexion, shade, tincture, cast, coloration, tone, key; primary color, secondary color, complementary color; coloring; spectrum, prism, spectroscope; pigment, paint, dye, wash, stain.

v color, dye, tinge, stain, tint, paint, wash; illuminate, emblazon.

adj colored, dyed, tinted; prismatic, chromatic; bright, vivid, intense, deep, rich, gorgeous; fresh, unfaded; gaudy, florid, garish, showy, flashy, glaring; mellow, harmonious, pearly, sweet, delicate, tender, refined; dull, gray.

429 [absence of color] **colorlessness** *n* neutral tint, black and white, chiaroscuro, monochrome; etiolation, pallor, paleness, discoloration.

v lose color, fade, turn pale, become colorless, pale; deprive of color, bleach, wash out, blanch, tarnish, etiolate, tone down, whiten.

adj uncolored, colorless, hueless, pale, pallid, faint, dull, dun, wan, sallow, dingy, ashy, gray, ashen, lackluster; discolored; light-colored, fair, blond, white.

430 **whiteness** *n* milkiness, frostiness, silveriness, pearliness; etiolation, albification, decoloration, colorlessness; albinism.

v whiten, bleach, blanch, etiolate, whitewash.

adj white, snowy, frosted, snow-white, milk-white, milky, chalky, pearly, ivory, silver, silvery, opaline, whitish, albinistic, etiolated, bleached, blanched, fair, light, wan, pallid, pale, lackluster, colorless, anemic, sallow, faint.

431 **blackness** *n* darkness, swarthiness, lividness; ink, ebony, coal, charcoal, pitch; obscurity.

v black, blacken, darken; blot, smutch, smut, smirch.

adj black, sable, somber, livid, dark, inky, ebony, pitchy, swarthy, sooty, dingy, dusky, murky; jet-black, pitch-black, black as coal, coal-black, kohl-black, black as night.

432 **gray** *n* grayness, neutral tint, silver, salt and pepper, dove color.

adj gray, iron-gray, silver, silvery, silverish, grayish, dun, drab, ashy, ashen, dove-colored, dapple-gray; grizzly, grizzled, hoary.

433 **brown** *n* brownness, beige, khaki.

adj brown, bay, dapple, auburn, nut-brown, chocolate, chestnut, cinnamon, russet, tawny, tan, brunette, mahogany, khaki, beige, ochre, sepia, hazel, brownish, coffee, cocoa, rust, roan, sorrel.

434 **red** *n* redness; blush, color.

v redden, blush, flush, get red in the face, turn color.

adj red, reddish, scarlet, crimson,

blood red, bloody, cherry-colored, vermilion, carmine, maroon, pink, hot-pink, rosy, ruby, salmon, wine-colored; red-faced, blushing, embarrassed, red as beet, red as a lobster, flushed, burning, fuming, flaming, inflamed; ruddy, glowing, blooming, warm, hot.

435 **green** *n* greenness, verdure, blue and yellow.

adj green, greenish, verdant, olive, pea-green, emerald, apple, Kelly green, blue-green, aquamarine, sea-green; grassy, verdurous; fresh, new, recent, young, innocent, naive, raw, unseasoned, immature, inexperienced, ignorant; sickly, wan, pale, livid; jealous, envious.

436 **yellow** *n* yellowness, jaundice.

v yellow, age, turn color, dry up.

adj yellow, yellowish, gold, golden, ocher, lemon, citrine, saffron, aureate, creamy, straw-colored, flaxen, blond, tawny, sallow; sordid, cheap; cowardly, *(informal)* chicken, craven, lily-livered, contemptible, despicable, mean, cringing, groveling; jaundiced.

437 **purple** *n* blue and red.

adj purple, purplish, lavender, lilac, magenta, orchid, violet, plum-colored, mauve.

438 **blue** *n* blueness.

adj blue, bluish, azure, marine blue, navy, aquamarine, greenish blue, sapphire, turquoise, cobalt, baby blue; depressed, down in the dumps, *(informal)* in the pits, *(informal)* down, low.

439 **orange** *n* red and yellow; flame.

adj orange, orangy, orangish, brass, copper, apricot, tangerine, gold, flame-colored.

440 **variegation** *n* striation, spottiness, streakiness, iridescence, play of colors.

v variegate, diversify, streak, stripe, checker, speckle, bespeckle, fleck, dapple; dot, striate, tattoo, inlay; embroider, quilt.

adj variegated, multi-colored, many-colored, kaleidoscopic; iridescent, prismatic, opaline, nacreous, pearly; pied, piebald, mottled; dappled, salt ad pepper, marbled, flecked, speckled, spotty, studded, freckled, flecky, spotted, diversified; striped, veined, lined, striated, streaked, brindled, banded, checked, checkered, plaid, mosaic, inlaid.

441 vision *n* sight, optics, eyesight; view, look, glance, ken, glimpse, peep, peek, gaze, stare, leer; contemplation, regard, survey; point of view, outlook, viewpoint, perspective, standpoint; perspicacity, discernment, perception, penetration.

v see, behold, discern, perceive, have in sight, descry, sight, make out, discover, distinguish, recognize spy, espy, catch a glimpse of, command a view of, witness; envision, contemplate; look, view, eye, survey, scan, inspect, run the eye over, glance around; observe, watch, watch for, peep, peer, peek, pry, take a peep, leer, ogle, glare.

adj visual, ocular, optic; clearsighted, eagle-eyed, discerning; visionary, farsighted.

adv on sight, at first sight, at a glance.

442 blindness *n* sightlessness; cataract; ignorance.

v be blind, not see; grope in the dark; blind, hoodwink, dazzle; screen, hide, mask.

adj blind, eyeless, sightless, unseeing, dark, purblind, stone-blind; dimsighted, undiscerning, ignorant.

adv blindly, blindfold, darkly.

443 [imperfect vision] **dimsightedness** *n* nearsightedness, farsightedness, purblindness, prebyopia, myopia, astigmatism, color blindness, cataract, ophthalmia; squint, cross-eye, strabismus, lazy eye, cockeye, swivel eye, goggle eyes.

fallacies of vision: refraction, distortion, illusion, mirage, phantasm, vision, specter, apparition, ghost; mirror, lens.

v be dimsighted, see double, wink, blink, squint, look askance, screw up the eyes.

adj dimsighted, purblind, myopic, astigmatic, nearsighted, farsighted, colorblind; blear-eyed, goggle-eyed, cockeyed, crosseyed.

444 spectator *n* beholder, observer, looker-on, onlooker, witness, eyewitness, bystander, passerby; sightseer, audience, crowd; spy, sentinel.

v witness, behold, look on.

445 optical instruments *n* lens, magnifying glass, microscope; spectacles, monocle, eyeglasses, glasses, contact lens, goggles, pince-nez; telescope, lorgnette, binoculars, spyglass, opera glasses; mirror, looking glass, reflector; prism, kaleidoscope, stereoscope.

446 visibility *n* perceptibility, discernibleness, distinctness, clearness, clarity, perceivability, conspicuousness, definition, sharp outline; appearance, manifestation.

v be visible, appear, open to the view, present itself, show itself, reveal itself, peep up, show up, turn up, start up, pop up, crop up; glimmer, loom; burst forth, burst upon the view, come into sight, come into view, come forth, come forward, attract attention.

adj visible, perceptible, discernible, perceivable, apparent, obvious, manifest, plain, clear, distinct, definite, well-defined, outlined, well-marked; recognizable, palpable, glaring, conspicuous, in full view, in full sight, in front of one's nose, under one's nose, before one's eyes.

447 invisibility *n* indistinctness, imperceptibility, invisibleness, indefiniteness; mystery, obscurity, delitescence, haziness, cloudiness; concealment; latency.

v be invisible; be hidden; escape notice; render invisible, conceal, hide.

adj invisible, imperceptible; not in sight, out of sight, out of view, unseen; inconspicuous, covert; dim, faint, mysterious, dark, obscure, confused, indistinct, indistinguishable, shadowy, indefinite, undefined, unmarked, blurry, blurred, unfocused, out of focus, misty, veiled; concealed, hidden.

448 appearance *n* phenomenon, sight, show, scene, view; prospect, vista, perspective, lookout, outlook, bird's-eye view, scenery, landscape, picture, tableau; display, exposure; pageant, spectacle; aspect, phase, seeming, shape, form, manifestation, guise, look, complexion, color, image, mien, air, cast, carriage, comportment, demeanor; presence; feature, trait, lines, outline, contour, face, countenance, physiognomy, visage, profile, outsides.

v appear, be visible, seem, look, show,

present; figure, cut a figure; present to the view.

adj apparent, seeming, ostensible.

adv apparently, to all appearance, ostensibly, seemingly, on the face of it, at first sight, to the eye.

449 disappearance *n* evanescence, eclipse; departure, exit; loss.

v disappear, vanish, dissolve, melt, melt away, fade, pass, pass out, go, depart, leave no trace, be gone.

adj disappearing, evanescent; departed, left; missing, lost, vanished.

Class IV
Intellectual Faculties

I. Formation of Ideas

450 intellect *n* rationality, mind, understanding, reason, faculties, judgment, sense, common sense, wits, brains, *(informal)* smarts; brain, head, pate, *(informal)* noodle, skull, *(informal)* upstairs.

v intellectualize, reason, understand, realize, ruminate; note, notice, mark, be aware of, take cognizance of.

adj intellectual, mental, cerebral, rational, sensical, commonsensical.

450a absence of intellect *n* want of intellect; inanity, imbecility, brutishness, brute instinct.

adj unintellectual, unintelligent, unrational, nonrational, empty-headed.

451 thought *n* abstraction, concept, conception, opinion, judgment, belief, idea, notion, tenet, conviction, speculation, consideration, contemplation; meditation, pondering, reflection, musing, cogitation, thinking; intention, design, purpose, intent; anticipation, expectation; consideration, attention, care, regard; trifle, mote.

v think, cogitate, meditate, reflect, muse, ponder, ruminate, contemplate; consider, regard, suppose, look upon, judge, esteem, deem, count, account; bear in mind, recollect, recall, remember; intend, mean, design, purpose; believe, suppose; anticipate, expect.

adj thoughtful, contemplative, meditative, reflective, pensive, deliberate; lost in thought, absorbed, engrossed in; careful, heedful, mindful, regardful, considerate, attentive; discreet, prudent, wary, cautious, circumspect.

452 absence of thought *n* incogitancy, vacancy of mind, thoughtlessness, fatuity, vacuity, emptiness; inattention.

v not think, make the mind a blank, *(informal)* turn off the brain, *(informal)* tune out.

adj vacant, unoccupied, empty; unthinking; inattentive, absent, *(informal)* turned off, *(informal)* tuned out; thoughtless, inconsiderate, unmindful, unheedful, imprudent; unreflective.

453 idea *n* thought, conception, theory, notion; observation, impression, apprehension, perception, brainstorm, brainchild, fancy, *(informal)* flash; opinion, view, belief, sentiment, judgment, supposition; plan, object, objective, aim.

adj ideational.

454 topic *n* subject, theme, thesis, subject-matter, food for thought; business, affair, argument.

adj topical, thematic.

adv under consideration, in question.

455 curiosity *n* interest, inquisitiveness, inquiring mind, thirst for knowledge; spying, prying, meddlesomeness.

spy, eavesdropper, gossip.

v be curious, take an interest in, stare, gape, spy, pry.

adj curious, inquisitive, inquiring, prying, spying, peeping, meddlesome, interested.

456 incuriosity *n* lack of interest, incuriousness, indifference, unconcern.

v have no curiosity, take no interest in.

adj incurious, uninquisitive, uninquiring, uninterested, indifferent, impassive, bored, apathetic.

457 attention *n* attending to, attentiveness, intentiveness, care, consideration, observation, heed, regard, mindfulness, notice, watchfulness, alertness; study, scrutiny; civility, courtesy, respect, politeness.

v be attentive, attend, observe, look, see, notice, remark, regard, pay attention, heed; examine, study, scrutinize.

adj attentive, observant, mindful, heedful, thoughtful, alive, alert, awake, on the watch, wary, circumspectful, watchful, careful; polite, courteous, respectful, deferential.

458 inattention *n* inattentiveness, inconsideration, heedlessness, unmindfulness, disregard, unconcern.

v be inattentive, overlook, disregard, pay no attention to, gloss over.

adj inattentive, unobservant, unmindful, unheeding, thoughtless, blind to, deaf to, napping, asleep, lost.

459 care *n* heed, caution, prudence, pains, anxiety, regard, attention, vigilance, carefulness, solicitude, circumspection, alertness, watchfulness, wakefulness; accuracy, exactness.

v be careful, take care.

adj careful, cautious, circumspect, watchful, vigilant, guarded, wary, prudent, tactful; painstaking, meticulous, discerning, exact, thorough, concerned, scrupulous, particular, finical, conscientious, attentive, heedful, thoughtful.

460 neglect *n* disregard, dereliction, negligence, remissness, carelessness, failure, omission, default, inattention, heedlessness, recklessness.

v neglect, disregard, ignore, slight, overlook, omit, be remiss, be negligent.

adj neglectful, disregardful, remiss, careless, negligent, unmindful, inattentive, indifferent, heedless, inconsiderate, thoughtless, imprudent; unwary, unguarded; neglecting, neglected, unheeded, uncared for, unobserved, unnoticed, unattended to.

461 inquiry *n* investigation, examination, study, scrutiny, exploration, research, search, pursuit; inquiring, questioning, interrogation; query, question.

inquirer, investigator, inquisitor, inspector.

v inquire, ask, question, interrogate, query, investigate, examine, seek, search, look for, study, consider.

adj inquiring, inquisitive, curious, scrutinizing, questioning, exploring; inquisitorial, exploratory, interrogative.

462 answer *n* reply, response, retort, rejoinder; discovery, solution; rationale.

v answer, reply, respond, rebut, re-

tort, rejoin; explain, interpret, discover, solve; satisfy, set at rest, atone for.

adj responsive; answerable, discoverable, soluble.

463 experiment *n* test, trial, examination, proof, assay, procedure; experimentation, research, investigation, analysis.

experimenter, analyzer, adventurer.

v experiment, try, test, examine, analyze, prove, assay, essay.

adj experimental, probative, analytic.

464 comparison *n* collation, association, relating, likening, correlation, comparative relation, setting side by side, juxtaposition.

v compare, collate, confront, place side by side, pit one against another, juxtapose, relate, correlate.

adj comparative, metaphorical, compared with; comparable.

465 discrimination *n* distinction, differentiation, diagnosis; appreciation, estimation, discernment, critique, judgment; nicety, refinement, taste.

v discriminate, distinguish, set apart, differentiate.

adj discriminating, critical, distinguishing, discriminative, discriminatory, choosy, picky; discerning, perceptive; tasteful, refined.

465a indiscrimination *n* indistinction, indistinctness, lack of discernment.

v be indiscriminate, not discriminate, confound, confuse.

adj indiscriminate, miscellaneous, undiscriminating.

466 measurement *n* survey, valuation, appraisement, assessment, estimate, estimation, reckoning, gauging; measure, standard, rule, gauge, scale.

v measure, survey, assess, rate, value, appraise, estimate.

adj measurable.

467 [on one side] **evidence** *n* facts, indication, sign, signal; ground, grounds, proof, testimony; information, deposition, affidavit, exhibit, citation, reference, confirmation, corroboration.

v be evident, evince, show, tell, cite, signal, indicate, imply, argue, bespeak; give evidence, testify, depose, witness.

adj evident, evidential, indicative, inferential, referential, corroborative, confirmatory.

468 counter-evidence *n* disproof, refutation, rebuttal, conflicting evidence, negation.

v rebut, refute, check, weaken, contravene, contradict, deny.

adj countervailing, contradictory, conflicting, unsupportive, uncorroborative

469 qualification *n* modification, limitation, mitigation, narrowing, restriction, coloring, allowance, consideration, extenuation, extenuating, circumstances condition, proviso, exception.

v qualify, modify, limit, mitigate, restrain, narrow, restrict, color, allow, allow for, make allowance for, consider, extenuate, except, make an exception, take into account, take into consideration.

adj qualified, qualifying, provided, conditional, extenuating, mitigating, admitting, supposing, with the proviso, provided that.

470 possibility *n* feasibility, practicality, likelihood, potentiality; contingency, chance.

v be possible, stand a chance, admit of, *(informal)* could be.

adj possible, imaginable, conceivable, credible, feasible, practical, performable, achievable, within reach, within the bounds of possibility, potential.

adv possibly, perhaps, perchance, peradventure, maybe.

471 impossibility *n* impracticality, unfeasibility, hopelessness.

v be impossible, have no chance.

adj impossible, not possible, inconceivable, incredible, unimaginable, unreasonable, unfeasible, impractical, unobtainable, unperformable, unachievable, beyond the bounds of reason, absurd, *(informal)* fat chance, *(informal)* no way.

472 probability *n* likelihood, likeliness, plausibility, tendency, prospect, good chance, reasonable, chance, expectation.

v be probable, point to, tend, imply, bid fair.

adj probable, likely, plausible, reasonable, presumable, well-founded, hopeful.

adv probably, in all probability, in all likelihood, most likely, presumably.

473 improbability *n* unlikelihood, bare possibility, implausibility, doubtfulness, questionableness.

v be improbable, not have much of a chance.

adj improbable, unlikely, implausible, doubtful, questionable, beyond all reasonable expectation.

474 certainty *n* fact, truth; infallibility, reliability, unquestionableness, inevitability, certitude, assurance, confidence, conviction.

v be certain, stand to reason, render certain, clinch, make sure; know.

adj certain, confident, sure, assured, convinced, satisfied, indubitable, indisputable, unquestionable, undeniable, incontestable, unimpeachable, irrefutable, unquestioned, incontrovertible, absolute, positive, plain, patent, obvious, clear; sure, inevitable, infallible, unfailing; fixed, agreed upon, settled, prescribed, determined, determinate, constant, stated, given; definite, particular, special, especial; reliable, trustworthy, dependable, trusty.

adv certainly, for certain, no doubt, doubtless, undoubtedly, *(informal)* sure enough.

475 uncertainty *n* insecurity, instability, unreliability, fallibility, danger; incertitude, doubt, doubtfulness, ambiguity, vagueness, questionableness, dubiousness; haziness, fogginess, obscurity; undependability, changeableness, variability. capriciousness, irregularity, fitfulness, chanciness.

v be uncertain, hesitate, flounder, waver; render uncertain, pose, puzzle, perplex, confuse, confound, bewilder; doubt, question.

adj uncertain, insecure, precarious, unsure, doubtful, unpredictable, problematical, unstable, unreliable, unsafe, fallible, perilous, dangerous; unassured, undecided, indeterminate, undetermined, unfixed, unsettled, indefinite, ambiguous, questionable, dubious; doubtful, vague, indistinct; undependable, changeable, variable, capricious, unsteady, irregular, fitful, desultory, chance, *(informal)* chancy.

476 reasoning *n* ratiocination, rationalism, dialectics; discussion, comment, argumentation, debate, disputation.

logic, induction, deduction, chain of thought, analysis, synthesis, syllogistic reasoning.

argument, case, proposition, terms, premises, postulate, data; inference, *argumentum ad hominem, paralipsis, a priori, a posteriori, reductio ad absurdum*, enthymeme, dilemma, on the horns of a dilemma.

reasoner, logician, dialectician, disputant, wrangler, arguer, debater, polemicist, casuist, rationalist.

arguments, reasons, pros and cons.

v to reason, discuss, argue, debate, dispute, wrangle; deduce, induce, infer, analyze, synthesize, postulate, propose, contend, demonstrate.

adj reasoning, rationalistic, dialectical, dialectic, argumentative, disputatious; logical, inductive, deductive, analytical, synthetic, syllogistic, inferential; demonstrable.

477 [the absence of reasoning] **intuition.** [false reasoning] **sophistry** *n* intuition, instinct, hunch, presentiment; insight, discernment, inspiration.

casuistry, jesuitry, perversion, equivocation, evasion, chicanery, quiddity, speciousness, *(informal)* bull, *(informal)* malarkey, bunk; false statement, fallacy, sophism.

sophist.

v intuit; reason falsely, pervert, quibble, equivocate, evade, mislead, gloss over, cavil, refine, subtilize, misrepresent, fence, beg the question.

adj intuitive, instinctive, instinctual. sophistical, equivocal, evasive, specious, fallacious, illogical, unsound, false, incorrect, untenable; inconsequential, weak, feeble, poor, flimsy, vague, nonsensical, absurd, foolish; frivolous, pettifogging, trifling, quibbling, nit-picking, subtle, over-retined.

adv intuitively, by intuition; illogically.

478 demonstration *n* proof, conclusiveness, example, verification, explanation.

v demonstrate, prove, establish, verify; evince, show, explain.

adj demonstrative, demonstrable, probative, conclusive, convincing; demonstrated, proven, proved, shown.

479 confutation *n* refutation, answer, disproof, invalidation, exposure.

v confute, refute, disprove, expose the error, overturn, invalidate.

adj confutable, refutable.

480 judgment *n* verdict, decree, decision, determination, conclusion, result, upshot, deduction, inference, assessment, opinion, estimate, criticism, critique; understanding, discrimination, discernment, perspicacity, sagacity, wisdom, intelligence, prudence, brains, taste, penetration, discretion, common sense.

judge, assessor, reviewer, critic, commentator; connoisseur.

v judge, estimate, consider, regard, esteem, appreciate, appraise, reckon, value; decide, determine, conclude, form an opinion, pass judgment; criticize, rate, rank; try, pass sentence upon, rule.

adj judicious, judicial, judgmental, determinate, conclusive; critical, discriminating, penetrating, perspicacious.

480a discovery *n* detection, determination, disclosure, trove, find.

v discover, learn of, ascertain, unearth, uncover, determine, ferret out, flush out, dig up; find out, detect, espy, descry, discern, see, notice, hit upon, stumble onto.

481 misjudgment *n* miscalculation, miscomputation, misconception, misinterpretation, misapprehension.

v misjudge, misconjecture, misconceive, misunderstand, misconstrue, misinterpret; overestimate, underestimate.

adj misjudging, ill-judging, wrongheaded, *(informal)* off base, wrong, in error.

482 overestimation *n* exaggeration, overvaluation, optimism; miscalculation.

v overestimate, overrate, overprize, overpraise, exaggerate, magnify, attach too much importance to, set too high a value on; miscalculate.

adj overestimated, overrated, inflated, pompous, pretentious.

483 underestimation *n* undervaluation, depreciation, detraction; modesty, self-depreciation; pessimism.

v underestimate, undervalue, under-rate, depreciate, disparage, detract, slight, minimize, make light of, make little of, disregard.

adj underestimating, depreciating, depreciative, deprecatory; underestimated, depreciated, unvalued, unprized; modest, pessimistic.

484 belief *n* opinion, view, tenet, doctrine, dogma, creed; certainty, conviction, assurance, confidence, persuasion, believing, trust, reliance; credence, credit, acceptance, faith, assent.

v believe, credit, give credence to, accept. have faith in, give assent, accept; know, see, realize, assume, presume; thick, opine, hold, conceive. consider; rely on, put one's trust on, have confidence in.

adj certain, sure, assured, positive, cocksure, satisfied, confident, convinced, secure; believing, trusting, confiding, credulous; believed, accredited, trusted, accepted; believable, credible, trustworthy.

485 disbelief, doubt *n* disbelief, incredulity; dissent, change of mind, retraction.

uncertainty, irresolution, hesitation, hesitancy, vacillation, misgiving, suspense; scruple, qualm, mistrust, distrust, suspicion, skepticism.

unbeliever, nonbeliever; skeptic.

v disbelieve, discredit, dissent, doubt, distrust, mistrust, suspect, have qualms; hesitate, waver, demur.

adj unbelieving, incredulous, doubtful, disputable, questionable, suspicious; uncertain, unsure; doubting, hesitating, hesitant, wavering, irresolute, dubious, skeptical.

486 credulity *n* credulousness, gullibility, infatuation, superstition, self-deception, self-delusion.

gull, dupe, *(informal)* sucker.

v be credulous, swallow.

adj credulous, believing, trusting, unsuspecting, gullible; simple, silly, childish, stupid; infatuated, superstitious.

487 incredulity *n* incredulousness, caution, wariness, suspicion, doubt, skepticism, disbelief.

nonbeliever, skeptic, heretic.

v be incredulous, distrust, doubt, suspect.

adj incredulous, cautious, wary; suspicious, dubious, doubtful, skeptical, unbelieving.

488 assent *n* acknowledgment, agreement, concurrence, acquiescence, consent, allowance, approval, concord, accord, approbation.

v assent, acquiesce, accede, concur, agree, fall in, acknowledge, admit, yield, allow; own, avow, confess.

adj assenting, agreeing, concurring, consenting, of one accord, of the same mind; agreed, acquiescent.

489 dissent *n* difference, discordance, dissension, disagreement, dissatisfaction; opposition, protest; nonconformity, separation.

dissenter, protester, rebel, radical, dissident, nonconformist.

v dissent, differ, disagree, protest, contradict; repudiate.

adj dissenting, negative; dissident, contradictory, disagreeing, opposing; nonconformist.

490 knowledge *n* enlightenment, erudition, wisdom, science, letters, information, learning, scholarship, lore; understanding, discernment, perception, apprehension, comprehension, judgment.

v know, be aware of; understand, discern, perceive, realize, fathom, apprehend, comprehend, *(informal)* dig; *(informal)* be hip; learn, discover.

adj knowing, aware of, cognizant of, acquainted with, privy to; discerning, perceptive, *(informal)* sharp, shrewd; knowledgeable, educated, enlightened, erudite, wise, instructed, learned, well-educated, bookish, well-read; known, recognized, received.

491 ignorance *n* illiteracy, unenlightenment, unawareness, unlearnedness, unacquaintance, unconsciousness, inexperience, darkness, blindness, incomprehension, simplicity, stupidity.

v be ignorant, know nothing, have no idea, be blind to.

adj ignorant, illiterate, unlettered, uneducated, uninstructed, untaught, untutored, uninformed, unenlightened, nescient; shallow, superficial; stupid, dumb, thick, dull.

492 scholar *n* savant, wise man, sage, academician, thinker, intellectual, bibliomaniac, bookworm, pedant; student, pupil, disciple, learner.

493 ignoramus *n* illiterate, know-nothing, blockhead, numskull, dullard, simpleton, dunce, ass, fool, bonehead, duffer, dolt, turkey, twerp, idiot, imbecile, cretin, moron, dimwit, *(informal)* jerk.

494 truth *n* fact, reality, verity, veracity; accuracy, precision, exactness.

v be true, be the case, have a true ring.

adj true, factual, actual, real, authentic, genuine, veracious, truthful, veritable; pure, natural; accurate, exact, faithful, correct, precise; agreeing; right, proper; legitimate, rightful; to the point, *(informal)* right on, *(informal)* where it's at, *(informal)* on target.

495 error *n* fallacy, misconception, misapprehension, misunderstanding, misinterpretation, misjudgment; aberration, inexactness, laxity; mistake, fault, blunder, slip, oversight, flaw, stumble, bungle; delusion, false, impression.

v err, be in error, mistake, blunder, slip, go astray, trip up; misconceive, misapprehend, misunderstand, misinterpret, miscalculate, misjudge.

adj erroneous, in error, fallacious, mistaken, incorrect, inaccurate, false, wrong, untrue, *(informal)* off base, *(informal)* off the mark.

496 maxim *n* proverb, aphorism, dictum, saying, adage, apothegm, motto, epigram, *mot juste,* truism, words of wisdom, axiom.

adj proverbial, aphoristic, axiomatic, truistic, *(informal)* corny, trite.

adv as they say, as the saying goes.

497 absurdity *n* nonsense, imbecility, foolishness, silliness, inanity, stupidity; farce, rhapsody, farrago, blunder, bathos; inconsistency, paradox, *non sequitur,* jargon, extravagance, exaggeration.

v be absurd, talk nonsense, play the fool.

adj absurd, nonsensical, ridiculous, silly, preposterous, foolish, inane, asinine, stupid, senseless, unreasonable, irrational, incongruous, self-contradictory, paradoxical, farcical, rhapsodic, bathetic, extravagant, exaggerated, bombastic, fantastic, meaningless.

498 intelligence. wisdom *n* intelligence, intellect, mind, capacity, understanding, discernment, reason, acumen, aptitude, penetration, brains, *(informal),* smarts; knowledge, news, information, tidings.

discretion, reasonableness, judgment, discernment, insight, sense, common sense, sagacity, insight, understanding, prudence; knowledge, information, learning, sapience, erudition, enlightenment.

v be intelligent; understand, discern, reason; be wise, discriminate.

adj intelligent, understanding, intellectual, quick, bright; astute, clever, sharp, alert, bright, apt, discerning, canny, shrewd, nimble, penetrating, piercing, on the ball.

wise, discerning, judicious, sage, sapient, sensible, sound, penetrating, sagacious, intelligent, perspicacious, profound, rational, prudent, cautious, politic, reasonable, thoughtful, reflective; learned, educated, erudite, schooled.

499 imbecility. folly *n* imbecility, want of intelligence, incompetence, incapacity, vacancy, dull understanding, meanness, simplicity, shallowness, stolidity, hebetude, puerility, fatuity, silliness, foolishness, driveling, stupidity, idiocy.

frivolity, irrationality, trifling, ineptitude, silliness, eccentricity, extravagance; rashness.

v be imbecilic.

be foolish, trifle, drivel, dote, ramble.

adj imbecile, imbecilic, idiotic, fatuous, driveling; vacant, mindless, witless, brainless, weak-headed, addlebrained, muddle-headed, dull-witted, feeble-minded, half-witted, dull, shallow, stolid, dim-witted, thick-skulled; shallow, weak, wanting, soft, sappy, stupid, obtuse, blunt, stolid, doltish, thick as a brick, asinine; childish, childlike, infantile, puerile, simple.

foolish, silly, senseless, irrational, insensate, nonsensical, inept, frivolous, trifling; eccentric, crazed, rash, thoughtless, giddy, obstinate, bigoted, narrowminded; foolish, unwise, injudicious, improper, unreasonable, ridiculous, stupid, asinine; ill-conceived, ill-advised, ill-judged, inexpedient, extravagant, frivolous, trivial, useless.

500 sage *n* wise man, master mind, thinker, philosopher, oracle, luminary, man of learning, expert, authority.

501 fool *n* simpleton, dolt, dunce, blockhead, nincompoop, ninny, numskull, ignoramus, booby, sap, dunderhead, dunderpate, idiot, natural, oaf, lout, loon, dullard; jester, buffoon, droll, zany, harlequin, clown; imbecile, moron, idiot, cretin.

502 sanity *n* soundness, mental balance, rationality, reason, sense, clearheadedness, lucidity, coherence, normality, sobriety, *(informal)* good head.

v be sane, *(informal)* have one's act together.

adj sane, rational, reasonable, sensible, clearheaded, level-headed, logical, sober, lucid, self-possessed, *(informal)* together.

503 insanity *n* disorder, imbalance, derangement, dementia, lunacy, madness, craziness, aberration; frenzy, raving, incoherence, delirium, delusion; *(informal)* oddity, eccentricity, twist, mania.

v be insane, become insane, lose one's senses, go mad, rave, rant, *(informal)* lose it.

adj insane, deranged, demented, lunatic, crazed, crazy, maniacal, mad, touched, cracked, unhinged, unsettled, daft, frenzied, possessed, delirious, far gone, wild, flighty, distracted, frantic, mad as a hatter, *(informal)* crackers, *(informal)* zonkers, *(informal)* nuts, *(informal)* zonko, *(informal)* weird, *(informal)* bananas, *(informal)* kaput.

504 madman *n* lunatic, maniac, bedlamite, raver, *(informal)* nut, *(informal)* weirdo, *(informal)* crazy; dreamer, romantic, rhapsodist, enthusiast, visionary, seer, fanatic.

505 memory *n* retention, retentiveness, remembrance, recollection, reminiscence, retrospect; recognition; reminder, hint, suggestion, keepsake, souvenir, memento, token, memorial.

v remember, recall, recollect, call up,

call to mind, bring to mind, think back upon, haunt one's thoughts, *(informal)* flash on; remind, suggest, hint, prompt, summon up, reminisce; retain, keep in mind, bear in mind, memorize, engrave in the mind, learn by heart; keep the memory alive.

adj reminiscent (of), mindful (of); fresh, alive, vivid; unforgotten, enduring, indelible, memorable, never to be forgotten, unforgettable, stirring, eventful.

506 oblivion *n* forgetfulness, short memory, slippery memory, untrustworthy memory, obliteration of the past, amnesia.

v forget, be forgetful, have a short memory, lose sight of, sink into oblivion; unlearn, efface from the memory, think no more of, consign into oblivion, banish from one's thoughts.

adj oblivious, forgetful, heedless, deaf to the past, insensible; out of mind, unremembered, forgotten, past recollection, buried, sunk into oblivion.

507 expectation *n* expectancy, anticipation, prospect, reckoning, calculation; suspense, waiting; hope, trust, assurance, confidence, reliance, presumption.

v expect, look for, look out for, look forward to, anticipate, await, hope for, wait for, foresee, prepare for, count on, rely on; predict, prognosticate, forecast.

adj expectant, watchful, vigilant, open-eyed, on tenterhooks, on one's toes, ready, in readiness, prepared, *(informal)* all set for; foreseen, long expected, prospective, in view, in sight, on the horizon, impending.

adv expectantly, on the watch, on edge, with bated breath.

508 nonexpectation *n* unforeseen occurrence, surprise, shock, blow, wonder, bolt out of the blue, astonishment; miscalculation, false expectation.

v not expect, be taken by surprise, catch unawares; burst upon, come out of nowhere, drop from the clouds; surprise, startle, stun, stagger, throw off one's guard, astonish.

adj nonexpectant, surprised, unwarned, unaware, off one's guard; unanticipated, unexpected, unlooked for, unforeseen; unheard of, startling; sudden.

adv unexpectedly, abruptly, suddenly, without warning.

509 [failure of expectation] **disappointment** *n* failure, defeat, frustration, unfulfillment, blighted hope, vain expectation, disillusion, *(informal)* comedown.

v be disappointed; disappoint, dash one's hopes, dash one's expectations, balk, jilt, tantalize; dumfound, disillusion, let down.

adj disappointed; disgruntled, disconcerted, aghast.

510 foresight *n* prudence, forethought, prevision, anticipation. precaution; forecast; prescience, fore-knowledge, prospect.

v foresee; look forward to, look ahead, look beyond; look into the future; see one's future, catch the lay of the land; anticipate, expect, assume, surmise, predict, forewarn.

adj anticipatory, prescient; far-sighted, prudent, provident; prospective, expectant.

511 prediction *n* prophecy, forecast, augury, prognostication, foretoken, portent, divination, soothsaying, presage.

v predict, foretell, prophesy, foresee, forecast, presage, augur, prognosticate, foretoken, portend, divine.

adj prophetic, oracular, portentous, premonitory.

512 omen *n* portent, foreboding, augury, sign, harbinger; sign of the times, symbol, warning.

513 oracle *n* prophet, prophetess, seer, soothsayer, augur, fortune-teller, witch, sibyl, necromancer, sorcerer, clairvoyant, interpreter.

514 supposition *n* assumption, presumption, condition, hypothesis, theory, postulate, proposition, thesis, theorem; conjecture, suggestion, guess, guesswork, suspicion, inkling, speculation.

v suppose, conjecture, surmise, suspect, guess, divine; theorize, speculate, presume, presuppose, assume, predicate; believe, take for granted; propound, put forth, propose, advance, hazard a suggestion, suggest.

adj assumed, given; conjectural, hypothetical, presumptive, theoretical, speculative, suggestive.

515 imagination *n* imaginativeness, fancy, invention, inspiration, creativity, originality, fiction, vision, fantasy, illusion, ideality, castles in the air, dreaming, dream, golden dreams; mental image, conception, idea, notion, thought, conceit, fancy, whim, figment, romance, vision, dream, chimera, shadow, illusion, phantasm, supposition, delusion; verve, vivacity, liveliness, animation.

v imagine, fancy, conceive, dream, idealize; create, originate, think up, devise, invent, coin, fabricate.

adj imaginative, fanciful, original, inventive, creative, visionary, ideal, unreal, illusory, unsubstantial, dreamy, dreamlike, romantic, fantastic, fabulous, chimerical, fantastical; vivacious, lively, animated; imaginable, conceivable, possible, believable; imagined.

II. Communication of Ideas

516 [idea to be conveyed] **meaning** *n* tenor, spirit, gist, trend, idea, purport, significance, signification, sense, import, denotation, conotation, interpretation; intent, intention, aim, object, purpose, design.

thing signified: matter, subject matter, substance, gist, argument.

v mean, signify, denote, conote, express, import, purport; convey, imply, indicate, point to, allude to, touch on, drive at, involve; declare, affirm, state; intend, aim, design, purpose.

adj meaning; meaningful, pointed, poignant, significant, expressive.

517 meaninglessness *n* unmeaningness, absence of meaning, senselessness, emptiness, empty words, rhetoric, platitude, nonsense, jargon, gibberish, jabber, rant, bombast, *(informal)* hot air; inanity, rigmarole, absurdity, ambiguity.

v mean nothing, jabber, rant, say nothing.

adj meaningless, senseless, nonsensical, inexpressive, vague, trivial, insignificant.

518 intelligibility *n* comprehensibility, clarity, clearness, lucidity, coherence, explicitness, persicuity, precision, plain-speaking.

v be intelligible; render, intelligible, clear up, simplify, elucidate, explain; understand, comprehend, take in, catch on, grasp, follow, master.

adj intelligible, understandable, comprehensible, clear, clear as day, lucid, luminous, transparent; plain, distinct, pointed, clear-cut, obvious, explicit, precise; graphic, illustrative, expressive.

519 unintelligibility *n* incomprehensibility, vagueness, obscurity, ambiguity, uncertainty, confusion.

v be unintelligible; render, unintelligible, conceal, darken, confuse, perplex, mystify, bewilder.

adj unintelligible, incomprehensible, indecipherable, unfathomable, inexplicable, inscrutable, insoluble, impenetrable; puzzling, enigmatic, obscure, muddy, dim, nebulous, mysterious, *(informal)* strange, *(informal)* weird; inexpressible, incommunicable, ineffable, unutterable.

520 equivocalness *n* ambiguity, uncertainty, questionableness, dubiousness, indeterminateness; double-meaning, word-play, double entendre, pun, play on words, conundrum, riddle, quibble; equivocation, duplicity, prevarication, white lie.

v be equivocal; have two meanings; equivocate, prevaricate.

adj equivocal, ambiguous, uncertain, doubtful, questionable, dubious, indeterminate; duplicitous, enigmatic, double-edged, deceptive, misleading.

521 figure of speech *n* phrase, expression, euphemism, manner of speaking, colloquialism, idiom, image; metaphor, simile, imagery, poetic device, poetics, figures of beauty.

v employ figures of speech; image, speak prettily.

adj figurative, idiomatic, colloquial, colorful, imagistic, poetic, expressive, allusive.

522 interpretation *n* definition, explanation, explication, elucidation, translation; exegesis, exposition, comment, commentary, gloss; solution, answer, meaning.

v interpret, define, explain, explicate,

elucidate, translate, shed light on, cast light on, decipher, decode, unravel, disentangle, gloss, annotate, expound, comment upon; construe, understand.

adj explanatory, expository, exegetical, interpretative, interpretive; interpretable, explicable, intelligible.

adv in explanation, that is to say, namely.

523 misinterpretation *n* misapprehension, misconception, misunderstanding, misreading, misconstruction, mistake; misrepresentation, perversion, exaggeration, false coloration, falsification, travesty.

v misinterpret, misapprehend, misconceive, misunderstand, misread, misconstrue, misapply, mistake; misrepresent, pervert, misstate, garble, falsify, distort, travesty, stretch the meaning, twist the meaning.

524 interpreter *n* translator, explainer, expounder, expositor, commentator, annotator, guide, critic; spokesman, speaker, representative.

525 manifestation *n* indication, expression, exposition, demonstration, showing, display, exhibition, declaration; materialization; openness, candor.

v make manifest, show, display, reveal, disclose, open, exhibit, evince, evidence, demonstrate, declare, express, make known; appear, be plain, come to light, materialize; indicate, point out.

adj manifest, evident, obvious, apparent, plain, clear, distinct, patent, open, palpable, visible, unmistakable, conspicuous, explicit; unreserved, downright, frank, plain spoken; barefaced, bold; manifested.

adv manifestly, openly, plainly, above board, in broad daylight, in plain sight.

526 latency *n* dormancy, latentness, quiescence, obscurity, darkness, hidden meaning, obscure meaning, undercurrent, suggestion, concealment; potentiality.

v be latent, lurk, smolder, underlie.

adj latent, dormant; lurking, secret, cryptic, veiled, hidden; potential; implied, implicit; allusive.

527 information *n* enlightenment, knowledge, news, data, facts, circumstances, situations, intelligence, advice; communication, notification, announcement, record; hint, suggestion, innuendo, inkling, whisper, insinuation.

informant, authority, intelligencer, reporter; informer, eavesdropper, detective, newsmonger; messenger.

guide, guidebook, handbook, manual, map, chart.

v inform, tell, acquaint with, impart to, make acquainted with, apprize, advise, enlighten; communicate, make known, express, mention, let fall, intimate, hint, insinuate, allude to, suggest; announce, report, give an account, disclose; know, learn, find out, get the scent of.

adj informed, communicated, reported, advised, apprized of, acquainted with, enlightened, published, *(informal)* filled in; declarative, expository, communicative.

528 concealment *n* hiding, secretion, ensconcing, sheltering, covering, burying, screening; keeping secret, secrecy, hiding, disguising, veiling, camouflaging, obscuring, dissembling, obfuscation, evasiveness; reticence, reserve, reservation, suppression, silence, secretiveness.

v conceal, hide, secrete, cover, put away, ensconce, bury, screen, shelter, keep out of sight, stow away; keep secret, hide, disguise, veil, cloak, mask, camouflage, obscure, obfuscate, dissemble, be evasive.

adj concealed, hidden, secret, private, privy, confidential, in secret, close, undercover, in hiding, in disguise, covert, mysterious; furtive, stealthy, surreptitious, secretive, evasive, clandestine; reserved, reticent, suppressed, uncommunicative.

adv secretly, in secret, in private, behind closed doors, on the sly; confidentially; stealthily.

529 disclosure *n* revelation, divulgence, exposition, exposure; exposé, uncovering, muckraking; acknowledgment, avowal, confession.

v disclose, discover, uncover, lay open, expose, bring to light, unmask; reveal, make known, divulge, show, tell, unveil, unmask, communicate; let slip, let drop, betray, blurt out; acknowledge,

allow, concede, grant, admit, own up, confess.

adj disclosed, revealed.

530 [means of concealment] **ambush** *n* ambuscade, lurking place, trap, snare, pitfall; hiding place, secret place, recess, hole, cubbyhole; screen, cover, shade, blinker, veil, curtain, cloak, cloud; mask, visor, disguise, masquerade.

v ambush, lie in wait for, set a trap for.

531 publication *n* issuance, distribution; announcement, proclamation, promulgation, propagation, pronouncement, declaration, disclosure, divulgence, advertisement, publicity; edition.

v publish, issue, distribute, print; make public, make known, announce, proclaim, promulgate, propagate, circulate, spread, disseminate, declare, disclose, divulge, advertise, publicize, get into print.

adj published; current, public, in circulation, in print, in black and white.

532 news *n* information, intelligence, tidings, report, rumor, scuttlebutt, hearsay, gossip, *(informal)* the word; newsstory, headlines, copy.

reporter, newsmonger, talebearer, gossip, tattler, informer.

v transpire, make news, make headlines; be rumored.

adj in the news, in the headlines, current, in circulation, in print.

533 secret *n* mystery; problem, question, difficulty, a confidence; unintelligibility.

adj secret, hidden, concealed, unrevealed, unknown, mysterious; reticent, secretive; private.

534 messenger *n* envoy, emissary, representative, intermediary, go-between, delegate, courier, runner, errand boy; intelligencer, reporter, newsmonger, spokesman, informant; forerunner, harbinger, herald, precursor.

535 affirmation *n* statement, profession, pronouncement, deposition, assertion, declaration; confirmation, ratification, endorsement; swearing, oath, affidavit; emphasis, dogmatism.

v affirm, state, assert, aver, avow, maintain, declare, swear, asseverate, depose, testify, say, pronounce; establish, confirm, ratify, approve, endorse, assent, acknowledge; swear, emphasize.

adj affirmative, declaratory, declarative, positive, assertive, emphatic, dogmatic; confirmative, corroborative, affirming, acquiescent.

536 negation. denial *n* nullification, invalidation.

disputation, confutation, contradiction, qualification; repudiation, rejection, abjuration, disavowal, disclaimer, recantation, retraction, rebuttal.

v negate, nullify, cancel, invalidate.

deny, dispute, controvert, contravene, oppose, gainsay, contradict, rebut; reject, renounce, abjure, disclaim, disavow; recant, revoke; refuse, repudiate, disown.

adj contradictory, negative.

537 teaching *n* instruction, education, pedagogy, pedagogics, edification, tutelage, tutorship; guidance, direction, preparation, schooling, learning, discipline; lesson, lecture, disquisition, discourse, explanation, harangue, homily, sermon, lore; doctrine, dogma, tenet, principle, rule, maxim, article of faith, creed, credo, belief, opinion.

v teach, instruct, edify, educate, inform, enlighten, prepare, discipline, train, drill, tutor, prime, coach, guide, direct, school, indoctrinate, inculcate, infuse, instill, imbue; expound, interpret, lecture, discourse, hold forth, sermonize, moralize.

adj educational, scholastic, academic, pedagogic, pedagogical, didactic; edifying, instructive.

538 misteaching *n* misinformation, misdirection, misguidance, perversion, sophistry, error.

v misteach, misinform, misinstruct, misdirect, misguide, pervert, mislead, misrepresent, confuse, bewilder, lie.

539 learning *n* acquisition of knowledge, acquirements, attainment, mental cultivation, scholarship, erudition, study, inquiry, questioning, search, pursuit of knowledge.

apprenticeship, tutelage, matriculation.

v learn, acquire, gain knowledge, memorize, master, study, grind, cram, *(informal)* book, read, peruse, pore

over, wade through, ingest, burn the midnight oil, *(informal)* pull an all-nighter.

adj studious, industrious; scholarly, scholastic, well-read, learned, erudite.

540 teacher *n* instructor, tutor, lecturer, professor, don, master, schoolmaster, guide, counselor, adviser, mentor; preacher, missionary, propagandist.

541 learner *n* scholar, student, pupil, apprentice, novice, neophyte, beginner; disciple, acolyte, follower.

542 school *n* academy, educational institution, college, university, institute, seminary, place of learning.

schoolbook, textbook, text, primer, grammar, reader, workbook.

adj scholastic, academic, collegiate.

543 veracity *n* truthfulness, frankness, truth, sincerity, candor, honesty, probity, fidelity, accuracy.

v speak the truth, *(informal)* level with, *(informal)* be straight with.

adj veracious, true, truthful, sincere, honest, honorable, candid, frank, open, straightforward, honest, scrupulous, punctilious, trustworthy.

544 falsehood *n* falsification, lie, fib, untruth, distortion, deception, misrepresentation, fabrication, fiction, sham; untruthfulness, lying, prevarication, duplicity, double dealing, deceitfulness, equivocation, dissembling, cunning, guile, insincerity, dishonesty, inaccuracy.

v lie, fib, falsify, prevaricate, misrepresent, deceive, *(informal)* come on to, doctor, feign, pretend, play false, dissemble, counterfeit, fabricate.

adj false, untrue, wrong, mistaken, incorrect, erroneous; untruthful, lying, mendacious, dishonest, deceitful, treacherous, faithless, insincere, hypocritical, disingenuous, unfaithful, cunning, perfidious, two-faced, recreant; deceptive, misleading, fallacious, spurious, fraudulent, bogus, phony, sham, counterfeit.

545 deception *n* deceiving, guiling, falseness, untruthfulness; artifice, sham, cheat, imposture, deceit, treachery, subterfuge, stratagem, ruse, hoax, fraud, trick, wile, snare, trap, illusion, delusion.

v deceive, mislead, lead astray, take

in, delude, cheat, cozen, dupe, gull, fool, bamboozle, hoodwink, *(informal)* con, trick, double-cross, defraud, outwit; entrap, ensnare, betray.

adj deceptive, misleading, delusive, illusory, fallacious, specious, untrue, false, deceitful; tricky, cunning, insidious.

546 untruth *n* falsehood, fib, lie, fiction, story, tale, tall tale, fabrication, fable, forgery, invention.

v make believe, pretend, feign, sham, fib, lie.

adj untrue, false, trumped up, unfounded, invented, fictitious, fabulous.

547 dupe *n* gull, pigeon, laughingstock, greenhorn, fool, sucker, puppet, *(informal)* nebbish.

v be deceived, be the dupe of, fall into a trap, go for the bait, bite, swallow.

adj credulous, gullible, unsuspecting, trusting.

548 deceiver *n* dissembler, hypocrite, sophist, liar, *(informal)* fast talker, storyteller, *(informal)* faker, *(informal)* phony, fraud, *(informal)* four-flusher, *(informal)*, shyster, confidence man, con man, cheat, swindler, imposter, pretender, humbug, adventurer, adventuress, serpent, snake in the grass.

549 exaggeration *n* overstatement, hyperbole, extravagance, coloring, coloration, embroidery; yarn, tale, *(informal)* shaggy dog story, *(informal)* fish story; tempest in a teacup, much ado about nothing, puffery, rant.

v exaggerate, magnify, amplify, expand, overestimate, overstate; heighten, color, embroider, puff up, fill out.

adj exaggerated, overwrought, bombastic, magniloquent, hyperbolic fabulous, extravagant, preposterous.

550 [means of communication] **indication** *n* symbolism, semiology; sign, symbol, index, indicator, pointer, note, token, symptom; type, mark, figure, emblem, insigne, cipher, device, representation; signal, beacon, alarm; feature, trait, characteristic, peculiarity, quality, earmark, cast; gesture, gesticulation, motion, cue, hint, clue, scent.

v indicate, denote, betoken, designate, signify, represent, stand for, typify, symbolize; note, mark, stamp; label, ticket; make a sign, signalize, signal, gesture, gesticulate; sign, seal, attest, underline, underscore, call attention to.

adj indicative, indicatory; connotative, denotative, typical, representative, symbolic, symbolical, characteristic, significant, emblematic.

551 record *n* trace, vestige, relic, remains; monument, achievement; account, chronicles, annals, history, note, register, memorandum, document, diary, log, journal, ledger.

v record, set down, place in the record, chronicle, enter, register, enter, list, enroll; commemorate, celebrate.

552 [suppression of sign] **obliteration** *n* erasure, cancelation, deletion, blot, effacement, extinction.

v obliterate, efface, expunge, erase, cancel, delete, blot out, rub out, strike out, wipe out, leave no trace.

adj obliterated, erased, blotted out; unrecorded.

553 recorder *n* notary, clerk, registrar, register, secretary, scribe, bookkeeper; annalist, historian, historiographer, chronicler, biographer, journalist, antiquarian, memorialist.

554 representation *n* depiction, imitation, illustration, delineation, expression, imagery, portraiture, figuration.

v represent, delineate, depict, portray, picture, figure, describe, trace, copy, illustrate, symbolize; personate, personify, play, mimic.

adj representative, imitiative, illustrative, figurative, symbolic, descriptive.

555 misrepresentation *n* distortion, exaggeration, misfiguration, falsification, bad likeness, caricature.

v misrepresent, distort, overdraw, exaggerate, falsify, caricature, daub.

556 painting *n* fine art, picture, depiction, representation, pictorialization, delineation, design, drawing, likeness, copy, imitation, fake, image.

art gallery, picture gallery, studio.

v paint, design, limn, draw, sketch, pencil, color; depict, represent.

adj pictorial, picturesque.

557 sculpture *n* carving, modeling, statuary; ceramics, potting.

statue, statuette, bust; cast, mold.

v sculpt, fashion, cast, mold, model, chisel, carve, cut, shape, form, figure, hew.

558 engraving *n* etching, chiseling, incising, plate engraving, photoengraving.

v engrave, grave, carve, incise, chisel, hatch, etch, stipple, print.

559 artist *n* painter, drawer, sketcher, designer, draftsman, cartoonist, caricaturist, sculptor, engraver.

560 language *n* speech, phraseology, style, expression, diction, jargon, dialect, terminology, vernacular, lingo, tongue.

literature, letters, belles, lettres humanities, classics, dead language.

linguist.

v express, say, express by words.

adj lingual, linguistic; dialect, vernacular, current, colloquial, slangy, polyglot, literary.

561 letter *n* character, hieroglyph, symbol, alphabet, consonant, vowel.

syllable, monosyllable, dissyllable, polysyllable.

spelling, orthography; phonetics; cipher, code; monogram, anagram.

v spell.

adj literal; alphabetical; syllabic; phonetic.

562 word *n* term, symbol, name, part of speech.

dictionary, vocabulary, lexicon, index, thesaurus, glossary.

etymology, derivation, philology, terminology, lexicography.

adj literal, verbal.

563 neology *n* neologism, new-fangled expression, *(informal)* hip expression, barbarism, corruption.

neologist, word coiner.

v coin words.

adj neologic, neological; colloquial, slang, *(informal)* hip, cant, barbarous.

564 nomenclature *n* naming; name, appellation, designation, epithet, nickname, *(informal)* moniker, *(informal)* handle, label, title, head, heading; style, proper name, surname, namesake.

v name, call, term, designate, denominate, style, entitle, dub, christen, baptize, nickname, characterize, specify, label.

adj titular, nominal.

565 misnomer *n* misnaming, malapropism; sobriquet, nickname, assumed name, alias, pen name, stage name, pseudonym, nom de plume, nom de guerre.

v misname, miscall, misterm; take an assumed name.

adj misnamed; soi-disant, self-styled; so-called.

566 phrase *n* expression, set phrase, turn of speech, idiom, tag phrase, figure of speech, euphemism, motto; phraseology.

v phrase, express, put into words, find the right words, arrange in words, voice, vocalize.

567 grammar *n* rules of language, usage, forms, style, formal features, constructions, parts of speech; accidence, syntax, inflection, case, declension, conjugation; grammar book, primer, rulebook.

grammarian.

adj grammatical, syntactic, syntactical.

568 solecism *n* ungrammatical, usage, bad grammar, faulty grammar, error, slip, inconsistency, impropriety.

v solecize.

adj ungrammatical, incorrect, inaccurate, faulty, inconsistent, improper.

569 style *n* diction, phraseology, wording; composition, mode of expression, choice of words, command of language, mode, manner, method, approach; kind, form, appearance, character, touch, characteristic, mark, signature, imprint, *(informal)* name.

v style, compose, express by words; write.

adj stylistic; characteristic; expressive.

570 perspicuity *n* clearness, clarity, lucidity, plainness, plain-speaking, distinctness, explicitness, exactness, intelligibility.

adj perspicuous, pellucid, clear, lucid, intelligible, plain, distinct, explicit, exact, definite, unequivocal.

571 obscurity *n* unintelligibility, involution, confusion, indistinctness, indefiniteness, ambiguity, vagueness, inexactness, impenetrability.

adj obscure, involved, confused, unintelligible, impenetrable, indefinite, vague, inexact, hidden, dark.

572 conciseness *n* brevity, summary, abridgment, terseness, pithiness, compression, tightness.

v be concise, condense, abridge, abstract, compress, tighten; come to the point.

adj concise, brief, compendious, short, terse, laconic, pithy, trenchant, succinct, compact, tight.

adv concisely, briefly, summarily, in short.

573 diffuseness *n* long-windedness, verbosity, wordiness, verbiage, looseness, exuberance, redundancy, profuseness, richness.

v be diffuse, enlarge, amplify, expand, inflate; meander, digress, ramble, run on and on.

adj diffuse, profuse, wordy, verbose, copious, exuberant; lengthy, long-winded, protracted, prolix, diffusive, roundabout; digressive, discursive, loose.

574 vigor *n* power, force, boldness, spirit, verve, heart, ardor, enthusiasm, raciness, glow, fire, warmth; loftiness, elevation, gravity, sublimity; eloquence, strong language.

adj vigorous, nervous, powerful, forcible, forceful, trenchant, biting, incisive, impressive; spirited, lively, glowing, sparkling, racy, bold, pungent, pithy; lofty, elevated, sublime, grand, weighty; eloquent, vehement, impassioned, passionate.

575 feebleness *n* weakness, enervation, frailty, faintness.

adj feeble, tame, weak, meager, vapid, insipid; trashy, poor, dull, dry, languid; prosy, prosaic, slight; careless, loose, slip-shod, wishy-washy, sloppy, slovenly; puerile, childish.

576 plainness *n* simplicity, homeliness, restraint, severity.

v speak plainly, speak directly, come straight to the point, be straightforward, not beat around the bush.

adj plain, simple, homely, homey, unadorned, unvarnished, neat, homespun; severe, chaste, pure.

adv in plain terms, in plain English; point-blank.

577 ornament *n* floridness, ornateness, elegance, grandiloquence, magniloquence, rhetorical flourish, declamation, rhetoric, flourish, fancy talk, *(informal)* big words; pretention, inflation, bombast, fustian, rant, fine writing, fine speaking.

v ornament, overcharge, talk big, talk fancy.

adj ornate, ornamented, beautified, florid, rich, flowery, fancy; euphuistic, euphemistic; sonorous, high sounding, inflated, swelling, turgid, pompous, pedantic, stilted, high-flown, sententious, rhetorical, declamatory, grandiose, grandiloquent, magniloquent, bombastic, flashy.

578 elegance *n* taste, good taste, propriety, correctness; lucidity, purity, grace, ease; gracefulness, euphony, gentility, cultivation, polish, refinement.

purist, classicist.

adj elegant, polished, classic, classical, fine, tasteful, proper, correct; chaste, pure, graceful, easy, readable, fluent, flowing, unaffected, natural, mellifluous, euphonious, felicitous, neat, well put.

579 inelegance *n* tastelessness, vulgarity, impropriety; bad diction, awkwardness, stiffness, turgidity, abruptness; barbarism, solecism, slang, mannerism, affectation, formality.

adj inelegant, graceless, ungraceful, harsh, abrupt, dry, stiff, cramped, formal, forced, labored, awkward, ponderous, turgid; artificial, mannered, affected, euphuistic; tasteless, barbarous, uncouth, rude, crude, vulgar.

580 voice *n* vocality, intonation, articulation, enunciation, distinctness, clearness, delivery; accent, accentuation, emphasis, stress; utterance, vocalization.

v voice, speak, utter; articulate, enunciate, vocalize, intone, pronounce, accent, accentuate, deliver.

adj vocal, oral; articulate, distinct, euphonious, melodious.

581 muteness n dumbness, silence, speechlessness; aphasia.

v be mute, be silent, be dumb; silence, muzzle, muffle, suppress, smother, gag, strike dumb, dumfound.

adj mute, silent, dumb, mum, tongue-tied; voiceless, speechless.

582 speech n talk, parlance, locution, conversation, parley, communication, prattle; talk, oration, address, discourse, lecture, recitation, sermon, harangue, tirade; oratory, eloquence, rhetoric, declamation.

speaker, spokesman, mouthpiece, orator, rhetorician.

v speak, utter, talk, voice, converse, communicate, pronounce, say, articulate; declaim, harangue, stump, spout, rant, lecture, sermonize, discourse, expatiate, soliloquize, address.

adj oral; talkative, conversational; declamatory.

583 [imperfect speech] **inarticulateness** n stammering, hesitation, muttering, mumbling, stuttering; reticence, taciturnity; speech impediment, aphasia.

v be inarticulate, stammer, hesitate, mutter, mumble, slur one's words, garble, sputter, hem and haw, whisper, croak, crack.

adj inarticulate, tongue-tied, speechless, voiceless, hesitant, reticent, taciturn.

584 loquacity n loquaciousness, volubility, talkativeness, verbosity, garulity, volubility; chatter, jabber, prattle, twaddle.

talker, chatterer, chatterbox, babbler, ranter.

v be loquacious, talk a mile a minute, pour forth, prate, chatter, babble, gab, run off at the mouth, jabber, jaw, gush.

adj loquacious, voluble, talkative, verbose, wordy, garrulous, chatty, chattering, glib, fluent, effusive.

585 taciturnity n silence, muteness, reserve, reticence, uncommunicativeness.

v be silent, keep silence, keep quiet, hold one's tongue, say nothing.

adj taciturn, silent, mute, mum, reserved, reticent, guarded, uncommunicative, close-mouthed, quiet.

586 public address n allocution, speech, formal speech, address, invocation.

v speak to, address; invoke, hail, salute; lecture, pronounce.

587 response n. See **answer 462.**

588 conversation n interlocution, colloquy, confabulation, talk, (informal) rap, discourse, verbal interchange, dialog, oral communication; chat, chit, chit-chat, small talk, table talk, idle talk, prattle, gossip; conference, parley, interview, audience, tête-à-tête, council, congress; palaver, debate, discussion.

v converse, confabulate, talk together, hold a conversation, carry on a conversation, engage in a discussion; bandy words, chat, chit-chat, gossip, tattle, prate; discourse with, confer with; talk it over, (informal) rap, (informal) chew the fat.

adj conversational, conversable; chatty, gossipy.

589 soliloquy n monolog, apostrophe, aside.

v soliloquize, talk to oneself, think out loud, apostrophize.

590 writing n chirography, penmanship, calligraphy, hand, script, longhand, shorthand, stenography; handwriting, signature, mark, hand; manuscript, MS., document, script, writ, author's copy, copy, original; composition, authorship, work, opus, book, volume, tome, publication, article, poetry, verse, literature.

writer, author, scribe, scrivener, clerk, copyist, secretary.

v write, pen, copy, transcribe; print, scribble, scrawl, scratch; compose, draw out, write down, set down, put pen to paper, take up the pen, take pen in hand.

adj written, in writing, in black and white.

591 printing n lettering, typography; type; composition, print, letterpress, text, matter; copy, impression, proof.

printer, compositor, reader, proofreader, copyeditor.

v print, compose; go to press, publish, bring out, issue.

adj typographical, printed.

592 correspondence n letter, epistle, missive, note, post card; communication, dispatch, bulletin, circular.

v correspond, communicate, write to, send a letter.

adj epistolary; in touch with, in communication with.

593 book *n* booklet; writing, work, volume, tome, opus, tract, treatise, brochure, handbook; novel, story; script, libretto; publication.

writer, author, essayist, editor; bookseller, publisher; librarian, bibliophile, bookworm.

594 description *n* narration, account, recounting, telling, recital, relation, statement, report, record; delineation, portrayal, characterization, representation, depiction, sketch, vignette.

v describe, set forth, narrate, account, recount, recite, rehearse, tell, relate, detail; picture, delineate, portray, characterize, limn, represent, depict.

595 dissertation *n* treatise, essay, thesis, theme, tract, discourse, disquisition, investigation, study, discussion, exposition; commentary, critique, criticism, review, article. commentator, critic, essayist, reviewer.

v discuss a subject, treat, examine, comment, criticize, explain.

596 compendium *n* abstract, précis, epitome, analysis, digest, compendium, brief, abridgment, abbreviation, condensation, summary; draft, note, synopsis, outline, syllabus, contents, prospectus; compilation, collection, album, anthology; extracts, cuttings, fragments, pieces; list, inventory, survey.

v abridge, abstract, précis, epitomize, summarize; abbreviate, shorten, condense, compress; compile, collect, note; list, inventory, survey.

adj compendious, synoptic, analytic, analytical.

597 poetry *n* poetics; verse, poesy, versification, rhyming, rhymes, making verses, metrics; doggerel.

poet, laureate, bard, troubadour, minstrel, versifier, rhymer, sonneteer, rhapsodist, poetaster.

v poeticize, sing, versify, rhyme, make verses, compose.

adj poetic, poetical, rhythmic, metrical, lyrical, tuneful, musical; beautiful, lovely, tender, sensitive.

598 prose *n* writing, fiction, imaginative writing, narrative prose.

v write prose.

adj prosy, unpoetic, rhymeless; prosaic, dull, flat, matter-of-fact, unimaginative, commonplace, humdrum, pedestrian, trite, hackneyed, mediocre, stock, ordinary; fictional.

599 the drama *n* the stage, the theater; theatricals, dramaturgy, playwriting; play, drama, stage-play, opera.

performance, acting, representation, impersonation, stage business, actor, actress, player, performer, thespian.

theater, playhouse, operahouse, amphitheater.

dramatist, playwriter, playwright.

v dramatize, act, play, perform, personate, act a part, put on the stage, enact.

adj dramatic, theatrical, histrionic, stagy.

Class V
Voluntary Powers
I. Individual Volition

600 will *n* volition, free will, freedom; choice, wish, desire, pleasure, disposition, inclination; intent, purpose, option; determination, resolution, resoluteness, decision, forcefulness; force of will, will power, self-control.

v will, see fit, think fit, decide, decree, determine, direct, command, bid.

adj willful, voluntary, volitional, intentional; free, optional, discretionary; autocratic, obdurate, adamant.

adv willfully, voluntarily, at will; of one's own accord, intentionally, deliberately.

601 necessity *n* obligation, compulsion, subjection; fate, destiny, fatality; inevitability, inevitableness, unavoidability, unavoidableness, irresistibility; requirement, requisite, demand; instinct, impulse.

v be obligated, be obliged, be fated; necessitate, compel, subject; require.

adj necessary, essential, requisite, needful; inevitable, unavoidable, ineluctable, irresistible, inexorable; compulsory; involuntary, instinctive, automatic, blind, mechanical.

adv necessarily, of necessity, willy nilly.

602 willingness *n* disposition, inclination, leaning, propensity, frame of mind, liking, humor, mood, vein, bent, penchant, aptitude; geniality, cordiality, good will; alacrity, readiness, eagerness, enthusiasm; assent, compliance, agreement.

v be willing, incline, lean to, mind, hold to, cling to; desire, acquiesce, assent, comply; find one's way to, give it a shot, *(informal)* take a swing at, *(informal)* lay into.

adj willing, fain, favorable, content, well disposed; ready, earnest, eager, desirous; genial, cordial.

adv willingly, freely, with pleasure, with all one's heart, graciously.

603 unwillingness *n* indisposition, disinclination, reluctance, dislike; aversion, indifference, slowness, lack of readiness, obstinacy; scrupulousness, hesitation, qualm, shrinking, holding back, recoil; averseness, dissent, refusal.

v be unwilling, dislike; demur, hesitate, shrink from, swerve, recoil; dissent, refuse.

adj unwilling, loath, reluctant, averse; laggard, backward, slow, slack, indifferent; scrupulous, hesitant.

adv unwillingly, grudgingly, against one's will, under protest.

604 resolution *n* determination, will, decision, strength of mind, resolve, firmness, energy, manliness, vigor, resoluteness; pluck, zeal, devotion; self-control, self-command, self-possession, self-reliance, self-restraint, self-denial; tenacity, perseverance, obstinacy, *(informal)* gumption.

v be resolute, resolve, will, determine, decide, make a resolution, conclude, fix, bring to a crisis, take a decisive step; stand firm, insist upon, make a point of, not give an inch.

adj resolute, firm, steadfast, resolved, purposeful, fixed, inflexible, bold, game, indomitable, relentless, tenacious, gritty, stern, irrevocable, obstinate.

adv resolutely, in earnest, earnestly, manfully.

604a perseverance *n* persistence, tenacity, resolution, doggedness, determination, steadfastness, indefatigability, pluck, stamina, backbone.

v persevere, persist, continue, keep on, last, stick it out, hang in there.

adj persevering, constant, steady, steadfast, persistent, tenacious, resolute, dogged, indefatigable, indomitable, staunch, true, game, *(informal)* tough.

605 irresolution *n* indecision, indetermination, instability, uncertainty; hesitation, hesitancy, vacillation, oscillation, changeableness, fluctuation, fickleness, weakness, frailty, timidity, cowardice.

v be irresolute, dawdle, dilly-dally, shilly-shally, hesitate, falter, waver, vacillate, change, fluctuate, blow hot and cold.

adj irresolute, indecisive, indeterminate, unstable, uncertain; hesitant, changeable, capricious, fickle, frail, feeble, weak, timid, *(informal)* soft, cowardly.

606 obstinacy *n* doggedness, persistence, pertinacity, resolution, intractability, firmness, immovability, inflexibility, obduracy, willfulness, perversity, stubbornness, mulishness; uncontrollability, wildness.

fixed idea, *idée fixe,* fanaticism, zealotry, infatuation, monomania; bigotry, intolerance, dogmatism.

bigot, dogmatist, zealot, fanatic.

v be obstinate, persist, die hard, fight, stick to an idea.

adj obstinate, dogged, persistent, pertinacious, resolute, intractable, firm, refractory, headstrong, willful, inflexible, immovable, perverse, stubborn, mulish, pig-headed; wayward, unruly, incorrigible, uncontrollable, wild; fanatic, zealous, monomaniacal; intolerant, dogmatic, arbitrary.

607 recantation *n* tergiversation, renunciation, abjuration, retraction, defection, apostasy, disavowal, revocation, reversal.

turncoat, apostate, renegade, deserter.

v recant, change one's mind, abjure, retract, renounce, disavow, revoke, defect, change sides.

adj changeful, irresolute, slippery, timeserving.

608 caprice *n* fancy, humor, whim, quirk, freak, fad, vagary, prank.

v be capricious.

adj capricious, erratic, eccentric, fitful, inconsistent, fanciful, whimsical, crotchety, freakish, wayward, wanton; contrary, captious, unreasonable, arbitrary, fickle; frivolous.

609 choice *n* selection, decision, pick, choosing, election, option, alternative, preference, predilection, desire.

v choose, select, elect, make a choice, prefer, pick cull, decide.

adj optional, discretional, preferential.

609a neutrality. absence of choice *n* neutrality, indifference; indecision, irresolution.

no choice, first come first served.

v be neutral, have no preference, waive, abstain.

take what's offered.

adj neutral, indifferent; indecisive, irresolute.

610 rejection *n* refusal, repudiation, renunciation; exclusion, elimination.

v reject, refuse, repudiate, decline, deny, rebuff, repel, renounce; discard, throw away, exclude, eliminate; jettison.

611 predetermination *n* premeditation, predeliberation, foregone conclusion; resolve, intention; fate, predestination, destiny.

v predetermine, predestine, premeditate, resolve beforehand, calculate.

adj aforethought; foregone.

adv advisedly, deliberately, intentionally.

612 impulse *n* sudden thought, flash, spurt, inspiration, improvisation.

v improvise, extemporize, flash on, hit on, come up with, pull out of a hat, pull out of the air; say what comes to mind.

adj impulsive, impromptu, spontaneous; extemporaneous.

adv extempore, extemporaneously; impromptu, offhand, impulsively.

613 habit *n* addiction, disposition, tendency, bent, wont; custom, prescription, practice, way, usage, wont, manner; prevalence, observance; conventionalism, conventionality, mode, fashion, vogue, conformity; rule, precedent, routine, rut, groove.

v habituate, inure, harden, season; accustom, familiarize; acclimate, accommodate; cling to, adhere to, acquire a habit, fall into a rut; be habitual, come into use, become a habit, take root.

adj habitual, customary, prescriptive, usual, general, ordinary, common, frequent, everyday, familiar, trite, commonplace, conventional, regular, set, stock, fixed, permanent; prevalent, current, fashionable; addictive.

adv habitually, as usual, as things go, as the world goes; as a rule, for the most part, generally.

614 disuse *n* desuetude, disusage, lack of practice.

v be unaccustomed, break a habit; disuse.

adj unaccustomed; unusual, original.

615 motive *n* reason, ground, principle, mainspring, purpose, cause, occasion, influence, impulse, instigation, spur, stimulus, incitement, incentive, inducement, consideration, temptation, motivation; intention, ulterior motive.

v motivate, induce, move, inspire, put up to, prompt, stimulate, spur, excite, arouse, rouse, incite, instigate; influence, sway, incline, dispose, lead, persuade, prevail upon, enlist, engage, invite, court, tempt, charm.

adj suasive, persuasive, seductive, attractive, provocative.

615a absence of motive *n* caprice, chance, absence of design.

v have no motive.

adj capricious, without rhyme or reason.

adv capriciously.

616 dissuasion *n* expostulation, remonstrance, deprecation, discouragement, damper, restraint, curb, check.

v dissuade, cry out against, remonstrate, expostulate, warn, disincline, indispose, shake, discourage, dishearten, disenchant; deter, hold back, restrain, repel, turn aside, wean from, damp, cool, chill, blunt.

adj dissuasive.

617 [ostensible motive, ground, or reason] **plea** *n* pretext, allegation, excuse; pretense, shallow excuse, lame excuse, makeshift.

v plead, allege, excuse, make a pretext of, pretend.

adj ostensible, alleged.

adv ostensibly, under the pretense of.

618 good *n* benefit, interest, service, behalf, advantage, improvement, gain, boot, profit, harvest; boon, blessing, good luck, prize, good fortune, windfall, godsend; prosperity, happiness, goodness.

v benefit, serve, profit, advantage.

adj commendable; useful, good, beneficial, advantageous.

619 evil *n* ill, harm, hurt, mischief, nuisance; damage, loss; disadvantage, drawback; disaster, accident, casualty, mishap, misfortune; calamity, catastrophe, tragedy, ruin, destruction, adversity; mental suffering, pain, anguish; outrage, wrong, injury, foul, play.

v be in trouble; harm, hurt, injure, ruin, destroy, torture.

adj evil, hurtful, injurious, harmful; disastrous, catastrophic, cataclysmic, tragic, ruinous.

620 intention *n* intent, purpose, project, undertaking, design, ambition, contemplation, view, proposal, meaning; object, aim, end, destination, mark, point, goal, target, prey, quarry, game; decision, determination, resolve, resolution, settled purpose.

v intend, mean, design, purpose, propose, contemplate, plan, expect, mediate, calculate, project, aim for, aim at, aspire at.

adj intentional, advised, express, determinate, bound for, bent upon, in view, in prospect.

adv intentionally, advisedly, wittingly, knowingly, purposely, on purpose, by design, pointedly; deliberately.

621 [absence of design] **chance** *n* destiny, lot, fate, luck, good luck, turn, *(informal)* break, *(informal)* jinx, fortune; speculation, venture, stake, shot in the dark, fluke; wager, gambling, betting. gambler, gamester, adventurer.

v chance, chance it, tempt fate, speculate, risk, venture, hazard, stake, wager, bet, place a bet, gamble, play for.

adj unintentional, accidental, random; fortuitous, lucky; speculative, venturesome.

adv unintentionally, unwittingly.

622 pursuit *n* pursuance, enterprise, undertaking, business, adventure, essay, quest, search.

v pursue, prosecute, follow, do, engage in, undertake, endeavor, seek, aim at, fish for, press on, go after, chase.

adj in quest of, in pursuit of.

623 avoidance *n* evasion, flight, escape, retreat, recoil, departure; abstention, abstinence, forbearance, inaction. avoider, shirker, quitter, truant; fugitive, refugee, runaway, deserter.

v avoid, shun, steer clear of, keep clear of, evade, elude, shirk, fly from, turn away from; abstain, refrain, eschew, leave alone, not get involved; shrink, hold back, retire, recoil, flinch, blink, shy, dodge, beat a retreat, turn tail, run for one's life, head for the hills, take flight, beat it out; desert, sneak off, shuffle off, slink away, steal away, slip, sneak, bolt, abscond.

adj elusive, evasive, escapist, fugitive.

624 relinquishment *n* surrender, resignation, yielding, waiver, waiving, abdication, leaving, desertion, withdrawal, secession, abandonment, renunciation.

v relinquish, surrender, give up, resign, yield, cede, waive, forswear, forgo, abdicate, leave, forsake, desert, renounce, quit, abandon, let go, resign, *(informal)* throw in the towel, call it quits, *(informal)* hang it up.

625 business *n* occupation, trade, craft, profession, calling, employment, vocation, pursuit; affair, matter, concern, transaction, undertaking; function, duty, office, position, part, role, capacity.

v employ oneself, undertake, turn one's hand to; be at work on, be engaged in, be occupied with.

adj businesslike; workaday, professional, official, functional; busy.

626 plan *n* scheme, plot, stratagem, policy, procedure, project, formula, method, system, organization, design, contrivance, device; drawing, sketch, draft, map, chart, diagram, representation; intrigue, cabal, conspiracy.

planner, designer, organizer, schemer, strategist, intriguer.

v plan, arrange, frame, scheme, plot, design, devise, contrive, invent, concoct, hatch; project, forecast; systematize, organize, cast, recast, lay groundwork.

adj procedural, formulaic, methodological, systematic, organizational; conspiratorial; strategic.

627 [path] **method** *n* road, procedure, way, means, manner, fashion, technique, process, course, route, track, beat, tack; door, gateway, channel, passage, avenue, means of access, approach.

adv how, in what way, in what manner; by what mode; one way or another, after this fashion.

628 mid-course *n* middle way, middle course, mean, golden mean; compromise, *(informal)* six of one and half a dozen of another, half measures, neutrality.

v steer a middle course, go straight; compromise, go half way, make a compromise.

adj moderate, midway; neutral, impartial.

629 circuit *n* roundabout way, digression, detour, loop, winding.

v go round about, make a circuit, detour, wind around, circle around; deviate, digress.

adj circuitous, indirect, roundabout; zigzag.

adv in a roundabout way, by an indirect course, indirectly.

630 requirement *n* requisite, requisition, need, necessity, wants, claim, demand, prerequisite; mandate, order, command, directive, injunction, charge, claim, precept.

v require, need, call for, have occasion for, necessitate, obligate; demand, request, need, order, enjoin, direct, ask.

adj requisite, necessary, essential, indispensable, needful; urgent, exigent, instant, crying.

adv of necessity.

631 instrumentality *n* mediation, intervention, medium, intermedium, vehicle, hand; aid; subservience.

go-between, intermediary, minister.

v mediate, minister, intervene; be instrumental, aid.

adj instrumental, useful, serviceable; intermediary, intermediate.

adv through, by, whereby, thereby, by the agency of, by dint of, by means of.

632 means *n* resources, wherewithal, way, ways and means, know how, ability; agency, method, approach; capital, provisions.

v have the means, find the means, possess the means.

adj instrumental.

adv by means of; herewith, therewith; wherewithal.

633 instrument *n* tool, implement, utensil, machinery, equipment.

adj instrumental; mechanical.

634 substitute *n* deputy, alternate, understudy, stand-in, proxy, *(informal)* sub, replacement.

v to substitute for, sub.

635 materials *n* raw materials, resources, stuff, stock, staples, supplies.

636 store *n* stock, fund, mine, supply, reserve, reservoir, *(informal)* stash; accumulation, hoard, storing, storage.

v store, put aside, lay away; store up, put up, hoard away, accumulate, amass, garner; reserve, husband, *(informal)* stash, hold back.

adj in store, in reserve, spare.

637 provision *n* supply, grist, resources, store, provender, stock, food; catering, providing, purveying, purveyance, supplying.

v make provision, provide, lay in, lay in a stock, lay in a store; supply, furnish, purvey, provision, cater, stock, store, replenish.

638 waste *n* consumption, expenditure, dissipation, diminution, decline, emaciation, exhaustion, loss, destruction, decay, impairment; misuse, prodigality, wasting; ruin, devastation, spoilation, desolation.

v waste, consume, spend, throw out, expend, squander, misuse, misspend, dissipate; destroy, wear away, erode, eat away, reduce, wear down, exhaust, enfeeble, wear out.

adj wasteful, prodigal, spendthrift; destructive; wasted, gone to waste.

639 sufficiency *n* adequacy, enough, competence.

v be sufficient, suffice, do, just do, satisfy; have enough.

adj sufficient, enough, adequate, ample, up to the mark, competent, commensurate, satisfactory.

adv sufficiently, amply.

640 insufficiency *n* inadequacy, incompetence, incompleteness, deficiency, imperfection, shortcoming; paucity, scarcity, dearth; dole, pittance; emptiness, poorness, depletion, flaccidity.

v be insufficient, not suffice, not do, fall short of, *(informal)* not cut it; want, lack, need, require, be in want.

adj insufficient, inadequate, too little, not enough, incomplete, deficient, imperfect, wanting, short, scarce, meager, poor, thin, sparse, scant; incompetent, perfunctory.

641 redundance *n* superfluity, superabundance, too much, too many, exuberance, profuseness, profusion, plenty, repletion, plethora, congestion, surfeit, overdose, overflow; excess, surplus; repetition, verbosity.

v superabound, overabound, swarm, overflow, run over, run riot, overrun, overdose, overload, overdo, overwhelm; supersaturate, gorge, glut, load, drench, inundate, deluge, flood; choke, cloy, suffocate, pile on, lay on thick, lavish.

adj redundant, exuberant, inordinate, superabundant, excessive, overmuch, replete, profuse, lavish; exorbitant, extravagant, overweening, *(informal)* much; superfluous, unnecessary, needless, over and above, spare, duplicate; repetitious, verbose.

adv over and above, over much, out of proportion, beyond bounds, over one's head.

642 importance *n* consequence, substance, weight, moment, prominence, consideration, significance, import, concern, emphasis, interest, momentousness, weightiness; gravity, seriousness, solemnity; pressure, urgency, stress.

v be important, deserve consideration, be worthy of notice, merit attention; attach importance, ascribe importance, value, care for, set store by; import, signify, matter, boot, carry weight; accentuate, emphasize, lay stress on; mark, underline, underscore.

adj important, consequential, weighty, momentous, prominent, considerable, significant, notable, salient; grave, serious, earnest, grand, solemn, impressive, commanding, imposing; urgent, pressing, critical, crucial, paramount, essential, vital, prime, primary, principal, all-important, capital, foremost, of vital importance; superior, considerable; significant, telling, trenchant, emphatic.

643 unimportance *n* insignificance, immateriality, triviality, paltriness, indifference, nothing, trifling; trumpery, trash, rubbish, frippery, chaff, bauble, trifle.

v be unimportant, not matter, matter little, signify little; make light of.

adj unimportant, of little account, of small importance, immaterial, unessential, nonessential, inconsequential, insignificant, inconsiderable, so-so; commonplace, ordinary, uneventful, mere, common; trifling, trivial, slight, slender, light, flimsy, shallow; frivolous, petty, niggling, piddling; poor, paltry, pitiful, sorry, mean, meager, shabby, beggarly, worthless, cheap, tawdry, trashy, gimmicky; unworthy of consideration, unworthy of notice; useless, of no account.

644 utility *n* usefulness, efficacy, helpfulness, service, use, stead, avail, help, aid; applicability, value, worth, productiveness.

v be useful, avail, serve, perform, help, aid, benefit; act a part, discharge a function, stand one in good stead.

adj useful, serviceable, functional, advantageous, valuable, productive, profitable, helpful, effectual, effective, efficacious, beneficial, salutary; applicable, available, practical, practicable, workable.

645 inutility *n* uselessness, inefficacy, ineptitude, inaptitude, inadequacy, inefficiency, unfruitfulness, futility, worthlessness, hopelessness.

v be useless, be of no help.

adj useless, unavailing, futile, inutile, fruitless, vain, ineffectual, profitless, bootless, valueless, worthless, hopeless; unserviceable, unusable, inoperative.

646 expedience *n* expediency, fitness, utility, suitability, profitability, advisability, propriety, appropriateness, desirability; opportunism, pragmatism, realism.

v be expedient, suit, befit, suit the occasion.

adj expedient, advantageous, opportune, fit, suitable, convenient, profitable, worthwhile, advisable, meet, proper, becoming, appropriate, desirable.

647 inexpedience *n* inexpediency, impropriety, unfitness, unsuitability, inappropriateness, undesirability; inconvenience, impracticality.

v be inexpedient, be inconvenient, hinder.

adj inexpedient, inopportune, unfit, unsuitable, disadvantageous, discommodious, unadvisable, unseemly, improper, unworkable, impractical, inconvenient, unprofitable, useless, worthless.

648 [good qualities] **goodness** *n* virtue, excellence, merit, value, worth; perfection, eminence, superiority, masterpiece, *chef d'oeuvre,* prime, flower, cream, elite, pick, pick of the litter, salt of the earth, *(informal)* A-1, *(informal)* tops, second to none; gem, jewel, treasure, one in a million; beneficence.

v be good, excel, transcend, stand the test, pass muster, challenge comparison, vie, emulate, rival, *(informal)* dwarf the competition; be beneficial, do good, profit, benefit, improve, be the making of, do a world of good, produce a good effect, do a good turn.

adj good, excellent, better, superior, above par, fine, genuine, true; best, choice, select, rare, invaluable, priceless, inestimable, superlative, perfect, inimitable, first-rate, first-class, very best, crack, prime, tip-top, capital, *(informal)* tops; beneficial, valuable, advantageous, profitable, edifying, salutary, serviceable; favorable, propitious.

649 [bad qualities] **badness** *n* harmfulness, hurtfulness, virulence, painfulness, abomination, pestilence, guilt, depravity, vice, evil, malignity, malevolence; bane, plague, evil star, ill wind, bad omen, *(informal)* jinx, *(informal)*

whammy; snake in the grass, skeleton in the closet, *(informal)* ghosts, *(informal)* demons; ill-treatment, annoyance, molestation, abuse, oppression, persecution, outrage, misusage, injury, damage.

v hurt, harm, injure, damage, pain; wrong, aggrieve, oppress, persecute, trample upon, tread upon, walk over, overburden; weigh down, run down; victimize, maltreat, molest, abuse, ill-use, bruise, scratch, maul, smite, do violence, do harm, stab, pierce.

adj hurtful, harmful, baleful, injurious, deleterious, detrimental, noxious, pernicious, mischievous; oppressive, burdensome, onerous, malign, malevolent; virulent, venomous, corrosive, poisonous, deadly, destructive; bad, ill, dreadful, horrid, horrible, dire, rank, foul, rotten, as low as one can go, *(informal)* the pits; evil, wrong, reprehensible, hateful, abominable, detestable, execrable, damnable, infernal, diabolical; vile, base, villainous, cruel, mean, low; deplorable, wretched, sad, grievous, lamentable, pitiable, pitiful, woeful, painful.

650 perfection *n* ideal, summit, paragon, model, standard, pattern, mirror; impeccability, faultlessness, excellence; masterpiece, master stroke; transcendence, superiority.

v perfect, bring to perfection, ripen, mature, complete, finish; be perfect, transcend.

adj perfect, faultless, immaculate, spotless, unblemished, impeccable, exquisite, consummate; in perfect condition, sound, intact; best, model, standard, inimitable, beyond all praise.

651 imperfection *n* deficiency, inadequacy, insufficiency, immaturity; fault, defect, weak point, weak spot, flaw, taint, blemish, weakness, shortcoming, drawback.

v be imperfect, have a defect, not pass muster, fall short.

adj imperfect, deficient, inadequate, insufficient, immature, defective, faulty, unsound, out of order, out of tune, warped, lame, frail, weak, crude, incomplete, below par, found wanting; indifferent, middling, ordinary, mediocre, average, so-so, tolerable, fair, passable, decent, not bad, bearable, better than nothing; inferior, secondary, second-rate, poor substitute.

652 cleanness n purity, purification, purgation, cleanliness; ablution, lavation; neatness, tidiness, orderliness; cathartic, purgative, laxative; detergent, disinfectant.

v clean, cleanse, purify, purge, expurgate, clarify, refine; wash, launder, scour, scrub, disinfect, fumigate, deodorize, ventilate; rout out, clear out, sweep out, make a clean sweep of, start fresh; neaten, tidy up, order, put things in order.

adj clean, pure, immaculate, spotless, stainless, unsullied, sweet; neat, spruce, tidy, trim, kempt.

653 uncleanness n impurity, defilement, contamination, taint; decay, putrefaction, corruption, mold, mildew, rot, dry rot; squalor, slovenliness, filth, dirt, smut, grime, mud, mire, muck, quagmire, slime.

v be unclean, rot, putrefy, fester, rankle, reek, stink, mold, go bad; dirty, soil, tarnish, spot, smear, blot, blur, smudge, smirch; besmear, befoul, splash, stain, sully, pollute, defile, debase, contaminate, taint, corrupt.

adj unclean, dirty, filthy, grimy, soiled; dusty, smutty, sooty, slimy; slovenly, untidy, sluttish, dowdy, unkempt, unscoured, squalid; nasty, coarse, foul, impure, offensive, abominable, beastly, reeky, fetid; moldy, musty, moth-eaten, bad, gone bad, rancid, rotten, corrupt, putrid, carious, fecal; gory, bloody; gross.

654 health n soundness, well-being, vigor, good health, bloom, color, vitality, robust health.

v be in health, be healthy, bloom, flourish, feel fine, feel good.

adj healthy, healthful, in health, well, sound, hearty, hale, strong, hardy, robust, vigorous, fit as a fiddle, in top shape, chipper, (informal) all together.

655 disease n illness, sickness, ill health, ailment, infirmity, indisposition, complaint, disorder, malady; delicacy, delicate, condition, decline, deterioration, decay.

v ail, suffer, be affected with, droop, flag, languish, sicken, pine, gasp, waste away, fail; take sick, take ill, come down with, contract a disease, catch a bug.

adj ill, sick, indisposed, not well, unwell, in poor health, in bad health, ailing, poorly, laid up, bed-ridden, out of sorts, under the weather, (informal) in bad shape; sickly, infirm, unsound, unhealthy, (informal) falling apart, weak, lame, decrepit; diseased, morbid, mangy, corrupt, contaminated, leprous.

656 salubrity n healthiness, healthfulness, wholesomeness.

v be salubrious, be good for, agree with.

adj salubrious, healthy, healthful, salutary, wholesome, sanitary, bracing, invigorating, benign, nutritious, tonic, hygienic.

657 insalubrity n unhealthiness, unsoundness.

v be unhealthy, not be good for, disagree with.

adj insalubrious, unhealthy, unwholesome, noxious, noisome, deleterious, pestilential, bad, harmful, virulent, venomous, poisonous, septic, toxic, deadly.

658 improvement n amelioration, amendment, emendation, correction, revision, reformation, restoration, repair, betterment, gain, advancement, elevation, increase, refinement, elaboration; acculturation, cultivation, civilization.

reformer, radical.

v improve, mend, amend, get better; ameliorate, better, amend, emend, correct, right, rectify, revise, reform, restore, repair; advance, progress, ascend, increase, fructify, ripen, mature; refine, enrich, elaborate; promote, cultivate, foster, enhance.

adj better, better off, all for the better; emendatory, corrective, reformative, restorative, improving, progressive, improved.

659 deterioration n debasement, recession, retrogradation, degeneracy, degeneration, degradation, deprivation, depravity, retrogression; detriment, damage, loss, injury, impairment, contamination, spoilage, corruption, adulteration; decline, declension, senility, decrepitude; decadence, decay, dilapidation, falling off, wear and tear, erosion, corrosion, rottenness, blight, atrophy, collapse.

v deteriorate, degenerate, fall off, wane, ebb, decline, droop, go down, go downhill, sink, go to seed, go to waste, lapse, break down, crack, shrivel, fade, wither, molder, rot, rankle, decay, go bad, rust, crumble, shake, totter, perish, die; taint, infect, contaminate, poison, canker, corrupt, pollute, vitiate, debase, degrade, adulterate; injure, impair, damage, harm, hurt, spoil, mar, despoil, dilapidate, waste, ravage; wound, maim, cripple, scotch, mangle, mutilate, disfigure, blemish, deface, warp; blight, rot, corrode, erode, wear away, wear out, sap, mine, undermine, shake the foundations of, break up, destroy, decimate.

adj deteriorated, unimproved, injured, degenerate, imperfect; battered, weathered, weather-beaten, all the worse for wear, stale, dilapidated, faded, shabby, threadbare, worn, far gone, *(informal)* had it; decayed, moth-eaten, worm-eaten, mildewed, rusty, moldy, seedy, time-worn, wasted, crumbling, moldering, rotten, blighted, tainted; decrepit, broken down, wornout, used up, out of commission, in a bad way, past cure, past hope, *(informal)* long gone.

660 restoration n reestablishment, replacement, reinstatement, renewal, rehabilitation, reconstruction, reproduction, rebuilding, renovation, revival; refreshment, resuscitation, revivification; renaissance, renascence, new birth, regeneration, reconversion; redress, retrieval, reclamation, recovery, resumption; repair, reparation, restitution, relief, deliverance, rectification, cure, healing; redemption.

v restore, recover, rally, revive, come round, pull through, get well, get over; reestablish, replace, rehabilitate, reinstate; reconstruct, rebuild, reproduce, reorganize, reconstitute, renew, renovate; redeem, reclaim, recover, retrieve, rescue, deliver; redress, recure; cure, heal, remedy, doctor, bring round; resuscitate, revive, reanimate, revivify, reinvigorate, refresh; recoup, make good, square, set to rights, correct, put in order; repair, retouch, patch up, fix.

adj restorative, recuperative, curative, remedial; restorable, remediable,

retrievable, curable; restored, convalescent, renascent, reborn.

661 relapse n lapse, falling back, retrogradation, deterioration, backsliding.

v relapse, lapse, fall back, slip back, sink back, suffer a relapse, fall again.

adj retrograde.

662 remedy n help, redress, solution, answer, panacea; cure, relief, medicine, treatment, restorative, specific, medication, ointment, balm; antidote, corrective, antitoxin, counteractive.

doctor, physician, surgeon.

v remedy, cure, heal, set right, put right, doctor, nurse, restore, recondition, repair, redress; counteract, remove, correct, right, solve.

adj remedial, restorative, corrective, palliative; medicinal, therapeutic, curative; soluble.

663 bane n curse, evil, plague, scourge, pain, nuisance, thorn in the side, pain in the neck; poison, virus, venom; fungus, mildew, dry rot, canker, cancer; sting, fang, thorn, bramble, briar, nettle.

adj baneful, bad, sinister, pernicious, evil, baleful, poisonous, venomous, ruinous, unwholesome, harmful, deadly.

664 safety n security, surety, impregnability, invulnerability; safeguard, safety valve, precaution, custody, safe keeping, preservation, protection.

protector, guardian, warden, preserver, custodian, watchdog, sentinel, scout.

v be safe; protect, take care of, care for, preserve, cover, screen, shelter, shroud, guard, defend, secure, house, garrison; watch, patrol, look out, take precautions.

adj safe, secure, snug, warm, sure, sound, on the safe side, out of danger; dependable, trustworthy, sure, reliable; cautious, wary, careful; defensible, tenable, invulnerable, impregnable, unassailable, safe and sound.

665 danger n hazard, insecurity, instability, precariousness, slipperiness, risk, peril, jeopardy, liability, exposure; injury, evil; warning, alarm, apprehension.

v be in danger, run into trouble, lay oneself open to, hang by a thread, totter;

endanger, expose to danger, imperil, jeopardize, adventure, venture, risk, hazard, threaten.

adj dangerous, hazardous, risky, perilous, precarious, unsafe, insecure, unstable, untrustworthy, unsteady, shaky, slippery, ominous, fearful, explosive, fraught with danger; defenseless, vulnerable, open, liable.

666 refuge *n* sanctuary, retreat, asylum, hiding place, stronghold, fortress, shelter, cover; anchor, mainstay, support, check, last resort, safeguard.

v seek refuge, take refuge, find refuge, take shelter, find safety.

667 pitfall *n* snare, trap, snag, ambush, snake in the grass, wolf in sheep's clothing, menace, complication, danger; slippery ground, weak foundation, rocks, reefs, sunken rocks, sand, quicksand, breakers, shoals, shallows, precipice, maelstrom.

668 warning *n* caution, notice, premonition, prediction, admonition, advice, lesson; alarm, omen, sign, signal, augury, portent, presage.

sentinel, sentry, watch, watchman, watchdog, patrol, scout, spy.

v warn, caution, admonish, forewarn; give notice, notify, appraise, inform; menace, threaten, portend.

adj premonitory, cautionary, advisory; ominous, portentous.

669 [indication of danger] **alarm** *n* alarum, alarm bell, tocsin, distress signal, siren, danger signal, hue and cry, SOS, cry, scream.

v alarm, sound the alarm, warn, cry out.

670 preservation *n* safekeeping, conservation; guarding, safeguard, shelter, protection, defense; maintenance, support, sustenance, continuance, retention, salvation.

v preserve, keep, conserve; guard, safeguard, shelter, shield, protect, defend, rescue; keep up, maintain, continue, support, uphold, sustain; retain, store, husband; cure, pickle, bottle, can.

adj preserved, unimpaired, uninjured, unhurt, safe, sound, intact; conservative, preservative.

671 escape *n* flight, evasion, loophole, retreat; reprieve, release, liberation; narrow escape, close call, near miss.

v escape, flee, abscond, fly, steal away, run away, *(informal)* take off, *(informal)* split; shun, fly, elude, evade, avoid.

adj stolen away, fled, *(informal)* cut out.

672 deliverance *n* extrication, disentanglement, rescue, reprieve, respite; liberation, release; emancipation, freedom; redemption, salvation.

v deliver, extricate, disentangle, rescue, reprieve, save, redeem; set free, liberate, release, emancipate, free; come to the rescue.

673 preparation *n* provision, plan, arrangement, anticipation, precaution, forecast, rehearsal; groundwork, homework, foundation, scaffolding; training, education, dissemination; readiness, ripeness, maturity.

v prepare, get ready, make ready, prime, arrange, make preparations, plan, devise, anticipate, lay the foundations, provide, order; mature, ripen, mellow, season, nurture; equip, arm, fit out, furnish; train, teach, prepare for, rehearse, make provision for, take steps, provide against.

adj prepatory, precautionary, provident, preparative, preparatory; provisional, preliminary; prepared, ready, available, all ready, handy; ripe, mature, mellow.

674 nonpreparation *n* unpreparedness, unreadiness; improvidence.

v be unprepared; extemporize, improvise.

adj unprepared, incomplete, premature, rudimental, embryonic, immature, unripe, raw, green, coarse, crude, rough, unhewn, untaught, fallow, unready; out of order, nonfunctional, *(informal)* on the fritz, in disrepair, *(informal)* out of whack; shiftless, improvident, thoughtless, careless, slack, remiss, happy-go-lucky.

675 essay *n* trial endeavor, effort, attempt, struggle, venture, adventure, speculation, experiment.

v essay, try, experiment; endeavor, strive, tempt, attempt, venture, adventure, speculate, tempt fortune, *(informal)* give it a go, *(informal)* take a shot at.

adj experimental, tentative, probationary; venturesome, adventurous, speculative.

adv experimentally, on trial.

676 undertaking *n* task, job, venture, engagement, compact, contract, enterprise; pilgrimage, quest.

v undertake, engage in, embark on, launch into, plunge into, volunteer; engage, promise, contract, take upon oneself, devote oneself to, determine, take up, take in hand; tackle, set about, fall to, begin, broach.

677 use *n* employ, exercise, application, appliance; disposal; consumption; agency, usefulness; benefit, recourse, resort, avail; utilization, utility, service, wear; usage.

v use, make use of, employ, put to use, put into operation, apply, set in motion, set to work; ply, work, wield, handle, manipulate; exert, exercise, practice, avail oneself of, profit by; resort to, have recourse to, recur to, take up, try; utilize, bring into play, press into service; use up, consume, expend, tax, task, wear.

adj useful, instrumental, utilitarian, subservient, employable, applicable, beneficial.

678 disuse *n* forbearance, abstinence; relinquishment, abandonment; desuetude.

v not use, do without, dispense with, let alone, forebear, abstain, spare, waive, neglect; keep back, reserve; disuse, lay up, shelve, set aside, put aside, leave off, have done with; supersede, discard, throw aside, relinquish, dismantle.

adj not in use, unemployed, unapplied; disused, unused, done with.

679 misuse *n* misusage, misemployment, misapplication, misappropriation; abuse, profanation, prostitution, desecration; waste.

v misuse, misemploy, misapply, misappropriate; abuse, profane, prostitute, desecrate; waste, squander, destroy; overwork, overtask, overtax.

680 action *n* movement, work, labor, performance, moving, working, performing, operation; deed, act, feat, exploit; conduct, behavior, procedure, execution; energetic activity, exercise, exertion, energy, effort; affair, encounter, meeting, engagement, conflict, combat, fight, battle.

actor, doer, worker.

v act, do, perform, execute, achieve, transact, enact; commit, perpetrate, inflict; exercise, prosecute, carry on, work, function, labor, operate, exert energy, be active; behave, conduct oneself, comport oneself; play, feign, fake, imitate.

adj in action, in operation, operative.

681 inaction *n* passivity, inactivity, idleness, solthfulness; waiting, mulling around, killing time; rest, repose,

v not act, not do, be inactive, abstain from doing, do nothing, let alone, let things take their course; stand aloof, refrain, pause, wait, bide one's time, cool one's heels, waste time, lie idle.

adj inactive, passive, idle, slothful; out of work.

682 activity *n* movement, hustle, bustle, stir, fuss, flurry, action, business; industry, assiduity, assiduousness, laboriousness, drudgery; diligence, perseverance, vigilance, wakefulness, restlessness, fidgetiness; briskness, liveliness, animation, life, vivacity, spirit, dash, energy; eagerness, zeal, ardor, vigor, abandon, exertion; earnestness, intentness, devotion.

v be active, busy oneself in, stir about, rouse oneself, speed, hasten, bustle, fuss, *(informal)* raise a ruckus; push, push ahead, *(informal)* step on it, *(informal)* move it, make progress; toil, plod, persist, persevere, hustle, *(informal)* hustle it, *(informal)* push; look sharp, keep moving, seize the opportunity, *carpe diem,* lose no time, dash off, make haste; have a hand in, trouble oneself about.

adj active, brisk, lively, busy as a bee, vivacious, alive, frisky; quick, prompt, ready, alert, spry, sharp, smart, awake, wide awake, eager, zealous; industrious, assiduous, diligent, vigilant; businesslike; restless, fussy, fidgety, busy.

683 inactivity *n* inaction, inertness, lull, quiescence; idleness, remissness, sloth, indolence, dawdling, laziness; dullness, languor, sluggishness, torpor, stupor, lethargy, procrastination.

idler, drone, dawdler, moper, lounger, loafer, sluggard, laggard, slumberer.

v be inactive, do nothing, dawdle, lag, hang back, slouch, loll, lounge, loaf, loiter, take it easy; fritter away time, idle, piddle, putter, dabble, dally, dilly-dally; languish, flag, relax; kill time, waste time.

adj inactive, motionless; indolent, lazy, slothful, idle, remiss, slack, inert, torpid, sluggish, languid, supine, heavy, dull, listless; laggard, slow, rusty, lackadaisical, irresolute; drowsy, lethargic, soporific, dreamy, dreamy-eyed.

684 haste *n* urgency, need, hurry, flurry, bustle, spurt, rush, dash, scramble, bustle, ado, precipitancy, precipitation; swiftness, celerity, alacrity, quickness, rapidity, dispatch, speed, expedition, promptitude, timeliness, promptness.

v haste, hasten, make haste, hurry, dash, push on, press on, press forward, scurry, bustle, scramble, rush, accelerate, urge, expedite, quicken, speed, precipitate, dispatch.

adj hasty, speedy, quick, hurried, swift, rapid, fast, fleet, brisk; precipitate, rash, foolhardy, reckless, indiscreet, thoughtless, headlong; testy, touchy, irascible, petulant, waspish, fretful, fiery, excitable, irritable, peevish.

685 leisure *n* spare time, free time, convenience, liberty, pause, stay, halt, lull, breather, *(informal)* letup, breathing spell, break, *(informal)* time out; interlude, vacation, holiday.

v have leisure, take one's time; rest, relax, repose.

adj leisure, spare, free; leisurely, slow, deliberate, quiet, calm, restful, peaceful, languid, easy, gradual.

686 exertion *n* effort, action, activity, endeavor, struggle, attempt, strain, trial, stress; labor, work, toil, travail; trouble, pain; energy.

v exert, exert oneself, labor, work, toil, sweat, drudge, strive, strain; work hard, rough it, buckle to, take pains, concentrate, spare no effort.

adj laborious, wearisome, burdensome, *(informal)* tough, *(informal)*

rough, strenuous, herculean, Sisyphean.

687 repose *n* rest, sleep, slumber; relaxation, breathing spell; halt, pause, respite, cessation; day of rest, Sabbath; holiday, vacation, recess.

v repose, rest; relax, unbend, slacken, catch one's breath, get one's wind, take a breather, pause; recline, lie down, go to bed, take a nap, go to sleep; take a holiday, go on vacation, shut up shop.

adj reposing, resting.

adv at rest.

688 fatigue *n* weariness, lassitude, tiredness, exhaustion, faintness; ennui, boredom, tedium, languor, yawning, drowsiness.

v be fatigued, yawn, droop, sink, flag, *(informal)* give out; gasp, pant, puff, blow, drop, swoon, faint; fatigue, tire, weary, exhaust, wear out; tax, task, strain; bore, tire, irritate, annoy.

adj fatigued, weary, drowsy, haggard, faint, exhausted, spent, tired, tired to death, worn out, *(informal)* gone; breathless.

689 refreshment *n* recovery of strength, restoration, revival, repair, relief.

v refresh, brace, strengthen, reinvigorate, revive, stimulate, freshen, cheer, enliven, reanimate; restore, repair, renew.

adj refreshing, restoring.

690 agent *n* doer, actor, performer, perpetrator, operator; practitioner, executioner, executor, executrix, minister, representative, deputy, servant, worker; participant, party to.

691 workshop *n* laboratory, factory, mill, mint, forge, studio; hive, beehive, seat of activity.

692 conduct *n* behavior, demeanor, action, actions, deportment, bearing, carriage, mien, manners; process, ways, practice, procedure, method; policy, tactics, strategy, plan; direction, management, execution, guidance, leadership, administration.

v conduct, behave, deport, act, bear; transact, execute, dispatch, discharge, proceed with, enact; direct, manage, carry on, supervise, regulate, administer, guide, lead.

adj procedural, practical, methodical, tactical, strategical, businesslike; directive, managerial, administrative, executive.

693 direction *n* guidance, advice, regulation, conduct, management, disposition, supervision, auspices, steerage, stewardship, ministration, administration, control, leadership, government, rule, command; order, command, instruction.

v direct, guide, advise, regulate, conduct, manage, control, dispose, supervise, overlook, steer, steward, pilot, minister, administer, legislate, lead, rule, govern, have charge of, command; order, instruct, prescribe.

adj directing, guiding, supervisory, managing, administering.

694 director *n* manager, governor, controller, superintendent, supervisor, overseer, inspector, foreman, surveyor, taskmaster, master, leader, boss; adviser, guide, pilot, captain, helmsman, driver; head, chief, principal, president, minister, official, functionary.

695 advice *n* counsel, opinion, recommendation, guidance, suggestion, persuasion, urging, exhortation; instruction, charge, injunction; admonition, warning, caution.

adviser, council, counselor, mentor.

v advise, give counsel to, suggest, recommend, prescribe, advocate, exhort, persuade; enjoin, enforce, charge, instruct; admonish, caution, warn; take counsel, confer, deliberate, discuss, consult, refer to; give counsel, offer counsel.

adj advisory, suggestive, persuasive, suasive; admonitory.

696 council *n* committee, court, chamber, cabinet, board, board of directors, advisory board, staff, syndicate, chapter; assembly, caucus, conclave, meeting, conference, session.

697 precept *n* direction, instruction, charge, prescript, prescription; golden rule, maxim, canon, law, code, act, statute, regulation, formula, form, technicality, rubric; order, command.

698 skill *n* skillfulness, dexterity, adroitness, expertness, proficiency, competence, facility, knack, mastery; accomplishment, acquirement, attainment, ability, craft; knowledge, wisdom, *savoir*

faire, tact, wit, sagacity, discretion, finesse, craftiness, cunning, management; cleverness, ingenuity, capacity, talent, talents, faculty, endowment, *forte,* turn, gift, genius; intelligence, sharpness, readiness, invention, inventiveness, aptness, aptitude, proclivity, capacity for, genius for, felicity, capability, qualification.

v be skillful, excel in, be master of, have a knack for; take advantage of.

adj skillful, dextrous, adroit, adept, expert, apt, handy, quick, deft, proficient, masterly, crack, first-rate, conversant; skilled, experienced, practiced, competent, efficient, qualified, capable, fit, fit for, trained, prepared, finished; clever, able, ingenious, felicitous, inventive; shrewd, sharp, smart, intelligent, cunning, tactful, discreet, wise, knowledgeable.

adv skillfully, artistically, with consummate skill.

699 unskillfulness *n* want of skill, incompetence, inability, inexpertness, maladroitness, ineptitude, clumsiness, awkwardness, carelessness, bumbling, bungling; indiscretion.

v be unskillful, blunder, bungle, boggle, fumble, botch, stumble.

adj unskillful, unskilled, inexpert, incompetent, unable, inapt, bungling, inept, maladroit, awkward, clumsy, gawky; unfit, ill-qualified, unhandy, not conversant; raw, rusty, out of practice.

700 expert *n* specialist, authority, mater, professional, connoisseur, veteran, old hand, old soldier; genius, mastermind, wizard, prodigy, *(informal)* pro.

701 bungler *n* blunderer, blunderhead, fumbler, duffer, clown, *(informal)* turkey, butter-fingers, greenhorn, amateur, rookie, novice, *(informal)* Sunday driver, *(informal)* armchair quarterback.

702 cunning *n* craftiness, skillfulness, shrewdness, artfulness, wiliness, subtlety, finesse, artifice, device, stratagem, intrigue, craft, guile, chicanery, duplicity, subterfuge, deceit, deceitfulness, slyness, deception; ability, skill, adroitness, expertness.

v be cunning, maneuver, contrive, manipulate, intrigue, finesse, surprise.

adj crafty, shrewd, artful, wily, subtle, tricky, foxy, politic, insidious, stealthy, Machiavellian, deceitful, duplicitous, sly, deceptive; canny, astute; ingenious, clever, skillful, sharp.

703 artlessness *n* simplicity, innocence, naivete, unworldliness, inexperience, inexposure, plainness, plain speaking, sincerity, honesty, openness, candor, matter of factness, bluntness.

v be artless, speak one's mind, come to the point, pull no punches.

adj artless, natural, simple, innocent, naive, childlike, unsuspicious, unworldly, unartificial, plain; sincere, frank, open, candid, honest, ingenuous, guileless, straightforward, aboveboard, point-blank, plain spoken, outspoken, blunt, direct, matter of fact.

adv in plain English, in simple words, without mincing words.

704 difficulty *n* dilemma, predicament, quandary, fix, exigency, emergency, crisis, trouble, problem, scrape, entanglement, strait, pass, pinch; reluctance, unwillingness, obstinacy, stubbornness; demur, objection, obstacle; labor, task, hard task, herculean task.

v be difficult, pose, perplex, bother, nonplus, hinder; encumber, embarrass, entangle.

adj difficult, hard, arduous, troublesome, irksome, laborious, formidable; awkward, unwieldy, unmanageable; fastidious, particular, stubborn, intractable, perverse; obscure, complex, intricate, delicate, uncertain, ticklish, critical; unfeasible, impractical, impossible, hopeless; austere, rigid.

705 facility *n* ease, easiness, capability, feasibility, practicability; flexibility, pliancy, smoothness, child's play.

v be easy, run smoothly, work well; facilitate, smooth, ease, lighten, free, clear, disencumber, disentangle, extricate, unravel.

adj easy, facile; feasible, practicable, within reach, accessible; manageable, tractable, pliant, smooth.

adv easily, readily, smoothly.

706 hindrance *n* impediment, deterrent, hitch, encumbrance, obstruction, check, stricture, restraint, hobble, obstacle, stumbling block; interuption, interference; impeding, stopping, stoppage, preventing.

v hinder, interrupt, check, impede, retard, encumber, delay, hamper, obstruct, trammel, cramp, handicap; block, thwart, frustrate, disconcert, prevent.

adj obstructive, intrusive; onerous, burdensome, cumbersome, obtrusive.

707 aid *n* help, support, succor, assistance, service, furtherance; relief, rescue, charity; assistant, helper, supporter, servant; patronage, championship, advocacy, favor, interest.

v aid, support, help, succor, assist, serve, abet, back, second; spell, relieve, rescue; sustain, uphold, prop, hold up, bolster; promote, facilitate, ease, advocate; be of help, give help, give assistance, oblige, accommodate, humor, encourage.

adj aiding, auxiliary, helpful, supportive; charitable; friendly, amicable, well-disposed, neighborly.

708 opposition *n* antagonism, hostility, resistance, counteraction; competition, enemy, foe, adversary, antagonist; opposing, resisting, combating.

v oppose, resist, combat, withstand, thwart, confront, contravene, interfere; hinder, obstruct, prevent, check; contradict, gainsay, deny, refuse, dissent.

adj adverse, antagonistic, contrary, at variance, at odds, anti, at issue, in opposition; unfavorable, unfriendly, hostile, inimical, resistant.

adv against, versus, counter to, in conflict with, at cross purposes; in spite, in defiance.

709 cooperation *n* concert, concurrence, agreement, concord, togetherness, harmony, unanimity; complicity, collusion, participation, combination, union, team-work; association, partnership, alliance, pool, coalition, confederation, fusion, fellowship, fraternity; unanimity, partisanship, spirit, party spirit, *esprit de corps*.

v cooperate, concur, combine, unite, pool, share, band together, pull together; act in concert, join forces, fraternize; conspire, be in league with; side with, go along with, join hands with, throw in one's lot with, rally round; participate, have a hand in.

adj cooperating, cooperative, participatory; in league, party to.

adv cooperatively, unanimously, shoulder to shoulder.

710 opponent *n* adversary, antagonist, competitor, rival, opposition; enemy, foe.

711 auxiliary *n* helper, aid, ally, assistant, confederate, collaborator, colleague, associate, partner, mate, friend.

712 party *n* group, gathering, assembly, assemblage, company, crew, band; clan, family, fellowship, community; body, faction, side, circle, clique, set, gang, claque, coterie, combination, ring, league, alliance, association.

v unite, join, band together, cooperate, assemble.

adj clannish, cliquish, communal, familial, fraternal.

713 discord *n* dissidence, dissonance, disagreement, clash, shock; variance, difference, dissension, misunderstanding, cross-purposes, odds, division, split, rupture, disruption, breach, schism, feud, conflict, struggle, argument, contention, quarrel, dispute, tiff, squabble, altercation, words; strife, outbreak.

v be discordant, disagree, clash, jar, conflict, differ, dissent, fall out, quarrel, dispute, squabble, wrangle, bicker, have words with; split, break, disunite, feud.

adj discordant, dissident, dissonant; divisive, disruptive; contentious, argumentative, quarrelsome, disputatious, fractious; at variance, at cross purposes.

714 concord *n* accord, harmony, sympathy, agreement, union, unison, unity, peace; amity, friendship, alliance, *detente*, understanding, togetherness, conciliation.

v agree, accord, harmonize with, fraternize, understand one another, concur, pull together; side with, sympathize with.

adj concordant, congenial, in accord; harmonious, sympathetic, friendly, fraternal, conciliatory.

adv with one voice, unanimously, in concert with.

715 defiance *n* daring, courage, courageousness, bravery, boldness; assertiveness, aggressiveness; antagonism, insubordination, recalcitrance, rebelliousness, insolence, resistance.

v defy, challenge, resist, dare, brave, flout, scorn, despise.

adj defiant, daring, courageous, brave, bold; resistant, insolent, rebellious, recalcitrant, contumacious, insubordinate, antagonistic.

adv in the face of, under one's very nose.

716 attack *n* onslaught, assault, offense, battery, onset, charge, encounter, aggression, incursion, invasion, sally, sortie, raid, foray; criticism, blame, censure, abuse.

assailant, aggressor, invader, attacker.

v assail, assault, molest, threaten, storm, charge, set upon, invade, bombard, beset, besiege, lay siege, storm; criticize, impugn, blame, censure, abuse; declare war, begin hostilities.

adj aggressive, offensive; critical, abusive.

adv on the offensive.

717 defense *n* guard, garrison, fortification, shield, shelter, screen, preservation, protection, guardianship, safeguard, security; justification, pleading, vindication.

v defend, guard, fortify, shield, shelter, screen, preserve, protect, keep safe, guard against, watch over, safeguard, secure; parry, repel, put to flight; uphold, maintain, justify, vindicate.

adj defensive, protective.

718 retaliation *n* reprisal, requital, retort, counterstroke, counterattack, retribution, reciprocation, reciprocity, recrimination, revenge, vengeance, reaction.

v retaliate, requite, retort, counterattack, revenge, repay, return, avenge.

adj retaliatory, vengeful, revengeful, retributive, reciprocal, reactive.

adv in retaliation.

719 resistance *n* opposition, withstanding, front, stand, oppugnance, reluctance, repulsion; interference, friction; insurrection, insurgence, rebellion.

v resist, withstand, stand up, stand;

confront, oppose, grapple with, rise up, revolt, rebel, repel, repulse.

adj resistant, refractory, recalcitrant, repulsive, repellent; stubborn, indomitable, obstinate.

720 contention *n* struggling, struggle, strife, discord, dissention, quarrel, disagreement, squabble, feud; rupture, break, falling out; opposition, belligerency, combat, conflict, competition, rivalry, contest; disagreement, dissension, debate, wrangle, altercation, dispute, argument, controversy.

v contend, struggle, strive, fight, battle, combat, vie, compete, rival; debate, dispute, argue, wrangle; assert, maintain, claim.

adj contentious, combative, belligerent, bellicose, warlike, quarrelsome, pugnacious; competitive.

721 peace *n* treaty, truce, accord, amity, harmony, concord; calm, quiet, tranquillity, peacefulness, calmness; order, security.

v be at peace; keep the peace; make peace.

adj peaceful, tranquil, placid, serene, calm, complacent; mellow, halcyon, pacific; peaceable, amicable, friendly, amiable, mild, gentle.

722 warfare *n* fighting, hostilities, war, combat, battle, ordeal; tactics, strategy, generalship.

v war, make war, wage war, fight, give fight, battle, do battle, combat, contend, cross swords.

adj warlike, contentious, belligerent, combative, bellicose, martial, military, militant.

adv to arms.

723 pacification *n* conciliation, reconciliation, accommodation, arrangement, adjustment, compromise; amnesty, peace offering, truce, armistice, suspension of hostilities.

v pacify, reconcile, propitiate, placate, conciliate, accommodate, appease, make peace; quiet, calm, tranquilize, assuage, still, smooth, moderate, ameliorate, mollify, meliorate, soothe, bury the hatchet.

adj pacific, conciliatory.

724 mediation *n* negotiation, arbitration, parley; intervention, intercession, interposition.

mediator, arbiter, arbitrator, peacemaker, go-between, negotiator, moderator, diplomat.

v mediate, intercede, intervene, interpose, interfere; step in, negotiate, arbitrate.

adj mediatory.

725 submission *n* nonresistance, obedience, compliance, acquiescence, yielding, submissiveness, pliancy; surrender, cessation, capitulation; resignation, passivity, docility.

v succumb, submit, yield, bend, acquiesce, resign, agree, obey, comply, bow, surrender, capitulate.

adj submissive, obedient, compliant, acquiescent, passive, docile, tame, humble.

726 combatant *n* fighter, contestant, disputant, battler, litigant, contender, competitor, militarist, soldier, warrior, polemic, candidate; antagonist, foe, enemy, opponent, rival, adversary, assailant, opposition, assailer, assailant, assaulter, opposer, opponent.

727 arms *n* weapons, weaponry, armaments, armor, ammunition, munitions, deadly weapons.

v arm, outfit, ready for battle, prepare for battle.

728 arena *n* battleground, battlefield, field of battle, theater, ring, lists; playhouse, amphitheater, stage, boards; Colosseum, gymnasium, playing field.

729 completion *n* culmination, finish, conclusion, close, termination, end, finale; upshot, result; final touch, crowning touch; consummation, accomplishment, achievement, fulfillment; performance, execution; perfection, thoroughness.

v complete, finish, end, conclude, close, terminate, finalize; consummate, perfect, accomplish, do, fulfill, achieve, effect, execute, enact, dispatch, discharge.

adj whole, entire, full, intact, unbroken, one, perfect; done, consummate, perfect, thorough, through-and-through.

adv completely, thoroughly; perfectly.

730 noncompletion *n* incompleteness, nonfulfilment, nonperformance; neglect, shortcoming.

v not complete, leave unfinished, leave undone; neglect, leg alone, let slip; fall short of.

adj incomplete, unfinished, sketchy.

731 success *n* progress, advance; hit, stroke, trump card; good fortune, good luck, luck, break; prosperity, achievement, fulfillment, accomplishment; ascendancy, mastery, conquest, victory, triumph; proficiency, skill, mastery.

v succeed, attain an end, secure an objective; progress, advance; accomplish, achieve, effect, complete; prosper, find fulfillment, fulfill oneself; master, conquer, triumph, surmount, overcome.

adj successful, prosperous, well-to-do; victorious, triumphant; masterful, proficient.

adv successfully, with flying colors, in triumph.

732 failure *n* unsuccessfulness, miscarriage, abortion, failing; neglect, omission, dereliction, non-performance; deficiency, insufficiency, defectiveness; blunder, mistake, fault, slip, mishap, scrape, mess, fiasco, breakdown; decline, decay, deterioration, loss; bankruptcy, insolvency, bust, dud.

v fail, come short, fall short, disappoint, miss the mark, miscarry, abort, blunder, botch, make a mess of, *(informal)* blow it, founder, flounder, sink, go amiss, go wrong, go hard with; fall off, dwindle, decline, fade, weaken, wane, give out, cease; desert, forsake.

adj unsuccessful, abortive, stillborn, fruitless, bootless, ineffectual, inefficient, insufficient, useless; lost, undone, bankrupt; wide of the mark, erroneous; frustrated, thwarted, foiled, defeated; defective, faulty.

adv unsuccessfully, in vain, to little purpose.

733 trophy *n* medal, prize, palm, laurel, honor, accolade, decoration, reward, recognition, triumph, celebration.

734 prosperity *n* well-being, success, fortune, wealth, affluence.

v prosper, thrive, flourish, rise, make one's way, flower, grow, blossom, bloom, fructify, succeed, *(informal)* make it.

adj prosperous, successful, wealthy, rich, well-to-do, well-off; favorable, propitious, fortunate, lucky, auspicious, golden, bright.

735 adversity *n* calamity, distress, catastrophe, crisis, disaster, failure; bad luck, hard times, misfortune, *(informal)* downers, *(informal)* bummers, trouble, hardship, pressure, affliction, wretchedness.

v go downhill, go to the dogs, decay, sink, decline, come to grief, *(informal)* hit the pits, fall on evil days.

adj adverse, unfavorable, unlucky, unfortunate; calamitous, disastrous, critical, dire, catastrophic; unprosperous, hapless, in a bad way, under a cloud, in adverse circumstances, down in the mouth.

adv adversely; if worst comes to worst.

736 mediocrity *n* average capacity, ordinariness, commonplaceness, insignificance, passableness, tolerableness, indifference, inferiority, paltriness, triviality; moderation, golden mean.

v jog on, get along.

adj mediocre, average, normal, ordinary, commonplace, run-of-the-mill, insignificant, tolerable, unimportant, indifferent, inferior, poor, slight, paltry; moderate, reasonable, temperate, respectable.

II. Intersocial Volition

737 authority *n* control, influence, jurisdiction, command, rule, sway, power, dominion, supremacy; expert, adjudicator, arbiter, judge, sovereign, ruler; warrant, justification, permit, permission, sanction, liberty, authorization.

v authorize, empower, commission, allow, permit, sanction, approve; warrant, justify, legalize, support, back; rule, sway, control, administer, govern.

adj authoritative, peremptory, magisterial, imperative, dogmatic, masterful; executive, administrative, sovereign, regnant, supreme, dominant, paramount, predominant, preponderant, influential, official, decisive, valid, absolute.

738 [absence of authority] **laxity** *n* laxness, looseness, slackness, lenience, toleration, relaxation, loosening, licence, freedom.

v be lax, tolerate, relax, give a free rein.

adj lax, loose, slack, remiss, lenient, negligent, careless, weak.

739 severity *n* seriousness, gravity, sternness, harshness, austerity, rigidity, rigorousness, strictness, stringency, relentlessness, abruptness, curtness; arbitrariness, absolutism, despotism, dictatorship, autocracy, tyranny, oppression; strength, force, brute force, coercion.

tyrant, disciplinarian, despot, taskmaster, oppressor, inquisitor.

v be severe, tyrannize, domineer, dominate, bully, inflict, wreak, be hard on, ill-treat, maltreat, oppress, trample on, crush, coerce.

adj severe, serious, grave, stern, harsh, austere, rigid, stiff, dour, rigorous, strict, strait-laced, stringent, relentless, hard, inexorable, abrupt, peremptory, curt, short; arbitrary, absolute, despotic, dictatorial, autocratic, tyrannical, oppressive, coercive, inquisitorial, ruthless, cruel, malevolent, arrogant.

adv severely, with a high hand, with a heavy hand.

740 lenience *n* leniency, tolerance, toleration, moderation, mildness, gentleness, favor, indulgence, forbearance, quarter, compassion, clemency, mercy.

v be lenient, tolerate, bear with, favor, indulge, allow.

adj lenient, tolerant, mild, easy, easygoing, gentle, tender, indulgent, compassionate, sympathetic, merciful.

741 command *n* order, ordinance, direction, bidding, injunction, charge, mandate, behest, ukase, commandment, requisition, requirement, instruction, dictum, act, fiat; demand, exaction, claim, request; control, mastery, disposal, rule, sway, power, domination.

v command, order, direct, bid, demand, charge, instruct, enjoin, require, impose; degree, enact, ordain, dictate, prescribe, appoint; claim, lay claim to.

adj commanding, authoritative.

742 disobedience *n* noncompliance, nonobservance, insubordination, contumancy, infraction, infringement, defiance, unruliness, rebelliousness, obstinacy, stubbornness, resistance, mutinousness, mutiny, rebellion.

insurgent, mutineer, rebel, revolutionary, rioter, traitor, *(informal)* radical.

v disobey, transgress, violate, disregard, defy, infringe, shirk, resist, mutiny, rebel, revolt.

adj disobedient, insubordinate, contumacious, defiant, refractory, unruly, fractious, rebellious, mutinous, obstinate, stubborn, unsubmissive, uncompliant, recalcitrant, insurgent, riotous.

743 obedience *n* observance, compliance, docility, tractability, deference, respect, duty, subservience, submissiveness, obsequiousness; allegiance, loyalty, fealty, homage, devotion.

v obey, comply, submit, follow, attend to, serve.

adj obedient, submissive, compliant, tractable, docile, deferential, respectful, dutiful, loyal, subservient.

adv obediently, in compliance with, in obedience to.

744 compulsion *n* coercion, constraint, duress, enforcement, conscription, force; impulse, necessity.

v compel, force, make, drive, coerce, constrain, enforce, impel, require, necessitate, oblige, motivate; subdue, subject, bend, bow, overpower.

adj compelling, compulsory, coercive, forcible, constraining; obligatory, necessary, unavoidable, inescapable, ineluctable, irresistible, inexorable.

adv by force, forcibly, on compulsion.

745 master *n* lord, commander, commandant, chief, head, leader, director, ruler, boss, authority.

746 servant *n* subject, retainer, follower, henchman, domestic, menial, help, helper, employee, worker, laborer.

v serve, function, answer, assist, help, aid, provide, cater, satisfy; wait on, attend.

747 [insignia of authority] **scepter** *n* regalia, staff, symbol, emblem, flag, badge; title.

748 freedom *n* liberty, independence, autonomy, noninterference; immunity, franchisement, franchise, privilege, latitude, scope; ease, facility; frankness, openness; familiarity, license, looseness, laxity.

v be free, have scope, do as one likes, do what one wants; free, liberate, permit, allow, set free.

adj free, independent, at large, loose, scot free; unconstrained, unconfined, unchecked, unhindered, unobstructed, unbound, uncontrolled, ungoverned, unchained, unfettered, unshackled, uncurbed, unbridled, unmuzzled; unrestricted, unlimited, unconditional; absolute; discretionary; wanton, rampant, irrepressible, unvanquished; immune, exempt, freed; autonomous.

adv freely.

749 subjection *n* dependence, subordination, thrall, thralldom, subjugation, bondage, serfdom, slavery, servitude, enslavement; service, employ, tutelage, constraint, yoke, submission, obedience.

v be subject, be at the mercy of, depend upon, fall prey to, play second fiddle to, serve, submit; subject, subjugate, master, tame, tread down, weigh down, enslave, enthral, rule.

adj subject, dependent, subordinate; under control, in harness.

750 liberation *n* disengagement, release, enlargement, emancipation, enfranchisement, deliverance, extrication, discharge, dismissal, acquittal, absolution.

v liberate, set free, free, disengage, release, emancipate, enfranchise, deliver, extricate, discharge, dismiss, unfetter, disenthrall, set loose, loose, let out, acquit, absolve.

adj liberated, freed.

751 restraint *n* restriction, circumscription, limitation, control, confinement, curb, check, suppression, constraint, repression.

v restrain, check, keep down, repress, curb, bridle, suppress, compel, hold, keep, constrain; restrict, circumscribe, confine, hinder.

adj restrained, constrained, restrictive, suppressive, repressive; imprisoned, pent up, under restraint.

752 prison *n* jail, gaol, cage, coop, pen, penitentiary, jailhouse, cell, block, dungeon, lock-up, stir, irons, *(informal)* calaboose; *(informal)* hoosegow, *(informal)* the joint, *(informal)* the big house.

753 keeper *n* custodian, guard *(informal)* screw, jailer, gaoler, warder, escort, body-guard; protector, guardian, governor, governess, teacher, tutor, nurse.

754 prisoner *n* captive, convict, con, jailbird.

v be imprisoned, stand convicted.

adj in prison, in custody, in chains, under wraps, in stir.

755 [vicarious authority] **commission** *n* delegation, consignment, assignment, deputation, legation, mission, embassy, agency, special committee; errand, charge, permit; appointment, nomination, charter.

v commission, delegate, consign, assign, charge, entrust, authorize; appoint, name, nominate, ordain; install, induct, invest, employ, empower.

756 abrogation *n* abolition, cancelation, annulment, repeal, retraction, revocation, remission, recision, nullification, invalidation.

v abrogate, abolish, cancel, annul, repeal, retract, revoke, rescind, nullify, void, invalidate.

adj null and void.

757 resignation *n* abjuration, renunciation, abdication, abandonment, desertion, relinquishment, retirement.

v resign, quit, give up, abjure, renounce, forgo, disclaim, abrogate, abandon, desert, relinquish, retire.

758 consignee *n* trustee, nominee, committee, delegation, delegate, commission; functionary, agent, representative, messenger.

759 deputy *n* substitute, proxy, delegate, representative, surrogate, alternate, second, assistant.

v stand for, represent, answer for.

760 permission *n* authorization, warrant, sanction, liberty, license, enfranchisement, franchise, leave, permit, liberty, freedom, allowance, consent, concession, tolerance, sufferance, indulgence, favor.

v permit, allow, let, tolerate, bear with, agree to, suffer, concede, accord, favor, humor, indulge; grant, empower, franchise, charter, confer, license, authorize, warrant, sanction.

adj permitted, permissive, indulgent, libertarian, tolerant; permissible, allowable, legal, legalized, lawful, legitimate.

761 prohibition *n* interdiction, injunction, prevention, embargo, ban, restriction, disallowance.

v prohibit, forbid, interdict, veto, disallow, bar, restrict, limit; prevent, hinder, preclude, obstruct.

adv prohibitive, proscriptive, restrictive; preventive.

762 consent *n* assent, acquiescence, acceptance, acknowledgment, permission, compliance, concurrence, agreement, approval; accord, concord, consensus, settlement, ratification, confirmation.

v consent, assent, agree, concur, permit, allow, let, yield, grant, comply, accede, acquiescence.

adj compliant, agreeable, amendable.

763 offer *n* proposal, proposition, overture, tender, bid; offering, gift.

v offer, present, proffer, tender; propose, give, move, put forward advance, invite, hold out, make a motion; hawk, merchandise, offer for sale.

adj for sale, in the open market.

764 refusal *n* rejection, spurning, denial, rebuff, repulse, repudiation; abnegation, protest, renunciation, disclaimer.

v refuse, decline, reject, spurn, turn down, deny, rebuff, repulse, repudiate; resist, repel, repudiate, renounce, disclaim, rescind, revoke.

adj noncompliant, dissident, recalcitrant, reluctant.

765 request *n* claim, demand, application, appeal, solicitation, petition, suit, entreaty, supplication, prayer.

v request, ask, ask for, beg, sue, petition, entreat, supplicate, solicit, beseech, plead, implore, require, demand, importune, clamor for.

adj importunate, clamorous, solicitous.

766 [negative request] **deprecation** *n* expostulation, intercession, mediation, protest, disapproval, remonstrance.

v deprecate, protest, expostulate, enter a protest, disapprove, remonstrate.

adj deprecatory, expostulatory, remonstrative; unsought.

767 petitioner *n* claimant, aspirant, postulant, seeker, solicitor, suitor, applicant, suppliant, supplicant; competitor, bidder; beggar, mendicant, panhandler, *(informal)* bum, *(informal)* streetwalker.

768 promise *n* undertaking, word, covenant, commitment, pledge, assurance, profession, vow, oath, guarantee, warranty, obligation, contract.

v promise, undertake, engage, enter into, bind oneself, commit oneself, pledge, agree, assure, warrant, guarantee, covenant, swear, give one's word; secure, give security, underwrite.

adj promissory, upon one's oath, on one's honor; promised, pledged, committed, bound, sworn.

769 compact *n* covenant, pact, contract, treaty, agreement, negotiation, bargain, arrangement, *(informal)* deal.

v contract, negotiate, bargain, stipulate, make terms; agree, engage, promise; complete, settle, confirm, subscribe, endorse.

adj compactual, contractual, promissory.

770 conditions *n* terms, articles, clauses, provisions, provisos, stipulations, promises, obligations, covenants.

v condition, stipulate, insist upon, contract, provide, bind, tie, oblige.

adj conditional, provisional.

adv conditionally, provisionally, on condition.

771 security *n* guarantee, warranty, bond, tie, pledge, promise, contract; mortgage, lien, pawn; stake, deposit, collateral, *(informal)* IOU, *(informal)* mark, promissory note; deed, bill of sale, receipt, certificate, title; sponsorship, surety, bail.

v give security, post bail, pawn, mortgage; guarantee, warrant, assure, promise; accept, endorse, underwrite, sponsor, stand for.

772 observance *n* performance, compliance, obedience, execution, discharge, acquittance, fulfillment, satisfaction, adhesion, acknowledgment, fidelity, faithfulness.

v observe, comply with, respect, abide by, acknowledge, adhere to, be faithful to, obey, act up to; meet, fulfill; carry out, execute, perform, satisfy, discharge.

adj observant, compliant, faithful, obedient, true, honorable; punctilious, scrupulous, as good as one's word.

adv faithfully.

773 nonobservance *n* evasion, failure, omission, noncompliance, neglect, negligence, laxity, laxness, carelessness, irresponsibility, disobedience; infringement, infraction, violation, transgression.

v fail, neglect, evade, omit, elude, ignore, disregard, discard, set at naught; infringe, transgress, violate, break.

adj nonobservant, lax, loose, disdainful, evasive, elusive, negligent, irresponsible, disobedient.

774 compromise *n* adjustment, negotiation, concession; compensation.

v compromise, bend, give and take, split the differences, come to an agreement, opt for the mean, adjust, arrange, settle.

775 acquisition *n* procurement, appropriation, gain, attainment, purchase, gift, find; profit, earnings, wages, winnings, income, proceeds, produce, crop, harvest, benefit.

v acquire, appropriate, gain, win, earn, attain, gather, collect; take over, take possession of, procure, secure, obtain, get, come into, receive, get hold of; profit, turn to profit.

adj profitable, advantageous, gainful, remunerative.

776 loss *n* damage, injury, privation, lapse, forfeiture, deprivation.

v lose, incur a loss, miss, mislay, let slip, forfeit; waste, get rid of.

adj lost, bereft, minus, deprived of, cut off, rid of; long lost, irretrievable.

777 possession *n* ownership, occupancy, holding, proprietorship, tenure, tenancy, control, custody; belonging.

v possess, own, have, hold, occupy, control, command, have to oneself, have in hand, belong to.

adj possessing, possessed of, in possession of, master of, in hand, at one's disposal; possessive, custodial.

777a exemption *n* exception, immunity, impunity, release.

v exempt, excuse, release; not have, be without.

adj exempt from, immune from, devoid of, without.

778 [joint possession] **participation** *n* partnership, co-ownership, joint tenancy, common holding, communion, community of possessions; communism, socialism, collectivism; cooperation.

participant, sharer, partner, co-partner, shareholder; communist, socialist.

v participate, partake, share, share in, go halves, split up, divide, have in common, own in common.

adj participatory, joint, common, collective, communal, communist, communistic, socialist, socialistic.

779 possessor *n* holder, occupant, tenant, lessee; proprietor, proprietress, master, mistress, owner.

780 property *n* possession, possessions, goods, effects, chattels, estate, belongings, assets, means, resources land, real estate, acreage; ownership, right; attribute, quality, characteristic, feature.

781 retention *n* keeping, holding, detention, custody, preservation, maintenance.

v retain, keep, hold, hold fast, secure, withhold, preserve, detain, reserve, maintain.

adj retentive.

782 relinquishment *n* renunciation, surrender, resignation, yielding, waiver, abdication, desertion, abandonment, quitting.

v relinquish, renounce, surrender, give up, resign, yield, cede, waive, forswear, forgo, abdicate, leave, forsake, desert, quit, abandon, let go, discard, cast off, dismiss, divest oneself.

adj cast off, done away with, left, forsworn, given up, left behind.

783 transfer *n* sale, lease, release, exchange, interchange; transference, transmission, changing hands.

v transfer, convey, assign, grant, consign, make over, hand over, pass, transmit, change, exchange, interchange, change hands; devolve, succeed.

adj transferable, conveyable, transmissive, exchangeable.

784 giving *n* bestowal, presentation, concession, delivery, consignment, dispensation, endowment, investiture, award; charity, almsgiving, liberality, generosity, philanthropy; gift, donation, present, boon, favor, grant, offering; allowance, contribution, donation, bequest, legacy; alms, largesse, bounty, help, gratuity; bribe, bait.

giver, granter, donor.

v give, bestow, confer, grant, accord, award, assign, entrust, consign; invest, allow, settle upon, donate, bequeath, leave; furnish, supply, help; afford, spare, favor with, lavish; deliver, hand, pass, turn over, present, give away, dispense, dispose of, give out, deal out, dole out, mete out, fork out; pay, render, impart.

adj charitable, beneficent, tributary, liberal, generous, philanthropic.

785 receiving *n* acquisition, reception, acceptance, admission, recipient, receiver, legatee, grantee, donee, beneficiary, pensioner.

v receive, take, acquire, admit, take in, accept; come into, fall to one, accrue.

adj receiving; received.

786 apportionment *n* allotment, consignment, assignment, allocation, distribution, dispensation, division, partition; portion, lot, share, measure, dose, dole, ration, ratio, proportion, quota, allowance.

v apportion, divide, distribute, dispense, allot, share, mete, portion out, parcel out, dole out, deal, carve, administer; partition, assign, appropriate, appoint.

adj distributive; respective.

787 lending *n* loan, advance, accommodation, mortgage, investment.

v lend, loan, advance, accommodate, lend on security, pawn; let, lease.

788 borrowing *n* pledging, pawning; appropriating, stealing, theft.

v borrow, pledge, pawn, borrow money; hire, rent, lease; appropriate, use, steal from, imitate.

789 taking *n* appropriation, capture, apprehension, seizure, abduction, dispossession, deprivation, expropriation, divestment, confiscation, eviction; extortion, theft; reprisal, recovery.

v take, catch, hook, nab, bag, pocket, receive, accept; reap, cull, pluck, gather; appropriate, assume, possess oneself of, help oneself to, commandeer, make free with; take away, abduct, steal, seize, snatch, snap up, capture, get hold of, take from, take away from, dispossess, expropriate, oust, eject, divest, confiscate, usurp, strip, fleece; retake, resume, recover.

adj predatory, rapacious, parasitic, greedy, ravenous.

790 restitution *n* return, restoration, reinvestment, rehabilitation, reparation, atonement, compensation, recovery.

v return, restore, give back, render, give up, let go; recoup, reimburse, compensate, reinvest, remit, rehabilitate, repair, make good, settle up; recover, get back, redeem, take back again.

adj compensatory, redemptive, recouperative.

791 stealing *n* theft, thievery, robbery, swindling, fraud, appropriation.

v steal, take, thieve, rob, pilfer, purloin, *(informal)* swipe, filch, embezzle, swindle, appropriate, fleece, defraud, *(informal)* rip off, *(informal)* screw.

adj thievish, light-fingered, piratical, predatory.

792 thief *n* robber, pilferer, filcher, rifler, crook, *(informal)* rip-off artist, cheat; burglar, house-breaker, second-story man, safecracker.

793 booty *n* spoils, plunder; prize, loot, catch, pickings, stolen goods, *(informal)* haul.

794 barter *n* exchange, trade, traffic, commerce, business, bargain; dealing, transaction, negotiation.

v barter, trade, exchange, traffic, bargain, swap, buy and sell, give and take, deal, haggle, negotiate, drive a bargain, transact.

adj commercial, mercantile; interchangeable, in trade, for sale, marketable.

795 purchase *n* buying, purchasing, acquisition; bargain, buy.

buyer, purchaser, shopper, customer, client, patron, clientele.

v purchase, buy, acquire, get, obtain, procure; shop, market, go shopping.

796 sale *n* selling, vendition, commerce, mercantilism, transaction, exchange, auction, trade.

seller, vendor, merchant.

v sell, trade, barter, vend, exchange, deal in, dispose, merchandise, hawk.

adj salable, marketable, vendible, for sale.

797 merchant *n* trader, dealer, seller, salesman, saleswoman, tradesman, shopkeeper, retailer, hawker, huckster, peddler, broker.

798 merchandise *n* goods, wares, commodity, articles, stock, produce, product, staple commodity, store, cargo.

v merchandise, sell.

799 market *n* mart, marketplace, fair, bazaar, business district, mall, shopping center, store, department store, establishment, place of business, office.

800 money *n* finance, accounts, funds, assets, wealth, supplies, ways and means, wherewithal, capital, almighty dollar, cash, currency, hard cash, *(informal)* bucks, change, small change, *(informal)* green, greenbacks; sum, amount, balance.

adj monetary, pecuniary, financial, fiscal.

801 treasurer *n* bursar, banker, purser, receiver, steward, trustee, accountant, paymaster, cashier, teller, financier.

802 treasury *n* bank, exchequer, strongbox, stronghold, coffer, chest, depository, purse, moneybag, safe, vault, cash box, cash register, till; securities, stocks, bonds, notes.

803 wealth *n* riches, fortune, opulence, affluence, easy circumstance, *(informal)* silver spoon, independence, competence, sufficiency, solvency; provision, livelihood, maintenance, means, resources, substance; income, capital, money.

v be wealthy, be rich.

adj wealthy, rich, affluent, well-off, well-to-do, comfortable.

804 poverty *n* indigence, penury, pauperism, destitution, want, need, neediness, lack, privation, distress, difficulties, straits, bad straits.

v be poor, want, lack, starve, live from hand to mouth, go to the dogs.

adj poor, indigent, destitute, poverty-stricken, needy, penniless, broke, *(informal)* bust, hard up, insolvent, seedy, beggarly.

805 credit *n* trust, score, tally, account, *(informal)* tab, bill.

creditor, lender, usurer.

v credit, accredit, entrust, keep an account with.

806 debt *n* obligation, liability, debit, score, duty, due.

debtor, borrower.

adj liable, answerable for, in debt; unpaid, in arrear.

807 payment *n* discharge, settlement, clearance, liquidation, satisfaction, reckoning, arrangement; acknowledgment, release, receipt, voucher; installment, remittance.

v pay, settle, liquidate, discharge, quit, acquit oneself of, reckon up, satisfy, compensate, reimburse, remunerate, recompense, make payment, square accounts, balance accounts, pay in full.

adj out of debt, solvent; straight, clear.

808 nonpayment *n* default, protest, repudiation; insolvency, bankruptcy, failure.

v not pay, default, fail, stop payment; run up bills.

adj in debt.

809 expenditure *n* outlay, expenses, disbursement, payment, costs, fees.

v expend, spend, pay out, disburse, *(informal)* fork out, lay out.

810 receipt *n* value received, acknowledgment of payment.
v receive, take, get, bring in.
adj profitable, remunerative.

811 accounts *n* money matters, finance, budget, bill, score, reckoning, account; statement, ledger, inventory, register, book, books, sheet; balance.
accountant, auditor, bookkeeper, financier.
v keep accounts, enter, post, book, credit, debit, balance.

812 price *n* amount, cost, expense, charge, figure, demand, damage, fare, hire, wages; worth, rate, value, valuation, appraisal; market price, quotation; bill, invoice.
v price, set a price, fix a price, appraise, assess, charge, demand, ask, require, exact; fetch, sell for, bring in, yield, accord.

813 discount *n* abatement, reduction, depreciation, allowance, qualification, rebate, sale.
v discount, put on sale, reduce, take off, allow, deduct, abate, rebate.

814 dearness *n* expensiveness, costliness, high price; overcharge, extravagance, exorbitance.
v be expensive, cost a lot; overcharge, bleed, fleece, extort.
adj dear, expensive, costly, precious; extravagant, exorbitant, unreasonable; priceless.

815 cheapness *n* low price, depreciation, bargain, value, *(informal)* steal, *(informal)* great buy.
v be cheap, cost little.
adj cheap, moderate, reasonable, inexpensive, dirt cheap.

816 liberality *n* generosity, munificence, bounty, bounteousness, hospitality, charity.
v be liberal, spend freely, give, spare no expense.
adj liberal, free, generous, bountiful, hospitable, munificent, beneficent, princely, charitable.

817 economy *n* frugality, thrift, thriftiness, saving, care, husbandry, retrenchment, parsimony.
v economize, save, retrench, husband.
adj economical, frugal, careful, thrifty, chary, parsimonious.

818 prodigality *n* unthriftiness, waste, wastefulness, profusion, profuseness, extravagance, profligacy, lavishness, squandering.
prodigal, spendthrift, squanderer.
v be prodigal, squander, lavish, misspend, waste, dissipate, fritter one's money.
adj prodigal, profuse, unthrifty, improvident, wasteful, profligate, extravagant, lavish.

819 parsimony *n* stinginess, illiberality, avarice, rapidity, rapacity, venality, cupidity, selfishness.
miser, niggard, churl, skinflint, codger, scrimp, *(informal)* tightwad, usurer, Scrooge.
v be parsimonious, grudge, begrudge, stint, pinch, hold back, withhold, starve, famish.
adj parsimonious, penurious, stingy, cheap, miserly, mean, pennywise, niggardly, tight, ungenerous, churlish, mercenary, venal, covetous, usurious, avaricious, greedy, rapacious, selfish.

Class VI
Words Relating to the Sentient and Moral Powers

I. Affections in General

820 affections *n* character, qualities, disposition, nature, spirit, temper, temperament, idiosyncrasy, habit, bent, bias, predisposition, proclivity, propensity, humor, mood, sympathy; soul, heart, inner man, essence; passion, driving spirit, ruling passion.
adj affected, characterized, formed, cast, molded, tempered, predisposed, prone, inclined, imbued; inborn, ingrained, deep-rooted.

adv at heart.

821 feeling *n* consciousness, impression; emotion, passion, sentiment, sensibility; sympathy, empathy; fervor, ardor, zeal, warmth, tenderness, sensitivity, sentimentality, susceptibility, pity; sentiment, opinion.

v feel, receive an impression, respond to.

adj feeling, emotional, sensitive, tender; sympathetic; emotional, impassioned, passionate, fervent, tender, sensitive; heart-felt, thrilling, rapturous, soul-stirring; moved, touched, affected.

adj heart and soul, from the bottom of one's heart.

822 sensibility *n* responsiveness, sensitiveness, awareness, susceptibility, impressibility, tenderness, sentimentality, sentimentalism; excitability; appreciation, understanding, moral sensibility.

v be sensitive, have a soft spot in one's heart.

adj sensitive, impressionable, susceptible, tender, warm-hearted, sentimental; excitable; aware, understanding, appreciative.

823 insensibility *n* insensitiveness, impassivity, apathy, coldness, callousness; imperturbable; dullness, boorishness.

v be insensitive, not care, be unaffected, have no interest in.

adj insensitive, unconscious, unaware; inattentive, indifferent, lukewarm; apathetic, impassive, unimpressionable; cold-blooded, cold-hearted, unmoved, unaffected, callous, thick-skinned, uncaring.

adv in cold blood.

824 excitation *n* excitation of feeling; mental excitation; galvanism, stimulation, provocation, inspiration, infection; animation, agitation, perturbation; fascination, intoxication, ravishment; irritation, anger, passion, thrill.

v excite, affect, touch, move, impress, interest, animate, inspire, infect, awake; evoke, provoke; stir up, wake up, light up; rouse, arouse, stir, fire, kindle, inflame; stimulate, quicken, sharpen, whet, wet the appetite, fan the fire, raise to a fervor; absorb, rivet, intoxicate, fascinate, enrapture; agitate, perturb, ruffle, fluster, disturb, startle, shock,

stagger, astound, electrify, galvanize; irritate.

adj excited, excitable, wrought up, overwrought, upset, hysterical, hot, red-hot, flushed, feverish, boiling, ebullient, seething, fuming, raging, raving, frantic, mad, distracted, beside oneself; exciting, warm, glowing, fervid, soul-stirring, thrilling, overwhelming, overpowering, sensational.

825 [excess of sensitiveness] **excitability** *n* impetuosity, vehemence, boisterousness, impatience, intolerance, irritability, restlessness, agitation; passion, excitement, fever, tumult, ebullition, tempest, fit, paroxysm, explosion, outburst, agony; violence, rage, fury, furor, desperation, madness, distraction, delirium, frenzy, hysterics.

v be impatient, lose patience, fuss, fidget; lose one's temper, flare up, burn, boil over, foam, fume, rage, rant, run wild, go mad, go into hysterics.

adj excitable, high-strung, nervous, irritable, impatient, intolerant; feverish, hysterical, delirious, mad; hurried, restless, fidgety, fussy; vehement, violent, wild, furious, fierce, fiery, hotheaded; overzealous, enthusiastic, impassioned, fanatical; rabid, clamorous, turbulent, tumultuous, boisterous; impulsive, impetuous, passionate, uncontrolled, uncontrollable, ungovernable, irrepressible, volcanic.

826 inexcitability *n* imperturbability, even temper, dispassion, patience, impassivity; coolness, calmness, composure, placidity, serenity, quietude; self-possession, self-restraint, stoicism; resignation, submission, sufferance, endurance, forbearance, fortitude, moderation, restraint.

v bear, endure, tolerate, suffer, put up with, reconcile oneself to, resign oneself to, brook, swallow, make the best of, stomach; compose, appease, propitiate, repress, calm down, cool down.

adj inexcitable, imperturbable, unsusceptible, dispassionate, enduring, stoical, staid, sober, sedate; easygoing, peaceful, placid, calm, cool; composed, collected, unruffled, content, resigned, subdued.

II. Personal Affections

827 pleasure *n* happiness, gladness, delectation, enjoyment, delight, joy, glee, cheer, cheerfulness, well-being, satisfaction, gratification, comfort, ease; felicity, bliss, enchantment, transport, rapture, ravishment, ecstasy, luxury, sensuality, voluptuousness.

v be pleased, joy, enjoy oneself, have one's head in the clouds, fall into raptures; be pleased with, derive pleasure from, take pleasure in, *(informal)* get into, delight in, rejoice in, indulge in, luxuriate in, relish, love, enjoy, like, *(informal)* dig, take a fancy to, take a shine to.

adj happy, blissful, joyful, gladsome, cheerful; comfortable, at ease, content; ecstatic.

adv happily, with pleasure.

828 pain *n* suffering, distress, torture, misery, dolor, anguish, agony, torment, throe, pang, ache, smart, twinge, stitch; displeasure, dissatisfaction, discomfort, discomposure, disquiet, malaise, inquietude, uneasiness, vexation, discontent, dejection, weariness; annoyance, irritation, worry, affliction, bore, bother, mortification, plague; care, solicitude, trouble, trial, ordeal, burden, load, fret; prostration, desolation, despair.

v suffer, afflict, torture, torment, distress, despair; hurt, harm, injure, trouble, grieve, disquiet, discomfort, discompose, worry, irritate, vex, mortify, plague.

adj uncomfortable, uneasy, weary; unhappy, infelicitous, poor, wretched, miserable, woebegone, careworn, cheerless, sorry, sorrowful, stricken, in tears, in despair.

829 pleasurableness *n* pleasantness, agreeableness, delectability, delight, congeniality; sprightliness, cheer, cheerfulness, liveliness; attraction, attractiveness, charm, fascination enchantment, witchery, seduction, winning ways, amenity, amiability; loveliness, beauty, brightness; goodness.

v be pleasurable, afford pleasure, offer pleasure, please, charm, delight, gladden, cheer; attract, invite, allure, stimulate, interest, captivate, fascinate, enchant, entrance, enrapture, bewitch, ravish, enravish, transport; agree with, satisfy, gratify; slake, satiate, quence; regale, refresh, treat, amuse.

adj pleasurable, pleasant, agreeable, enjoyable, delightful, congenial, amiable; comfortable, cordial, genial, gladsome, sweet, delectable, nice, dainty, delicate, delicious, luscious, luxurious, voluptuous, sensual; attractive, lovely, beautiful, seductive, rapturous, ecstatic, beatific, heavenly; fair, sunny, bright; gay, sprightly, merry, cheery, cheerful, lively, vivacious.

830 painfulness *n* trouble, care, trial, affliction, blow, burden, curse, mishap, misfortune, adversity; annoyance, nuisance, grievance, bore, bother, vexation, mortification; wound, sore, sore subject, thorn in the side, skeleton in the closet; sorry sight, heavy news, bad news; affront, insult, offense.

v pain, hurt, wound, sadden, displease, annoy, trouble, disturb, cross, perplex, irk, vex, mortify, worry, plague, bother, pester, harass, badger, bait, heckle, irritate, anger, persecute, provoke; harrow, torment, torture; affront, insult, give offense, offend, maltreat, mistreat; sicken, disgust, revolt, nauseate, repel, shock, horrify, appal.

adj painful, hurtful, dolorous; unpleasant, disagreeable, unpalatable, bitter, distasteful; unwelcome, undesirable, obnoxious; dismal, dreary, melancholy, grievous, piteous, woeful, rueful, mournful, deplorable, pitiable, lamentable, pathetic; invidious, vexatious, troublesome, irksome, wearisome, worrisome; intolerable, insufferable, unsupportable, unbearable, unendurable, grim, dreadful, fearful, frightful, dire, odious, hateful, repulsive, repellant, abhorrent, horrid, horrible, offensive, nauseous, loathsome, vile, hideous; sore, severe, grave, hard, harsh, cruel; ruinous, disastrous, calamitous, tragic; burdensome, onerous, oppressive, cumbersome.

adv painfully.

831 content *n* contentment, complacency, satisfaction, ease, serenity, comfort; conciliation, resignation.

v gratify, satisfy, set at ease, comfort, appease, conciliate, reconcile.

adj contented, complacent, satisfied,

sanguine, comfortable; assenting, acceding, resigned, willing, agreeable.

adv to one's heart's content.

832 discontent *n* discontentment, dissatisfaction, uneasiness, disquietude, restlessness, displeasure.

v be discontented, repine, regret, fret, chafe, grumble; dissatisfy, disappoint, disconcert.

adj discontented, dissatisfied, displeased, uneasy, restless, dejected, malcontent, regretful, down in the dumps.

833 regret *n* sorrow, lamentation, grief; remorse, penitence, contrition, repentance.

v regret, deplore, lament, feel sorry about, grieve at, bemoan, bewail, rue, mourn for, repent.

adj regretful, sorry, lamentable, rueful; penitent, contrite.

834 relief *n* deliverance, alleviation, ease, assuagement, mitigation, comfort, solace, consolation; help, assistance, aid.

v relieve, ease, alleviate, assuage, mitigate, allay, comfort, soothe, lessen, abate, diminish; cheer, comfort, console; aid, help, assist, succor, refresh, remedy, support.

adj soothing, consoling, assuaging, comforting, palliative, curative.

835 aggravation *n* worsening, heightening, intensification, exaggeration; *(informal)* annoyance, irritation, vexation.

v aggravate, worsen, intensify, heighten, increase, make serious, make grave.

adj worse, intensified, irritated.

adv from bad to worse, out of the frying pan and into the fire.

836 cheerfulness *n* geniality, high spirits, liveliness, vivacity, joviality, jocularity, mirth, merriment, exhilaration.

v cheer, gladden, enliven, inspirit, delight, rejoice, exhilarate, animate, encourage; shout, applaud, acclaim, salute.

adj cheery, gay, blithe, happy, lively, spirited, sprightly, joyful, joyous, mirthful, buoyant, sparkling, vivacious, gleeful, sunny, jolly; pleasant, bright, gay, winsome, gladdening, cheery, cheering, inspiring, animating, hearty, robust.

adv cheerfully.

837 dejection *n* depression, heaviness, heavy heart, melancholy, sadness, dumps, doldrums, despondency, gloom, weariness, disgust, despair, hopelessness.

v be dejected, lose heart, frown, mope, droop, despond, brood over, sink, despair.

adj unhappy, depressed, dispirited, disheartened, discouraged, despondent, *(informal)* down, downhearted, sad, melancholy, lugubrious, heartsick, dismal, gloomy, miserable, desolate; pessimistic, cynical.

adv with a long face, with tears in one's eyes.

838 rejoicing *n* exaltation, triumph, jubilation, reveling, merrymaking, celebration, paean; smile, smirk, grin, giggle, titter, laughter, guffaw, shout, peal of laughter.

v rejoice, congratulate oneself, clap one's hands, dance, skip, sing, hurrah, cry for joy, leap with joy, exalt, triumph; smile, smirk, grin, giggle, titter, chuckle, cackle, laugh, crow, burst out, shout, split, roar, shake one's sides, split one's sides.

adj jubilant, exultant, triumphant, flushed, *(informal)* high, elated, laughing, convulsed with laughter.

839 lamentation *n* lament, howl, wail, wailing, complaint, moan, moaning, groan, sob, sigh; dirge, elegy, monody, threnody.

v lament, bewail, bemoan, deplore, grieve, scream, sob, cry, weep, mourn over, sorrow over.

adj lamenting, in mourning, sorrowful, mournful, lamentable, tearful, plaintive.

840 amusement *n* enjoyment, entertainment, recreation, diversion, relaxation, pastime, pleasure, playing, festivity.

v amuse, entertain, cheer, divert, enliven, interest; amuse oneself, play, sport, make merry.

adj amusing, entertaining, diverting, relaxing, pleasant, witty, jovial, jolly, playful.

841 weariness *n* ennui, lassitude, fatigue, exhaustion, boredom; tedium, monotony, dullness.

v weary, tire, fatigue, bore, exhaust.

adj wearisome, tiresome, boring, tedious, irksome, monotonous, humdrum, dull, prosaic, trying; weary, drowsy, exhausted, tired, wearied, fatigued; uninterested, impatient, dissatisfied.

842 wit *n* drollery, facetiousness, pleasantry, repartee, cleverness, humor, fun; understanding, intelligence, sagacity, wisdom, intellect, mind, sense.

v joke, jest, banter, pun.

adj witty, quick, quick-witted, nimble, sharp, clever, facetious, whimsical, pleasant, humorous, playful, sparkling, scintillating; intelligent, sagacious, wise, perceptive, insightful.

843 dullness *n* heaviness, flatness, stupidity, obtuseness, lack of originality, banality.

v be dull, blunt, deaden, benumb.

adj dull, uninteresting, unimaginative, dry, prosaic, matter-of-fact, commonplace, boring, tedious, dreary, vapid; stupid stolid, slow, flat.

844 humorist *n* wit, wag, comedian, comedienne, joker, jester, wisecracker, epigrammatist, punster, buffoon, clown, fool, satirist, lampooner, cutup, funnyman.

845 beauty *n* loveliness, pulchritude, elegance, grace, gracefulness, comeliness, seemliness, fairness, attractiveness, brilliance, radiance, splendor, gorgeousness, magnificence, sublimity.

v beautify.

adj beautiful, handsome, comely, seemly, attractive, lovely, pretty, fair, fine, elegant, beauteous, graceful, pulchritudinous, brilliant, radiant, gorgeous, magnificent; artistic, aesthetic, picturesque.

846 ugliness *n* homeliness, inelegance, unsightliness, distortion, disfigurement, deformity, frightfulness.

v deface, disfigure, distort.

adj ugly, displeasing, hard-featured, unlovely, unsightly, unseemly, homely; hideous, gruesome, repulsive, offensive, revolting, terrible, base, vile, squalid, gross, monstrous, heinous; disagreeable, unpleasant, objectionable.

847 ornament *n* ornamentation, adornment, decoration, embellishment, frills, finery.

v ornament, embellish, adorn, decorate, beautify.

adj ornamental, decorative; ornamented, ornate, embellished, beautified.

848 blemish *n* disfigurement, deformity, defect, flaw, fault, taint, blot, spot, speck.

v stain, sully, spot, taint, tarnish, injur, mar, damage, deface, impair.

adj disfigured, injured, imperfect, discolored, freckled, pitted.

849 simplicity *n* plainness, homeliness; clarity, chasteness, restraint, severity, lack of adornment, lack of affectation.

v simplify, uncomplicate, clarify, strip to essentials, get back to basics.

adj simple, plain, homely, natural, unadorned, unaffected, unembellished, neat, unassuming, unpretentious; chaste, severe; clear, straightforward, lucid.

850 [good taste] taste *n* good taste, delicacy, refinement, polish, elegance, grace, discrimination, culture, cultivation.

v show taste, appreciate, judge, criticize, discriminate.

adj tasteful, in good taste, decorous, attractive, cultivated, cultured, refined, discriminative, polished, felicitous, appropriate, suitable, apt, becoming, pleasing.

adj tastefully, elegantly.

851 [bad taste] vulgarity *n* bad taste, barbarism, coarseness, lack of decorum, ill-breeding, boorishness; gaudiness, tawdriness, finery, frippery, tinsel.

v be vulgar; vulgarize.

adj vulgar, in bad taste, unrefined, boorish, common, coarse, ill-bred, ill-mannered, ignoble, mean, plebeian, crude, rude, shabby; gaudy, tawdry, flashy, garish, crass, showy, *(informal)* tacky.

852 fashion *n* custom, style, vogue, mode, rage, craze; conventionality, conformity; society, polite society, beau monde; manners, breeding, air, demeanor, *savoir-faire,* gentility, decorum, propriety, etiquette.

v be fashionable, be the rage; fashion, adapt, suit, fit, adjust; make, shape, frame, form, mold.

adj fashionable, in vogue, à la mode, all the rage; modish, stylish, conventional, customary; well-bred, well-mannered, civil, polite, courteous, polished, refined, genteel, decorous.

853 ridiculousness *n* outrageousness, silliness, absurdity.

v be ridiculous, make a fool of oneself, play the fool.

adj absurd, preposterous, extravagant, asinine, laughable, nonsensical, silly, funny, ludicrous, droll, comical, farcical, outlandish, outrageous, fantastic.

854 fop *n* fine gentleman, dandy, *(informal)* dude, coxcomb, beau, man about town, prig, jackanapes.

855 affectation *n* affectedness, pretense, pretention, airs, mannerisms, unnaturalness, display, show, sham, feigning, simulation, foppery.

v affect, act a part, put on airs, pretend, assume, feign, counterfeit, simulate, pose, attitudinize.

adj affected, pretentious, ostentatious, feigned, artificial, stilted, mannered, stagey, theatrical, modish, unnatural.

856 ridicule *n* derision, scoffing, mockery, gibes, jeers, taunts, raillery; satire, burlesque, sneer, banter, wit, irony.

v ridicule, deride, banter, chaff, twit, mock, taunt, make fun of, sneer at, burlesque, satirize, rail at, lampoon jeer at, scoff at *(informal)* put down.

adj derisory, derisive, sarcastic, ironic, ironical, burlesque, mocking.

857 [object and cause of ridicule] **laughing-stock** *n* butt, game, fair game, fool, dupe, original, oddity, queer fish, square, straight, buffoon.

858 hope *n* confidence, trust, reliance, faith, assurance; expectation, expectancy, anticipation, aspiration, longing, desire, dream, wish.

v hope, trust, rely on, lean on, have faith in; hope for, expect, presume, anticipate; long for, desire.

adj hopeful, expectant, sanguine, optimistic, confident; probable, promising, propitious, reassuring, encouraging, cheering, inspiriting.

859 hopelessness *n* despair, desperation, despondency, dejection, pessimism.

v despair, give up hope, despond.

adj hopeless, despairing, desperate, despondent, forlorn, disconsolate; irremediable, remediless, unremedial, incurable.

860 fear *n* apprehension, consternation, dismay, alarm, trepidation, dread, terror, fright, horror, panic; anxiety, solicitude, suspicion, misgiving, concern; awe, reverence, veneration.

v fear, be afraid of, apprehend, distrust, dread; revere, venerate, reverence.

adj fearful, afraid, apprehensive, dismayed, alarmed, frightened, terrified, horrified, aghast, terror-stricken, horror-stricken, panic-stricken; anxious, concerned, solicitous, suspicious; fearful, awesome, awe-inspiring; awful, dreadful, terrible.

861 courage *n* fearlessness, dauntlessness, intrepidity, guts, fortitude, pluck, spirit, nerve, heroism, daring, audacity, bravery, mettle, valor, hardihood, bravado, gallantry.

v dare, venture, look danger in the face, take heart, take the bull by the horns.

adj courageous, fearless, dauntless, intrepid, *(informal)* gutsy, spirited, stout-hearted, resolute, bold, heroic, daring, audacious, brave, valorous, enterprising, adventurous, gallant.

862 cowardice *n* fear, poltroonery, dastardliness, faint-heartedness, yellow streak, dread, timidity, baseness, abject fear.

coward, poltroon, craven, sneak, lily-liver, *(informal)* chicken.

v be cowardly, cower, skulk, quail, hide.

adj cowardly, fearful, craven, dastardly, pusillanimous, recreant, timid, timorous, faint-hearted, lily-livered, chicken-hearted, fearful, afraid, scared, spineless, *(informal)* chicken.

863 rashness *n* haste, impetuosity, recklessness, impulsiveness, heedlessness, thoughtlessness, imprudence, indiscretion, audacity, carelessness, foolhardiness.

v be rash, plunge.

adj rash, hasty, impetuous, reckless,

headlong, precipitate, impulsive, thoughtless, heedless, imprudent, indiscreet, careless, unwary, foolhardy, presumptuous, audacious.

864 caution *n* prudence, discretion, circumspection, heed, care, wariness, heedfulness, vigilance, forethought; warning, admonition, advice, injunction, counsel.

v be cautious, take care; warn, admonish, advise, counsel.

adj cautious, prudent, heedful, careful, watchful, discreet, wary, vigilant, alert, provident chary, circumspect, guarded.

865 desire *n* longing, fancy, craving, yearning, wish, want, need, hunger, appetite, thirst; request, wish, ambition, aspiration; love, passion, lust.

v desire, wish for, long for, crave, want, wish, covet, fancy; ask, request, solicit; lust for.

adj desirous, desiring, craving, wishful, hungry, thirsty, covetous, fervent, ardent, lustful.

866 indifference *n* unconcern, listlessness, apathy, insensibility, coolness, insensitiveness, inattention.

v be indifferent, take no interest in, have no heart for, spurn, disdain.

adj indifferent, unconcerned, listless, apathetic, cool, cold, lukewarm, insensitive, inattentive.

867 dislike *n* disinclination, disrelish, distaste, disgust, repugnance, antipathy, antagonism, aversion, hatred, horror, loathing.

v dislike, disrelish, be averse to, be disinclined, be reluctant, have no taste for; disgust, repel, nauseate, hate, loathe.

adj disliking, disinclined, averse, loath; dislikable, distasteful, disagreeable, offensive, repulsive, repugnant, repellent, abhorrent, nauseating, disgusting, loathsome.

868 fastidiousness *n* nicety; hypercriticism; discernment, discrimination, judiciousness, keenness, perspicacity.

v be fastidious, split hairs.

adj fastidious, nice, dainty, delicate; hard to please, finicky, hypercritical, fussy, querulous, meticulous, exacting, scrupulous, proper, priggish, prim; discerning, discriminative, judicious, keen, sharp, perspicacious, sagacious.

869 satiety *n* repletion, saturation, glut, surfeit; disgust, weariness.

v sate, satiate, saturate, cloy, glut, stuff, gorge, surfeit; gall, disgust, bore, tire, weary.

adj satiated, glutted, stuffed, gorged, surfeited; disgusted, bored, tired, weary.

870 wonder *n* surprise, marvel, astonishment, stupefaction, amazement, awe, admiration, bewilderment, puzzlement.

v wonder, think, speculate, conjecture, meditate, ponder, question; marvel, admire, be surprised, start, stare, startle, astonish, amaze, astound, stagger, stupefy, bewilder, dumfound.

adj marvelous, wonderful, extraordinary, remarkable, awesome, startling, wondrous, miraculous, astonishing, amazing, astounding, unique, curious, strange, odd, peculiar; astonished, surprised, aghast, agog, startled, breathless, awe-struck, spell-bound, lost in wonder, amazed, fascinated, bewildered.

871 expectance *n* expectancy, expectation.

v expect, foresee, assume, not be surprised, make nothing of.

adj expecting, expectant, relied on, expected, figured on, foreseen.

872 prodigy *n* phenomenon, wonder, marvel, miracle; freak, monstrosity, spectacle, curiosity; genius, intellectual giant, wizard, mastermind, expert, sage, child genius, wunderkind.

873 repute *n* estimation, reputation, account, regard, report; name, standing, distinction, credit, respect, respectability, dignity, greatness, eminence, honor, renown.

v consider, esteem, account, hold, regard, deem, reckon; be held in high repute, be distinguished.

adj reputed, regarded, accounted; reputable, respected, respectable, esteemed, celebrated, distinguished, dignified, honored, renowned, eminent.

874 disrepute *n* disgrace, dishonor, disfavor, discredit, ill repute, low repute, bad name, shame, degradation, obloquy, debasement, ignominy, infamy, stain, spot, blot, tarnish, taint.

v disgrace oneself, have a bad name, shame, disgrace, dishonor, tarnish, stain, taint, blot.

adj disreputable, base, low, unsavory, shady, unworthy, disgraced, vile, ignominious, dishonorable, opprobrious, shameful, disgraceful, infamous, tainted, tarnished.

875 nobility *n* distinction, eminence, stateliness, majesty, grandeur, dignity, loftiness, profundity, highmindedness; rank, condition, high birth, gentility, quality, royalty, aristocracy, lord, lady.

v be noble; ennoble.

adj noble, exalted, honorable, dignified, imposing, stately; titled, aristocratic, patrician, high-born.

876 commonalty *n* the common people, the lower classes, commoners, multitude, proletariat, populace, rank and file, bourgeoisie, general public, citizenry, peasantry, crowd, herd, rabble.

adj common, mean, low, base, ignoble, vulgar, homely, plebeian, proletarian, low-born, obscure, rustic, boorish, uncivilized.

877 title *n* honor, name, designation, decoration.

adj titled.

878 pride *n* self-respect, self-assurance, self-esteem, conceit, vanity, egotism, arrogance, vainglory, self-importance; insolence, haughtiness, superciliousness, presumption.

v be proud, presume, swagger, give oneself airs.

adj proud, high-minded, dignified, stately, noble, imposing, honorable, creditable; self-assured, self-satisfied, contented, egotistical, vain, conceited, arrogant, haughty, smug, overbearing, over-confident, snobbish, supercilious, presumptuous.

879 humility *n* modesty, humbleness, meekness, lowliness, submissiveness.

v lower, abase, debase, degrade, humiliate, mortify, shame, subdue, crush, break.

adj humble, low, lowly, unassuming, plain, common, poor, meek, modest,

submissive, unpretentious; respectful, polite, courteous.

adj with downcast eyes, on bended knee.

880 vanity *n* pride, conceit, self-esteem, self-complacency, egotism, self-admiration, self-love, self-glorification; hollowness, emptiness, sham, triviality.

v be vain, have too high an opinion of oneself, inflate, puff up.

adj vain, conceited, egotistical, self-complacent, proud, vainglorious, arrogant, overweening, inflated; useless, hollow, trifling, trivial.

881 modesty *n* humility, diffidence, timidity, bashfulness; moderation, decency, propriety, simplicity, chastity, prudery, prudishness.

v be modest, retire, give way to, stay in the background.

adj modest, humble, diffident, timid, timorous, bashful, sheepish, shy; moderate, humble, unpretentious, decent, becoming, proper, inextravagant, unostentatious, retiring, unassuming, unobtrusive; demure, prudish, chaste, pure, virtuous.

adv modestly, humbly, quietly, privately, without ceremony.

882 ostentation *n* pretention, pretentiousness, semblance, show, showiness, pretense, display, pageantry, pomp, pompousness, flourish, splendor.

v show off, parade, display, exhibit, blazon forth, emblazon, flaunt.

adj ostentatious, pretentious, showy, flashy, grand, pompous, garish, gaudy, flaunting, high-sounding, sumptuous, theatrical, dramatic, solemn, majestic, ceremonious, punctilious, over-blown.

adv with a flourish.

883 celebration *n* ceremony, ceremonial, commemoration, solemnization, observance, memorialization, festival, festivity.

v celebrate, commemorate, observe, keep; proclaim, announce; praise, extol, laud, glorify, honor, applaud, commend; solemnize, ritualize.

adj celebrational, commemorative, honorific, commendatory; celebrated, famous, renowned, illustrious, eminent, famed.

adv in honor of, in commemoration of, in celebration of.

884 boasting *n* bragging, swaggering, braggadocio, bravado.

boaster, braggart, blusterer, *(informal)* windbag.

v exaggerate, brag, vaunt, swagger, crow, strut, talk big.

adj boasting, boastful, pretentious, vainglorious, elated, exultant, jubilant, triumphant.

885 [undue assumption of superiority] **insolence** *n* boldness, rudeness, disrespect, impertinence, impudence, haughtiness, arrogance, audacity, abusiveness, contemptuousness.

v be insolent, swagger, assume, presume, take liberties, ride roughshod over.

adj insolent, bold, rude, disrespectful, impertinent, impudent, brazen, brassy, haughty, arrogant, audacious, presumptuous, overbearing, abusive, contemptuous, insulting.

886 servility *n* submissiveness, obsequiousness, abasement, slavishness, cringing, fawning, meanness, baseness, groveling, sycophancy, slavery.

toady, sycophant, boot-licker, *(informal)* apple-polisher, *(informal)* brown-noser.

v be servile, cringe, bow, stoop, kneel, toady, fawn, lick the boots of; sneak, crawl, crouch, cower.

adj servile, obsequious, slavish, cringing, fawning, sycophantic, groveling, sniveling, mealy-mouthed, abject, base, mean.

887 blusterer *n* swaggerer, braggart, boaster, windbag, bully, ruffian, rowdy, redneck.

III. Sympathetic Affections

888 friendship *n* amity, friendliness, harmony, concord, fellow-feeling, sympathy, good will, affection; companionship, comradeship, fellowship, fraternity, intimacy.

v be friendly, have an acquaintance with, keep company with, know, sympathize with, befriend, make friends with.

adj friendly, kind, kindly, amiable

neighborly, brotherly, cordial, genial, well-disposed, benevolent, kind-hearted, affectionate; helpful, advantageous, propitious; acquainted, familiar, intimate.

adv amicably, with open arms.

889 enmity *n* unfriendliness, dislike, discord, ill will, antagonism, animosity, hostility, malevolence, hatred.

v be at odds with.

adj inimical, unfriendly, alienated, estranged, hostile.

890 friend *n* companion, acquaintance, crony, chum, pal, mate, fellow, bosom buddy, intimate, confidant; well-wisher, patron, supporter, backer, advocate, partisan, defender, sympathizer; ally, associate.

891 enemy *n* foe, adversary, opponent, antagonist, attacker.

892 sociality *n* sociableness, gregariousness, social interaction, social intercourse, comradeship, camaraderie, companionship, cordiality, good fellowship, conviviality.

v be sociable, consort with, fraternize, welcome.

adj sociable, gregarious, social, warm, genial, cordial, friendly, convivial, amicable, clubbish, chummy, neighborly, hospitable.

893 seclusion. exclusion *n* privacy, retirement, withdrawal, solitude, sequestration, retreat, isolation, hiding, secrecy. elimination, prohibition, exception, omission, preclusion, rejection, ejection, expulsion, banishment, ostracism, exile.

recluse, hermit, cenobite, outcast, castaway, pariah, wastrel, foundling.

v seclude oneself, retire, withdraw, retreat, sequester, isolate, hide. exclude, eliminate, prohibit, reject, eject, expel.

adj secluded, retired, withdrawn, sequestered, private, isolated, solitary, excluded, eliminated, prohibited, omitted, precluded, rejected, ejected, repulsed, banished, ostracized, exiled.

894 courtesy *n* civility, sociability, politeness, good manners, good behavior, affability, gentility, graciousness, courtliness, respect.

v be courteous, behave well.

adj courteous, civil, polite, well-mannered, well-bred, gentlemanly, gallant, urbane, debonair, affable, gracious, courtly, respectful, obliging.

895 discourtesy *n* disrespect, ill-breeding, bad manners, tactlessness, rudeness, impudence, vulgarity.

v be discourteous.

adj discourteous, ill-bred, ill-mannered, ill-behaved, ungentlemanly, uncivil, impolite, ungracious, vulgar, crude, disrespectful, rude.

896 congratulations *n* felicitation, compliment, salute, salutation.

v congratulate, offer congratulations, salute.

adj congratulatory; complimentary.

897 love *n* affection, liking, regard, friendliness, kindness, kindliness, tenderness, fondness, devotion, warmth, attachment, yearning, passion, rapture, adoration, idolatry.

lover, admirer, suitor, adorer, wooer; beau, sweetheart, flame, love, truelove, paramour, boyfriend, girlfriend, ladylove, idol, darling, angel, beloved.

v love, like, be fond of, have affection for, be enamored of, be in love with, cherish, adore, revere, adulate, idolize.

adj loving, smitten, affectionate, tender, fond, attached, enamored, devoted, amorous, passionate, adoring; lovable, adorable, winning, enchanting, bewitching.

898 hate *n* dislike, aversion, animosity, hatred, antipathy, detestation, loathing, abhorrence, odium, horror, repugnance.

v hate, dislike, detest, abhor, loathe, despise, execrate, abominate.

adj hateful, detestable, odious, abominable, loathsome, abhorrent, repugnant, invidious, obnoxious, offensive, disgusting, nauseating, revolting, vile, repulsive; hating, averse from, set against, bitter, spiteful, malicious.

899 favorite *n* pet, minion, idol, jewel, spoiled child, apple of one's eye, man after one's own heart; love, dear, darling, honey, sweetheart.

900 resentment *n* displeasure, pique, umbrage, animosity, bitterness, envy, jealousy, anger, wrath, indignation.

v resent, take offense, bristle over, chafe, fume, frown, pout, snarl, gnash, growl, scowl, glower, grouch, bear a grudge.

adj resentful, offended, bitter, worked up, angry, wrathful, irate, indignant; envious, jealous.

901 irascibility *n* irritability, excitability, sensitivity.

v be irascible, quick to fly off the handle, have a temper.

adj irascible, testy, short-tempered, hot-tempered, quick-tempered, touchy, temperamental, irritable, snappish, petulant, overly sensitivie, choleric.

901a sullenness *n* moodiness, moroseness, churlishness, sluggishness.

v be sullen, frown, scowl, sulk, pout.

adj silent, reserved, sulky, morose, moody, ill-humored, sour, vexatious, bad-tempered, surly, cross, grumpy, peevish, perverse; gloomy, dismal, cheerless, overcast, somber, mournful, dark; slow, sluggish, dull stagnant.

902 [expression of affection or love] **endearment** *n* embrace, caress, hug, kiss, blandishment, dalliance, love token.

v endear, embrace, caress, blandish, flirt, dally.

adj endearing.

903 marriage *n* wedding, nuptials, matrimony, wedlock; union, alliance, association, confederation.

married man, married woman, husband, wife, spouse, mate, partner, consort, better half, *(informal)* old man, *(informal)* old lady.

v marry, tie the knot, take to the altar, wive, couple.

adj married, wed, united.

904 celibacy *n* sexual abstinence; bachelorhood.

celibate, unmarried man, bachelor, unmarried woman, spinster, old maid, virgin, maiden; priest.

adj celibate, unmarried.

905 divorce *n* marital separation, legal separation; separation, disunion, isolation.

v divorce, *(informal)* split up, separate, isolate.

adj divorced, separated, *(informal)* split up.

906 benevolence *n* kindness, kindliness, humanity, tenderness, kindheartedness, unselfishness, generosity, liberality, charity, philanthropy, altruism.

good Samaritan, sympathizer, altruist.

v wish well, take an interest in, treat well, comfort, benefit, assist, aid.

adj benevolent, kind, kindly, well-disposed, kind-hearted, humane, tender, tender-hearted, unselfish, generous,, liberal, benevolent, obliging, charitable, philanthropic, altruistic.

907 malevolence *n* ill will, enmity, rancor, resentment, malice, maliciousness, spite, spitefulness, grudge, hate, hatred, venom.

v bear ill will.

adj malevolent, malicious, resentful, spiteful, begrudging, hateful, venomous, vicious, hostile, ill-natured, evil-minded, rancorous.

908 malediction *n* curse, swear, imprecation, denunciation, cursing, damning, damnation, execration; slander.

v curse, swear, imprecate, denounce, damn, execrate; slander.

909 threat *n* menace, danger, indication, portent, foreboding, prognostication; intimidation.

v threaten, menace, endanger, indicate, presage, impend, portend, augur, forebode, foreshadow, prognosticate; frighten, denounce, intimidate, cow, badger.

adj threatening, menacing, endangering, impending, arguring, foreshadowing, foreboding, ominous, inauspicious, sinister, frightening, intimidating.

910 philanthropy *n* humaneness, compassion, humanitarianism, benevolence, helpfulness, munificence, public spirit, charity.

philanthropist, humanitarian, patriot.

adj philanthropic, humanitarian, benevolent, munificent, altruistic, public spirited, civic minded, charitable.

911 misanthropy *n* hatred of mankind, incivism.

misanthrope, man-hater; misogynist, woman-hater.

adj misanthropic, antisocial, uncivil.

912 benefactor *n* succorer, patron, supporter, contributor, friend.

913 evildoer *n* wrongdoer, troublemaker, subversive, oppressor, destroyer.

914 pity *n* sympathy, compassion, commiseration, condolence, mercy.

v pity, commiserate, feel sorry for, be sorry for, sympathize with, feel for.

adj pitying, compassionate, sympathetic, touched, moved, affected, feeling.

914a pitilessness *n* cruelty, meanness, ruthlessness, hard-heartedness.

v have no pity for.

adj pitiless, merciless, cruel, mean, unmerciful, ruthless, implacable, relentless, inexorable, hard-hearted, stony.

915 condolence *n* lamentation, sympathy, consolation.

v condole with, console, sympathize, lament.

916 gratitude *n* thanks, thankfulness, appreciation, indebtedness.

v be grateful, thank, appreciate.

adj grateful, appreciative, thankful, obliged, beholding, indebted, in one's debt.

917 ingratitude *n* thanklessness, unthankfulness.

ingrate.

v be ungrateful.

adj ungrateful, unthankful, unmindful, thankless.

918 forgiveness *n* pardon, excuse, indulgence, remission, reprieve, amnesty, grace, absolution.

v forgive, pardon, excuse, absolve reprieve, acquit.

adj forgiving.

919 revenge *n* vengeance, retaliation, requital, reprisal, retribution, vindictiveness, vengefulness.

avenger, vindicator, nemesis.

v revenge, avenge, retaliate, requite, vindicate.

adj revengeful, vengeful, vindictive, spiteful, malevolent, resentful, malicious, malignant, unforgiving, implacable.

920 jealousy *n* envy, resentment; suspicion; watchfulness, vigilance.

v be jealous.

adj jealous, envious, resentful; suspicious; solicitous, watchful, vigilant.

921 envy *n* jealousy, enviousness, grudge, covetousness.

v envy, covet, begrudge, resent.

adj envious, covetous, jealous, begrudging.

IV. Moral Affections

922 right *n* virtue, justice, fairness, integrity, equity, equitableness, uprightness, rectitude, morality, morals, goodness, honor, lawfulness; accuracy, truth.

v be right; do right.

adj right, just, good, equitable, moral, fair, upright, honest, lawful; correct, proper, suitable, fit; correct, true, accurate; genuine, legitimate, rightful.

adv righteously, rightfully, lawfully, rightly, justly, fairly, equitably.

923 wrong *n* evil, wickedness, misdeed, sin, vice, immorality, iniquity, inequity, injustice, unlawfulness.

adj wrong, injure, harm, maltreat, abuse, oppress, cheat, defraud, dishonor.

adj wrong, bad, evil, wicked, sinful, immoral, iniquitous, reprehensible, unjust, crooked, dishonest; erroneous, inaccurate, incorrect, false, untrue, mistaken; improper, unappropriate, unfit; awry, amiss, out of order.

adv wrongly, wickedly, sinfully.

924 claim *n* due, right, privilege, prerogative, prescription, demand, sanction, warrant, license.

claimant, appellant.

v claim, deserve, have the right, be entitled.

adj claiming, having a right to, privileged, prescribed, sanctioned allowed, licensed, authorized, due.

925 [absence of right] **unrightfulness** *n* impropriety, illegitimacy, presumption.

usurper, pretender.

v be unentitled.

adj unrightful, having no right to unentitled, unauthorized, unwarranted, illegitimate, not licensed.

926 duty *n* obligation, function, responsibility, onus, burden, business; conscience, moral imperative, sense of duty; homage, respect, reverence.

v do one's duty, behoove, become, befit, beseem; observe, perform, fulfill, discharge.

adj obligatory, binding, imperative, incumbent, under obligation, obliged, bound, tied, duty bound; dutiful, respectful, docile, submissive, deferential, reverential, obedient.

927 dereliction of duty *n* nonobservance, nonperformance, neglect, failure, carelessness, fault, infraction, violation, transgression.

v neglect, slight, fail, violate.

adj undutiful, negligent, careless, at fault, failing, in violation.

927a exemption *n* immunity, impunity, privilege, freedom, exception, excuse, dispensation.

v exempt, excuse, release, acquit, discharge, free.

adj exempt, immune, privileged, freed, excepted, excused, unbound.

928 respect *n* esteem, deference, regard, consideration, estimation, veneration, reverence, homage, honor, admiration, approbation, approval, affection, feeling; respects, regards, duty; regard, consideration, attention, devotion.

v honor, revere, reverence, esteem, venerate, regard, consider, defer to, admire, adulate, adore, love; regard, heed, attend, notice, consider.

adj respectful, courteous, polite, well-mannered, well-bred, civil, deferential; respected, estimable, venerable, admirable; respecting, heeding, considering, regarding, attending.

929 disrespect *n* discourtesy, impoliteness, rudeness, crudeness, incivility, impudence, impertinence, irreverence, derision.

v hold in disrespect, be disrespectful, insult, deride, scoff, mock, sneer, jeer, deride, ridicule, scorn.

adj disrespectful, discourteous, impolite, rude, crude, uncivil, impudent, impertinent, irreverent insulting, derisive, scornful.

930 contempt *n* scorn, disdain, derision, contumely; dishonor, disgrace, shame.

v feel contempt for, contemn, scorn, disdain, deride, despise.

adj contemptible, despicable, mean, low, miserable, abject, base, vile; contemptuous, scornful, disdainful, derisive; dishonorable, disgraceful, shameful.

931 approbation n approval, sanction, esteem, admiration, commendation.

v approbate, approve, esteem, value, honor, admire, appreciate, sanction, endorse, commend, praise.

adj commendatory, complimentary, laudatory; approved, praised, in high esteem, in favour; praiseworthy, commendable, good, meritorious, estimable, creditable.

932 disapprobation n disapproval, dislike, disesteem, odium, disparagement, deprecation, denunciation, censure.

v disapprove, dislike, object to, frown upon, censure, blame, reproach, reprove, admonish, berate.

adj disapproving, disparaging, reproachful, defamatory, denunciatory, condemnatory.

933 flattery n adulation, charming, lipservice, (informal) brown-nosing, fawning, flunkeyism, sycophancy.

v flatter, curry favor, slobber over, (informal) lay it on thick, wheedle, fawn, court, (informal) brown-nose, pander to, overpraise.

adj flattering, adulatory, honeymouthed, smooth-tongued, servile, sycophantic.

934 detraction n detracting, disparagement, belittling, defamation, vilification, calumny, abuse, slander, aspersion, deprecation.

v detract, run down, criticize, decry, disparage, blacken, belittle, depreciate, cast aspersions, defame, malign, abuse, slander, vilify.

adj detracting, disparaging, belittling, derogatory, depreciating, calumnious, abusive, slanderous, vilifying, scurrilous.

935 flatterer n adulator, toady, flunkey, (informal) apple-polisher, fawner, sycophant, (informal) brown-noser, bootlicker, opportunist, courtier.

936 detractor n reprover, critic, carper, slanderer, (informal) hatchet man, backbiter, defamer, castigator, satirist, cynic, reviler.

937 vindication n exoneration, exculpation, acquittal; justification, warrant, support, defense.

apologist, vindicator, defender.

v vindicate, exonerate, acquit, clear; uphold, justify, maintain, defend, support.

adj vindicating, vindicated, exonerated, exonerating, exculpatory, acquitted; justified, warranted, supported.

938 accusation n arraignment, indictment, charge, incrimination, impeachment; accusal, blaming, inculpation, charging, imputation.

accuser, prosecutor, plaintiff; relator, informer; appellant.

v charge; arraign, indict, charge, incriminate, impeach; blame, inculpate, charge, involve, point to, impute.

adj accused, accusing, accusatory, accusative, incriminatory, imputative.

939 probity n honesty, uprightness, virtue, rectitude, integrity.

v be honorable.

adj honest, honorable, virtuous, upright, scrupulous, high-principled.

940 improbity n dishonesty, wickedness, immorality, evil.

v be dishonest, play false.

adj dishonest, dishonorable, unscrupulous, immoral, wicked, evil.

941 knave n rogue, rascal, blackguard, sneak, villain, scoundrel.

942 disinterestedness n impartiality, fairness, lack of bias, unselfishness, generosity, liberality.

v be disinterested.

adj disinterested, unbiased, unprejudiced, unselfish, impartial, fair, generous, liberal.

943 selfishness n self-interest, selfseeking, self-love, egoism, egotism, solipsism, illiberality, parsimony, stinginess, meanness.

v be selfish, cultivate one's own garden, look after oneself, feather one's own nest.

adj selfish, self-centered, self-indulgent, self-interested, self-seeking, egotistical, solipsistic, illiberal, parsimonious, stingy, cheap, mean.

944 virtue *n* virtuousness, goodness, uprightness, morality, ethics, probity, rectitude, integrity; excellence, merit, quality, asset; innocence, chastity, purity.
v be virtuous, have the virtue of.
adj virtuous, right, upright, moral, righteous, good, chaste, pure.

945 vice *n* fault, sin, depravity, iniquity, immorality, wickedness; blemish, blot, imperfection, defect.
v sin, err, transgress, trespass.
adj vicious, immoral, depraved, profligate, wicked, sinful, sinning, corrupt, bad, iniquitous, reprehensible, blameworthy, censurable, wrong, improper; spiteful, malignant, malicious, malevolent; faulty, defective; ill-tempered, bad-tempered, refractory.

946 innocence *n* purity, virtue, virtuousness, faultlessness, spotlessness; guiltlessness, blamelessness; uprightness, honesty; naïveté, simplicity, artlessness, guilelessness, ingenuousness.
v be innocent.
adj innocent, pure, untainted, sinless, virtuous, virginal, blameless, faultless, impeccable, spotless, immaculate; guiltless, blameless; upright, honest, forthright; naïve, simple, unsophisticated, artless, guileless, ingenuous.

947 guilt *n* guiltiness, culpability, criminality; sinfulness.
v be guilty.
adj guilty, culpable, to blame, in fault.

948 good man *n* model, paragon, hero, soldier, saint, salt of the earth, *(informal)* ace.

949 bad man *n* wrong-doer, evil-doer, sinner, scoundrel, miscreant, villain, wretch, monster, devil, demon, scum of the earth.

950 penitence *n* contrition, atonement, compunction, repentance, remorse, regret.
penitent, prodigal son.
v be penitent, repent, rue, regret.
adj penitent, sorry, contrite, repenting; repentant, atoning, amending, remorseful, regretful; penitential.

951 impenitence *n* irrepentance, obduracy, hardness of heart.
v be impenitent, show no remorse.

adj impenitent, uncontrite, not sorry, obdurate, unrepentant, remorseless; unrepenting, unrepented, unatoned; irreclaimable.

952 atonement *n* satisfaction, reparation, compensation, amends, quittance; redemption, expiation, reclamation, conciliation, propitiation.
v atone, atone for; give satisfaction, satisfy, make amends; expiate, propitiate, reclaim, redeem, repair, absolve, purge, shrive, do penance, repent.
adj atoning, propitiating, propitiatory, redemptive, expiating, expiatory.

953 temperance *n* moderation, self-restraint, self-control, continence; sobriety, even-temperednes, calmness, coolness, detachment, dispassion.
vegetarian; teetotaler; abstainer.
v be temperate, abstain, forbear, restrain.
adj temperate, moderate, self-controlled, self-restrained, frugal, sparing; sober, calm, cool, detached, dispassionate.

954 intemperance *n* excess, exorbitance, inordinateness, extravagance; indulgence, high living, self-indulgence, epicurism, epicureanism, sybaritism; inabstinence, alcoholism.
v be intemperate, indulge, wallow in.
adj intemperate, excessive, exorbitant, inordinate, extravagant; indulgent, self-indulgent, epicurean.

954a sensualist *n* sybarite, voluptuary, pleasure-seeker, epicure, epicurean, libertine, hedonist.

955 asceticism *n* puritanism, austerity, abstemiousness, self-abnegation, self-denial, total abstinence, self-motification.
ascetic, anchorite, puritan, martyr; hermit, recluse.
v abstain, deny oneself, fast, starve.
adj ascetic, puritanical, austere, abstemious, rigorous, rigid, stern, severe, harsh, strict, self-denying, self-mortifying.

956 fasting *n* day of fasting; going hungry, starving oneself, starvation.
v fast, starve, famish.
adj fasting, starving, unfed; starved, half-starved, hungry.

957 gluttony n greed, greediness, voracity; epicurism, gormandizing, gulosity, crapulence, over-eating, (informal) piggishness.

glutton, epicure, cormorant, hog, (informal) pig.

v be gluttonous, hog; overeat, gorge, stuff oneself, make a pig of oneself, guzzle, bolt, devour, engorge, gobble up.

adj gluttonous, greedy, voracious; epicurean, gormandizing, crapulent, swinish, (informal) piggish.

958 sobriety n abstinence, teetotalism.

teetotaler, abstainer.

v be sober, abstain, take the pledge.

adj sober, unintoxicated, on the wagon, (informal) straight, (informal) dry, dry as a bone.

959 drunkenness n intemperance, drinking, inebriety, insobriety, intoxication, alcoholism.

drunkard, sot, tippler, drinker, inebriate, dipsomaniac, alcoholic, (informal) boozer, (informal) lush, (informal) juicer.

v be drunk, drink, imbibe, booze, guzzle, swill, soak, sot, lush, drink like a fish, hit the bottle.

adj drunk, drunken, sotted, intoxicated, inebriated, tipsy, tight, (informal) potted, (informal) stewed, (informal) stewed to the gills, dead drunk, (informal) plowed, (informal) plastered, (informal) tanked, (informal) wasted, (informal) juiced, (informal) blown away, (informal) high, (informal) flying, (informal) feeling no pain.

960 purity n cleanness; decency, decorum, delicacy; continence, chastity, innocence, modesty, virtue, virginity; simplicity, genuineness, faultlessness, perfection; guiltlessness, honesty, uprightness.

virgin, vestal virgin.

v be pure.

adj pure, decent, delicate; innocent, continent, chaste, virginal, modest, virtuous, undefiled, unsullied, unstained, untainted, uncorrupted, clean, spotless, immaculate; simple, genuine, faultless, perfect; honest, upright; unmixed, unadulterated, uncontaminated

961 impurity n indecency, indelicacy; incontinence, immodesty, lewdness, concupiscence, prurience, lechery; grossness, obscenity, ribaldry, smut, bawdry; uncleanness, adulteration, contamination, defilement; fault, flaw, imperfection; guilt, sin, sinfulness.

v be impure.

adj impure, indecent, indelicate; incontinent, immodest, unchaste, concupiscent, lewd, prurient, lecherous; gross, obscene, ribald, dirty, smutty, bawdy; unclean, sullied, defiled, contaminated, adulterated, tainted, stained, corrupted, jaded; faulty, flawed, imperfect; guilty, sinning, sinful, wicked.

962 libertine n rake, roué, debauchee, lecher, sensualist, voluptuary, profligate, seducer, deceiver, courtesan, prostitute, strumpet, harlot, whore, street-walker, trollop, hussy, bitch, slut, minx.

963 legality n legitimacy, legitimateness, lawfulness; duty, obligation.

law, code, constitution, charter, statute, regulation, decree, order.

v legalize; legislate, enact, ordain, decree, codify, formulate, pass a law.

adj legal, legitimate, authorized, licit, lawful, legalized, legislated; constitutional.

964 illegality n illegitimacy, unlawfulness, illicitness, lawlessness.

v be illegal, offend against the law, violate the law.

adj illegal, unlawful, illegitimate, illicit, contraband, unconstitutional, unchartered, unwarranted, unauthorized, unlicensed, proscribed, prohibited, outlawed, criminal; lawless, arbitrary, despotic, unanswerable, unaccountable.

965 [executive] jurisdiction n judicature, authority, power, right, control; territory, range, magistracy.

v judge, sit in judgment; administer.

adj jurisdictive, judicial, administrative; inquisitorial.

966 tribunal n court, courtroom, board, bench, court of law, court of justice, bar of justice, judgment seat, dock, forum, witness-chair.

967 judge n justice, judiciary, magistrate, judicator, adjudicator, jurist, juror; moderator, arbiter, arbitrator, umpire, referee.

v judge, adjudge, determine, hear a cause, try a case, pass sentence.

adj judicial, judicious, juridical, legal, juristic, judicatory, jurisdictive.

968 lawyer *n* attorney, attorney-at-law, counselor, barrister, solicitor, pleader, counsel, advocate, counselor-at-law, legal adviser; prosecutor, prosecuting attorney, district attorney, public prosecutor, attorney general.

bar, legal profession.

v practice law, be called to the bar, plead, read the law.

adj learned in the law.

969 lawsuit *n* suit, action, cause, dispute, contention; case, debate, litigation, legal proceedings, legal action, legal process, trial, debate, pleadings, argument, argumentation, disputation, prosecution; writ, summons, subpoena, affidavit, suitor, party to a suit, litigant, verdict, decision; precedent.

v go to the law, sue, file a claim, bring to trial, put on trial, serve, serve with a writ, cite, arraign, prosecute, bring an action against, indict, impeach, attach, summon.

adj litigious.

970 acquittal *n* clearance, exculpation, exoneration, absolution, discharge, pardon; impunity, immunity.

v acquit, exculpate, exonerate, clear, absolve, pardon; discharge, release, liberate, set free.

adj acquitted, cleared, exculpated, exonerated; discharged, released, set free.

971 condemnation *n* conviction, guilty verdict, proscription.

v condemn, convict, find guilty, damn, doom, proscribe; stand condemned.

adj condemned, condemnatory, convicted

972 punishment *n* sentence, judgment, penalty, retribution, discipline, chastisement, castigation, reproof, correction.

v punish, inflict punishment, correct, discipline, penalize, reprove, castigate, chasten, administer correction. scold, berate, jail, incarcerate, execute, torture, banish, flog, whip, lash, scourge.

adj punishing, punitive, castigatory,

penalized, penalizing; punished, castigated.

973 reward *n* recompense, prizes, desert, compensation, pay, remuneration, requital, merit; bounty, premium, bonus; reparation, redress; retribution, reckoning, amends.

v reward, recompense, requite, compensate, pay, remunerate.

adj rewarding, remunerative, compensatory, retributive, reparatory; rewarded.

974 penalty *n* punishment, retribution, pain, pains, penance; fine, forfeit, damages, sequestration, incarceration, confiscation.

v penalize, punish; fine, confiscate, sequester; penalized, punished.

975 scourge *n* punishment, flogging; affliction, calamity, plague, bane, pest, nuisance; whip, lash, strap, throng, rod, cane, stick; prison, house of correction.

gaoler, jailer, executioner, hangman.

976 deity *n* divinity, god, godhead, omnipotence, providence, lord, the almighty, supreme being, first cause, prime mover, author, creator, the infinite, the eternal, the all-powerful, the all-merciful, omnipresence.

adj divine, godly, almighty, holy, hallowed, sacred, heavenly, celestial, sacrosanct; superhuman, supernatural, spiritual, ghostly, unearthly.

977 angel *n* glorified spirit, beneficent spirit, ministering spirit, heavenly spirit, winged being, seraph, cherub, archangel, helper, spirit, guardian; *(informal)* friend, patron, protector, guardian angel, love.

adj angelic, seraphic, cherubic, spiritual, ethereal; pure, good righteous, ideal, beautiful; *(informal)* adorable, entrancing, transporting, rapturous, lovely, enrapturing.

978 devil *n* Satan, Lucifer, Beelzebub; tempter, evil one, evil spirit, serpent, prince of darkness, demon, evil incarnate.

diabolism, satanism.

adj devilish, satanic, diabolic, infernal, hellish.

979 fabulous spirit *n* god, goddess, fairy, fay, sylph, faun, nymph, nereid, dryad, sea-maid, oread, naiad, mermaid, kelpie, nixie, sprite, pixie, elf.
adj fabulous, mythological, imaginary, sylphic.

980 demon *n* demonology; devil, fiend, evil spirit, incubus, monster, succubus, succuba, fury, harpy, ghoul, vampire, ogre, gnome, imp, kobold, dwarf, urchin, troll, sprite, bad fairy, leprechaun; ghost, specter, apparition, spirit, shade, shadow, vision, hobgoblin, wraith, spook, banshee, siren, satyr.
adj demonic, supernatural, weird, uncanny, unearthly, spectral, ghostly, ghostlike, elfin, fiendish, impish, haunted.

981 heaven *n* kingdom of heaven, kingdom of god, heavenly kingdom, paradise, nirvana; celestial bliss, glory.
adj heavenly, celestial, supernal, unearthly, paradisaic, paradisical, beatific, elysian, blissful, beautiful, divine, blessed, beautified, glorified.

982 hell *n* Gehenna, inferno, Hades, Erebus, pandemonium, abyss, limbo; [*informal*] torment, torture, pain, agony, suffering.
adj hellish, infernal, stygian, satanic, diabolic, devilish; [*informal*] painful, agonizing, excruciating, horrifying, unendurable.

983 theology *n* theosophy, divinity, hagiography, theologics, theism, monotheism, religion, religious persuasion, dogma, creed, credo, doctrine, tenent, articles of faith.
theologian, theologue, divine.
adj theological, religious, theosophical, hagiological.

983a orthodoxy *n* soundness; strictness, faithfulness, adherence, observance; truth, true faith, religious truth.
adj orthodox, sound, strict, faithful, catholic, doctrinal, authoritative, official, traditional; scriptural, divine, Christian; conventional, established, approved, prescriptive, prevailing, customary.

984 heterodoxy *n* unorthodoxy, nonconformity, iconoclasm, doubt, skepticism, recusancy, dissent, misbelief, error, heresy, schism, apostasy.
pagan, heathen, dissenter, nonconformist, skeptic, heretic, atheist.
adj heterodox, nonconformist, nonconforming, iconoclastic, doubting, skeptical, unscriptural, unorthodox, uncanonical, recusant, dissenting, misbelieving, heretical, schismatic.

985 revelation *n* disclosure, discovery, expression, declaration, expression, utterance, publication, admission, convession, acknowledgment; enlightenment, proclamation, announcement; Christian Revelation. Scriptures, Word of God.
adj revelatory; instructive; confessional.

986 religious writings *n* Scriptures, *Bible,* Old Testament, New Testament, The Vedas, Upanishads, Bhagavad Gita, Koran, Alcoran, Avesta.

987 piety *n* godliness, devoutness, devotion, humility, veneration, sanctity, grace, holiness; reverence, regard, respect.
believer, devotee, pietist, righteous man.
v be pious, have faith; believe, revere, venerate, sanctify, consecrate.
adj pious, devout, godly, reverent, religious, holy, sacred, pietistic, saintly; devoted, humble, reverential.

988 impiety *n* irreverence, irreligion, scoffing, profaneness, profanity, blasphemy, desecration, sacrilege, sin, sinfulness; hypocrisy, cant, sanctimony, sanctimoniousness.
sinner, scoffer, blasphemer, sacrilegist, hypocrite.
v be impious, scoff, swear, profane, blaspheme, desecrate, revile, commit sacrilege.

989 irreligion *n* ungodliness, laxity, impiety, indifference, apathy, skepticism, doubt, disbelief, incredulity, agnosticism, freethinking, atheism, infidelity.
skeptic, doubter, nonbeliever, agnostic, cynic, freethinker, atheist, infidel, heathen.
v be irreligious, doubt, disbelieve, lack faith, question.
adj irreligious, godless, ungodly, un-

holy, unhallowed, undevout; skeptical, doubting, unbelieving, indifferent, apathetic, incredulous, freethinking, agnostic, atheistic, faithless; worldly, earthly, unspiritual.

990 worship *n* reverence, homage, adoration, honor; regard, idolizing, idolatry, deification; prayer, supplication, petition; service, celebration, rites.

worshiper, congregation, suppliant, communicant, celebrant.

v worship, adore, adulate, idolize, deify, love, like; pray, kneel, bow, fall on one's knees; invoke, supplicate, offer prayers, petition; praise, bless, laud, glorify, magnify, sing praises.

adj worshiping, revering, adoring, honoring; worshipful, reverential, honorific, celebrational.

991 idolatry *n* idolism, idolatrousness, idolization, fetishism, idol-worship, deification, demonology; blind adoration, extravagant love, fervor, ardency, enchantment, hero worship.

idol, image, icon, symbol, statue, false god, pagan deity.

v idolize, worship idols, idolatrize, worship, glorify, put on a pedestal, canonize, deify, apotheosize; dote upon, treasure, prize.

adj idolatrous, idol-worshiping, pagan, fetishistic; adoring, impassioned, lovesick.

992 sorcery *n* occultism, magic, witchery, enchantment, witchcraft, spell, necromancy, divination, charm, conjuration, bewitchery, spiritualism.

v practice sorcery, conjure, charm, enchant, bewitch, divine, entrance, mesmerize, cast a spell, call up spirits, raise spirits.

adj magic, magical, bewitching, enchanting, charming, incantory, weird, cabalistic, talismanic; charmed, bewitched, enchanted.

993 spell *n* charm, incantation, exorcism, voodoo, trance, rapture, suggestion, jinx, hocus-pocus, mumbo-jumbo, abracadabra.

994 sorcerer *n* magician, conjuror, necromancer, wizard, witch, exorcist, charmer, medicine man, shaman, medium, clairvoyant, mesmerist, soothsayer, guru.

995 churchdom *n* church, ministry, priesthood, sisterhood, prelacy, hierarchy.

v call, ordain, consecrate, bestow, elect.

adj ecclesiastical, clerical, priestly, pastoral, ministerial, hierarchical.

996 clergy *n* clerical, ministry, priesthood, the cloth, clergyman, divine, ecclesiastic, churchman, pastor, shepherd, minister, preacher, parson, father, reverend, priest, rabbi.

v receive the call, take orders.

adj clerical; ordained.

997 laity *n* fold, flock, congregation, assembly, brethren, people; layman, parishioner.

v secularize.

adj lay, laical, secular, civil, temporal.

998 rite *n* ceremony, observance, function, service, procedure, form, usage.

v perform a rite.

adj ritualistic, ceremonial.

999 canonicals *n* religious garments, vestments, robe, gown, surplice.

1000 temple *n* place of worship, house of god, cathedral, church, chapel, meetinghouse, synagogue, tabernacle, mosque, shrine, pantheon; monastery, priory, abbey, friary, convent, nunnery, cloister; parsonage, rectory, vicarage.

adj churchly, cloistered, monastic.

Index

A

A.M. *n* 125

abandon *n* 682; *v* 293, 624, 757, 782

abandonment *n* 624, 678, 757, 782

abase *v* 308, 879

abasement *n* 308, 886

abate *v* 36, 174, 287, 813, 834

abatement *n* 36, 813

abbreviate *v* 38, 201, 596

abbreviated *adj* 201

abbreviation *n* 38, 201, 596

abdicate *v* 624, 782

abdication *n* 624, 757, 782

abduct *v* 789

abduction *n* 789

aberrant *adj* 83, 279

aberration *n* 20a, 83, 279, 291, 495, 503

abet *v* 707

abeyance *n* 142

abhor *v* 898

abhorrence *n* 898

abhorrent *adj* 830, 867, 898

abide *v* 1, 110, 141, 143, 186

abide by *v* 772

abiding *adj* 110, 141, 150

ability *n* 79, 157, 632, 698, 702

abject *adj* 207, 886, 930

abject fear *n* 862

abjuration *n* 536, 607, 757

abjure *v* 536, 607, 757

ablaze *adj* 382, 420

able *adj* 157, 698

able-bodied *adj* 159

ablution *n* 652

abnegation *n* 764

abnormal *adj* 83

abnormality *n* 83

abode *n* 189

abolish *v* 756

abolition *n* 756

abominable *adj* 649, 653, 898

abominate *v* 898

abomination *n* 649

aboriculture *n* 371

aboriginal *adj* 124

abort *v* 732

abortion *n* 732

abortive *adj* 732

about *adv* 9, 32, 227

aboutface *adv* 283

above all *adv* 33

aboveboard *adj* 246, 703; *adv* 525

above par *adj* 648

abracadabra *n* 993

abrade *v* 330

abrasion *n* 331, 330

abreast *adv* 236

abridge *v* 36, 201, 572, 596

abridged *adj* 201

abridgement *n* 36, 201, 572, 596

abrogate *v* 756, 757

abrogation *n* 756

abrupt *adj* 113, 173, 217, 579, 739

abruptly *adv* 508

abruptness *n* 113, 579, 739

abscond *v* 623, 671

absence *n* 187

absence of choice *n* 609a

absence of design *n* 615a

absence of influence *n* 175a

absence of intellect *n* 450a

absence of meaning *n* 517

absence of motive *n* 615a

absence of smell *n* 399

absence of thought *n* 452

absence of time *n* 107

absent *v* 293; *adj* 187, 452

absenteeism *n* 187

absent oneself *v* 187

absolute *adj* 1, 31, 52, 104, 474, 737, 739, 748

absolutely *adv* 31

absolution *n* 750, 918, 970

absolutism *n* 739

absolve *v* 750, 918, 952, 970

absorb *v* 48, 296, 824

absorbed *adj* 451

absorption *n* 296

abstain *v* 623, 678, 953, 955, 958, 609a

abstainer *n* 953, 958

abstain from doing *v* 681

abstemious *adj* 955

abstemiousness *n* 955

abstention *n* 623

abstinence *n* 623, 678, 958

abstract *n* 596; *v* 78, 572, 596; *adj* 2, 4

109

abstraction *n* 451
absurd *adj* 47, 471, 477, 497, 853
absurdity *n* 497
absurdity *n* 517, 853
abundance *n* 31, 102
abundant *adj* 31
abundantly *adv* 31
abuse *n* 694, 697, 716, 934; *v* 649, 679, 716, 923, 934
abusive *adj* 716, 885, 934
abusiveness *n* 885
abutment *n* 199
abut on *v* 199
abysmal *adj* 208
abyss *n* 180, 198, 208, 982
academic *adj* 537, 542
academician *n* 492
academy *n* 542
accede *v* 488, 762
acceding *adj* 831
accelerate *v* 132, 173, 274, 684
acceleration *n* 274
accent *n* 580; *v* 580
accentuate *v* 580, 642
accentuation *n* 580
accept *v* 76, 82, 484, 771, 785, 789
acceptance *n* 484, 762, 785
acceptance into *n* 76
accepted *adj* 484
access *n* 197, 286
accessible *adj* 260, 705
accession *n* 37
accessory *n* 39, 88; *adj* 37, 88
accidence *n* 567
accident *n* 156, 619
accidental *adj* 6, 156, 621
acclaim *v* 836
acclimate *v* 613
acclivitous *adj* 305

acclivity *n* 217, 305
accolade *n* 733
accommodate *v* 23, 613, 707, 723, 787
accommodate oneself to *v* 82
accommodation *n* 723, 787
accompaniment *n* 88
accompaniment *n* 39
accompanist *n* 416
accompany *v* 88, 120, 416
accompanying *adj* 88
accomplish *v* 52, 161, 729, 731
accomplishment *n* 698, 729, 731
accord *n* 23, 178, 488, 714, 721, 762; *v* 23, 413, 714, 760, 784, 812
accordance *n* 16, 23, 178
accordant *adj* 23
accordingly *adv* 8
accord with *v* 16
account *n* 551, 594, 805, 811, 873; *v* 451, 594, 873
accountable *adj* 177
accountant *n* 801, 811
accounted *adj* 873
account for *v* 155
accounting for *n* 155
accounts *n* 811
accounts *n* 800
accouterments *n* 225
accredit *v* 805
accredited *adj* 484
accretion *n* 35
accrue *v* 37, 785
acculturation *n* 658
accumulate *v* 37, 72, 636
accumulation *n* 72, 636
accuracy *n* 459, 494, 543, 922

accurate *adj* 246, 494, 922
accusal *n* 938
accusation *n* 938
accusative *adj* 938
accusatory *adj* 938
accused *adj* 938
accuser *n* 938
accusing *adj* 938
accustom *v* 613
ace *n* 948
acerbate *v* 397
acerbic *adj* 397
acerbity *n* 397
ache *n* 378, 828; *v* 378
achievable *adj* 470
achieve *v* 161, 680, 729, 731
achievement *n* 161, 551, 729, 731
aching *n* 378
acid *adj* 397
acidify *v* 397
acidity *n* 397
acidulate *v* 397
acidulous *adj* 397
acknowledge *v* 488, 529, 535, 772
acknowledgment *n* 488, 529, 762, 772, 807, 985
acknowledgment of payment *n* 810
acme *n* 206, 210
acolyte *n* 541
acoustics *n* 402
acquaintance *n* 890
acquainted *adj* 888
acquainted with *adj* 490, 527
acquaint with *v* 527
acquiesce *v* 488, 602, 725, 762
acquiescence *n* 488, 725, 762
acquiescent *adj* 488, 535, 725

acquire *v* 539, 775, 785, 795
acquire a habit *v* 613
acquirement *n* 698
acquirements *n* 539
acquisition *n* 775
acquisition *n* 785, 795
acquisition of knowledge *n* 539
acquit *v* 750, 918, 927a, 937, 970
acquit oneself of *v* 807
acquittal *n* 970
acquittal *n* 750, 937
acquittance *n* 772
acquitted *adj* 937, 970
acreage *n* 342, 780
acres *n* 342
acrid *adj* 392, 395, 397
acridity *n* 392, 397
acridness *n* 395
act *n* 680, 697, 741; *v* 170, 599, 680, 692
act a part *v* 599, 644, 855
act in concert *v* 709
acting *n* 599
action *n* 680
action *n* 264, 682, 686, 692, 969
actions *n* 692
activate *v* 175
active *adj* 171, 359, 682
activity *n* 682
activity *n* 171, 264, 686
actor *n* 599, 680, 690
actress *n* 599
actual *adj* 1, 118, 494
actuality *n* 1
actually *adv* 1
act up to *v* 772
acumen *n* 498
acute *adj* 171, 173, 253, 375, 410, 410
acute angle *n* 244
acutely *adv* 31
acuteness *n* 173, 253

adage *n* 496
adamant *adj* 600
adamantine *adj* 323
adapt *v* 23, 852
adaptability *n* 149
adaptable *adj* 82, 149
adapt to *v* 82
add *v* 37, 85
addendum *n* 37, 39
addiction *n* 613
addictive *adj* 613
addition *n* 37
addition *n* 35, 39
additional *adj* 35, 37, 39
addle-brained *adj* 499
address *n* 189, 582, 586; *v* 582, 586
add to *v* 35
add up *v* 37, 85
add up to *v* 50
add water *v* 337
adept *adj* 698
adequacy *n* 639
adequate *adj* 157, 639
adhere *v* 46, 199
adherence *n* 46, 983a
adhere to *v* 613, 772
adhering *adj* 46
adhesion *n* 46, 772
adhesive *adj* 46, 327, 352
adhesiveness *n* 46, 352
adieu n 293
ad infinitum adv 104
adjacent *adj* 197
adjoin *v* 197, 199
adjoining *adj* 197
adjourn *v* 133
adjournment *n* 133
adjudge *v* 967
adjudicator *n* 737, 967
adjunct *n* 39
adjunct *n* 37, 88
adjust *v* 23, 27, 58, 774, 852
adjustable *adj* 149
adjustment *n* 723, 774

administer *n* 965; *v* 692, 693, 737, 786, 965
administer correction *v* 972
administering *adj* 693
administration *n* 692, 693
administrative *adj* 692, 737, 965
admirable *adj* 928
admiration *n* 870, 928, 931
admire *v* 870, 928, 931
admirer *n* 897
admission *n* 76, 296, 785, 985
admit *v* 54, 76, 296, 488, 529, 785
admit of *v* 470
admittance *n* 296
admitting *adj* 469
admixture *n* 41
admonish *v* 668, 695, 864, 932
admonition *v* 668, 695, 864
admonitory *adj* 695
ado *n* 315, 684
adolescence *n* 131
adolescent *adj* 131
adorable *adj* 897, 977
adoration *n* 897, 990
adore *v* 897, 928, 990
adorer *n* 897
adoring *adj* 897, 990, 991
adorn *v* 847
adornment *n* 847
adrift *adj* 10, 44, 73; *adv* 44
adroit *adj* 698
adroitness *n* 698, 702
adulate *v* 897, 928, 990
adulation *n* 933
adulator *n* 935
adulatory *adj* 933
adult *adj* 131

adulterate *v* 41, 659
adulterated *adj* 337, 961
adulteration *n* 41, 659, 961
adulthood *n* 131
adumbrate *v* 422
adumbration *n* 421
advance *n* 282, 286, 731, 787; *v* 35, 109, 282, 307, 514, 658, 731, 763, 787
advanced *adj* 128, 282
advanced age *n* 128
advanced guard *n* 234
advancement *n* 282, 658
advancing *adj* 282
advantage *n* 33, 618; *v* 618
advantageous *adj* 618, 644, 646, 648, 775, 888
advent *n* 121, 286, 292
adventitious *adj* 6, 8, 156
adventure *n* 151, 622, 675; *v* 665, 675
adventurer *n* 463, 548, 621
adventuress *n* 548
adventurous *adj* 675, 861
adversary *n* 708, 710, 726, 891
adverse *adj* 708, 735
adversely *adv* 735
adversity *n* 735
adversity *n* 619, 830
advertise *v* 531
advertisement *n* 531
advice *n* 695
advice *n* 527, 668, 693, 864
advisability *n* 646
advisable *adj* 646
advise *v* 527, 693, 695, 864
advised *adj* 527, 620

advisedly *adv* 611, 620
adviser *n* 540, 694, 695
advisory *adj* 668, 695
advisory board *n* 696
advocacy *n* 707
advocate *n* 890, 968; *v* 695, 707
aerate *v* 338
aerial *adj* 267, 338
aeriform *adj* 338
aeronautical *n* 267
aeronautics *n* 267
aesthetic *adj* 845
afar *adj* 196; *adv* 196
affability *n* 894
affable *adj* 894
affair *n* 151, 454, 625, 680
affairs *n* 151
affect *v* 9, 175, 176, 824, 855
affectation *n* 855
affectation *n* 579
affected *adj* 579, 820, 821, 855, 914
affectedness *n* 855
affection *n* 888, 897, 928
affectionate *adj* 888, 897
affections *n* 820
affidavit *n* 467, 535, 969
affiliated *adj* 9, 11
affiliation *n* 11
affinity *n* 9, 17, 216, 288
affirm *v* 516, 535
affirmation *n* 535
affirmative *adj* 535
affirming *adj* 535
affix *n* 39; *v* 37, 43
afflict *v* 828
affliction *n* 735, 828, 830, 975
affluence *n* 734, 803
affluent *adj* 803
afford *v* 784

afford pleasure *v* 829
affront *n* 830; *v* 830
afire *adj* 382
aflame *adj* 382
afloat *adj* 1, 267
aforementioned *adj* 116
aforethought *adj* 611
afraid *adj* 860, 862
afresh *adv* 104, 123
aft *adv* 235
after *adj* 117; *adv* 63, 117, 235, 281
aftermath *n* 65
afternoon *n* 126
afterpiece *n* 65
aftertaste *n* 390
after the flood *adv* 59
after this fashion *adv* 627
afterthought *n* 65
afterwards *adv* 117
again *adv* 104
again and again *adv* 104
against *adv* 708; *prep* 179
against one's will *adv* 603
against the grain *adv* 256
age *n* 128
age *n* 106, 108, 124; *v* 124, 435
aged *adj* 124, 128, 130
agency *n* 170
agency *n* 632, 677, 755
agent *n* 690
agent *n* 153, 758
agglomerate *n* 46
aggrandize *v* 35, 194
aggrandizement *n* 35, 37, 194
aggravate *n* 173, 835
aggravation *n* 835
aggregate *n* 50, 72; *v* 50
aggregation *n* 46, 72
aggression *n* 716
aggressive *adj* 716

aggressiveness *n* 715
aggressor *n* 716
aggrieve *v* 649
aghast *adj* 509, 860, 870
agile *adj* 274
agitate *v* 315, 824
agitated *adj* 149, 315
agitation *n* 315
agitation *n* 59, 149, 171, 173, 824, 825
aglow *adj* 420
agnostic *adj* 989
agnosticism *n* 989
ago *adv* 122
agog *adj* 870
agonize *v* 378
agonizing *adj* 982
agony *n* 378, 825, 828, 982
agrarian *adj* 371
agree *v* 23, 82, 178, 488, 714, 725, 762, 768, 769
agreeable *adj* 23, 82, 377, 413, 762, 829, 831
agreeableness *n* 829
agreed *adj* 488
agreed upon *adj* 474
agreeing *adj* 23, 413, 488, 494
agreement *n* 23
agreement *n* 16, 17, 82, 178, 242, 488, 602, 709, 714, 762, 769
agree to *v* 760
agree with *v* 656, 829
agricultural *adj* 371
agriculture *n* 371
agrobiology *n* 371
agrology *n* 371
agronomics *n* 371
agronomy *n* 371
ahead *adv* 234, 280, 282, 303
aid *n* 707
aid *n* 631, 644, 711,

834; *v* 215, 631, 644, 707, 746, 834, 906
aiding *adj* 707
ail *v* 655
ailing *adj* 655
ailment *n* 655
aim *n* 278, 453, 516, 620; *v* 278, 516
aim at *v* 278, 620, 622
aim for *v* 620
air *n* 338
air *n* 349, 415, 448, 852; *v* 338
aircraft *n* 273
airing *n* 266
airman *n* 269
air-pipe *n* 351
airplane *n* 273
airs *n* 855
airtight *adj* 261
air travel *n* 267
airy *adj* 4, 320, 334, 338
ait *n* 346
ajar *adj* 260
akimbo *adj* 244
akin *adj* 11
akin to *adj* 17
alacrity *n* 132, 274, 602, 684
à la mode *adj* 852
alarm *n* 669
alarm *n* 550, 665, 668, 860; *v* 669
alarm bell *n* 669
alarmed *adj* 860
alarum *n* 669
albeit *adv* 30
albification *n* 430
albinism *n* 430
albinistic *adj* 430
album *n* 596
alchemy *n* 144
alcoholic *n* 959
alcoholism *n* 954, 959
Alcoran *n* 986
alert *adj* 457, 498, 682, 864

alertness *n* 457, 459
algebra *n* 85
algebraic *adj* 85
alias *n* 565
alien *adj* 10, 57
alienated *adj* 889
alight *v* 265, 292, 306, 342
aligned *adj* 216
alignment *n* 278
alike *adj* 17
alive *adj* 359, 375, 457, 505, 682
alive and kicking *adj* 359
all *adv* 50
allay *v* 834
all but *adv* 32
all day long *adv* 110
allegation *n* 617
allege *v* 617
alleged *adj* 617
allegiance *n* 743
all-embracing *adj* 76
all-encompassing *adj* 78
alleviate *v* 174, 834
alleviation *n* 834
all for the better *adj* 658
alliance *n* 9, 11, 178, 709, 712, 714, 903
allied *adj* 9, 11, 216
allied to *adj* 17
allied with *adj* 178
all-important *adj* 642
all in all *adv* 50
all-inclusive *adj* 78
all manner of kinds *adj* 81
allocation *n* 786
allocution *n* 586
all of a sudden *adv* 113
all one *adj* 27
allot *v* 51, 60, 786
allotment *n* 60, 786
all over *adv* 180
allow *v* 469, 488, 529,

737, 740, 748, 760, 762, 784, 813

allowable *adj* 760

allowance *n* 469, 488, 760, 784, 786, 813

allowed *adj* 924

allow for *v* 469

alloy *n* 41, 48

all-purpose *adj* 148

all ready *adj* 673

all set for *adj* 507

all the livelong day *adv* 110

all the rage *adj* 852

all the time *adv* 106

all the worse for wear *adj* 659

allude to *v* 516, 527

allure *v* 288, 829

alluring *adj* 288

allusive *adj* 521, 526

alluvial *adj* 342

ally *n* 711, 890; *v* 174

almanac *n* 114

almighty *adj* 157, 976

almighty dollar *n* 800

almost *adv* 32

alms *n* 784

almsgiving *n* 784

aloft *n* 267

alone *adj* 87

alongside *adv* 236

a long way off *adv* 196

a long while back *adv* 122

along with *adv* 37, 88

aloud *adv* 404

alphabet *n* 561

alphabetical *adj* 561

already *adv* 116, 122

also *adv* 37

alter *v* 15, 140

alteration *n* 20a, 140

altercation *n* 713, 720

altered *adj* 15, 20a

alter ego *n* 17

alternate *n* 534, 759; *v* 12, 20a, 70, 138,

147, 149 *adj* 12, 70, 138

alternately *adv* 138

alternation *n* 138, 145, 149, 314

alternative *n* 147, 609

alter one's course *v* 279

although *adv* 30, 179

altitude *n* 206

altogether *adv* 50, 52

altruism *n* 906

altruist *n* 906

altruistic *adj* 906, 910

always *adv* 16, 112

amalgam *n* 41, 48

amalgamate *v* 41, 48

amalgamation *n* 41, 48

amass *v* 50, 72, 636

amateur *n* 701

amaze *v* 870

amazed *adj* 870

amazement *n* 870

amazing *adj* 870

amazingly *adv* 31

amber *n* 356a

ambergris *n* 356a

ambiguity *n* 475, 517, 519, 520, 571

ambiguous *adj* 475, 520

ambition *n* 620, 865

amble *v* 275

ambrosial *adj* 394

ambuscade *n* 530

ambush *n* 530

ambush *n* 667; *v* 530

ameliorate *v* 658, 723

amelioration *n* 658

amenable *adj* 762

amend *v* 658

amending *adj* 950

amendment *n* 658

amends *n* 30, 952, 973

amenity *n* 829

amiability *n* 829

amiable *adj* 721, 829, 888

amicable *adj* 707, 721, 892

amicably *adv* 888

amid *adv* 41, 228

amidst *adv* 41

amiss *adj* 923

amity *n* 714, 721, 888

ammunition *n* 727

amnesia *n* 506

amnesty *n* 723, 918

among *adv* 41, 228

amongst *adv* 41, 228

amorous *adj* 897

amorphism *n* 241

amorphous *adj* 241

amount *n* 25, 26, 800, 812

amount to *v* 50

amphitheater *n* 599, 728

ample *adj* 31, 180, 192, 202, 639

amplification *n* 194

amplify *v* 194, 549, 573

amplitude *n* 102, 192, 202

amplitudinous *adj* 192

amply *adv* 31, 639

amputate *v* 38

amputation *n* 38

amuse *v* 829, 840

amusement *n* 840

amuse oneself *v* 840

amusing *adj* 840

anachronism *n* 115

anachronism *n* 135

anachronistic *adj* 115

anagram *n* 561

analogous *adj* 12, 17, 216

analogy *n* 9, 17, 216

analysis *n* 49, 60, 463, 476, 596

analytic *adj* 85, 463, 596

analytical *adj* 476, 596

analyze *v* 49, 463, 476

analyzer *n* 463

anarchic *adj* 59
anarchism *n* 59
anarchy *n* 59
anatomic *adj* 329
anatomical *adj* 329
anatomy *n* 329, 357, 368
ancestral *adj* 166
ancestry *n* 122, 166
anchor *n* 666
anchorage *n* 184
anchorite *n* 955
ancient *adj* 124
ancient times *n* 122
and *adv* 37
and everywhere *adv* 186
and so forth *adv* 37
anemic *adj* 430
anesthesia *n* 376
anesthetic *adj* 376
anesthetize *v* 376, 381
anew *adv* 104, 123
angel *n* 977
angel *n* 164, 897
angelic *adj* 977
anger *n* 824, 900; *v* 830
angle *n* 244; *v* 244
angry *adj* 382, 900
anguish *n* 378, 619, 828
angular *adj* 244
angularity *n* 244
anility *n* 128
animal *n* 366
animal *adj* 366
animalistic *adj* 364, 366
animality *n* 364
animal kingdom *n* 366
animal life *n* 357, 364
animal physiology *n* 368
animate *v* 382, 824, 836; *adj* 357
animated *adj* 171, 382, 515
animated nature *n* 357
animate matter *n* 357
animating *adj* 836

animation *n* 359, 515, 682, 824
animosity *n* 889, 898, 900
ankle-deep *adj* 209
annalist *n* 553
annal(s) *n* 114
annals *n* 551
annex *n* 39; *v* 37
annexation *n* 37, 43
annihilate *v* 2
annihilation *n* 2, 162
annotate *v* 522
annotator *n* 524
announce *v* 527, 531, 883
announcement *n* 527, 531, 985
annoy *v* 688, 830
annoyance *n* 649, 828, 830, 835
annul *v* 756
annulment *n* 756
anoint *v* 332
anointment *n* 332, 355
anomalous *adj* 59, 83
anomaly *n* 59, 83
anon *adv* 132
another *adj* 15
another time *n* 119
answer *n* 462
answer *n* 479, 522, 662; *v* 462, 746
answerable *adj* 177, 462
answerable for *adj* 806
answer for *v* 759
antagonism *n* 14, 24, 179, 708, 715, 867, 889
antagonist *n* 708, 710, 726, 891
antagonistic *adj* 14, 24, 179, 708, 715
antagonize *v* 14, 179
antecedence *n* 116
antecedence *n* 62

antecedent *n* 64, 116; *adj* 62, 116
antedate *v* 115, 116
antediluvian *adj* 124
antemeridian *n* 125
anterior *adj* 62, 116, 234
anteriority *n* 116
anthology *n* 596
anthracite *n* 388
anthropology *n* 368
anti *adj* 708
anticipate *v* 115, 121, 132, 451, 507, 510, 673, 858
anticipation *n* 121, 132, 451, 507, 510, 673, 858
anticipatory *adj* 132, 510
antidote *n* 662
antipathy *n* 14, 289, 867, 898
antipodal *adj* 237
antipodean *adj* 14
antipodes *n* 14
antiquarian *n* 553
antiquarianism *n* 124
antiquated *adj* 124
antique *adj* 124
antiquity *n* 122, 124
antisocial *adj* 911
antithesis *n* 14, 218, 237
antithetical *adj* 14, 237
antitoxin *n* 662
anxiety *n* 459, 860
anxious *adj* 860
any *adj* 25
apace *adv* 274
apart *adj* 44, 87; *adv* 44
apathetic *adj* 383, 456, 823, 866, 989
apathy *n* 823, 866, 989
ape *v* 19
aperture *n* 260
apex *n* 8, 67, 210

aphasia *n* 581, 583
aphorism *n* 496
aphoristic *adj* 496
apiece *adv* 79
aping *n* 19
apologist *n* 937
apostasy *n* 607, 984
apostate *n* 607
a posteriori *n* 476
apostrophe *n* 589
apostrophize *v* 589
apothegm *n* 496
apotheosize *v* 991
appal *v* 830
apparel *n* 225; *v* 225
apparent *adj* 446, 448, 525
apparently *adv* 448
apparition *n* 4, 443, 980
appeal *n* 411, 765
appear *v* 446, 448, 525
appearance *n* 448
appearance *n* 220, 240, 446, 569
appease *v* 174, 723, 826, 831
appellant *n* 924, 938
appellation *n* 564
append *v* 37
appendage *n* 39, 65
appendix *n* 39
appertain to *v* 9, 56
appetite *n* 865
appetizing *adj* 394
applaud *v* 836, 883
apple *adj* 435
apple of one's eye *n* 899
apple-polisher *n* 886, 935
appliance *n* 677
applicability *n* 644
applicable *adj* 644, 677
applicant *n* 767
application *n* 677, 765
apply *v* 677
appoint *v* 741, 755, 786
appointment *n* 755

apportion *v* 44, 51, 60, 73, 786
apportionment *n* 786
apportionment *n* 60, 73
apposite *adj* 23
apposition *n* 23, 199
appraisal *n* 812
appraise *v* 466, 480, 668, 812
appraisement *n* 466
appreciate *v* 394, 480, 850, 916, 931
appreciation *n* 465, 822, 916
appreciative *adj* 822, 916
apprehend *v* 490, 860
apprehension *n* 453, 490, 665, 789, 860
apprehensive *adj* 860
apprentice *n* 541
apprenticeship *n* 539
apprize *v* 527
apprized of *adj* 527
approach *n* 286
approach *n* 197, 569, 627, 632; *v* 121, 152, 286
approaching *adj* 286
approbate *v* 931
approbation *n* 931
approbation *n* 488, 928
appropriate *v* 775, 786, 788, 789, 791; *adj* 79, 134, 646, 850
appropriateness *n* 646
appropriating *n* 788
appropriation *n* 775, 789, 791
approval *n* 488, 762, 928, 931
approve *v* 535, 737, 931
approved *adj* 931, 983a
approximate *v* 17, 197; *adj* 17, 197, 286
approximation *n* 9, 17, 19, 286
apricot *adj* 439

a priori *n* 476
apt *adj* 23, 498, 698, 850
aptitude *n* 176, 498, 602, 698
aptness *n* 176, 698
aqua *n* 337
aquamarine *v* 435, 438
aquatics *n* 267
aqueduct *n* 350
aqueous *adj* 337
arable *adj* 371
arbiter *n* 724, 737, 967
arbitrariness *n* 739
arbitrary *adj* 83, 606, 608, 739, 964
arbitrate *v* 174, 724
arbitration *n* 724
arbitrator *n* 724, 967
arc *n* 245
arcade *n* 245
arced *adj* 245
arch *n* 245, 250; *v* 245; *adj* 31
archaic *adj* 124
archaism *n* 124
archangel *n* 977
arched *adj* 245, 250
archetype *n* 22
archipelago *n* 346
architect *n* 164
architecture *n* 161, 329
arch over *v* 245
arctic *adj* 383
ardency *n* 991
ardent *adj* 382, 865
ardor *n* 382, 574, 682, 821
arduous *adj* 704
area *n* 181
arena *n* 728
arenose *adj* 330
areola *n* 247
argue *v* 24, 467, 476, 720
arguer *n* 476
argument *n* 454, 476, 516, 713, 720, 969

argumentation *n* 476, 969

argumentative *adj* 476, 713

arguments *n* 476

argumentum ad hominem *n* 476

aria *n* 413

arid *adj* 169, 340

aridity *n* 340

arise *v* 151, 305

aristocracy *n* 875

aristocratic *adj* 875

arithmetic *n* 85

arithmetical *adj* 85

arithmetic operations *n* 85

arm *n* 343; *v* 157, 673, 727

armaments *n* 727

armistice *n* 723

armlet *n* 247

armor *n* 727

arms *n* 727

army *n* 72

aroma *n* 400

aromatic *adj* 400

around *adv* 227

arouse *v* 175, 382, 615, 824

arraign *v* 938, 969

arraignment *n* 938

arrange *v* 58, 60, 626, 673, 774

arranged *adj* 60

arrange in a series *v* 69

arrange in words *v* 566

arrangement *n* 60

arrangement *n* 58, 673, 723, 769

arrangement *n* 807

array *n* 58, 102; *v* 60, 225

arrest *v* 142

arrival *n* 292

arrive *v* 151, 265, 292, 342

arrogance *n* 878, 885

arrogant *adj* 739, 878, 885, 880

artery *n* 350

artful *adj* 702

artfulness *n* 702

art gallery *n* 556

article *n* 3, 316, 590, 595

article of faith *n* 537

articles *n* 770, 798

articles of faith *n* 983

articulate *v* 580, 582; *adj* 580

articulation *n* 43, 580

artifice *n* 545, 702

artificial *adj* 579, 855

artificial light *n* 423

artist *n* 559

artist *n* 416

artistic *adj* 845

artistically *adv* 698

artless *adj* 703, 946

artlessness *n* 703

artlessless *n* 946

as a consequence *adv* 154

as a matter of course *adv* 82

as a rule *adv* 613

ascend *v* 35, 305, 658

ascendancy *n* 33, 157, 175, 731

ascendant *adj* 305

ascending *adj* 217

ascension *n* 305

ascent *n* 305

ascent *n* 35, 217

ascertain *v* 480a

ascetic *n* 955; *adj* 955

asceticism *n* 955

as chance will have it *adv* 156

ascribe importance *v* 642

ascribe to *v* 155

ascription *n* 155

as good as one's word *adj* 772

ash *n* 388

ashen *adj* 429, 432

ashes *n* 362

ashore *adv* 342

ashy *adj* 429, 432

aside *n* 589

as if *adv* 17

as if it were *adv* 17

asinine *adj* 497, 499, 853

as it happens *adv* 151

as it were *adv* 17

ask *v* 461, 630, 765, 812, 865

askance *adv* 217

askew *adj* 217, 243; *adv* 217

ask for *v* 765

asleep *adj* 458

as low as one can go *adj* 649

as matters stand *adv* 8

aspect *n* 183, 220, 448

aspects *n* 5

asperity *n* 256

aspersion *n* 934

asphalt *n* 356a

asphyxiate *v* 361

aspirant *n* 767

aspiration *n* 858, 865

aspire at *v* 620

asquint *adj* 217

as regards *adv* 9

ass *n* 493

assail *v* 716

assailant *n* 716, 726

assailer *n* 726

assassin *n* 165, 361

assassination *n* 361

assault *n* 716; *v* 716

assaulter *n* 726

assay *n* 463; *v* 463

assemblage *n* 72

assemblage *n* 43, 102, 712

assemble *v* 50, 72, 72, 712

assembled *adj* 72

assembly *n* 43, 72, 696, 712, 997

assent *n* 488

assent *n* 23, 82, 178, 484, 602, 762; *v* 82, 488, 535, 602, 762

assenting *adj* 488, 831

assert *v* 535, 720

assertion *n* 535

assertive *adj* 535

assertiveness *n* 715

assess *v* 466, 812

assessment *n* 466, 480

assessor *n* 480

asset *n* 944

assets *n* 780, 800

asseverate *v* 535

assiduity *n* 682

assiduous *adj* 682

assiduousness *n* 682

assign *v* 60, 755, 783, 784, 786

assignment *n* 155, 755, 786

assign to *v* 155

assimilate *v* 16, 144

assimilation *n* 144

assist *v* 707, 746, 834, 906

assistance *n* 707, 834

assistant *n* 707, 711, 759

associate *n* 88, 711, 890; *v* 9, 41, 43, 72, 216

associated *adj* 9

associated with *adj* 88

associate with *v* 88

association *n* 9, 72, 88, 464, 709, 712, 903

assortment *n* 60, 72

assuage *v* 174, 723, 834

assuagement *n* 174, 834

assuaging *adj* 834

assume *v* 484, 510, 514, 789, 855, 871, 885

assumed *adj* 514

assumed name *n* 565

assumption *n* 514

assurance *n* 474, 484, 507, 768, 858

assure *v* 768, 771

assured *adj* 474, 484

asteroids *n* 318

as the saying goes *adv* 496

as the world goes *adv* 613

as they say *adv* 496

as things go *adv* 151, 613

astigmatic *adj* 443

astigmatism *n* 443

astonish *v* 508, 870

astonished *adj* 870

astonishing *adj* 870

astonishingly *adv* 31

astonishment *n* 508, 870

astound *v* 824, 870

astounding *adj* 870

astral *adj* 318

astray *adv* 279

astringent *adj* 195, 397

astronaut *n* 269

astute *adj* 498, 702

asunder *adj* 44; *adv* 44

as usual *adv* 613

as well as *adv* 37

asylum *n* 666

asymmetrical *adj* 241

asymmetry *n* 241, 243

at a different time *adv* 119

at a distance *adj* 196

at a glance *adv* 441

at all events *adv* 30

at all times *adv* 136

at a low ebb *adj* 308

at an angle *adv* 217

at any rate *adv* 30

at a snail's pace *adv* 275

at a standstill *adj* 265

at bottom *adv* 5

at cross purposes *adj* 713; *adv* 59, 708

at ease *adj* 827

at fault *adj* 927

at first sight *adv* 441, 448

at full gallop *adv* 274

at full speed *adv* 274

at half speed *adv* 275

at hand *adj* 152, 197

at heart *adv* 82

atheism *n* 989

atheist *n* 984, 989

atheistic *adj* 989

athletic *adj* 159

at intervals *adv* 70

at issue *adj* 708

at its height *adv* 33

at large *adj* 748

atlas *n* 86

at last *adv* 67, 133

at length *adv* 133, 200

atmosphere *n* 338

atmospheric *adj* 338

at no time *adv* 107

at odds *adj* 708

atoll *n* 346

atom *n* 32, 180a

atomization *n* 336

atomize *v* 336

atonal *adj* 410, 414

atonality *n* 410, 414

at once *adv* 132

atone *v* 30, 952

atone for *v* 462, 952

atonement *n* 952

atonement *n* 790, 950

at one's disposal *adj* 777

at one's fingertips *adv* 197

at one's leisure *adv* 133

at one with *adj* 178

atoning *adj* 950, 952

at present *adv* 118

at random *adv* 156

at regular intervals *adv* 58

at rest *adj* 265; *adv* 687

atrophy *n* 195, 659

at short notice *adv* 132
at sight *adv* 132
at some other time *adv* 119
at some time or other *adv* 119
attach *v* 37, 43, 969
attached *adj* 897
attach importance *v* 642
attachment *n* 37, 39, 43, 88, 897
attach too much importance to *v* 482
attack *n* 716
attacker *n* 716, 891
attain *v* 292, 775
attain an end *v* 731
attain majority *v* 131
attainment *n* 292, 539, 698, 775
attempt *n* 675, 686; *v* 675
attend *v* 186, 281, 418, 457, 746, 928
attendance *n* 186
attendant *n* 88; *adj* 88
attending *n* 418; *adj* 186, 928
attending to *n* 457
attend regularly *v* 136
attend to *v* 743
attention *n* 457
attention *n* 451, 459, 928
attentive *adj* 451, 457, 459
attentiveness *n* 457
attenuate *v* 195
attenuation *n* 195, 330
attest *v* 550
at that instant *adv* 119
at that time *adv* 119
at the eleventh hour *adv* 133
at the heels *adv* 235
at the least *adv* 32
at the present time *adv* 118

at the same time *adv* 30, 120
at the top of one's lungs *adv* 404
at the top of one's voice *adv* 404
at this moment *adv* 118
at this time *adv* 118
at times *adv* 136
attire *n* 225
attitude *n* 8, 183, 240
attitudinize *v* 855
attorney *n* 968
attorney-at-law *n* 968
attorney general *n* 968
attract *v* 288, 829
attract attention *v* 446
attracting *adj* 288
attraction *n* 288
attraction *n* 829
attractive *adj* 288, 615, 829, 845, 850
attractiveness *n* 288, 829, 845
attributable *adj* 155
attribute *n* 780
attributed *adj* 155
attribute to *v* 155
attribution *n* 155
attrition *n* 331
attunement *n* 413
at variance *adj* 24, 708, 713
at will *adv* 600
at work *adj* 170
auburn *adj* 433
auction *n* 796
audacious *adj* 861, 863, 885
audacity *n* 861, 863, 885
audibility *n* 402, 418
audible *adj* 402
audience *n* 444, 588
audition *n* 418
auditor *n* 418, 811
auditory *adj* 418
auger *n* 262

augment *v* 35, 37
augmentation *n* 35, 39, 194
augur *n* 513; *v* 511, 909
auguring *adj* 909
augury *n* 511, 512, 668
au naturel adj 226
aureate *adj* 435
aureole *n* 420
auricular *adj* 418
aurora *n* 420
auscultation *n* 418
auspices *n* 175, 693
auspicious *adj* 134, 734
austere *adj* 704, 739, 955
austerity *n* 739, 955
authentic *adj* 494
author *n* 153, 164, 590, 593, 976
authoritative *adj* 175, 737, 741, 983a
authority *n* 737
authority *n* 157, 175, 500, 527, 700, 745, 965
authorization *n* 737, 760
authorize *v* 157, 737, 755, 760
authorized *adj* 924, 963
author's copy *n* 590
authorship *n* 161, 590
autocracy *n* 739
autocratic *adj* 600, 739
automatic *adj* 601
automobile *n* 272
autonomous *adj* 748
autonomy *n* 748
autopsy *n* 363
autumn *n* 126
auxiliary *n* 711
auxiliary *adj* 37, 707
avail *n* 644, 677; *v* 644
available *adj* 260, 644, 673
avail oneself of *v* 677
avarice *n* 819

avaricious *adj* 819
avenge *v* 718, 919
avenger *n* 919
avenue *n* 302, 627
aver *v* 535
average *n* 29; *adj* 29,
    651, 736
average capacity *n* 736
averse *adj* 289, 603,
    867
averse from *adj* 898
averseness *n* 603
aversion *n* 289, 603,
    867, 898
Avesta *n* 986
aviate *v* 267
aviation *n* 267
aviational *adj* 267
aviator *n* 269
aviatrix *n* 269
avoid *v* 287, 623, 671
avoidance *n* 623
avoider *n* 623
avow *v* 488, 535
avowal *n* 529
await *v* 121, 152, 507
awake *v* 404, 824; *adj*
    457, 682
award *n* 784; *v* 784
aware *adj* 375, 822
awareness *n* 822
aware of *adj* 490
away *adj* 187, 196; *adv*
    196
awe *n* 860, 870
a wee bit *adv* 32
awe-inspiring *adj* 860
awesome *adj* 860, 870
awe-struck *adj* 870
awful *adj* 395, 403, 860
awhile *adv* 111
awkward *adj* 579, 699,
    704
awkwardness *n* 579,
    699
awl *n* 262
awning *n* 223, 424
awry *adj* 217, 243, 923

ax *v* 44
axiom *n* 496
axiomatic *adj* 496
axis *n* 153, 222

B

baa *v* 412
babble *v* 348, 584
babbler *n* 584
babe *n* 129
babe in arms *n* 129
baby *n* 129
baby blue *adj* 438
babyish *adj* 129
bachelor *n* 904
bachelorhood *n* 904
back *n* 235; *v* 707, 737;
    adj 235
back and forth *adv* 314
backbiter *n* 936
backbone *n* 5, 221,
    604a
back down *v* 283
backer *n* 164, 890
backfire *n* 277
backfiring *adj* 277
background *n* 196, 235
backlash *n* 145, 277
back out *v* 283
backside *n* 235
backsliding *n* 283, 661
backward *adj* 133, 603;
    adv 133
backwards *adv* 283
backwater *n* 283
bad *adj* 34, 397, 401,
    649, 653, 657, 663,
    923, 945
bad diction *n* 579
bad fairy *n* 980
badge *n* 747
badger *v* 830, 909
bad grammar *n* 568
bad likeness *n* 555
bad luck *n* 735
bad man *n* 949
bad manners *n* 895
bad name *n* 874

badness *n* 649
bad news *n* 830
bad odor *n* 401
bad omen *n* 649
bad smell *n* 401
bad straits *n* 804
bad taste *n* 851
bad tasting *adj* 395
bad-tempered *adj*
    901a, 945
bad timing *n* 135
bag *v* 789
bail *n* 771
bait *n* 784; *v* 288, 830
bake *v* 384
baker's dozen *n* 98
baking *adj* 382
balance *n* 27, 29, 40,
    150, 242, 800, 811; *v*
    27, 30, 811
balance accounts *v* 807
balanced *adj* 27, 150,
    242
balance out *v* 30, 179
bale *n* 190
baleful *adj* 649, 663
balk *v* 509
ball *n* 249
ballast *n* 30
balloon *n* 273
ball-shaped *adj* 249
balm *n* 356, 662
balustrade *n* 232
bamboozle *v* 545
ban *n* 761
banal *adj* 209
banality *n* 209, 843
bananas *adj* 503
band *n* 72, 247, 416,
    417, 712
bandage *n* 223, 263
banded *adj* 440
band together *v* 709,
    712
bandy *v* 148, 315
bandy words *v* 588
bane *n* 663
bane *n* 165, 649, 975

baneful *adj* 663

bang *n* 406; *v* 276

bang into *v* 276

banish *v* 55, 185, 297, 972

banished *adj* 893

banish from one's thoughts *v* 506

banishment *n* 185, 297, 893

bank *n* 217, 802

banker *n* 801

bankrupt *adj* 732

bankruptcy *v* 732, 808

banshee *n* 980

banter *n* 856; *v* 842, 856

baptize *v* 564

bar *n* 215, 346, 968; *v* 55, 261, 761

barb *n* 253; *v* 253

barbarism *n* 563, 579, 851

barbarous *adj* 241, 563, 579

barbed *adj* 253

bard *n* 597

bare *v* 226, 260; *adj* 226

barefaced *adj* 525

barely *adv* 32

barely audible *adj* 405

bareness *n* 226

bare possibility *n* 473

barf *v* 297

bargain *n* 769, 794, 795, 815; *v* 769, 794

barge *n* 271, 273

bark *n* 223; *v* 412

bar of justice *n* 966

barrel *n* 249

barrelhouse *n* 415

barren *adj* 158, 169

barrenness *n* 158, 169

barricade *n* 232

barrier *n* 232, 261

barrister *n* 968

barter *n* 794

barter *n* 148; *v* 148, 794, 796

base *n* 211

base *n* 208, 215; *v* 215; *adj* 34, 207, 211, 649, 846, 874, 876, 886, 930

based on *adj* 19, 211

baseless *adj* 2, 4

baseness *n* 862, 886

bashful *adj* 881

bashfulness *n* 881

basic *adj* 5, 42, 211

basics *n* 66

basin *n* 252, 343, 344

basis *n* 211, 215

bask in *v* 377

batch *n* 25, 72

bathetic *adj* 497

bathos *n* 497

batter *v* 162, 276

battered *adj* 659

battery *n* 716

battle *n* 680, 722; *v* 720, 722

battlefield *n* 728

battleground *n* 728

battler *n* 726

battle with words *v* 148

bauble *n* 643

bawdry *n* 961

bawdy *adj* 961

bawl *v* 411

bay *n* 343; *v* 412; *adj* 433

bayonet *n* 262; *v* 361

bayou *n* 343

bazaar *n* 799

be *v* 1

be absent *v* 187

be absurd *v* 497

beacon *n* 550

be active *v* 680, 682

be affected with *v* 655

be afraid of *v* 860

be agitated *v* 315

beak *n* 250

be alive *v* 359

be all ears *v* 418

beam *n* 420; *v* 420

be an example *v* 22

bear *v* 215, 270, 692, 826

bearable *adj* 651

bear a grudge *v* 900

bear a resemblance *v* 17

bearer *n* 271

bear fruit *v* 161

bear ill will *v* 907

bearing *n* 9, 278, 692

bearings *n* 183

bear in mind *v* 451, 505

bear no resemblance *v* 18

bear off *v* 279

be artless *v* 703

bear upon *v* 9

bear with *v* 740, 760

beast *n* 366

beastly *adj* 653

beast of burden *n* 271

beasts of the field *n* 366

beat *n* 104, 138, 314, 627; *v* 138, 276, 314, 315, 330, 406, 407

beat a retreat *v* 623

beat back *v* 289

beatific *adj* 829, 981

beatified *adj* 981

beat it out *v* 623

be at odds with *v* 889

be at peace *v* 721

be attendant on *v* 281

be attentive *v* 457

be at the mercy of *v* 749

beat time *v* 114

beat up *v* 352

be at work on *v* 625

beau *n* 897, 854

beau monde *n* 852

beauteous *adj* 845

beautified *adj* 577, 847

beautiful *adj* 242, 597, 829, 845, 977, 981

beautify *v* 845, 847

beauty *n* 845

beauty *n* 242, 829
be averse to *v* 867
be aware of *v* 450, 490
be beforehand *v* 132
be behind *v* 235
be beneficial *v* 648
be blind *v* 442
be blind to *v* 491
be blunt *v* 254
bebop *n* 415
be born *v* 359
be bound for *v* 278
be brittle *v* 328
be broad *v* 202
be called to the bar *v* 968
becalm *v* 265
be capricious *v* 608
be careful *v* 459
because *adv* 153, 155
be cautious *v* 864
be central *v* 222
be certain *v* 474
be cheap *v* 815
be cheek to cheek *v* 236
becloud *v* 421, 422
be cold *v* 383
become *v* 144, 926
become a habit *v* 613
become colorless *v* 429
become insane *v* 503
become large *v* 192
become little *v* 193
become old *v* 124
become small *v* 195
becoming *adj* 646, 850, 881
be composed of *v* 54
be concise *v* 572
be contiguous *v* 199
be contrary *v* 14
be converted into *v* 144
be courteous *v* 894
be cowardly *v* 862
be credulous *v* 486
be cunning *v* 702
be curious *v* 455
be curved *v* 245

bed *n* 204
be dark *v* 421
bedazzle *v* 420
be deaf *v* 419
be deceived *v* 547
be dejected *v* 837
be dense *v* 321
bedew *v* 339
be difficult *v* 704
be diffuse *v* 573
be dim *v* 422
be dimsighted *v* 443
be disappointed *v* 509
be discontented *v* 832
be discordant *v* 414, 713
be discourteous *v* 895
be dishonest *v* 940
be disinclined *v* 867
be disinterested *v* 942
be disrespectful *v* 929
be distant *v* 196
be distinguished *v* 873
bedlamite *n* 504
bed-ridden *adj* 655
be drunk *v* 959
bedtime *n* 126
be due to *v* 154
be dull *v* 843
be dumb *v* 581
be early *v* 132
be easy *v* 705
beehive *n* 691
be elastic *v* 325
bee line *n* 246
Beelzebub *n* 978
be enamored of *v* 897
be engaged in *v* 625
be entitled *v* 924
be equivocal *v* 520
be evasive *v* 528
be evident *v* 467
be expedient *v* 646
be expeditious *v* 134
be expensive *v* 814
be exterior *v* 220
be extraneous *v* 57
be faithful to *v* 772

befall *v* 151
be fashionable *v* 852
be fastidious *v* 868
be fated *v* 601
be fatigued *v* 688
be firm *v* 150
befit *v* 23, 646, 926
be fluid *v* 333
be fond of *v* 897
be foolish *v* 499
before *adj* 62; *adv* 62, 116, 234, 280
beforehand *adv* 116, 132
before long *adv* 132
before now *adv* 122
before one's eyes *adj* 446
be forgetful *v* 506
befoul *v* 653
be fragrant *v* 400
be free *v* 748
befriend *v* 888
be friendly *v* 888
beg *v* 765
be general *v* 78
beget *v* 161
beggar *n* 767
beggarly *adj* 643, 804
begin *v* 66, 676
begin at the beginning *v* 66
begin hostilities *v* 716
beginner *n* 541
beginning *n* 66
be gluttonous *v* 957
be gone *v* 449
be good *v* 648
be good for *v* 656
be grateful *v* 916
be great *v* 31
begrudge *v* 819, 921
begrudging *adj* 907, 921
beg the question *v* 277, 477
be guilty *v* 947
be habitual *v* 613

behalf *n* 618
be haphazard *v* 139
be hard on *v* 739
behave *v* 680, 692
behave well *v* 894
behavior *n* 680, 692
behead *v* 361
be healthy *v* 654
be heavy *v* 319
be held in high repute *v* 873
behemoth *n* 192
behest *n* 741
be hidden *v* 447
behind *adv* 63, 235, 281
behind closed doors *adv* 528
behind time *adv* 133
be hip *v* 490
behold *v* 441, 444
beholder *n* 444
beholding *adj* 916
be honorable *v* 939
behoove *v* 926
be horizontal *v* 213
be hot *v* 382
be identical *v* 13
beige *n* 433; *adj* 433
be ignorant *v* 491
be illegal *v* 964
be ill timed *v* 135
be imbecilic *v* 499
be impatient *v* 825
be impenitent *v* 951
be imperfect *v* 651
be impious *v* 988
be important *v* 642
be impossible *v* 471
be impotent *v* 158
be imprisoned *v* 754
be improbable *v* 473
be impure *v* 961
be inactive *v* 172, 265, 681, 683
be inarticulate *v* 583
be in a state *v* 7
be inattentive *v* 458

be incomplete *v* 53
be inconvenient *v* 647
be incredulous *v* 487
be in danger *v* 665
be indifferent *v* 866
be indiscriminate *v* 465a
be in error *v* 495
be inert *v* 172
be inexpedient *v* 647
be inferior *v* 34
be infinite *v* 104
be influential *v* 175
be infrequent *v* 137
be in front *v* 234
being *n* 1, 3, 359
be in health *v* 654
be inherent *v* 5
be in league with *v* 709
be in love with *v* 897
be innocent *v* 946
be inodorous *v* 399
be insane *v* 503
be insensible *v* 376
be insensitive *v* 823
be inside *v* 221
be insolent *v* 885
be instantaneous *v* 113
be instrumental *v* 631
be insufficient *v* 640
be intelligent *v* 498
be intelligible *v* 518
be intemperate *v* 954
be interior *v* 221
be intrinsic *v* 5
be in trouble *v* 619
be inverted *v* 218
be invisible *v* 447
be in want *v* 640
be irascible *v* 901
be irregular *v* 139
be irreligious *v* 989
be irresolute *v* 605
be jealous *v* 920
be large *v* 192
be late *v* 133
belated *adj* 133
be latent *v* 526

be lax *v* 738
belch out *v* 297
be left *v* 40
be left over *v* 40
be lenient *v* 740
be liable *v* 177
be liberal *v* 816
belief *n* 484
belief *n* 451, 453, 537
believable *adj* 484, 515
believe *v* 451, 484, 514, 987
believed *adj* 484
believer *n* 987
believing *n* 484; *adj* 484, 486
be light *v* 320
be little *v* 193, 934
belittling *n* 934; *adj* 934
belles lettres *n* 560
bellicose *adj* 720, 722
bellied *adj* 250
belligerency *n* 720
belligerent *adj* 720, 722
belling *n* 412
bellow *v* 404, 411, 412
bellwether *n* 64
belly *n* 221
be located *v* 183
be long *v* 200
belonging *n* 777
belongings *n* 780
belonging to *adj* 9
belong to *v* 9, 56, 777
be loquacious *v* 584
be loud *v* 404
beloved *n* 897
be low *v* 207; *adv* 207
below par *adj* 651
belowstairs *adv* 207
belt *n* 247, 276
be made up of *v* 54
be master of *v* 698
bemoan *v* 833, 839
be modest *v* 881
be mute *v* 581
be narrow *v* 203

bench *n* 966
bend *n* 217, 244, 245; *v* 217, 244, 245, 278, 279, 311, 324, 325, 725, 744, 774
bend an ear *v* 418
bending *n* 245
bend over *v* 308
bend to *v* 176
be near *v* 197
beneath *adv* 207
benefactor *n* 912
beneficence *n* 648
beneficent *adj* 784
beneficent spirit *n* 977
beneficial *adj* 618, 644, 648, 677
beneficiary *n* 785
beneficient *adj* 816
benefit *n* 618, 677, 775; *v* 618, 644, 648, 906
be negligent *v* 460
be neutral *v* 609a
benevolence *n* 906
benevolence *n* 910
benevolent *adj* 888, 906, 906, 910
benign *adj* 656
be noble *v* 875
be no more *v* 360
bent *n* 176, 602, 613, 820; *adj* 244
bents *n* 5
bent upon *adj* 620
benumb *v* 376, 381, 385, 843
benumbed *adj* 381
be numerous *v* 102
be obligated *v* 601
be obliged *v* 601
be oblique *v* 217
be obstinate *v* 606
be occupied with *v* 625
be odorless *v* 399
be of help *v* 707
be of no help *v* 645
be old *v* 124
be one's fortune *v* 151

be one's lot *v* 151
be on the side *v* 236
be opaque *v* 426
be opportune *v* 134
be opposite *v* 237
be owing to *v* 154
be parsimonious *v* 819
be part of *v* 56
be penitent *v* 950
be perfect *v* 650
be pious *v* 987
be plain *v* 525
be pleased *v* 827
be pleased with *v* 827
be pleasurable *v* 829
be poor *v* 804
be possible *v* 470
be powerful *v* 157
be present *v* 186
be probable *v* 472
be prodigal *v* 818
be proud *v* 878
be pungent *v* 392
be pure *v* 960
bequeath *v* 784
bequest *n* 784
be rare *v* 137
be rash *v* 863
berate *v* 932, 972
bereft *adj* 776
be regular *v* 82
be related to *v* 11
be reluctant *v* 867
be remiss *v* 460
be resolute *v* 604
be rich *v* 803
be ridiculous *v* 853
be right *v* 922
be rumored *v* 532
be safe *v* 664
be salubrious *v* 656
be sane *v* 502
be savory *v* 394
beseech *v* 765
beseem *v* 926
be selfish *v* 943
be sensible *v* 375
be sensitive *v* 822

be sensitive to *v* 375
be servile *v* 886
beset *v* 716
be severe *v* 739
be sharp *v* 253
be short *v* 201
beside *adv* 83, 236
be side by side *v* 236
beside oneself *adj* 824
besides *adv* 37
beside the mark *adj* 10
besiege *v* 716
be silent *v* 403, 581, 585
be similar *v* 17
be situated *v* 183
be skillful *v* 698
be small *v* 32
besmear *v* 653
be sober *v* 958
be sociable *v* 892
be sorry for *v* 914
bespeak *v* 132, 467
be specific *v* 79
bespeckle *v* 440
best *adj* 648, 650
be still *v* 265, 403
bestow *v* 784, 995
bestowal *n* 784
be straight *v* 246
be straightforward *v* 576
be straight with *v* 543
bestride *v* 206
be subject *v* 749
be subsequent to *v* 117
be sufficient *v* 639
be suitable *v* 134
be sullen *v* 901a
be superior *v* 33
be surprised *v* 870
bet *v* 621
be taken *v* 360
be taken by surprise *v* 508
be tasteless *v* 391
be temperate *v* 953
be that as may *adv* 30
be the case *v* 494
be the dupe of *v* 547

be the effect of *v* 154
be the making of *v* 648
be the rage *v* 852
be thick *v* 202
be thin *v* 203
betimes *adv* 132
betoken *v* 550
be transient *v* 111
be transparent *v* 425
betray *v* 529, 545
be true *v* 494
be true for everyone *v* 78
better *v* 658; *adj* 648, 658
better half *n* 903
betterment *n* 658
better off *adj* 658
better than nothing *adj* 651
betting *n* 621
between *adv* 228
betwixt *adv* 228
betwixt and between *adv* 228
be unaccustomed *v* 614
be unaffected *v* 823
be uncertain *v* 475
be unclean *v* 653
be uncomfortable *v* 83
be unentitled *v* 925
be unequal *v* 28
be ungrateful *v* 917
be unhealthy *v* 657
be uniform *v* 16
be unimportant *v* 643
be unintelligible *v* 519
be universal *v* 78
be unlike *v* 18
be unnecessary *v* 57
be unpalatable *v* 395
be unprepared *v* 674
be unproductive *v* 169
be unsavory *v* 395
be unskillful *v* 699
be unwilling *v* 603
be useful *v* 644
be useless *v* 645
be vain *v* 880

beverage *n* 298
be vertical *v* 212
be violent *v* 173
be virtuous *v* 944
be visible *v* 446, 448
be vulgar *v* 851
bevy *n* 72
bewail *v* 833, 839
be weak *v* 160
be wealthy *v* 803
bewilder *v* 475, 519, 538, 870
bewildered *adj* 870
bewilderment *n* 870
be willing *v* 602
be wise *v* 498
bewitch *v* 829, 992
bewitched *adj* 992
bewitchery *n* 992
bewitching *adj* 897, 992
be without *v* 777a
be worthy of notice *v* 642
beyond *adv* 33
beyond all bounds *adv* 31
beyond all praise *adj* 650
beyond all reasonable expectation *adj* 473
beyond bounds *adv* 641
beyond compare *adj* 33; *adv* 31
beyond measure *adv* 31
beyond one's depth *adv* 208
beyond the bounds of reason *adj* 471
beyond the mark *adv* 303
Bhagavad Gita *n* 986
bias *n* 176, 820; *v* 175, 217
Bible *n* 986
bibliomaniac *n* 492
bibliophile *n* 593
bicker *v* 315, 713

bicycle *n* 272
bid *n* 763; *v* 600, 741
bidder *n* 767
bidding *n* 741
bide *v* 133, 141
bide one's time *v* 681
bid fair *v* 472
bier *n* 363
biformity *n* 89
bifurcate *v* 91, 244; *adj* 244
bifurcated *adj* 91
bifurcation *n* 91, 244
big *adj* 31, 192
bigot *n* 606
bigoted *n* 499
bigotry *n* 606
big words *n* 577
bike *n* 272
biker *n* 268
biking *n* 266
bill *n* 805, 811, 812
bill of sale *n* 771
billow *n* 348
billows *n* 341
billygoat *n* 373
binary *adj* 89
bind *v* 9, 43, 45, 770
binding *adj* 926
bind oneself *v* 768
bind together *v* 43
binoculars *n* 445
binomial *adj* 89
biographer *n* 553
biologist *n* 357
biology *n* 357
bipartite *adj* 91
bird *n* 366
bird's-eye view *n* 448
birds of a feather *n* 17
birth *n* 66
bisect *v* 91
bisected *adj* 91
bisection *n* 91
bisection *n* 68
bit *n* 32, 51, 390
bit by bit *adv* 26, 51, 275

bitch *n* 374, 962
bite *n* 392; *v* 298, 378, 385, 547
bite into *v* 298
biting *adj* 171, 392, 574
bitter *adj* 383, 392, 395, 397, 830, 898, 900
bitter cold *adj* 383
bitterly *adv* 31, 383
bitterness *n* 392, 900
bitumen *n* 356a
bituminous coal *n* 388
bivouac *v* 184
bizarre *adj* 83
black *v* 431; *adj* 421, 431
black and white *n* 429
black as coal *adj* 431
black as night *adj* 431
blackball *v* 55
blacken *v* 431, 934
blackguard *n* 941
blackness *n* 431
blackness *n* 421
blame *n* 716; *v* 716, 932, 938
blameless *adj* 946
blamelessness *n* 946
blameworthy *adj* 945
blaming *n* 938
blanch *v* 429, 430
blanched *adj* 430
bland *adj* 174, 391, 395
blandish *v* 902
blandishment *n* 902
blandness *n* 391, 395
blank *n* 2, 4; *adj* 2, 4
blanket *n* 223
blaspheme *v* 988
blasphemer *n* 988
blasphemy *n* 988
blast *n* 173, 349, 404, 406; *v* 349
blast furnace *n* 386
blatter *v* 412
blaze *n* 382, 420; *v* 382, 420

blazing *adj* 382, 420
blazon forth *v* 882
bleach *v* 429, 430
bleached *adj* 430
bleak *adj* 383
blear-eyed *adj* 443
bleary *adj* 422
bleat *v* 412
bleed *v* 378, 814
bleeding *n* 299
blemish *n* 848
blemish *n* 651, 945; *v* 659
blend *n* 48; *v* 41, 41, 48, 352, 413
blending *n* 48, 413
bless *v* 990
blessed *adj* 981
blessing *n* 618
blight *n* 659; *v* 659
blighted *adj* 659
blighted hope *n* 509
blimp *n* 273
blind *n* 424; *v* 442; *adj* 442, 601
blind adoration *n* 991
blindfold *adv* 442
blindly *adv* 442
blindness *n* 442
blindness *n* 491
blind to *adj* 458
blink *v* 443, 623
blinker *n* 530
bliss *n* 827
blissful *adj* 827, 981
blister *n* 250
blithe *adj* 836
bloated *adj* 194, 250
block *n* 192, 321, 752; *v* 706
blockade *n* 261; *v* 261
blockhead *n* 493, 501
block up *v* 261
blond *adj* 429, 435
blood *n* 11
blood red *adj* 434
blood relation *n* 11
bloodshed *n* 361

bloodthirsty *adj* 361
bloody *adj* 361, 434, 653
bloom *n* 654; *v* 161, 367, 654, 734
blooming *adj* 161, 434
blossom *v* 161, 367, 734
blot *n* 552, 848, 874, 945; *v* 431, 653, 874
blot out *v* 552
blotted out *adj* 552
blow *n* 276, 349, 508, 830; *v* 347, 349, 688
blow great guns *v* 349
blow hard *v* 349
blow hot and cold *v* 605
blown away *adj* 959
blow one's brains out *v* 361
blow one's chance *v* 135
blow out *v* 421
blow over *v* 122
blow-up *n* 173; *v* 173, 194, 349
blubber *n* 356
blue *n* 438
blue *adj* 438
blue and red *n* 437
blue and yellow *n* 435
blue-green *adj* 435
blueness *n* 438
blue sky *n* 338
bluff *adj* 173
bluish *adj* 438
blunder *n* 495, 497, 732; *v* 495, 699, 732
blunderer *n* 701
blunderhead *n* 701
blunt *v* 376, 616, 843; *adj* 172, 246, 254, 499, 703
bluntness *n* 254
bluntness *n* 703
blur *v* 422, 653
blurred *adj* 447
blurry *adj* 422, 447
blurt out *v* 529
blush *n* 434; *v* 434

blushing *adj* 434
bluster *v* 173
blusterer *n* 887
blusterer *n* 884
blustering *adj* 173
boar *n* 373
board *n* 204, 298, 696, 966
boarder *n* 188
board of directors *n* 696
boards *n* 728
boaster *n* 884, 887
boastful *adj* 884
boasting *n* 884
boasting *adj* 884
boat *n* 273
boating *n* 267
boat ride *n* 267
bob *v* 309, 315
bodiless *adj* 4, 317
bodiliness *n* 3
bodily *adj* 3, 316, 364
bodily pleasure *n* 377
body *n* 3, 50, 72, 202, 316, 362, 372, 712
body-guard *n* 753
body in *v* 316
body politic *n* 372
bog *n* 345
boggle *v* 699
boggy *adj* 345
bogus *adj* 544
bohemian *n* 268
boil *n* 250; *v* 173, 315, 336, 353, 382, 384
boiling *n* 336, 353; *adj* 824
boil over *v* 173, 825
boisterous *adj* 173, 404, 825
boisterousness *n* 173, 825
bold *adj* 525, 574, 604, 715, 861, 885
boldness *n* 574, 715, 885
bolster *v* 215, 707

bolt *v* 43, 261, 274, 298, 623, 957
bolt out of the blue *n* 508
bolt upright *adj* 212
bombard *v* 716
bombast *n* 517, 577
bombastic *adj* 497, 549, 577
bond *n* 9, 45, 771; *v* 45
bondage *n* 749
bonds *n* 802
bonehead *n* 493
bones *n* 362
bonus *n* 973
booby *n* 501
book *n* 593
book *n* 590, 811; *v* 539, 811
bookish *adj* 490
bookkeeper *n* 553, 811
booklet *n* 593
books *n* 811
bookseller *n* 593
bookworm *n* 492, 593
boom *n* 215, 404, 408; *v* 404
boomerang *n* 145, 277; *v* 277
booming *n* 408
boon *n* 618, 784
boorish *adj* 851, 876
boorishness *n* 823, 851
boot *n* 618; *v* 642
bootless *adj* 158, 645, 732
bootlicker *n* 886, 935
booty *n* 793
booze *v* 959
boozer *n* 959
bop *n* 415
border *n* 231, 232, 233; *v* 199, 231
bordering *adj* 197
border upon *v* 197
bore *n* 828, 830; *v* 260, 688, 841, 869
bored *adj* 456, 869
boredom *n* 688, 841

borer *n* 262
boring *adj* 275, 841, 843
borrow *v* 788
borrower *n* 806
borrowing *n* 788
borrow money *v* 788
bosom *n* 208
bosom buddy *n* 890
boss *n* 694, 745
bossed *adj* 250
botanic *adj* 367
botanical *adj* 369
botanic garden *n* 369
botanist *n* 357
botany *n* 369
botany *n* 357
botch *v* 699, 732
both *adj* 89
bother *n* 828, 830; *v* 704, 830
bottle *v* 670
bottom *n* 208, 211; *adj* 211
bottomless *adj* 208
bottomless pit *n* 208
bough *n* 51
bounce *n* 159
bound *n* 309; *v* 229, 233, 274, 309; *adj* 768, 926
boundary *n* 232, 233
boundary line *n* 233
bound for *adj* 278, 620
boundless *adj* 104, 180
boundlessness *n* 105
bounds *n* 233
bounteousness *n* 816
bountiful *adj* 816
bounty *n* 784, 816, 973
bourgeois *adj* 29
bourgeoisie *n* 876
bout *n* 138
bow *n* 245, 308; *v* 245, 308, 725, 744, 886, 990
bowed *adj* 245, 250

bowed instruments *n* 417

bowels *n* 221

boxcar *n* 272

boy *n* 129, 373

boyfriend *n* 897

boyhood *n* 127

boyish *adj* 129

brace *n* 89, 215; *v* 159, 215, 689

bracelet *n* 247

bracing *adj* 656

bracket *n* 45, 215; *v* 43, 89

brag *v* 884

braggadocio *n* 884

braggart *n* 884, 887

bragging *n* 884

braid *v* 219

brain *n* 450

brainchild *n* 453

brainless *adj* 499

brains *n* 450, 480, 498

brainstorm *n* 453

brake *v* 275

bramble *n* 663

branch *n* 51

branching *n* 291

branch off *v* 291

brand *v* 384

brand-new *adj* 123

branny *adj* 330

brass *adj* 439

brass band *n* 417

brass instruments *n* 417

brassy *adj* 885

bravado *n* 861, 884

brave *v* 715; *adj* 715, 861

bravery *n* 715, 861

brawl *v* 411

brawny *adj* 192

bray *v* 412

brazen *adj* 885

breach *n* 44, 198, 260, 713

breadth *n* 202

breadth *n* 202

break *n* 44, 53, 70, 106, 140, 142, 198, 621, 685, 720, 731; *v* 44, 51, 70, 328, 713, 773, 879

breakability *n* 328

breakable *adj* 328

break a habit *v* 614

break bread *v* 298

breakdown *n* 162, 732; *v* 304, 659

breaker *n* 348

breakers *n* 667

breakfast *v* 298

break ground *v* 66

break in *v* 294

breaking down *n* 49

breaking up *n* 162

break in upon *v* 70, 135

break of day *n* 125

break off *v* 142

break one's neck *v* 360

break out *v* 66

break the ground *v* 116

breakup *n* 67, 146; *v* 44, 73, 162, 659

breast *n* 250

breath *n* 359, 405

breathe *v* 1, 349, 359, 405

breathe new life into *v* 163

breathe one's last *v* 360

breather *n* 70; *n* 685

breathing space *n* 180

breathing spell *n* 685, 687

breathless *adj* 688, 870

breath of air *n* 338, 349

breath of life *n* 359

bred *adj* 370

breed *n* 75, 167; *v* 161, 370

breeding *n* 370, 852

breeze *n* 338, 349

breezy *adj* 338, 349

brethren *n* 997

brevity *n* 201, 572

brewing *adj* 152

briar *n* 663

bribe *n* 784

bridge *n* 45; *v* 45

bridge over *v* 43

bridle *v* 370, 751

brief *n* 596; *adj* 111, 201, 572

briefly *adv* 111, 572

brig *n* 273

brigantine *n* 273

bright *adj* 420, 428, 498, 734, 829, 836

brightness *n* 420, 829

brilliance *n* 845

brilliancy *n* 420

brilliant *adj* 416, 845

brim *n* 231

brimful *adj* 52

brimming *adj* 52

brindled *adj* 440

brine *n* 341; *v* 392

bring *v* 270

bring about *v* 153

bring an action against *v* 969

bring back to life *v* 163

bring forth *v* 161

bring in *v* 296, 810, 812

bring into *v* 144

bring into focus *v* 222

bring into play *v* 677

bring into relation with *v* 9

bring low *v* 308

bring out *v* 74, 591

bring round *v* 660

bring to a crisis *v* 604

bring to a focus *v* 74

bring to an end *v* 67

bring to a point *v* 74

bring to a standstill *v* 142

bring to bear upon *v* 170

bring together *v* 72

bring to life *v* 359

bring to light *v* 529

bring to mind *v* 505

bring to pass *v* 153
bring to perfection *v* 650
bring to trial *v* 969
bring up *v* 161, 235
bring up the rear *v* 235
brink *v* 231
brisk *adj* 111, 274, 682, 684
briskness *n* 682
bristle over *v* 900
bristling *adj* 253
bristly *adj* 256
brittle *adj* 328
brittleness *n* 328
broach *v* 153, 676
broach *adj* 78, 202
broadcast *adj* 73
broad daylight *n* 420
broadside *n* 236; *adv* 236
brochure *n* 593
broil *v* 382, 384
broke *adj* 804
broken *adj* 70
broken down *adj* 659
broker *n* 797
brood *n* 167
brood over *v* 837
brook *v* 826
brother *n* 27
brotherhood *n* 11, 17, 72
brotherly *adj* 888
brown *n* 433
brown *adj* 433
brownish *adj* 433
brownness *n* 433
brown-nose *v* 933
brown-noser *n* 886, 935
brown-nosing *n* 933
browse *v* 264
bruise *v* 649
brunette *adj* 433
brunt *n* 66
brush *v* 379
brush aside *v* 297
brushing *n* 379

brushwood *n* 388
brusque *adj* 173
brutal *adj* 173
brutality *n* 173
brute *n* 366
brute creation *n* 366
brute force *n* 739
brute instinct *n* 450a
brute matter *n* 316, 358
brutishness *n* 450a
bubble *n* 353
bubble *n* 353; *v* 315, 348, 353
bubbling *n* 353
bubbly *adj* 348, 353
buck *n* 309, 373
buckle *n* 243, 248; *v* 43, 243
buckle to *v* 686
bud *n* 66; *v* 161, 194, 300
budding *adj* 127
budge *v* 264
budget *n* 811
buff *v* 255
buffet *v* 276, 315
buffoon *n* 501, 844, 857
buggy *n* 272
build *n* 240; *v* 161, 235, 240
building *n* 161
built on *adj* 211
bulb *n* 249
bulbous *adj* 250
bulge *n* 250; *v* 250
bulk *n* 31, 50, 202
bulk containers *n* 191
bulky *adj* 192, 202
bull *n* 373, 477
bulletin *n* 592
bully *n* 887; *v* 739
bum *v* 266
bum around *v* 266
bumbling *n* 699
bumming around *n* 266
bump *n* 250, 276
bump against *v* 276
bunch *n* 250

bunchy *adj* 250
bungle *n* 495; *v* 699
bungler *n* 701
bungling *n* 699; *adj* 699
bunk *n* 477
buoyancy *n* 320
buoyant *adj* 320, 325, 836
burden *n* 190, 319, 828, 830, 926
burdensome *adj* 319, 649, 686, 706, 830
burglar *n* 792
burial *n* 363; *adj* 363
burial ground *n* 363
buried *adj* 208, 506
buried in *adj* 229
burlesque *n* 21, 856; *v* 856; *adj* 856
burn *v* 382, 384, 825
burnable *adj* 388
burn in *v* 384
burning *adj* 382, 434
burnish *v* 255
burnished *adj* 420
burnt *adj* 384
burn the midnight oil *v* 539
burp out *v* 297
burrow *v* 184
bursar *n* 801
burst *n* 113, 406; *v* 44, 173, 328
burst forth *v* 66, 194, 446
burst in *v* 294
burst out *v* 838
burst upon *v* 508
burst upon the view *v* 446
bury *v* 229, 363, 528
burying *n* 528
bury the hatchet *v* 723
bush *n* 367
bushy *adj* 256
business *n* 625
business *n* 454, 622, 682, 794, 926

business district *n* 799

businesslike *adj* 58, 625, 682, 692

bust *n* 557, 732

bustle *n* 171, 315, 682, 684; *v* 315, 682, 684

bustling *adj* 151

busy *adj* 151, 625, 682

busy as a bee *adj* 682

busy oneself in *v* 682

but *adv* 30

butcher *n* 361; *v* 361

butchery *n* 361

butt *n* 857; *v* 276

butt against *v* 276

butter *n* 356

butter-fingers *n* 701

butt in *v* 135

buttocks *n* 235

button *n* 250; *v* 43

button up *v* 261

buttress *n* 215

buy *n* 795; *v* 795

buy and sell *v* 794

buyer *n* 795

buying *n* 795

buzz *v* 409, 412

buzzing *n* 409

by *adv* 631

by accident *adv* 156

by and by *adv* 132

by an indirect course *adv* 629

by chance *adv* 156

by degrees *adv* 26

by design *adv* 620

by dint of *adv* 631; *prep* 157

by fits and starts *adv* 70, 139, 315

by force *adv* 159, 173, 744

bygone *adj* 122

by installments *adv* 51

by intuition *adv* 477

by means of *adv* 170, 631, 632

by no means *adv* 32

by rule *adv* 82

bystander *n* 444

by storm *adv* 173

by the agency of *adv* 631

by the by *adv* 10, 134

by the way *adv* 10, 134

by turns *adv* 138

by virtue of *prep* 157

C

cabal *n* 626

cabalistic *adj* 992

cabinet *n* 696

cackle *v* 412, 838

cacophonous *adj* 410, 414

cadaver *n* 362

cadaverous *adj* 362

cadence *n* 402

caesura *n* 70, 198

cage *n* 752; *v* 370

calamitous *adj* 735, 830

calamity *n* 619, 735, 975

calcination *n* 384

calculable *adj* 85

calculate *v* 85, 611, 620

calculation *n* 85, 507

calculus *n* 85

calefaction *n* 384

calendar *n* 86, 114

caliber *n* 26

call *v* 564, 995

call attention to *v* 550

call for *v* 630

calligraphy *n* 590

calling *n* 625

call it quits *v* 67, 624

callous *adj* 823

callousness *n* 823

callow *adj* 127

call to mind *v* 505

call up *v* 505

call up spirits *v* 992

calm *n* 174, 265, 721; *v* 174, 723; *adj* 174, 265, 403, 685, 721, 826, 953

calm down *v* 826

calmness *n* 174, 265, 721, 826, 953

caloric *n* 382

caloricity *n* 382

calorimeter *n* 389

calumnious *adj* 934

calumny *n* 934

camaraderie *n* 892

camouflage *v* 528

camouflaging *n* 528

can *v* 670

canal *n* 350

cancel *v* 536, 552, 756

cancelation *n* 552, 756

cancel out *v* 179

cancer *n* 663

candid *adj* 246, 543, 703

candidate *n* 726

candied *adj* 396

candle *n* 423

candor *n* 525, 543, 703

candy *v* 396

cane *n* 975

canker *n* 663; *v* 659

cankerworm *n* 165

canny *adj* 498, 702

canon *n* 697

canonicals *n* 999

canonize *v* 991

canopy *n* 223

cant *n* 988; *adj* 563

canticle *n* 413

cap *n* 261, 263; *v* 33, 206

capability *n* 157, 175, 698, 705

capable *adj* 157, 698

capacious *adj* 180, 192

capacity *n* 157, 159, 180, 192, 498, 625, 698

capacity for *n* 698

cape *n* 250

caper *n* 309; *v* 309

capillary *adj* 205

capital *n* 632, 800, 803;
  adj 210, 642, 648
capitulate *v* 725
capitulation *n* 725
caprice *n* 608
caprice *n* 615a
capricious *adj* 139,
  149, 475, 605, 608,
  615a
capriciously *adv* 139,
  615a
capriciousness *n* 139,
  149, 475
capsule *n* 273
captain *n* 269, 694
captious *adj* 608
captivate *v* 829
captive *n* 754
capture *n* 789; *v* 789
car *n* 272
caravan *n* 266
carbon *n* 21, 90, 388
carbonaceous *adj* 388
carbonization *n* 384
carcass *n* 362
cardinal points *n* 278
care *n* 459
care *n* 451, 457, 817,
  828, 830, 864
careen *v* 217
care for *v* 642, 664
careful *adj* 451, 457,
  459, 664, 817, 864
carefulness *n* 459
careless *adj* 460, 575,
  674, 738, 863, 927
carelessness *n* 460, 699,
  773, 863, 927
caress *n* 902; *v* 902
careworn *adj* 828
cargo *n* 190, 798
caricature *n* 21, 555; *v*
  19, 555
caricaturist *n* 559
carious *adj* 653
carmine *adj* 434
carnage *n* 361
carpe diem v 134, 682

carper *n* 936
carriage *n* 271, 272,
  448, 692
carrier *n* 271
carrion *n* 362
carry *v* 215, 270
carry on *v* 143, 680, 692
carry on a conversation
  v 588
carry out *v* 772
carry weight *v* 175, 642
cart *n* 272
cartoonist *n* 559
carve *v* 44, 240, 557,
  558, 786
carving *n* 557
cascade *n* 348
case *n* 7, 232, 476, 567,
  969; *v* 223
case in point *n* 82
cash *n* 800
cash box *n* 802
cashier *n* 801
cash register *n* 802
cast *n* 21, 75, 176, 240,
  428, 448, 550, 557; *v*
  73, 240, 284, 557,
  626; *adj* 820
cast a shadow *v* 424
cast a spell *v* 992
cast aspersions *v* 934
castaway *n* 893
cast down *v* 308
cast forth *v* 73
castigate *v* 972
castigated *adj* 972
castigation *n* 972
castigator *n* 936
castigatory *adj* 972
castles in the air *n* 515
cast light on *v* 522
cast light upon *v* 420
cast off *v* 297, 782; *adj*
  782
cast over *v* 353
casualty *n* 619
casuist *n* 476
casuistry *n* 477

cataclysm *n* 162
cataclysmic *adj* 619
catacomb *n* 363
catafalque *n* 363
catalog *n* 86; *v* 60
catalyst *n* 153
cataract *n* 442, 443
catastrophe *n* 619, 735
catastrophic *adj* 619,
  735
catch *n* 793; *v* 789
catch a bug *v* 655
catch a glimpse of *v* 441
catch fire *v* 384
catch on *v* 518
catch one's breath *v* 687
catch the lay of the land
  v 510
catch unawares *v* 508
category *n* 75
cater *v* 637, 746
catering *n* 637
caterwaul *v* 412
cathartic *n* 652
cathedral *n* 1000
catholic *adj* 78, 983a
catholicity *n* 78
cattle car *n* 272
caucus *n* 696
causal *adj* 153, 156
causality *n* 153
causation *n* 153, 170
cause *n* 153
cause *n* 66, 615, 969; *v*
  153, 161
caused by *adj* 154
cause sensation *v* 375
cauterization *n* 384
cauterize *v* 384
caution *n* 864
caution *n* 459, 487,
  668, 695; *v* 668, 695
cautionary *adj* 668
cautious *adj* 451, 459,
  487, 498, 664, 864
cavalcade *n* 266
cave *n* 189, 221, 252
cave in *n* 304

cavern *n* 252
cavernous *adj* 252
cavil *v* 477
cavity *n* 252
caw *v* 412
cease *v* 142, 265, 360, 732
ceaseless *adj* 112
ceaselessness *n* 112
cede *v* 624, 782
ceiling *n* 223
celebrant *n* 990
celebrate *v* 551, 883
celebrated *adj* 873, 883
celebration *n* 883
celebration *n* 733, 838, 990
celebrational *adj* 883, 990
celerity *n* 274, 684
celestial *adj* 318, 976, 981
celestial bliss *n* 981
celestial spaces *n* 318
celibacy *n* 904
celibate *n* 904; *adj* 904
cell *n* 189, 357, 752
cement *v* 46, 48, 323
cemetery *n* 363
cenobite *n* 893
censurable *adj* 945
censure *n* 716, 932; *v* 716, 932
census *n* 85
centenary *n* 98
center *n* 29, 68, 74, 221, 222; *v* 290
center of gravity *n* 222
center on *v* 74
central *adj* 68, 222
centrality *n* 222
centralization *n* 48, 222
centralize *v* 48, 222
centrally *adv* 222
central part *n* 208
centrifugal *adj* 291
century *n* 98, 108
ceramics *n* 557

cerebral *adj* 450
ceremonial *n* 883; *adj* 240, 998
ceremonious *adj* 240, 882
ceremony *n* 240, 883, 998
certain *adj* 79, 246, 474, 484
certainly *adv* 474
certainty *n* 474
certainty *n* 484
certificate *n* 771
certitude *n* 474
cessation *n* 142
cessation *n* 261, 265, 360, 687, 725
chafe *v* 378, 384, 832, 900
chaff *n* 643; *v* 856
chain *n* 69; *v* 43
chain of thought *n* 476
chaise *n* 272
chalk *n* 342
chalky *adj* 430
challenge *v* 715
challenge comparison *v* 648
chamber *n* 696
chamber group *n* 416
chamber music *n* 415
chamber orchestra *n* 416
champaign *n* 344
championship *n* 707
chance *n* 156, 621
chance *n* 152, 470, 615a; *v* 151, 156, 621; *adj* 475
chance it *v* 621
chanciness *n* 475
chancy *adj* 156, 475
change *n* 140
change *n* 20a, 144, 147, 800; *v* 15, 20a, 140, 146, 147, 605, 783
changeable *adj* 140, 144, 149, 475, 605

changeableness *n* 149
changeableness *n* 111, 140, 475, 605
changed *adj* 15, 20a, 140
change direction *v* 279
changeful *adj* 607
change hands *v* 783
changelessness *n* 150
change of mind *n* 485
change one's mind *v* 607
changeover *n* 144
change sides *v* 607
changing hands *n* 783
channel *n* 260, 302, 350, 627; *v* 259
chaos *n* 59, 162, 241
chaotic *adj* 59, 241
chap *n* 373
chapel *n* 1000
chapter *n* 696
character *n* 5, 7, 561, 569, 820
characteristic *n* 79, 550, 569, 780; *adj* 5, 15, 79, 550, 569
characterization *n* 594
characterize *v* 564, 594
characterized *adj* 820
charcoal *n* 388, 431
charge *n* 630, 695, 697, 716, 741, 755, 812, 938; *v* 52, 190, 695, 716, 741, 755, 812, 938, 938, 938
charging *n* 938
charitable *adj* 707, 784, 816, 906, 910
charity *n* 707, 784, 816, 906, 910
charm *n* 829, 992, 993; *v* 288, 615, 829, 992
charmed *adj* 992
charmer *n* 994
charming *n* 933; *adj* 992
charnel house *n* 363
chart *n* 183, 527, 626

charter *n* 755, 963; *v* 760

chary *adj* 817, 864

chase *v* 622

chase away *v* 289

chasm *n* 208, 260

chaste *adj* 242, 576, 578, 849, 881, 944, 960

chasten *v* 972

chasteness *n* 849

chastisement *n* 972

chastity *n* 881, 944, 960

chat *n* 588; *v* 588

chattels *n* 780

chatter *n* 584; *v* 584

chatterbox *n* 584

chatterer *n* 584

chattering *adj* 584

chatty *adj* 584, 588

cheap *adj* 435, 643, 815, 819, 943

cheapness *n* 815

cheat *n* 545, 548, 792; *v* 545, 923

check *n* 179, 616, 666, 706, 751; *v* 179, 233, 275, 468, 706, 708, 751

checked *adj* 440

checker *v* 440

checkered *adj* 440

checklist *n* 86

cheek *n* 236

cheek by jowl *adv* 236

cheer *n* 827, 829; *v* 411, 689, 829, 834, 836, 840

cheerful *adj* 827, 829

cheerfully *adv* 836

cheerfulness *n* 836

cheerfulness *n* 827, 829

cheering *adj* 836, 858

cheerless *adj* 828, 901a

cheery *adj* 829, 836, 836

chemistry *n* 144

cherish *v* 897

cherry-colored *adj* 434

cherub *n* 129, 977

cherubic *adj* 977

chest *n* 802

chestnut *adj* 433

chew *v* 298

chewing *n* 298

chew the fat *v* 588

chiaroscuro *n* 429

chicanery *n* 477, 702

chick *n* 129

chicken *n* 862; *adj* 862

chicken-hearted *adj* 862

chief *n* 694, 745

chiefly *adv* 31

child *n* 129, 167

childbirth *n* 163

child genius *n* 872

childhood *n* 127

childish *adj* 129, 486, 499, 575

childlike *adj* 499, 703

children *n* 167

child's play *n* 705

chill *v* 383, 385, 616; *adj* 383

chilled *adj* 385

chilliness *n* 383

chilly *adj* 383

chime *n* 408; *v* 407, 413

chimera *n* 515

chimerical *adj* 515

chimney *n* 351

chink *n* 198; *v* 408

chip *n* 32; *v* 44, 195

chip off the old block *n* 17, 167

chipper *adj* 654

chirography *n* 590

chirp *v* 412

chirrup *v* 412

chisel *v* 240, 557, 558

chiseling *n* 558

chit *n* 588

chit-chat *n* 588; *v* 588

chock-full *adj* 52

chocolate *adj* 433

choice *n* 609

choice *n* 600; *adj* 648

choice of words *n* 569

choir *n* 416

choke *v* 261, 361, 641

choleric *adj* 901

chomp *v* 298

choose *v* 609

choosing *n* 609

choosy *adj* 465

chop *v* 44

choppy seas *n* 348

chop up *v* 201

choral *adj* 415, 416

choral music *n* 415

chorus *n* 411, 416

christen *v* 564

Christian *adj* 983a

Christian Revelation *n* 985

chromatic *adj* 428

chronicle *n* 114; *v* 114, 551

chronicler *n* 553

chronicles *n* 551

chronological *adj* 114

chronological error *n* 115

chronology *n* 114

chronometer *n* 114

chronometry *n* 114

chubby *adj* 194

chuck *v* 284, 412

chuckle *v* 838

chug *v* 298

chum *n* 890

chummy *adj* 892

church *n* 995, 1000

churchdom *n* 995

churchman *n* 996

churl *n* 819

churlish *adj* 819

churlishness *n* 901a

churn *v* 315, 352

cilia *n* 205

cinder *n* 388

cinerary *adj* 363

cinnamon *adj* 433

cipher *n* 84, 550, 561
circle *n* 181, 247, 712;
  v 227, 247, 311
circle around *v* 312, 629
circling *n* 311; *adj* 248
circuit *n* 629
circuit *n* 181, 230, 247,
  279, 311; *v* 311
circuitous *adj* 279, 311,
  629
circuitously *adv* 279
circular *n* 592; *adj* 245,
  247, 249, 311
circularity *n* 247
circularity *n* 311
circular motion *n* 311
circulate *v* 531
circulation *n* 311, 312
circumference *n* 230
circumjacent *adj* 227
circumnavigate *v* 311
circumnavigation *n* 311
circumscribe *v* 76, 195,
  221, 229, 232, 233,
  751
circumscribed *adj* 229
circumscription *n* 229
circumscription *n* 751
circumspect *adj* 451,
  459, 864
circumspectful *adj* 457
circumspection *n* 459,
  864
circumstance *n* 8
circumstance *n* 151
circumstances *n* 7, 527
circumstantial *adj* 8
circumvention *n* 311
citation *n* 467
cite *v* 467, 969
citizen *n* 188
citizenry *n* 876
citrine *adj* 435
civic *adj* 372
civic minded *adj* 910
civil *adj* 852, 894, 928,
  997
civility *n* 457, 894

civilization *n* 372, 658
clack *v* 407, 412
clad *adj* 225
claim *n* 924
claim *n* 630, 741, 765;
  v 720, 741, 924
claimant *n* 767, 924
claiming *adj* 924
claim relationship with *v*
  11
clairvoyant *n* 513, 994
clamber *v* 305
clammy *adj* 352
clamor *n* 404, 411
clamor for *v* 765
clamorous *adj* 404,
  411, 765, 825
clamorousness *n* 404
clamp *v* 43
clan *n* 72, 75, 712
clandestine *adj* 528
clang *n* 404, 408; *v* 404
clangor *n* 404, 408
clank *v* 410
clannish *adj* 712
clap one's hands *v* 838
claque *n* 712
clarify *v* 74, 652, 849
clarity *n* 446, 518, 570,
  849
clash *n* 276, 713; *v* 24,
  179, 406, 713
clashing *n* 179, 410;
  adj 24, 410
clasp *v* 43, 46
class *n* 75
class *n* 51, 58
classic *adj* 242, 578
classical *adj* 242, 578
classical music *n* 415
classicist *n* 578
classics *n* 560
classification *n* 60
classify *v* 60
clatter *v* 407
clauses *n* 770
clay *n* 362

clean *v* 42, 652; *adj*
  652, 960
cleanliness *n* 652
cleanness *n* 652
cleanness *n* 960
clean out *v* 297
cleanse *v* 652
clean sweep *n* 146
clear *v* 705, 937, 970;
  adj 42, 413, 420,
  425, 446, 474, 518,
  525, 570, 807, 849
clearance *n* 807, 970
clear as day *adj* 518
clear-cut *adj* 518
cleared *adj* 970
clearheaded *adj* 502
clearheadedness *n* 502
clearness *n* 425, 446,
  518, 570, 580
clear out *v* 297, 652
clear-sighted *adj* 441
clear stage *n* 134
clear up *v* 518
cleave *v* 44, 46, 91, 259
cleft *n* 198, 260; *adj* 91
clemency *n* 740
clergy *n* 996
clergyman *n* 996
clerical *n* 996; *adj* 995,
  996
clerk *n* 553, 590
clever *adj* 498, 698,
  702, 842
cleverness *n* 698, 842
click *v* 406
client *n* 795
clientele *n* 795
cliff *n* 212, 306
climactic *adj* 8, 377
climate *n* 181, 338
climax *n* 8, 67, 210,
  377; *v* 210
climb *v* 305
climb upward *v* 305
clime *n* 181, 338
clinch *v* 43, 474
cling *v* 46

cling to *v* 602, 613
clink *v* 408, 410
clip back *v* 201
clique *n* 712
cliquish *adj* 712
cloak *n* 530; *v* 528
clock *n* 114
clockwork *n* 80
clod *n* 192
clogging *n* 261
close *n* 67, 729; *v* 67, 261, 729; *adj* 17, 43, 186, 197, 199, 203, 321, 528
close at hand *adj* 121
close by *adj* 152
close call *n* 671
closed *adj* 261
closely packed *adj* 72
close-mouthed *adj* 585
closeness *n* 186, 197, 203
close of the day *n* 126
close quarters *n* 197
close to *adv* 197
close upon *adv* 117, 197
close up shop *v* 142
closure *n* 261
clothe *v* 225
clothed *adj* 223, 225
clothes *n* 225
clothing *n* 223, 225
cloud *n* 353
cloud *n* 353, 424, 530; *v* 353, 421, 422
clouded *adj* 426
cloudiness *n* 353, 422, 426, 447
cloudless *adj* 420
cloud over *v* 422
cloudy *adj* 353, 421, 422, 424, 426
cloven *adj* 91
clown *n* 501, 701, 844
cloy *v* 376, 641, 869
cloying *adj* 396
club *n* 74

clubbish *adj* 892
cluck *v* 412
clue *n* 550
clump *n* 72, 250
clumsiness *n* 699
clumsy *adj* 699
cluster *n* 72; *v* 72
clutter *n* 407
coach *n* 272; *v* 537
coagulate *v* 321
coagulation *n* 321
coal *n* 388, 431
coal-black *adj* 431
coalesce *v* 13, 48
coalescence *n* 48
coalescent *adj* 13
coalition *n* 709
coarse *adj* 241, 256, 329, 410, 653, 674, 851
coarseness *n* 329, 851
coast *n* 231, 342; *v* 267
coat *n* 204; *v* 204, 224
coating *n* 223, 224, 332
cobalt *adj* 438
cock *n* 373
cockcrow *n* 125
cockeye *n* 443
cockeyed *adj* 443
cocksure *adj* 484
cocoa *adj* 433
code *n* 561, 697, 963
codger *n* 819
codify *v* 963
coequal *adj* 27
coerce *v* 739, 744
coercion *n* 739, 744
coercive *adj* 739, 744
coeval *adj* 120
coexist *v* 120, 199
coexistence *n* 88, 120
coexisting *adj* 120
coexist with *v* 88
coextension *n* 216
coextensive *adj* 216
coffee *adj* 433
coffer *n* 802
coffin *n* 363

cogency *n* 157
cogitate *v* 451
cogitation *n* 451
cognizant of *adj* 490
cohere *v* 46, 321
coherence *n* 46
coherence *n* 502, 518
coherent *adj* 321
cohesion *n* 46, 327
cohesive *adj* 46, 321, 327
cohesiveness *n* 46, 327
coil *n* 248, 311; *v* 245, 248
coiled *adj* 248
coin *v* 515
coincide *v* 13, 199
coincidence *n* 120
coincident *adj* 13, 120
coinciding *adj* 13
coin words *v* 563
coke *n* 388
cold *n* 383
cold *adj* 383, 866
cold-blooded *adj* 383, 823
cold-hearted *adj* 823
coldly *adv* 383
coldness *n* 383, 823
cold storage *n* 387
collaborate *v* 178
collaboration *n* 178
collaborative *adj* 178
collaborator *n* 711
collapse *n* 158, 195, 659; *v* 158, 195, 304
collar *n* 247
collate *v* 464
collateral *n* 771; *adj* 6, 216
collation *n* 464
colleague *n* 711
collect *v* 72, 596, 775
collected *adj* 826
collection *n* 72, 102, 596
collective *adj* 78, 778
collectively *adv* 50

collectivism *n* 778

college *n* 542

collegiate *adj* 542

collide with *v* 276

collision *n* 179, 276

colloquial *adj* 521, 560, 563

colloquialism *n* 521

colloquy *n* 588

collusion *n* 709

colonize *v* 184

color *n* 428

color *n* 434, 448, 654; *v* 428, 469, 549, 556

coloration *n* 428, 549

colorblind *adj* 443

color blindness *n* 443

colored *adj* 428

colorful *adj* 521

coloring *n* 428, 469, 549

colorless *adj* 429, 430

colorlessness *n* 429

colorlessness *n* 430

colossal *adj* 192, 206

Colosseum *n* 728

column *n* 69, 266

combat *n* 173, 680, 720, 722; *v* 708, 720, 722

combatant *n* 726

combating *n* 708

combative *adj* 173, 720, 722

combination *n* 48

combination *n* 41, 54, 709, 712

combine *v* 41, 48, 87, 178, 709

combined *adj* 48

combo *n* 416

combustible *n* 388; *adj* 384, 388

combustion *n* 384

come about *v* 151

come after *v* 63, 117

come ashore *v* 342

come before *v* 62, 116, 280

come between *v* 228

come close to *v* 197

comedian *n* 844

comedienne *n* 844

come-down *n* 509; *v* 306

come down with *v* 655

come first *v* 33, 62, 280

come forth *v* 446

come forward *v* 446

come from *v* 154

come in *v* 294

come in its turn *v* 138

come in sequence *v* 281

come into *v* 775, 785

come into play *v* 170

come into sight *v* 446

come into the world *v* 359

come into use *v* 613

come into view *v* 446

comeliness *n* 242, 845

comely *adj* 845

come near *v* 121

come of age *v* 131

come on *v* 121, 152

come on to *v* 544

come out of *v* 295

come out of nowhere *v* 508

come round *v* 151, 660

come round again *v* 138

come short *v* 732

come short of *v* 34, 304

come straight to the point *v* 576

come to *v* 50, 292, 359

come to a close *v* 67

come to an agreement *v* 774

come together *v* 72, 290

come to grief *v* 735

come to light *v* 525

come to nothing *v* 169, 304

come to pass *v* 151

come to rest *v* 184

come to the front *v* 234

come to the point *v* 79, 572, 703

come to the rescue *v* 672

comets *n* 318

come up short *v* 304

come up to *v* 27

come up with *v* 612

comfort *n* 377, 827, 831, 834; *v* 831, 834, 834, 906

comfortable *adj* 23, 377, 803, 827, 829, 831

comforting *adj* 834

comical *adj* 853

coming *n* 292; *adj* 121, 152

coming after *n* 63, 281

coming and going *n* 314

coming before *n* 62

coming beforehand *n* 280

coming together *n* 290

command *n* 741

command *n* 157, 630, 693, 697, 737; *v* 157, 206, 600, 693, 741, 777

commandant *n* 745

command a view of *v* 441

commandeer *v* 789

commander *n* 269, 745

commanding *adj* 642, 741

commandment *n* 741

command of language *n* 569

commemorate *v* 551, 883

commemoration *n* 883

commemorative *adj* 883

commence *v* 66

commencement *n* 66

commend *v* 883, 931

commend *v* 883, 931
commendable *adj* 618, 931
commendation *n* 931
commendatory *adj* 883, 931
commensurate *adj* 23, 639
comment *n* 476, 522; *v* 595
commentary *n* 522, 595
commentator *n* 480, 524, 595
comment upon *v* 522
commerce *n* 794, 796
commercial *adj* 794
commingle *v* 41
commiserate *v* 914
commiseration *n* 914
commission *n* 755
commission *n* 758; *v* 737, 755
commit *v* 680
commitment *n* 768
commit oneself *v* 768
commit sacrilege *v* 988
commit suicide *v* 361
committed *adj* 768
committee *n* 696, 758
commodity *n* 798
common *adj* 34, 78, 82, 613, 643, 778, 851, 876, 879
commonalty *n* 876
commonalty *n* 34
commoners *n* 876
common holding *n* 778
common law *n* 124
commonly *adv* 136
commonness *n* 34
commonplace *adj* 29, 34, 598, 613, 643, 736, 843
commonplaceness *n* 736
common run *n* 78
common sense *n* 450, 480, 498

commonsensical *adj* 450
commonweal *n* 372
commonwealth *n* 372
commotion *n* 315
communal *adj* 712, 778
communicant *n* 990
communicate *v* 527, 529, 582, 592
communicated *adj* 527
communication *n* 43, 527, 582, 592
communicative *adj* 527
communion *n* 778
communism *n* 778
communist *n* 778; *adj* 778
communistic *adj* 778
community *n* 188, 372, 712
community of possessions *n* 778
commutation *n* 147, 148
commute *v* 147, 148
compact *n* 769
compact *n* 202, 676; *v* 201; *adj* 43, 195, 201, 202, 321, 572
compactness *n* 195
compactual *adj* 769
companion *n* 890
companion piece *n* 237
companionship *n* 888, 892
company *n* 72, 88, 186, 712
comparable *adj* 464
comparative *adj* 26, 464
comparative anatomy *n* 368
comparative physiology *n* 368
comparative relation *n* 464
compare *v* 216, 464
compared with *adj* 464
comparison *n* 464

comparison *n* 9, 216
compartment *n* 51
compass *n* 26; *v* 227
compassion *n* 740, 910, 914
compassionate *adj* 740, 914
compatible *adj* 23, 413
compel *v* 157, 601, 744, 751
compelling *adj* 744
compendious *adj* 76, 201, 572, 596
compendium *n* 596
compendium *n* 195, 596
compensate *v* 30, 179, 790, 807, 973
compensating *adj* 30
compensation *n* 30
compensation *n* 774, 790, 952, 973
compensatory *adj* 30, 790, 973
compete *v* 720
competence *n* 157, 639, 698, 803
competency *n* 157
competent *adj* 157, 639, 698
competition *n* 708, 720
competitive *adj* 720
competitor *n* 710, 726, 767
compilation *n* 54, 72, 596
compile *v* 72, 596
complacency *n* 831
complacent *adj* 721, 831
complain *v* 411
complaint *n* 655, 839
complement *n* 39, 88, 237
complementary *adj* 12, 237
complementary color *n* 428
complete *v* 52, 67, 142,

292, 650, 729, 731, 769; *adj* 31, 50, 52

completely *adv* 31, 50, 52, 729

completeness *n* 52

completeness *n* 50

completion *n* 729

completion *n* 142, 261

complex *adj* 59, 482, 704

complexion *n* 7, 428, 448

compliance *n* 82, 602, 725, 743, 762, 772

compliant *adj* 82, 725, 743, 762, 772

complicate *v* 61

complicated *adj* 59, 248

complication *n* 59, 667

complications *n* 154

complicity *n* 709

compliment *n* 896

complimentary *adj* 896, 931

comply *v* 82, 602, 725, 743, 762

comply with *n* 772

component *n* 56

component *n* 51

component part *n* 56

comportment *n* 448

comport oneself *v* 680

compose *v* 54, 161, 174, 415, 569, 590, 591, 597, 826

composed *adj* 826

composite *n* 48; *adj* 41

composition *n* 54

composition *n* 48, 569, 590, 591

compositor *n* 591

composure *n* 174, 826

compound *n* 48, 232; *v* 41

comprehend *v* 54, 76, 490, 518

comprehensibility *n* 518

comprehensible *adj* 518

comprehension *n* 76, 490

comprehensive *adj* 56, 76, 78, 192

compress *v* 195, 201, 321, 572, 596

compressed *adj* 201

compressible *adj* 322

compression *n* 195, 572

comprise *v* 76

compromise *n* 774

compromise *n* 29, 30, 68, 628, 723; *v* 628, 774

compulsion *n* 744

compulsion *n* 601

compulsory *adj* 601, 744

compunction *n* 950

computable *adj* 85

computation *n* 85

compute *v* 85

comradeship *n* 888, 892

con *n* 754; *v* 545

concatenation *n* 43

concave *adj* 252

concavity *n* 252

concavity *n* 308

conceal *v* 223, 447, 519, 528

concealed *adj* 447, 528, 533

concealment *n* 528

concealment *n* 447, 526

concede *v* 529, 760

conceit *n* 515, 878, 880

conceited *adj* 878, 880

conceivable *adj* 470, 515

conceive *v* 66, 168, 484, 515

concentrate *v* 72, 222, 290, 686

concentric *adj* 222

concept *n* 451

conception *n* 451, 453, 515

conceptual *adj* 2

concern *n* 9, 625, 642, 860; *v* 9

concerned *adj* 459, 860

concerning *adv* 9

concert *n* 178, 709

concert artist *n* 416

concertize *v* 416

concession *n* 760, 774, 784

conciliatory *adj* 723

conciliate *v* 723, 831

conciliation *n* 714, 723, 831, 952

conciliatory *adj* 714

concise *adj* 201, 572

concisely *adv* 572

conciseness *n* 572

conciseness *n* 201

conclave *n* 72, 696

conclude *v* 67, 480, 604, 729

concluded *adj* 67

concluding *adj* 67

conclusion *n* 65, 67, 154, 480, 729

conclusive *adj* 67, 478, 480

conclusiveness *n* 478

concoct *v* 626

concomitance *n* 120

concomitant *n* 88; *adj* 88, 120

concomitants *n* 154

concord *n* 413, 714

concord *n* 23, 413, 488, 709, 721, 762, 888

concordance *n* 413

concordant *adj* 413, 714

concourse *n* 72, 290

concrete *adj* 3

concretion *n* 321

concupiscence *n* 961

concupiscent *adj* 961

concur *v* 120, 178, 290, 488, 709, 714, 762

concurrence *n* 178

concurrence *n* 23, 120, 290, 488, 709, 762

concurrent *adj* 120, 178, 290

concurrently *adv* 120

concurring *adj* 488

condemn *v* 971

condemnation *n* 971

condemnatory *adj* 932, 971

condemned *adj* 971

condensation *n* 195, 201, 321, 339, 596

condense *v* 195, 201, 321, 572, 596

condensed *adj* 201

condiment *n* 393

condition *n* 7, 8, 469, 514, 875; *v* 770

conditional *adj* 8, 469, 770

conditionally *adv* 8, 770

conditions *n* 770

condolence *n* 915

condolence *n* 914

condole with *v* 915

conduce *v* 176, 178

conduce to *v* 153

conducive *adj* 176

conduct *n* 692

conduct *n* 680, 693; *v* 270, 692, 693

conduct oneself *v* 680

conductor *n* 271

conduct to *v* 278

conduit *n* 350

conduit *n* 302

confabulate *v* 588

confabulation *n* 588

confederate *n* 711

confederation *n* 709, 903

confer *v* 695, 760, 784

conference *n* 588, 696

confer power *v* 157

confer with *v* 588

confess *v* 488, 529

confession *n* 529, 985

confessional *adj* 985

confidant *n* 890

confidence *n* 474, 484, 507, 533, 858

confidence man *n* 548

confident *adj* 474, 484, 858

confidential *adj* 221, 528

confidentially *adv* 528

confiding *adj* 484

configuration *n* 240

confine *n* 233; *v* 195, 229, 233, 751

confined *adj* 203, 229

confinement *n* 229, 751

confirm *v* 535, 769

confirmation *n* 467, 535, 762

confirmative *adj* 535

confirmatory *adj* 467

confiscate *v* 789, 974

confiscation *n* 789, 974

conflict *n* 24, 680, 713, 720; *v* 713

conflicting *adj* 14, 24, 179, 468

conflicting evidence *n* 468

conflict with *v* 179

confluence *n* 43, 290

confluent *adj* 290, 413

conflux *n* 72, 290

conform *v* 82

conformable to rule *adj* 82

conformity *n* 82

conformity *n* 16, 23, 80, 240, 613, 852

conform to *v* 16, 82

confound *v* 61, 465a, 475

confront *v* 234, 464, 708, 719

confuse *v* 41, 59, 61, 185, 465a, 475, 519, 538

confused *adj* 59, 447, 571

confusion *n* 59, 519, 571

confutable *adj* 479

confutation *n* 479

confutation *n* 536

confute *v* 479

congeal *v* 321, 385

congelation *n* 385

congenial *adj* 23, 413, 714, 829

congeniality *n* 829

congenital *adj* 5

congestion *n* 641

conglomerate *n* 72, 321

conglomeration *n* 41, 46, 72

congratulate *v* 896

congratulate oneself *v* 838

congratulations *n* 896

congratulatory *adj* 896

congregate *v* 72

congregation *n* 72, 990, 997

congress *n* 72, 290, 588

congruity *n* 23

congruous *adj* 23

conical *adj* 253

conjectural *adj* 514

conjecture *n* 514; *v* 514, 870

conjoin *v* 41, 45

conjoined *adj* 413

conjugation *n* 567

conjunction *n* 8, 43

conjuration *n* 992

conjure *v* 992

conjuror *n* 994

con man *n* 548

connect *v* 9, 43, 45, 216

connected *adj* 9, 11

connection *n* 9, 11, 43, 45, 46

connective *n* 45

connoisseur *n* 480, 700

connotation *adj* 516

connotative *n* 550
connote *v* 516
conquer *v* 731
conquest *n* 731
consanguineous *adj* 11
consanguinity *n* 11
conscience *n* 926
conscientious *adj* 246, 459
conscious *adj* 375
consciousness *v* 375, 821
conscription *n* 744
consecrate *v* 987, 995
consecutive *adj* 63, 69
consecutively *adv* 69
consecutiveness *n* 69
consensus *n* 762
consent *n* 762
consent *n* 23, 178, 488, 760; *v* 762
consenting *adj* 488
consequence *n* 62, 63, 65, 154, 642
consequent *adj* 63
consequential *adj* 642
consequently *adv* 154
conservation *n* 141, 670
conservative *adj* 670
conserve *v* 670
consider *v* 451, 461, 469, 480, 484, 873, 928
considerable *adj* 31, 192, 642
considerate *adj* 451
consideration *n* 451, 457, 469, 615, 642, 928
considering *adj* 928
consign *v* 270, 755, 783, 784
consignee *n* 758
consignment *n* 755, 784, 786
consign to oblivion *n* 506

consign to the grave *v* 363
consistency *n* 16, 23
consistent *adj* 16, 23, 413
consistent with *adv* 82
consist in *v* 1
consist of *v* 54
consolation *n* 834, 915
console *v* 834, 915
consolidate *n* 46, 48, 321
consolidation *n* 46, 321
consoling *adj* 834
consonance *n* 413
consonant *n* 561; *adj* 23, 413
consort *n* 903; *v* 41
consort with *v* 88, 892
conspicuous *adj* 446, 525
conspicuousness *n* 446
conspiracy *n* 626
conspiratorial *adj* 626
conspire *v* 178, 709
constancy *n* 16, 80, 112, 141, 150
constant *adj* 16, 69, 80, 110, 136, 138, 141, 150, 474, 604a
constant flow *n* 69
constantly *adv* 112, 136
constellations *n* 318
consternation *n* 860
constipation *n* 261
constituent *n* 51, 56
constitute *v* 54, 56, 161
constituting *adj* 54
constitution *n* 5, 7, 54, 329, 963
constitutional *n* 266; *adj* 963
constrain *v* 744, 751
constrained *adj* 751
constraining *adj* 744
constraint *n* 744, 749, 751
constrict *v* 195

construct *v* 161, 240
construction *n* 5, 161, 240, 329
constructions *n* 567
constructive *adj* 161
construe *v* 522
consult *v* 695
consume *v* 638, 677
consummate *v* 67, 729; *adj* 31, 52, 67, 650, 729
consummately *adv* 31
consummation *n* 67, 729
consumption *n* 162, 638, 677
contact *n* 199, 379
contact lens *n* 445
contain *v* 54, 76
container *n* 191
contaminate *v* 653, 659
contaminated *adj* 655, 961
contamination *n* 653, 659, 961
contemn *v* 930
contemplate *v* 441, 451, 620
contemplation *n* 441, 451, 620
contemplative *adj* 451
contemporaneous *adj* 120
contemporaneousness *n* 120
contemporary *adj* 120
contempt *n* 930
contemptible *adj* 435, 930
contemptuous *adj* 885, 930
contemptuousness *n* 885
contend *v* 476, 720, 722
contender *n* 726
content *n* 831
content *adj* 602, 826, 827

contented *adj* 831, 878
contention *n* 720
contention *n* 713, 969
contentious *adj* 713, 720, 722
contentment *n* 831
contents *n* 190
contents *n* 56, 221, 596
contest *n* 720
contestant *n* 726
contiguity *n* 199
contiguity *n* 197
contiguous *adj* 199
contiguousness *n* 199
continence *n* 953, 960
continent *n* 342; *adj* 960
continental *adj* 342
contingency *n* 151, 156, 470
contingent *adj* 8, 177
continual *adj* 136, 138
continually *adv* 136
continuance *n* 143
continuance *n* 110, 117, 200, 670
continuation *n* 63, 65, 143
continue *v* 1, 106, 110, 136, 143, 604a, 670
continuing *adj* 143
continuity *n* 69
continuity *n* 16, 58, 143, 150
continuous *adj* 69, 112, 143
continuously *adv* 69, 112
continuousness *n* 69
contort *v* 243, 248
contortion *n* 243
contour *n* 230, 448
contraband *adj* 964
contract *n* 676, 768, 769, 771; *v* 36, 195, 676, 769, 770
contract a disease *v* 655
contracted *adj* 195

contracting *adj* 195
contraction *n* 195
contraction *n* 36, 261
contractual *adj* 769
contradict *v* 14, 468, 489, 536, 708
contradiction *n* 14, 218, 536
contradictory *adj* 14, 468, 489, 536
contraposition *n* 218, 237
contrariety *n* 14
contrariety *n* 15, 179, 218
contrary *adj* 14, 179, 608, 708
contrast *n* 14, 15; *v* 15
contrasted *adj* 14
contrast with *v* 14
contravene *v* 14, 468, 536, 708
contribute *v* 153, 176, 178
contribution *n* 784
contributor *n* 912
contrite *adj* 833, 950
contrition *n* 833, 950
contrivance *n* 626
contrive *v* 161, 626, 702
control *n* 157, 175, 693, 737, 741, 751, 777, 965; *v* 157, 175, 693, 737, 777
controller *n* 694
controversy *n* 720
controvert *v* 536
contumacious *adj* 715, 742
contumancy *n* 742
contumely *n* 930
conundrum *n* 520
convalescent *adj* 660
convene *v* 72
convenience *n* 685
convenient *adj* 646
convention *n* 72, 80, 240

conventional *adj* 80, 82, 240, 246, 613, 852, 983a
conventionalism *n* 613
conventionality *n* 82, 613, 852
converge *v* 197, 290
convergence *n* 290
convergent *adj* 290
conversable *adj* 588
conversant *adj* 698
conversation *n* 588
conversation *n* 582
conversational *adj* 582, 588
converse *v* 582, 588; *adj* 14, 237
conversion *n* 144
conversion *n* 140, 218
convert *v* 140
convertibility *n* 13
convertible *adj* 144, 149
convert into *v* 144
convex *adj* 250
convexity *n* 250
convey *v* 270, 516, 783
conveyable *adj* 783
conveyance *n* 272
conveyor *n* 271
convict *n* 754; *v* 971
convicted *adj* 971
conviction *n* 451, 474, 484, 971
convinced *adj* 474, 484
convincing *adj* 478
convivial *adj* 892
conviviality *n* 892
convoluted *adj* 59, 248
convolution *n* 248
convolution *n* 59, 312
convoy *v* 88
convulse *v* 61, 173, 315, 378
convulsed with laughter *adj* 838
convulsion *n* 59, 146, 173, 315, 378

convulsive *adj* 173, 315, 378
coo *v* 412
cook *v* 384, 384
cool *v* 338, 385, 616; *adj* 174, 383, 826, 866, 953
cool down *v* 826
cooled *adj* 385
cooling *n* 385
coolness *n* 383, 826, 866, 953
cool one's heels *v* 681
coop *n* 752
cooperate *v* 178, 709, 712
cooperating *adj* 709
cooperation *n* 709
cooperation *n* 23, 178, 778
cooperative *adj* 178, 709
cooperatively *adv* 709
coordinate *v* 60
co-ownership *n* 778
co-partner *n* 778
copious *adj* 168, 573
copper *adj* 439
copula *n* 45
copy *n* 21
copy *n* 13, 19, 22, 90, 532, 556, 590, 591; *v* 19, 554, 590
copyeditor *n* 591
copying *n* 19
copyist *n* 590
cord *n* 247
cordial *adj* 377, 602, 829, 888, 892
cordiality *n* 602, 892
core *n* 5, 68, 208, 222
cork *n* 263; *v* 261
corkscrew *n* 248, 262, 311
cork up *v* 261
cormorant *n* 957
corner *n* 244
cornered *adj* 244

corny *adj* 496
corollary *n* 39
corona *n* 247
coronet *n* 247
corporal *adj* 3
corporality *n* 3, 364
corporate *adj* 43
corporeal *adj* 3, 316, 364
corporeality *n* 316
corpse *n* 362
corpselike *adj* 362
corpulence *n* 192
corpulent *adj* 192, 194
corral *n* 232
correct *v* 246, 658, 660, 662, 972; *adj* 246, 494, 578, 922, 922
correction *n* 658, 972
corrective *n* 662; *adj* 658, 662
correctness *n* 578
correlate *v* 12, 464
correlation *n* 12
correlation *n* 9, 464
correlative *adj* 12, 216
correspond *v* 12, 23, 592
correspondence *n* 592
correspondence *n* 12, 13, 17, 23, 216
correspondent *adj* 23
corresponding *adj* 12, 17, 216
correspond to *v* 216
corroboration *n* 467
corroborative *adj* 467, 535
corrode *v* 659
corrosion *n* 659
corrosive *adj* 649
corrugate *v* 258
corrugation *n* 256
corrupt *v* 653, 659; *adj* 653, 655, 945
corrupted *adj* 961
corruption *n* 49, 563, 653, 659

corse *n* 362
cortege *n* 266
coruscate *v* 420
coruscation *n* 420
cosmic *adj* 318
cosmonaut *n* 269
cosmopolitan *adj* 372
cost *n* 812
cost a lot *v* 814
costliness *n* 814
cost little *v* 815
costly *adj* 814
costs *n* 809
costume *n* 225
cote *n* 232
coterie *n* 712
cough *v* 349
could be *v* 470
council *n* 696
council *n* 72, 588, 695
counsel *n* 695, 864, 968; *v* 864
counselor *n* 540, 695, 968
counselor-at-law *n* 968
count *v* 85, 451
count among *v* 76
countenance *n* 448
counter *adj* 14
counteract *v* 30, 179, 662
counteracting *adj* 179
counteraction *n* 179
counteraction *n* 708
counteractive *n* 662
counterattack *n* 718; *v* 718
counterbalance *n* 27; *v* 30
counterblast *n* 179
counter-evidence *n* 468
counterfeit *n* 21; *v* 19, 544, 855; *adj* 19, 544
countering *adj* 237
counter maneuver *n* 179
counterpart *n* 17, 21, 237
counterpoint *n* 413

counterpoise *n* 30; *v* 30, 179
counterrevolution *n* 146
counterstroke *n* 718
counter to *adv* 708
countervail *v* 30
countervailing *adj* 468
countless *adv* 104
count on *v* 507
country *n* 181, 189
county *n* 181
coup *n* 146
coup de grace n 361
coup d'état n 146
couple *n* 89, 100; *v* 43, 89, 903
coupled *adj* 89
coupled with *adj* 88
couple with *v* 88
coupling *n* 43
courage *n* 861
courage *n* 715
courageous *adj* 715, 861
courageousness *n* 715
courier *n* 271, 534
course *n* 109
course *n* 58, 106, 264, 278, 348, 627
course of time *n* 109
coursing *n* 361
court *n* 696, 966; *v* 615, 933
courteous *adj* 457, 852, 879, 894, 928
courtesan *n* 962
courtesy *n* 894
courtesy *n* 457
courtier *n* 935
courtliness *n* 894
courtly *adj* 894
court of justice *n* 966
court of law *n* 966
courtroom *n* 966
cove *n* 343
covenant *n* 768, 769; *v* 768
covenants *n* 770

cover *n* 223, 263, 424, 530, 666; *v* 30, 204, 223, 224, 225, 424, 528, 664
covered *adj* 223
covering *n* 223
covering *n* 220, 225, 528
coverlet *n* 223
cover over *v* 223
covert *adj* 447, 528
covet *v* 865, 921
covetous *adj* 819, 865, 921
covetousness *n* 921
cow *n* 374; *v* 909
coward *n* 862
cowardice *n* 862
cowardice *n* 172, 605
cowardly *adj* 435, 605, 862
cower *v* 862, 886
coxcomb *n* 854
cozen *v* 545
crack *n* 44, 70, 113, 198, 259; *v* 44, 328, 406, 583, 659; *adj* 648, 698
cracked *adj* 410, 503
cracked bell *n* 408a
crackers *adj* 503
crackle *v* 406
crack of doom *n* 121
cradle *n* 66, 127
craft *n* 625, 698, 702
craftiness *n* 698, 702
craftsmanship *n* 161
crafty *adj* 702
craggy *adj* 253, 256
cram *v* 194, 539
crammed *adj* 52
cramp *n* 378; *v* 158, 160, 195, 706
cramped *adj* 579
cranny *n* 198
crapulence *n* 957
crapulent *adj* 957
crash *n* 276; *v* 406

crashpad *n* 189
crass *adj* 851
crater *n* 208, 252
crave *v* 865
craven *n* 862; *adj* 435, 862
craving *n* 276, 865; *adj* 865
crawl *v* 109, 275, 886
craze *n* 852
crazed *adj* 499, 503
craziness *n* 503
crazy *n* 504; *adj* 503
creak *v* 410
creaking *n* 410; *adj* 410
cream *n* 356, 648
creamy *adj* 352, 435
crease *n* 258; *v* 258
create *v* 153, 515
creation *n* 161, 318
creative *adj* 153, 161, 515
creativity *n* 168, 515
creator *n* 153, 164, 976
creature *n* 3, 366, 372
credence *n* 484
credible *adj* 470, 484
credit *n* 805
credit *n* 484, 873; *v* 484, 805, 811
creditable *adj* 878, 931
credo *n* 537, 983
credulity *n* 486
credulous *adj* 484, 486, 547
credulousness *n* 486
creed *n* 484, 537, 983
creep *v* 109, 275, 380
creeper *n* 367
creeping thing *n* 366
cremate *v* 363
cremation *n* 363, 384
crescent *n* 245; *adj* 245
crescent-shaped *adj* 245
cretin *n* 493, 501
crevice *n* 198

crew *n* 72, 269, 712
crick *n* 378
criminal *adj* 964
criminality *n* 947
crimson *adj* 434
cringe *v* 886
cringing *n* 886; *adj* 435, 886
crinkle *v* 256, 258
cripple *v* 158, 659
crippled *adj* 158
crisis *n* 8, 134, 151, 704, 735
crisp *adj* 328
criss-cross *v* 219
critic *n* 480, 524, 595, 936
critical *adj* 8, 465, 480, 642, 704, 716, 735
criticism *n* 480, 595, 716
criticize *v* 480, 595, 716, 850, 934
critique *n* 465, 480, 595
croak *v* 412, 583
croaking *adj* 410
crony *n* 890
crook *n* 244, 245, 792; *v* 217, 245, 279
crooked *adj* 217, 243, 244, 279, 923
crookedness *n* 243
croon *v* 416
crop *n* 154, 775; *v* 201
crop up *v* 151, 446
cross *n* 41; *v* 41, 179, 219, 302, 830; *adj* 41, 901a
crossed *adj* 219
cross-eye *n* 443
crosseyed *adj* 443
cross-fire *n* 148
crossing *n* 219
crossing *adj* 219
cross-purposes *n* 713
crossroad *n* 219
cross swords *v* 722
crotch *n* 244

crotchety *adj* 608
crouch *v* 207, 886
crouched *adj* 207
crow *v* 412, 838, 884
crowd *n* 72, 102, 444, 876; *v* 72, 102, 197
crowded *adj* 72, 102
crown *n* 247; *v* 210
crowning *adj* 33, 67
crowning point *n* 210
crowning touch *n* 729
crucial *adj* 642
crude *adj* 53, 579, 651, 674, 851, 895, 929
crudeness *n* 929
cruel *adj* 649, 739, 830, 914a
cruelly *adv* 31
cruelty *n* 914a
cruise *n* 267; *v* 267
cruiser *n* 273
crumb *n* 32, 330
crumble *v* 49, 160, 162, 328, 330, 659
crumbling *adj* 124, 659
crumbly *adj* 330
crumbs *n* 40
crumple *v* 256, 258
crumple up *v* 195
crunch *v* 298
crush *n* 72; *v* 162, 195, 330, 739, 879
crush out *v* 162
crust *n* 223
crustacean *n* 366
crutch *n* 215
cry *n* 411
cry *n* 669; *v* 411, 412, 839
cry for joy *v* 838
crying *n* 411, 412; *adj* 411, 630
cry out *v* 411, 669
cry out against *v* 616
crypt *n* 363
cryptic *adj* 526
crystalline *adj* 425

crystallization *n* 321, 323
crystallize *v* 321
cubbyhole *n* 530
cube *v* 93
cuckoo *v* 412
cue *n* 550
cull *v* 609, 789
culminate *v* 210
culmination *n* 65, 206, 210, 261, 729
culpability *n* 947
culpable *adj* 947
cultivate *v* 371, 375, 658
cultivated *adj* 850
cultivate one's own garden *v* 943
cultivation *n* 371, 578, 658, 850
culture *n* 850
cultured *adj* 850
culvert *n* 350
cumbersome *adj* 319, 706, 830
cumbrous *adj* 319
cunning *n* 702
cunning *n* 544, 698; *adj* 544, 545, 698
cup *n* 252
cupidity *n* 819
cupola *n* 250
cupped *adj* 252
curable *adj* 660
curative *adj* 660, 662, 834
curb *n* 179, 616, 751; *v* 174, 179, 275, 751
curd *n* 354
curdle *v* 397
curdled *adj* 397
cure *n* 660, 662; *v* 660, 662, 670
curfew *n* 126
curiosity *n* 455
curiosity *n* 872
curious *adj* 455, 461, 870

curiously *adv* 31

curl *n* 245, 248; *v* 245, 248, 258

currency *n* 800

current *n* 338, 348; *adj* 1, 78, 118, 151, 531, 532, 560, 613

curry *v* 331, 392

curry favor *v* 933

curse *n* 663, 830, 908; *v* 908

cursing *n* 908

cursory *adj* 209

curt *adj* 201, 739

curtail *v* 38

curtailed *adj* 201

curtailment *n* 38, 201

curtain *n* 424, 530; *v* 424

curtness *n* 739

curtsy *n* 308; *v* 308

curvature *n* 245

curve *n* 217, 245, 245; *v* 245, 279

curved *adj* 245

custodial *adj* 777

custodian *n* 664, 753

custody *n* 664, 777, 781

custom *n* 80, 124, 613, 852

customarily *adv* 136

customariness *n* 82

customary *adj* 80, 82, 124, 136, 613, 852, 983a

customer *n* 795

cut *n* 44, 70, 198, 240, 257, 259, 276, 378; *v* 44, 240, 257, 259, 361, 371, 385, 557

cut across *v* 302

cut adrift *v* 44, 297

cut a figure *v* 448

cut away *v* 38

cutback *n* 38; *v* 38, 201; *adj* 201

cut down *v* 195, 361

cut in two *v* 91

cut off *v* 38, 44, 361; *adj* 776

cut open *v* 260

cut out *v* 293

cut short *v* 142, 201

cutter *n* 273

cutthroat *n* 361

cutting *adj* 253, 383

cutting edge *n* 253

cuttings *n* 596

cut to pieces *v* 361

cut to ribbons *v* 361

cutup *n* 844; *v* 44

cycle *n* 138, 247

cyclic *adj* 138

cyclical *adj* 138

cyclically *adv* 138

cycling *n* 266

cyclist *n* 268

cyclone *n* 312, 315, 349

cyclonic *adj* 349

cylinder *n* 249

cylindrical *adj* 249

cylindricality *n* 249

cynic *n* 165, 936, 989

D

dab *n* 32, 276; *v* 276

dabble *v* 683

dad *n* 166

dado *n* 211

daft *adj* 503

daily *adv* 136

dainty *adj* 394, 829, 868

dale *n* 252

dalliance *n* 902

dally *v* 683, 902

damage *n* 619, 649, 659, 776, 812; *v* 649, 659, 848

damages *n* 974

damn *v* 908, 971

damnable *adj* 649

damnation *n* 908

damning *n* 908

damp *v* 339, 616; *adj* 339

dampen *v* 408a

dampened *adj* 408a

damper *n* 408a, 616

dampness *n* 339

dam up *v* 261

dance *n* 309; *v* 309, 315, 838

dance all night *v* 309

dandy *n* 854

danger *n* 665

danger *n* 475, 667, 909

dangerous *adj* 475, 665

danger signal *n* 669

dangle *v* 214

dangler *n* 281

dangling *adj* 214

dank *adj* 339

dankness *n* 339

dapple *v* 440; *adj* 433

dappled *adj* 440

dapple-gray *adj* 432

dare *v* 715, 861

daring *n* 715, 861; *adj* 715, 861

dark *adj* 421, 422, 431, 442, 447, 571, 901a

darken *v* 353, 421, 422, 431, 519

darkened *adj* 421, 422

darkish *adj* 422

darkly *adv* 442

darkness *n* 421

darkness *n* 426, 431, 491, 526

darling *n* 897, 899

dart *v* 274

dash *n* 32, 41, 274, 310, 682, 684; *v* 41, 274, 276, 310, 684

dash off *v* 274, 682

dash one's expectations *v* 509

dash one's hopes *v* 509

dastardliness *n* 862

dastardly *adj* 862

data *n* 476, 527

date *n* 106; *v* 114

daub *v* 555

decode v 522
decoloration n 430
decompose v 49
decomposed adj 49
decomposition n 49
decorate v 847
decoration n 733, 847, 877
decorative adj 847
decorous adj 850, 852
decorum n 852, 960
decoy v 288
decrease n 36
decrease n 38, 195, 283; v 36, 38, 193, 195
decreased adj 36
decreasing adj 36
decree n 480, 963; v 600, 741, 963
decrement n 40a
decrepit adj 124, 158, 160, 655, 659
decrepitude n 128, 158, 160, 659
decry v 934
deduce v 476
deduct v 38, 813
deductible adj 38
deduction n 38
deduction n 40a, 65, 476, 480
deductive adj 476
deed n 680, 771
deem v 451, 873
deep n 341; adj 208, 404, 428
deepen v 35, 208
deepness n 208
deep-rooted adj 820
deep-seated adj 208, 221
deep-sounding adj 408
deep-toned adj 408
deface v 241, 659, 846, 848
defacement n 241
defalcation n 304

defamation n 934
defamatory adj 932
defame v 934
defamer n 936
default n 304, 460, 808; v 808
defeat n 509
defeated adj 732
defect n 40a, 53, 651, 848, 945; v 607
defection n 607
defective adj 53, 651, 732, 945
defectiveness n 732
defend v 664, 670, 717, 937
defender n 890, 937
defense n 717
defense n 670, 937
defenseless adj 665
defensible adj 664
defensive adj 717
defer v 133
deference n 743, 928
deferential adj 457, 743, 926, 928
defer to v 928
defiance n 715
defiance n 742
defiant adj 715, 742
deficiency n 28, 34, 53, 304, 640, 651, 732
deficient adj 28, 34, 53, 304, 640, 651
deficit n 53
defile v 653
defiled adj 961
defilement n 653, 961
define v 233, 522
definite adj 79, 233, 246, 446, 474, 570
definition n 446, 522
definitive adj 67
deflect v 245, 279
deflection n 245, 291
deform v 241, 243
deformed adj 243

deformity n 241, 243, 846, 848
defraud v 545, 791, 923
defrost v 382
deft adj 698
defunct adj 2, 360
defy v 715, 742
degeneracy n 659
degenerate v 659; adj 659
degeneration n 659
degradation n 308, 659, 874
degrade v 308, 659, 879
degraded adj 207
degree n 26
degree n 58, 71
deification n 990, 991
deify v 990, 991
deity n 976
dejected adj 832
dejection n 837
dejection n 828, 859
delay n 133; v 133, 142, 706
delayed adj 133
delectability n 394, 829
delectable adj 394, 829
delectation n 827
delegate n 534, 758, 759; v 270, 755
delegation n 755, 758
delete v 552
deleterious adj 649, 657
deletion n 552
deliberate v 695; adj 174, 275, 383, 451, 685
deliberately adv 133, 600, 611, 620
deliberateness n 174, 275
delicacy n 160, 655, 850, 960
delicate adj 160, 203, 328, 329, 394, 428, 704, 829, 868, 960

delicate condition *n* 655
delicious *adj* 394, 829
delight *n* 377, 827, 829; *v* 829, 836
delightful *adj* 377, 829
delight in *v* 827
delineate *v* 554, 594
delineation *n* 554, 556, 594
deliquescence *n* 335
deliquescent *adj* 335
delirious *adj* 503, 825
delirium *n* 503, 825
delitescence *n* 447
deliver *v* 270, 580, 660, 672, 750, 784
deliverance *n* 672
deliverance *n* 660, 750, 834
delivery *n* 580, 784
dell *n* 252
delude *v* 545
deluge *n* 72, 348; *v* 337, 348, 641
delusion *n* 495, 503, 515, 545
delusive *adj* 545
delve *v* 252
demand *n* 601, 630, 741, 765, 812, 924; *v* 630, 741, 765, 812
demeanor *n* 448, 692, 852
demented *adj* 503
dementia *n* 503
demi- *adj* 91
demi-lune *adj* 245
demise *n* 360
demolish *v* 162
demolition *n* 162
demon *n* 980
demon *n* 949, 978
demonic *adj* 980
demonology *n* 980, 991
demonstrable *adj* 476, 478
demonstrate *v* 476, 478, 525

demonstrated *adj* 478
demonstration *n* 478
demonstration *n* 525
demonstrative *adj* 478
demur *n* 704; *v* 485, 603
demure *adj* 881
den *n* 189
dendrology *n* 369
denial *n* 536
denial *n* 764
denominate *v* 564
denotation *n* 516
denotative *adj* 550
denote *v* 516, 550
denounce *v* 908, 909
dénouement *n* 65, 67
dense *adj* 72, 202, 275, 321, 365, 376
denseness *n* 202
density *n* 321
density *n* 202
dent *v* 252, 257
dented *adj* 252
denunciation *n* 908, 932
denunciatory *adj* 932
deny *v* 468, 536, 610, 708, 764
deny oneself *v* 955
deodorize *v* 652
depart *v* 66, 185, 293, 302, 360, 449
departed *adj* 2, 449
department *n* 51, 75
department store *n* 799
depart this life *v* 360
departure *n* 293
departure *n* 287, 360, 449, 623
departure from *n* 279
depend *v* 214
dependable *adj* 474, 664
dependence *n* 749
dependent *adj* 214, 749
depend upon *v* 154, 749
depict *v* 554, 556, 594

depiction *n* 554, 556, 594
deplane *v* 292
depletion *n* 640
deplorable *adj* 649, 830
deplore *v* 833, 839
deport *v* 270, 692
deportation *n* 270
deportment *n* 692
depose *v* 467, 535
deposit *n* 771
deposition *n* 467, 535
depository *n* 191, 802
depraved *adj* 945
depravity *n* 649, 659, 945
deprecate *v* 766
deprecation *n* 766
deprecation *n* 616, 932, 934
deprecatory *adj* 483, 766
depreciate *v* 36, 483, 934
depreciated *adj* 483
depreciating *adj* 483, 934
depreciation *n* 36, 483, 813, 815
depreciative *adj* 483
depress *v* 207, 252, 308
depressed *adj* 207, 308, 438, 837
depressing *adj* 383
depression *n* 308
depression *n* 207, 208, 252, 837
deprivation *n* 659, 776, 789
deprived of *adj* 776
deprive of *v* 38
deprive of color *v* 429
depth *n* 208
deputation *n* 755
deputy *n* 759
deputy *n* 634, 690
derange *v* 59, 61, 185
deranged *adj* 59, 503

derangement *n* 61

derangement *n* 59, 185, 503

dereliction *n* 460, 732

dereliction of duty *n* 927

deride *v* 856, 929, 930

derision *n* 856, 929, 930

derisive *adj* 856, 929, 930

derisory *adj* 856

derivable from *adj* 154

derivation *n* 154, 155, 562

derivative *adj* 154

derived from *adj* 154

derive from *v* 155

derive pleasure from *v* 827

derogatory *adj* 934

descend *v* 217, 306, 310

descendant *n* 167

descending *n* 306; *adj* 217, 306

descent *n* 306

descent *n* 153

describe *v* 554, 594

description *n* 594

descriptive *adj* 554

descry *v* 441, 480a

desecrate *v* 679, 988

desecration *n* 679, 988

desert *n* 180, 344, 973; *v* 623, 624, 732, 757, 782

deserter *n* 607, 623

desertion *n* 624, 757, 782

deserve *v* 924

deserve consideration *v* 642

design *n* 22, 451, 516, 556, 620, 626; *v* 451, 516, 556, 620, 626

designate *v* 79, 550, 564

designation *n* 564, 877

designer *n* 559; 626

desirability *n* 646

desirable *adj* 646

desire *n* 865

desire *n* 600, 609, 858; *v* 602, 858, 865

desiring *adj* 865

desirous *adj* 602, 865

desist *v* 67, 142, 265

desolate *v* 162; *adj* 837

desolation *n* 162, 638, 828

despair *n* 828, 837, 859; *v* 828, 837, 859

despairing *adj* 859

desperate *adj* 173, 859

desperately *adv* 31

desperation *n* 825, 859

despicable *adj* 435, 930

despise *v* 715, 898, 930

despoil *v* 659

despond *v* 837, 859

despondency *n* 837, 859

despondent *adj* 837, 859

despot *n* 739

despotic *adj* 739, 964

despotism *n* 739

dessication *n* 340

destination *n* 67, 620

destine *v* 152

destined *adj* 152

destiny *n* 121, 152, 601, 611, 621

destitute *adj* 804

destitution *n* 804

destroy *v* 2, 162, 619, 638, 659, 679

destroyed *adj* 162

destroyer *n* 165

destroyer *n* 913

destroy oneself *v* 361

destruction *n* 162

destruction *n* 146, 173, 619, 638

destructive *adj* 162, 638, 649

desuetude *n* 614, 678

desultory *adj* 59, 70, 279, 475

detach *v* 44, 47

detached *adj* 10, 47, 953

detachment *n* 44, 291, 953

detail *v* 79, 594

details *n* 32, 79

detain *v* 781

detect *v* 480a

detection *n* 480a

detective *n* 527

detention *n* 781

deter *v* 616

detergent *n* 652

deteriorate *v* 36, 195, 659

deteriorated *adj* 659

deterioration *n* 659

deterioration *n* 36, 283, 655, 661, 732

determinate *adj* 474, 480, 620

determination *n* 150, 278, 480, 600, 604, 620, 480a, 604a

determine *v* 79, 153, 278, 480, 600, 604, 676, 967, 480a

determined *adj* 474

deterrent *n* 706

detest *v* 898

detestable *adj* 649, 898

detestation *n* 898

detonate *v* 173

detonation *n* 406

detour *n* 245, 279, 629; *v* 629

detract *v* 483, 934

detracting *n* 934; *adj* 934

detraction *n* 934

detraction *n* 483

detractor *n* 936

detrain *v* 292

detriment *n* 659

detrimental *adj* 649

deuce *n* 89
devastate *v* 162
devastation *n* 162, 638
develop *v* 153, 161,
194, 282, 313, 367
developing *adj* 127
development *n* 35, 144,
154, 161, 194, 282,
313
developmental *adj* 35
deviant *adj* 15
deviate *v* 20a, 140, 245,
279, 291, 629
deviating *adj* 15, 279
deviation *n* 279
deviation *n* 20a, 140,
245, 291
device *n* 550, 626, 702
devil *n* 978
devil *n* 949, 980; *v* 392
devilish *adj* 978, 982
devise *v* 515, 626, 673
devoid *adj* 187
devoid of *adj* 777a
devolve *v* 783
devoted *adj* 897, 987
devotee *n* 987
devote oneself to *v* 676
devotion *n* 604, 682,
743, 897, 928, 987
devour *v* 162, 298, 957
devout *adj* 987
devoutness *n* 987
dew *n* 339
dewy *adj* 339
dexterity *n* 698
dextral *adj* 238
dextrous *adj* 698
diabolic *adj* 978, 982
diabolical *adj* 649
diabolism *n* 978
diagnosis *n* 465
diagonal *adj* 217
diagram *n* 626
dialect *n* 560
dialectic *adj* 476, 560
dialectical *adj* 476
dialectician *n* 476

dialects *n* 476
dialog *n* 588
diameter *n* 202
diametrically opposite
adj 237
diaphanous *adj* 425
diaphanousness *n* 425
diaphragm *n* 68
diary *n* 114, 551
dichotomy *n* 91
dictate *v* 741
dictatorial *adj* 739
dictatorship *n* 739
diction *n* 560, 569
dictionary *n* 86
dictum *n* 496, 741
didactic *adj* 537
die *n* 22; *v* 2, 67, 142,
360, 659
die hard *v* 606
die out *v* 2, 142
differ *v* 15, 489, 713
difference *n* 15
difference *n* 18, 24, 28,
291, 489, 713
different *adj* 15, 18
differentiate *v* 18, 79,
465
differentiation *n* 465
different time *n* 119
differ from *v* 14, 18
difficult *adj* 704
difficulties *n* 804
difficulty *n* 704
difficulty *n* 177, 533
diffidence *n* 881
diffident *adj* 881
diffuse *v* 73; *adj* 73,
573
diffused *adj* 186
diffuseness *n* 573
diffusion *n* 73, 186
diffusive *adj* 73, 573
dig *v* 208, 252, 259,
490, 827
digest *n* 596; *v* 384
digestible *adj* 299, 390
dig in *v* 298

digit *n* 84
dignified *adj* 873, 875,
878
dignity *n* 873, 875
digress *v* 279, 573, 629
digression *n* 279, 629
digressive *adj* 279, 573
dig to daylight *v* 260
dig up *v* 480a
dike *n* 198, 259, 350
dilapidate *v* 659
dilapidated *adj* 659
dilapidation *n* 162, 659
dilate *v* 35, 194, 322
dilation *n* 322
dilatory *adj* 133
dilemma *n* 476, 704
diligence *n* 682
diligent *adj* 682
dilly-dally *v* 133, 605,
683
dilly-dallying *n* 133
dilute *v* 160, 203, 337
diluted *adj* 203
dim *v* 421; *adj* 405,
422, 426, 447, 519
dimensions *n* 31, 192
diminish *v* 36, 38, 103,
174, 195, 834
diminished *adj* 34, 103
diminution *n* 36, 195,
638
diminution of number *n*
103
diminutive *adj* 32, 193
diminutiveness *n* 32,
193
dimness *n* 422
dimness *n* 343, 421
dimple *n* 252
dim-sighted *adj* 442,
443
dimsightedness *n* 443
dimwit *n* 493
dimwitted *adj* 254, 499
din *n* 404
dine *v* 298
dingdong *n* 407, 408

dingy *adj* 421, 422, 429, 431

dining *n* 298

dint *n* 252

dip *n* 217, 252, 300, 306, 308, 310; *v* 300, 310, 337

diplomat *n* 724

dipsomaniac *n* 959

dire *adj* 649, 735, 830

direct *v* 175, 278, 537, 600, 630, 692, 693, 741; *adj* 246, 278, 703

directing *adj* 693

direction *n* 278, 693

direction *n* 183, 537, 692, 697, 741

directive *n* 630; *adj* 692

direct line *n* 246

directly *adv* 132, 278

directness *n* 246

director *n* 694

director *n* 745

directory *n* 86

dirge *n* 363, 839

dirigible *n* 273

dirt *n* 342, 653

dirt cheap *adj* 815

dirty *v* 653; *adj* 653, 961

disability *n* 158

disable *v* 158

disabled *adj* 158

disadvantage *n* 619

disadvantageous *adj* 647

disagree *v* 24, 291, 489, 713

disagreeable *adj* 24, 830, 846, 867

disagreeing *adj* 24, 489

disagreement *n* 24

disagreement *n* 10, 15, 47, 489, 713, 720

disagree with *v* 657

disallow *v* 761

disallowance *n* 761

disappear *v* 2, 4, 360, 449

disappearance *n* 449

disappearing *adj* 449

disappoint *v* 509, 732, 832

disappointed *adj* 509

dissapointment *n* 509

disapprobation *n* 932

disapproval *n* 766, 932

disapprove *v* 766, 932

disapproving *adj* 932

disarm *v* 158

disarrange *v* 61

disarray *n* 59, 61

disaster *n* 619, 735

disastrous *adj* 619, 735, 830

disavow *n* 536; *v* 607

disavowal *n* 536, 607

disband *v* 44, 73

disbelief *n* 485

disbelief *n* 485, 487, 989

disbelieve *v* 485, 989

disburse *v* 809

disbursement *n* 809

discard *v* 297, 610, 678, 773, 782

discern *v* 441, 480a, 490, 498

discernible *adj* 446

discernibleness *n* 446

discerning *adj* 441, 459, 465, 490, 498, 868

discernment *n* 441, 465, 477, 480, 490, 498, 868

discharge *n* 284, 295, 297, 299, 406, 750, 772, 807, 970; *v* 284, 295, 297, 692, 729, 750, 772, 807, 926, 927a, 970

discharge a function *v* 644

discharged *adj* 970

disciple *n* 492, 541

disciplinarian *n* 739

discipline *n* 58, 537, 972; *v* 537, 972

disclaim *n* 536; *v* 757, 764

disclaimer *n* 536, 764

disclose *v* 525, 527, 529, 531

disclosed *adj* 529

disclosure *n* 529

disclosure *n* 480a, 531, 985

discoloration *n* 429

discolored *adj* 429, 848

discomfort *n* 378, 828; *v* 828

discommodious *adj* 647

discompose *v* 61, 828

discomposure *n* 61, 828

disconcert *v* 61, 706, 832

disconcerted *adj* 509

disconnect *v* 44, 70

disconnected *adj* 10, 70

disconnectedness *n* 70

disconnection *n* 10, 44, 47

disconsolate *adj* 859

discontent *n* 832

discontent *n* 828

discontented *adj* 832

discontentment *n* 832

discontinuance *n* 142

discontinuation *n* 142

discontinue *v* 44, 70, 142, 265

discontinuity *n* 70

discontinuity *n* 44, 53

discontinuous *adj* 44, 70

discord *n* 414, 713

discord *n* 24, 59, 410, 720, 889

discordance *n* 489

discordant *adj* 24, 410, 414, 713

discount *n* 813
discount *n* 40a; *v* 813
discourage *v* 616
discouraged *adj* 837
discouragement *n* 616
discourse *n* 537, 582, 588, 595; *v* 537, 582
discourse with *v* 588
discourteous *adj* 895, 929
discourtesy *n* 895
discourtesy *n* 929
discover *v* 441, 462, 480a, 490, 529
discoverable *adj* 462
discovery *n* 480a
discovery *n* 462, 985
discredit *n* 874; *v* 485
discreet *adj* 451, 698, 864
discrepancy *n* 15, 24
discretion *n* 480, 498, 698, 864
discretional *adj* 609
discretionary *adj* 600, 748
discriminate *v* 15, 465, 498, 850
discriminating *adj* 465, 480
discrimination *n* 465
discrimination *n* 15, 480, 850, 868
discriminative *adj* 15, 465, 850, 868
discriminatory *adj* 465
discursive *adj* 279, 573
discuss *v* 476, 695
discuss a subject *v* 595
discussion *n* 476, 588, 595
disdain *n* 930; *v* 866, 930
disdainful *adj* 773, 930
disease *n* 655
disease *n* 378
diseased *adj* 655
disembark *v* 292, 342

disembarkation *n* 292
disenchant *v* 616
disencumber *v* 705
disengage *v* 44, 750
disengagement *n* 44, 750
disentangle *v* 42, 44, 60, 522, 672, 705
disentanglement *n* 672
disenthrall *v* 750
disestablish *v* 185
disesteem *n* 932
disfavor *n* 874
disfigure *v* 241, 243, 659, 846
disfigured *adj* 848
disfigurement *n* 241, 243, 846, 848
disgrace *n* 874, 930; *v* 874
disgraced *adj* 874
disgraceful *adj* 874, 930
disgrace oneself *v* 874
disgruntled *adj* 509
disguise *n* 530; *v* 528
disguising *n* 528
disgust *n* 837, 867, 869; *v* 289, 395, 830, 867, 869
disgusted *adj* 869
disgusting *adj* 867, 898
dishabille *n* 226
dishearten *v* 616
disheartened *adj* 837
disheartening *adj* 383
disheveled *adj* 73
dishonest *adj* 544, 923, 940
dishonesty *n* 544, 940
dishonor *n* 874, 930; *v* 874, 923
dishonorable *adj* 874, 930, 940
disillusion *n* 509; *v* 509
disinclination *n* 603, 867
disincline *v* 616

disinclined *adj* 867
disinfect *v* 652
disinfectant *n* 652
disingenuous *adj* 544
disintegrate *v* 330
disintegration *n* 330
disinter *v* 363
disinterested *adj* 942
disinterestedness *n* 942
disinterment *n* 363
disjoin *v* 44, 47, 51
disjoined *adj* 44
disjunction *n* 44
disjunction *n* 10, 47, 49, 70
disjunctive *adj* 44
dislikable *adj* 867
dislike *n* 867
dislike *n* 289, 603, 889, 898, 932; *v* 603, 867, 898, 932
disliking *adj* 867
dislocate *v* 44, 61
dislocation *n* 44, 61, 185
dislodge *v* 185, 297
dislodgment *n* 297
dismal *adj* 830, 837, 901a
dismantle *v* 162, 678
dismay *n* 860
dismayed *adj* 860
dismemberment *n* 44
dismiss *v* 750, 782
dismissal *n* 750
dismount *v* 292, 306
disobedience *n* 742
disobedience *n* 773
disobedient *adj* 742, 773
disobey *v* 742
disorder *n* 59
disorder *n* 61, 173, 241, 315, 503, 655; *v* 59, 61, 185
disordered *adj* 241
disorderly *adj* 59, 173

disorganization *n* 61

disorganize *v* 61, 162

disorganized *adj* 59

disown *n* 536

disparage *v* 483, 934

disparagement *n* 932, 934

disparaging *adj* 932, 934

disparate *adj* 18, 24, 28

disparity *n* 15, 18, 24, 28, 291

dispassion *n* 826, 953

dispassionate *adj* 826, 953

dispatch *n* 592, 684; *v* 361, 684, 692, 729

dispel *v* 73, 162

dispensation *n* 784, 786, 927a

dispense *v* 73, 784, 786

dispense with *v* 678

disperse *v* 44, 49, 73, 291

dispersed *adj* 73

dispersion *n* 73

dispersion *n* 44, 186

dispirited *adj* 837

dispiriting *adj* 383

displace *v* 61, 185, 270

displaced *adj* 185

displacement *n* 185

displacement *n* 140

display *n* 448, 525, 855, 882; *v* 525, 882

displease *v* 289, 830

displeased *adj* 832

displeasing *adj* 846

displeasure *n* 828, 832, 900

disposal *n* 60, 677, 741

dispose *v* 60, 176, 615, 693, 796

dispose of *v* 784

disposition *n* 58, 60, 176, 600, 602, 613, 693, 820

dispossess *v* 789

dispossession *n* 789

disproof *n* 468, 479

disproportion *n* 24

disproportionate *adj* 24

disprove *v* 479

disputable *adj* 485

disputant *n* 476, 726

disputation *n* 476, 536, 969

disputatious *adj* 476, 713

dispute *n* 536, 713, 720, 969; *v* 24, 476, 713, 720

disputing *adj* 24

disqualify *v* 158

disquiet *n* 149, 315, 828; *v* 828

disquietude *n* 149, 832

disquisition *n* 537, 595

disregard *n* 458, 460; *v* 458, 460, 483, 742, 773

disregardful *adj* 460

disregard of time *n* 115

disrelish *n* 867; *v* 867

disreputable *adj* 874

disrepute *n* 874

disrespect *n* 929

disrespect *n* 885, 895

disrespectful *adj* 885, 895, 929

disrobe *v* 226

disrobed *adj* 226

disruption *n* 162, 713

disruptive *adj* 713

dissatisfaction *n* 489, 828, 832

dissatisfied *adj* 832, 841

dissatisfy *v* 832

dissect *v* 44, 49

dissection *n* 49

dissemble *v* 528, 544

dissembler *n* 548

dissembling *n* 528, 544

disseminate *v* 73, 531

dissemination *n* 73, 673

dissension *n* 24, 489, 713, 720

dissent *n* 489

dissent *n* 485, 603, 984; *v* 291, 485, 489, 603, 708, 713

dissenter *n* 489, 984

dissenting *adj* 24, 489, 984

dissention *n* 720

dissertation *n* 595

dissever *v* 44

dissidence *n* 24, 713

dissident *n* 489; *adj* 489, 713, 764

dissimilar *adj* 18

dissimilarity *n* 18

dissimilarity *n* 15, 28

dissimilitude *n* 18

dissipate *v* 162, 638, 818

dissipation *n* 73, 638

dissociate *v* 44

dissociation *n* 10, 44

dissolution *n* 49, 162, 335, 360

dissolvable *adj* 335

dissolve *v* 2, 4, 49, 162, 335, 360, 449

dissonance *n* 24, 410, 414, 713

dissonant *adj* 24, 410, 414, 713

dissuade *v* 616

dissuasion *n* 616

dissuasive *adj* 616

dissyllable *n* 561

distance *n* 196

distance *n* 198, 200, 235

distanced *adj* 10

distant *adj* 196

distaste *n* 867

distasteful *adj* 830, 867

distend *v* 194

distention *n* 194

distill *v* 336

distillation *n* 336

distinct *adj* 402, 446, 518, 525, 570, 580

distinction *n* 15, 31, 465, 873, 875

distinctive *adj* 15

distinctive feature *n* 79

distinctness *n* 446, 570, 580

distinguish *v* 15, 441, 465

distinguished *adj* 206, 873

distinguishing *adj* 465

distort *v* 217, 243, 523, 555, 846

distorted *adj* 243

distortion *v* 243

distortion *n* 443, 544, 555, 846

distracted *adj* 503, 824

distraction *n* 825

distress *n* 735, 804, 828; *v* 828

distress signal *n* 669

distribute *v* 60, 73, 531, 786

distribution *n* 60, 73, 531, 786

distributive *adj* 786

district attorney *n* 968

distrust *n* 485; *v* 485, 487, 860

disturb *v* 61, 185, 315, 824, 830

disturbance *n* 59, 61, 315

disunion *n* 24, 44, 59, 905

disunite *v* 44, 713

disusage *n* 614

disuse *n* 614, 678

disuse *v* 614, 678

disused *adj* 678

ditch *n* 198, 259, 350

ditto *n* 21; *adv* 104

dive *n* 208, 310; *v* 310

diverge *v* 20a, 291

divergence *n* 291

divergence *n* 15, 18, 24, 73, 279

divergency *n* 20a

divergent *adj* 15, 24, 291

divers *adj* 15

diverse *adj* 15, 81

diversified *adj* 15, 16a, 18, 20a, 81, 440

diversify *v* 15, 18, 140, 440

diversion *n* 140, 279, 840

diversity *n* 15, 16a, 18, 81

divert *v* 279, 840

diverting *adj* 840

divest *v* 226, 789

divestment *n* 789

divest oneself *v* 782

divide *v* 44, 44, 51, 60, 73, 85, 91, 291, 778, 786

divided *adj* 51

divide into four parts *v* 97

divide into three parts *v* 94

divide in two *v* 91

divination *n* 511, 992

divine *n* 996; *v* 511, 514, 992; *adj* 976, 981, 983a

divinity *n* 976, 983

division *n* 44, 51, 60, 73, 75, 198, 291, 713, 786

divisive *adj* 713

divorce *n* 905

divorce *n* 44; *v* 44, 905

divorced *adj* 905

divulge *v* 529, 531

divulgence *n* 529, 531

do *v* 161, 170, 622, 639, 680, 729

do a good turn *v* 648

do as one likes *v* 748

do away with *v* 162, 297, 361

do a world of good *v* 648

do battle *v* 722

docile *adj* 725, 743, 926

docility *n* 725, 743

dock *n* 966

doctor *n* 662; *v* 544, 660, 662

doctrinal *adj* 983a

doctrine *n* 484, 537, 983

document *n* 551

dodge *v* 264, 279, 623

doe *n* 374

doer *n* 680, 690

doff *v* 226

dog *n* 373

dogged *adj* 150, 640a, 606

doggedness *n* 150, 604a, 606

doggerel *n* 597

dogma *n* 484, 537, 983

dogmatic *adj* 535, 606, 737

dogmatism *n* 535, 606

dogmatist *n* 606

do good *v* 648

do harm *v* 649

doing *adj* 151

doings *n* 151

doldrums *n* 837

dole *n* 32, 640, 786

dole out *v* 60, 73, 784, 786

dolor *n* 378, 828

dolorous *adj* 378, 830

dolt *n* 493, 501

doltish *adj* 499

domain *n* 75, 181

dome *n* 250

domestic *n* 746; *adj* 188, 221, 370

domestic animals *n* 366

domesticate *v* 184, 370

domesticated *adj* 370

domestication *n* 370

domicile *n* 189

dominance *n* 175

dominant *adj* 175, 737

dominate *v* 175, 739

domination *n* 741

domineer *v* 739

dominion *n* 157, 737

don *n* 540

donate *v* 784

donation *n* 784

done *adj* 729

done away with *adj* 782

donee *n* 785

done with *adj* 678

donor *n* 784

do nothing *v* 169, 681, 683

doom *n* 152, 360, 421; *v* 152, 971

doomsday *n* 121

do one's duty *v* 926

door *n* 231, 232, 260, 627

doorway *n* 232, 260

do over *v* 144

do penance *v* 952

do right *v* 922

dormancy *n* 526

dormant *adj* 172, 265, 526

dose *n* 25, 786

dot *n* 32; *v* 440

dote *v* 499

dote upon *v* 991

double *n* 17, 90, 147; *v* 90, 258; *adj* 90, 147

double-cross *v* 545

doubled *adj* 90

double dealing *n* 544

double-edged *adj* 520

double entendre *n* 520

double-meaning *n* 520

doubleness *n* 89

doubling *n* 90

doubt *n* 485

doubt *n* 475, 487, 984,

989; *v* 475, 485, 487, 989

doubter *n* 989

doubtful *adj* 473, 475, 485, 487, 520

doubtfulness *n* 473, 475

doubting *adj* 485, 984, 989

doubtless *adv* 474

dough *n* 354

doughy *adj* 324, 354

dour *adj* 739

douse *v* 310, 337

dove color *n* 432

dove-colored *adj* 432

dovetail *v* 23, 219

do violence *v* 649

dowdy *adj* 653

do what one wants *v* 748

do without *v* 678

down *v* 298; *adj* 837; *adv* 207

downfall *n* 162, 306

downhearted *adj* 837

downhill *n* 217; *adj* 217

down in the dumps *adj* 438, 832

down in the mouth *adj* 735

downright *adj* 525; *adv* 31

downstairs *adv* 207

downward *adv* 207

downy *adj* 255, 256

dozen *n* 98

drab *adj* 432

draft *n* 208, 349, 596, 626

draftsman *n* 559

drafty *adj* 349

drag *n* 285; *v* 109, 275, 285, 288, 307

drag on *v* 110

drag out *v* 110, 133

drag up *v* 307

drain *n* 295, 350; *v* 295, 297, 340

drainage *n* 295, 340

drain into *v* 348

drake *n* 373

drama *n* 599

dramatic *adj* 599, 882

dramatist *n* 599

dramatize *v* 599

dramaturgy *n* 599

drape *v* 225

drapery *n* 225

draught *n* 298

draw *n* 27; *v* 153, 230, 285, 288, 301, 556

draw a curtain *v* 424

draw aside *v* 279

drawback *n* 177, 619, 651

drawer *n* 559

draw forth *v* 301

draw in *v* 195

drawing *n* 285, 556, 626

drawing and quartering *n* 361

drawl *v* 275

drawn *adj* 27

draw near *v* 121, 286

drawn game *n* 27

draw out *v* 110, 133, 200, 301, 590

draw to a close *v* 67

draw together *v* 72

dread *n* 860, 862; *v* 860

dreadful *adj* 649, 830, 860

dreadfully *adv* 31

dream *n* 4, 515, 515, 858; *v* 515

dreamer *n* 504

dreaming *n* 515

dreamlike *adj* 515

dreamy *adj* 4, 515, 683

dreamy-eyed *adj* 683

dreary *adj* 16, 830, 843

dredge *v* 307

dregs *n* 40

drench *v* 337, 339, 348, 641

dress *n* 225
dress *v* 225
dressed *adj* 225
dribble *v* 295, 348
drift *n* 176, 278, 349; *v* 176, 264, 267, 279, 287
drift away *v* 287
drill *n* 262; *v* 260, 537
drink *n* 298; *v* 298, 959
drinkable *adj* 299
drinker *n* 959
drinking *n* 296, 298, 959
drink like a fish *v* 959
drink one's fill *v* 298
drink up *v* 298
drip *v* 295, 348
dripping *n* 356
drive *n* 266, 284; *v* 276, 284, 744
drive a bargain *v* 794
drive at *v* 516
drive away *v* 289
drive in *v* 300
drivel *n* 499
driveling *n* 499; *adj* 499
driver *n* 268, 694
driving *n* 266
driving spirit *n* 820
drizzle *n* 32, 348; *v* 348
drizzly *adj* 348
droll *n* 501; *adj* 853
drollery *n* 842
drone *n* 683
droning *n* 407
droop *v* 306, 655, 659, 688, 837
drooping *adj* 160
drop *n* 32, 306; *v* 158, 160, 306, 310, 348, 688
drop by drop *adv* 26
drop dead *v* 360
drop down *v* 306
drop down dead *v* 360

drop from the clouds *v* 508
drop in the ocean *n* 32
droplet *n* 32
drop off *v* 283, 360
drop out *v* 283
dropsical *adj* 194
dropsy *n* 194
drought *n* 340
droves *n* 102
drown *v* 337, 361, 376
drowsiness *n* 688
drowsy *adj* 683, 688, 841
drudge *v* 686
drudgery *n* 682
drug *v* 381
drugged *adj* 381
drum *n* 249; *v* 407
drumming *n* 407
drunk *adj* 959
drunkard *n* 959
drunken *adj* 959
drunkenness *n* 959
dry *v* 340; *adj* 340, 575, 579, 843, 958
dryad *n* 979
dry as a bone *adj* 340, 958
dry land *n* 342
dryness *n* 340
dry rot *n* 653, 663
dry up *v* 340, 435
dual *adj* 89
dualism *n* 89
duality *n* 89
dub *v* 564
dubious *adj* 475, 485, 487, 520
dubiousness *n* 475, 520
ducking *n* 310
duct *n* 350, 351
ductile *adj* 324
ductility *n* 324
dud *n* 732
dude *n* 854
due *n* 806, 924; *adj* 924
duet *n* 415

due to *adj* 154, 155
duffer *n* 493, 701
dulcet *adj* 413
dull *v* 254, 381, 422; *adj* 160, 172, 254, 275, 337, 376, 381, 422, 428, 429, 491, 499, 575, 598, 683, 841, 843, 901a
dullard *n* 493, 501
dulled *adj* 381
dullness *n* 843
dullness *n* 172, 254, 683, 823, 841
dull understanding *n* 499
dull-witted *adj* 499
dumb *adj* 491, 581
dumb animal *n* 366
dumbness *n* 581
dumfound *v* 509, 581, 870
dumps *n* 837
dumpy *adj* 193, 201, 202
dun *adj* 429, 432
dunce *n* 493, 501
dunderhead *n* 501
dunderpate *n* 501
dungeon *n* 752
dunk *v* 310, 337
dunking *n* 310
duo *n* 415
dupe *n* 547
dupe *n* 486, 857; *v* 545
duplex *adj* 89
duplexity *n* 89
duplicate *n* 13, 21, 90; *v* 19, 90, 104; *adj* 19, 90, 641
duplicated *adj* 90
duplication *n* 90
duplication *n* 19, 104
duplicitous *adj* 520, 702
duplicity *n* 520, 544, 702
durability *n* 110

durability *n* 112, 141, 150

durable *adj* 106, 110, 141, 150

duration *n* 106, 200

duress *n* 744

during *adv* 106

dusk *n* 126, 421

duskiness *n* 421, 422

dusky *adj* 431

dust *n* 330, 362

dusty *adj* 330, 653

dutiful *adj* 743, 926

duty *n* 926

duty *n* 625, 743, 806, 928, 963

duty bound *adj* 926

dwarf *n* 980; *adj* 193

dwarfish *adj* 193

dwell *v* 186, 188, 265

dweller *n* 188

dwelling *n* 189

dwindle *v* 36, 195, 732

dwindling *n* 36

dye *n* 428; *v* 428

dyed *adj* 428

dying *n* 360

dying day *n* 360

dynamic *adj* 171

E

each *adv* 79

each to each *adv* 79

each to his own *adv* 79

eager *adj* 602, 682

eagerness *n* 602, 682

eagle-eyed *adj* 441

ear *n* 418

earlier *adv* 116

earliness *n* 132

early *adj* 132; *adv* 121, 132

earmark *n* 550

earn *v* 775

earnest *adj* 602, 642

earnestly *adv* 604

earnestness *n* 682

earnings *n* 775

ear-piercing *adj* 410

earshot *n* 197

ear-splitting *adj* 404

earth *n* 318, 342, 362

earthly *adj* 318, 342, 989

earthy *adj* 342

ease *n* 377, 578, 705, 748, 827, 831, 834; *v* 705, 707, 834

easily *adv* 705

easiness *n* 705

easy *adj* 275, 578, 685, 705, 740

easy circumstance *n* 803

easy going *adj* 174, 740, 826

eat *v* 298

eatable *adj* 299

eat away *v* 638

eating *n* 298

eating *n* 296

eavesdrop *v* 418

eavesdropper *n* 418, 455, 527

ebb *n* 36; *v* 36, 195, 283, 287, 659

ebb and flow *n* 314

ebbing *n* 36

ebon *adj* 431

ebony *n* 431

ebullience *n* 171

ebullient *adj* 171, 382, 824

ebullition *n* 171, 173, 315, 825

eccentric *adj* 83, 499, 608

eccentricity *n* 83, 499, 503

ecclesiastic *n* 996

ecclesiastical *adj* 995

echo *n* 21, 104; *v* 104, 277, 402, 408

echoing *n* 408

eclipse *n* 421, 449; *v* 33, 422

economical *adj* 817

economize *v* 817

economy *n* 817

economy *n* 58

ecstasy *n* 377, 827

ecstatic *adj* 377, 827, 829

ecumenical *adj* 78

eddy *n* 312, 348

edge *n* 231

edge *n* 233; *v* 231

edgewise *adv* 217

edging *n* 231

edible *adj* 299

edification *n* 537

edify *v* 537

edifying *adj* 537, 648

edition *n* 531

editor *n* 593, 805

educate *v* 537

educated *adj* 490, 498

education *n* 537, 673

educational *adj* 537

educational institution *n* 542

eel *n* 248

efface *v* 552

efface from the memory *v* 506

effacement *n* 552

effect *n* 154

effect *n* 65; *v* 153, 729, 731

effective *adj* 157, 175, 644

effects *n* 780

effectual *adj* 170, 644

effervesce *v* 173, 315, 353

effervescence *n* 171, 173, 315, 353

effervescent *adj* 338, 353

efficacious *adj* 157, 170, 644

efficacy *n* 157, 644

efficient *adj* 157, 170, 698

effigy *n* 21

effluence *n* 295
effluvium *n* 398
effort *n* 675, 680, 686
effulgence *n* 420
effulgent *adj* 420
effusion *n* 295, 297, 299
effusive *adj* 584
egalitarian *adj* 29, 78
egg *n* 153
egg-shaped *adj* 247, 249
ego *n* 5
egoism *n* 943
egotism *n* 878, 880, 943
egotistical *adj* 878, 880, 943
egregiously *adv* 31
egress *n* 295
egress *n* 302
eight *n* 98
eject *v* 185, 297, 789, 893
ejected *adj* 893
ejection *n* 297
ejection *n* 185, 301, 893
eke out *v* 110
elaborate *v* 658
elaboration *n* 658
elapse *v* 109
elapsed *adj* 122
elastic *adj* 277, 324, 325
elasticity *n* 325
elasticity *n* 159, 277, 324
elated *adj* 838, 884
elbow *n* 244
elbow-grease *n* 331
elbowroom *n* 180
elder *n* 130; *adj* 128
elderly *adj* 124, 128
eldership *n* 128
eldest *adj* 128
elect *v* 609, 995
election *n* 609
electricity *n* 388
electric light *n* 423
electrify *v* 824

electrocute *v* 361
electrocution *n* 361
electronic music *n* 415
electronic sound reproduction *n* 402
elegance *n* 578
elegance *n* 577, 845, 850
elegant *adj* 578, 845
elegantly *adv* 850
elegy *n* 363, 839
element *n* 51, 56, 153, 211
elemental *adj* 42, 211
elementary *adj* 42
elements *n* 66
elephant *n* 192
elevate *v* 206, 235, 307
elevated *adj* 206, 307, 574
elevation *n* 307
elevation *n* 206, 574, 658
eleven *n* 98
elf *n* 979
elfin *adj* 980
elicit *v* 153, 301
eliminate *v* 38, 42, 55, 103, 297, 299, 301, 610, 893
eliminated *adj* 893
elimination *n* 42, 55, 103, 297, 299, 301, 610, 893
elite *n* 648
ellipse *n* 247
elliptic *adj* 247
elliptical *adj* 247
elongate *v* 200
elongation *n* 196, 200
eloquence *n* 574, 582
eloquent *adj* 574
elsewhere *adv* 187
elucidate *v* 74, 518, 522
elucidation *n* 522
elude *v* 623, 671, 773
elusive *adj* 623, 773
elysian *adj* 981

emaciated *adj* 203
emaciation *n* 638
emanate *v* 295, 299
emanate from *v* 154
emanation *n* 295, 299, 398
emancipate *v* 672, 750
emancipation *n* 195, 672, 750
emasculate *v* 158
emasculated *adj* 158
embalm *v* 363
embargo *n* 761
embark *v* 66, 267, 293
embarkation *n* 293
embark on *v* 676
embarrass *v* 704
embarrassed *adj* 434
embassy *n* 755
embed *v* 221
embedded *adj* 221, 229
embellish *v* 847
embellished *adj* 847
embellishment *n* 847
ember *n* 388
embezzle *v* 791
emblazon *v* 428, 882
emblem *n* 550, 747
emblematic *adj* 550
embody *v* 50, 54, 76, 82, 316
embosomed *adj* 229
emboss *v* 250
embrace *n* 902; *v* 54, 76, 902
embroider *v* 440, 549
embroidery *n* 549
embroil *v* 61
embryo *n* 153
embryology *n* 368
embryonic *adj* 66, 153, 674
emend *v* 658
emendation *n* 658
emendatory *adj* 658
emerald *adj* 435
emerge *v* 295
emergence *n* 295

emergency *n* 8, 151, 704

emigrant *n* 268

eminence *n* 31, 33, 206, 648, 873, 875

eminent *adj* 206, 873, 883

eminently *adv* 33

emissary *n* 534

emission *n* 297

emit sound *v* 402

emotion *n* 821

emotional *adj* 821

empathy *n* 821

emphasis *n* 535, 580, 642

emphasize *v* 535, 642

emphatic *adj* 535, 642

emphatically *adv* 31

employ *n* 677, 749; *v* 677, 755

employable *adj* 677

employee *n* 746

employ figures of speech *v* 521

employment *n* 625

employ oneself *v* 625

empower *v* 157, 737, 755, 760

emptiness *n* 2, 187, 209, 452, 517, 640, 880

empty *v* 185, 297; *adj* 2, 4, 187, 209, 298, 452

empty-headed *adj* 450a

empty vessel *n* 362

empty words *n* 517

emulate *v* 19, 648

enact *v* 599, 680, 692, 729, 741, 963

enamored *adj* 897

encamp *v* 184

encampment *n* 184

encase *v* 223

enchant *v* 829, 992

enchanted *adj* 992

enchanting *adj* 897, 992

enchantment *n* 827, 829, 991, 992

encircle *v* 76, 220, 227, 247

enclose *v* 227, 232

enclosure *n* 232

enclosure *n* 229

encompass *v* 76, 227

encore *adv* 104

encounter *n* 276, 680, 716; *v* 151

encourage *v* 707, 836

encouraging *adj* 858

encroach *v* 303

encroachment *n* 303

encumber *v* 319, 704, 706

encumbrance *n* 706

end *n* 67

end *n* 65, 142, 152, 154, 360, 620, 729; *v* 67, 142, 360, 729

endanger *v* 665, 909

endangering *adj* 909

endear *v* 902

endearing *adj* 902

endearment *n* 902

endeavor *n* 675, 686; *v* 622, 675

ended *adj* 67

endemic *adj* 79

endless *adj* 102, 104, 112

endlessness *n* 105, 112

end of the day *n* 126

end one's days *v* 360

endorse *v* 535, 769, 771, 931

endorsement *n* 535

endow *v* 157

endowment *n* 698, 784

end result *n* 161

end to end *adj* 199

endurance *n* 112, 141, 150, 826

endure *v* 1, 106, 110, 112, 141, 151, 826

enduring *adj* 110, 141, 150, 505, 826

endwise *adv* 212

enemy *n* 891

enemy *n* 708, 710, 726

energetic *adj* 157, 171, 359

energetic activity *n* 680

energize *v* 171

energized *adj* 171

energy *n* 171

energy *n* 157, 159, 173, 359, 604, 680, 682, 686

enervate *v* 158, 160

enervation *n* 575

enfeeble *v* 160, 638

enfold *v* 229

enforce *v* 695, 744

enforcement *n* 744

enfranchise *v* 750

enfranchisement *n* 750, 760

engage *v* 132, 288, 615, 676, 768, 769

engage in *v* 622, 676

engage in a discussion *v* 588

engagement *n* 676, 680

engender *v* 161

engorge *v* 957

engrave *v* 259, 558

engrave in the mind *v* 505

engraver *n* 559

engraving *n* 558

engrossed in *adj* 451

enhance *v* 307, 658

enigmatic *adj* 519, 520

enjoin *v* 630, 695, 741

enjoy *v* 377, 394, 827

enjoyable *adj* 829

enjoyment *n* 827, 840

enjoy oneself *v* 827

enlarge *v* 31, 35, 35, 194, 573

enlargement *n* 35, 37, 194, 750

enlighten *v* 420, 527, 537

enlightened *adj* 490, 527

enlightenment *n* 490, 498, 527, 985

enlist *v* 615

enliven *v* 689, 836, 840

enmity *n* 889

enmity *n* 907

ennervation *n* 160

ennoble *v* 875

ennui *n* 688, 841

enormity *n* 102, 192

enormous *adj* 31, 192

enormously *adv* 31

enormousness *n* 31, 192

enough *n* 639; *adj* 639; *adv* 31

enplane *v* 293

enrapture *v* 824, 829

enrapturing *adj* 977

enravish *v* 829

enrich *v* 658

enroll *v* 551

ensconce *v* 528

ensconced *adj* 184

ensconcing *n* 528

ensemble *n* 416, 417

enslave *v* 749

enslavement *n* 749

ensnare *v* 545

ensue *v* 63, 151

ensuing *adj* 117

entangle *v* 43, 61, 219, 704

entangled *adj* 59

entanglement *n* 59, 219, 704

enter *v* 294, 551, 811

enter a protest *v* 766

enter into *v* 56, 768

enterprise *n* 622, 676

enterprising *adj* 861

entertain *v* 840

entertaining *adj* 840

entertainment *n* 840

enthral *v* 749

enthusiasm *n* 574, 602

enthusiast *n* 504

enthusiastic *adj* 825

enthymeme *n* 476

enticing *adj* 288

entire *adj* 50, 52, 729

entirely *adv* 31, 50

entirety *n* 50, 52

entitle *v* 564

entity *n* 1

entomb *v* 363

entombment *n* 363

entomology *n* 368

entrain *v* 293

entrance *n* 294; *v* 829, 992

entrancing *adj* 977

entrap *v* 545

entreat *v* 765

entreaty *n* 411, 765

entrée *n* 296

entrust *v* 755, 784, 805

entry *n* 294, 296

entwine *v* 43, 248

enumerate *v* 85

enumeration *n* 85

enunciate *v* 580

enunication *n* 580

envelope *n* 232

envious *adj* 435, 900, 920, 921

enviousness *n* 921

environ *v* 227

environment *n* 227

environs *n* 227

envision *v* 441

envoy *n* 534

envy *n* 921

envy *n* 900, 920; *v* 921

eon *n* 108

ephemeral *adj* 111

ephemerality *n* 111

epicure *n* 945a 957

epicurean *n* 945a; *adj* 954, 957

epicureanism *n* 954

epicurism *n* 954, 957

epigram *n* 496

epigrammatist *n* 844

epilog *n* 65

episode *n* 39, 70, 151

episodic *adj* 228

epistle *n* 592

epistolary *adj* 592

epithet *n* 564

epitome *n* 193, 596

epitomize *v* 201, 596

epoch *n* 106, 108

equal *n* 27; *v* 27; *adj* 13, 27, 30 216, 242

equality *n* 27

equality *n* 13

equalization *n* 30

equalize *v* 27, 30

equally *adv* 27

equal to *adj* 157

equate *v* 216

equation *n* 30, 216

equator *n* 68

equestrian *n* 268

equidistance *n* 68

equidistant *adj* 68

equilibrium *n* 27, 150

equip *v* 225, 673

equipment *n* 225, 633

equipose *n* 27

equitable *adj* 246, 922

equitableness *n* 922

equitably *adv* 922

equity *n* 922

equivalance *n* 27

equivalent *n* 27, 30, 147; *adj* 12, 13, 27, 30, 216

equivocal *adj* 477, 520

equivocalness *n* 520

equivocate *v* 477, 520

equivocation *n* 477, 520, 544

era *n* 106, 108

eradicate *v* 103, 162, 301

eradication *n* 301

erase *v* 162, 331, 552

every once in a while
adv 136
every other *adj* 138
every which way *adv*
227
every whit *adv* 52
evict *v* 297
eviction *n* 297, 789
evidence *n* 467
evidence *v* 525
evident *adj* 467, 525
evidential *adj* 467
evil *n* 619
evil *n* 649, 663, 665,
923, 940; *adj* 619,
649, 663, 923, 940
evildoer *n* 913
evil-doer *n* 949
evil incarnate *n* 978
evil-minded *adj* 907
evil one *n* 978
evil spirit *n* 978, 980
evil star *n* 649
evince *v* 467, 478, 525
evoke *v* 153, 824
evolution *n* 313
evolution *n* 161
evolutional *adj* 313
evolutionary *adj* 313
evolve *v* 301, 313
evolved from *adj* 154
evolvement *n* 313
ewe *n* 374
exacerbate *v* 173
exacerbation *n* 173
exact *v* 812; *adj* 17, 21,
459, 494, 570
exacting *adj* 868
exaction *n* 741
exactness *n* 13, 80, 459,
494, 570
exaggerate *v* 194, 482,
549, 555, 884
exaggerated *adj* 194,
497, 549
exaggeration *n* 549
exaggeration *n* 482,
497, 523, 555, 835

exalt *v* 35, 307, 838
exaltation *n* 307, 838
exalted *adj* 206, 875
examination *n* 461, 463
examine *v* 457, 461,
463, 595
example *n* 22, 82, 478
exasperate *v* 173
exasperation *n* 173
excavate *v* 208, 252
excavation *n* 252
exceed *v* 33, 303
exceeding *adj* 33
exceedingly *adv* 31
excel *v* 33, 648
excel in *v* 698
excellence *n* 33, 648,
650, 944
excellent *adj* 33, 648
except *v* 469; *adv* 38,
83
excepted *adj* 927a
excepting *adv* 38
exception *n* 55, 83, 469,
777a, 893, 927a
exceptional *adj* 20, 79,
83
excess *n* 40, 641, 954
excessive *adj* 31, 641,
954
excessively *adv* 31
exchange *n* 12, 147,
148, 783, 794, 796; *v*
12, 147, 148, 783,
794, 796
exchangeable *adj* 783
exchequer *n* 802
excise *v* 38
excitability *n* 825
excitability *n* 173, 822,
901
excitable *adj* 382, 684,
822, 824, 825
excitation *n* 824
excitation of feeling *n*
824
excite *v* 171, 173, 375,
377, 615, 824

excite an impression *v*
375
excited *adj* 173, 382,
824
excitement *n* 825
exciting *adj* 824
exclaim *v* 411
exclamation *n* 411
exclude *v* 55, 610, 893
excluded *adj* 57, 893
exclusion *n* 5, 77, 893
exclusion *n* 610
exclusive *adj* 55, 79
exclusive of *adv* 38
excrete *v* 299
excretion *n* 299
excruciating *adj* 982
exculpate *v* 970
exculpated *adj* 970
exculpation *n* 937, 970
exculpatory *adj* 937
excursion *n* 226, 302,
311
excursionist *n* 268
excuse *n* 617, 918,
927a; *v* 617, 777a,
918, 927a
excused *adj* 927a
execrable *adj* 649
execrate *v* 898, 908
execration *n* 908
execute *v* 361, 416,
680, 692, 729, 772,
972
execution *n* 361, 680,
692, 729, 772
executioner *n* 165, 361,
690; 975
executive *adj* 692, 737
executor *n* 690
executrix *n* 690
exegesis *n* 522
exegetical *adj* 522
exemplar *n* 22
exemplary *adj* 82
exemplification *n* 82
exempt *v* 777a, 927a;
adj 748, 927a

exempt from *adj* 777a
exemption *n* 777a, 927a
exercise *n* 170, 677, 680; *v* 677, 680
exert *v* 171, 677, 686
exert energy *v* 680
exert force *v* 288
exertion *n* 686
exertion *n* 171, 680, 682
exert oneself *v* 686
exhalation *n* 299, 398
exhale *v* 299
exhaust *v* 158, 638, 688, 841
exhausted *adj* 2, 158, 688, 841
exhaustion *n* 158, 638, 688, 841
exhaustive *adj* 52
exhibit *n* 467; *v* 525, 882
exhibition *n* 525
exhilarate *v* 836
exhilaration *n* 836
exhort *v* 695
exhortation *n* 695
exhumation *n* 363
exhume *v* 363
exigency *n* 8, 704
exigent *adj* 630
exiguity *n* 203
exile *n* 55, 185, 297, 893; *v* 55, 185, 297
exiled *adj* 893
exist *v* 1, 359
existence *n* 1
existence *n* 1, 359
existent *adj* 1
existing *adj* 118
exit *n* 293, 295, 449
exodus *n* 293
exonerate *v* 937, 970
exonerated *adj* 937, 970
exonerating *adj* 937
exoneration *n* 937, 970
exorbitance *n* 814, 954

exorbitant *adj* 31, 641, 814, 954
exorbitantly *adv* 31
exorcism *n* 993
exorcist *n* 994
exotic *adj* 10, 83
expand *v* 31, 35, 192, 194, 202, 322, 549, 573
expanded *adj* 194
expanse *n* 105, 180, 192
expansion *n* 194
expansion *n* 35, 180, 322
expansive *adj* 180, 194, 202
expatiate *v* 582
expect *v* 121, 451, 507, 510, 620, 858, 871
expectance *n* 871
expectancy *n* 507, 858, 871
expectant *adj* 507, 510, 858, 871
expectantly *adv* 507
expectation *n* 507
expectation *n* 121, 451, 472, 858, 871
expectations *n* 152
expected *adj* 871
expecting *adj* 871
expedience *n* 646
expediency *n* 646
expedient *n* 147; *adj* 646
expedite *v* 132, 684
expedition *n* 132, 266, 684
expeditious *adj* 132, 274
expel *v* 185, 284, 297, 893
expend *v* 638, 677, 809
expenditure *n* 809
expenditure *n* 638
expense *n* 812
expenses *n* 809
expensive *adj* 814

expensiveness *n* 814
experience *v* 151
experienced *adj* 698
experiment *n* 463
experiment *n* 675; *v* 463, 675
experimental *adj* 463, 675
experimentally *adv* 675
experimentation *n* 463
experimenter *n* 463
experiment with *v* 140
expert *n* 700
expert *n* 500, 737, 872; *adj* 698
expertness *n* 698, 702
expiate *v* 952
expiating *adj* 952
expiation *n* 952
expiatory *adj* 952
expiration *n* 67, 360
expire *v* 67, 109, 360
expired *adj* 122
explain *v* 462, 478, 518, 522, 595
explainer *n* 524
explanation *n* 155, 478, 522, 537
explanatory *adj* 522
explicable *adj* 522
explicate *v* 522
explication *n* 522
explicit *adj* 518, 525, 570
explicitness *n* 518, 570
explode *v* 173
exploit *n* 680
exploration *n* 461
exploratory *adj* 461
exploring *adj* 461
explosion *n* 173, 404, 406, 825
explosive *adj* 173, 665
expose *n* 529; *v* 226, 260, 529
exposed *adj* 177, 226, 260, 338
expose oneself to *v* 177

expose the error *v* 479
expose to danger *v* 665
exposition *n* 522, 525, 529, 595
expositor *n* 524
expository *adj* 522, 527
expostulate *v* 616, 766
expostulation *n* 616, 766
expostulatory *adj* 766
exposure *n* 448, 479, 529, 665
expound *v* 522, 537
expounder *n* 524
express *v* 516, 525, 527, 560, 566; *adj* 620
express by words *v* 560, 569
expression *n* 521, 525, 554, 560, 566, 985, 985
expressive *adj* 516, 518, 521, 569
expropriate *v* 789
expropriation *n* 789
expulsion *n* 185, 297, 893
expunge *v* 162, 552
expurgate *v* 652
exquisite *adj* 394, 650
exquisitely *adv* 31
extant *adj* 1
extemporaneous *adj* 612
extemporaneously *adv* 612
extempore *adv* 612
extemporize *v* 612, 674
extend *v* 35, 194, 200
extended *adj* 200, 202
extend to *v* 196, 200
extension *n* 35, 65, 180, 194
extensive *adj* 31, 76, 180
extensively *adv* 180
extent *n* 26, 106, 180, 200, 202, 233
extenuate *v* 469

extenuating *adj* 469
extenuating
  circumstances *n* 469
extenuation *n* 469
exterior *n* 220; *adj* 220
exteriority *n* 220
exterminate *v* 162
extermination *n* 301
external *adj* 6, 57, 220
externality *n* 57
externally *adv* 220
externals *n* 6
extinct *adj* 2, 122, 162, 360
extinction *n* 2, 162, 360, 421, 552
extinguish *v* 162, 385, 421
extirpate *v* 301
extirpation *n* 301
extol *v* 883
extort *v* 814
extortion *n* 789
extra *adj* 37
extract *v* 301
extraction *n* 301
extracts *n* 596
extradite *v* 270
extradition *n* 270
extraneous *adj* 6, 10, 57, 220
extraneousness *n* 57
extraneousness *n* 6
extraordinary *adj* 31, 83, 870
extravagance *n* 497, 499, 549, 814, 818, 954
extravagant *adj* 31, 497, 499, 549, 641, 814, 818, 853, 954
extravagant love *n* 991
extravagantly *adv* 31
extreme *n* 67; *adj* 31
extremely *adv* 31
extremity *n* 67
extricate *v* 301, 672, 705, 750

extrication *n* 301, 672, 750
extrinsic *adj* 6, 57, 220
extrinsicality *n* 6
extrinsicality *n* 57
extrinsically *adv* 6
exuberance *n* 573, 641
exuberant *adj* 573, 641
exude *v* 295
exultant *adj* 838, 884
eye *n* 247; *v* 441
eye for an eye *n* 30
eyeglasses *n* 445
eyeless *adj* 442
eyesight *n* 441
eyewitness *n* 444
eyot *n* 346

F

fable *n* 546
fabric *n* 7
fabricate *v* 161, 515, 544
fabrication *n* 161, 544, 546
fabulous *adj* 2, 515, 546, 549, 979
fabulous spirit *n* 979
façade *n* 220, 234
face *n* 220, 234, 448; *v* 223, 224, 234
facet *n* 220
facetious *adj* 842
facetiousness *n* 842
face to face *adv* 237
facile *adj* 705
facilitate *v* 705, 707
facility *n* 705
facility *n* 157, 698, 748
facing *n* 223; *adj* 237
facsimile *n* 13, 21, 90
fact *n* 1, 151, 474, 494
faction *n* 712
factious *adj* 24
factory *n* 691
facts *n* 467, 527
factual *adj* 494
faculties *n* 450

faculty *n* 698
fad *n* 608
faddish *adj* 123
faddishness *n* 123
fade *v* 4, 111, 124, 160, 287, 360, 422, 429, 449, 659, 732
faded *adj* 659
fail *v* 160, 304, 360, 655, 732, 773, 808, 927
failing *n* 732; *adj* 53, 128, 927
failure *n* 732
failure *n* 304, 460, 509, 735, 773, 808, 927
fain *adj* 602
faint *v* 158, 688; *adj* 32, 160, 203, 405, 422, 429, 430, 447, 688
faint-hearted *adj* 862
faint-heartedness *n* 862
faintly *adv* 32
faintness *n* 405
faintness *n* 575, 688
faint sound *n* 405
fair *n* 799; *adj* 174, 246, 429, 430, 651, 829, 845, 922, 942
fair game *n* 857
fairly *adv* 922
fairness *n* 174, 845, 922, 942
fairy *n* 979
faith *n* 484, 858
faithful *adj* 17, 21, 494, 772, 983a
faithfully *adv* 772
faithfulness *n* 772, 983a
faithless *adj* 544, 989
fake *n* 556; *v* 680; *adj* 19
fake god *n* 991
faker *n* 548
fall *n* 126, 162, 217, 283, 306, 348, 360; *v* 162, 306, 310, 360

fallacious *adj* 4, 477, 495, 544, 545
fallacy *n* 4, 477, 495
fall again *v* 661
fall away *v* 195
fall back *v* 145, 283, 287, 661
fall behind *v* 281, 283
fallibility *n* 475
fallible *adj* 475
fall in *v* 488
falling *n* 306; *adj* 217
falling back *n* 145, 287, 661
falling-off *n* 36, 659
falling out *n* 720
falling short *n* 304
fall into a rut *v* 613
fall into a trap *v* 547
fall into raptures *v* 827
fall off *v* 36, 659, 732
fall on evil days *v* 735
fall on one's knees *v* 990
fall out *v* 151, 713
fallow *adj* 674
fall prey to *v* 749
fall short *v* 304, 651, 732
fall short of *v* 28, 34, 53, 640, 730
fall through *v* 304
fall to *v* 151, 298, 676
fall to one *v* 785
fall to one's lot *v* 156
fall to pieces *v* 162
fall under *v* 76
false *adj* 19, 477, 495, 544, 545, 546, 923
false coloration *n* 523
false expectation *n* 508
false god *n* 991
falsehood *n* 544
falsehood *n* 546
false impression *n* 495
falseness *n* 545
false statement *n* 477
falsification *n* 523, 544, 555

falsify *v* 523, 544, 555
falter *v* 605
famed *adj* 883
familial *adj* 11, 166, 712
familiar *adj* 613, 888
familiarity *n* 748
familiarize *v* 613
family *n* 11, 75, 166, 167, 712
family likeness *n* 17
famish *v* 819, 956
famous *adj* 883
famously *adv* 31
fan *v* 338, 349, 385
fanatic *n* 504, 606; *adj* 606
fanatical *adj* 825
fanaticism *n* 606
fanciful *adj* 149, 515, 608
fancy *n* 453, 515, 608, 865; *v* 515, 865; *adj* 577
fancy talk *n* 577
fang *n* 663
fantastic *adj* 83, 497, 515, 853
fantastical *adj* 515
fantasy *n* 515
fan the fire *v* 173, 824
far *adj* 196
far and wide *adv* 180
far away *adj* 196; *adv* 196
farce *n* 497
farcical *adj* 497, 853
far cry to *n* 196
fare *n* 298, 812
farewell *n* 293
farfetched *adj* 10
far gone *adj* 503, 659
farm *v* 371
farming *n* 371
farness *n* 196
far off *adj* 196; *adv* 196
farrago *n* 41, 497

farsighted *adj* 441, 443, 510
farsightedness *n* 443
fascinate *v* 288, 824, 829
fascinated *adj* 870
fascination *n* 824, 829
fashion *n* 852
fashion *n* 7, 123, 613, 627; *v* 240, 557, 852
fashionable *adj* 123, 613, 852
fashionableness *n* 123
fast *v* 955, 956; *adj* 43, 150, 274, 684; *adv* 43
fast as a bullet *adj* 274
fasten *v* 43, 45, 150
fastidious *adj* 704, 868
fastidiousness *n* 868
fasting *n* 956
fasting *adj* 956
fast talker *n* 548
fat *n* 356; *adj* 192, 194
fatal *adj* 162, 360, 361
fatality *n* 360, 601
fat chance *adj* 471
fate *n* 121, 156, 601, 611, 621
father *n* 166, 996
fatherhood *n* 166
fatherland *n* 189
fathership *n* 166
fathom *v* 490
fathomless *adj* 208
fatigue *n* 688
fatigue *n* 841; *v* 688, 841
fatigued *adj* 688, 841
fatten *v* 194, 298
fattiness *n* 354
fatty *adj* 354
fatuity *n* 452, 499
fatuous *adj* 499
faucet *n* 263
fault *n* 70, 495, 651, 732, 848, 927, 945, 961

faultless *adj* 50, 650, 946, 960
faultlessness *n* 650, 946, 960
faulty *adj* 568, 651, 732, 945, 961
faulty grammar *n* 568
faun *n* 979
fauna *n* 357, 366
favor *n* 707, 740, 760, 784; *v* 740, 760
favorable *adj* 134, 602, 648, 734
favorite *n* 899
favor with *v* 784
fawn *v* 886, 933
fawner *n* 935
fawning *n* 886, 933; *adj* 886
fay *n* 979
fealty *n* 743
fear *n* 860
fear *n* 862; *v* 860
fearful *adj* 665, 830, 860, 862
fearfully *adv* 31
fearless *adj* 861
fearlessness *n* 861
feasibility *n* 470, 705
feasible *adj* 470, 705
feast on *v* 298, 377
feat *n* 680
feather one's own nest *v* 943
feathery *adj* 320
feature *n* 56, 79, 448, 550, 780
features *n* 5
fecal *adj* 653
fecund *adj* 168, 365
fecundity *n* 168
feeble *adj* 32, 158, 160, 203, 337, 477, 575, 605
feeble-minded *adj* 499
feebleness *n* 575
feebleness *n* 158
feed *v* 298, 388

feel *n* 379; *v* 375, 379, 821
feel contempt for *v* 930
feel fine *v* 654
feel for *v* 914
feel good *v* 654
feeling *n* 821
feeling *n* 375, 379, 928; *adj* 821, 914
feeling no pain *adj* 959
feel pain *v* 378
feel pleasure *v* 377
feel sorry about *v* 833
feel sorry for *v* 914
fees *n* 809
feign *v* 544, 546, 680, 855
feigned *adj* 855
feigning *n* 855
felicitation *n* 896
felicitous *adj* 23, 578, 698, 850
felicity *n* 698, 827
fell *v* 162, 213, 308
fellow *n* 17, 27, 88, 373, 890; *adj* 88
fellow creature *n* 372
fellow-feeling *n* 888
fellow man *n* 372
fellowship *n* 709, 712, 888
female *n* 374; *adj* 374
female animal *n* 374
feminine *adj* 374
femininity *n* 374
fen *n* 345
fence *n* 232; *v* 277, 477
fence in *v* 229
ferment *n* 59, 171, 173, 315, 320; *v* 173, 315, 353, 397
fermentation *n* 171, 315, 353
fermented *adj* 397
ferocious *adj* 173
ferocity *n* 173
ferret out *v* 480a
fertile *adj* 168, 371

fertility *n* 168
fertilize *v* 168
fervent *adj* 382, 821, 865
fervid *adj* 382, 824
fervor *n* 382, 821, 991
fester *v* 653
festival *n* 883
festivity *n* 840, 883
fetch *v* 270, 812
fetid *adj* 401, 653
fetidness *n* 401
fetishism *n* 991
fetishistic *adj* 991
fetor *n* 401
fetter *v* 43
feud *n* 713, 720; *v* 713
fever *n* 382, 825
feverish *adj* 824, 825
few *n* 100; *adj* 32, 103, 137
few and far between *adj* 103
fewness *n* 103
fewness *n* 32
fiasco *n* 732
fiat *n* 741
fib *n* 544, 546; *v* 544, 546
fiber *n* 205
fibrous *adj* 205
fickle *adj* 149, 605, 608
fickleness *n* 605
fiction *n* 515, 544, 546, 598
fictional *adj* 598
fictitious *adj* 546
fidelity *n* 543, 772
fidget *v* 825
fidgetiness *n* 149, 682
fidgety *adj* 149, 682, 825
field *n* 344
field of battle *n* 728
fields *n* 344
fiend *n* 980
fiendish *adj* 980
fierce *adj* 173, 825

fiery *adj* 382, 684, 825
fiery furnace *n* 386
fifty *n* 98
fifty-fifty chance *n* 156
fifty-fifty split *n* 91
fight *n* 680; *v* 606, 720, 722
fighter *n* 726
fighting *n* 173, 722
figment *n* 515
figuration *n* 554
figurative *adj* 521, 554
figure *n* 84, 550, 812; *v* 240, 448, 554, 557
figured on *adj* 871
figure of speech *n* 521
figure of speech *n* 566
figures of beauty *n* 521
filament *n* 205
filch *v* 791
filcher *n* 792
file *n* 69, 86, 266, 330; *v* 38, 60, 69, 195, 255, 330
file a claim *v* 969
filial *adj* 167
filiation *n* 11
filigree *n* 219
filing *n* 330
fill *v* 52, 186, 190, 224
filled in *adj* 527
fill in *v* 52
filling *n* 224
fill out *v* 194, 549
fill up *v* 52, 261
fill up the time *v* 106
film *n* 204, 427
filminess *n* 426
filmy *adj* 204, 329, 426
filth *n* 653
filthy *adj* 653
final *adj* 67
finale *n* 65, 67, 360, 729
final gasp *n* 360
finality *n* 67
finalize *v* 729
finally *adv* 67, 151

final stage *n* 67
final touch *n* 729
finance *n* 800, 811
financial *adj* 800
financier *n* 801, 811
find *n* 480a, 775; *v* 151
find fulfillment *v* 731
find guilty *v* 971
find oneself *v* 186
fine one's way to *v* 602
find out *v* 480a, 527
find refuge *v* 666
find safety *v* 666
find the means *v* 632
find the right words *v* 566
find vent *v* 295
fine *n* 974; *v* 974; *adj* 32, 203, 322, 329, 578, 648, 845
fine art *n* 556
fine gentleman *n* 854
fineness *n* 329
fine powder *n* 330
finery *n* 847, 851
fine speaking *n* 577
finesse *n* 698, 702; *v* 702
fine writing *n* 577
finger *v* 379
fingering *n* 379
finical *adj* 459
finicky *adj* 868
finish *n* 65, 67, 142, 242, 729; *v* 52, 67, 142, 650, 729
finished *adj* 242, 698
finishing stroke *n* 361
fire *n* 171, 382, 423, 574; *v* 384, 388, 420, 824
fired *adj* 384
fire off *v* 284
fire place *n* 386
fireproof *adj* 385
firewood *n* 388
firing *n* 388, 406

firm *adj* 43, 150, 323, 604, 606
firmament *n* 318
firmly *adv* 43
firmness *n* 150, 323, 604, 606
first *adj* 66; *adv* 66
first and foremost *adv* 66
first blush *n* 125
first cause *n* 153, 976
first-class *adj* 648
first come first served *n* 607, 609a
first move *n* 66
first rank *n* 234
first-rate *adj* 33, 648, 698
first step *n* 66
firth *n* 343
fiscal *adj* 800
fish *n* 366
fish for *v* 622
fishing *n* 361
fish story *n* 549
fish up *v* 307
fissure *n* 44, 198, 260
fit *n* 7, 173, 315, 825; *v* 23, 852; *adj* 646, 698, 922
fit as a fiddle *adj* 654
fit for *adj* 698
fitful *adj* 70, 139, 149, 475, 608
fitfully *adv* 139
fitfulness *n* 139, 475
fitness *n* 646
fit out *v* 225, 673
fits *n* 315
five, etc. *n* 98
five *n* 98
fivefold division *n* 99
fix *n* 704; *v* 43, 60, 150, 184, 604, 660
fix a price *v* 812
fixed *adj* 5, 141, 150, 240, 265, 474, 604, 613

fixed idea *n* 606
fixedness *n* 150
fixity *n* 150, 265
fix the time *v* 114
fizzle *v* 353, 409
fjord *n* 343
flabby *adj* 324
flaccid *adj* 160, 324, 326
flaccidity *n* 160, 324, 326, 640
flag *n* 747; *v* 160, 275, 655, 683, 688
flaky *adj* 204
flame *n* 382, 420, 423, 439, 897; *v* 382, 897
flame-colored *adj* 439
flaming *adj* 434
flammable *adj* 384, 388
flank *n* 236; *v* 236
flanked *adj* 236
flanking *adj* 236
flap *n* 214; *v* 214, 315
flare *n* 420; *v* 173, 420
flare up *v* 420, 825
flash *n* 113, 420, 453, 612; *v* 113, 420
flash on *v* 505; *v* 612
flashy *adj* 428, 577, 851, 882
flat *n* 344; *adj* 172, 207, 213, 251, 337, 391, 395, 598, 843
flat as a pancake *adj* 251
flatlands *n* 207
flatness *n* 251
flatness *n* 207, 213, 391, 843
flatten *v* 213, 251, 255
flatter *v* 933
flatterer *n* 935
flattering *adj* 933
flattery *n* 933
flatulent *adj* 334, 338
flaunt *v* 882
flaunting *adj* 882
flavor *n* 390, 394; *v* 390

flavored *adj* 390
flavorful *adj* 390, 394
flavorfulness *n* 394
flavoring *n* 393
flavorless *adj* 395
flavorlessness *n* 395
flavory *adj* 390
flaw *n* 70, 198, 495, 651, 848, 961
flawed *adj* 961
flaxen *adj* 435
fleck *v* 440
flecked *adj* 440
flecky *adj* 440
fled *adj* 671
flee *v* 671
fleece *n* 223; *v* 789, 791, 814
fleet *n* 273; *adj* 274, 684
fleeting *adj* 111
flesh *n* 364
flesh and blood *n* 3, 316, 364
fleshiness *n* 354
fleshly *adj* 364
fleshy *adj* 354
flexibility *n* 324, 705
flexible *adj* 324
flexure *n* 245
flicker *n* 315; *v* 315, 420, 422
flickering *adj* 139
flier *n* 269
flier *n* 269
flight *n* 267, 274, 287, 293, 623, 671
flighty *adj* 149, 503
flimsiness *n* 4, 209, 425
flimsy *adj* 160, 209, 322, 324, 425, 477, 643
flinch *v* 623
fling *n* 284; *v* 284
flip out *v* 173
flipside *n* 235
flirt *v* 902

flit *v* 109, 111, 264, 266, 274

flitting *adj* 111, 266

float *v* 267, 320

floating *adj* 405

flock *n* 72, 997; *v* 72

flocks and herds *n* 366

flog *v* 972

flogging *n* 975

flood *n* 72, 121, 348; *v* 641

flood gate *n* 233, 350

floor *n* 204; *v* 213

flop *v* 315

flora *n* 357, 367, 369

floriculture *n* 371

florid *adj* 428, 577

floridness *n* 577

flounce *v* 309, 315

flounder *v* 149, 314, 315, 475, 732

flourish *n* 577, 882; *v* 367, 654, 734

flourish of trumpets *n* 404

floury *adj* 330

flout *v* 715

flow *n* 264, 348; *v* 109, 214, 264, 333, 347, 348

flower *n* 648; *v* 161, 734

flowerage *n* 367

flowering *n* 161

flowery *adj* 577

flow from *v* 154

flow in *v* 294

flowing *n* 348; *adj* 405, 578

flow into *v* 348

flow out *v* 295, 348

flow out of *v* 295

flow over *v* 348

fluctuate *v* 149, 314, 605

fluctuating *adj* 149

fluctuation *n* 149, 314, 605

flue *n* 351

fluency *n* 333

fluent *adj* 333, 348, 578, 584

fluffy *adj* 256

fluid *n* 337; *adj* 333, 337

fluidity *n* 333

fluke *n* 156, 621

flukey *adj* 156

flunkey *n* 935

flunkeyism *n* 933

flurry *n* 682, 684

flush *n* 382, 420; *v* 382, 434

flushed *adj* 434, 824, 838

flush out *v* 480a

fluster *v* 824

flute *v* 259

fluted *adj* 259

flutter *n* 315; *v* 315, 422

flux *n* 109, 144, 264, 348

flux and reflux *n* 314

fly *v* 109, 111, 267, 287, 328, 671

fly back *v* 277

fly from *v* 623

flying *n* 274, 267; *adj* 111, 267, 959

fly over *v* 267

fly to pieces *v* 328

foam *n* 353; *v* 173, 315, 353, 825

foaming *n* 353

foamy *adj* 353

focal *adj* 222

focus *n* 74

focus *v* 74

focus on *v* 222

fodder *n* 362

foe *n* 708, 710, 726, 891

fog *n* 353, 424

fogginess *n* 422, 475

foggy *adj* 422, 426, 353

foil *n* 14

foiled *adj* 732

fold *n* 258

fold *n* 232, 997; *v* 258

folded *adj* 258

foliage *n* 367

foliation *n* 367

folk *n* 372

folk music *n* 415

follow *v* 19, 63, 281, 518, 622, 743

follow after *v* 117

follower *n* 117, 541, 746

follow in a line *v* 69

following *n* 63, 117, 281; *adj* 63, 117, 281

follow in the steps of *v* 281

follow in the wake of *v* 281

follow the rules *v* 82

folly *n* 499

fond *adj* 897

fondle *v* 379

fondling *n* 379

fondness *n* 897

font *n* 153

food *n* 298, 637

food for thought *n* 454

food for worms *n* 362

fool *n* 501

fool *n* 493, 547, 844, 857; *v* 545

foolhardiness *n* 863

foolhardy *adj* 684, 863

foolish *adj* 477, 497, 499

foolishness *n* 497, 499

foot *n* 211

footing *n* 8, 71, 183, 215

fop *n* 854

foppery *n* 855

for *adv* 155

for a long time *adv* 110

for a time *adv* 111

foray *n* 716

forbear *v* 678, 953
forbearance *n* 623, 678, 740, 826
forbears *n* 122
forbid *v* 761
force *n* 157, 159, 170, 171, 173, 574, 739, 744; *v* 157, 744
forced *adj* 10, 579
forceful *adj* 157, 159, 171, 574
forcefulness *n* 600
force of will *n* 600
for certain *adv* 474
forcible *adj* 171, 574, 744
forcibly *adv* 744
ford *v* 302
fore *adj* 234
forebode *v* 909
foreboding *n* 512, 909; *adj* 909
forecast *n* 510, 511, 673; *v* 507, 511, 626
forefather *n* 130
forefront *n* 234
foregoing *adj* 62, 116, 122
foregone *adj* 611
foregone conclusion *n* 611
foreground *n* 234
foreign *adj* 10, 57, 220
foreign body *n* 57
foreign parts *n* 196
foreign substance *n* 57
fore-knowledge *n* 510
foreman *n* 694
foremost *adj* 33, 66, 234, 642
forenoon *n* 125
foreordain *v* 152
forerun *v* 62, 116, 280
forerunner *n* 64, 116, 534
foresee *v* 121, 507, 510, 511, 871
foreseen *adj* 507, 871

foreshadow *v* 909
foreshadowing *adj* 909
foresight *n* 510
forestall *v* 132
forestry *n* 371
foretell *v* 511
forethought *n* 510, 864
foretoken *n* 511; *v* 511
forever *adv* 16, 112
forewarn *v* 510, 668
foreword *n* 64
forfeit *n* 974; *v* 776
forfeiture *n* 776
for form's sake *adv* 82
forge *n* 386, 691
forge ahead *v* 282
forgery *n* 19, 21, 546
forget *v* 506
forgetful *adj* 506
forgetfulness *n* 506
forgive *v* 918
forgiveness *n* 918
forgiving *adj* 918
forgo *v* 624, 757, 782
for good *adv* 106, 141
for good and all *adv* 141
forgotten *adj* 122, 506
fork *n* 244; *v* 91, 244, 291
forked *adj* 244
for keeps *adv* 106
forking *n* 91, 291
fork out *v* 784
forlorn *adj* 859
form *n* 240
form *n* 7, 21, 54, 80, 329, 448, 569, 697, 998; *v* 54, 56, 60, 144, 161, 240, 557, 852
formal *adj* 80, 82, 240, 242, 383, 579
formal features *n* 567
formality *n* 240, 579
formal speech *n* 586
form an opinion *v* 480
formation *n* 161, 240

formative *adj* 127, 153, 161
formative years *n* 127
form a whole *v* 50
formed *adj* 820
former *adj* 62, 116, 122
formerly *adv* 122
former times *n* 122
formidable *adj* 704
form into a sphere *v* 249
formless *adj* 241
formlessness *n* 241
form part of *v* 56
forms *n* 567
formula *n* 80, 240, 626, 697
formulaic *adj* 80, 626
formulate *v* 963
forsake *v* 624, 732, 782
for sale *adj* 763, 794, 796
forswear *v* 624, 782
forsworn *adj* 782
forte n 698
forth *adv* 282
forthcoming *adj* 152
for the moment *adv* 111
for the most part *adv* 613
for the sake of conformity *adv* 82
for the time being *adv* 106
forthright *adj* 246, 946
forthwith *adv* 132
fortification *n* 717
fortify *v* 159, 717
fortitude *n* 826, 861
fortress *n* 666
fortuitous *adj* 134, 156, 621
fortunate *adj* 134, 734
fortune *n* 152, 156, 621, 734, 803
fortune-teller *n* 513
forum *n* 966
forward *adj* 234; *adv* 282

fossil fuel *n* 388
foster *v* 658
foul *adj* 401, 649, 653
foulness *n* 401
foul play *n* 619
foul smell *n* 401
found *v* 153, 215
foundation *n* 153, 211, 215, 673
founded on *adj* 211
founder *n* 164; *v* 732
foundling *n* 893
found wanting *adj* 651
fount *n* 153
fountain *n* 153
four *n* 95; *adj* 95, 96
four-flusher *n* 548
fourfold *adj* 95, 96
fourfold division *n* 97
fourth *adj* 96
fourthly *adv* 96
fourth part *n* 97
four times *adv* 96
fowls of the air *n* 366
foxy *adj* 702
fracas *n* 59
fraction *n* 100a
fraction *n* 32, 51, 84
fractional *adj* 51, 84
fractional part *n* 100a
fractious *adj* 713, 742
fracture *n* 44, 70
fragile *adj* 160, 203, 328
fragility *n* 160, 328
fragment *n* 32, 51
fragmentary *adj* 51
fragments *n* 596
fragrance *n* 400
fragrant *adj* 377, 400
frail *adj* 158, 160, 203, 328, 605, 651
frailty *n* 158, 160, 328, 575, 605
frame *n* 7, 231, 240, 329; *v* 161, 626, 852
frame of mind *n* 602
framework *n* 329

franchise *n* 748, 760; *v* 760
franchisement *n* 748
frangible *adj* 328
frank *adj* 246, 525, 543, 703
frankness *n* 543, 748
frantic *adj* 173, 503, 824
fraternal *adj* 712, 714
fraternity *n* 11, 709, 888
fraternize *v* 709, 714, 892
fratricide *n* 361
fraud *n* 545, 548, 791
fraudulent *adj* 544
fraught *adj* 52
fraught with danger *adj* 665
fray *v* 331
freak *n* 156; *v* 608, 872
freaked *adj* 173
freakish *adj* 608
freckled *adj* 440, 848
free *v* 672, 705, 748, 750, 927a; *adj* 44, 600, 685, 748, 816
freed *adj* 748, 750, 927a
freedom *n* 748
freedom *n* 600, 672, 738, 760, 927a
freely *adv* 602, 748
free space *n* 180
free spirit *n* 268
free swinging *n* 214
freethinker *n* 989
freethinking *n* 989; *adj* 989
free time *n* 685
free will *n* 600
freeze *v* 376, 383, 385
freezer *n* 387
freezing *adj* 383
freight *n* 190
freighter *n* 271, 273
frenzied *adj* 173, 503

frenzy *n* 503, 825
frequency *n* 136
frequent *adj* 104, 136, 613
frequently *adv* 136
fresh *adj* 123, 428, 435, 505
freshen *v* 338, 689
freshness *n* 123
fresh wind *n* 349
fret *n* 828; *v* 378, 832
fretful *adj* 684
fretwork *n* 219
friability *n* 330
friction *n* 331
friction *n* 179, 719
fridge *n* 387
friend *n* 890
friend *n* 711, 912, 977
friendliness *n* 888, 897
friendly *adj* 707, 714, 721, 888, 892
friendship *n* 888
friendship *n* 714
fright *n* 860
frighten *v* 909
frightened *adj* 860
frightening *adj* 909
frightful *adj* 830
frightfully *adv* 31
frightfulness *n* 846
frigid *adj* 158, 383
frigidaire *n* 387
frigidity *n* 383
frills *n* 847
fringe *n* 231
frippery *n* 643, 851
frisk *n* 309; *v* 309
frisky *adj* 309, 682
fritter away time *v* 683
fritter one's money *v* 818
frivolity *n* 4, 209, 499
frivolous *adj* 4, 477, 499, 608, 643
frizz *v* 248
frizzle *v* 248, 258

from all points of the compass *adv* 180

from bad to worse *adv* 835

from beginning to end *adv* 52

from first to last *adv* 52

from head to foot *adv* 52

from pole to pole *adv* 180

from side to side *adv* 314

from the beginning *adv* 66

from the bottom of one's heart *adv* 821

from the four corners of the world *adv* 180

from this time *adv* 121

from time to time *adv* 136

from top to bottom *adv* 52

front *n* 234

front *n* 719; *v* 234; *adj* 234

frontage *n* 234

frontal *adj* 234

frontier *n* 233

fronting *adj* 237

frontispiece *n* 64, 234

front rank *n* 234

frost-bitten *adj* 383

frosted *adj* 426, 430

frostiness *n* 430

frosty *adj* 383

froth *n* 353; *v* 353

frothy *adj* 353

frown *v* 837, 900, 901a

frown upon *v* 932

frozen *adj* 381, 383, 385

fructification *n* 161

fructify *v* 168, 658, 734

frugal *adj* 817, 953

frugality *n* 817

fruit *n* 154, 367

fruitful *adj* 168

fruitfulness *n* 168

fruition *n* 161

fruitless *adj* 158, 645, 732

frustrate *v* 706

frustrated *adj* 732

frustration *n* 509

fry *v* 384

fuel *n* 388

fuel *v* 388

fuel oil *n* 388

fugitive *n* 268, 623; *adj* 623

fulfill *v* 52, 161, 168, 729, 772, 926

fulfilled *adj* 52

fulfillment *n* 161, 729, 731, 772

fulfill oneself *v* 731

full *adj* 31, 50, 52, 52, 404, 729

full-blown *adj* 194

full circle *n* 311

full-flavored *adj* 392, 394

full grown *adj* 131, 192, 194

fullness *n* 31, 52, 131

full of incident *adj* 151

full turn *n* 311

fully *adv* 31, 52

fulminate *v* 404

fulsome *adj* 401

fumble *v* 61, 699

fumbler *n* 701

fume *n* 398, 401; *v* 173, 382, 825, 900

fumigate *v* 652

fuming *adj* 434, 824

fun *n* 842

function *n* 170, 625, 926, 998; *v* 680, 746

functional *adj* 625, 644

functionary *n* 694, 758

fund *n* 636

fundamental *adj* 5, 211, 215

fundamentally *adv* 31

fundamental part *n* 211

funds *n* 800

funeral *n* 363; *adj* 363

funeral rites *n* 363

funereal *adj* 363

fungus *n* 663

funish *v* 784

funnel *n* 350, 351

funny *adj* 853

funnyman *n* 844

fur *n* 223

furcation *n* 291

furious *adj* 173, 382, 825

furiously *adv* 31

furnace *n* 386

furnish *v* 637, 673

furor *n* 825

furrow *n* 259

furrow *v* 259

furrowed *adj* 259

further *adv* 37

furtherance *n* 707

furthermore *adv* 37

furtive *adj* 528

fury *n* 173, 825, 980

fuse *v* 43, 48, 384

fusion *n* 48, 384, 709

fuss *n* 315, 682; *v* 682, 825

fussy *adj* 682, 825, 868

fustian *n* 577

fustiness *n* 401

fusty *adj* 401

futile *adj* 158, 645

futility *n* 645

future *n* 117, 152; *adj* 121

future events *n* 152

futurism *n* 123

G

gab *v* 584

gad about *v* 266

gadding *adj* 266

gadding about *n* 266

gag *v* 403, 581

gaggle *v* 412

gain *n* 618, 658, 775; *v* 775

gainful *adj* 775

gain ground *v* 282

gain knowledge *v* 539

gain on *v* 286

gainsay *v* 536, 708

gait *n* 264

galaxy *n* 318

gale *n* 349

gall *v* 378, 869

gallant *adj* 861, 894

gallantry *n* 861

gallimaufry *n* 41

gallop *v* 111

galvanism *n* 824

galvanize *v* 824

gamble *n* 156; *v* 621

gambler *n* 621

gambling *n* 156, 621

game *n* 366, 620, 857; *adj* 604, 604a

gamester *n* 621

gaming *n* 156

gander *n* 373

gang *n* 72, 712

gaol *n* 752

gaoler *n* 753

gap *n* 70, 196, 198, 260

gape *v* 198, 260, 455

gaping *adj* 208, 260

garb *n* 225; *v* 225

garble *v* 523, 583

garden *v* 371, 371

gardening *n* 371

garish *adj* 428, 851, 882

garland *n* 247

garner *v* 636

garrison *n* 717; *v* 664

garrote *n* 361; *v* 361

garroter *n* 361

garrulity *n* 584

garrulous *adj* 584

gas *n* 388; *v* 361

gaseity *n* 334

gaseous *adj* 334, 336

gaseousness *n* 334

gash *n* 198

gasification *n* 336

gasify *v* 336

gas lamp *n* 423

gasoline *n* 356, 388

gasp *v* 349, 655, 688

gassing *n* 361

gate *n* 232, 260

gateway *n* 232, 260, 627

gather *v* 72, 258, 775, 789

gathering *n* 72, 712

gathering place *n* 74

gather together *v* 290

gaudiness *n* 851

gaudy *adj* 428, 851, 882

gauge *n* 466

gauging *n* 466

gaunt *adj* 203

gauze *n* 424

gauziness *n* 425

gauzy *adj* 425

gawky *adj* 699

gay *adj* 829, 836

gaze *n* 441

gazette *n* 86

gear *n* 225

Gehenna *n* 982

gelding *n* 373

gelid *adj* 383

gem *n* 648

genealogy *n* 69, 166

general *adj* 78, 613

generality *n* 78

generalization *n* 78

generalize *v* 78

generally *adv* 613

general public *n* 372, 876

generalship *n* 722

generate *v* 161, 168

generation *n* 11, 108, 161, 163

generative *adj* 153, 161, 168

generator *n* 164

generic *adj* 78

generosity *n* 784, 816, 906, 942

generous *adj* 784, 816, 906, 942

genesis *n* 66, 153, 161

genial *adj* 382, 602, 829, 888, 892

geniality *n* 602, 836

genius *n* 698, 700, 872

genius for *n* 698

genteel *adj* 852

gentility *n* 578, 852, 875, 894

gentle *adj* 174, 275, 405, 721, 740

gentleman *n* 373

gentlemanly *adj* 894

gentleness *n* 174, 740

gentlewoman *n* 374

genuflect *v* 308

genuflection *n* 308

genuine *adj* 494, 648, 922, 960

genuineness *n* 960

genus *n* 75

geography *n* 183

geology *n* 358

germ *n* 66, 153

germinate *v* 194, 367

gestation *n* 161

gesticulate *v* 550

gesticulation *n* 550

gesture *n* 550; *v* 550

get *v* 775, 795, 810

get a footing *v* 184

get a head start *v* 132

get along *v* 282, 736

get back *v* 790

get back to basics *v* 849

get better *v* 658

get between *v* 228

get closer to *v* 286

get close to *v* 286

get down *v* 306

get down to particulars *v* 79

get going *v* 66, 276, 284

get hold of *v* 775, 789
get into *v* 827
get into print *v* 531
get on *v* 282
get one's wind *v* 687
get over *v* 660
get ready *v* 673
get red in the face *v* 434
get rid of *v* 297, 776
get the scent of *v* 527
get through *v* 67
get to *v* 292
get to the heart of *v* 222
get under way *v* 293
get up *v* 305
get well *v* 660
ghost *n* 362, 980; 443
ghostlike *adj* 980
ghostly *adj* 976, 980
ghoul *n* 980
giant *n* 192
gibberish *n* 517
gibes *n* 856
giddy *adj* 499
gift *n* 698, 763, 775, 784
gigantic *adj* 31, 159, 192, 206
giggle *n* 838; *v* 838
gimmicky *adj* 643
gird *v* 43, 227
girdle *n* 232, 247
girl *n* 129, 374
girlfriend *n* 897
girlhood *n* 127
girlish *adj* 129
gist *n* 5, 516
give *n* 325; *v* 324, 325, 763, 784, 816
give a free rein *v* 738
give a hearing to *v* 418
give an account *v* 527
give and take *v* 148, 774, 794
give a new turn to *v* 140
give assent *v* 484
give assistance *v* 707
give a start to *v* 276

give audience to *v* 418
give away *v* 784
give back *v* 790
give birth to *v* 163, 359
give counsel *v* 695
give counsel to *v* 695
give credence to 484
give energy *v* 171
give entrance to *v* 296
give evidence *v* 467
give fight *v* 722
give help *v* 707
give in *v* 82, 360
give it a shot *v* 602
given *adj* 474, 514
give no quarter *v* 361
give notice *v* 668
given time *n* 134
given up *adj* 782
give offense *v* 830
give oneself airs *v* 878
give one's word *v* 768
give out *v* 732, 784
give out a smell *v* 398
give out sound *v* 402
give pleasure *v* 377
giver *n* 784
give rise to *v* 153
give satisfaction *v* 952
give security *v* 768, 771
give up *v* 624, 757, 782, 790
give up hope *v* 859
give up the ghost *v* 360
give way *v* 160, 328
give way to *v* 881
giving *n* 784
glacial *adj* 383
glaciation *n* 385
gladden *v* 829, 836
gladdening *adj* 836
glade *n* 252
gladness *n* 827
gladsome *adj* 827, 829
glance *n* 441
glance around *v* 441
glare *v* 420, 441
glaring *adj* 428, 446

glaringly *adv* 31
glass *n* 389
glasses *n* 445
glassy *adj* 255, 420
glaze *v* 255
gleam *n* 420; *v* 420
glee *n* 827
gleeful *adj* 836
glen *n* 252
glib *adj* 584
glide *v* 264, 267
glider *n* 273
gliding *n* 267
glimmer *v* 420, 422, 446
glimmering *n* 420
glimpse *n* 441
glint *n* 420
glisten *v* 420
glitter *v* 420
gloat over *v* 377
globe *n* 249, 318
globe-trotter *n* 268
globular *adj* 249
globularity *n* 249
globule *n* 249
gloom *n* 837
gloominess *n* 422
gloomy *adj* 421, 422, 837, 901a
glorified *adj* 981
glorified spirit *n* 977
glorify *v* 883, 990, 991
glory *n* 420, 981
gloss *n* 255, 522; *v* 522
glossary *n* 562
gloss over *v* 458, 477
glossy *adj* 255, 420
glow *n* 382, 420, 574; *v* 382
glower *v* 900
glowing *adj* 382, 434, 574, 824
glue *v* 46
gluey *adj* 352
glut *n* 869; *v* 641, 869
glutinosity *n* 352
glutinous *adj* 327, 352

glutted *adj* 869
glutton *n* 957
gluttonous *adj* 957
gluttony *n* 957
gnarled *adj* 256
gnash *v* 900
gnaw *v* 298, 378
gnome *n* 980
go *v* 264, 293, 302, 449
go about *v* 218
go adrift *v* 279
go after *v* 117, 281, 622
goal *n* 67, 620
go along with *v* 709
go amiss *v* 732
go around *v* 247, 311
go ashore *v* 342
go astray *v* 279, 495
go away *v* 293, 302
go back *v* 287
go back to *v* 104
go bad *v* 653, 659
gobble *v* 412
gobble up *v* 957
go before *v* 116, 280
go beserk *v* 173
go-between *n* 534, 631, 724
go beyond *v* 303
go boating *v* 267
go by *v* 109
go by the rules *v* 82
god *n* 976, 979
goddess *n* 979
godhead *n* 976
godless *adj* 989
godliness *n* 987
godly *adj* 976, 987
go down *v* 306, 659
go downhill *v* 659, 735
godsend *n* 618
go forth *v* 293
go for the bait *v* 547
goggle-eyed *adj* 443
goggle eyes *n* 443
goggles *n* 445
go half way *v* 628
go halves *v* 91; *v* 778

go hand in hand with *v* 178
go hard with *v* 732
going *n* 264
going back *n* 145
going hungry *n* 956
going on *adj* 53, 151
go into hysterics *v* 825
gold *adj* 435, 439
golden *adj* 435, 734
golden dreams *n* 515
golden mean *n* 29, 628, 736
golden opportunity *n* 134
golden rule *n* 697
golden years *n* 128
go mad *v* 503, 825
gone *adj* 2, 122, 360
gone bad *adj* 397, 653
gone by *adj* 122, 124
gone to waste *adj* 638
good *n* 618
good *adj* 52, 394, 618, 648, 922, 931, 944, 977
good behavior *n* 894
goodbye *n* 293
good chance *n* 472
good fellowship *n* 892
good fortune *n* 618, 731
good head *n* 502
good health *n* 654
good luck *n* 618, 621, 731
goodly *adj* 31
good man *n* 948
good manners *n* 894
goodness *n* 648
goodness *n* 618, 829, 922, 944
goods *n* 780, 798
good samaritan *n* 906
good taste *n* 578, 850
good will *n* 602, 888
gooey *adj* 396
go off *v* 173
go on *v* 106, 143

go on forever *v* 104, 112
go on vacation *v* 687
go out *v* 142
go over *v* 218
go over again *v* 104
go over the same ground *v* 104
go pit-a-pat *v* 315
gore *v* 260
gorge *n* 198; *v* 641, 869, 957
gorged *adj* 869
gorgeous *adj* 428, 845
gorgeousness *n* 845
gormandizing *n* 957; *adj* 957
go round about *v* 629
gory *adj* 361, 653
go shopping *v* 795
go side by side *v* 120
gossamer *n* 205
gossamery *adj* 329
gossip *n* 455, 532, 588; *v* 588
gossipy *adj* 588
go straight *v* 246, 628
go the way of all flesh *v* 360
go through *v* 151, 302
go to *v* 278
go to bed *v* 687
go to press *v* 591
go to seed *v* 659
go to sleep *v* 687
go to the dogs *v* 162, 735, 804
go to the law *v* 969
go to waste *v* 659
go to wrack and ruin *v* 162
gouge *n* 262; *v* 252
go up *v* 305
govern *v* 693, 737
governess *n* 753
government *n* 693
governor *n* 694, 753
go wild *v* 173
gown *n* 999

go wrong *v* 732
grab *v* 379
grace *n* 242, 578, 845, 850, 918, 987
graceful *adj* 578, 845
gracefulness *n* 242, 578, 845
graceless *adj* 579
gracious *adj* 894
graciously *adv* 602
graciousness *n* 894
gradation *n* 26, 58, 69
grade *n* 26, 58, 71, 217, 305, 306
grade crossing *n* 219
gradual *adj* 26, 69, 275, 685
gradually *adv* 26, 69, 275
graduate *v* 60, 69
graduation *n* 60
graft *v* 184, 300
grain *n* 5, 256, 329, 330
graininess *n* 330
grammar *n* 567
grammar *n* 542
grammar book *n* 567
grammarian *n* 567
grammatical *adj* 567
grand *adj* 574, 642, 882
grandchildren *n* 167
grandeur *n* 875
grandfather *n* 130, 166
grandiloquence *n* 577
grandiloquent *adj* 577
grandiose *adj* 577
grandmother *n* 130, 166
grandsire *n* 130, 166
grant *n* 784; *v* 529, 760, 762, 783, 784
grantee *n* 785
granter *n* 784
granular *adj* 330
granularity *n* 330
granulate *v* 330
granulation *n* 330
granule *n* 32

graphic *adj* 518
grapple with *v* 719
grasp *v* 518
grass *n* 367
grassland *n* 344
grassy *adj* 435
grate *v* 330, 378, 410, 414
grateful *adj* 916
grater *n* 330
gratification *n* 827
gratify *v* 829, 831
grating *n* 219, 410; *adj* 410, 414
gratitude *n* 916
gratuity *n* 784
grave *n* 363; *v* 558; *adj* 642, 739, 830
grave clothes *n* 363
gravestone *n* 363
graveyard *n* 363
gravitate *v* 306, 319
gravitate toward *v* 176
gravitation *n* 319
gravitational *adj* 288
gravity *n* 319
gravity *n* 288, 574, 642, 739
gray *n* 432
gray *n* 422; *adj* 128, 422, 428, 429, 432
graybeard *n* 130
gray hairs *n* 128
grayish *adj* 432
grayness *n* 422, 432
graze *v* 199
graze over *v* 379
grazing over *n* 379
grease *n* 355, 356; *v* 255, 332, 355
greasiness *n* 355
greasing *n* 332
greasy *adj* 355
great *adj* 31, 192
greaten *v* 35
greater *adj* 33
greatest *adj* 33
greatly *adv* 31

greatness *n* 31
greatness *n* 33, 192, 873
great waters *n* 341
greed *n* 957
greediness *n* 957
greedy *adj* 789, 819, 957
green *n* 435
green *adj* 123, 127, 435, 674
greenbacks *n* 800
greenhorn *n* 547, 701
greenish *adj* 435
greenish blue *adj* 438
greenness *n* 123, 435
greens *n* 367
gregarious *adj* 892
gregariousness *n* 892
gridiron *n* 219
grief *n* 833
grievance *n* 830
grieve *v* 828, 839
grieve at *v* 833
grievous *adj* 649, 830
grievously *adv* 31
grill *v* 384
grille *n* 219
grim *adj* 830
grimace *v* 243
grime *n* 653
grimy *adj* 653
grin *n* 838; *v* 838
grind *v* 195, 253, 330, 331, 410, 539
grinder *n* 330
grinding *n* 410
grindstone *n* 330
grip *n* 378
gripe *n* 378; *v* 378
grist *n* 637
gristly *adj* 327
grit *n* 327, 330
gritty *adj* 330, 604
grizzled *adj* 432
grizzly *adj* 432
groan *n* 839; *v* 411

groove *n* 259, 613; *v* 259

grope in the dark *v* 442

gross *adj* 653, 846, 961

grossness *n* 961

grouch *v* 900

ground *n* 181, 211, 215, 342, 467, 615; *v* 215

grounded on *adj* 211

groundless *adj* 4

grounds *n* 342, 344, 467

groundswell *n* 315

groundwork *n* 60, 64, 153, 211, 673

group *n* 72, 372, 416, 417, 712; *v* 60, 72

groupings *n* 60

grove *n* 252

grovel *v* 207, 275

groveling *n* 886; *adj* 207, 435, 886

grow *v* 35, 144, 194, 282, 367, 734

grow dim *v* 422

grow from *v* 154

growing *adj* 35

grow into *v* 144

growl *v* 412, 900

growling *n* 412

grown up *adj* 131

growth *n* 35, 144, 161, 194, 250, 282, 365

grow up *v* 131

grudge *n* 907, 921; *v* 819

grudgingly *adv* 603

gruesome *adj* 846

gruff *adj* 254, 410

grumble *v* 407, 411, 832

grumbling *n* 407

grumpy *adj* 901a

grunt *v* 412

guarantee *n* 768, 771; *v* 768, 771

guard *n* 717, 753; *v* 664, 670, 717

guard against *v* 717

guarded *adj* 459, 585, 864

guardian *n* 664, 753, 977

guardian angel *n* 977

guardianship *n* 717

guarding *n* 670

guerilla *n* 361

guess *n* 514; *v* 514

guesswork *n* 514

guffaw *n* 838

guidance *n* 537, 692, 693, 695

guide *n* 524, 527, 540, 694; *v* 537, 692, 693

guidebook *n* 527

guiding *adj* 693

guile *n* 544, 702

guileless *adj* 703, 946

guilelessness *n* 946

guiling *n* 545

guillotine *v* 361

guilt *n* 947

guilt *n* 649, 961

guiltiness *n* 947

guiltless *adj* 946

guiltlessness *n* 946, 960

guilty *adj* 947, 961

guilty verdict *n* 971

guise *n* 448

gulf *n* 343

gulf *n* 198, 343

gull *n* 486, 547; *v* 545

gulley *n* 259

gullibility *n* 486

gullible *adj* 486, 547

gully *n* 350

gulosity *n* 957

gulp *v* 298

gulp down *v* 298

gum *n* 356a

gummy *adj* 327, 352, 356a

gun down *v* 361

gunshot *n* 197

gurgle *v* 348, 353, 408

gurgling *n* 353

guru *n* 994

gush *n* 295, 348; *v* 295, 348, 584

gush out *v* 295

gust *n* 349; *v* 349

gusto *n* 390

gut *v* 162

guts *n* 221, 861

gutsy *adj* 861

gutter *n* 259, 350

guttural *adj* 410

guzzle *v* 957, 959

gymnasium *n* 728

gypsy *n* 268

gyration *n* 312

H

habit *n* 613

habit *n* 5, 820

habitat *n* 189

habitation *n* 189

habitation *n* 189

habitual *adj* 82, 104, 136, 613

habitually *adv* 136, 613

habituate *v* 613

hack *v* 44

hackneyed *adj* 598

hack up *v* 201

Hades *n* 982

haggard *adj* 203, 688

haggle *v* 794

hagiography *n* 983

hagiological *adj* 983

hail *v* 586

hair *n* 205

hair's breadth *n* 197

hairy *adj* 256

halcyon *adj* 721

hale *adj* 654

half a dozen *n* 98

half a hundred *n* 98

half and half *adj* 27, 41

half measures *n* 628

half-moon *n* 245

half-starved *adj* 956

halfway *adj* 68; *adv* 68

half-witted *adj* 499

hallowed *adj* 976
halo *n* 420
halt *n* 142, 685, 687; *v* 142, 160, 265, 275
halve *v* 91
halved *adj* 91
halving *n* 91
hammer *v* 104
hammered instruments *n* 417
hamper *v* 706
hamstring *v* 158
hand *n* 236, 372, 590, 590, 631; *v* 784
handbook *n* 527, 593
handful *n* 25, 32
handicap *v* 706
hand in hand *adv* 88
handle *n* 564; *v* 379, 677
handling *n* 379
hand of death *n* 360
hand over *v* 270, 783
hands *n* 269
handsome *adj* 845
handwriting *n* 590
handy *adj* 197, 673, 698
hang *v* 214, 361
hang a turn *v* 140
hang back *v* 683
hang by a thread *v* 665
hanging *n* 361; *adj* 214
hanging down *n* 214
hang in there *v* 604a
hang it up *v* 624
hangman *n* 975
hang over *v* 152
hang together *v* 46, 178
hap *n* 156; *v* 156
haphazard *adj* 139, 156
haphazardness *n* 139
hapless *adj* 735
happen *v* 1, 151
happening *n* 8, 151; *adj* 151
happily *adv* 827
happiness *n* 618, 827

happy *adj* 23, 134, 827, 836
happy-go-lucky *adj* 674
harangue *n* 537, 582; *v* 582
harass *v* 830
harbinger *n* 64, 512, 534
hard *adj* 159, 323, 376, 397, 704, 739, 830
hard and fast law *n* 80
hard as a rock *adj* 323
hard as nails *adj* 323
hard by *adv* 197
hard cash *n* 800
hard coal *n* 388
harden *v* 48, 159, 321, 323, 613
hardening *n* 321, 385
hard-featured *adj* 846
hard-hearted *adj* 914a
hard-heartedness *n* 914a
hardihood *n* 861
hardiness *n* 159
hardly *adv* 32, 137
hardly ever *adv* 137
hardness *n* 323
hardness of hearing *n* 419
hardness of heart *n* 951
hard of hearing *adj* 419
hardship *n* 735
hard task *n* 704
hard times *n* 735
hard to please *adj* 868
hard up *adj* 804
hardy *adj* 159, 654
harlequin *n* 501
harlot *n* 962
harm *n* 619; *v* 619, 649, 659, 828, 923
harmful *adj* 619, 649, 657, 663
harmfulness *n* 649
harmless *adj* 158
harmonious *adj* 23,

242, 413, 416, 428, 714
harmoniousness *n* 413
harmonious sounds *n* 415
harmonize *v* 23, 82, 413
harmonize with *v* 714
harmony *n* 23, 58, 242, 413, 415, 709, 714, 721, 888
harness *v* 43, 225
harping *n* 104; *adj* 104
harp on *v* 104
harpy *n* 980
harrow *v* 371, 830
harsh *adj* 410, 414, 579, 739, 830, 955
harshness *n* 410, 414, 739
hart *n* 373
harvest *n* 154, 618, 775
harvest time *n* 126
hash *n* 59
haste *n* 684
haste *n* 132, 863; *v* 274, 684
hasten *v* 132, 274, 310, 682, 684
hastily *adv* 132
hasty *adj* 684, 863
hatch *n* 260; *v* 161, 558, 626
hatchet man *n* 936
hate *n* 898
hate *n* 907; *v* 867, 898
hateful *adj* 649, 830, 898, 907
hating *adj* 898
hatred *n* 867, 889, 898, 907
hatred of mankind *n* 911
haughtiness *n* 878, 885
haughty *adj* 878, 885
haul *n* 190; *v* 190, 285
hauling *n* 285
haunt *n* 74, 189
haunted *adj* 980

heavenly *adj* 318, 829, 976, 981

heavenly bodies *n* 318

heavenly kingdom *n* 981

heavenly spirit *n* 977

heavens *n* 180, 318

heaviness *n* 202, 319, 837, 843

heavy *n* 202; *adj* 172, 194, 319, 683

heavy as lead *adj* 319

heavy heart *n* 837

heavy news *n* 830

hebetude *n* 499

heckle *v* 830

hedge *n* 232

hedge in *v* 229

hedonist *n* 954a

heed *n* 457, 459, 864; *v* 418, 457, 928

heedful *adj* 451, 457, 459, 864

heedfulness *n* 864

heeding *n* 418; *adj* 928

heedless *adj* 460, 506, 863

heedlessness *n* 458, 460, 863

heel *n* 211; *v* 279

he him *n* 373

height *n* 206

height *n* 26, 125, 210, 307

heighten *v* 35, 206, 307, 549, 835

heightening *n* 835

heinous *adj* 846

heir *n* 167

heirs *n* 121, 167

helicopter *n* 273

hell *n* 982

hellish *adj* 978, 982

helmsman *n* 269, 694

help *n* 644, 662, 707, 746, 784, 834; *v* 215, 644, 707, 746, 784, 834

helper *n* 707, 711, 746, 977

helpful *adj* 644, 707, 888

helpfulness *n* 644, 910

helpless *adj* 158

helplessness *n* 158

help oneself to *v* 789

helter skelter *adv* 59

hem *n* 231; *v* 43, 231, 258

hem and haw *v* 149, 583

hemi- *adj* 91

hem in *v* 227

hemisphere *n* 181

hemorrhage *n* 299

hen *n* 374

hence *adv* 155

henceforth *adv* 121

henchman *n* 746

her *n* 374

herald *n* 64, 534; *v* 116, 280

herb *n* 367

herbaceous *adj* 367

herbage *n* 367

herbal *adj* 367, 369

Herculean *adj* 159

herculean *adj* 686

herculean task *n* 704

herd *n* 876; *v* 72

here *adv* 186

hereabouts *adv* 183

hereafter *n* 121, 152; *adv* 121

here and there *adv* 182, 183

here below *adv* 318

hereditary *adj* 5, 154

heredity *n* 167

heresy *n* 984

heretic *n* 487, 984

heretical *adj* 984

heretofore *adv* 122

herewith *adv* 88, 632

heritage *n* 11, 121, 122

hermetically sealed *adj* 261

hermit *n* 893, 955

hero *n* 948

heroic *adj* 861

heroism *n* 861

hero worship *n* 991

hesitancy *n* 485, 605

hesitant *adj* 485, 583, 603, 605

hesitate *v* 475, 485, 583, 603, 605

hesitating *adj* 485

hesitation *n* 485, 583, 603, 605

heterodox *adj* 984

heterodoxy *n* 984

heterogeneity *n* 10, 16a, 291

heterogeneous *adj* 10, 15, 41, 81

hew *v* 44, 240, 557

hiatus *n* 198

hiburnal *adj* 383

hidden *adj* 447, 526, 528, 533, 571

hidden meaning *n* 526

hide *n* 223; *v* 442, 447, 528, 862, 893

hideous *adj* 830, 846

hiding *n* 528, 893

hiding place *n* 189, 530, 666

hie *v* 264, 274

hierarchical *adj* 995

hierarchy *n* 995

hieroglyph *n* 561

high *adj* 206, 410, 838, 959

high birth *n* 875

high-born *adj* 875

high caliber *n* 33

higher *adj* 33

highest *adj* 210

high-flown *adj* 577

high living *n* 954

highly seasoned *adj* 392

high-minded *adj* 878

highmindedness *n* 875

high note *n* 409

horizontal *adj* 213, 251, 308

horizontality *n* 213

horizontally *adv* 213

horrible *adj* 649, 830

horribly *adv* 31

horrid *adj* 649, 830

horrified *adj* 860

horrify *v* 830

horrifying *adj* 982

horror *n* 860, 867, 898

horror-stricken *adj* 860

horseback riding *n* 266

horseman *n* 268

horsemanship *n* 266

horse-shoe *n* 245

horsewoman *n* 268

horticultural *adj* 369

horticulture *n* 371

hose *n* 348, 350

hospitable *adj* 816, 892

hospitality *n* 816

host *n* 72, 102

hostile *adj* 14, 24, 383, 708, 889, 907

hostilities *n* 173, 722

hostility *n* 708, 889

hot *adj* 382, 392, 434, 824

hot air *n* 517

hotchpotch *n* 41

hotheaded *adj* 825

hotness *n* 392

hot pink *adj* 434

hot-tempered *adj* 901

hourly *adv* 136

house *v* 184, 664

housebreak *v* 370

house-breaker *n* 792

housebroken *adj* 370

house of correction *n* 975

house of god *n* 1000

housing *n* 189

hover *v* 152, 206, 305

hover about *v* 264

hover around *v* 264

how *adv* 627

howbeit *adv* 30

however *adv* 30

howl *n* 411, 839; *v* 411, 412

howling *n* 412

hub *n* 222

hubbub *n* 315, 404, 411

huckster *n* 797

huddle *v* 72

hue *n* 428

hue and cry *n* 411, 669

hueless *adj* 429

hug *n* 902; *v* 46

huge *adj* 31, 192, 206

hugeness *n* 192

hulky *adj* 192

hullabaloo *n* 411

hum *n* 405; *v* 405, 407, 412

human *adj* 372

human being *n* 372

human community *n* 372

humane *adj* 906

humaneness *n* 910

humanitarian *n* 910; *adj* 372, 910

humanitarianism *n* 910

humanities *n* 560

humanity *n* 372, 906

humankind *n* 372

human race *n* 372

human species *n* 372

humble *adj* 34, 725, 879, 881, 987

humbleness *n* 879

humbly *adv* 881

humbug *n* 548

humdrum *adj* 275, 598, 841

humid *adj* 337, 339

humidity *n* 339

humiliate *v* 879

humility *n* 879

humility *n* 881, 987

hummocky *adj* 250

humor *n* 5, 176, 602, 608, 820, 842; *v* 707, 760

humorist *n* 844

humorous *adj* 842

hump *n* 250

hunch *n* 250, 477

hundred *n* 98

hunger *n* 865

hungry *adj* 865, 956

hunt *v* 361

hunting *n* 361

hurdle *v* 309

hurl *v* 284

hurly-burly *n* 315

hurrah *v* 838

hurricane *n* 349

hurried *adj* 684, 825

hurry *n* 684; *v* 132, 274, 310, 684

hurt *n* 378, 619; *v* 378, 619, 649, 659, 828, 830

hurtful *adj* 619, 649, 830

hurtfulness *n* 649

hurtle *v* 276, 309

hurtle over *v* 310

husband *n* 903; *v* 636, 670, 817

husbandry *n* 371, 817

hush *n* 403; *v* 174, 265, 403

hushed *adj* 403

husky *adj* 405

hussy *n* 962

hustle *n* 682; *v* 276, 315, 682

hybrid *n* 41; *adj* 41

hydrous *adj* 337

hygienic *adj* 656

hyperbola *n* 245

hyperbole *n* 549

hyperbolic *adj* 549

hypercritical *adj* 868

hypercriticism *n* 868

hypertension *n* 315

hypocrisy *n* 988

hypocrite *n* 548, 988

hypocritical *adj* 544
hypothesis *n* 514
hypothetical *adj* 514
hysterical *adj* 173, 824, 825

I

ice *v* 385
ice box *n* 387
ice chest *n* 387
ice house *n* 387
iciness *n* 383
icing *n* 385
icon *n* 991
iconoclasm *n* 984
iconoclast *n* 165
iconoclastic *adj* 984
icthyology *n* 368
icy *adj* 383
idea *n* 453
idea *n* 451, 515, 516
ideal *n* 650; *adj* 2, 515, 977
ideality *n* 515
idealize *v* 515
ideational *adj* 453
idée fixe n 606
identical *adj* 13, 17
identically *adv* 13
identity *n* 13
identity *n* 17, 27
idiocy *n* 499
idiom *n* 521, 566
idiomatic *adj* 79, 521
idiosyncracy *n* 820
idiosyncrasies *n* 5
idiosyncrasy *n* 79, 83, 176
idiosyncratic *adj* 5
idiot *n* 493, 501, 501
idiotic *adj* 499
idle *v* 683; *adj* 681, 683
idleness *n* 681, 683
idler *n* 683
idle talk *n* 588
idol *n* 897, 899, 991
idolatrize *v* 991
idolatrous *adj* 991

idolatrousness *n* 991
idolatry *n* 991
idolatry *n* 897, 990
idolism *n* 991
idolization *n* 991
idolize *v* 897, 990, 991
idolizing *n* 990
idol-worship *n* 991
idol-worshiping *adj* 991
if *adv* 8
iffy *adj* 156
if it so happen *adv* 8
if so *adv* 8
if worst comes to worst *adv* 735
ignite *v* 384
ignoble *adj* 207, 851, 876
ignominious *adj* 874
ignominy *n* 874
ignoramus *n* 493
ignoramus *n* 501
ignorance *n* 491
ignorance *n* 442
ignorant *adj* 435, 442, 491
ignore *v* 460, 773
ill *n* 619; *adj* 649, 655
ill-advised *adj* 499
ill-behaved *adj* 895
ill-bred *adj* 851, 895
ill-breeding *n* 851, 895
ill-conceived *adj* 499
illegal *adj* 964
illegality *n* 964
illegitimacy *n* 925, 964
illegitimate *adj* 925, 964
ill-fashioned *adj* 243
ill-flavored *adj* 395
ill health *n* 655
ill-humored *adj* 901a
illiberal *adj* 32, 943
illiberality *n* 819, 943
illicit *adj* 964
illicitness *n* 964
illiteracy *n* 491
illiterate *n* 493; *adj* 491

ill-judged *adj* 499
ill-judging *adj* 481
ill-made *adj* 243
ill-mannered *adj* 851, 895
ill-natured *adj* 907
illness *n* 655
illogical *adj* 47, 477
illogically *adv* 477
ill-proportioned *adj* 243
ill-qualified *adj* 699
ill repute *n* 874
ill-tempered *adj* 945
ill-timed *adj* 135
ill-treat *v* 739
ill-treatment *n* 649
illuminate *v* 420, 423, 428
illumination *n* 420
illumine *v* 420
ill-use *v* 649
illusion *n* 4, 443, 515, 545
illusory *adj* 4, 515, 545
illustrate *v* 82, 554
illustration *n* 82, 554
illustrative *adj* 82, 518, 554
illustrious *adj* 883
ill will *n* 889, 907
ill wind *n* 649
image *n* 17, 21, 448, 521, 556, 991; *v* 521
imagery *n* 521, 554
imaginable *adj* 470, 515
imaginary *adj* 4, 979
imagination *n* 515
imaginative *adj* 2, 515
imaginativeness *n* 515
imaginative writing *n* 598
imagine *v* 515
imagined *adj* 515
imagistic *adj* 521
imbalance *n* 15, 28, 503
imbalanced *adj* 28

imbecile *n* 493, 501; *adj* 499
imbecilic *adj* 499
imbecility *n* 499
imbecility *n* 450a, 497, 499
imbibe *v* 296, 959
imbibition *n* 298
imbue *v* 41, 300, 537
imbued *adj* 820
imitate *v* 19, 680, 788
imitation *n* 19
imitation *n* 21, 554, 556; *adj* 19
imitative *adj* 17, 19, 554
immaculate *adj* 650, 652, 946, 960
immaterial *adj* 4, 317, 643
immateriality *n* 317
immateriality *n* 643
immature *adj* 53, 123, 127, 435, 651, 674
immaturity *n* 53, 123, 651
immeasurability *n* 105
immeasurably *adv* 31
immediate *adj* 132
immediately *adv* 113, 132
immemorial *adj* 124
immense *adj* 31, 104, 192
immensity *n* 31, 192
immerse *v* 300, 310, 337
immersed in *adj* 229
immersion *n* 300, 310
immigrant *n* 268
immigrate *v* 266
immigration *n* 266
imminent *adj* 152, 286
immobile *adj* 172
immobility *n* 141, 150, 172, 265
immobilize *v* 265
immoderately *adv* 31

immodest *adj* 961
immodesty *n* 961
immoral *adj* 923, 940, 945
immorality *n* 923, 940, 945
immortal *adj* 112
immortalize *v* 112
immovability *n* 141, 150, 606
immovable *adj* 150, 606
immune *adj* 748, 927a
immune from *adj* 777a
immunity *n* 748, 777a, 927a, 970
immutability *n* 141, 150
immutable *adj* 110, 150
imp *n* 980
impact *n* 276, 379
impair *v* 659, 848
impairment *n* 638, 659
impale *v* 260
impart *v* 784
impartial *adj* 246, 628, 942
impartiality *n* 942
impart to *v* 527
impassable *adj* 261
impasse *n* 151
impassionate *adj* 383
impassioned *adj* 574, 821, 825, 991
impassive *adj* 456, 823
impassivity *n* 823, 826
impatience *n* 825
impatient *adj* 825, 841
impeach *v* 938, 969
impeachment *n* 938
impeccability *n* 650
impeccable *adj* 650, 946
impede *v* 179, 275, 706
impediment *n* 177, 706
impeding *n* 706
impel *v* 175, 264, 276, 284, 744
impend *v* 121, 152, 909

impending *adj* 121, 152, 286, 507, 909
impenetrability *n* 321, 571
impenetrable *adj* 261, 321, 323, 519, 571
impenetrable to light *adj* 426
impenitence *n* 951
impenitent *adj* 951
imperative *adj* 737, 926
imperceptibility *n* 447
imperceptible *adj* 193, 447
imperceptibly *adv* 32
imperfect *adj* 34, 53, 304, 640, 651, 659, 848, 961
imperfection *n* 651
imperfection *n* 28, 34, 53, 304, 640, 945, 961
imperfectly *adv* 32
imperil *v* 665
imperishable *adj* 112
impermanence *n* 111
impermanent *adj* 111
impermeability *n* 321
impermeable *adj* 261, 321
impersonate *v* 19
impersonation *n* 19, 599
impertinence *n* 885, 929
impertinent *adj* 885, 929
imperturbability *n* 826
imperturbable *n* 823; *adj* 383, 826
impervious *adj* 261
impervious to light *adj* 426
impetuosity *n* 173, 825, 863
impetuous *adj* 173, 825, 863
impetus *n* 276, 284
impiety *n* 988

impiety n 989
impish adj 980
implacable adj 914a, 919
implant v 300
implantation n 300
implanted adj 5
implausibility n 473
implausible adj 473
implement n 633
implicit adj 526
implied adj 526
implore v 765
implosion n 276
imply v 467, 472, 516
impolite adj 895, 929
impoliteness n 929
import n 516, 642; v 296, 516, 642
importance n 642
importance n 31, 62, 175
important adj 31, 33, 175, 642
importation n 296, 300
importunate adj 765
importune v 765
impose v 741
imposing adj 642, 875, 878
impossibility n 471
impossible adj 471, 704
imposter n 548
imposture n 545
impotence n 158
impotence n 160, 169, 175a
impotent adj 158, 160, 175a
impractical adj 471, 647, 704
impracticality n 471, 647
imprecate v 908
imprecation n 908
impregnability n 664
impregnable adj 159, 664

impregnate v 168, 300
impress v 175, 375, 824
impressibility n 375, 822
impressible adj 324
impression n 375, 453, 591, 821
impressionable adj 822
impressive adj 574, 642
imprint n 569
imprison v 229
inprisoned adj 229, 751
improbability n 473
improbable adj 473
improbity n 940
impromptu adj 612; adv 612
improper adj 499, 568, 647, 923, 945
improper time n 135
impropriety n 568, 579, 647, 925
improve v 282, 648, 658
improved adj 658
improvement n 658
improvement n 282, 618
improvidence n 674
improvident adj 674, 818
improving adj 658
improvisation n 612
improvise v 416, 612, 674
imprudence n 863
imprudent adj 452, 460, 863
impudence n 885, 895, 929
impudent adj 885, 929
impugn v 716
impulse n 276, 612
impulse n 284, 601, 615, 744
impulsion n 284
impulsive adj 149, 612, 825, 863
impulsively adv 612

impulsiveness n 863
impunity n 777a, 927a, 970
impure adj 653, 961
impurity n 961
impurity n 653
imputation n 155, 938
imputative adj 938
impute v 938
impute to v 155
in a bad way adj 659, 735
in abeyance adv 172
inability n 158, 699
in a body adv 50
inabstinence n 954
inaccessible adj 196
in accord adj 714
in accordance with adj 23; adv 82
inaccuracy n 544
inaccurate adj 495, 568, 923
in a column adv 69
inaction n 681
inaction n 623, 683; adj 170, 680
inactive adj 172, 265, 681, 683
inactivity n 683
inactivity n 172, 681
in addition adv 37
inadequacy n 28, 34, 640, 645, 651
inadequate adj 28, 158, 640, 651
inadmissible adj 55
in advance adv 62, 234, 280
in adverse circumstances adj 735
in a fair way to adj 176
in a great measure adv 31
in a jiffy adv 113
in a line adj 69
in all aspects adv 52

infanticide *n* 361

infantile *adj* 129, 499

infantlike *adj* 129

infatuated *adj* 486

infatuation *n* 486, 606

in fault *adj* 947

in favour *adj* 931

infect *v* 659, 824

infection *n* 824

infelicitous *adj* 828

infer *v* 476

inference *n* 65, 476, 480

inferential *adj* 467, 476

inferior *adj* 28, 34, 651, 736

inferiority *n* 34

inferiority *n* 28, 736

infernal *adj* 649, 978, 982

inferno *n* 982

infertile *adj* 169

infertility *n* 169

infidel *n* 989

infidelity *n* 989

infiltrate *v* 41, 294

infiltration *n* 41, 294, 302

infinite *adj* 31, 102, 104, 180

infinitely *adv* 31, 104

infiniteness *n* 105

infinitesimal *adj* 32, 193

infinitude *n* 105

infinity *n* 105

infinity *n* 112, 180

infirm *adj* 158, 160, 655

infirmity *n* 158, 160, 655

in fits *adv* 315

inflame *v* 171, 173, 384, 824

inflamed *adj* 434

in flames *adj* 382

inflammable *adj* 385

inflate *v* 194, 322, 349, 573, 880

inflated *adj* 482, 577, 880

inflation *n* 322, 577

inflect *v* 245

inflection *n* 567

inflexibility *n* 141, 246, 323, 606

inflexible *adj* 323, 604, 606

inflict *v* 680, 739

inflict pain *v* 378

inflict punishment *v* 972

in flight *adj* 267

influence *n* 175

influence *n* 153, 170, 615, 737; *v* 62, 153, 170, 176, 615

influential *adj* 157, 175, 176, 737

influx *n* 294

in force *adj* 170

inform *v* 527, 537, 668

informality *n* 83

informant *n* 527, 534

information *n* 527

information *n* 467, 490, 498, 532

informed *adj* 527

informer *n* 527, 532, 938

infraction *n* 83, 303, 742, 773, 927

infrequency *n* 137

infrequency *n* 103

infrequent *adj* 103, 137

infrequently *adv* 137

infringe *v* 303, 742, 773

infringement *n* 303

infringement *n* 83 742, 773

in front *adv* 234, 280

in front of one's nose *adj* 446

in full sight *adj* 446

in full view *adj* 446

infuriate *v* 173

infuse *v* 41, 300, 537

infusion *n* 41, 300

in future *adv* 121

ingathering *n* 72

ingenious *adj* 698, 702

ingenuity *n* 698

ingenuous *adj* 703, 946

ingenuousness *n* 946

ingest *v* 296, 539

ingestion *n* 296, 298

in good taste *adj* 850

in good time *adv* 152

ingraft *v* 300

ingrained *adj* 5, 221, 820

ingrate *n* 917

ingratitude *n* 917

ingredient *n* 51, 56, 211

ingress *n* 294

ingress *n* 302

inhabit *v* 184, 186, 188, 189

inhabitant *n* 188

inhabiting *adj* 186

inhale *v* 398

in hand *adj* 777

inharmonious *adj* 24, 414

inharmoniousness *n* 414

in harmony with *adj* 23

in harness *adj* 749

in health *adj* 654

inherence *n* 5

inherent *adj* 5, 221

inherited *adj* 5

in hiding *adj* 528

in high esteem *adj* 931

in honor of *adv* 883

inhumation *n* 363

inimical *adj* 708, 889

inimitable *adj* 20, 33, 648, 650

iniquitous *adj* 923, 945

iniquity *n* 923, 945

initial *adj* 66

initiate *v* 66, 296

initiation *n* 66, 296

initiative *n* 66

in its infancy *adv* 66
in its own sweet time *adv* 152
in its turn *adv* 58
inject *v* 300
injection *n* 296, 300
injudicious *adj* 499
injunction *n* 630, 695, 741, 761, 864
injur *v* 848
injure *v* 619, 649, 659, 828, 923
injured *adj* 659, 848
injurious *adj* 619, 649
injury *n* 173, 619, 649, 659, 665, 776
injustice *n* 173, 923
ink *n* 431
in keeping with *adj* 23; *adv* 82
inkling *n* 514, 527
inky *adj* 431
inlaid *adj* 221, 440
inlands *n* 342
inlay *v* 440
in league *adj* 709
inlet *n* 260, 343
in lieu of *adv* 147
inmate *n* 188
in moderation *adv* 174
inmost *adj* 221
in motion *adj* 264
in mourning *adj* 839
innate *adj* 5, 221
inner *adj* 221
inner coating *n* 224
inner man *n* 820
innermost *adj* 221
innermost recesses *n* 221
inner part *n* 221
innocence *n* 946
innocence *n* 703, 944, 960
innocent *adj* 435, 703, 946, 960
in no respect *adv* 32
in no time *adv* 113

innovate *v* 140
innovation *n* 20a, 123, 140
innovative *adj* 140
innuendo *n* 527
in obedience to *adv* 743
inoculate *v* 300
inoculation *n* 300
inodorousness *n* 399
in one's birthday suit *adj* 226
in one's debt *adj* 916
in operation *adj* 170, 680
inoperative *adj* 158, 645
inopportune *adj* 135, 647
inopportuneness *n* 135
in opposition *adj* 708
in order *adj* 58; *adv* 58
inordinate *adj* 31, 641, 954
inordinately *adv* 31
inordinateness *n* 954
inorganic *adj* 358
inorganic matter *n* 358
in part *adv* 32, 51
in particular *adv* 79
in perfect condition *adj* 650
in place of *adv* 147
in plain English *adv* 576, 703
in plain sight *adv* 525
in plain terms *adv* 576
in play *adj* 170
in poor health *adj* 655
in possession of *adj* 777
in preparation *adj* 53
in presence of *adv* 186
in print *adj* 531, 532
in prison *adj* 754
in private *adv* 528
in progress *adj* 53
in prospect *adj* 121, 152, 620
in proximity *adj* 186

in pursuit of *adj* 622
input *n* 175
in question *adv* 454
in quest of *adj* 622
inquietude *n* 828
inquire *v* 461
inquirer *n* 461
inquiring *n* 461; *adj* 455, 461
inquiring mind *n* 455
inquiry *n* 461
inquiry *n* 539
inquisitive *adj* 455, 461
inquisitiveness *n* 455
inquisitor *n* 461, 739
inquisitorial *adj* 461, 739, 965
in rapport *adj* 413
in readiness *adj* 507
in reality *adv* 1
in relief *adj* 250
in reserve *adj* 636
in retaliation *adv* 718
inroad *n* 294
in rotation *adv* 138
insalubrious *adj* 657
insalubrity *n* 657
insane *adj* 173, 503
insanity *n* 503
inscrutable *adj* 519
in secret *adj* 528; *adv* 528
insect *n* 366
insecure *adj* 475, 665
insecurity *n* 475, 665
insensate *adj* 499
insensibility *n* 376, 823
insensibility *n* 866
insensible *adj* 376, 381, 506
insensitive *adj* 376, 823, 866
insensitiveness *n* 823, 866
inseparability *n* 46
inseparable *adj* 43, 46
insert *v* 221, 228, 300
insertion *n* 300

insertion *n* 37, 228, 294, 296

in short *adv* 572

inside *n* 221; *adj* 221

inside out *adj* 218

insidious *adj* 545, 702

insight *n* 477, 498; *adj* 507

insightful *adj* 842

insigne *n* 550

insignificance *n* 32, 643, 736

insignificant *adj* 4, 32, 517, 643, 736

in simple words *adv* 703

insincere *adj* 544

insincerity *n* 544

insinuate *v* 527

insinuate oneself *v* 294

insinuation *n* 228, 294, 300, 527

insipid *adj* 337, 391, 575

insipidity *n* 391

insist upon *v* 604, 770

in snatches *adv* 70

insobriety *n* 959

insolence *n* 885

insolence *n* 715, 878

insolent *adj* 715, 885

insoluble *adj* 321, 519

insolvency *n* 732, 808

insolvent *adj* 804

in some degree *adv* 26

in some place *adv* 182

inspect *v* 441

inspector *n* 694; 461

inspiration *n* 477, 515, 612, 824

inspire *v* 615, 824

inspiring *adj* 836

inspirit *v* 836

inspiriting *adj* 858

in spite *adv* 708

in spite of *prep* 179

instability *n* 149, 475, 605, 665

install *v* 184, 755

installation *n* 184

installment *n* 807

instance *n* 82

instant *n* 113; *adj* 113, 118, 630

instantaneous *adj* 111, 113, 132

instantaneously *adv* 113, 132

instantaneousness *n* 113

instead *adv* 147

instigate *v* 615

instigation *n* 170, 615

instill *v* 41, 300, 537

instinct *n* 477, 601

instinctive *adj* 5, 477, 601

instinctual *adj* 5, 477

in stir *adj* 754

institute *n* 542; *v* 153, 161

in store *adj* 152, 636

instruct *v* 537, 693, 695, 741

instructed *adj* 490

instruction *n* 537, 693, 695, 697, 741

instructive *adj* 537, 985

instructor *n* 540

instrument *n* 633

instrument *adj* 415

instrumental *adj* 176, 416, 631, 632, 633, 677

instrumentalist *n* 416

instrumentality *n* 631

instrumentality *n* 170

instrumental music *n* 415

insubordinate *adj* 715, 742

insubordination *n* 715, 742

insubstantiality *n* 2, 317

in succession *adv* 69

in such and such a place *adv* 183

in such wise *adv* 8

insufferable *adj* 830

insufficiency *n* 640

insufficiency *n* 53, 304, 651, 732

insufficient *adj* 28, 32, 304, 640, 651, 732

insufficiently *adv* 32

insular *adj* 10, 44, 87, 346

insularity *n* 44

insulate *v* 44, 87

insulation *n* 44

insult *n* 830; *v* 830, 929

insulting *adj* 885, 929

insurgence *n* 719

insurgent *n* 742; *adj* 742

insurrection *n* 719

insusceptibility *n* 376

in suspense *adv* 172

intact *adj* 50, 52, 141, 650, 670, 729

intactness *n* 52

intaglio *n* 22

intangible *adj* 2, 4, 317

in tears *adj* 828

integer *n* 84

integral *adj* 50

integral part *n* 56

integrate *v* 50

integrity *n* 50, 922, 939, 944

intellect *n* 450

intellect *n* 498, 842

intellectual *n* 492; *adj* 450, 498

intellectual giant *n* 872

intellectualize *v* 450

intelligence *n* 498

intelligence *n* 480, 498, 527, 532, 698, 842

intelligencer *n* 527, 534

intelligent *adj* 498, 698, 842

intelligibility *n* 518

intelligibility *n* 570
intelligible *adj* 518, 522, 570
intemperance *n* 954
intemperance *n* 959
intemperate *adj* 954
intend *v* 451, 516, 620
intense *adj* 31, 171, 382, 428
intensely *adv* 31
intensification *n* 835
intensified *adj* 835
intensify *v* 35, 171, 835
intensity *n* 26, 31, 171, 173, 382
intent *n* 451, 516, 600, 620
intention *n* 620
intention *n* 278, 451, 516, 611, 615
intentional *adj* 600, 620
intentionally *adv* 600, 611, 620
intentiveness *n* 457
intentness *n* 682
inter *v* 363
interact *v* 12
intercalation *n* 228
intercede *v* 724
intercession *n* 724, 766
interchange *n* 148
interchange *n* 12, 219, 783; *v* 12, 147, 148, 783
interchangeability *n* 148
interchangeable *adj* 12, 148, 794
intercourse *n* 148
interdepend *v* 12
interdependence *n* 12
interdict *v* 761
interdiction *n* 761
interest *n* 455, 618, 642, 707; *v* 288, 824, 829, 840
interested *adj* 455
interfere *v* 228, 708, 724

interference *n* 179, 228, 706, 719
interfere with *v* 179
interim *n* 106, 198
interior *n* 221, 342; *adj* 221
interiority *n* 221
interjacence *n* 228
interjacent *adj* 228
interject *v* 228
interjection *n* 228
interlace *v* 41, 43, 219
interlaced *adj* 219
interlard *v* 41
interlarding *n* 41
interlineation *n* 228
interlink *v* 219
interlocation *n* 228
interlocution *n* 588
interlude *n* 106, 198, 685
intermediary *n* 534, 631; *adj* 631
intermediate *adj* 29, 68, 631
intermedium *n* 631
interment *n* 363
interminable *adj* 104, 112, 200
intermission *n* 70, 106
intermittence *n* 138
intermittent *adj* 70, 138
intermittently *adv* 138
intern *v* 221
internal *adj* 5, 221
internally *adv* 221
interpenetrate *v* 228
interpenetration *n* 228
interpolate *v* 41, 228
interpolation *n* 41, 228, 300
interpose *v* 70, 228, 724
interposition *n* 37, 228, 724
interpret *v* 462, 522, 537
interpretable *adj* 522
interpretation *n* 522

interpretation *n* 155, 516
interpretative *adj* 522
interpreter *n* 524
interpreter *n* 513
interpretive *adj* 522
interregnum *n* 106, 142, 198
interrogate *v* 461
interrogation *n* 461
interrogative *adj* 461
interrupt *v* 70, 142, 198, 706
interrupted *adj* 70
interruption *n* 61, 70, 142, 198, 706
intersect *v* 219
intersection *n* 219
interspace *n* 198, 221
intersperse *v* 228
interspersion *n* 228
interstice *n* 198
intertwine *v* 41, 43, 219
intertwined *adj* 219
interval *n* 198
interval *n* 53, 70, 106, 196
intervene *v* 70, 198, 228, 631, 724
intervening *adj* 228
intervention *n* 228, 631, 724
interview *n* 588
interweave *v* 41, 43, 219
in the altogether *adj* 226
in the background *adv* 235
in the blood *adj* 5
in the bud *adv* 66
in the buff *adj* 226
in the cards *adj* 152
in the course of *adv* 106
in the course of things *adv* 151
in the event of *adv* 8
in the face of *adv* 715

in the first place *adv* 66

in the foreground *adv* 234

in the fourth place *adv* 96

in the genes *adj* 5

in the headlines *adj* 532

in the interim *adv* 106

in the lead *adv* 234

in the long run *adv* 29, 152

in the main *adv* 50

in the matter of *adv* 9

in the meantime *adv* 106

in the middle *adv* 68

in the midst of *adv* 41

in the news *adj* 532

in the nick of time *adv* 134

in the open air *adv* 338

in the open market *adj* 763

in the rear *adv* 235, 281

in the same category *adj* 9

in the thick of *adv* 228

in the third place *adv* 93

in the vanguard *adv* 280

in the wide open spaces *adv* 338

in the wind *adj* 152

intimacy *n* 888

intimate *n* 890; *v* 527; *adj* 197, 221, 888

intimately *adv* 43

in time *adv* 109, 152

intimidate *v* 909

intimidating *adj* 909

intimidation *n* 909

intolerable *adj* 830

intolerance *n* 606, 825

intolerant *adj* 606, 825

intonation *n* 402, 580

intone *v* 580

in top shape *adj* 654

in touch with *adj* 592

in tow *adj* 285

intoxicate *v* 824

intoxicated *adj* 959

intoxication *n* 824, 959

intractability *n* 606

intractable *adj* 606, 704

in trade *adj* 794

intrepid *adj* 861

intrepidity *n* 861

intricate *adj* 248, 704

intrigue *n* 626, 702; *v* 702

intriguer 626

intrinsic *adj* 5, 221

intrinsicality *n* 5

intrinsically *adv* 5

in triumph *adv* 731

introduce *v* 62, 228, 280, 296, 300

introduction *n* 64, 66, 296, 300

introductory *adj* 62, 64, 66, 116

intrude *v* 135, 228, 294

intrusion *n* 57, 135, 228, 294

intrusive *adj* 228, 706

intuit *v* 477

intuition *n* 477

intuition *n* 477

intuitive *adj* 477

intuitively *adv* 477

in turn *adv* 58, 138

intwine *v* 219

in two shakes (of a lamb's tail) *adv* 113

inundate *v* 337, 348, 641

inundation *n* 348

in unison *adj* 413

inure *v* 613

inutile *adj* 645

inutility *n* 645

invade *v* 294, 716

invader *n* 716

in vain *adv* 732

invalidate *v* 158, 479, 536, 756

invalidation *n* 479, 536, 756

invaluable *adj* 648

invariability *n* 16, 141

invariable *adj* 5, 16, 110, 141, 150

invariably *adv* 16, 82

in various places *adv* 182

invasion *n* 294, 716

invent *v* 515, 626

invented *adj* 546

invention *n* 515, 546, 698

inventive *adj* 515, 698

inventiveness *n* 168, 698

inventor *n* 164

inventory *n* 86, 596, 811; *v* 596

inverse *n* 237; *adj* 218, 237

inversely *adv* 218

inversion *n* 218

inversion *n* 14, 140, 145

invert *v* 14, 61, 218

inverted *adj* 59, 218

invest *v* 157, 755, 784

invested *adj* 225

investigate *v* 461

investigation *n* 461, 463, 595

investigator *n* 461

investiture *n* 784

investment *n* 787

inveterate *adj* 124

invidious *adj* 830, 898

in view *adj* 507, 620

invigorate *v* 159, 171

invigorating *adj* 171, 656

invigoration *n* 159

invincible *adj* 159

inviolate *adj* 141

in violation *adj* 927

invisibility *n* 447

invisible *adj* 193, 447

invisibleness *n* 447

invite v 288, 615, 763, 829

invocation n 586

in vogue adj 852

invoice n 812

invoke v 72, 586, 990

involuntary adj 601

involution n 248, 571

involve v 516, 938

involved adj 59, 248, 571

invulnerability n 664

invulnerable adj 664

inward adj 221; adv 221

in what manner adv 627

in what way adv 627

in writing adj 590

iota n 32

irascibility n 901

irascible adj 382, 684, 901

irate adj 900

iridescence n 440

iridescent adj 429, 440

irk v 830

irksome adj 704, 830, 841

iron v 255

iron-gray adj 432

ironic adj 856

ironical adj 856

irons n 752

irony n 856

irradiate v 420

irrational adj 497, 499

irrationality n 499

irreclaimable adj 951

irreconcilability n 10

irreconcilable adj 24

irrecoverable adj 122

irrefutable adj 246, 474

irregular adj 16a, 59, 70, 81, 83, 139, 243, 256, 475

irregularity n 139

irregularity n 16a, 59, 83, 256, 475

irregularly adv 59, 139

irrelation n 10

irrelevancy n 175a

irrelevant adj 10

irreligion n 989

irreligion n 988

irreligious adj 989

irremediable adj 859

irrepentance n 951

irrepressible adj 173, 748, 825

irresistibility n 601

irresistible adj 159, 601, 744

irresolute adj 149, 485, 605, 607, 609a, 683

irresolution n 605

irresolution n 149, 172, 314, 485, 609a

irrespective adj 10

irresponsibility n 773

irresponsible adj 773

irretrievable adj 776

irreverence n 929, 988

irreverent adj 929

irrevocable adj 604

irrigate v 348

irrigation n 348

irritability n 825, 901

irritable adj 684, 825, 901

irritate v 173, 289, 688, 824, 828, 830

irritated adj 835

irritation n 824, 828, 835

irruption n 294

island n 346

isle n 346

islet n 346

isolate v 44, 79, 87, 893, 905

isolated adj 10, 44, 87, 893

isolation n 44, 893, 905

issuance n 531

issue n 154, 167, 295; v 73, 151, 295, 531, 591

issue from v 154

issues n 151

itch v 380

itching n 380; adj 380

itchy adj 380

items n 79

iterate v 104

iteration n 90, 104, 136

iterative adj 104

itinerant n 268; adj 266

J

jabber n 517, 584; v 517, 584

jackanapes n 854

jaded adj 961

jag v 257

jagged adj 244

jail n 752; v 972

jailbird n 754

jailer n 753; 975

jailhouse n 752

jangle v 410

jar n 315; v 24, 410, 414, 713

jargon n 497, 517, 560

jarring adj 410, 414

jaundice n 435, 436

jaundiced adj 435

jaunt n 266

jaw v 584

jazz n 415

jealous adj 435, 900, 920, 921

jealousy n 920

jealousy n 900, 921

jeopardize v 665

jeer v 929

jeer at v 856

jeers n 856

jeopardy n 665

jerk n 285, 315, 493; v 285, 315

jerky adj 315

jest v 842

jester n 501, 844
jesuitry n 477
jet n 273, 348; v 267, 348
jet-black adj 431
jet-setter n 268
jetting adj 267
jettison v 610
jetty n 250
jewel n 648, 899
jibe v 23
jilt v 509
jingle v 408
jinx n 621; n 993
job n 676
jocularity n 836
jog n 315; v 276
joggle v 315
jog on v 736
join v 37, 41, 43, 45, 72, 87, 88, 199, 290, 712
joined adj 43
join forces v 709
join hands with v 709
joining n 37, 43, 290
joint n 43; adj 43, 88, 178, 778
jointly adv 43
joint tenancy n 778
joke v 842
joker n 844
jolly adj 836, 840
jolt n 315; v 276, 315
jostle v 179, 276, 315
jot n 32
jounce v 315
journal n 114, 551
journalist n 553
journey n 266
journey n 302; v 266
journeyer n 268
journeying adj 266
jovial adj 840
joviality n 836
jowl n 236
joy n 377, 827; v 827

joyful adj 377, 827, 836
joyous adj 836
jubilant adj 838, 884
jubilation n 838
judge n 967
judge n 480, 737, 965; v 451, 480, 850, 965, 967
judgment n 480
judgment n 450, 451, 453, 465, 490, 498, 972
judgmental adj 480
judgment seat n 966
judicator n 965, 967
judicatory adj 967
judicature n 965
judicial adj 480, 965, 967
judiciary n 967
judicious adj 174, 480, 498, 868, 967
judiciousness n 174, 868
juice v 354
juiced adj 959
juiceless adj 340
juicer n 959
juicy adj 333, 337, 339
jumble n 41, 59; v 41, 59, 61
jumbo jet n 273
jump n 305, 309; v 309, 310
junction n 43
junction n 41, 45, 48
juncture n 8, 43, 134
jungle n 59
junior adj 127
juridical adj 967
jurisdiction n 965
jurisdiction n 737
jurisdictive adj 965, 967
jurist n 967
juristic adj 967
juror n 967

just adj 246, 922
just as adv 17
just do v 639
justice n 922, 967
justification n 717, 737, 937
justified adj 937
justify v 717, 737, 937
just in time adv 134
justly adv 922
just now adv 123
jut out v 250
juvenile adj 127
juvenility n 123, 127
juxtapose v 464

K

kaleidoscope n 445
kaleidoscopic adj 440
kaput adj 503
karma n 152
keen adj 171, 253, 375, 868
keen blast n 349
keenness n 868
keep n 298; v 141, 143, 670, 751, 781, 883
keep accounts v 811
keep alive v 359
keep an account with v 805
keep apart v 44
keep away v 187
keep back v 678
keep clear of v 623
keep cold v 385
keep company with v 888
keep down v 751
keeper n 753
keep going v 143
keep hold v 150
keeping n 781
keeping out n 55
keeping secret n 528
keep in mind v 505
keep moving v 264, 682

keep on *v* 136, 143, 604a
keep on one's toes *v* 264
keep out *v* 55
keep out of sight *v* 528
keep pace with *v* 27, 120, 178
keep quiet *v* 265, 403, 585
keep safe *v* 717
keepsake *n* 505
keep secret *v* 528
keep silence *v* 585
keep the memory alive *v* 505
keep the peace *v* 721
keep up *v* 141, 143, 670
Kelly green *adj* 435
kelpie *n* 979
kempt *adj* 652
ken *n* 441
kernel *n* 68, 222
kerosene *n* 356, 388
kerosene lamp *n* 423
ketch *n* 273
key *n* 346, 428
keyhole *n* 260
khaki *n* 433; *adj* 433
kick *n* 276
kick up a row *v* 173
kid *n* 129
kill *v* 361
killer *n* 165
killing *n* 361
killing time *n* 681
kill time *v* 106, 683
kiln *n* 386
kind *n* 75, 569; *adj* 888, 906
kind-hearted *adj* 888, 906
kindheartedness *n* 906
kindle *v* 153, 171, 173, 384, 420, 824
kindliness *n* 897, 906
kindling *n* 388
kindly *adj* 888, 906
kindness *n* 897, 906

kindred *n* 11; *adj* 11
kinfolk *n* 11
kingdom of god *n* 981
kingdom of heaven *n* 981
kinsman *n* 11
kiss *n* 902
kith and kin *n* 11
knack *n* 698
knave *n* 941
knead *v* 324, 379
kneading *n* 379
knee *n* 244
knee-deep *adj* 209
kneel *v* 308, 886, 990
knell *n* 363
knife *n* 262
knife edge *n* 253
knit *v* 43, 259
knob *n* 249, 250
knock *n* 276; *v* 276, 406
knock down *v* 213
knot *n* 219, 321; *v* 219
knotted *adj* 59, 256
know *v* 474, 484, 490, 527, 888
know how *n* 632
knowing *adj* 490
knowingly *adv* 620
knowledge *n* 490
knowledge *n* 498, 527, 698
knowledgeable *adj* 490, 698
known *adj* 490
know no bounds *v* 104
know-nothing *n* 493; *v* 491
knuckle *n* 244
kobold *n* 980
kohl-black *adj* 431
Koran *n* 986

L

label *n* 564; *v* 550, 564
labor *n* 680, 686, 704; *v* 680, 686
laboratory *n* 691

labored *adj* 579
laborer *n* 746
laborious *adj* 686, 704
laboriousness *n* 682
labyrinth *n* 59, 248
labyrinthine *adj* 248
lace *n* 219; *v* 43
lack *n* 804; *v* 34, 53, 304, 640, 804
lackadaisical *adj* 683
lack faith *v* 989
lacking *adj* 53, 187, 304
lackluster *adj* 422, 429, 430
lack of adornment *n* 849
lack of affectation *n* 849
lack of bias *n* 942
lack of connection *n* 10
lack of decorum *n* 851
lack of discernment *n* 465a
lack of feeling *n* 376, 381
lack of interest *n* 456
lack of originality *n* 843
lack of practice *n* 614
lack of readiness *n* 603
lack of uniformity *n* 16a
laconic *adj* 572
lacquer *n* 356a; *v* 356a
lad *n* 129
lade *v* 190
lading *n* 190
ladle *v* 270
lady *n* 374, 875
ladylove *n* 897
lag *v* 275, 281, 683
laggard *n* 683; *adj* 603, 683
lagoon *n* 343
laical *adj* 997
laid low *adj* 160
laid up *adj* 655
laim *v* 158
lair *n* 189
laity *n* 997

lay up *v* 678
lay waste *v* 162
laziness *n* 683
lazy *adj* 275, 683
lazy eye *n* 443
lead *n* 234; *v* 116, 176, 615, 692, 693
lead astray *v* 545
leaden *adj* 422
leader *n* 64, 694, 745
leadership *n* 692, 693
leading *n* 280; *adj* 66
lead the way *v* 62, 66, 280
leaf *n* 204
leafage *n* 367
league *n* 712
leak *n* 198; *v* 295
leakage *n* 295
lean *v* 176, 217; *adj* 203
leaning *n* 176, 217, 602; *adj* 176
leanness *n* 203
lean on *v* 858
lean to *v* 602
leap *n* 309
leap *n* 305, 310; *v* 309, 310
leaping *adj* 309
leap with joy *v* 838
learn *v* 490, 527, 539
learn by heart *v* 505
learned *adj* 490, 498, 539
learned in the law *adj* 968
learner *n* 541
learner *n* 492
learning *n* 539
learning *n* 490, 498, 537
learn of *v* 480a
lease *n* 783; *v* 787, 788
leash *v* 43
leave *n* 760; *v* 44, 185, 293, 302, 624, 782, 784

leave alone *v* 623
leaven *n* 320; *v* 320
leave no trace *v* 449, 552
leave off *v* 142, 678
leave out *v* 55
leaves *n* 367
leave-taking *n* 287, 293
leave undone *v* 730
leave unfinished *v* 730
leaving *n* 624
leavings *n* 40
lecher *n* 962
lecherous *adj* 961
lechery *n* 961
lecture *n* 537, 582; *v* 537, 582, 586
lecturer *n* 540
ledge *n* 215, 250
ledger *n* 86, 551, 811
lee *n* 236
leer *n* 441; *v* 441
lee side *n* 236
leeway *n* 180
left *n* 239
left *adj* 40, 449, 782
left behind *adj* 782
left hand *n* 239
left-handed *adj* 239
leftover *n* 40; *adj* 40
left side *n* 239
legacy *n* 784
legal *adj* 760, 963, 967
legal action *n* 969
legal adviser *n* 968
legality *n* 963
legalize *v* 737, 963
legalized *adj* 760, 963
legal proceedings *n* 969
legal process *n* 969
legal profession *n* 968
legal separation *n* 905
legatee *n* 785
legation *n* 755
legislate *v* 693, 963
legislated *adj* 963
legitimacy *n* 963
legitimate *adj* 494, 760, 922, 963

legitimateness *n* 963
leguminous *adj* 367
leisure *n* 685
leisure *adj* 685
leisureliness *n* 275
leisurely *adj* 275, 685; *adv* 133, 275
lemon *adj* 435
lend *v* 787
lend an ear *v* 418
lender *n* 805
lending *n* 787
lend on security *v* 787
length *n* 200
lengthen *v* 110, 133, 200
lengthened *adj* 200
lengthiness *n* 200
lengthwise *adv* 200
lengthy *adj* 200, 573
lenience *n* 740
lenience *n* 174, 738
leniency *n* 740
lenient *adj* 174, 738, 740
lenity *n* 174
lens *n* 443, 445
leprechaun *n* 980
leprous *adj* 655
less *adj* 34; *adv* 34, 38
lessee *n* 779
lessen *v* 36, 174, 195, 834
lessening *n* 36, 195
lesser *adj* 34
lesson *n* 537, 668
let *v* 760, 762, 787
let alone *v* 678, 681, 730
let down *v* 308, 509
let drop *v* 308, 529
let fall *v* 308, 527
let fly *v* 284
let go *v* 624, 782, 790
lethal *adj* 162, 360, 361
lethargic *adj* 683
lethargy *n* 683
let in partial light *v* 427
let out *v* 750

let slip *v* 529, 730, 776
letter *n* 561
letter *n* 592
letter carrier *n* 271
lettering *n* 591
letterpress *n* 591
letters *n* 490, 560
let the opportunity slip by *v* 135
let things take their course *v* 681
levee *n* 72
level *n* 26, 27, 213, 251; *v* 16, 27, 162, 213, 251, 255, 308; *adj* 16, 27, 207, 213, 251, 255
level at *v* 278
level-headed *adj* 502
level with *v* 543
leverage *n* 175
leviathan *n* 192
levity *n* 320
lewd *adj* 961
lewdness *n* 961
lexicography *n* 562
lexicon *n* 562
liability *n* 177
liability *n* 665, 806
liable *adj* 176, 177, 665, 806
liar *n* 548
liberal *adj* 784, 816, 906, 942
liberality *n* 816
liberality *n* 784, 906, 942
liberate *v* 44, 672, 748, 750, 970
liberated *adj* 750
liberation *n* 750
liberation *n* 671, 672
libertarian *adj* 760
libertine *n* 962
libertine *n* 954a
liberty *n* 685, 737, 748, 760, 760
librarian *n* 593

libretto *n* 593
licence *n* 738
license *n* 748, 760, 924; *v* 760
licensed *adj* 924
licit *adj* 246, 963
lick the boots of *v* 886
lid *n* 223, 261, 263
lie *n* 544, 546; *v* 183, 213, 538, 544 546
lie around *v* 220
lie down *v* 213, 687
lie flat *v* 207, 213
lie idle *v* 681
lie in *v* 1
lie in wait for *v* 530
lie low *v* 207
lien *n* 771
lie still *v* 265
life *n* 359
life *n* 151, 171, 682
lifeblood *n* 5, 359
life-giving *adj* 168
lifeless *adj* 172, 360
lifelessness *n* 172
lifelike *adj* 17, 21
lifetime *n* 108
lift *n* 307; *v* 235, 307
lift up *v* 235, 307
light *n* 420
light *n* 7; *v* 292, 384, 420, 423; *adj* 320, 322, 420, 430, 643
light bulb *n* 423
light-colored *adj* 429
lighten *v* 320, 420, 705
lightening *n* 420
light-fingered *adj* 791
light-footed *adj* 274
lightness *n* 320
light of day *n* 420
light on *v* 156
light up *v* 824
like *v* 394, 827, 897, 990; *adj* 17, 216
like a shot *adv* 113
like a ton of bricks *adj* 319

likelihood *n* 470, 472
likeliness *n* 472
likely *adj* 176, 177, 472
likeness *n* 17, 21, 216, 556
likening *n* 464
like two peas in a pod *n* 17
likewise *adv* 37
liking *n* 602, 897
lilac *adj* 437
lily-liver *n* 862
lily-livered *adj* 435, 862
limb *n* 51
limber *adj* 324
limbo *n* 982
limit *n* 233
limit *n* 67, 71; *v* 195, 229, 233, 469, 761
limitation *n* 229, 469, 751
limited *adj* 103, 203, 233
limitless *adj* 104, 180
limitlessness *n* 105
limn *v* 556, 594
limp *v* 160, 275; *adj* 53, 158, 160, 324, 326
limpid *adj* 425
limpidity *n* 425
limpness *n* 326
line *n* 69, 278; *v* 224
lineage *n* 11, 69, 122, 166
lineal *adj* 166, 200
linear *adj* 69, 200, 246
lined *adj* 224, 440
line of march *n* 278
liner *n* 273
lines *n* 230, 448
linger *v* 133, 275
lingering *adj* 110
lingo *n* 560
lingual *adj* 560
linguist *n* 560
linguistic *adj* 560

liniment *n* 356
lining *n* 224
link *n* 45
link *n* 9, 43; *v* 9, 43, 45, 219
linkage *n* 43
link up *v* 43, 219
linseed oil *n* 356
lip *n* 231
lip-service *n* 933
liquefaction *n* 335
liquefaction *n* 333, 384
liquefy *v* 333, 335, 384
liquefying *n* 335
liquid *n* 337; *adj* 333, 337
liquidate *v* 807
liquidation *n* 807
liquid containers *n* 191
liquidity *n* 333
list *n* 86
list *n* 217, 596; *v* 551, 596
listen *v* 418
listener *n* 418
listening *n* 418
listing *n* 86
listless *adj* 683, 866
listlessness *n* 866
lists *n* 728
literal *adj* 561, 562
literally *adv* 19
literary *adj* 560
literature *n* 560, 590
litigant *n* 726, 969
litigation *n* 969
litigious *adj* 969
litter *n* 167; *v* 61
little *adj* 32, 193
little by little *adv* 26, 275
littleness *n* 193
littleness *n* 32, 201
little one *n* 129
live *n* 374; *v* 1, 141, 186, 188, 359; *adj* 359

live from hand to mouth *v* 804
livelihood *n* 803
liveliness *n* 515, 682, 829, 836
lively *adj* 309, 359, 375, 515, 574, 682, 829, 836
live off *v* 298
live on *v* 298
livery *n* 225
livestock *n* 366
live through *v* 151
livid *adj* 431, 435
lividness *n* 431
living being *n* 364
living beings *n* 357
living thing *n* 366
load *n* 190, 319, 828; *v* 52, 190, 319, 641
loaf *v* 683
loafer *n* 683
loan *n* 787; *v* 787
loath *adj* 603, 867
loathe *v* 867, 898
loathing *n* 867, 898
loathsome *adj* 395, 830, 867, 898
local *adj* 183
locale *n* 182, 183
locality *n* 182, 183
locate *v* 183, 184
located *adj* 183, 184
locate oneself *v* 184
location *n* 184
location *n* 183
loch *n* 343
lock *n* 350; *v* 43
lock-up *n* 752
locomotion *n* 264
locomotive *n* 271
locution *n* 582
lodge *v* 184, 186
lodger *n* 188
lodging *n* 189
loft *v* 235
loftiness *n* 206, 574, 875

lofty *adj* 206, 574
log *n* 114, 388, 551
logic *n* 23, 476
logical *adj* 23, 476, 502
logician *n* 476
loiter *v* 133, 275, 683
loitering *n* 133
loll *v* 683
lone *adj* 87
long *adj* 200; *adv* 110
long ago *adv* 110, 122
long dozen *n* 98
longevity *n* 110, 128
long expected *adj* 507
long for *v* 858, 865
longhand *n* 590
longing *n* 858, 865
longitude *n* 200
longitudinal *adj* 200
longitudinally *adv* 200
long lost *adj* 776
long shot *n* 137
longstanding *adj* 110
long-winded *adj* 573
long-windedness *n* 573
look *n* 441, 448; *v* 441, 448, 457
look after oneself *v* 943
look ahead *v* 510
look askance *v* 443
look beyond *v* 510
look danger in the face *v* 861
looker-on *n* 444
look for *v* 461, 507
look forward *v* 121
look forward to *v* 507, 510
looking back *adj* 122
looking glass *n* 445
look into the future *v* 510
look like *v* 17
look on *v* 186, 444
lookout *n* 448
look out for *v* 507
look sharp *v* 682
look upon *v* 451

loom *v* 152, 446
looming *adj* 152
loon *n* 501
loop *n* 245, 247, 629
loophole *n* 671
loose *v* 44, 750; *adj* 44,
　47, 279, 573, 575,
　738, 748, 773
loosen *v* 47
looseness *n* 47, 573,
　738, 748
loosening *n* 47, 738
loot *n* 793
lop *v* 371
loquacious *adj* 584
loquaciousness *n* 584
loquacity *n* 584
lord *n* 745, 875, 976
lore *n* 490, 537
lorgnette *n* 445
lose *v* 776
lose an opportunity *v*
　135
lose color *v* 429
lose ground *v* 283
lose heart *v* 837
lost it *v* 503
lose no time *v* 682
lose one's senses *v* 503
lose one's temper *v* 825
lose patience *v* 825
lose sight of *v* 506
loss *n* 776
loss *n* 40a, 449, 619,
　638, 659, 732
loss of life *n* 360
lost *adj* 2, 449, 458,
　732, 776
lost in thought *adj* 451
lost in wonder *adj* 870
lot *n* 25, 152, 621, 786
lottery *n* 156
loud *adj* 404
loudly *adv* 404
loudness *n* 404
loud noise *n* 404
lough *n* 343
lounge *v* 683

lounger *n* 683
lout *n* 501
lovable *adj* 897
love *n* 897
love *n* 865, 897, 899,
　977; *v* 827, 928, 990
loveliness *n* 829, 845
lovely *adj* 242, 377,
　597, 829, 845, 977
lover *n* 897
lovesick *adj* 991
love token *n* 902
loving *adj* 897
low *v* 412; *adj* 32, 207,
　405, 438, 649, 874,
　876, 879, 930
low-born *adj* 876
lower *v* 207, 308, 879;
　adj 34
lowering *n* 308
lowland *n* 344
lowlands *n* 207
lowliness *n* 879
lowly *adj* 207, 879
low-lying *adj* 207
lowness *n* 207
low price *n* 815
low quality *n* 34
low relief *n* 250
low repute *n* 874
loyal *adj* 743
loyalty *n* 743
lubricate *v* 255, 332,
　355
lubrication *n* 332
lubrication *n* 255, 355
lubricity *n* 255, 355
lucent *adj* 420
lucid *adj* 425, 502, 518,
　570, 849
lucidity *n* 420, 425,
　502, 518, 570, 578
Lucifer *n* 978
luck *n* 152, 156, 621,
　731
lucky *adj* 134, 621, 734
ludicrous *adj* 853
lug *v* 285

lugubrious *adj* 837
lukewarn *adj* 382, 823,
　866
lull *n* 142, 265, 403,
　683, 685; *v* 174, 265
lull to sleep *v* 265
lumber *v* 275
luminary *n* 423
luminary *n* 500
luminosity *n* 420
luminous *adj* 420, 518
lump *n* 50, 51, 72, 192,
　321
lumpish *adj* 192, 319
lump together *v* 72
lunacy *n* 503
lunar *adj* 245, 318
lunatic *n* 504; *adj* 503
lunch *v* 298
lunge *n* 276
lurch *n* 306; *v* 306
lure *v* 288
lurid *adj* 421, 422
lurk *v* 526
lurking *adj* 526
lurking place *n* 530
luscious *adj* 394, 396,
　829
lush *n* 959; *v* 959; *adj*
　337, 365, 396
lust *n* 865
luster *n* 420
lust for *v* 865
lustful *adj* 865
lustihood *n* 159
lustrous *adj* 420
luxuriate *v* 377
luxuriate in *v* 827
luxurious *adj* 377,
　829
luxuriousness *n* 377
luxury *n* 377, 827
lying *n* 544; *adj* 544
lying down *n* 213
lymph *n* 337

M

ma *n* 166
ma'am *n* 374
Machiavellian *adj* 702
machinery *n* 633
macrocosm *n* 318
mad *adj* 173, 503, 824, 825
madam *n* 374
madame *n* 374
mad as a hatter *adj* 503
madden *v* 173
madman *n* 504
madness *n* 503, 825
maelstrom *n* 312, 348, 667
magenta *adj* 437
magic *n* 992; *adj* 992
magical *adj* 992
magician *n* 994
magisterial *adj* 737
magistracy *n* 965
magistrate *n* 967
magnetic *adj* 288
magnetism *n* 288
magnetize *v* 288
magnificence *n* 845
magnificent *adj* 192, 845
magnify *v* 35, 194, 482, 549, 990
magnifying glass *n* 445
magniloquence *n* 577
magniloquent *adj* 549, 577
magnitude *n* 25, 31, 192
mahogany *adj* 433
maiden *n* 129, 904; *adj* 66
maim *v* 158, 659
main *n* 341, 350
mainly *adv* 31
mainspring *n* 153, 615
mainstay *n* 666
maintain *v* 141, 143, 170, 215, 535, 670, 717, 720, 781, 937

maintain course *v* 143
maintenance *n* 141, 143, 170, 670, 781, 803
majestic *adj* 882
majesty *n* 875
major *adj* 33
majority *n* 33, 100, 131
make *n* 240; *v* 54, 56, 144, 161, 744, 852
make a choice *v* 609
make a circuit *v* 629
make a clean sweep of *v* 652
make a complete circle *v* 311
make a compromise *v* 628
make acquainted with *v* 527
make a fool of oneself *v* 853
make a fresh start *v* 66
make a generalization *v* 78
make allowance for *v* 469
make amends *v* 30, 952
make a mess of *v* 732
make a motion *v* 763
make an addition to *v* 37
make an end of *v* 67
make an exception *v* 469
make a noise *v* 402
make a pig of oneself *v* 957
make a place for *v* 184
make a point of *v* 604
make a pretext of *v* 617
make a resolution *v* 604
make a sign *v* 550
make a U-turn *v* 311
make believe *v* 546
make faces *v* 243
make for *v* 278
make free with *v* 789
make friends with *v* 888
make fun of *v* 856

make good *v* 660, 790
make grave *v* 835
make haste *v* 132, 682, 684
make headlines *v* 532
make headway *v* 282
make known *v* 525, 527, 529, 531
make light of *v* 483, 643
make little of *v* 483
make loose *v* 47
make manifest *v* 525
make merry *v* 840
make music *v* 415, 416
make news *v* 532
make nothing of *v* 871
make obeisance *v* 308
make one sick *v* 395
make one's way *v* 734
make out *v* 441
make over *v* 783
make payment *v* 807
make peace *v* 721, 723
make preparations *v* 673
make productive *v* 168
make progress *v* 282, 682
make provision *v* 637
make provision for *v* 673
make public *v* 531
make pungent *v* 392
maker *n* 164
make ready *v* 673
make sail *v* 267
make serious *v* 835
makeshift *n* 147, 617
make solid *v* 150
make strides *v* 282
make sure *v* 150, 474
make terms *v* 769
make the best of *v* 826
make the mind a blank *v* 452
make time *v* 132
make-up *n* 54
make up for *v* 30
make use of *v* 677
make verses *v* 597

make war v 722
making verses n 597
maladroit adj 699
maladroitness n 699
malady n 655
malaise n 378, 828
malapropism n 565
malarkey n 477
malcontent adj 832
male n 373; adj 373
male animal n 373, 374
malediction n 908
malevolence n 907
malevolence n 649, 889
malevolent adj 649,
　739, 907, 919, 945
malformation n 243
malformed adj 243
malice n 907
malicious adj 898, 907,
　919, 945
maliciousness n 907
malign v 934; adj 649
malignant adj 919, 945
malignity n 649
mall n 799
malleability n 149, 324
malleable adj 82, 149,
　324
maltreat v 649, 739,
　830, 923
mamma n 166
mammal n 366
mammoth n 192; adj
　31
man n 373
man n 372
man about town n 854
man after one's own
　heart n 899
manage v 58, 692, 693
manageable adj 705
management n 692,
　693, 698
manager n 694
managerial adj 692
managing adj 693
mandate n 630, 741

maneuver v 702
manfully adv 604
mangle v 659
mangy adj 655
man-hater n 911
manhood n 131, 373
mania n 503
maniac n 504
maniacal adj 503
manifest adj 446, 525
manifestation n 525
manifestation n 446,
　448
manifested adj 525
manifestly adv 525
manifold adj 15, 81,
　102
manipulate v 379, 677,
　702
manipulation n 379
mankind n 372
mankind n 372
manliness n 604
manly adj 131, 373
manner n 569, 613, 627
mannered adj 579, 855
mannerism n 79, 83,
　579
mannerisms n 855
manner of speaking n
　521
manners n 692, 852
man of learning n 500
mantle n 424
manual n 527
manufacture n 161; v
　161
manuscript n 590
many adj 100, 102
many-colored adj 440
many-sided adj 81
map n 183, 527, 626
mar v 659, 848
marble n 249
marbled adj 440
march n 266
marches n 233
marching band n 417

march of time n 109
mare n 374
margin n 231
marine adj 341
marine blue adj 438
mariner n 269
mariner n 269
marital separation n 905
maritime adj 267, 341
mark n 26, 71, 550,
　569, 590, 620; v 450,
　550, 642
marked adj 79
market n 799
market v 795
marketable adj 794,
　796
marketplace n 799
market price n 812
mark the time v 114
mark time v 114, 265
maroon adj 434
marquee n 223
marriage n 903
marriage n 43
marriageable adj 131
married adj 903
married man n 903
married woman n 903
marrow n 5, 221
marry v 43, 48, 903
marsh n 345
marshal v 60
marshy adj 339, 345
mart n 799
martial adj 722
martyr n 955
marvel n 870, 872; v
　870
marvelous adj 31, 870
marvelously adv 31
masculine adj 373
masculinity n 373
mash v 324, 352, 354
mask n 223, 424, 530; v
　442, 528
masquerade n 530

mass *n* 25, 31, 50, 72, 102, 192, 321
massacre *n* 361; *v* 361
massage *v* 379
massaging *n* 379
massive *adj* 192, 319, 321
massy *adj* 192
master *n* 745
master *n* 129, 540, 694, 700, 779; *v* 518, 539, 731, 749
masterful *adj* 731, 737
masterly *adj* 698
master mind *n* 500, 700, 872
master of *adj* 777
masterpiece *n* 648, 650
master stroke *n* 650
mastery *n* 698, 731, 741
mastic *n* 356a
masticate *v* 298
mastication *n* 298
mat *n* 219; *v* 219
match *n* 17, 27; *v* 17, 23, 27
matchless *adj* 33
mate *n* 17, 27, 711, 890, 903; *v* 89
material *n* 316; *adj* 3, 316
material existence *n* 3
materialism *n* 316
materialist *n* 316
materialistic *adj* 3, 316
materiality *n* 316
materiality *n* 3
materialization *n* 525
materialize *v* 316, 525
materials *n* 635
materials *n* 316
maternal *adj* 166
maternity *n* 11, 166
mates *n* 269
matins *n* 125
matriarch *n* 130
matriarchal *adj* 166
matricide *n* 361

matriculation *n* 539
matrimony *n* 903
matrix *n* 22
matted *adj* 219
matter *n* 3, 316, 516, 591, 625; *v* 642
matter little *v* 643
matter of fact *n* 1; *adj* 598, 703, 843
matter of factness *n* 703
matters *n* 151
matting *n* 219
mature *v* 144, 650, 658, 673; *adj* 673
mature years *n* 128
maturity *n* 124, 128, 131, 673
maul *v* 649
mausoleum *n* 363
mauve *adj* 437
maxim *n* 496
maxim *n* 537, 697
maximum *n* 210
maybe *adv* 470
maze *n* 248
mazy *adj* 248
meadow *n* 344
meager *adj* 32, 53, 103, 203, 575, 640, 643
meagerness *n* 203
mealy *adj* 330
mealy-mouthed *adj* 886
mean *n* 29
mean *n* 68, 628; *v* 451, 516, 620; *adj* 29, 32, 34, 68, 207, 435, 643, 649, 819, 851, 876, 886, 914a, 930, 943
meander *v* 248, 264, 266, 279, 573
meandering *n* 248
meaning *n* 516
meaning *n* 522, 620; *adj* 516
meaningful *adj* 516
meaningless *adj* 497, 517

meaninglessness *n* 517
meanness *n* 32, 34, 499, 886, 914a, 943
mean nothing *v* 517
means *n* 632
means *n* 627, 780, 803
means of access *n* 627
meantime *adv* 106
meanwhile *adv* 106
measurable *adj* 466
measure *n* 25, 26, 174, 413, 466, 786; *v* 106, 466
measured *adj* 174
measure for measure *n* 30
measureless *adj* 104
measurement *n* 466
measurement *n* 25
measure time *v* 114
meaty *adj* 354
mechanical *adj* 601, 633
medal *n* 733
meddlesome *adj* 455
meddlesomeness *n* 455
medial *adj* 68
median *n* 29; *adj* 68
meditate *v* 620, 631, 724
mediation *n* 724
mediation *n* 631, 766
mediator *n* 724
mediatory *adj* 724
medication *n* 662
medicinal *adj* 662
medicine *n* 662
medicine man *n* 994
mediocre *adj* 28, 29, 34, 598, 651, 736
mediocrity *n* 736
mediocrity *n* 28, 34
meditate *v* 451, 870
meditation *n* 451
meditative *adj* 451
medium *n* 29, 631, 994
medley *n* 41
meek *adj* 879

meekness n 879
meet v 23, 72, 199, 290, 772; adj 646
meeting n 43, 72, 199, 290, 680, 696
meetinghouse n 1000
meet up with v 151
meet with v 151
melancholy n 837; adj 830, 837
mélange n 41
melee n 59
meliorate v 174, 723
mellifluence n 413
mellifluous adj 413, 578
mellow v 144, 673; adj 128, 413, 428, 673, 721
melodic adj 413
melodious adj 377, 413, 580
melodiousness n 413
melody n 413
melody n 415
melt v 111, 144, 335, 384, 449
melt away v 4, 449
melting n 335, 384
member n 51, 56
membrane n 204
membranous adj 204
memento n 505
memento mori n 363
memorable adj 505
memorandum n 551
memorial n 505
memorialist n 553
memorialization n 883
memorize v 505, 539
memory n 505
memory n 122
menace n 667, 909; v 668, 909
menacing adj 909
menagerie n 72
mend v 658
mendacious adj 544

mendicant n 767
menial n 746
mental adj 450
mental balance n 502
mental cultivation n 539
mental excitation n 824
mental image n 515
mental suffering n 619
mention v 527
mentor n 540, 695
mephitic adj 401
mercantile adj 794
mercantilism n 796
mercenary adj 819
merchandise n 798
merchandise v 763, 796, 798
merchant n 797
merchant n 796
merchant ship n 273
merciful adj 740
merciless adj 914a
mercurial adj 149, 264
mercury n 389
mercy n 740, 914
mere n 343; adj 643
merely adv 32
merge v 48, 300
merge in v 56
merge into v 144
meridian n 125, 181
merit n 648, 944, 973
merit attention v 642
meritorious adj 931
mermaid n 979
merriment n 836
merry adj 829
merrymaking n 838
mesh n 219
mesmerist n 994
mesmerize v 992
mess n 59, 61, 162, 732
messenger n 534
messenger n 271, 527, 758
mess up v 59
messy adj 59
metallurgy n 358

metamorphose v 140
metamorphosis n 140
metaphor n 521
metaphorical adj 464
mete v 786
meteors n 318
mete out v 784
meter n 413
method n 627
method n 58, 60, 569, 626, 632, 692
methodical adj 58, 60, 692
methodically adv 58
methodological adj 626
methodology n 58
meticulous adj 459, 868
metrical adj 597
metrics n 597
mettle n 861
mew v 412
miasmic adj 401
microcosm n 193
microscope n 445
microscopic adj 32, 193
mid adj 68
mid-course n 628
midcourse n 68
midday n 125
middle n 68
middle n 29, 208, 222; adj 29, 68, 222; adv 222
middle class adj 29
middle course n 628
middle ground n 68, 174
middlemost adj 222
middle of the road n 174
middle way n 628
middling adj 32, 651
midmost adj 68
midnight n 126
midnight n 421
mid-point n 29, 68
midriff n 68

midst *n* 68, 208, 222; *adv* 222

midsummer 125

midway *adj* 628; *adv* 68

mien *n* 448, 692

might *n* 31, 157, 159, 173

mightily *adv* 31

mighty *adj* 31, 157, 159, 192, 192

migrate *v* 266

migration *n* 266

migratory *adj* 266

mild *adj* 174, 382, 391, 721, 740

mildew *n* 653, 663

mildewed *adj* 659

mildness *n* 174, 740

militant *adj* 722

militarist *n* 726

military *adj* 722

military band *n* 417

milkiness *n* 427, 430

milk-white *adj* 430

milky *adj* 352, 427, 430

mill *n* 330, 691

millennium *n* 108, 121

millions *n* 372

mimic *v* 19, 554

mimicry *n* 19

mince *v* 275

mince steps *v* 275

mind *n* 450, 498, 842; *v* 602

mindblower *n* 137

mindful *adj* 451, 457

mindfulness *n* 457

mindful (of) *adj* 505

mindless *adj* 499

mine *n* 636; *v* 252, 260, 659

mineral *adj* 358

mineral kingdom *n* 358

mineralogy *n* 358

mineral world *n* 358

mingle *v* 41

mingling *n* 41

miniature *adj* 32, 193

minimize *v* 483

minion *n* 899

minister *n* 631, 690, 694, 996; *v* 631, 693

ministerial *adj* 995

ministering spirit *n* 977

ministration *n* 693

ministry *n* 995, 996

minor *n* 129; *adj* 32, 34

minority *n* 34, 127

minstrel *n* 416, 597

mint *n* 22, 691

minus *adj* 776; *adv* 38, 187

minuscule *adj* 32

minute *adj* 32, 193

minutiae *n* 32

minx *n* 962

miracle *n* 872

miraculous *adj* 870

mirage 443

mire *n* 653

mirror *n* 445, 650; *v* 19; 443

mirth *n* 836

mirthful *adj* 836

misanthrope *n* 165

misanthropic *adj* 911

misanthropy *n* 911

misapplication *n* 679

misapply *v* 523, 679

misapprehend *v* 495, 523

misapprehension *n* 481, 495, 523

misappropriate *v* 679

misappropriation *n* 679

misbelieve *n* 984

misbelieving *adj* 984

miscalculate *v* 482, 495

miscalculation *n* 481, 482, 508

miscall *v* 565

miscarriage *n* 732

miscarry *v* 732

miscellaneous *adj* 15, 41, 465a

miscellaneousness *n* 78

miscellany *n* 41, 72, 78

mischief *n* 619

mischievous *adj* 649

miscomputation *n* 481

misconceive *v* 481, 495, 523

misconception *n* 481, 495, 523

misconjecture *v* 481

misconstruction *n* 523

misconstrue *v* 481, 523

miscreant *n* 949

misdate *n* 115; *v* 115

misdated *adj* 115

misdeed *n* 923

misdirect *v* 538

misdirection *n* 538

misemploy *v* 679

misemployment *n* 679

miser *n* 819

miserable *adj* 828, 837, 930

miserably *adv* 31, 32

miserly *adj* 819

misery *n* 828

misfiguration *n* 555

misfortune *n* 619, 735, 830

misgiving *n* 485, 860

misguidance *n* 538

misguide *v* 538

mishap *n* 619, 732, 830

misinform *v* 538

misinformation *n* 538

misinstruct *v* 538

misinterpret *v* 481, 495, 523

misinterpretation *n* 523

misinterpretation *n* 481, 495

misjudge *v* 481, 495

misjudging *adj* 481

misjudgment *n* 481

misjudgment *n* 495

mislay v 61, 776

mislead v 477, 538, 545

misleading adj 520, 544, 545

mismatch n 24; v 15

mismatched adj 24

misname v 565

misnamed adj 565

misnaming n 565

misnomer n 565

misogynist n 911

misplace v 61, 185

misplaced adj 115, 185

misplacement n 115, 185

misproportion n 241, 243

misread v 523

misreading n 523

misrepresent v 277, 477, 523, 538, 544, 555

misrepresentation n 555

misrepresentation n 523, 544

miss n 129, 374; v 776

misshape v 243

misshapen adj 241, 243

missing adj 187, 449

missing link n 53

mission n 755

missionary n 540

missive n 592

misspend v 638, 818

misstate v 523

miss the mark v 732

mist n 353, 422, 424, 427; v 353

mistake n 495, 523, 732; v 495, 523

mistaken adj 495, 544, 923

misteach v 538

misteaching n 538

mister n 373

misterm v 565

mistime v 135

mistimed adj 135

mistiness n 422, 426

mistreat v 830

mistress n 779

mistrust n 485; v 485

misty adj 353, 422, 426, 447

misunderstand v 481, 495, 523

misunderstanding n 495, 523, 713

misusage n 649, 679

misuse n 679

misuse n 638; v 638, 679

mite n 32

mitigate v 174, 469, 834

mitigating adj 469

mitigation n 174, 469, 834

mix n 41, 48; v 41, 48, 61

mixed adj 41

mixture n 41

mixture n 48

moan n 839; v 411

moaning n 411, 839

moat n 259, 350

mob n 72, 102

mobile adj 149, 264

mobility n 149, 264

mobilization n 264

mobilize v 264

mock v 19, 856, 929; adj 17, 19

mockery n 856

mocking n 19; adj 856

mode n 7, 569, 613, 852

model n 21, 22, 80, 240, 650, 948; v 144, 240, 557; adj 650

modeled after adj 19

modeled on adj 19

modeling n 557

model oneself on v 19

mode of expression n 569

moderate v 174, 275, 723; adj 174, 275, 628, 736, 815, 881, 953

moderately adv 174

moderation n 174

moderation n 275, 736, 740, 826, 881, 953

moderator n 724, 967

modern adj 123

modernism n 123

modernity n 123

modernize v 123

modest adj 483, 879, 881, 960

modestly adv 881

modesty n 881

modesty n 483, 879, 960

modicum n 32

modification n 20a, 140, 469

modified adj 15, 20a

modify v 15, 20a, 140, 469

modish adj 852, 855

modulate v 140

modulation n 140, 413

module n 22, 273

moist adj 337, 339

moisten v 337, 339

moisture n 339

mold n 7, 21, 22, 240, 329, 557, 653; v 144, 240, 557, 653, 852

moldable adj 324

molded adj 820

molder v 659

moldering adj 659

moldy adj 653, 659

molecule n 32

molest v 649, 716

molestation n 649

mollification n 324

mollify v 174, 324, 723

mollusk n 366

molten adj 384

mom n 166

moment *n* 113, 642
momentary *adj* 111, 113
momentous *adj* 642
momentousness *n* 642
monetary *adj* 800
money *n* 800
money *n* 803
moneybag *n* 802
money matters *n* 811
mongrel *n* 41; *adj* 41
moniker *n* 564
monochrome *n* 429
monocle *n* 445
monody *n* 839
monogram *n* 561
monolog *n* 589
monomania *n* 606
monomaniacal *adj* 606
monosyllable *n* 561
monotheism *n* 983
monotonous *adj* 16, 27, 104, 841
monotony *n* 16, 27, 104, 841
monsoon *n* 349
monster *n* 192, 949, 980
monstrosity *n* 192, 243, 872
monstrous *adj* 31, 192, 846
monstrously *adv* 31
monument *n* 363, 551
moo *v* 412
mood *n* 7, 176, 602, 820
moodiness *n* 901a
moods *n* 5
moody *adj* 901a
moon *n* 420, 423
moonbeam *n* 420
moor *n* 344; *v* 43
moored *adj* 184, 186
mooring *n* 184
mope *v* 837
moper *n* 683
moral *adj* 922, 944
moral imperative *n* 926

morality *n* 922, 944
moralize *v* 537
morals *n* 922
moral sensibility *n* 822
morass *n* 345
moratorium *n* 133
morbid *adj* 655
more *adv* 33, 37
more or less *adj* 25
moreover *adv* 37
more than one *adj* 100
morgue *n* 363
morn *n* 125
morning *n* 125
morning *n* 125
morningtide *n* 125
moron *n* 493, 501
morose *adj* 901a
moroseness *n* 901a
morphology *n* 368
morrow *n* 121
morsel *n* 32, 390
mortal *n* 372; *adj* 111, 361, 372
mortal coil *n* 362
mortality *n* 111, 360, 372
mortal remains *n* 362
mortar and pestle *n* 330
mortgage *n* 771, 787; *v* 771
mortification *n* 828, 830
mortify *v* 828, 830, 879
mortuary *n* 363; *adj* 363
mosaic *adj* 81, 440
moss *n* 345
most *adv* 31
most likely *adv* 472
mote *n* 32, 451
moth-eaten *adj* 653, 659
mother *n* 166, 192
mother earth *n* 342
motherhood *n* 166
motherland *n* 189
motion *n* 264

motion *n* 550
motionless *adj* 172, 265, 683
motivate *v* 615, 744
motivation *n* 615
motive *n* 615
motive power *n* 264
mot juste *n* 496
motley *adj* 16a, 41, 81
motorboat *n* 273
motorcar *n* 272
motorcycle *n* 272
motoring *n* 266
motorscooter *n* 272
mottled *adj* 440
motto *n* 496, 566
mound *n* 192
mount *v* 206, 305
mountain *n* 192, 250
mourn for *v* 833
mournful *adj* 830, 839, 901a
mourn over *v* 839
mouth *n* 231, 343
mouthful *n* 25, 32
mouthpiece *n* 582
movable *adj* 264, 270
movableness *n* 264
move *n* 264, 270; *v* 175, 264, 266, 270, 302, 615, 763, 824
move away from *v* 287
move back *v* 287
moved *adj* 821, 914
movement *n* 264, 680, 682
move off *v* 293
move out *v* 293
move quickly *v* 274
mover *n* 164
move slowly *v* 275
move to the center *v* 29
move towards *v* 286
moving *n* 266, 680; *adj* 264
mow *v* 371
Mr. *n* 373
Ms. *n* 374

much *adj* 641; *adv* 31
much ado about nothing *n* 549
much the same *adj* 17, 27
muck *n* 653
muckraking *n* 529
mud *n* 345, 653
muddle *n* 59; *v* 61
muddle-headed *adj* 499
muddy *adj* 339, 345, 352, 519
muffle *v* 403, 408a, 590
muffled *adj* 405, 408a
muffled drums *n* 408a
muffler *n* 408a
muggy *adj* 339
mulish *adj* 606
mulishness *n* 606
mulling around *n* 681
multi-colored *adj* 440
multifarious *adj* 16a, 81
multifold *adj* 81
multiformity *n* 81
multiple *adj* 102
multiplication *n* 168
multiplicity *n* 102
multiply *v* 35, 85, 102, 163, 168
multiply by four *v* 96
multiplying by four *n* 96
multi-purpose *adj* 148
multitude *n* 102
multitude *n* 31, 72, 100, 876
multitudes *n* 372
multitudinous *n* 102; *adj* 102
mum *n* 166; *adj* 581 585
mumble *v* 583
mumbling *n* 583
mumbo-jumbo *n* 993
mummify *v* 363
mummy *n* 166
munch *v* 298
mundane *adj* 318
munificence *n* 816, 910

munificent *adj* 816, 910
munitions *n* 727
murder *n* 361; *v* 361
murderer *n* 361
murderous *adj* 361
murk *n* 421
murkiness *n* 421
murky *adj* 421, 422, 426, 431
murmur *n* 405; *v* 348, 405
murmured *adj* 405
muscular *adj* 159
muse *v* 451
mushiness *n* 326
mushy *adj* 324, 339
music *n* 415
musical *adj* 413, 415, 416, 597
musical instruments *n* 417
musicalness *n* 413
musician *n* 416
musing *n* 451
muster *n* 72; *v* 72, 85
mustiness *n* 401
musty *adj* 401, 653
mutability *n* 149
mutable *adj* 149
mutation *n* 140
mute *n* 408a; *v* 408a; *adj* 403, 581, 585
muted *adj* 405, 408a
muteness *n* 581
muteness *n* 403, 585
mutilate *v* 38, 241, 361, 659
mutilation *n* 38, 241
mutineer *n* 742
mutinous *adj* 742
mutinousness *n* 742
mutiny *n* 146, 742; *v* 742
mutter *v* 405, 583
muttering *n* 583
mutual *adj* 12, 148
mutuality *n* 12
muzzle *v* 158, 403, 581

myopia *n* 443
myopic *adj* 443
mysterious *adj* 208, 447, 519, 528, 533
mystery *n* 447, 533
mystify *v* 519

N

nab *v* 789
nacreous *adj* 427, 440
nadir *n* 211
naiad *n* 979
naive *adj* 435, 703, 946
naivete *n* 703, 946
naked *adj* 226
nakedness *n* 226
name *n* 13, 562, 564, 569, 873, 877; *v* 564, 755
namely *adv* 522
namesake *n* 564
naming *n* 564
nannygoat *n* 374
nap *n* 256
naphtha *n* 356
napping *adj* 458
narrate *v* 594
narration *n* 594
narrative prose *n* 598
narrow *v* 195, 203, 469; *adj* 32, 203
narrow escape *n* 671
narrowing *n* 469
narrow-minded *adj* 32, 499
narrow-mindedness *n* 32
narrowness *n* 203
narrowness *n* 203
nascent *adj* 66
nasty *adj* 395, 653
natal *adj* 66
nation *n* 188
national *adj* 372
native *n* 188; *adj* 188
nativity *n* 66
natural *n* 501; *adj* 82, 494, 578, 703, 849

natural causes *n* 360

natural gas *n* 388

natural harbor *n* 343

natural history *n* 357

naturalist *n* 357

natural light *n* 423

natural philosophy *n* 316

natural world *n* 357

nature *n* 5, 80, 176, 318, 357, 820

naught *n* 4, 101

nauseate *v* 395, 830, 867

nauseating *adj* 401, 867, 898

nauseous *adj* 395, 401, 830

nautical *adj* 267

naval *adj* 267

navel *n* 222

navigable *adj* 267

navigate *v* 267

navigation *n* 267

navigator *n* 269

navy *n* 273; *adj* 438

near *v* 286; *adj* 17, 121, 152, 186, 197, 199; *adv* 197

nearly *adv* 32

near miss *n* 671

nearness *n* 197

nearness *n* 9, 186, 286

near side *n* 239

nearsighted *adj* 443

nearsightedness *n* 443

near the mark *adv* 32

neat *adj* 58, 576, 578, 652, 849

neaten *v* 652

neatness *n* 652

nebbish *n* 547

nebula *n* 353

nebulosity *n* 353, 422

nebulous *adj* 422, 519

necessarily *adv* 154, 601

necessary *adj* 601, 630, 744

necessitate *v* 601, 630, 744

necessity *n* 601

necessity *n* 630, 744

neck and neck race *n* 27

necklace *n* 247

necromancer *n* 513, 994

necromancy *n* 992

need *n* 630, 684, 804, 865; *v* 630, 640

needful *adj* 601, 630

neediness *n* 804

needle *n* 253, 262

needless *adj* 641

needy *adj* 804

negate *v* 536

negation *n* 536

negation *n* 468

negative *n* 22; *adj* 14, 84, 489, 536

neglect *n* 460

neglect *n* 730, 732, 773, 927; *v* 53, 460, 678, 730, 773, 927

neglected *adj* 460

neglectful *adj* 460

neglecting *adj* 460

negligence *n* 460, 773

negligent *adj* 460, 738, 773, 927

negotiate *v* 724, 769, 794

negotiation *n* 724, 769, 774, 794

negotiator *n* 724

neigh *v* 412

neighbor *v* 197

neighborhood *n* 197, 227

neighboring *adj* 197

neighborly *adj* 707, 888, 892

nemesis *n* 919

neologic *adj* 563

neological *adj* 563

neologism *n* 563

neologist *n* 563

neology *n* 563

neophyte *n* 541

nereid *n* 979

nerve *n* 159, 861; *v* 159

nervous *adj* 574, 825

nescient *adj* 491

ness *n* 250

nest *n* 189

nestle *v* 186

net *n* 219; *v* 219

nethermost *adj* 211

netting *n* 219

nettle *n* 663

network *n* 219

neutral *adj* 29, 609a, 628

neutrality *n* 690a

neutrality *n* 29, 609a, 628

neutralization *n* 179

neutralize *v* 30, 179

neutral tint *n* 429, 432

never *adv* 107

never-ending *adj* 104, 112

nevermore *adv* 107

nevertheless *adv* 30

never to be forgotten *adj* 505

new *adj* 18, 123, 146, 435

new birth *n* 660

newborn *adj* 129

newfangled *adj* 83, 123, 140

new-fangled expression *n* 563

newfangledness *n* 123

newly *adv* 123

newness *n* 123

news *n* 532

news *n* 498, 527

newsmonger *n* 527, 532, 534

newsstory *n* 532

New Testament *n* 986

next *adj* 63; *adv* 117
next generation *n* 127
next world *n* 152
nibble *v* 298
nice *adj* 394, 829, 868
nice distinction *n* 15
nicety *n* 465, 868
niche *n* 182, 221, 244
nick *n* 257; *v* 257
nickname *n* 564, 565; *v* 564
nick of time *n* 134
niggard *n* 819
niggardly *adj* 819
niggling *adj* 643
nigh *adj* 197; *adv* 197
night *n* 421
nightfall *n* 126
nihilist *n* 165
nil *n* 4
nimble *adj* 274, 498, 842
nincompoop *n* 501
nine *n* 98
ninny *n* 501
nip *n* 392; *v* 385
nip in the bud *v* 361
nipping *adj* 383
nipple *n* 250
nippy *adj* 392
nirvana *n* 981
nit-picking *adj* 477
nixie *n* 979
nobility *n* 875
nobility *n* 33
noble *adj* 31, 875, 878
nobody *n* 101
no choice *n* 609a
nocturnal *adj* 421
node *n* 250
no doubt *adv* 474
nodular *adj* 250
nodulation *n* 256
nodule *n* 250
noise *n* 402, 404, 414
noiseless *adj* 403
noisily *adv* 404
noisome *adj* 401, 657

noisy *adj* 404
nomad *n* 268
nomadic *adj* 264, 266
nomadism *n* 266
nom de guerre *n* 565
nom de plume *n* 565
nomenclature *n* 564
nominal *adj* 564
nominate *v* 755
nomination *n* 755
nominee *n* 758
no more *adj* 360
no more than *adv* 32
nonadhesion *n* 47
nonadhesive *adj* 47
nonappearance *n* 187
nonattendance *n* 187
nonbeliever *n* 485, 487, 989
noncohesive *adj* 47
noncompletion *n* 730
noncompletion *n* 53, 304
noncompliance *n* 742, 773
noncompliant *adj* 764
nonconforming *adj* 984
nonconformist *n* 489, 984; *adj* 489, 984
nonconformity *n* 16a, 24, 79, 83, 489, 984
none *n* 101
nonentity *n* 2
nonessential *adj* 57, 643
nonetheless *adv* 30
nonexistence *n* 2
nonexistent *adj* 2, 187
nonexpectant *adj* 508
nonexpectation *n* 508
nonextension *n* 180a
nonfulfillment *n* 730
nonfunctional *adj* 674
nonimitation *n* 20
noninterference *n* 748
nonlinear *adj* 245
nonobservance *n* 773

nonobservance *n* 83, 742, 927
nonobservant *adj* 773
nonpayment *n* 808
nonperformance *n* 730, 732, 927
nonplus *n* 704
nonpreparation *n* 674
nonrational *adj* 450a
non-relation *n* 10
nonresidence *n* 187
nonresistance *n* 725
nonresonance *n* 408a
nonresonant *adj* 408a
nonsense *n* 497, 517
nonsensical *adj* 477, 497, 499, 517, 853
non sequitur *n* 497
nontranslucent *adj* 426
nontransparency *n* 426
nontransparent *adj* 426
noodle *n* 450
nook *n* 182, 221, 244
noon *n* 125
noon *n* 125
noonday *n* 125
noontide *n* 125
noontime *n* 125
normal *adj* 5, 29, 82, 736
normalcy *n* 80
normality *n* 502
normal state *n* 80
nose *n* 250
not a bit *adv* 32
notable *adj* 31, 642
notably *adv* 31
not act *v* 681
not a jot *adv* 32
notary *n* 553
not at all *adv* 32
not a whit *adv* 32
not bad *adj* 651
not beat around the bush *v* 576
not be good for *v* 657
not be surprised *v* 871
not care *v* 823

notch n 257
notch n 244; v 257
notched adj 257
not come up to v 28, 34
not come up to snuff v
    28
not complete v 730
not conversant adj 699
not curved adj 246
not cut it v 640
not discriminate v 465a
not do v 640, 681
note n 550, 551, 592,
    596; v 450, 550, 596
not enough adj 640
notes n 802
noteworthy adj 31
not exist v 2
not expect v 508
not germane adj 57
not get involved v 623
not give an inch v 604
not have v 777a
not have much of a
    chance v 473
not hear v 419
not here adj 187
nothing n 4, 101, 643
nothingness n 2, 4
notice n 457, 668; v
    450, 457, 480a, 928
notification n 527
notify v 668
no time n 107
not in adj 187
not included in adj 55
not in sight adj 447
not in the least adv 32
not in use adj 678
notion n 451, 453, 515
not licensed adj 925
not many adj 103
not matter v 643
not often adv 137
not pass muster v 34,
    651
not pay v 808
not pertinent adj 10

not possible adj 471
not present adj 187, 187
not quite adv 32
not reach v 304
not see v 442
not smell v 399
not sorry adj 951
not straight adj 243
not suffice v 640
not the same adj 15
not think v 452
not true adj 243
not use v 678
not well adj 655
not with it adj 246
notwithstanding adv 30
nourishment n 298, 359
novel n 593; adj 18,
    123
novelty n 18, 123
novice n 541, 701
now adv 118
nowadays adv 118
now and then adv 136
no way adj 471
noway adv 32
nowhere adv 187
nowise adv 32
now or never adv 134
noxious adj 649, 657
nozzle n 250
nuance n 15
nub n 68, 222
nubile adj 131
nuclear power n 388
nucleus n 68, 153, 222
nude adj 226
nudity n 226
nuisance n 619, 663,
    830, 975
null and void adj 756
nullification n 536, 756
nullify v 2, 30, 179,
    536, 756
nullity n 4
numb v 376; adj 376,
    381
number n 84

number v 85
number among v 76
numbering n 85
numberless adj 104
numbers n 102
numbing adj 383
numbness n 381
numbness n 376
numerable adj 85
numeral n 84; adj 84,
    85
numeration n 85
numerical adj 85
numerous adj 100, 102
numskull n 493, 501
nuptials n 903
nurse n 753; v 662
nursery n 127
nursling n 129
nurture v 235, 673
nut n 504
nutbrown adj 433
nutriment n 298, 359
nutrition n 298
nutritious adj 299, 656
nutritive adj 299
nuts adj 503
nutshell n 32

O

oaf n 501
oath n 535, 768
obduracy n 606, 951
obdurate adj 600, 951
obedience n 743
obedience n 725, 749,
    772
obedient adj 725, 743,
    772, 926
obediently adv 743
obeisance n 308
obese adj 192, 194
obesity n 192
obey v 725, 743, 772
obey the rules v 82
obfuscate v 528
obfuscation n 528

offhand *adv* 132, 612

office *n* 170, 625, 799

official *n* 694; *adj* 625, 737, 983a

offing *n* 196

off one's guard *adj* 508

off-set *n* 30; *v* 30, 179

offshoot *n* 39, 51, 65, 154

offside *n* 238

offspring *n* 154, 167

off the mark *adj* 495

of late *adv* 122, 123

of little account *adj* 643

of long standing *adj* 124

of necessity *adv* 601, 630

of no account *adj* 643

of old *adv* 122

of one accord *adj* 488

of one mind *adj* 178

of one's own accord *adv* 600

of other times *adj* 124

of small importance *adj* 643

oft *adv* 136

often *adv* 104, 136

oftentimes *adv* 136

of the same mind *adj* 488

oft-repeated *adj* 136

of various kinds *adj* 16a

of vital importance *adj* 642

of yore *adv* 122

ogle *v* 441

ogre *n* 980

oil *n* 356

oil *n* 355; *v* 255, 332, 355

oil burner *n* 386

oiliness *n* 355

oiling *n* 332

oil lamp *n* 423

oily *adj* 255, 355

oink *v* 412

ointment *n* 355, 356, 662

old *adj* 124, 128, 130

old age *n* 124, 128

older *adj* 128

old-fashioned *adj* 124

old hand *n* 700

old lady *n* 166, 903

old maid *n* 904

old man *n* 130, 166, 903

oldness *n* 124

old soldier *n* 700

Old Testament *n* 986

old woman *n* 130

oleaginous *adj* 355

olive *adj* 435

olive oil *n* 356

omen *n* 512

omen *n* 668

ominous *adj* 665, 668, 909

omission *n* 53, 55, 460, 732, 773, 893

omit *v* 55, 460, 773

omitted *adj* 893

omnipotence *n* 157, 976

omnipotent *adj* 104, 157

omnipresence *n* 186, 976

omnipresent *adj* 186

on *adv* 125, 282

on a bed of roses *adv* 377

on account of *adv* 155

on a large scale *adv* 31

on a level with *adj* 27

on a line with *adv* 278

on all sides *adv* 227

on a moment's notice *adv* 113

on an equal footing with *adj* 27

on a par with *adj* 27

on bended knee *adv* 879

once and for all *adv* 67

once more *adv* 90, 104

on compulsion *adv* 744

on condition *adv* 770

on dry land *adv* 342

one *n* 372; *adj* 13, 52, 87, 729

one and the same *adj* 27

one by one *adv* 44

on edge *adv* 507

one in a million *n* 648

on end *adv* 212

oneness *n* 87

one of a kind *adj* 20

onerous *adj* 649, 706, 830

oneself *n* 13

one's own *n* 11

one's own flesh and blood *n* 11

one step at a time *adv* 275

on every side *adv* 227

one way or another *adv* 627

on fire *adj* 382

on foot *adj* 170

ongoing *adj* 53

on land *adv* 342

onlooker *n* 444

only *adv* 32

only just *adv* 32

only so far *adv* 233

on no account *adv* 32

on no occasion *adv* 107

on one's back *adv* 213

one one's honor *adj* 768

on one side *adv* 217, 236

on one's own time *adv* 133

on one's toes *adj* 507

on purpose *adv* 620

onset *n* 66, 716

on sight *adv* 441

onslaught *n* 716

on target *adj* 494

on tenterhooks *adj* 507

on that occasion *adv* 119

on the average *adv* 29
on the ball *adj* 498
on the brink of *adv* 121
on the dot *adv* 132
on the eve of *adv* 121
on the face of it *adv* 448
on the face of the earth *adv* 180, 318
on the go *adv* 264
on the horizon *adj* 152, 507
on the horns of a dilemma *n* 476
on the instant *adv* 132
on the march *adv* 264
on the move *adv* 264
on the offensive *adv* 716
on the other hand *adv* 30
on the point of *adv* 121
on the road *adj* 264, 266
on the road to *adv* 278
on the safe side *adj* 664
on the sly *adv* 528
on the spot *adv* 132, 134
on the spur of the moment *adv* 113, 132, 134
on the wagon *adj* 958
on the wane *adj* 36
on the watch *adj* 457; *adv* 507
on the whole *adv* 50
on time *adj* 132; *adv* 132
ontology *n* 1
on trial *adv* 675
onus *n* 926
onward *adv* 282
ooze *v* 295, 348
oozing *n* 295
oozy *adj* 352
opacity *n* 426
opacity *n* 353
opalescence *n* 427

opalescent *adj* 427
opaline *adj* 430, 440
opaque *adj* 422, 426
opaqueness *n* 426
ope *v* 260
open *v* 66, 194, 198, 260, 525; *adj* 177, 260, 338, 525, 543, 665, 703
open air *n* 338
open-eyed *adj* 507
open field *n* 134
opening *n* 260
opening *n* 66, 198, 260
open into *v* 348
openly *adv* 525
openness *n* 525, 703, 748
open space(s) *n* 180
open to the view *v* 446
opera *n* 599
opera glasses *n* 445
operahouse *n* 599
operate *v* 161, 170, 680
operatic *adj* 415, 416
operation *n* 170, 680
operation *adj* 170, 680
operator *n* 690
ophthalmia *n* 443
opine *v* 484
opinion *n* 451, 453, 480, 484, 537, 695, 821
opponent *n* 710
opponent *n* 726, 891
opportune *adj* 134, 646
opportunely *adv* 134
opportuneness *n* 134
opportunism *n* 646
opportunist *n* 935
opportunity *n* 134
oppose *v* 14, 179, 237, 536, 708, 719
opposed *adj* 14
opposer *n* 726
opposing *n* 708; *adj* 14, 237, 489

opposite *n* 237; *adj* 14, 218, 237
oppositeness *n* 14
opposite poles *n* 237
opposite side *n* 237
opposition *n* 237, 708
opposition *n* 14, 24, 218, 489, 710, 719, 720, 726
opposition *n* 179
oppress *v* 649, 739, 923
oppression *n* 649, 739
oppressive *adj* 382, 421, 649, 739, 830
oppressor *n* 739, 913
opprobrious *adj* 874
oppugnance *n* 719
opt for the mean *v* 774
optic *adj* 441
optical instruments *n* 445
optics *n* 420, 441
optimism *n* 482
optimistic *adj* 858
option *n* 600, 609
optional *adj* 600, 609
opulence *n* 803
opus *n* 590, 593
oracle *n* 513
oracle *n* 500
oracular *adj* 511
oral *adj* 580, 582
oral communication *n* 588
orange *n* 439
orange *adj* 439
orangish *adj* 439
orangy *adj* 439
oration *n* 582
orator *n* 582
oratory *n* 582
orb *n* 181, 247
orbit *n* 247
orchestra *n* 416, 417
orchestral *adj* 415
orchestral music *n* 415
orchid *adj* 437

ordain v 741, 755, 963, 995

ordained adj 996

ordeal n 722, 828

order n 58

order n 63, 75, 242, 630, 693, 697, 721, 741, 963; v 58, 630, 652, 673, 693, 741

ordered adj 60, 242

ordering n 60

orderliness n 58, 652

orderly adj 58, 60

order of succession n 63

ordinance n 741

ordinariness n 736

ordinary adj 82, 598, 613, 643, 651, 736

ordinary condition n 80

oread n 979

organic adj 357

organic chemistry n 357

organic remains n 357

organisms n 357

organization n 60, 161, 329, 626

organizational adj 329, 626

organize v 60, 161, 626

organized adj 58

organizer n 626

orgasm n 173, 377

orgasmic adj 173, 377

orifice n 260

origin n 66, 153

original n 22, 590, 857; adj 20, 79, 83, 153, 515, 614

originality n 18, 20, 83, 123, 168, 515

originate v 66, 153, 515

originate from v 154

originate in v 154

origination n 153

originator n 164

ornament n 577, 847

ornament v 577, 847

ornamental adj 847

ornamentation n 847

ornamented adj 577, 847

ornate adj 577, 847

ornateness n 577

ornithology n 368

orthodox adj 82, 983a

orthodoxy n 983a

orthography n 561

oscillate v 149, 314

oscillating adj 149, 314

oscillation n 314

oscillation n 138, 149, 605

ossification n 323

ossify n 323

ostensible adj 448, 617

ostensibly adv 448, 617

ostentation n 882

ostentatious adj 855, 882

ostracism n 893

ostracized adj 893

other adj 15

other side of the coin n 235

other time n 119

otherwordly adj 317

oust v 297, 789

out adj 187; adv 220

out and out adv 52

outbound adj 295

outbreak n 66, 173, 295, 713

outburst n 173, 295, 825

outcast n 893

outcome n 63, 65, 154

outcry n 404, 411

outdated adj 124

outdo v 33, 303

outer adj 220

outer edges n 233

outer space n 180

outfit n 225; v 225, 727

outflank v 236

outgoing adj 295

outgrow v 194

outgrowth n 65, 154

outing n 266

out in the open adv 338

outlandish adj 10, 83, 853

outlast v 110

outlawed adj 964

outlay n 809

outlet n 260

outline n 230

outline n 240, 448, 596; v 230

outlined adj 446

outlive v 110, 141

outlook n 441, 448

outlying adj 196, 220

outmoded adj 124

outnumber v 102

out of all proportion adv 31

out of commission adj 659

out of danger adj 664

out of date adj 124

out of debt adj 807

out of doors adv 338

out-of-fashion adj 124

out of focus adj 447

out of its element adj 185

out of joint adj 24

out of mind adj 506

out of one's depth adv 208

out of order adj 59, 651, 674, 923

out of place adj 59, 115, 185

out of practice adj 699

out of proportion adj 241; adv 641

out of shape adj 243

out of sight adj 447

out of sorts adj 655

out of step adj 24

out-of-style adj 124

out of the frying pan and into the fire adv 835

out-of-the-way *adj* 10, 196

out of tune *adj* 24, 414, 651

out of view *adj* 447

out of work *adj* 681

outpost *n* 196

outpouring *n* 295

outrage *n* 173, 619, 649

outrageous *adj* 31, 853

outrageousness *n* 853

outrank *v* 33

outride *v* 303

outrigger *n* 215

outright *adv* 52

outrival *v* 33

outrun *v* 303

outset *n* 66, 293

outside *n* 220; *adj* 220

outsides *n* 448

outside time *n* 107

outskirts *n* 196, 227

outspoken *adj* 703

outspread *adj* 202

outstretched *adj* 200, 202

outstrip *v* 33, 303

outward *adj* 220, 295

outwards *adv* 220

outweigh *v* 33, 175

outwit *v* 545

oval *n* 247; *adj* 247

oven *n* 386

over *adj* 40, 67; *adv* 33, 122, 220, 237

overabound *v* 641

over again *adv* 90, 104

over against *adv* 237

over and above *adj* 641; *adv* 33, 37, 641

over and done with *adv* 67

over and over *adv* 104

overbearing *adj* 878, 885

over-blown *adj* 882

overburden *v* 649

overcast *v* 421; *adj* 421, 422, 901a

overcharge *n* 814; *v* 577, 814

overcome *v* 731

over-confident *adj* 878

overdo *v* 641

overdose *n* 641; *v* 641

overdraw *v* 555

overdue *adj* 115, 133

overeat *v* 957

over-eating *n* 957

overestimate *v* 481, 482, 549

overestimated *adj* 482

overestimation *n* 482

overflow *n* 641; *v* 348, 641

overgrown *adj* 192, 194

overhang *v* 206

overhanging *adj* 206

overhear *v* 418

overlay *v* 223, 356a

overload *v* 641

overlook *v* 458, 460, 693

overlying *adj* 206

overly sensitive *adj* 901

overmatch *v* 28

overmuch *adj* 641; *adv* 641

over one's head *adv* 208, 641

overpower *v* 744

overpowering *adj* 824

overpraise *v* 482, 933

overprize *v* 482

overrate *v* 482

overrated *adj* 482

overreach *v* 303

over-refined *adj* 477

override *v* 175

overripe *adj* 128

overrun *v* 194, 303, 641

overseer *n* 694

overshoot *v* 303

oversight *n* 495

oversimplification *n* 78

overspread *v* 223

overstate *v* 549

overstatement *n* 549

overstep *v* 303

overtask *v* 679

overtax *v* 679

over the way *adv* 237

overthrow *n* 146, 162, 308; *v* 162, 308

overture *n* 763

overturn *n* 146, 218, 308; *v* 162, 218, 308, 479

overvaluation *n* 482

overweening *adj* 641, 880

overwhelm *v* 641

overwhelming *adj* 824

overwork *v* 679

overwrought *adj* 549, 824

overzealous *adj* 825

ovoid *adj* 249

owing to *adj* 154, 155

own *v* 488, 777

owner *n* 779

ownership *n* 777, 780

own in common *v* 778

own up *v* 529

P

P.M. *n* 126

pace *n* 264; *v* 106

pacific *adj* 174, 721, 723

pacification *n* 723

pacification *n* 174

pacify *v* 174, 723

pack *n* 72

pack it up *v* 293

pact *n* 23, 769

pad *n* 189; *v* 194, 224

padding *n* 224, 263

paddle *v* 267

paddock *n* 232

paean *n* 838

pagan *n* 984; *adj* 991

pagan deity *n* 991

pageant *n* 448
pageantry *n* 882
pain *n* 378, 828
pain *n* 619, 663, 686, 974, 982; *v* 649, 830
painful *adj* 378, 649, 830, 982
painfully *adv* 31, 830
painfulness *n* 830
painfulness *n* 649
pain in the neck *n* 663
pains *n* 459, 974
painstaking *adj* 459
paint *n* 428; *v* 428, 556
painter *n* 559
painting *n* 556
pair *n* 17, 89; *v* 89
pair off *v* 89
pal *n* 890
palatability *n* 394
palatable *adj* 377, 390, 394
palaver *n* 588
pale *n* 232, 233; *v* 422, 429; *adj* 422, 429, 430, 435
paleness *n* 422, 429
paleontology *n* 368
paling *n* 232
pall *n* 363; *v* 376, 395
palliative *adj* 174, 662, 834
pallid *adj* 429, 430
pallor *n* 429
palm *n* 733
palmer *n* 268
palpability *n* 379
palpable *adj* 3, 316, 379, 446, 525
palpitate *v* 315
palpitation *n* 315
palsied *adj* 160
paltriness *n* 32, 643, 736
paltry *adj* 32, 34, 643, 736
panacea *n* 662
pandemonium *n* 59, 982

pander to *v* 933
pang *n* 378, 828
panhandler *n* 767
panic *n* 860
panic-stricken *adj* 860
pant *v* 349, 382, 688
pap *n* 250
papa *n* 166
paper *v* 223
par *n* 27
parabola *n* 245
parade *v* 882
paradigm *n* 22
paradisaic *adj* 981
paradise *n* 981
paradisical *adj* 981
paradox *n* 497
paradoxical *adj* 497
paragon *n* 650, 948
paralipsis n 476
parallel *n* 17; *v* 9,17, 19, 216; *adj* 17, 216, 242
parallelism *n* 216
parallelism *n* 13, 17, 23, 242
paralysis *n* 158, 376
paralytic *adj* 158, 376
paralyze *v* 158, 376
paralyzed *adj* 158
paramount *adj* 33, 642, 737
paramour *n* 897
paraphrase *n* 19, 21
parasitic *adj* 789
parasol *n* 223, 424
parboil *v* 384
parcel out *v* 60, 786
parch *v* 340, 382, 384
parched *adj* 340
pardon *n* 918, 970; *v* 918, 970
pare *v* 38, 195, 204
pared back *adj* 103
pare down *v* 38, 201
parentage *n* 166
parentage *n* 11
parental *adj* 166

parenthesis *n* 70
parenthetical *adj* 10, 228
parenthetically *adv* 10, 228
pariah *n* 893
parishioner *n* 997
parity *n* 27
parlance *n* 582
parley *n* 582, 588, 724
parody *n* 19, 21; *v* 19
paroxysm *n* 173, 825
parricide *n* 361
parry *v* 717
parsimonious *adj* 817, 819, 943
parsimony *n* 819
parsimony *n* 817, 943
parson *n* 996
part *n* 51
part *n* 56, 100a, 625; *v* 44, 51, 291
partake *v* 778
part company *v* 44
partial *adj* 28
partially *adv* 32, 51
participant *n* 690, 778
participate *v* 56, 709, 778
participation *n* 778
participation *n* 709
participatory *adj* 709, 778
particle *n* 32, 330
particular *n* 151; *adj* 79, 459, 474, 704
particularity *n* 79
particularize *v* 79
particularly *adv* 31, 33
particulars *n* 79
parting *n* 44
partisan *n* 890
partisanship *n* 709
partition *n* 786; *v* 51, 786
partly *adv* 51
partner *n* 711, 778, 903

partnership *n* 88, 178, 709, 778

part of speech *n* 562

parts of speech *n* 567

party *n* 712

party *n* 72, 372

party spirit *n* 709

party to *n* 690; *adj* 709

party to a suit *n* 969

pass *n* 7, 8, 151, 704; *v* 33, 109, 122, 264, 270, 302, 449, 783, 784

passable *adj* 651

passableness *n* 736

passably *adv* 32

passage *n* 302

passage *n* 144, 260, 267, 270, 627

pass a law *v* 963

pass away *v* 2, 67, 111, 122, 142, 360

pass by *v* 109

passed away *adj* 122

passenger *n* 268

passerby *n* 444

passing *n* 360; *adj* 111

passing time *n* 109

pass into *v* 144

passion *n* 173, 382, 820, 821, 824, 825, 865, 897

passionate *adj* 382, 574, 821, 825, 897

passive *adj* 172, 681, 725

passiveness *n* 172

passivity *n* 172, 681, 725

pass judgment *v* 480

pass muster *v* 648

pass off *v* 151

pass on *v* 360

pass out *v* 449

pass out of *v* 295

pass over *v* 55

pass sentence *v* 967

pass sentence upon *v* 480

pass through *v* 302

pass time *v* 106

past *adj* 122

past cure *adj* 659

paste *n* 354; *v* 46

past hope *adj* 659

pastiche *n* 41

pastime *n* 840

pastiness *n* 352

pastor *n* 996

pastoral *adj* 995

past recollection *adj* 506

past time *n* 122

pasturage *n* 344

pasture *n* 344

pasty *adj* 354, 391

pat *n* 276; *v* 276; *adj* 23

patch up *v* 660

patchwork *n* 41; *adj* 16a

pate *n* 450

patent *adj* 474, 525

paternal *adj* 166

paternity *n* 11, 166

path *n* 260, 278, 302

pathetic *adj* 830

pathless *adj* 261

patience *n* 826

patriarch *n* 130

patriarchal *adj* 166

patrician *adj* 875

patriot *n* 910

patrol *v* 664, 668

patron *n* 795, 890, 912, 977

patronage *n* 175, 707

patronize *v* 136

patter *v* 407

pattern *n* 22, 240, 650

pattern after *v* 19

paucity *n* 32, 103, 640

pauperism *n* 804

pause *n* 70, 142, 198, 265, 685, 687; *v* 70, 142, 265, 681, 687

paw *v* 379

pawn *n* 771; *v* 771, 787, 788

pawning *n* 788

pay *n* 973; *v* 784, 807, 973

pay attention *v* 457

pay in full *v* 807

paymaster *n* 801

payment *n* 807

payment *n* 809

pay no attention to *v* 458

pay out *v* 809

pea *n* 249

peace *n* 721

peace *n* 265, 403, 714

peaceable *adj* 721

peaceful *adj* 174, 265, 685, 721, 826

peacefulness *n* 174, 721

peacemaker *n* 724

peace offering *n* 723

pea-green *adj* 435

peak *n* 206, 210

peaked *adj* 253

peal *n* 404; *v* 404, 407

peal of bells *n* 407

peal of laughter *n* 838

pearliness *n* 427, 430

pearly *adj* 427, 428, 430, 440

pear-shaped *adj* 249

peasantry *n* 876

peat *n* 388

peck at *v* 298

peculiar *adj* 5, 79, 83, 870

peculiarities *n* 5

peculiarity *n* 83, 550

peculiarly *adv* 31, 33

pecuniary *adj* 800

pedagogic *adj* 537

pedagogical *adj* 537

pedagogies *n* 537

pedagogy *n* 537

pedant *n* 492

pedantic *adj* 577

peddler *n* 797

pedestal *n* 211
pedestrian *n* 268; *adj* 598
pedigree *n* 69
peek *n* 441; *v* 441
peel *n* 204, 223; *v* 204, 226
peep *n* 441; *v* 441
peephole *n* 260
peeping *adj* 455
peep of day *n* 125
peep up *v* 446
peer *n* 27; *v* 441
peevish *adj* 684, 901a
peg *n* 250
pellet *n* 249
pellucid *adj* 425, 570
pelt *v* 276
pen *n* 232, 752; *v* 590
penalize *v* 972, 974
penalized *v* 974; *adj* 972
penalizing *adj* 972
penalty *n* 974
penalty *n* 972
penance *n* 974
penchant *n* 177, 602
pencil *v* 556
pendant *n* 214
pendent *adj* 214
pendulous *adj* 214
pendulum *n* 214
penetrate *v* 294, 302
penetrating *adj* 480, 498
penetration *n* 294, 302, 441, 480, 498
penitence *n* 950
penitence *n* 833
penitent *n* 950; *adj* 833, 950
penitential *adj* 950
penitentiary *n* 752
penmanship *n* 590
pen name *n* 565
penniless *adj* 804
pennywise *adj* 819
pensioner *n* 785

pensive *adj* 451
pent up *adj* 751
penumbra *n* 421
penurious *adj* 819
penury *n* 804
people *n* 188, 372, 997; *v* 102
people the world *v* 163
pep *n* 171
pepper *n* 393; *v* 392
peppery *adj* 392
peradventure *adv* 470
perambulate *v* 264
perambulation *n* 266
perceivability *n* 446
perceivable *adj* 446
perceive *v* 375, 441, 490
perceptibility *n* 446
perceptible *adj* 446
perception *n* 418, 441, 453, 490
perceptive *adj* 375, 465, 490, 842
perch *n* 189; *v* 184, 186
perchance *adv* 156, 470
percolation *n* 295
percussion *n* 417
perdition *n* 162
peregrination *n* 266
peremptory *adj* 737, 739
perennial *adj* 69
perfect *v* 650, 729; *adj* 31, 52, 104, 648, 650, 729, 960
perfection *n* 650
perfection *n* 52, 648, 729, 960
perfectly *adv* 729
perfidious *adj* 544
perforate *v* 260
perforated *adj* 260
perforation *n* 260
perforator *n* 262
perform *v* 161, 170,

415, 416, 599, 644, 680, 772, 926
performable *adj* 470
performance *n* 161, 599, 680, 729, 772
perform a rite *v* 998
performer *n* 416, 599, 690
performing *n* 680
perfume *n* 400; *v* 400
perfumed *adj* 400
perfunctory *adj* 53, 640
perhaps *adv* 470
peril *n* 665
perilous *adj* 475, 665
perimeter *n* 230
period *n* 108
period *n* 71, 106, 138, 198, 200
periodic *adj* 70, 138
periodical *adj* 138
periodically *adv* 138
periodicity *n* 138
peripatetic *adj* 266
periphery *n* 230
perish *v* 2, 162, 360, 659
perishable *adj* 111
permanence *n* 141
permanence *n* 16, 110, 150
permanent *adj* 106, 110, 141, 150, 613
permanently *adv* 141
permeable *adj* 260
permeate *v* 186, 228, 302
permeation *n* 186, 228, 302
permissible *adj* 760
permission *n* 760
permission *n* 737, 762
permissive *adj* 760
permit *n* 737, 755, 760; *v* 737, 748, 760, 762
permitted *adj* 760
permutation *n* 140, 148
pernicious *adj* 649, 663

perpendicular *adj* 212, 246

perpendicularity *n* 212

perpetrate *v* 680

perpetrator *n* 690

perpetual *adj* 104, 110, 112, 136, 143, 150

perpetually *adv* 112, 136

perpetuate *v* 112, 143

perpetuation *n* 143

perpetuity *n* 112

perpetuity *n* 105

perplex *v* 475, 519, 704, 830

perplexed *adj* 59

perplexity *n* 59

persecute *v* 649, 830

persecution *n* 649

perseverance *n* 604a

perseverance *n* 143, 150, 604, 682

persevere *v* 604a, 682

persevering *adj* 604a

persicuity *n* 518

persist *v* 106, 110, 141, 143, 604a, 606, 682

persistence *n* 110, 141, 143, 604a, 606

persistent *adj* 141, 143, 604a, 606

person *n* 3, 372

personage *n* 372

personal *adj* 5, 79, 372

personality *n* 5, 13, 79

personate *v* 19, 554, 599

personify *v* 554

personnel *n* 56

persons *n* 372

perspective *n* 183, 441, 448

perspicacious *adj* 480, 498, 868

perspicacity *n* 441, 480, 868

perspicuity *n* 570

perspicuous *adj* 570

perspiration *n* 299, 339

perspire *v* 299, 339

persuade *v* 175, 615, 695

persuasion *n* 175, 484, 695

persuasive *adj* 615, 695

pertain to *v* 9

pertinacious *adj* 150, 606

pertinacity *n* 150, 606

pertinent *adj* 23

perturb *v* 61, 824

perturbation *n* 61, 315, 824

peruse *v* 539

pervade *v* 186

pervasion *n* 186

pervasive *adj* 186

pervasiveness *n* 186

perverse *adj* 606, 704, 901a

perversion *n* 477, 523, 538

perversity *n* 606

pervert *v* 477, 523, 538

pessimism *n* 483, 859

pessimist *n* 165

pessimistic *adj* 483, 837

pest *n* 975

pester *v* 830

pestilence *n* 649

pestilential *adj* 657

pet *n* 899

petite *adj* 32

petition *n* 765, 990; *v* 765, 990

petitioner *n* 767

petrification *n* 321, 323

petrify *v* 321, 323

petroleum *n* 356, 388

pettifogging *adj* 477

pettiness *n* 32

petty *adj* 32, 643

petulant *adj* 684, 901

phantasm *n* 443, 515

phantom *n* 4

phase *n* 7, 8, 71, 448

phenomenon *n* 151, 448, 872

philanthropic *adj* 784, 906, 910

philanthropist *n* 910

philanthropy *n* 910

philanthropy *n* 784, 906

philology *n* 562

philosopher *n* 500

phonetic *adj* 561

phonetics *n* 402, 561

phonology *n* 402

phony *n* 548; *adj* 19, 544

phosphorescence *n* 423

phosphorescent *adj* 420, 423

photoengraving *n* 558

photography *n* 420

phrase *n* 566

phrase *n* 521; *v* 566

phraseology *n* 560, 566, 569

physical *adj* 3, 173, 316

physical elements *n* 316

physical gratification *n* 377

physical insensibility *n* 381

physicality *n* 316

physical science *n* 316

physician *n* 662

physicist *n* 316

physics *n* 316

physiognomy *n* 448

physiology *n* 357

physique *n* 364

phytology *n* 369

pick *n* 609, 648; *v* 609

picket *v* 43

pickings *n* 793

pickle *n* 7; *v* 392, 670

pick of the litter *n* 648

pickup *n* 274

picky *adj* 465

pictorial *adj* 556

pictorialization *n* 556

picture n 448, 556; v 554, 594

picture gallery n 556

picturesque adj 556, 845

piddle v 683

piddling adj 643

piebald adj 440

piece n 51

piecemeal adv 51

pieces n 596

piece together v 43

pied adj 440

pierce v 260, 378, 385, 649

piercer n 262

pierce the ears v 404

piercing adj 404, 410, 498

pietist n 987

pietistic adj 987

piety n 987

pig n 957

pigeon n 547

pigeonhole n 182

piggish adj 957

piggishness n 957

pig-headed adj 606

pigment n 428

pigmy adj 193

pile n 72, 256

pile on v 641

pile up v 37

pilfer v 791

pilferer n 792

pilgrim n 268

pilgrimage n 266, 676

pill n 249

pilot n 269, 694; v 693

pimple n 250

pin n 253, 262, 263; v 43, 45

pince-nez n 445

pinch n 8, 704; v 195, 378, 385, 819

pinched adj 203

pinch hit v 147

pine v 655

pinhole n 260

pink adj 434

pinnacle n 206, 210

pioneer n 64

pious adj 987

pipe n 350

piquancy n 392, 394

piquant adj 392

pique n 900

piratical adj 791

pirouette n 312

pit n 208, 252, 363

pitapat n 407

pitch n 26, 210, 356a, 402, 413, 431; v 284, 306, 314

pitch black adj 421, 431

pitchy adj 431

piteous adj 830

piteously adv 31

pitfall n 667

pitfall n 530

pith n 5, 221

pithiness n 572

pithy adj 572, 574

pitiable adj 649, 830

pitiful adj 643, 649

pitiless adj 914a

pitilessness n 914a

pit one against another v 464

pittance n 640

pitted adj 848

pity n 914

pity n 821; v 914

pitying adj 914

pivot n 43, 153, 222; v 312

pivotal adj 222

pixie n 979

placate v 723

place n 182

place n 8, 58, 71, 183, 184; v 60, 184

place a bet v 621

place before v 62

placed adj 184

place in the record v 551

place of business n 799

place of departure n 293

place of learning n 542

place of worship n 1000

place side by side v 464

place together v 72

placid adj 721, 826

placidity n 826

plagiarism n 19

plaque n 649, 663, 828, 975; v 828, 830

plaid adj 440

plain n 344

plain adj 16, 246, 446, 474, 518, 525, 570, 576, 703, 849, 879

plainly adv 525

plainness n 576

plainness n 570, 703, 849

plainsong n 413

plain-speaking n 518, 570, 703

plain spoken adj 525, 703

plaint n 411

plaintiff n 938

plaintive adj 839

plait n 219, 258; v 219, 258

plan n 626

plan n 60, 453, 673, 692; v 60, 620, 626, 673

plane n 213, 251; v 255, 267, 273; adj 213, 251

planets n 318

planning n 60

plant v 184, 300, 371

plant life n 357, 365, 367

plastered adj 959

plastic adj 324

plasticity n 324

plat v 219

plate n 22, 251; v 204

plateau n 344

plate engraving *n* 558
platitude *n* 517
platter *n* 204, 251
plausibility *n* 472
plausible *adj* 472
play *n* 170, 175, 180,
   599; *v* 170, 416, 554,
   599, 680, 840
played out *adj* 67
player *n* 416, 599
play false *v* 544, 940
play for *v* 621
playful *adj* 840, 842
playhouse *n* 599, 728
playing *n* 840
playing field *n* 728
play of colors *n* 440
play on words *n* 520
play second fiddle to *v*
   749
play the fool *v* 497, 853
play the notes *v* 416
play truant *v* 187
play with *v* 140
playwright *n* 599
playwriter *n* 599
playwriting *n* 599
plea *n* 617
plea *n* 411
plead *v* 617, 765, 968
pleader *n* 968
pleading *n* 717
pleadings *n* 969
pleasant *adj* 829, 836,
   840, 842
pleasantness *n* 829
pleasantry *n* 842
please *v* 829
pleasing *adj* 413, 850
pleasing combination *n*
   413
pleasing sounds *n* 415
pleasurable *adj* 377,
   829
pleasurableness *n* 829
pleasure *n* 377
pleasure *n* 827

pleasure *n* 377, 600,
   840
pleasure-seeker *n* 954a
pleat *n* 258; *v* 258
plebeian *adj* 851, 876
pledge *n* 177, 768, 771;
   v 768, 788
pledged *adj* 768
pledging *n* 788
plenty *n* 641
plethora *n* 641
pliability *n* 324
pliable *adj* 324
pliancy *n* 324, 705, 725
pliant *adj* 324, 705
plight *n* 7, 8
plod *v* 275, 682
plot *n* 626; *v* 626
plough *v* 371
plow *v* 259, 371
plowed *adj* 959
pluck *n* 150, 604, 604a,
   861; *v* 789
plucked instruments *n*
   417
pluck out *v* 301
plug *n* 261, 263; *v* 261
plugging *n* 261
plug up one's ears *v* 419
plumb *adj* 212
plum-colored *adj* 437
plump *adj* 192
plumpness *n* 192
plunder *n* 793
plunge *n* 310
plunge *n* 300; *v* 208,
   300, 310, 337, 863
plunge into *v* 676
plural *adj* 100
plurality *n* 100
plus *adv* 37
ply *n* 258; *v* 677
pock *n* 250
pocket *v* 789
poesy *n* 597
poet *n* 597
poetaster *n* 597
poetic *adj* 521, 597

poetical *adj* 597
poetic device *n* 521
poeticize *v* 597
poetics *n* 521, 597
poetry *n* 597
poetry *n* 590
poignancy *n* 392
poignant *adj* 516
point *n* 8, 26, 32, 71,
   180a, 182, 253, 620;
   v 253, 278
point-blank *adj* 703;
   adv 278, 576
pointed *adj* 201, 253,
   516, 518
pointedly *adv* 31, 620
pointedness *n* 253
pointer *n* 550
point of departure *n* 293
point of view *n* 441
point out *v* 525
points of the compass *n*
   278
point to *v* 155, 472,
   516, 938
point toward *v* 278
poison *v* 659, 663
poisonous *adj* 649,
   657, 663
polar *adj* 210, 383
polarity *n* 89, 179, 218,
   237
pole *n* 222
polemic *n* 726
polemicist *n* 476
poles apart *adv* 237
policy *n* 626, 692
polish *n* 255, 578, 850;
   v 255, 331
polished *adj* 255, 578,
   850, 852
polite *adj* 383, 457,
   852, 879, 894, 928
politeness *n* 457, 894
polite society *n* 852
politic *adj* 498, 702
poll *n* 85; *v* 85
pollute *v* 653, 659

poltroon n 862
poltroonery n 862
polyglot adj 560
polyp n 250
polyphony n 413
polysyllable n 561
pommel n 249
pomp n 882
pompous adj 482, 577, 882
pompousness n 882
pond n 343
ponder v 451, 870
pondering n 451
ponderous adj 319, 579
pool n 343, 709; v 709
poor adj 34, 477, 575, 640, 643, 736, 804, 828, 879
poorer adj 34
poorly adj 655
poorly timed adj 135
poorness n 34, 640
poor substitute adj 651
pop n 166, 406
pop music n 415
pop off v 360
populace n 72, 876
popular music n 415
populate v 102
population n 188, 372
populous adj 72, 102
pop up v 446
porch n 231, 260
pore over v 539
porous adj 260
port n 239
portable adj 270
portal n 231, 260
portend v 511, 668, 909
portent n 511, 512, 668, 909
portentous adj 511, 668
porter n 271; 532
portion n 51, 100a, 786
portion out v 786
portly adj 192
portrait n 21

portraiture n 554
portray v 554, 594
portrayal n 594
pose n 183; v 475, 704, 855
position n 8, 71, 183, 625
positive adj 1, 31, 84, 246, 474, 484, 535
possess v 777
possessed adj 503
possessed of adj 777
possessing adj 777
possession n 777
possession n 780
possessions n 780
possessive adj 777
possess oneself of v 789
possessor n 779
possess the means v 632
possibility n 470
possibility n 2, 156
possible adj 2, 177, 470, 515
possibly adv 470
post n 183; v 184, 274, 811
post bail v 771
post card n 592
postdate v 115
posterior n 235; adj 117, 235
posteriority n 117
posteriority n 63
posterity n 167
posterity n 121
posthaste adv 274
posthumous adj 117
postman n 271
post meridian n 126
post mortem examination n 363
postpone v 133
postponement n 133
postscript n 65
postulant n 767
postulate n 476, 514; v 476

posture n 8, 183, 240
potable adj 298
pot-bellied adj 194
potency n 157, 159
potent adj 157, 159, 171, 175
potential n 2; adj 2, 470, 526
potentiality n 470, 526
potion n 298
potpourri n 41
potted adj 959
potting n 557
pound n 232; v 330
pour v 333, 348
pour forth v 584
pour in v 294
pour out v 295, 348
pour out of v 295
pout v 900, 901a
poverty n 804
poverty-stricken adj 804
powder n 330
powdery adj 330
power n 157
power n 159, 171, 175, 404, 574, 737, 741, 965; v 388
powerful adj 157, 159, 171, 175, 404, 574
powerfully adv 31, 157
powerless adj 158, 160
powerlessness n 158, 175a
practicability n 705
practicable adj 644, 705
practical adj 170, 470, 644, 692
practicality n 470
practically adv 5
practice n 613, 692; v 677
practiced adj 698
practice law v 968
practice sorcery v 992
practitioner n 690

225 **presentation**

pragmatism *n* 646
prairie *n* 344
praise *v* 883, 931, 990
praised *adj* 931
praiseworthy *adj* 931
prance *v* 315
prank *n* 608
prate *v* 584, 588
prattle *n* 582, 584, 588
pray *n* 990
prayer *n* 411, 765, 990
preacher *n* 540, 996
preamble *n* 64
precarious *adj* 111,
  475, 665
precariousness *n* 665
precaution *n* 510, 664,
  673
precautionary *adj* 673
precede *v* 62, 116, 280
precedence *n* 62, 280
precedence *n* 116
precedent *n* 22, 64, 80,
  613, 969; *adj* 62
preceding *adj* 62, 116
precept *n* 697
precept *n* 630
precincts *n* 227
precious *adj* 31, 814
precipice *n* 212, 306,
  667
precipitancy *n* 684
precipitate *v* 684; *adj*
  132, 684, 863
precipitately *adv* 132
precipitation *n* 132, 684
precipitous *adj* 217,
  306
précis *n* 596; *v* 596
precise *adj* 494, 518
precision *n* 80, 494, 518
preclude *v* 761
precluded *adj* 893
preclusion *n* 893
precocious *adj* 132
precocity *n* 132
precursor *n* 64

precursor *n* 62, 116,
  280, 534
precursory *adj* 64, 116
predatory *adj* 789, 791
predecessor *n* 64, 116
predeliberation *n* 611
predestination *n* 611
predestine *v* 152, 611
predetermination *n*
  611
predetermine *v* 611
predicament *n* 8, 183,
  704
predicate *v* 514
predict *v* 507, 510, 511
prediction *n* 511
prediction *n* 668
predilection *n* 177, 609
predisposed *adj* 820
predisposition *n* 176,
  820
predominance *n* 33,
  175
predominant *adj* 175,
  737
predominate *v* 33, 175
pre-eminence *n* 33, 206
pre-eminent *adj* 33,
  206
pre-eminently *adv* 31,
  33
pre-engage *v* 132
pre-existence *n* 116
pre-existent *adj* 116
preface *n* 64; *v* 62
prefatory *adj* 62, 64
prefer *v* 609
preference *n* 62, 609
preferential *adj* 609
prefix *n* 64; *v* 62
prehistoric *adj* 124
prelacy *n* 995
preliminary *adj* 62, 64,
  673
prelude *n* 64, 66
premature *adj* 132,
  135, 674
prematurely *adv* 132

prematurity *n* 132
premeditate *v* 611
premeditation *n* 611
premises *n* 476
premium *n* 973
premonition *n* 668
premonitory *adj* 511,
  668
preordain *v* 152
preparation *n* 673
preparation *n* 60, 64,
  537
preparative *adj* 673
preparatory *adj* 62, 673
prepare *v* 60, 537, 673
prepared *adj* 507, 673,
  698
prepare for *v* 507, 673
prepare for battle *v* 727
prepatory *adj* 673
preponderance *n* 33,
  175
preponderant *adj* 737
preposterous *adj* 497,
  549, 853
preposterously *adv* 31
prepubescence *n* 131
prerequisite *n* 630
prerogative *n* 924
presage *n* 511, 668; *v*
  116, 511, 909
presbyopia *n* 443
prescience *n* 510
prescient *adj* 510
prescribe *v* 693, 695,
  741
prescribed *adj* 474, 924
prescript *n* 697
prescription *n* 613, 697,
  924
prescriptive *adj* 124,
  613, 983a
presence *n* 186
presence *n* 1, 448
present *n* 784; *v* 448,
  763, 784; *adj* 118,
  186
presentation *n* 784

present events n 151
presentiment n 477
present itself v 446
presently adv 132
present the music v 416
present time n 118
present to the view v 448
preservation n 670
preservation n 141,
  664, 717, 781
preservative adj 670
preserve v 141, 143,
  664, 670, 717, 781
preserved adj 670
preserver n 664
president n 694
press n 72; v 255, 319
press forward v 684
press in v 300
pressing adj 642
press into service v 677
press on v 622, 684
press onward v 282
pressure n 175, 319,
  642, 735
presto adv 113
presumable adj 472
presumably adv 472
presume v 484, 514,
  858, 878, 885
presumption n 507,
  514, 878, 925
presumptive adj 514
presumptuous adj 863,
  878, 885
presuppose v 514
pretend v 544, 546,
  617, 855
pretender n 548, 925
pretense n 617, 855,
  882
pretention n 577, 855,
  882
pretentious adj 482,
  855, 882, 884
pretentiousness n 882
pretext n 617
pretty adj 845; adv 31

pretty well adv 31, 32
prevail v 33, 78, 175
prevailing adj 78, 983a
prevail upon v 615
prevalence n 33, 78,
  175, 613
prevalent adj 1, 78,
  175, 613
prevaricate v 520, 544
prevarication n 520,
  544
prevent v 706, 708, 761
preventing n 706
prevention n 761
preventive adj 761
previous adj 116
previously adv 116
prevision n 510
prey n 620
price n 812
price v 812
priceless adj 33, 648,
  814
prick n 253; v 260, 378,
  380
pricking n 380
prickle n 253
prickly adj 253, 256
prick up one's ears v 418
pride n 878
pride n 880
priest n 904, 996
priesthood n 995, 996
priestly adj 995
prig n 854
priggish adj 868
prim adj 868
primal adj 66, 153
primary adj 153, 642
primary color n 428
prime n 125, 648; v
  537, 673; adj 84,
  642, 648
prime mover n 153, 976
prime of day n 125
primer n 542, 567
primeval adj 124
primitive adj 124

primordial adj 124
princely adj 816
prince of darkness n 978
principal n 694; adj
  642
principally adv 33
principle n 5, 80, 153,
  211, 537, 615
print n 591; v 531, 558,
  590, 591
printed adj 591
printer n 591
printing n 591
prior adj 62, 116
priority n 62, 116, 280
prior to adv 116
prism n 428, 445
prismatic adj 428, 440
prison n 752
prison n 975
prisoner n 754
pristine adj 122
privacy n 893
private adj 79, 221,
  528, 533, 893
privately adv 881
privation n 776, 804
privilege n 748, 924,
  927a
privileged adj 924,
  927a
privy adj 528
privy to adj 490
prize n 618, 733, 793,
  973; v 991
probability n 472
probability n 156
probable adj 472, 858
probably adv 472
probationary adj 675
probative adj 463, 478
probe n 262
probity n 939
probity n 543, 944
problem n 533, 704
problematical adj 59,
  475

procedural *adj* 80, 626, 692

procedure *n* 80, 463, 626, 627, 680, 692, 998

proceed *v* 109, 282, 302

proceed from *v* 154

proceeding *n* 151, 282; *adj* 53

proceeds *n* 775

proceed with *v* 692

process *n* 627, 692

procession *n* 69, 266

proclaim *v* 531, 883

proclamation *n* 531, 985

proclivity *n* 176, 698, 820

procrastinate *v* 133

procrastination *v* 133, 683

procreate *v* 161, 168

procreation *n* 161, 168

procreative *adj* 168

procreator *n* 166

procure *v* 775, 795

procurement *n* 775

prod *v* 276

prodigal *n* 818; *adj* 638, 818

prodigality *n* 818

prodigality *n* 638

prodigal son *n* 950

prodigious *adj* 31

prodigy *n* 872

prodigy *n* 700

produce *n* 775, 798; *v* 153, 161, 168

produce a good effect *v* 648

produce nothing *v* 169

producer *n* 164

producer *n* 153

product *n* 84, 154, 161, 798

production *n* 161

production *n* 153

productive *adj* 153, 161, 168, 644

productiveness *n* 168

productiveness *n* 644

productivity *n* 168

proem *n* 64

profanation *n* 679

profane *v* 679, 988

profaneness *n* 988

profanity *n* 988

profession *n* 535, 625, 768

professional *n* 700; *adj* 625

professor *n* 540

proffer *v* 763

proficiency *n* 698, 731

proficient *adj* 698, 731

profile *n* 230, 236, 448; *v* 230

profit *n* 618, 775; *v* 618, 648, 775

profitability *n* 646

profitable *adj* 644, 646, 648, 775, 810

profit by *v* 677

profitless *adj* 645

profligacy *n* 818

profligate *n* 962; *adj* 818, 945

profound *adj* 31, 208, 498

profundity *n* 208, 875

profuse *adj* 102, 573, 641, 818

profuseness *n* 573, 641, 818

profusion *n* 102, 641, 818

progenitor *n* 166

progeny *n* 167

prognosticate *v* 507, 511, 909

prognostication *n* 511, 909

progress *n* 144, 264, 282, 731; *v* 282, 658, 731

progression *n* 282

progression *n* 58, 69

progressive *adj* 69, 282, 658

prohibit *v* 761, 893

prohibited *adj* 893, 964

prohibition *n* 761

prohibition *n* 55, 893

prohibitive *adj* 761

project *n* 620, 626; *v* 250, 284, 620, 626

projection *n* 250, 284

proletarian *adj* 876

proletariat *n* 876

prolific *adj* 161, 168

prolix *adj* 573

prolog *n* 64

prolong *v* 35, 110, 133, 143, 200

prolongation *n* 110, 133, 143

prolonged *adj* 110

promenade *n* 266

prominence *n* 206, 250, 307, 642

prominent *adj* 206, 250, 642

prominently *adv* 31, 33

promiscuous *adj* 41

promise *n* 768

promise *n* 771; *v* 676, 768, 769, 771

promised *adj* 768

promises *n* 770

promising *adj* 858

promissory *adj* 768, 769

promissory note *n* 771

promontory *n* 250

promote *v* 176, 658, 707

prompt *v* 505, 615; *adj* 132, 682

promptitude *n* 132, 684

promptness *n* 684

promulgate *v* 531

promulgation *n* 531

prone *adj* 207, 213, 820

proneness n 176, 207, 213

pronounce v 535, 580, 582, 586

pronouncement n 531, 535

proof n 463, 467, 478, 591

proofreader n 591

prop n 215; v 707

propagandist n 540

propagate v 161, 531

propagation n 168, 531

propane n 356, 388

propel v 264, 284

propensity n 176, 177, 602, 820

proper adj 79, 494, 578, 646, 868, 881, 922

proper name n 564

proper time n 134

property n 780

prophecy n 511

prophesy v 511

prophet n 513

prophetess n 513

prophetic adj 511

propinquity n 197

propitiate v 723, 826, 952

propitiating adj 952

propitiation n 952

propitiatory adj 952

propitious adj 134, 648, 734, 858, 888

proportion n 9, 242, 786

proportionate adj 413

proportions n 180, 192

proposal n 620, 763

propose v 476, 514, 620, 763

proposition n 476, 514, 763

propound v 514

proprietor n 779

proprietorship n 777

proprietress n 779

propriety n 578, 646, 852, 881

propulsion n 284

propulsion n 276

propulsive adj 284

propulsive force n 284

prop up v 215

prosaic adj 575, 598, 841, 843

pros and cons n 476

proscenium n 234

proscribe v 971

proscribed adj 964

proscription n 971

proscriptive adj 761

prose n 598

prosecute v 622, 680, 969

prosecuting attorney n 968

prosecution n 969

prosecutor n 938, 968

prospect n 121, 448, 472, 507, 510

prospective adj 507, 510

prospectively adv 121

prospects n 152

prospectus n 596

prosper v 731, 734

prosperity n 734

prosperity n 618, 731

prosperous adj 731, 734

prostitute n 962; v 679

prostitution n 679

prostrate v 213, 308; adj 207, 213, 308

prostration n 158, 207, 213, 308, 828

prosy adj 575, 598

protect v 664, 670, 717

protected adj 223

protection n 175, 664, 670, 717

protective adj 717

protecter n 664, 753, 977

protest n 489, 764, 766, 808; v 489, 766

protestor n 489

protoplasm n 357

prototype n 22

prototype n 80

protract v 110, 133, 200

protracted adj 110, 200, 573

protraction n 110, 133, 143

protrude v 250

protrusion n 250

protuberance n 250

protuberant adj 250

proud adj 878, 880

prove v 151, 463, 478

proved adj 478

proven adj 478

provender n 298, 637

proverb n 496

proverbial adj 496

provide v 637, 673, 746, 770

provide against v 673

provided adj 469; adv 8

provided that adj 469

providence n 976

provident adj 510, 673, 864

providential adj 134

providing n 637

province n 75, 181

provincial adj 181, 246

provision n 637

provision n 673, 803; v 637

provisional adj 8, 111, 673, 770

provisionally adv 8, 770

provisions n 298, 632, 770

proviso n 469

provisos n 770

provocation n 824
provocative adj 615
provoke v 153, 824, 830
prowl v 266
proximate adj 63, 197
proximation n 197
proximity n 186, 197, 199
proxy n 634, 759
prudence n 459, 480, 498, 510, 864
prudent adj 451, 459, 498, 510, 864
prudery n 881
prudish adj 881
prudishness n 881
prune v 38, 201
prurience n 961
prurient adj 961
pry v 441, 455
prying n 455; adj 455
pseudo adj 17
pseudonym n 565
psychical adj 317
puberty n 127, 131
pubescence n 131
pubescent adj 131
public n 372; adj 260, 372, 531
public address n 586
publication n 531
publication n 161, 590, 593, 985
publicity n 531
publicize v 531
public prosecutor n 968
public spirit n 910
public spirited adj 910
publish v 531, 591
published adj 527, 531
publisher n 593
pucker n 258; v 258, 259
puerile adj 129, 499, 575
puerility n 499
puff n 349; v 349, 688
puffery n 549

puffiness n 194
puff up v 194, 549, 880
pugnacious adj 720
puissance n 157
puissant adj 159
puke v 297
pulchritude n 845
pulchritudinous adj 845
pull n 288, 319; v 267, 285, 288, 301, 319
pull an all-nighter v 539
pulling n 285, 301
pull no punches v 703
pull out v 301
pull out of a hat v 612
pull out of the air v 612
pull the shade v 424
pull through v 660
pull together v 178, 709, 714
pull to pieces v 162
pull up v 142, 301
pulp n 354; v 354
pulpiness n 354
pulpy adj 354
pulsate v 138, 314, 315
pulsating adj 314, 315
pulsation n 138, 314
pulse n 138, 314
pulverization n 330
pulverize v 330
pulverulence n 330
pump n 348; v 349
pun n 520; v 842
punch n 22, 276; v 276
puncher n 262
punctilious adj 543, 772, 882
punctual adj 132, 138
punctuality n 132, 138
punctually adv 132
puncture v 260
pungency n 392
pungent adj 392, 394, 398, 574
punish v 972, 974
punished v 974; adj 972

punishing adj 972
punishment n 972
punishment n 974, 975
punitive adj 972
punster n 844
punt v 267
puny adj 193
pupil n 492, 541
puppet n 547
purblind adj 442, 443
purblindness n 443
purchase n 795
purchase n 775; v 795
purchaser n 795
purchasing n 795
pure adj 42, 494, 576, 578, 652, 881, 944, 946, 960, 977
purely adv 32
purgation n 652
purgative n 652
purge v 297, 652, 952
purification n 42, 652
purify v 42, 652
purist n 578
puritan n 955
puritanical adj 955
puritanism n 955
purity n 960
purity n 42, 578, 652, 944, 946
purlieus n 227
purloin n 791
purple n 437
purple adj 437
purplish adj 437
purport n 516; v 516
purpose n 451, 516, 600, 615, 620; v 451, 516, 620
purposeful adj 604
purposely adv 620
purr v 412
purring n 412
purse n 802
purser n 801
pursuance n 622

pursue *v* 143, 286, 281, 622
pursuit *n* 622
pursuit *n* 461, 625
pursuit of knowledge *n* 539
purvey *v* 637
purveyance *n* 637
purveying *n* 637
push *n* 276, 284; *v* 276, 284, 682
push ahead *v* 682
push aside *v* 297
push away *v* 297
push back *v* 289
push on *v* 684
pusillanimous *adj* 862
pustule *n* 250
put *v* 184
put about *v* 311
put an end to *v* 67
put an end to oneself *v* 361
put aside *v* 55, 636, 678
put away *v* 528
put down *v* 856
put forth *v* 514
put forward *v* 763
put in *v* 300
put in motion *v* 284
put in order *v* 660
put in the place of *v* 147
put into operation *v* 677
put into shape *v* 60
put into words *v* 566
put off *v* 133, 226
put on airs *v* 855
put on a pedestal *v* 991
put one's trust on *v* 484
put on sale *v* 813
put on the brakes *v* 275
put on the stage *v* 599
put on trial *v* 969
put out *v* 385, 421
put out of order *v* 59
put out to sea *v* 293
put pen to paper *v* 590
putrefaction *n* 49, 653

putrefy *v* 653
putrid *adj* 401, 653
put right *v* 246, 662
put straight *v* 246
putter *v* 683
put things in order *v* 652
put to death *v* 361
put to flight *v* 717
put together *v* 43
put to sea *v* 267
put to the sword *v* 361
put to use *v* 677
putty *n* 356a
put up *v* 161, 235, 636
put up to *v* 615
put up with *v* 151, 826
puzzle *v* 475
puzzlement *n* 870
puzzling *adj* 519

Q

quack *v* 412
quadrilateral *adj* 95
quadripartite *adj* 97
quadripartition *n* 97
quadrisection *n* 97
quadruped *n* 366
quadruple *adj* 96
quadruplicate *v* 96
quadruplication *n* 96
quadrupling *n* 96
quaff *v* 298
quaggy *adj* 345
quagmire *n* 345, 653
quail *v* 862
quaint *adj* 83
quake *v* 314, 315, 383
qualification *n* 469
qualification *n* 140, 536, 698, 813
qualified *adj* 469, 698
qualify *v* 140, 174, 469
qualifying *adj* 469
qualities *n* 820
quality *n* 5, 33, 176, 550, 780, 875, 944
qualm *n* 485, 603
quandary *n* 704

quantitative *adj* 25
quantity *n* 25
quantity *n* 31, 72, 102
quarrel *n* 713, 720; *v* 24, 713
quarrelsome *adj* 713, 720
quarry *n* 620
quarter *n* 95, 97, 181, 236, 740; *v* 97, 184
quartered *adj* 97
quartering *n* 97
quarter of a hundred *n* 98
quarters *n* 189
quartet *n* 95, 415, 416
quasi *adv* 17
quaternity *n* 95
quaver *n* 315, 407, 408; *v* 314, 315
queer *adj* 83
queer fish *n* 857
quell *v* 265
quench *v* 385, 829
querulous *adj* 868
query *n* 461; *v* 461
quest *n* 622, 676
quester *n* 268
question *n* 461, 533; *v* 461, 475, 870, 989
questionable *adj* 473, 475, 485, 520
questionableness *n* 473, 475, 520
questioning *n* 461, 539; *adj* 461
quibble *n* 520; *v* 477
quibbling *adj* 477
quick *adj* 111, 274, 498, 682, 684, 698, 842
quick as lightning *adj* 274
quicken *v* 132, 170, 173, 274, 359, 684, 824
quickly *adv* 132

quickness *n* 132, 274, 684

quicksand *n* 667

quick-tempered *adj* 901

quick to fly off the handle *v* 901

quick-witted *adj* 842

quiddity *n* 477

quid pro quo n 30

quiescence *n* 150, 172, 265, 403, 526, 683

quiescent *adj* 172, 265, 403

quiet *n* 174, 403, 721; *v* 174, 723; *adj* 174, 403, 585, 685

quietly *adv* 881

quietude *n* 265, 826

quietus *n* 360

quilt *n* 223; *v* 440

quinquepartite *adj* 99

quinquesection *n* 99

quintessence *n* 5

quintet *n* 415

quirk *n* 83, 608

quit *v* 293, 624, 757, 782, 807

quite *adv* 52

quits *n* 27; *adj* 27

quittance *n* 952

quitter *n* 623

quitting *n* 782

quiver *n* 315, 407; *v* 277, 314, 315, 383

quota *n* 786

R

rabbi *n* 996

rabble *n* 876

rabid *adj* 825

race *n* 11, 75, 188, 274, 348; *v* 274

raciness *n* 574

rack *n* 378

racket *n* 315, 404, 407, 414

racy *adj* 574

radial *adj* 291

radiance *n* 420, 845

radiant *adj* 291, 420, 423, 845

radiate *v* 291, 420

radiation *n* 73, 291, 420

radical *n* 489, 658, 742; *adj* 52

radioactivity *n* 420

rage *n* 825, 852; *v* 173, 825

raging *adj* 173, 824

ragtime *n* 415

raid *n* 716

rail *n* 232

rail at *v* 856

railing *n* 232

raillery *n* 856

raiment *n* 225

rain *n* 348; *v* 348

rain cats and dogs *v* 348

rainfall *n* 348

rain hard *v* 348

rain in buckets *v* 348

rain in torrents *v* 348

rainy *adj* 348

raise *v* 35, 161, 235, 250, 307, 370

raised *adj* 250

raise one's voice *v* 411

raise spirits *v* 992

raise to a fervor *v* 824

raise up *v* 206

raising *n* 307, 370

rake *n* 962; *v* 371

rake out *v* 301

rally *v* 660

rallying point *n* 74

rally round *v* 709

ram *n* 373

ramble *v* 266, 279, 499, 573

rambler *n* 268

rambling *adj* 47, 266, 279

ramification *n* 51, 291

ramify *v* 291

ram in *v* 300

rammer *n* 263

rampage *v* 173

rampant *adj* 173, 175, 307, 748

ramrod *n* 263

ramshackle *adj* 124

ranch *v* 370

ranching *n* 370

rancid *adj* 397, 401, 653

rancidity *n* 401

rancor *n* 907

rancorous *adj* 907

random *adj* 156, 621

range *n* 26, 69, 180, 196, 200, 278, 386, 965; *v* 60, 196, 266

rank *n* 26, 58, 69, 71, 875; *v* 58, 60, 480; *adj* 365, 401, 649

rank and file *n* 876

rankle *v* 653, 659

rankness *n* 401

rant *n* 517, 549, 577; *v* 503, 517, 582, 825

ranter *n* 584

rap *n* 276, 406, 588; *v* 276, 406, 588

rapacious *adj* 789, 819

rapacity *n* 819

rapid *adj* 274, 684

rapidity *n* 274, 684, 819

rapids *n* 348

rapture *n* 827, 897, 993

rapturous *adj* 821, 829, 977

rare *adj* 20, 83, 103, 137, 322, 648

rarefaction *n* 322

rarefy *v* 322

rarely *adv* 137

rare occurrence *n* 137

rarity *n* 137, 322

rascal *n* 941

rash *n* 72; *adj* 499, 684, 863

rashness *n* 863

rashness *n* 499

rasp *n* 330; *v* 330, 331

rasping *n* 410; *adj* 410
ratatat *n* 407
rate *n* 26, 264, 812; *v* 466, 480
rather *adv* 32
ratification *n* 535, 762
ratify *v* 535
ratio *n* 9, 26, 786
ratiocination *n* 476
ration *n* 786
rational *adj* 450, 498, 502
rationale *n* 155, 462
rationalism *n* 476
rationalist *n* 476
rationalistic *adj* 476
rationality *n* 450, 502
rations *n* 298
rattle *v* 407
raucousness *n* 410
ravage *v* 162, 659
ravager *n* 165
rave *v* 503
ravel *v* 219
raveled *adj* 59
raveling *n* 59
ravenous *adj* 789
raver *n* 504
ravine *n* 198, 259
raving *n* 503; *adj* 173, 824
ravish *v* 829
ravishment *n* 824, 827
raw *adj* 378, 383, 435, 674, 699
raw materials *n* 635
ray *n* 420
raze *n* 162
razor edge *n* 253
razor sharp *adj* 253
reach *n* 26, 196, 200; *v* 27, 270
reach a point *v* 292
reaching *n* 292
reach to *v* 196, 200
react *v* 179, 277, 287
reaction *n* 145, 179, 276, 277, 287, 718

reactionary *adj* 179, 277
reactive *adj* 718
read *v* 539
readable *adj* 578
reader *n* 542, 591
readily *adv* 705
readiness *n* 132, 602, 673, 698
read the law *v* 968
ready *adj* 507, 602, 673, 682
ready for battle *v* 727
real *adj* 1, 494
real estate *n* 342, 780
realism *n* 646
reality *n* 1, 494
realize *v* 450, 484, 490
realm *n* 181
reanimate *v* 163, 359, 660, 689
reanimation *n* 163
reap *v* 371, 789
reappear *v* 104
reappearance *n* 104, 163
reappearing *adj* 163
rear *n* 235
rear *n* 235; *v* 161, 235, 307; *adj* 235
rearguard *n* 235
rear rank *n* 235
rearward *adv* 235
reason *n* 450, 498, 502, 615; *v* 450, 498
reasonable *adj* 174, 472, 498, 502, 736, 815
reasonable chance *n* 472
reasonableness *n* 174; 498
reasoner *n* 476
reason falsely *v* 477
reasoning *n* 476
reasoning *adj* 476
reasons *n* 476
reason why *n* 155
reassuring *adj* 858

rebate *n* 813; *v* 813
rebel *n* 165, 489; *v* 146, 719, 742
rebellion *n* 146, 719, 742
rebellious *adj* 146, 715, 742
rebelliousness *n* 715, 742
reborn *adj* 660
rebound *n* 145, 277; *v* 145, 277
rebuff *n* 277, 289, 764; *v* 289, 610, 764
rebuild *v* 660
rebuilding *n* 660
rebut *v* 462, 468, 536
rebuttal *n* 468, 536
recalcitrance *n* 715
recalcitrant *adj* 715, 719, 742, 764
recall *v* 451, 505
recant *v* 536, 607
recantation *n* 607
recantation *n* 536
recapitulate *v* 104
recapitulation *n* 104
recast *v* 140, 146, 626
recede *v* 283, 287
receipt *n* 810
receipt *n* 771, 807
receive *v* 76, 296, 775, 785, 789, 810
receive an impression *v* 821
received *adj* 490, 785
receive pleasure *v* 377
receiver *n* 191, 785, 801
receive the call *v* 996
receiving *n* 785
receiving *adj* 785
recent *adj* 122, 123, 435
recentness *n* 123
receptacle *n* 191
reception *n* 296

reception *n* 76, 292, 785

recess *n* 198, 244, 530, 687

recesses *n* 221

recession *n* 287

recession *n* 283, 659

recipient *n* 785

reciprocal *adj* 12, 148, 718

reciprocally *adv* 12

reciprocate *v* 12, 148

reciprocation *n* 12, 148, 718

reciprocity *n* 12, 148, 718

recision *n* 756

recital *n* 594

recitation *n* 582

recite *v* 85, 594

reckless *adj* 684, 863

recklessness *n* 460, 863

reckon *v* 85, 480, 873

reckoning *n* 85, 466, 507, 807, 811, 973

reckon up *v* 807

reclaim *v* 660, 952

reclamation *n* 660, 952

reclination *n* 213

recline *v* 213, 687

recluse *n* 893, 955

recognition *n* 505, 733

recognizable *adj* 446

recognize *v* 441

recognized *adj* 490

recoil *n* 277

recoil *n* 145, 283, 287, 603, 623; *v* 145, 179, 277, 287, 325, 603, 623

recollect *v* 451, 505

recollection *n* 505

recommend *v* 695

recommendation *n* 695

recompense *n* 973; *v* 30, 807, 973

reconcilable *adj* 23

reconcile *v* 723, 831

reconcile oneself to *v* 826

reconciliation *n* 723

recondition *v* 662

reconstitute *v* 660

reconstruct *v* 660

reconstruction *n* 660

reconversion *n* 660

record *n* 551

record *n* 86, 527, 594; *v* 60, 551

recorder *n* 53

recount *v* 594

recounting *n* 594

recoup *v* 660, 790

recouperative *adj* 790

recourse *n* 677

recover *v* 660, 789, 790

recovery *n* 660, 789, 790

recovery of strength *n* 689

recreant *adj* 544, 862

recreation *n* 840

recrimination *n* 718

rectification *n* 660

rectify *v* 246, 658

rectilinear *adj* 246

rectitude *n* 922, 939, 944

recumbency *n* 213

recuperative *adj* 660

recur *v* 104, 136, 138

recure *v* 660

recurrence *n* 104, 136

recurrent *adj* 70, 104, 138

recurring *adj* 104, 136, 138

recur to *v* 677

recurve *v* 245

recusancy *n* 984

recusant *adj* 984

red *n* 434

red *adj* 434

red and yellow *n* 439

red as a lobster *adj* 434

red as beet *adj* 434

redden *v* 434

reddish *adj* 434

redeem *v* 30, 147, 660, 672, 790, 952

redemption *n* 660, 672, 952

redemptive *adj* 790, 952

redesign *v* 140

red-faced *adj* 434

red-hot *adj* 824

redneck *n* 887

redness *n* 434

redolence *n* 398, 400

redolent *adj* 398, 400

redouble *v* 35, 90

redress *n* 660, 662, 973; *v* 660, 662

reduce *v* 38, 103, 195, 201, 308, 638, 813

reduced *adj* 34, 103, 201

reduce to *v* 144

reduce to a square *v* 95

reducible *adj* 38

reductio ad absurdum n 476

reduction *n* 36, 103, 144, 195, 201, 813

reduction to power *n* 330

redundance *n* 641

redundance *n* 104

redundancy *n* 573

redundant *adj* 104, 641

reduplicate *v* 90

reduplication *n* 90

re-echo *v* 408

reed instruments *n* 417

reef *n* 346

reefs *n* 667

reek *v* 401, 653

reeking *adj* 382, 401

reeky *adj* 653

reel *v* 314, 315

reestablish *v* 660

reestablishment *n* 660

refashion *v* 163

referable *adj* 155
referable to *adj* 9
referee *n* 967; *v* 174
reference *n* 9, 467
reference to *n* 155
referential *adj* 467
refer to *v* 9, 155, 695
refine *v* 477, 652, 658
refined *adj* 428, 465, 850, 852
refinement *n* 465, 578, 658, 850
reflect *v* 19, 420, 451
reflection *n* 420, 451
reflective *adj* 451, 498
reflector *n* 445
reflex *n* 145, 276, 277; *adj* 283
reflexion *n* 21
refluent *adj* 283
reflux *n* 283
reform *v* 144, 658
reformation *n* 658
reformative *adj* 658
reformer *n* 658
refraction *n* 279, 291, 420, 443
refractory *adj* 606, 719, 742, 945
refrain *v* 623, 681
refresh *v* 159, 338, 385, 660, 689, 829, 834
refreshing *adj* 689
refreshment *n* 689
refreshment *n* 159, 660
refrigerate *v* 383, 385
refrigeration *n* 385
refrigerator *n* 387
refuge *n* 666
refugee *n* 268, 623
refusal *n* 764
refusal *n* 603, 610
refuse *n* 40; *v* 536, 603, 610, 708, 764
refutable *adj* 479
refutation *n* 468, 479
refute *v* 468, 479
regale *n* 829

regalia *n* 747
regard *n* 441, 451, 457, 459, 873, 897, 928, 987, 990; *v* 9, 418, 451, 457, 480, 873, 928
regarded *adj* 873
regardful *adj* 451
regarding *n* 418; *adj* 928
regards *n* 928
regenerate *v* 163
regeneration *n* 163, 660
regenerative *adj* 163
reggae *n* 415
regicide *n* 361
regiment *n* 72
regimentals *n* 225
region *n* 181
regional *adj* 181
register *n* 86, 114, 551, 553, 811; *v* 60, 114, 551
registrar *n* 553
regnant *adj* 737
regress *n* 287; *v* 145, 283, 287
regression *n* 283
regression *n* 287
regressive *adj* 283
regret *n* 833
regret *n* 950; *v* 832, 833, 950
regretful *adj* 832, 833, 950
regular *adj* 16, 58, 60, 80, 138, 240, 242, 613
regular as clockwork *adj* 138
regularity *n* 138
regularity *n* 16, 58, 80, 138, 242
regularly *adv* 138
regulate *v* 58, 60, 174, 692, 693
regulation *n* 80

regulation *n* 693, 697, 963
regurgitate *v* 297, 348
regurgitation *n* 297
rehabilitate *v* 660, 790
rehabilitation *n* 660, 790
rehash *v* 104
rehearsal *n* 673
rehearse *v* 104, 594, 673
reign *n* 175
reimburse *v* 790, 807
reinforce *v* 37, 159
reinforcement *n* 39
reinstate *v* 660
reinstatement *n* 660
reinvest *v* 790
reinvestment *n* 790
reinvigorate *v* 660, 689
reiterate *v* 104, 136
reiteration *n* 104, 136
reject *v* 55, 297, 536, 610, 764, 893
rejected *adj* 893
rejection *n* 610
rejection *n* 55, 297, 536, 764, 893
rejoice *v* 836, 838
rejoice in *v* 827
rejoicing *n* 838
rejoin *v* 72, 462
rejoinder *n* 462
rekindle *v* 384
relapse *n* 661
relapse *v* 145, 287, 661
relate *v* 12, 216, 464, 594
related *adj* 9, 11
relate to *v* 9
relating *n* 464
relating to *adj* 9
relation *n* 9
relation *n* 11, 594
relationship *n* 9, 11
relative *n* 11; *adj* 9
relative to *adj* 9
relator *n* 938

relax v 47, 160, 275, 324, 683, 685, 687, 738

relaxation n 47, 160, 174, 687, 738, 840

relaxed adj 47, 160, 174

relaxing adj 840

release n 360, 671, 672, 750, 777a, 783, 807; v 672, 750, 777a, 927a, 970

released adj 970

relegate v 55, 270

relegation n 270

relent v 324

relentless adj 604, 739, 914a

relentlessness n 739

relevant adj 9

reliability n 150, 474

reliable adj 150, 246, 474, 664

reliance n 484, 507, 858

relic n 40, 124, 551

relics n 362

relied on adj 871

relief n 834

relief n 250, 660, 662, 689, 707

relieve v 707, 834

religion n 983

religious adj 983, 987

religious garments n 999

religious persuasion n 983

religious truth n 983a

religious writings n 986

relinquish v 624, 678, 757, 782

relinquishment n 624, 782

relinquishment n 678, 757

relish n 377, 390, 393,

394; v 377, 394, 827

relocate v 184

reluctance n 603, 704, 719

reluctant adj 603, 764

rely on v 484, 507, 858

remain v 1, 40, 106, 110, 141, 186, 265

remainder n 40

remaining adj 40

remains n 40, 362, 551

remake v 144

remark v 457

remarkable adj 31, 870

remarkably adv 31

remediable adj 660

remedial adj 660, 662

remediless adj 859

remedy n 662

remedy v 660, 662, 834

remember v 451, 505

remembrance n 505

remind v 505

reminder n 505

reminisce v 505

reminiscence n 505

reminiscent (of) adj 505

remiss adj 460, 674, 683, 738

remission n 756, 918

remissness n 460, 683

remit v 790

remittance n 807

remnant n 40

remodel v 140, 144, 146

remonstrance n 616, 766

remonstrate v 616, 766

remonstrative adj 766

remorse n 833, 950

remorseful adj 950

remorseless adj 951

remote adj 10, 196

remote cause n 153

remoteness n 196

remote past n 122

removable adj 38

removal n 38, 185, 270, 287, 293, 301

remove n 196; v 2, 38, 185, 270, 301, 662

removed adj 196

remunerate v 30, 807, 973

remuneration n 973

remunerative adj 775, 810, 973

renaissance n 660

renascence n 660

renascent adj 163, 660

rend v 44

render v 144, 784, 790

render blunt v 254

render certain v 474

render concave v 252

render curved v 245

render few v 103

render general v 78

render horizontal v 213

render insensible v 376

render intelligible v 518

render invisible v 447

render oblique v 217

render powerless v 158

render sensible v 375

render straight v 246

render uncertain v 475

render unintelligible v 519

render violent v 173

rendezvous n 74

renegade n 607

renew v 90, 123, 163, 660, 689

renewal n 90, 163, 660

renounce v 536, 607, 610, 624, 757, 764, 782

renovate v 123, 163, 660

renovated adj 123

renovation n 123, 163, 660

renown n 31, 873

renowned adj 873, 883

rent *n* 44, 198, 260; *v* 788

renunciation *n* 607, 610, 624, 757, 764, 782

reorganize *v* 144, 660

repair *n* 658, 660, 689; *v* 658, 660, 662, 689, 790, 952

reparation *n* 30, 660, 790, 952, 973

reparatory *adj* 973

repartee *n* 842

repay *v* 718

repeal *n* 756; *v* 756

repeat *v* 90, 104, 136

repeated *adj* 104

repeatedly *adv* 104, 136

repel *v* 289, 610, 616, 717, 719, 764, 830, 867

repellant *adj* 830

repellent *adj* 289, 719, 867

repelling *adj* 289

repent *v* 833, 950, 952

repentance *n* 833, 950

repentant *adj* 950

repenting *adj* 950

repercussion *n* 145

repetition *n* 104

repetition *n* 17, 90, 136, 143, 641

repetitious *adj* 104, 641

repetitive *adj* 104

repine *v* 832

replace *v* 63, 147, 660

replacement *n* 147, 634, 660

replenish *v* 52, 637

replete *adj* 52, 641

repletion *n* 641, 869

replica *n* 13, 19, 21

reply *n* 462; *v* 462

report *n* 532, 594, 873; *v* 527

reported *adj* 527

reporter *n* 527, 532, 534

repose *n* 687

repose *n* 265, 681; *v* 265, 685, 687

reposing *adj* 687

repository *n* 191

reprehensible *adj* 649, 923, 945

represent *v* 147, 550, 554, 556, 594, 759

representation *n* 554

representation *n* 17, 19, 21, 550, 556, 594, 599, 626

representative *n* 147, 524, 534, 690, 758, 759; *adj* 17, 550, 554

representing *adj* 17

repress *v* 179, 751, 826

repression *n* 179, 751

repressive *adj* 751

reprieve *n* 133, 671, 672, 918; *v* 672, 918

reprint *n* 21

reprisal *n* 148, 718, 789, 919

reproach *v* 932

reproachful *adj* 932

reproduce *v* 19, 104, 163, 168, 660

reproduction *n* 163

reproduction *n* 13, 19, 21, 104, 660

reproductive *adj* 163

reproof *n* 972

reprove *v* 932, 972

reprover *n* 936

reptile *n* 366

repudiate *v* 55, 489, 536, 610, 764

repudiation *n* 55, 536, 610, 764, 808

repugnance *n* 867, 898

repugnant *adj* 867, 898

repulse *n* 145, 277, 289, 764; *v* 289, 719, 764

repulsed *adj* 893

repulsion *n* 289

repulsion *n* 719

repulsive *adj* 289, 395, 719, 830, 846, 867, 898

reputable *adj* 246, 873

reputation *n* 873

repute *n* 873

reputed *adj* 873

request *n* 765

request *n* 741, 865; *v* 630, 765, 865

require *v* 601, 630, 640, 741, 744, 765, 812

requirement *n* 630

requirement *n* 601, 741

requisite *n* 601, 630; *adj* 601, 630

requisition *n* 630, 741

requital *n* 30, 148, 718, 919, 973

requite *v* 148, 718, 919, 973

rescind *v* 44, 756, 764

rescue *n* 672, 707; *v* 660, 670, 672, 707

research *n* 461, 463

resemblance *n* 13, 17, 216

resemble *v* 17, 197

resembling *adj* 17

resent *v* 900, 921

resentful *adj* 900, 907, 919, 920

resentment *n* 900

resentment *n* 907, 920

reservation *n* 528

reserve *n* 528, 585, 636; *v* 636, 678, 781

reserved *adj* 383, 528, 585, 901a

reservoir *n* 191, 343, 636

reside *v* 188

residence *n* 189

resident *n* 188; *adj* 186

residual *adj* 40

residue *n* 40
residuum *n* 40
resign *v* 624, 725, 757, 782
resignation *n* 757
resignation *n* 624, 725, 782, 826, 831
resigned *adj* 826, 831
resign oneself to *v* 826
resilience *n* 325
resiliency *n* 325
resilient *adj* 325
resin *n* 356a
resin *v* 356a
resinous *adj* 356a
resist *v* 179, 708, 715, 719, 742, 764
resistance *n* 719
resistance *n* 179, 708, 715, 742
resistant *adj* 323, 327, 708, 715, 719
resisting *n* 708
resolute *adj* 150, 604, 604a, 606, 861
resolutely *adv* 604
resoluteness *n* 150, 600, 604
resolution *n* 604
resolution *n* 144, 150, 600, 604a, 606, 620
resolve *n* 604, 611, 620; *v* 604
resolve beforehand *v* 611
resolved *adj* 604
resolve into *v* 144
resolve into its elements *v* 49
resonance *n* 408
resonance *n* 277, 402, 404
resonant *adj* 402, 408
resort *n* 677
resort to *v* 677
resound *v* 402, 404, 408
resounding *adj* 404, 408

resources *n* 632, 635, 637, 780, 803
respect *n* 928
respect *n* 457, 743, 873, 894, 926, 987; *v* 772
respectability *n* 873
respectable *adj* 736, 873
respected *adj* 873, 928
respectful *adj* 457, 743, 879, 894, 926, 928
respecting *adj* 928
respective *adj* 79, 786
respectively *adv* 79
respects *n* 928
respiration *n* 359
respire *v* 349, 359
respite *n* 106, 133, 142, 198, 672, 687
resplendent *adj* 420
respond *v* 277, 462
respond to *v* 821
response *n* 587
response *n* 179, 276, 277, 462
responsibility *n* 177, 926
responsible *adj* 177
responsive *adj* 375, 462
responsiveness *n* 375, 822
rest *n* 265
rest *n* 40, 70, 142, 211, 360, 681, 687; *v* 70, 142, 265, 685, 687
restate *v* 104
restatement *n* 104
restful *adj* 265, 685
resting *adj* 687
restitution *n* 790
restitution *n* 660
restless *adj* 149, 264, 682, 825, 832
restlessness *n* 149, 264, 315, 682, 825, 832
restorable *adj* 660

restoration *n* 660
restoration *n* 123, 145, 163, 658, 689, 790
restorative *n* 662; *adj* 163, 658, 660, 662
restore *v* 123, 145, 159, 163, 658, 660, 662, 689, 790
restored *adj* 123, 660
restore equilibrium *v* 27
restoring *adj* 689
restrain *v* 179, 195, 229, 233, 370, 469, 616, 751, 953
restrained *adj* 229, 751
restraint *n* 751
restraint *n* 55, 179, 229, 576, 616, 706, 826, 849
restrict *v* 233, 469, 751, 761
restricted *adj* 203
restriction *n* 469, 751, 761
restrictive *adj* 751, 761
restructure *v* 140
result *n* 63, 65, 480, 729
result from *v* 154
resulting *adj* 117
resulting from *adj* 154
resume *v* 104, 789
resumption *n* 660
resurgent *adj* 163
resurrect *v* 163
resurrection *n* 163
resuscitate *v* 163, 660
resuscitation *n* 163, 660
retailer *n* 797
retain *v* 150, 505, 670, 781
retainer *n* 746
retake *v* 789
retaliate *v* 148, 718, 919
retaliation *n* 718
retaliation *n* 30, 148, 919
retaliatory *adj* 718
retard *v* 133, 275, 706

retardation *n* 133
retch *v* 297
retention *n* 781
retention *n* 505, 670
retentive *adj* 781
retentiveness *n* 505
reticence *n* 528, 583, 585
reticent *adj* 528, 533, 583, 585
reticulated *adj* 260
reticulation *n* 219
retinue *n* 69
retire *v* 283, 287, 293, 623, 757, 881, 893
retired *adj* 893
retirement *n* 283, 287, 757, 893
retiring *adj* 881
retort *n* 148, 462, 718; *v* 148, 462, 718
retouch *v* 660
retract *v* 607, 756
retraction *n* 485, 536, 607, 756
retreat *n* 74, 189, 283, 287, 623, 666, 671, 893; *v* 145, 283, 893
retrench *v* 38, 201, 817
retrenchment *n* 38, 201, 817
retribution *n* 718, 919, 972, 973, 974
retributive *adj* 718, 973
retrievable *adj* 660
retrieval *n* 660
retrieve *v* 660
retroactive *adj* 122
retrogradation *n* 145, 659, 661
retrograde *adj* 283, 661
retrogression *n* 145, 283, 659
retrogressive *adj* 283
retrospect *n* 505
retrospection *n* 122, 145
retrospective *adj* 122

retrospectively *adv* 122
return *n* 145, 283, 287, 790; *v* 104, 138, 145, 283, 718, 790
returning *n* 145
return to *v* 104
reunion *n* 43, 72
revamp *v* 140
reveal *v* 260, 525, 529
revealed *adj* 529
reveal itself *v* 446
revelation *n* 985
revelation *n* 529
revelatory *adj* 985
revel in *v* 377
reveling *n* 838
revenge *n* 919
revenge *n* 718; *v* 718, 919
revengeful *adj* 718, 919
reverberant *adj* 104, 408
reverberate *v* 277, 408
reverberating *adj* 104, 408
reverberation *n* 104, 277, 407, 408
revere *v* 860, 897, 928, 987
reverence *n* 860, 926, 928, 987, 990; *v* 860, 928
reverend *n* 996
reverent *adj* 987
reverential *adj* 926, 987, 990
revering *adj* 990
reversal *n* 14, 140, 218, 287, 607
reverse *n* 235, 237; *v* 145, 218; *adj* 14, 218, 237
reversion *n* 145
reversion *n* 218
revert *v* 14, 104, 145, 283, 287
reverting *n* 145
review *n* 595

reviewer *n* 480, 595
revile *v* 988
reviler *n* 936
revise *v* 658
revision *n* 658
revival *n* 163, 660, 689
revive *v* 163, 359, 660, 689
revivification *n* 163, 660
revivify *v* 159, 163, 660
revocation *n* 607, 756
revoke *v* 536, 607, 756, 764
revolt *n* 146; *v* 146, 289, 719, 742, 830
revolting *adj* 846, 898
revolution *n* 146
revolution *n* 138, 140, 218, 312
revolutionary *adj* 146, 742
revolutionize *v* 146
revolve *v* 138, 312
revolving *adj* 312
revulsion *n* 145, 146, 218, 277
reward *n* 973
reward *n* 733; *v* 973
rewarded *adj* 973
rewarding *adj* 973
rhapsodic *adj* 497
rhapsodist *n* 504, 597
rhapsody *n* 497
rhetoric *n* 517, 577, 582
rhetorical *adj* 577
rhetorical flourish *n* 577
rhetorician *n* 582
rheumy *adj* 337
rhyme *v* 597
rhymeless *adj* 598
rhymer *n* 597
rhymes *n* 597
rhyme with *v* 17
rhyming *n* 597
rhythm *n* 104, 138, 413
rhythm *n* 413

rhythmic *adj* 104, 138, 597

rhythmical *adj* 138

rib *n* 215

ribald *adj* 961

ribaldry *n* 961

ribbed *adj* 259

rich *adj* 394, 413, 428, 577, 734, 803

riches *n* 803

richly *adv* 31

richness *n* 573

rickety *adj* 160

ricochet *n* 145, 277; *v* 277

riddle *n* 520; *v* 260

ride *n* 226

rider *n* 39, 268

ride roughshod over *v* 885

ride the waves *v* 267

ridge *n* 250, 346

ridicule *n* 856

ridicule *v* 856, 929

ridiculous *adj* 497, 499

ridiculousness *n* 853

rid of *adj* 776

rife *adj* 78, 175

rifler *n* 792

rift *n* 44, 198, 260

rig *n* 272

rigging *n* 225

right *n* 238, 922

right *n* 780, 924, 965; *v* 246, 658, 662; *adj* 494, 922, 944

right ahead *adv* 234

right and left *adv* 180, 227

right angle *n* 244

righteous *adj* 944, 977

righteously *adv* 922

righteous man *n* 987

rightful *adj* 494, 922

rightfully *adv* 922

right hand *n* 238

right-handed *adj* 238

rightly *adv* 922

right now *n* 118

right on *adj* 494

right side *n* 238

rigid *adj* 82, 150, 240, 323, 704, 739, 955

rigidity *n* 141, 323, 739

rigmarole *n* 517

rigor mortis *n* 360

rigorous *adj* 739, 955

rigorousness *n* 739

rig out *v* 225

rill *n* 348

rim *n* 231

rimple *n* 258; *v* 258

rind *n* 223

ring *n* 247, 408, 712, 728; *v* 408

ringing *n* 408; *adj* 413

ring in the ear *v* 408

ring in the ears *v* 404

riot *n* 59, 173; *v* 173

rioter *n* 742

riotous *adj* 59, 173, 742

ripe *adj* 128, 673

ripe age *n* 128

ripen *v* 144, 650, 658, 673

ripeness *n* 124, 131, 673

ripen into *v* 144

ripe old age *n* 128

rip open *v* 260

rip out *v* 301

ripple *n* 258, 314, 315, 348; *v* 258, 314

rise *n* 35, 217, 282, 305; *v* 35, 146, 305, 734

rise above *v* 31

rise from *v* 154

rise up *v* 146, 206, 719

rising *n* 146, 305; *adj* 217, 305

rising ground *n* 217

risk *n* 665; *v* 621, 665

risky *adj* 665

rite *n* 998

rites *n* 990

ritualistic *adj* 998

ritualize *v* 883

rival *n* 710, 726; *v* 648, 720

rivalry *n* 720

rive *v* 44

river *n* 348

river *n* 348

rivet *v* 43, 824

rivulet *n* 348

road *n* 278, 302, 627

road to ruin *n* 162

roam *v* 266

roan *adj* 433

roar *n* 404, 408, 411; *v* 173, 404, 411, 412, 838

roaring *n* 404

roast *v* 384

rob *v* 791

robber *n* 792

robbery *n* 791

robe *n* 999; *v* 225

robust *adj* 159, 654, 836

robust health *n* 654

rock *n* 342, 415

rock and roll band *n* 416

rocks *n* 667

rod *n* 215, 975

roe *n* 374

rogue *n* 941

role *n* 625

roll *n* 407

roll *n* 86, 248, 249, 312, 408; *v* 248, 255, 264, 314, 348, 407

roll call *n* 85

roller *n* 249

rolling pin *n* 249

rolling seas *n* 348

roll into a ball *v* 249

roll on *v* 264

romance *n* 515

romantic *n* 504; *adj* 515

romp *v* 173

roof *n* 223

rookie n 701
room n 180
roomy adj 180
roost n 189; v 186
root n 153; v 184
rooted adj 124, 184
root out v 301
ropy adj 205
rosin n 356a; v 356a
rosy adj 434
rot n 49, 653; v 49,
    653, 659
rotary adj 312
rotate v 312
rotating adj 312
rotation n 312
rotation n 138, 145
rotten adj 160, 401,
    649, 653, 659
rottenness n 659
rotund adj 249
rotundity n 249
rotundity n 247
roué n 962
rough adj 16a, 173,
    241, 254, 256, 329,
    397, 410, 674
roughen v 256
rough-hewn adj 256
rough it v 686
roughness n 256
roughness n 254
rough seas n 348
rough up v 256
round n 69, 138; v 245,
    247, 249; adj 247,
    249, 254
roundabout adj 279,
    311, 573, 629; adv
    279
roundabout way n 629
round and round adv
    138, 248
rounded adj 245, 247,
    254
rounded inward adj 252
roundness n 247, 249
round number n 84

round the edge v 254
rouse v 175, 615, 824
rouse oneself v 682
rousing adj 171
route n 302, 627
routine n 16, 58, 80,
    138, 613; adj 16, 138
rout out v 652
rove v 266, 279
rover n 268
roving n 266; adj 266
row n 59, 69; v 267
rowdy n 887
royalty n 875
rpm n 138
rub v 255, 331, 379
rubadub n 407
rubbery adj 325
rubbing n 331, 379
rubbish n 643
rub out v 331, 552
rubric n 697
ruby adj 434
ruckus n 59
ruddy adj 434
rude adj 173, 241, 579,
    851, 885, 895, 929
rudeness n 885, 895,
    929
rudimental adj 66, 674
rudiments n 66
rue v 833, 950
rueful adj 830, 833
ruffian n 887
ruffle n 258; v 59, 256,
    258, 824
rugged adj 241, 256
ruin n 162, 619, 638; v
    162, 619
ruinous adj 162, 619,
    663, 830
ruins n 40
rule n 80, 157, 175,
    240, 466, 537, 613,
    693, 737, 741; v 157,
    480, 693, 737, 749
rulebook n 567
ruler n 737, 745

rules of language n 567
ruling passion n 820
rumble n 408; v 59, 407
rumbling n 407
ruminate v 450, 451
rumor n 532
rump n 235
rumple v 256, 258
rumus n 59
run n 264; 109, 264,
    274, 333, 348
run abreast v 27
run against v 276
run amuck v 173
runaway n 623
run away v 287, 671
run counter to v 179
run down v 649, 934;
    adj 124
run for one's life v 623
run headlong v 173
run into v 276
run into trouble v 665
run its course v 67, 109,
    122
runner n 271, 534
running water n 348
run off at the mouth v
    584
run of the mill adj 29,
    736
run on and on v 573
run out v 67
run over v 641
run parallel v 178
run riot v 173, 641
run smoothly v 705
run the eye over v 441
run the fingers over v
    379
run the risk of v 177
run through v 186, 361
run up against v 179
run up bills v 808
run wild v 173, 825
rupture n 44, 713, 720;
    v 44
ruse n 545

rush *n* 72, 274, 310,
348, 684; *v* 173, 274,
310, 684
russet *adj* 433
rust *v* 659; *adj* 433
rustic *adj* 876
rustle *v* 409
rusty *adj* 659, 683, 699
rut *n* 259, 613
ruthless *adj* 739, 914a

S

Sabbath *n* 687
sable *adj* 431
saboteur *n* 361
saccharine *adj* 396
saccharinity *n* 396
sacred *adj* 976, 987
sacrilege *n* 988
sacrilegist *n* 988
sacrosanct *adj* 976
sad *adj* 649, 837
sadden *v* 830
sadly *adv* 31
sadness *n* 837
safe *n* 802; *adj* 664,
670
safe and sound *adj* 664
safecracker *n* 792
safeguard *n* 664, 666,
670, 717; *v* 670, 717
safekeeping *n* 664, 670
safety *n* 664
safety valve *n* 664
saffron *adj* 435
sag *v* 245
sagacious *adj* 498, 842,
868
sagacity *n* 480, 498,
698, 842
sage *n* 500
sage *n* 492, 872; *adj*
498
sail *n* 267; *v* 267
sailboat *n* 273
sailing *n* 267; *adj* 267
sailor *n* 269
saint *n* 948

saintly *adj* 987
salable *adj* 796
salad oil *n* 356
sale *n* 796
sale *n* 783, 813
salesman *n* 797
saleswoman *n* 797
salient *adj* 250, 642
sallow *adj* 429, 430,
435
sally *n* 716; *v* 293
salmon *adj* 434
salt *n* 393; *v* 392
salt and pepper *n* 432;
adj 440
salt of the earth *n* 648,
948
salt water *n* 341
salty *adj* 392
salubrious *adj* 656
salubrity *n* 656
salutary *adj* 644, 648,
656
salutation *n* 896
salute *n* 896; *v* 586,
836, 896
salvation *n* 670, 672
salve *n* 356
salvo *n* 406
sameness *n* 13, 16, 17,
104
sample *n* 82
sanctify *v* 987
sanctimoniousness *n*
988
sanctimony *n* 988
sanction *n* 737, 760,
924, 931; *v* 737, 760,
931
sanctioned *adj* 924
sanctity *n* 987
sanctuary *n* 666
sand *n* 330, 667; *v* 255
sand bar *n* 209
sanded *adj* 255
sandiness *n* 330
sandpaper *v* 255
sandy *adj* 330

sane *adj* 246, 502
sanguine *adj* 831, 858
sanitary *adj* 656
sanity *n* 502
sans adv 187
sap *n* 5, 501; *v* 162, 659
sapience *n* 498
sapient *adj* 498
sapless *adj* 340
sapphire *adj* 438
sappy *adj* 333, 499
sarcastic *adj* 856
sarcophagous *n* 363
sash *n* 247
Satan *n* 978
satanic *adj* 978, 982
satanism *n* 978
sate *v* 869
satiate *v* 376, 829, 869
satiated *adj* 869
satiety *n* 869
satire *n* 856
satirist *n* 844, 936
satirize *v* 856
satisfaction *n* 772, 807,
827, 831, 952
satisfactory *adj* 639
satisfied *adj* 474, 484,
831
satisfy *v* 462, 639, 746,
772, 807, 829, 831,
952
saturate *v* 52, 339, 869
saturated *adj* 52
saturation *n* 869
satyr *n* 980
sauce *n* 393
saunter *n* 266; *v* 266,
275
sauté *v* 384
savage *adj* 173
savant *n* 492
save *v* 672, 817; *adv*
38, 83
saving *n* 817
savoir faire n 698,
852
savor *n* 390; *v* 390, 394

savoriness *n* 394
savory *adj* 390, 394
saw *n* 257; *v* 44
say *n* 175; *v* 535, 560, 582
saying *n* 496
say nothing *v* 517, 585
say what comes to mind *v* 612
scabrous *adj* 256
scaffolding *n* 673
scald *v* 384
scale *n* 69, 71, 204, 466; *v* 305
scale the heights *v* 305
scallop *n* 257; *v* 257
scalpel *n* 262
scaly *adj* 204
scamper *v* 274
scan *v* 441
scant *adj* 32, 137, 640
scantiness *n* 103, 203
scanty *adj* 32,103
scarce *adj* 32, 103, 137, 640
scarcely *adv* 32, 137
scarcity *n* 32, 103, 640
scared *adj* 862
scarify *v* 257
scarlet *adj* 434
scatter *v* 61, 73, 291
scattered *adj* 73
scene *n* 448
scenery *n* 448
scent *n* 398, 550; *v* 398, 400
scented *adj* 400
scentless *adj* 399
scepter *n* 747
schedule *n* 86
scheme *n* 626; *v* 626
schemer *n* 626
schism *n* 713, 984
schismatic *adj* 984
scholar *n* 492
scholar *n* 541
scholarly *adj* 539
scholarship *n* 490, 539

scholastic *adj* 537, 539, 542
school *n* 542
school *v* 537
schoolbook *n* 542
schoolboy *n* 129
schooled *adj* 498
schoolgirl *n* 129
schooling *n* 537
schoolmaster *n* 540
schooner *n* 273
science *n* 490
science of existence *n* 1
science of light *n* 420
science of living beings *n* 357
science of matter *n* 316
science of sound *n* 402
science of the mineral kingdom *n* 358
scintilla *n* 32, 420
scintillate *v* 420
scintillating *adj* 842
scintillation *n* 420
scion *n* 167
scoff *v* 929, 988
scoff at *v* 856
scoffer *n* 988
scoffing *n* 856, 988
scold *v* 972
scoop *n* 262; *v* 252
scoop out *v* 252
scope *n* 26, 180, 748
scorch *v* 384
scorched *adj* 384
score *n* 98, 259, 805, 806, 811; *v* 259
scores *n* 102
scorn *n* 930; *v* 715, 929, 930
scornful *adj* 929, 930
scotch *v* 659
scot free *adj* 748
scoundrel *n* 941, 949
scour *v* 331, 652
scourge *n* 975
scourge *v* 663, 972
scour the country *v* 266

scout *n* 664, 668
scowl *v* 900, 901a
scraggly *adj* 256
scramble *n* 59, 684; *v* 684
scrap *n* 32
scrape *n* 704, 732; *v* 38, 195, 255, 330, 331
scratch *n* 257, 259; *v* 257, 331, 380, 590, 649
scratching *n* 380; *adj* 410
scratchy *adj* 380
scrawl *v* 590
scrawny *adj* 203
scream *n* 411, 669; *v* 404, 410, 411, 839
screech *v* 411, 412
screeching *n* 412; *adj* 414
screen *n* 223, 424, 530, 717; *v* 424, 442, 528, 664, 717
screening *n* 528
screw *n* 243; *v* 43, 243
screw up the eyes *v* 443
scribble *v* 590
scribe *n* 553, 590
scrimp *v* 819
script *n* 590, 593
scriptural *adj* 983a
Scriptures *n* 985, 986
scrivener *n* 590
Scrooge *n* 819
scrub *v* 331, 652
scruple *n* 485
scrupulous *adj* 246, 459, 543, 603, 772, 868, 939
scrupulousness *n* 603
scrutinize *v* 457
scrutinizing *adj* 461
scrutiny *n* 457, 461
scull *v* 267
sculpt *v* 557
sculptor *n* 559
sculpture *n* 557

scum of the earth *n* 949
scurrilous *adj* 934
scurry *v* 684
scuttle *v* 162
scuttlebutt *n* 532
sea *n* 341
sea dog *n* 269
seafaring *adj* 267
seafaring man *n* 269
sea-girt *adj* 346
seagoing *adj* 267, 341
sea-green *adj* 435
seal *n* 22; *v* 261, 550
sealing *n* 261
sealing wax *n* 356a
seam *n* 43; *v* 259
sea-maid *n* 979
seaman *n* 269
sear *v* 384
search *n* 461, 539, 622;
   v 461
season *n* 106, 106; *v*
   41, 392, 393, 613,
   673
seasonable *adj* 134
seasoned *adj* 392
seasoning *n* 41, 393
seat *v* 184
seat of activity *n* 691
secession *n* 624
seclude *v* 55, 87
secluded *adj* 893
seclude oneself *v* 893
seclusion *n* 893
seclusion *n* 55
second *n* 113, 759; *v*
   707 *adj* 90
secondary *adj* 32, 34,
   651
secondary color *n* 428
second hand *adj* 19
second-rate *adj* 34, 651
second-story man *n* 792
second thoughts *n* 65
second to none *n* 648
secrecy *n* 528, 893
secret *n* 533

secret *adj* 221, 526,
   528, 533
secretary *n* 553, 590
secrete *v* 299, 528
secretion *n* 299, 528
secretive *adj* 528, 533
secretiveness *n* 528
secretly *adv* 528
secret place *n* 530
sect *n* 75
section *n* 51, 75
sectional *adj* 51
secular *adj* 997
secularize *v* 997
secure *v* 43, 132, 664,
   717, 768, 775, 781;
   adj 43, 150, 484, 664
secure an objective *v*
   731
securities *n* 802
security *n* 771
security *n* 664, 717,
   721
sedate *adj* 826
seducer *n* 962
seduction *n* 829
seductive *adj* 288, 615,
   829
see *v* 441, 457,
   480a;484
seed *n* 32, 153; *v* 371
see double *v* 443
seedy *adj* 160, 659, 804
see fit *v* 600
seeing that *adv* 8
seek *v* 461, 622
seeker *n* 268, 767
seek refuge *v* 666
seem *v* 448
seeming *n* 448; *adj* 448
seemingly *adv* 448
seemliness *n* 845
seemly *adj* 845
see one's future *v* 510
seer *n* 130, 504, 513
seesaw *adv* 314
seethe *v* 382
see the light *v* 359

seething *adj* 824
see-through *adj* 425
segment *n* 51, 100a
segregate *v* 44, 55
segregated *adj* 47
segregation *n* 44, 55
seize *v* 789
seize the day *v* 134
seize the opportunity *v*
   134, 682
seize the time *v* 134
seizure *n* 789
seldom *adv* 137
select *v* 609; *adj* 648
selection *n* 609
self *n* 13; *adj* 13
self-abnegation *n* 955
self-admiration *n* 880
self-assurance *n* 878
self-assured *adj* 878
self-centered *adj* 943
self-command *n* 604
self-complacency *n* 880
self-complacent *adj* 880
self-contradictory *adj*
   497
self-control *n* 600, 604,
   953
self-controlled *adj* 953
self-deception *n* 486
self-delusion *n* 486
self-denial *n* 604, 955
self-denying *adj* 955
self-depreciation *n* 483
self-esteem *n* 878, 880
self-glorification *n* 880
self-importance *n* 878
self-indulgence *n* 954
self-indulgent *adj* 943,
   954
self-interest *n* 943
self-interested *adj* 943
selfish *adj* 32, 819, 943
selfishness *n* 943
selfishness *n* 32, 819
self-love *n* 880, 943
self-luminous *adj* 423
self-mortifying *adj* 955

set a trap for *v* 530

set at rest *v* 462

set down *v* 551, 590

set fire to *v* 384

set foot on dry land *v* 342

set forth *v* 293, 594

set forward *v* 293

set free *v* 44, 672, 748, 750, 970; *adj* 970

set going *v* 276

set in motion *v* 66, 284, 677

set in one's ways *adj* 5

set loose *v* 750

setoff *n* 30

set one's sights on *v* 278

set on fire *v* 384

set out *v* 60, 66, 293

set phrase *n* 566

set right *v* 662

set sail *v* 293

set store by *v* 642

set the fashion *v* 62

setting side by side *n* 464

settle *v* 60, 150, 184, 265, 306, 769, 774, 807

settled *adj* 67, 184, 474

settle down *v* 184, 265

settled purpose *n* 620

settlement *n* 23, 184, 762, 807

settle up *v* 790

settle upon *v* 784

set too high a value on *v* 482

set to rights *v* 660

set to work *v* 677

set up *v* 153, 161, 307

set upon *v* 716

seven *n* 98

sever *v* 44, 291

several *n* 100; *adj* 100, 102

severally *adv* 44, 79

severance *n* 44, 291

severe *adj* 242, 576, 739, 830, 849, 955

severely *adv* 31, 739

severity *n* 739

severity *n* 173, 576, 849

sew *v* 43

sewer *n* 350

sex *n* 377

sextet *n* 415

sexual *adj* 377

sexual abstinence *n* 904

sexual failure *n* 158

sexuality *n* 377

shabby *adj* 34, 643, 659, 851

shade *n* 424

shade *n* 15, 26, 223, 362, 421, 422, 428, 530, 980; *v* 421, 422, 424

shading off *adj* 26

shadow *n* 4, 21, 281, 421, 424, 515, 980; *v* 281, 353, 421, 422

shadowiness *n* 422

shadowy *adj* 4, 421, 422, 424, 447

shady *adj* 421, 424, 426, 874

shaft *n* 208, 351

shaggy *adj* 256

shaggy dog story *n* 549

shake *n* 315; *v* 160, 314, 315, 383, 404, 407, 616, 659

shake one's sides *v* 838

shake the foundations of *v* 659

shake up *v* 315

shaking *adj* 315

shaky *adj* 160, 315, 665

shallow *n* 209; *adj* 209, 491, 499, 643

shallow excuse *n* 617

shallowness *n* 209

shallowness *n* 499

shallows *n* 667

sham *n* 544, 545, 855, 880; *v* 546; *adj* 544

shaman *n* 994

shamble *v* 275, 315

shame *n* 874, 930; *v* 874, 879

shameful *adj* 874, 930

shape *n* 448; *v* 240, 557, 852

shapeless *adj* 241

shapelessness *n* 241

shapeliness *n* 242

shapely *adj* 242

share *n* 786; *v* 709, 778, 786

shareholder *n* 778

share in *v* 56, 778

sharer *n* 778

sharp *adj* 171, 173, 217, 253, 375, 392, 397, 404, 410, 416; *adj* 490, 498, 682, 698, 702, 842, 868

sharp edged *adj* 253

sharpen *v* 171, 173, 253, 375, 824

sharpness *n* 253

sharpness *n* 392, 397, 410, 698

sharp outline *n* 446

shatter *v* 44, 158, 162, 328

shattered *adj* 160

shave *v* 195, 201, 204, 255

she *n* 374

shear *v* 195, 201

sheathe *v* 225

shed *n* 223; *v* 73

shed light on *v* 522

shed light upon *v* 420

sheen *n* 420

sheeny *adj* 420

sheepish *adj* 881

sheer *adj* 52, 425

sheerness *n* 425

sheet *n* 204, 223, 811

shelf *n* 215

shell *n* 363

shellac *n* 356a; *v* 356a

shellfish *n* 366

shelter *n* 666, 670, 717; *v* 528, 664, 670, 717

sheltering *n* 528

shelve *v* 133, 678

shepherd *n* 996

shield *n* 223, 717; *v* 670, 717

shift *n* 140, 147, 270; *v* 140, 144, 264, 270, 279

shifting *n* 144; *adj* 264

shiftless *adj* 674

shilly-shally *v* 133, 605

shimmer *n* 420; *v* 420

shine *v* 420

shiny *adj* 255, 420

ship *n* 273

ship *n* 271; *v* 190

shipment *n* 190

ship out *v* 293

shipping *n* 267

shipshape *adj* 58

shirk *v* 623, 742

shirker *n* 623

shiver *v* 315, 328, 383

shivering *adj* 383

shoal *n* 209

shoals *n* 667

shock *n* 276, 315, 508, 713; *v* 824, 830

shockingly *adv* 31

shoot *n* 378; *v* 194, 274, 284, 361, 367, 378

shoot ahead of *v* 303

shooting *n* 361, 378

shoot up *v* 250, 367

shop *v* 795

shopkeeper *n* 797

shopper *n* 795

shopping center *n* 799

shore *n* 231, 342

shore up *v* 215

short *adj* 28, 53, 201, 572, 640, 739

shortcoming *n* 304

shortcoming *n* 28, 34, 53, 640, 651, 730

short distance *n* 197

shorten *v* 36, 38, 201, 596

shortened *adj* 201

shortening *n* 36, 38, 201

shorthand *n* 590

short-lived *adj* 111

shortly *adv* 132

short memory *n* 506

shortness *n* 201

short of *adj* 53; *adv* 32, 34, 38

short-tempered *adj* 901

shot *n* 284

shot in the dark *n* 621

shoulder *n* 236; *v* 215, 276

shoulder to shoulder *adv* 709

shout *n* 411, 838; *v* 404, 411, 836, 838

shout at the top of one's lungs *v* 411

shove *n* 276; *v* 276, 284

shove in *v* 300

shovel *v* 270

shove off *v* 267, 293

show *n* 448, 855, 882; *v* 448, 467, 478, 525, 529

shower *n* 348

shower down *v* 348

showery *adj* 348

showiness *n* 882

showing *n* 525

show itself *v* 446

shown *adj* 478

show no remorse *v* 951

show off *v* 882

show taste *v* 850

show up *v* 446

showy *adj* 428, 851, 882

shred *n* 32

shrewd *adj* 490, 498, 698, 702

shrewdness *n* 702

shriek *n* 411; *v* 411

shrill *adj* 203, 404, 410

shrillness *n* 410

shrink *v* 36, 195, 283, 287, 623

shrink from *v* 603

shrinking *n* 36, 195, 603

shrive *v* 952

shrivel *v* 195, 659

shroud *n* 363; *v* 664

shrub *n* 367

shrubbery *n* 367

shrunk *adj* 195

shrunken *adj* 195

shudder *v* 383

shuffle *v* 149, 275, 315

shuffle off *v* 623

shuffle off the mortal coil *v* 360

shun *v* 623, 671

shunt *v* 279

shut *v* 261; *adj* 261

shutout *n* 101; *v* 55

shutter *n* 424

shutting up *n* 261

shut up *v* 261, 403

shut up shop *v* 687

shy *v* 283, 623; *adj* 881

shyster *n* 548

sibilant *adj* 409

sibilation *n* 409

sibyl *n* 513

sick *adj* 655

sicken *v* 289, 395, 655, 830

sickening *adj* 395

sickly *adj* 160, 435, 655

sickness *n* 655

side *n* 236

side *n* 712

side by side *adv* 88, 236

side effects *n* 154

sidelong *adj* 236; *adv* 217, 236

sideways *adv* 217, 236
side with *v* 709, 714
sidle *v* 217, 236
sift *v* 42, 60
sifting *n* 42
sigh *n* 839
sight *n* 441, 448; *v* 441
sightless *adj* 442
sightlessness *n* 442
sightseer *n* 268, 444
sign *n* 467, 512, 550, 668; *v* 550
signal *n* 467, 550, 668; *v* 467, 550
signalize *v* 550
signally *adv* 31
signature *n* 569, 590
significance *n* 516, 642
significant *adj* 516, 550, 642
signification *n* 516
signify *v* 516, 550, 642
signify little *v* 643
sign of the times *n* 512
silence *n* 403
silence *n* 265, 528, 581, 585; *v* 403, 581
silent *adj* 265, 403, 581, 585, 901a
silent as the grave *adj* 403
silently *adv* 403
silhouette *n* 230
silken *adj* 255
silky *adj* 255
silliness *n* 497, 499, 853
silly *adj* 486, 497, 499, 853
silver *n* 432; *adj* 430, 432
silverness *n* 430
silverish *adj* 432
silvery *adj* 413, 430, 432
similar *adj* 17, 21, 216
similarity *n* 17
similarity *n* 9, 13, 27

simile *n* 17, 521
similitude *n* 17, 21
simmer *v* 315, 382, 384
simple *adj* 42, 486, 499, 576, 703, 849, 946, 960
simpleness *n* 42
simpleton *n* 493, 501
simplicity *n* 849
simplicity *n* 491, 499, 576, 703, 881, 946, 960
simplification *n* 78
simplify *v* 42, 78, 518, 849
simply *adv* 32
simulate *v* 19, 855
simulating *adj* 17
simulation *n* 19, 855
simultaneity *n* 120
simultaneous *adj* 120
simultaneously *adv* 120
simultaneousness *n* 120
sin *n* 923, 945, 961, 988; *v* 945
since *adv* 8, 117, 155
sincere *adj* 543, 703
sincerity *n* 543, 703
since the occasion presents itself *adv* 134
sinewy *adj* 159
sinful *adj* 923, 945, 961
sinfully *adv* 923
sinfulness *n* 947, 961, 988
sing *v* 416, 597, 838
singe *v* 384
singer *n* 416
singing *n* 412; *adj* 413
single *adj* 42, 87
singlehanded *adj* 87
singleness *n* 87
single out *v* 79
singly *adv* 87
sing out *v* 411
sing praises *v* 990
singular *adj* 79, 83, 87

singularity *n* 79, 87
singularly *adv* 31
sinister *adj* 663, 909
sinistral *adj* 239
sink *v* 162, 208, 306, 308, 360, 659, 688, 732, 735, 837
sink back *v* 661
sinking *n* 306
sink into oblivion *v* 506
sinless *adj* 946
sinner *n* 949, 988
sinning *adj* 945, 961
sinuosity *n* 248
sip *n* 298, 390
siphon *n* 350
sir *n* 373
sire *n* 166
siren *n* 669, 980
sisterhood *n* 11, 72, 995
Sisyphean *adj* 686
site *n* 183
sit in judgment *v* 965
situate *v* 183, 184
situated *adj* 183
situation *n* 183
situation *n* 7, 8, 151, 182, 184
situations *n* 527
six *n* 98
six of one and half a dozen of another *n* 628; *adj* 27
sizable *adj* 192
size *n* 192
size *n* 25, 31, 200
skeletal *adj* 203
skeleton *n* 40, 362
skeleton in the closet *n* 649, 830
skeptic *n* 485, 487, 984, 989
skeptical *adj* 485, 487, 984, 989
skepticism *n* 485, 487, 984, 989
sketch *n* 594, 626; *v* 230, 556

sketcher *n* 559
sketchy *adj* 53, 730
skill *n* 698
skill *n* 79, 702, 731
skilled *adj* 698
skillful *adj* 698, 702
skillfully *adv* 698
skillfulness *n* 698, 702
skin *n* 220, 223
skin-deep *adj* 209
skinflint *n* 819
skinniness *n* 203
skinny *adj* 203
skip *n* 198; *v* 309, 838
skipper *n* 269
skirt *n* 231; *v* 231, 236
skirting *n* 231; *adj* 236
skulk *v* 862
skull *n* 450
sky *n* 318, 338
skyscraping *adj* 206
slab *n* 204, 251
slack *adj* 47, 160, 172, 275, 603, 674, 683, 738
slacken *v* 47, 275, 687
slackness *n* 275, 738
slake *v* 174, 829
slam *n* 276; *v* 276
slander *n* 908, 934; *v* 908, 934
slanderer *n* 936
slanderous *adj* 934
slang *n* 579; *adj* 563
slangy *adj* 560
slant *n* 217; *v* 217
slantwise *adv* 217
slap *n* 276; *v* 276
slash *v* 44
slaughter *n* 361; *v* 361
slaughtering *n* 361
slavery *n* 749, 886
slavish *adj* 886
slavishness *n* 886
slayer *n* 361
sleek *v* 255; *adj* 255
sleep *n* 687
sleeping *adj* 172, 265

sleeping car *n* 272
slender *adj* 32, 203, 643
slenderize *v* 203
slenderness *n* 32, 203
slice *n* 204; *v* 44, 204
slick *adj* 355
slide *v* 109, 264, 306
slight *v* 460, 483, 927; *adj* 432, 209, 322, 575, 643, 736
slightly *adv* 32
slightness *n* 4, 32, 203
slim *v* 203; *adj* 203
slime *n* 653
slimness *n* 203
slimy *adj* 352, 355, 653
sling *v* 284
slink away *v* 623
slip *n* 32, 306, 495, 568, 732; *v* 109, 306, 495, 623
slip back *v* 661
slipperiness *n* 665
slippery *adj* 255, 355, 607, 665
slippery ground *n* 667
slippery memory *n* 506
slip-shod *adj* 575
slit *n* 44, 198, 259, 260; *v* 44
sliver *n* 32
slobber over *v* 933
sloop *n* 273
slope *n* 217, 306; *v* 217
sloping *adj* 217, 306
sloppy *adj* 345, 575
slot *n* 260
sloth *n* 133, 172, 275, 683
slothful *adj* 681, 683
slothfulness *n* 681
slouch *v* 207, 217, 275, 683
slough *n* 345
slovenliness *n* 653
slovenly *adj* 59, 575, 653

slow *v* 275, 420; *adj* 133, 172, 275, 603, 683, 685, 843, 901a
slowly *adv* 133, 275
slowness *n* 275
slowness *n* 133, 603
sluggard *n* 683
sluggish *adj* 172, 275, 683, 901a
sluggishness *n* 275, 683, 901a
sluice *n* 350
slumber *n* 687
slumberer *n* 683
slump *v* 306
slur one's words *v* 583
slushy *adj* 352
slut *n* 962
sluttish *adj* 653
sly *adj* 702
slyness *n* 702
smack *n* 32, 276, 390; *v* 390
smack the lips *v* 390
small *adj* 32, 193
small change *n* 800
smallness32
smallness *n* 193
small number *n* 103
small quantity *n* 32, 103
small talk *n* 588
smart *n* 378, 828; *v* 378; *adj* 682, 698
smarts *n* 450, 498
smash *v* 162
smatch *n* 390; *v* 390
smear *v* 653
smell *n* 398, 400; *v* 398, 401
smell bad *v* 401
smell of *v* 398
smell rotten *v* 401
smell sweet *v* 400
smelly *adj* 398
smile *n* 838; *v* 838
smirch *v* 431, 653
smirk *n* 838; *v* 838
smite *v* 649

smitten *adj* 897

smoggy *adj* 426

smoke *v* 382, 392

smoking *adj* 382

smoky *adj* 426

smolder *v* 382, 526

smoldering *adj* 172

smooth *v* 16, 174, 255, 705, 723; *adj* 174, 213, 251, 255, 705

smoothly *adv* 705

smoothness *n* 255

smoothness *n* 251, 705

smooth-tongued *adj* 933

smother *v* 361, 581

smudge *v* 653

smug *adj* 878

smut *n* 653, 961; *v* 431

smutch *v* 431

smutty *adj* 653,961

snag *n* 667

snaggy *adj* 253

snake *n* 248

snake in the grass *n* 548, 649, 667

snaky *adj* 248

snap *n* 406

snap *n* 277; *v* 44, 328, 406

snap back *v* 277

snappish *adj* 901

snap up *v* 789

snare *n* 530, 545, 667

snarl *v* 412, 900

snatch *n* 32; *v* 789

sneak *n* 941; *v* 275, 623, 862, 886

sneak off *v* 623

sneer *n* 856; *v* 929

sneer at *v* 856

sneeze *v* 409

sniff *v* 398

snip *v* 44

snippet *n* 32

sniveling *adj* 886

snobbish *adj* 878

snort *v* 412

snout *n* 250

snow-white *adj* 430

snowy *adj* 430

snuff *v* 398

snuff out *v* 421

snug *adj* 261, 664

soak *v* 337, 339, 959

soak up *v* 340

soap *n* 356

soar *v* 31, 206, 267, 303, 305

sob *n* 839; *v* 411, 839

sobbing *n* 411

sober *v* 174; *adj* 174, 246, 502, 826, 953, 958

sobriety *n* 958

sobriety *n* 502, 953

sobriquet *n* 565

so-called *adj* 565

sociability *n* 894

sociable *adj* 892

sociableness *n* 892

social *adj* 372, 892

social interaction *n* 892

social intercourse *n* 892

socialism *n* 778

socialist *n* 778; *adj* 778

socialistic *adj* 778

sociality *n* 892

society *n* 188, 372, 852

society of men *n* 372

sodden *v* 339; *adj* 337

soft *adj* 255, 324, 345, 403, 405, 413, 499

soft as butter *adj* 324

soft coal *n* 388

soften *v* 174, 324

softening *n* 324

softness *n* 324

softness *n* 160, 326

soggy *adj* 337, 339

soi-disant adj 565

soil *n* 181, 342; *v* 653

soiled *adj* 653

sojourn *v* 186

solace *n* 834

solar *adj* 318

solar energy *n* 388

solar system *n* 180, 318

solder *v* 43, 46

soldier *n* 726, 948

sole *n* 211; *adj* 87

solecism *n* 568

solecism *n* 579

solecize *v* 568

solemn *adj* 403, 642, 882

solemnity *n* 642

solemnization *n* 883

solemnize *v* 883

solicit *v* 765, 865

solicitation *n* 411, 765

solicitor *n* 767, 968

solicitous *adj* 411, 765, 860, 920

solicitude *n* 459, 828, 860

solid *adj* 16, 52, 150, 202, 321, 323

solidarity *n* 52

solid body *n* 321

solidification *n* 321, 385

solidify *v* 46, 48, 321

solidity *n* 150, 321

solidness *n* 321

soliloquize *v* 582, 589

soliloquy *n* 589

solipsism *n* 943

solipsistic *adj* 943

solitary *adj* 87, 893

solitude *n* 893

solo *n* 415; *adj* 87; *v* 416

soloist *n* 416

solubility *n* 333

soluble *adj* 333, 335, 462, 662

solubleness *n* 335

solution *n* 462, 522, 662

solve *v* 462, 662

solvency *n* 803

solvent *adj* 335, 807

specify v 79, 564
specimen n 82
specious adj 477, 545
speciousness n 477
speck n 32, 848
speckle v 440
speckled adj 440
spectacle n 448, 872
spectacles n 445
spectator n 444
specter n 980; 443
spectral adj 2, 4, 980
spectroscope n 428
spectrum n 428
speculate v 155, 514, 621, 675, 870
speculation n 156, 451, 514, 621, 675
speculative adj 514, 621, 675
speech n 582
speech n 560, 586
speech impediment n 583
speechless adj 403, 581, 583
speechlessness n 403, 590
speed n 264, 274, 684; v 274, 682, 684
speedily adv 132
speediness n 132
speed up v 274
speedy adj 274, 684
spell n 993
spell n 106, 198, 992; v 561, 707
spell-bound adj 870
spelling n 561
spend v 638, 809
spend freely v 816
spendthrift adj 638, 818
spend time v 106
spent adj 158, 160, 688
spew v 297

sphere n 26, 181, 249, 318; v 249
spherical adj 249
sphericity n 249
spheroid n 249
spice n 41, 393; v 392
spiced adj 392
spick and span adj 123
spicy adj 392, 400
spigot n 263
spike n 253, 263; v 260
spiked adj 253
spiky adj 253
spill v 348
spin n 266; v 312
spin a melody v 416
spin around v 312
spindly adj 203
spine n 253
spineless adj 862
spinelessness n 172
spinning n 312
spin out v 200
spinster n 904
spiny adj 253
spiral n 248, 311; adj 248
spirit n 5, 171, 359, 516, 574, 682, 709, 820, 861, 977, 980
spirited adj 171, 574, 836, 861
spiritual adj 2, 317, 976, 977
spiritualism n 992
spirituality n 317
spit v 260
spite n 907
spiteful adj 898, 907, 919, 945
spitefulness n 907
splash n 348; v 337, 348, 653
splendid adj 420
splendor n 420, 845, 882
splice v 43, 219

splint n 215
splinter n 32; v 44, 328
splintery adj 328
split n 44, 713; v 44, 91, 293, 328, 713, 838
split down the middle v 91
split hairs v 868
split one's sides v 838
split the difference v 29
split the differences v 774
split the eardrums v 404, 419
split up v 778, 905; adj 51, 905
spoil v 397, 659
spoilage n 659
spoilation n 638
spoiled adj 397
spoiled child n 899
spoiler n 165
spoils n 793
spokesman n 524, 534, 582
sponge v 339, 340
sponginess n 354
sponsor v 771
sponsorship n 771
spontaneous adj 612
spook n 980
spoonful n 25, 32
sporadic adj 103, 137, 139
sport v 840
spot n 182, 848, 874; v 653, 848
spotless adj 650, 652, 946, 960
spotlessness n 946
spotted adj 440
spottiness n 440
spotty adj 440
spouse n 903
spout n 348, 350; v 295, 348, 582

sprawl *v* 200, 213, 306

spray *n* 353

spread *n* 180, 291; *v* 73, 194, 291, 531; *adj* 73

spreading *n* 73, 194

spread out *v* 35, 194

spread the sails *v* 267

spread to *v* 196

sprightliness *n* 829

sprightly *adj* 829, 836

spring *n* 153, 159, 309, 325, 348; *v* 274, 309, 325

spring back *v* 277, 325

spring from *v* 154

springiness *n* 325

springtime *n* 125

spring up *v* 367

springy *adj* 309, 325

sprinkle *v* 73, 337

sprinkling *n* 32, 41

sprite *n* 979, 980

sprout *v* 35, 194, 367

spruce *adj* 652

spry *adj* 682

spun-out *adj* 110

spur *n* 250, 253, 615; *v* 615

spurious *adj* 544

spurn *v* 764, 866

spurning *n* 764

spurt *n* 274, 348, 612, 684; *v* 348

sputter *v* 348, 583

spy *n* 444, 455; *v* 441, 455

spyglass *n* 445

spying *n* 455; *adj* 455

squabble *n* 713, 720; *v* 713

squad *n* 72

squadron *n* 72

squalid *adj* 653, 846

squall *n* 349

squalor *n* 653

squander *v* 162, 638, 679, 818

squanderer *n* 818

squandering *n* 818

square *n* 857; *v* 30, 95, 660; *adj* 246

square accounts *v* 807

square one *n* 66

square-rigger *n* 273

square with *v* 23

squash *v* 162, 195, 352, 354, 409

squashy *adj* 345

squat *v* 184; *adj* 193, 201, 202, 207

squawking *adj* 410

squeak *v* 411, 412

squeal *v* 411

squeeze *v* 195, 348, 354

squeeze out *v* 301

squeezing *n* 195, 301

squelch *v* 162

squint *n* 443; *v* 443

squirt *n* 348

squishy *adj* 324

stab *v* 260, 361, 649

stability *n* 150

stability *n* 16, 110, 141

stabilization *n* 150

stabilize *v* 150

stable *adj* 110, 141, 150, 265

staff *n* 215, 696, 747

staff of life *n* 359

stag *n* 373

stage *n* 26, 71, 106, 204, 728

stage business *n* 599

stage name *n* 565

stage-play *n* 599

stagey *adj* 855

stagger *n* 275, 314, 315, 508, 824, 870

stagnant *adj* 265, 901a

stagnate *v* 265

stagnation *n* 265

stagy *adj* 599

staid *adj* 826

stain *n* 428, 874; *v* 428, 653, 848, 874

stained *adj* 961

stainless *adj* 652

stake *n* 621, 771; *v* 621

stale *adj* 124, 659

stalk *n* 215

stall *v* 133

stallion *n* 373

stalwart *adj* 192

stamina *n* 159, 604a

stammer *v* 583

stammering *n* 583

stamp *n* 7, 22; *v* 240, 550

stamp out *v* 162, 385

stand *n* 71, 211, 719; *v* 106, 110, 141, 719

stand a chance *v* 177, 470

stand aloof *v* 681

standard *n* 22, 26, 80, 466, 650; *adj* 29, 82, 650

standardization *n* 16

standardize *v* 58

stand as an example *v* 82

stand as opposites *v* 237

stand at the head *v* 66

stand by *v* 186

stand condemned *v* 971

stand convicted *v* 754

stand erect *v* 212

stand fast *v* 141, 265

stand firm *v* 150, 265, 604

stand for *v* 147, 550, 759, 771

stand immobile *v* 265

stand-in *n* 634

stand in front *v* 234

standing *n* 8, 26, 71, 110, 183, 873

stand next to *v* 197

stand one in good stead *v* 644

stand out *v* 250
standpoint *n* 183, 441
stand still *v* 265
stand straight and tall *v* 212
stand the test *v* 648
stand to reason *v* 474
stand up *v* 719
stand upright *v* 212
stand up straight *v* 212
staple commodity *n* 798
staples *n* 635
starboard *n* 238
starchy *adj* 352
stare *n* 441; *v* 455, 870
stark *adj* 31
stark-naked *adj* 226
stars *n* 423
start *n* 66, 293; *v* 66, 151, 276, 284, 293, 309, 870
start again *v* 66
start fresh *v* 652
starting point *n* 66, 293
startle *v* 508, 824, 870
startled *adj* 870
startling *adj* 508, 870
start over *v* 66
start up *v* 250, 446
starvation *n* 956
starve *v* 385, 804, 819, 955, 956
starved *adj* 956
starving *adj* 956
starving oneself *n* 956
stash *n* 636; *v* 636
state *n* 7
state *n* 188; *v* 516, 535
stated *adj* 474
stateliness *n* 875
stately *adj* 875, 878
statement *n* 535, 594, 811
station *n* 26, 71, 183; *v* 184
stationary *adj* 265
statistical *adj* 85

statistics *n* 85
statuary *n* 557
statue *n* 557, 963, 991
statuette *n* 557
stature *n* 206
status *n* 7, 8, 71
statute *n* 697; 963
staunch *adj* 150, 604a
stave in *v* 252
stay *n* 133, 215, 685; *v* 1, 133, 141, 142, 186, 265
stay away *v* 187
stay in the background *v* 881
stay together *v* 46
stead *n* 644
steadfast *adj* 150, 604, 604a
steadfastness *n* 150, 604a
steadiness *n* 138, 150
steady *adj* 80, 138, 150, 604a
steal *v* 275, 789, 791
steal a march on *v* 132
steal away *v* 623, 671
steal from *v* 788
stealing *n* 791
stealing *n* 788
stealthily *adv* 528
stealthy *adj* 528, 702
steam *n* 353; *v* 267, 336, 353
steamer *n* 273
steaming *n* 336
steam press *v* 255
steam up *v* 353
steamy *adj* 353
steel *v* 159
steep *v* 337; *adj* 217, 306
steepness *n* 217
steer *n* 373; *v* 693
steerage *n* 693
steer a middle course *v* 628

steer clear of *v* 279, 623
steer for *v* 278
steersman *n* 269
stench *n* 401
stencil *n* 21
stenography *n* 590
stentorian *adj* 404, 411
step *n* 71, 264
step by step *adv* 26, 58, 69, 275
step in *v* 724
steppe *n* 344
stereoscope *n* 445
sterile *adj* 158, 169
sterility *n* 169
stern *adj* 604, 739, 955
sternness *n* 739
stew *v* 382, 384
steward *n* 801; *v* 693
stewardship *n* 693
stewed *adj* 959
stewed to the gills *adj* 959
stick *n* 215, 975; *v* 46, 260
stick fast *v* 150, 265
stick in *v* 300
stickiness *n* 46, 352, 396
stick it out *v* 604a
stick out *v* 250
stick to *v* 143
stick to an idea *v* 606
stick up *v* 250
sticky *adj* 46, 327, 352, 396
stiff *adj* 240, 579, 739
stiff breeze *n* 349
stiffen *v* 323
stiffness *n* 246, 579
stifle *v* 361, 403
stifled *adj* 405
stifling *adj* 382
stiletto *n* 262
still *v* 174, 403, 723; *adj* 174, 265, 403; *adv* 30

still-born *adj* 732
stillness *n* 265, 403
stilted *adj* 307, 577, 855
stilts *n* 215
stimulate *v* 171, 173, 382, 615, 689, 824, 829
stimulating *adj* 171
stimulation *n* 824
stimulus *n* 615
sting *v* 378, 380, 663
stinginess *n* 819, 943
stinging *n* 380; *adj* 392
stingy *adj* 819, 943
stink *n* 401; *v* 401, 653
stinking *adj* 401
stinky *adj* 401
stint *v* 819
stipple *v* 558
stipulate *v* 769, 770
stipulations *n* 770
stir *n* 264, 315, 682, 752; *v* 264, 315, 375, 382, 824
stir about *v* 682
stirring *adj* 151, 505
stir up *v* 173, 824
stitch *n* 43, 378, 828; *v* 43
stock *n* 11, 25, 635, 636, 637, 798; *v* 637; *adj* 598, 613
stocks *n* 802
stock-still *adj* 265
stockyard *n* 232
stoical *adj* 383, 826
stoicism *n* 826
stoke *v* 388
stolen away *adj* 671
stolen goods *n* 793
stolid *adj* 499, 843
stolidity *n* 499
stomach *v* 826
stone-blind *adj* 442
stone-deaf *adj* 419
stone's throw *n* 197

stony *adj* 914a
stoop *v* 217, 306, 886
stop *n* 133, 142, 360; *v* 67, 70, 142, 261, 265, 403
stopcock *n* 263
stopgap *n* 147
stoppage *n* 142, 261, 706
stop payment *v* 808
stopper *n* 263
stopper *n* 261
stopping *n* 142, 263, 706
stop short *v* 142, 265
stop up *v* 261
stopwatch *n* 114
storage *n* 636
storage areas *n* 191
store *n* 636
store *n* 31, 637, 798, 799; *v* 72, 636, 637, 670
store up *v* 636
storing *n* 636
storm *n* 173, 315, 348, 349; *v* 173, 349, 716
stormy *adj* 173, 349
story *n* 204, 546, 593
storyteller *n* 548
stout *adj* 159, 192
stout-hearted *adj* 861
stoutness *n* 159
stove *n* 386
stow away *v* 528
strabismus *n* 443
straggle *v* 279
straggler *n* 268
straggling *adj* 59
straight *n* 857; *adj* 212, 246, 278, 807, 958; *adv* 132, 278
straighten *v* 246
straighten out *v* 60
straightforward *adj* 543, 703, 849; *adv* 278

straight line *n* 246
straightness *n* 246
straightway *adv* 132
strain *n* 402, 413, 415, 686; *v* 42, 686, 688
strait *n* 704
strait-laced *adj* 739
straitness *n* 203
straits *n* 343, 804
strand *n* 205, 205
strange *adj* 10, 83, 519, 870
strangely *adv* 31
strangle *v* 158, 361
strangulation *n* 361
strap *n* 975; *v* 43
strapper *n* 192
strapping *adj* 159
stratagem *n* 545, 626, 702
strategic *adj* 626
strategical *adj* 692
strategist *n* 626
strategy *n* 692, 722
stratified *adj* 204
stratosphere *n* 338
stratum *n* 204, 213
straw-colored *adj* 435
stray *v* 279; *adj* 73, 279
streak *n* 259, 420; *v* 440
streaked *adj* 440
streakiness *n* 440
stream *n* 347
stream *n* 264, 347, 348, 420; *v* 72, 264, 333, 348, 349
streamy *adj* 348
street-walker *n* 962
strength *n* 159
strength *n* 25, 26, 31, 157, 171, 327, 364, 739
strengthen *v* 157, 159, 171, 689
strengthening *n* 159
strength of mind *n* 604
strenuous *adj* 686

stress *n* 580, 642, 686
stretch *n* 180; *v* 194, 200, 325
stretch out *v* 200
stretch the meaning *v* 523
stretch to *v* 196, 200
strew *v* 73
strewn *adj* 73
striate *v* 440; *adj* 440
striated *adj* 259
striation *n* 440
stricken *adj* 828
strict *adj* 82, 739, 955, 983a
strictness *n* 739, 983a
stricture *n* 706
stride *n* 264
stride forward *v* 282
stridency *n* 410
strident *adj* 410
strife *n* 713, 720
strike *v* 170, 276
strike a balance *v* 27
strike dumb *v* 581
strike out *v* 552
strike up *v* 416
strike while the iron is hot *v* 134
strikingly *adv* 31
string *n* 69; *v* 43
stringency *n* 739
stringent *adj* 739
strings *n* 417
string together *v* 69
stringy *adj* 200, 205, 327
strip *v* 226, 789
stripe *v* 440
striped *adj* 440
stripling *n* 129
strip to essentials *v* 849
strive *v* 675, 686, 720
stroke *n* 276, 731; *v* 379
stroking *n* 379
stroll *n* 266; *v* 264
strong *adj* 31, 150, 157,

159, 171, 323, 327, 392, 401, 654
strongbox *n* 802
stronghold *n* 666, 802
strong language *n* 574
strongly *adv* 159
strong smelling *adj* 398, 401
strop *v* 253
structural *adj* 329
structure *n* 329
structure *n* 7
struggle *n* 675, 686, 713, 720; *v* 720
struggling *n* 720
strumpet *n* 962
strut *v* 884
stubble *n* 40
stubborn *adj* 150, 327, 606, 704, 719, 742
stubbornness *n* 150, 327, 606, 704, 742
stubby *adj* 201
stud *n* 250
studded *adj* 253, 440
student *n* 492, 541
studio *n* 556, 691
studious *adj* 539
study *n* 457, 461, 539, 595; *v* 457, 461, 539
stuff *n* 3, 635; *v* 190, 194, 224, 376, 869
stuffed *adj* 869
stuff in *v* 300
stuffing *n* 190, 224, 263
stuff oneself *v* 957
stuff up *v* 261
stumble *n* 495; *v* 306, 315, 699
stumble on *v* 156
stumble onto *v* 480a
stumbling block *n* 706
stump *n* 40; *v* 582
stumpy *adj* 201
stun *v* 376, 404, 419, 508
stunned *adj* 419

stunted *adj* 193, 195, 201
stupefaction *n* 870
stupefy *v* 376, 870
stupendous *adj* 31, 192
stupendously *adv* 31
stupid *adj* 275, 486, 491, 497, 499, 843
stupidity *n* 491, 497, 499, 843
stupor *n* 683
sturdy *adj* 150, 159
stuttering *n* 583
stygian *adj* 982
style *n* 569
style *n* 7, 560, 564, 567, 852; *v* 564, 569
stylish *adj* 123, 852
stylishness *n* 123
stylistic *adj* 569
styptic *adj* 397
suasive *adj* 615, 695
sub *n* 634; *v* 147, 634
subdivide *v* 44
subdivision *n* 44, 51, 75, 100a
subdue *v* 744, 879
subdued *adj* 826
subject *n* 454, 746; *v* 601, 744, 749; *adj* 177, 749
subjection *n* 749
subjection *n* 34, 601
subjective *adj* 5
subject-matter *n* 454, 516
subjoin *v* 37
subjugate *v* 749
subjugation *n* 749
sublimation *n* 307
sublime *adj* 206, 574
sublimity *n* 206, 574, 845
sublunary *adj* 318
submerge *v* 310, 337
submerged *adj* 208

submersion *n* 208, 300, 310

submicroscopic *adj* 193

submission *n* 725

submission *n* 749, 826

submissive *adj* 725, 743, 879, 926

submissiveness *n* 725, 743, 879, 886

submit *v* 725, 743, 749

subordinate *adj* 34, 749

subordination *n* 34, 749

subpar *adv* 34

subpoena *n* 969

subscribe *v* 769

subsequence *n* 117

subsequent *adj* 63, 117

subsequently *adv* 63, 117

subservience *n* 631, 743

subservient *adj* 176, 677, 743

subside *v* 36, 287, 360

subsidiary *adj* 176

subsist *v* 1, 141, 359

subsistence *n* 1, 298

subsoil *n* 221

substance *n* 3, 25, 221, 316, 516, 642, 803

substanceless *adj* 209

substantial *adj* 1, 3, 316, 321

substantiality *n* 3

substantiality *n* 316

substantially *adv* 5

substantive *adj* 1, 3

substitute *n* 634

substitute *n* 147, 759; *v* 147

substitute for *v* 147

substitution *n* 147

substratum *n* 204, 221

substructure *n* 211

subterfuge *n* 545, 702

subtilize *v* 477

subtle *adj* 320, 329, 477, 702

subtlety *n* 15, 702

subtract *v* 36, 38, 85

subtracted *adj* 38

subtracting *adj* 38

subtraction *n* 36, 38

suburbs *n* 227

subversion *n* 14, 146, 162, 218

subversive *n* 913; *adj* 162

subvert *v* 162, 218

succeed *v* 63, 117, 731, 734, 783

succeeding *adj* 63, 117

success *n* 731

success *n* 734

successful *adj* 731, 734

successfully *adv* 731

succession *n* 63, 69, 117

successive *adj* 69, 117

successor *n* 117

succinct *adj* 572

succor *n* 707; *v* 707, 834

succorer *n* 912

succuba *n* 980

succubus *n* 980

succulent *adj* 337, 352

succumb *v* 725

sucker *n* 486, 547

sucking *n* 296

suction *n* 296

sudden *adj* 111, 113, 132, 508

sudden impulse *n* 276

suddenly *adv* 113, 132, 508

suddenness *n* 111, 113, 132

sudden thought *n* 612

suds *n* 353

sue *v* 765, 969

suet *n* 356

suffer *v* 378, 655, 760, 826, 828

sufferance *n* 760, 826

suffer a relapse *v* 661

suffering *n* 378, 828, 982

suffice *v* 639

sufficiency *n* 639

sufficiency *n* 31, 803

sufficient *adj* 31, 639

sufficiently *adv* 639

suffix *n* 39, 65

suffocate *v* 361, 641

suffocating *adj* 382, 401

suffocation *n* 361

suffuse *v* 41

suffusion *n* 41

sugar *v* 396

sugariness *n* 396

sugary *adj* 396

suggest *v* 505, 514, 527, 695

suggestion *n* 505, 514, 526, 527, 695, 993

suggestive *adj* 514, 695

suicidal *adj* 361

suicide *n* 361, 361

suit *n* 225, 765, 969; *v* 23, 646, 852

suitability *n* 134, 646

suitable *adj* 134, 646, 850, 922

suitable time *n* 134

suite *n* 69

suiting *adj* 413

suitor *n* 767, 897, 969

suit the occasion *v* 134, 646

sulk *v* 901a

sulky *adj* 901a

sullenness *n* 901a

sullied *adj* 961

sully *v* 653, 848

sultry *adj* 382

sum *n* 50, 84, 800; *v* 37, 85

summarily *adv* 132, 572

summarize *v* 596

summary *n* 572, 596

summer *n* 125
summertime *n* 125
summit *n* 210
summit *n* 206, 650
summon *v* 969
summons *n* 969
summon up *v* 505
sumptuous *adj* 882
sun *n* 420, 423
sunbeam *n* 420
sundown *n* 126
sundry *adj* 102
sunglasses *n* 424
sunk *adj* 208
sunken *adj* 252
sunken rocks *n* 667
sunk into oblivion *adj* 506
sunny *adj* 382, 420, 829, 836
sunrise *n* 125, 420
sunset *n* 126
sunshade *n* 223, 424
sunshine *n* 420
sunup *n* 125
sup *v* 298
superabound *v* 641
superabundance *n* 641
superabundant *adj* 641
superannuation *n* 124, 128
supercilious *adj* 878
superciliousness *n* 878
superficial *adj* 209, 220, 491
superficiality *n* 209
superficies *n* 220
superfluity *n* 40, 641
superfluous *adj* 40, 57, 641
superfluousness *n* 57
superhuman *adj* 976
superimpose *v* 223
superintendent *n* 694
superior *adj* 33, 642, 648
superiority *n* 33

superiority *n* 28, 62, 648, 650
superlative *adj* 33, 648
superlatively *adv* 31, 33
supernal *adj* 210, 981
supernatural *adj* 976, 980
supersaturate *v* 641
supersede *v* 147, 678
superstition *n* 486
superstitious *adj* 486
supervise *v* 692, 693
supervision *n* 693
supervisor *n* 694
supervisory *adj* 693
supination *n* 213
supine *adj* 207, 213, 683
supping *n* 298
supplant *v* 147
supplanting *n* 147
supple *adj* 324
supplement *n* 37, 39, 65; *v* 37
supplemental *adj* 37
supplementary *adj* 37
suppliant *n* 767, 990
supplicant *n* 767
supplicate *v* 765, 990
supplication *n* 765, 990
supplies *n* 635, 800
supply *n* 636, 637; *v* 637, 784
supplying *n* 637
support *n* 215
support *n* 153, 666, 670, 707, 937; *v* 170, 215, 670, 707, 737, 834, 937
supported *adj* 215, 937
supporter *n* 215, 707, 890, 912
supporting *adj* 215
supportive *adj* 707
suppose *v* 451, 514
supposing *adj* 469

supposition *n* 514
supposition *n* 453, 515
suppress *v* 581, 751
suppressed *adj* 528
suppression *n* 162, 528, 751
suppressive *adj* 751
supremacy *n* 33, 737
supreme *adj* 31, 33, 210, 737
supreme being *n* 976
supremely *adv* 31, 33
sure *adj* 246, 474, 484, 664
sure enough *adv* 474
surety *n* 664, 771
surf *n* 348, 353
surface *n* 220, 329
surfeit *n* 641, 869; *v* 869
surfeited *adj* 869
surge *n* 348; *v* 72
surgeon *n* 662
surly *adj* 901a
surmise *v* 510, 514
surmount *v* 206, 303, 305, 731
surname *n* 564
surpass *v* 33, 303
surpassingly *adv* 33
surplice *n* 999
surplus *n* 40, 641
surprise *n* 137, 508, 870; *v* 508, 702
surprised *adj* 508, 870
surprisingly *adv* 31
surrender *n* 624, 725, 782; *v* 624, 725, 782
surreptitious *adj* 528
surrogate *n* 759
surround *v* 227, 229
surrounding *adj* 227
surroundings *n* 7, 227
survey *n* 441, 466, 596; *v* 441, 466, 596
surveyor *n* 594
survival *n* 110

survive v 1, 40, 110, 141

surviving adj 40

susceptibility n 176, 177, 821, 822

susceptible adj 375, 822

suspect v 485, 487, 514

suspend v 133, 142, 214

suspended adj 214

suspense n 485, 507

suspension n 214

suspension n 133, 142

suspension of hostilities n 723

suspicion n 485, 487, 514, 860, 920

suspicious adj 485, 487, 860, 920

sustain v 143, 159, 170, 215, 670, 707

sustenance n 298, 670

swab v 340

swaddle v 225

swagger v 878, 884, 885

swaggerer n 887

swaggering n 884

swain n 373

swallow v 298, 486, 547, 826

swamp n 345; v 162

swampy adj 345

swap n 148; v 148, 794

swarm n 72; v 72, 102, 641

swarming adj 72

swarm with v 102

swarthiness n 431

swarthy adj 431

swash v 348

swathe v 225

sway n 157, 175, 737, 741; v 175, 217, 315, 615, 737

swear n 908; v 535, 768, 908, 988

swearing n 535

sweat n 299; v 299, 382, 686

sweep n 180, 245; v 245, 274

sweep along v 264

sweep away v 162

sweeping adj 52, 76

sweep out v 652

sweet adj 377, 396, 413, 428, 652, 829

sweeten v 396

sweetened adj 396

sweetheart n 897, 899

sweetness n 396

sweet scent n 400

sweet scented adj 400

sweet smell n 400

sweet smelling adj 400

sweet-sounding adj 413

sweet sounds n 413, 415

swell n 348, 404; v 194, 367, 404

swelling n 194, 250; adj 250, 577

swell up v 250

swelter v 382

sweltering adj 382

swerve v 140, 279, 291, 603

swerving n 279

swift adj 274, 684

swiftly adv 274

swiftness n 111, 274, 684

swill v 959

swim v 320

swim in v 377

swindle v 791

swindler n 548

swindling n 791

swing n 180, 415; v 214, 314

swinging adj 214

swinish adj 957

swivel v 312

swivel eye n 443

swollen adj 194, 250

swoon v 158, 688

swoop down v 306

sworn adj 768

sybarite n 954a

sybaritism n 954

sycophancy n 886, 933

sycophant n 886, 935

sycophantic adj 886, 933

syllabic adj 561

syllable n 561

syllabus n 596

syllogistic adj 476

syllogistic reasoning n 476

sylph n 979

sylphic adj 979

symbol n 84, 512, 550, 561, 562, 747, 991

symbolic adj 550, 554

symbolical adj 550

symbolism n 550

symbolize v 550, 554

symmetrical adj 27, 58, 242, 413

symmetry n 242

symmetry n 27, 58

sympathetic adj 714, 740, 821, 914

sympathize v 915

sympathizer n 890, 906

sympathize with v 714, 888, 914

sympathy n 714, 820, 821, 888, 914, 915

symphonic adj 415

symphonic music n 415

symphonious adj 413

symphonize v 413

symphony n 413

symphony orchestra n 416

symptom n 550

synagogue n 1000

synchronism n 120

synchronize v 120

synchronized adj 413

take up one's abode v 189

take upon oneself v 676

take up quarters v 184

take up the pen v 590

take what's offered v 607

take wing v 266, 267

taking n 789

taking nourishment n 298

tale n 546, 549

talebearer n 532

talent n 79, 698

talents n 698

talismanic adj 992

talk n 582, 588; v 582

talk a mile a minute v 584

talkative adj 582, 584

talkativeness n 584

talk big v 577, 884

talker n 584

talk fancy v 577

talk it over v 588

talk nonsense v 497

talk together v 588

talk to oneself v 589

tall adj 200, 206

tallness n 206

tallow n 356

tall tale n 546

tally n 86, 805; v 23, 85

tallying n 85

tame v 174, 370, 749; adj 172, 370, 575, 725

taming n 370

tamper with v 140

tan adj 433

tang n 390, 392, 394

tangerine adj 439

tangibility n 3

tangible adj 3, 316

tangle v 61, 219

tangled adj 59

tanked adj 959

tanker n 273

tantalize v 509

tantamount adj 27

tap n 263, 276; v 260, 276, 406

taper n 423; v 203

tapering adj 253

taper to a point v 253

tapping n 407

tar n 356a

tardiness n 133, 275

tardy adj 133, 275

target n 620

tarn n 343

tarnish n 874; v 429, 653, 848, 874

tarnished adj 874

tarpaulin n 223

tarry v 110, 133

tarrying n 133

tart adj 397

tartness n 397

task n 676, 704; v 677, 688

taskmaster n 694, 739

taste n 390, 850

taste n 394, 465, 480, 578; v 298, 390, 394

taste bad v 395

tasteful adj 465, 578, 850

tastefully adv 850

taste good v 394

taste great v 394

tasteless adj 337, 391, 395, 579

tastelessness n 391

tastelessness n 395, 579

tastiness n 394

tasty adj 377, 390, 394

tattle v 588

tattler n 532

tattoo v 440

taunt v 856

taunts n 856

taut adj 43

tautological adj 104

tautology n 104

tawdriness n 851

tawdry adj 643, 851

tawny adj 433, 435

tax v 677, 688

teach v 537, 673

teacher n 540

teacher n 753

teaching n 537

team-work n 709

tear v 44, 173, 274

tearful adj 839

tear out v 301

tears n 411

tear to pieces v 44

tear up v 162

teasing n 377

teat n 250

technicality n 697

technique n 627

tedious adj 275, 841, 843

tedium n 688, 841

teem v 168

teeming adj 72, 102, 168

teem with v 102

teenage adj 131

teenage years n 131

teeter v 160, 275, 315

teetering adj 160

teetotaler n 953, 958

teetotalism n 958

telescope n 445

telethermometer n 389

tell v 85, 467, 527, 529, 594

teller n 801

telling n 594; adj 642

temper n 5, 7, 323, 820; v 174, 323, 324

temperament n 5, 176, 820

temperamental adj 901

temperance n 953

temperance n 174

temperate *adj* 174, 736, 953

temperateness *n* 174

temperature *n* 382

tempered *adj* 820

tempest *n* 173, 315, 349, 825

tempest in a teacup *n* 549

tempestuous *adj* 349

temple *n* 1000

temporal *adj* 111, 997

temporarily *adv* 111

temporary *adj* 111

tempt *v* 615, 675

temptation *n* 615

tempter *n* 978

tempt fate *v* 621

tempt fortune *v* 675

ten *n* 98

tenable *adj* 664

tenacious *adj* 46, 150, 327, 604, 604a

tenacity *n* 327

tenacity *n* 150, 604, 604a

tenancy *n* 777

tenant *n* 188, 779; *v* 186

tend *v* 176, 278, 472

tendencies *n* 5

tendency *n* 176

tendency *n* 177, 278, 472, 613

tender *n* 763; *v* 763; *adj* 324, 378, 428, 597, 740, 821, 822, 897, 906

tender age *n* 127

tender-hearted *adj* 906

tenderness *n* 378, 821, 822, 897, 906

tender years *n* 127

tending *adj* 176

tendril *n* 205, 248

tend toward *v* 278

tenet *n* 451, 484, 537, 983

tenor *n* 7, 26, 278, 516

tensile *adj* 325

tension *n* 159

tent *n* 223

tentative *adj* 675

tenuity *n* 322

tenuous *adj* 322

tenure *n* 777

tepid *adj* 382

tergiversation *n* 607

term *n* 71

term *n* 106, 108, 198, 200, 233, 562; *v* 564

terminal *adj* 67, 233

terminate *v* 67, 142, 729

termination *n* 67, 142, 233, 261, 729

terminology *n* 560, 562

terminus *n* 233

terms *n* 476, 770

terrain *n* 342

terrestrial *adj* 318, 342

terrible *adj* 846, 860

terribly *adv* 31

terrified *adj* 860

territorial *adj* 181, 342

territory *n* 181, 965

terror *n* 860

terror-stricken *adj* 860

terse *adj* 572

terseness *n* 572

tertiary *adj* 92

test *n* 463; *v* 463

testify *v* 467, 535

testimony *n* 467

testy *adj* 684, 901

tête-à-tête *n* 588

tether *v* 43

tetrad *n* 95

text *n* 22, 542, 591

textbook *n* 542

texture *n* 256, 329

textured *adj* 256

thank *v* 916

thankful *adj* 916

thankfulness *n* 916

thankless *adj* 917

thanklessness *n* 917

thanks *n* 916

that being the case *adv* 8

thatch *n* 223

that is to say *adv* 522

thaw *v* 335, 382, 384

thawing *n* 335

the all-merciful *n* 976

the all-powerful *n* 976

the almighty *n* 976

theater *n* 599, 728

theatrical *adj* 599, 855, 882

theatricals *n* 599

the cloth *n* 996

the common people *n* 876

the converse *n* 14

the drama *n* 599

the eternal *n* 976

theft *n* 788, 789, 791

the future *n* 121

the infinite *n* 976

the inverse *n* 14

theism *n* 983

the latest thing *n* 123

the lead *n* 62, 280

the like *n* 17

the lower classes *n* 876

thematic *adj* 454

theme *n* 413, 454, 595

then *adv* 119

thence *adv* 155

theologian *n* 983

theological *adj* 983

theologics *n* 983

theologue *n* 983

theology *n* 983

the open *n* 338

the opposite *n* 14

theorem *n* 514

theoretical *adj* 514

theorize *v* 155, 514

theory *n* 155, 453, 514

theosophical *adj* 983

throw in one's lot with *v* 709

throw in the towel *v* 624

throw off one's guard *v* 508

throw of the dice *n* 156

throw open *v* 260

throw out *v* 55, 297, 638

throw out of gear *v* 61

throw out of whack *v* 61

throw up *v* 297

thrust *n* 276, 284; *v* 276

thrust in *v* 300

thud *n* 406, 408a; *v* 408a

thug *n* 361

thumb *v* 379

thump *n* 276, 408a; *v* 276, 408a

thumper *n* 192

thumping *adj* 192

thunder *n* 404, 408; *v* 173, 404

thundering *adj* 192, 404

thunderousness *n* 404

thus *adv* 8

thus far *adv* 233

thus far and no further *adv* 233

thwack *n* 276; *v* 276

thwart *v* 706, 708

thwarted *adj* 732

tick *v* 407

ticket *v* 550

tickle the palate *v* 390, 394

tickle the tastebuds *v* 390

tickling *n* 380

ticklish *adj* 380, 704

tidal *adj* 348

tide *n* 348

tides *n* 341

tidiness *n* 652

tidings *n* 498, 532

tidy *adj* 58, 652

tidy up *v* 652

tie *n* 9, 11, 27, 45, 771; *v* 9, 43, 45, 770

tied *adj* 926

tier *n* 69, 204

tiered *adj* 204

ties of blood *n* 11

tie the hands *v* 158

tie the knot *v* 903

tie up *v* 342

tie up in knots *v* 158

tiff *n* 713

tight *adj* 43, 46; *adj* 261, 572, 819, 959

tighten *v* 572

tightness *n* 572

till *n* 802; *v* 371; *adv* 106

tillage *n* 371

till the soil *v* 371

tilt *n* 217, 306; *v* 217, 244, 306

tilted *adj* 217

tilt over *v* 218

tilt up *v* 307

timber *n* 413

timbre *n* 408

time *n* 106

time *n* 108; *v* 106

time-honored *adj* 124

time immemorial *n* 122

timeless *adj* 112

timelessness *n* 112

timeliness *n* 134, 684

timely *adj* 106, 132, 134

timeout *n* 106

timepiece *n* 114

timeserving *adj* 607

timetable *n* 114

time to come *n* 121

timeworn *adj* 124, 659

timid *adj* 605, 862, 881

timidity *n* 605, 862, 881

timorous *adj* 862, 881

tincture *n* 41, 428; *v* 41

tinge *n* 32, 41, 428; *v* 41, 428

tingle *v* 378, 380

tininess *n* 32, 193

tinsel *n* 851

tint *n* 26, 428; *v* 428

tinted *adj* 428

tintinnabulation *n* 408

tiny *adj* 32, 193

tippler *n* 959

tipsy *adj* 959

tiptop *adj* 210, 648

tirade *n* 582

tire *v* 688, 841, 869

tired *adj* 688, 841, 869

tiredness *n* 688

tired to death *adj* 688

tiresome *adj* 841

tissue *n* 329

tit for tat *n* 30

titillation *n* 377, 380

title *n* 877

title *n* 564, 747, 771

titled *adj* 875, 877

title page *n* 66

titter *n* 838; *v* 838

titular *adj* 564

to a certain degree *adv* 32

toady *n* 886, 935; *v* 886

to a large extent *adv* 31

to all appearance *adv* 448

to all intents and purposes *adv* 27, 52

to and fro *adv* 314

to arms *adv* 722

to a small extent *adv* 32

toast *v* 384

to blame *adj* 947

to boot *adv* 37

to come *adj* 121, 152

to crown all *adv* 33

tocsin *n* 669

toddler *n* 129

together *adj* 46, 502; *adv* 120

togetherness *n* 709, 714

together with *adv* 37, 88

togs *n* 225

toil *n* 686; *v* 682, 686

token *n* 505, 550

tolerable *adj* 32, 651, 736

tolerableness *n* 736

tolerance *n* 740, 760

tolerant *adj* 740, 760

tolerate *v* 738, 740, 760, 826

toleration *n* 738, 740

to little purpose *adv* 732

toll *v* 407

tomb *n* 363

tombstone *n* 363

tomcat *n* 373

tome *n* 590, 593

tomorrow *n* 121, 152; *adv* 121

tone *n* 7, 26, 159, 402, 428

tone color *n* 413

tone down *v* 429

tongue *n* 560

tongue-tied *adj* 581, 583

tonic *adj* 656

tonnage *n* 192

too *adv* 37

tool *n* 633

too late *adv* 133

too little *adj* 640

tools for pulverization *n* 330

too many *n* 641

too much *n* 641

to one's heart's content *adv* 831

too soon *adv* 132

tooth *n* 257

toothed *adj* 257

top *n* 206, 210, 223, 261; *v* 33, 210; *adj* 210

topic *n* 454

topical *adj* 183, 454

topmost *adj* 210

topographical *adj* 183

topography *n* 183

topple *v* 28, 162, 306

topsy-turvy *adj* 59, 218

torch *n* 423

to reason *v* 476

torment *n* 378, 828; *v* 378, 828, 830

tornado *n* 312, 315, 349

torpid *adj* 172, 683

torpor *n* 172, 683

torrent *n* 348

torrid *adj* 382

tortuous *adj* 248

torture *n* 378, 828, 982; *v* 378, 619, 828, 830, 972

torturous *adj* 378

to some degree *adv* 32

to some extent *adv* 26

toss *n* 284; *v* 284, 314, 315

tossup *n* 156

to substitute for *v* 634

tot *n* 129

total *n* 50, 84; *v* 37; *adj* 31, 50

total abstinence *n* 955

total destruction *n* 2

total eclipse *n* 421

totality *n* 50, 52

totally *adv* 31, 50, 52

to the eye *adv* 448

to the four winds *adv* 180

to the letter *adv* 19

to the minute *adv* 132

to the point *adj* 494

to the quick *adv* 375

totter *v* 160, 275, 314, 315, 659, 665

tottering *adj* 160

touch *n* 379

touch *n* 41, 375, 569; *v* 9, 197, 199, 375, 379, 824

touchable *adj* 316

touched *adj* 503, 821, 914

touching *n* 199; *adj* 199

touch on *v* 516

touchstone *n* 211

touchy *adj* 684, 901

tough *adj* 46, 323, 327

toughness *n* 327

tour *n* 266, 302; *v* 266

tourist *n* 268

tourniquet *n* 263

tow *v* 285

towage *n* 285

toward *adv* 278

tower *v* 31, 206, 305

towering *adj* 31, 192, 206

towing *n* 285

townsman *n* 188

toxic *adj* 657

trace *n* 551; *v* 230, 554

tracery *n* 219

trace to *v* 155

track *n* 627

tract *n* 181, 593, 595

tractability *n* 743

tractable *adj* 324, 705, 743

tractile *adj* 285, 324

tractility *n* 324

traction *n* 285

trade *n* 148, 625, 794, 796; *v* 148, 794, 796

trader *n* 797

tradesman *n* 797

trade wind *n* 349

tradition *n* 124

traditional *adj* 124, 983a

traffic *n* 794; *v* 794

tragedy *n* 619

tragic *adj* 619, 830

trail *n* 65; *v* 214, 275, 285, 286, 281

train *n* 65, 69, 214, 235, 271, 272, 281; *v* 285, 370, 537, 673

trained *adj* 698

training *n* 673

traipse *v* 275

trait *n* 448, 550

traitor *n* 742

trammel *v* 706

tramp *n* 268

trample on *v* 739

trample out *v* 162

trample upon *v* 649

trance *n* 993

tranquil *adj* 174, 265, 721

tranquilization *n* 174

tranquilize *v* 265, 723

tranquillity *n* 265, 721

transact *v* 680, 692, 794

transaction *n* 151, 625, 794, 796

transcend *v* 31, 33, 303, 648, 650

transcendence *n* 33, 650

transcendent *adj* 33

transcribe *v* 590

transcript *n* 21

transcription *n* 21

transfer *n* 783

transfer *n* 21, 270; *v* 185, 270, 783

transferable *adj* 270, 783

transference *n* 270

transference *n* 140, 783

transfiguration *n* 140

transfigure *v* 140

transform *v* 140

transformable *adj* 140, 149

transformation *n* 140, 144

transfuse *v* 41

transfusion *n* 41

transgress *n* 303, 742, 773, 945

transgression *n* 303, 773, 927

transience *n* 111

transient *adj* 111, 264

transit *n* 144, 270

transition *n* 144, 270

transitional *adj* 264

transitoriness *n* 111

transitory *adj* 111

translate *v* 522

translation *n* 522

translator *n* 524

translucent *adj* 425

transluscence *n* 425

transmissible *adj* 270

transmission *n* 270, 302, 783

transmissive *adj* 783

transmit *v* 270, 783

transmit light *v* 425

transmittable *adj* 270

transmutable *adj* 144

transmutation *n* 140, 144

transmute *v* 140

transparence *n* 425

transparency *n* 425

transparent *adj* 337, 425, 518

transpire *v* 532

transplant *v* 270

transplantation *n* 270

transport *n* 270, 827; *v* 270, 829

transportable *adj* 270

transportation *n* 272

transporter *n* 271

transporting *adj* 977

transposal *n* 218

transpose *v* 148, 185, 218, 270

transposition *n* 140, 148, 185, 218, 270

transverse *adj* 217, 219

trap *n* 530, 545, 667

trappings *n* 225

trash *n* 643

trashy *adj* 209, 575, 643

travail *n* 686

travel *n* 266; *v* 266

traveler *n* 268

traveling *n* 266; *adj* 264, 266

traverse *v* 266, 302

travesty *n* 21, 523; *v* 19, 523

trawler *n* 273

treacherous *adj* 544

treachery *n* 545

tread *n* 264

tread down *v* 749

tread upon *v* 649

treasure *n* 648; *v* 991

treasurer *n* 801

treasury *n* 802

treat *v* 595, 829

treatise *n* 593, 595

treatment *n* 662

treat well *v* 906

treaty *n* 23, 721, 769

treble *v* 93; *adj* 93

trebly *adv* 93

tree *n* 367

trellis *n* 219

tremble *v* 149, 160, 315, 383

tremendously *adv* 31

tremor *n* 315

tremulous *adj* 149, 315

trench *n* 259

trenchant *adj* 171, 253, 572, 574, 642

trend *n* 176, 278, 516

trendiness *n* 123

trendy *adj* 123

trepidation *n* 860

trespass *n* 303; *v* 303, 945

trestle *n* 215

triad *n* 92

trial *n* 463, 675, 686, 828, 830, 969

triality *n* 92

tribe *n* 72, 75

tribunal *n* 966

tributary *n* 348; *adj* 784

trice *n* 113

trick *n* 545; *v* 545

trickle *n* 348; *v* 295, 348

trickly *adj* 348

tricky *adj* 545, 702

trifle *n* 32, 451, 643; *v* 499

trifling *n* 499, 643; *adj* 4, 32, 477, 499, 643, 880

triform *adj* 92

trill *v* 407

trim *n* 231, 240; *v* 27, 231; *adj* 652

trimming *n* 231

trinity *n* 92

trio *n* 92, 415, 416

trip *n* 266, 302, 306; *v* 306, 309

tripartition *n* 94

triple *v* 93; *adj* 93

triplet *n* 92

triplicate *adj* 93

triplication *n* 93

triplicity *n* 93

tripling *n* 93

triply *adv* 93

trip the light fantastic toe *v* 309

trip up *v* 495

trisect *v* 94

trisection *n* 94

trite *adj* 496, 598, 613

triumph *n* 731, 733, 838; *v* 731, 838

triumphant *adj* 731, 838, 884

trivial *adj* 32, 209, 499, 517, 643, 880

triviality *n* 32, 209, 643, 736, 880

troll *n* 980

trollop *n* 962

troop *n* 72

trophy *n* 733

tropical *adj* 382

troubadour *n* 597

trouble *n* 59, 686, 704, 735, 828, 830; *v* 61, 828, 830

troublemaker *n* 913

trouble oneself about *v* 682

troublesome *adj* 59, 704, 830

trough *n* 252, 259, 350

trove *n* 480a

truant *n* 623

truce *n* 142, 721, 723

truck *n* 271, 272; *v* 264

trudge *v* 275

true *adj* 1, 17, 246, 246, 494, 543, 648, 772, 922, 604

true faith *n* 983a

truelove *n* 897

true to life *adj* 17

truism *n* 496

truistic *adj* 496

truly *adv* 31

trump card *n* 731

trumped up *adj* 546

trumpery *n* 643

truncate *v* 201, 241

truncation *n* 241

trunk *n* 50

truss *n* 215

trust *n* 484, 507, 805, 858; *v* 858

trusted *adj* 484

trustee *n* 758, 801

trusting *adj* 484, 486, 547

trustworthy *adj* 474, 484, 543, 664

trusty *adj* 474

truth *n* 494

truth *n* 1, 474, 543, 922, 983a

truthful *adj* 494, 543

truthfulness *n* 543

try *v* 463, 480, 675, 677

try a case *n* 967

trying *adj* 841

tube *n* 350, 351

tubed instruments *n* 417

tuck *n* 258; *v* 258

tuck in *v* 300

tug *n* 285; *v* 285

tugboat *n* 273

tumble *n* 306; *v* 162, 306, 315

tumid *adj* 194

tumult *n* 59, 315, 825

tumultuous *adj* 59, 173, 404, 825

tundra *n* 344

tune *n* 413, 415; *v* 413

tuned out *adj* 452

tuneful *adj* 413, 597

tunefulness *n* 413

tuneless *adj* 414

tune out *v* 452

tunnel *n* 350; *v* 252, 260

turbulence *n* 173, 315

turbulent *adj* 59, 173, 825

turf *n* 388

turgid *adj* 194, 577, 579

turgidity *n* 579

turkey *n* 493

turmoil *n* 59, 173, 315

turn *n* 7, 134, 138, 140, 176, 245, 311, 621,

698; *v* 49, 140, 245, 248, 279, 311, 312

turn about *v* 218

turn a circle *v* 311

turn a deaf ear to *v* 419

turn and turn about *adv* 148

turn around *v* 311

turn aside *v* 140, 279, 616

turn away *v* 297

turn away from *v* 623

turn back *v* 145, 283

turncoat *n* 607

turn color *v* 434, 435

turn down *v* 764

turned *adj* 397

turned off *adj* 452

turning *n* 311

turning point *n* 8, 67, 134, 145, 153, 210, 233

turn into *v* 144

turn off the brain *v* 452

turn of speech *n* 566

turn of the tide *n* 145, 218

turn one's hand to *v* 625

turn on the juice *v* 274

turn out *v* 151, 297

turn over *v* 218, 270, 784

turn pale *v* 429

turn tail *v* 623

turn the scale *v* 28

turn the stomach *v* 395

turn the tide *v* 28, 145

turn to dust *v* 360

turn to profit *v* 775

turn topsy-turvy *v* 61, 218

turn up *v* 151, 156, 446

turn upside down *v* 14, 61

turquoise *adj* 438

tutelage *n* 537, 539, 749

tutor *n* 540, 753; *v* 537

tutorship *n* 537

twaddle *n* 584

twain *adj* 89

twang *n* 402, 408

tweak *v* 378

twelve *n* 98

twenty *n* 98

twenty-five *n* 98

twerp *n* 493

twice *adv* 90

twilight *n* 126

twin *n* 17; *adj* 17, 88, 89, 90

twine *v* 219, 248

twine round *v* 227

twinge *n* 378, 828; *v* 378

twinkle *v* 113, 422

twinkling *n* 113

twins *n* 89

twirl *n* 248; *v* 248, 311, 312

twist *n* 243, 248, 503; *v* 43, 219, 243, 248, 279, 311

twisted *adj* 248

twister *n* 315, 349

twist the meaning *v* 523

twit *v* 856

twitch *n* 378; *v* 378

twitter *n* 315; *v* 315, 412

two *n* 89; *adj* 89

two-faced *adj* 544

twofold division *n* 91

two or more *n* 100

two-sided *adj* 89

type *n* 5, 17, 22, 75, 550, 591; *v* 240

typical *adj* 82, 550

typify *v* 550

typographical *adj* 591

typography *n* 591

tyrannical *adj* 739

tyrannize *v* 739

tyrant *n* 739

U

ubiquity *n* 186

ubiquitous *adj* 186

ugliness *n* 846

ugliness *n* 243

ugly *adj* 846

ukase *n* 741

ulterior *adj* 121

ulterior motive *n* 615

ultimate *adj* 67

ultimately *adv* 117, 121, 133

ululation *n* 412

umbra *n* 421

umbrage *n* 900

umbrageous *adj* 421, 422

umbrella *n* 223, 424

umpire *n* 967; *v* 174

unable *adj* 158, 699

unaccompanied *adj* 87

unaccountable *adj* 964

unaccustomed *adj* 614

unachievable *adj* 471

unacquaintance *n* 491

unadorned *adj* 576, 849

unadulterated *adj* 42, 960

unadvisable *adj* 647

unaffected *adj* 578, 823, 849

unallied *adj* 10

unalterability *n* 141

unalterable *adj* 150

unanimity *n* 23, 709

unanimously *adv* 709, 714

unanswerable *adj* 964

unanticipated *adj* 508

unapplied *adj* 678

unapproachable *adj* 196

unappropriate *adj* 923

unartificial *adj* 703
unassailable *adj* 664
unassuming *adj* 849, 879, 881
unassured *adj* 475
unatoned *adj* 951
unattached *adj* 44
unattended *adj* 87
unattended to *adj* 460
unauthorized *adj* 925, 964
unavailing *adj* 645
unavoidability *n* 601
unavoidable *adj* 601, 744
unavoidableness *n* 601
unaware *adj* 508, 823
unawareness *n* 491
unbearable *adj* 830
unbegotten *adj* 2
unbeliever *n* 485
unbelieving *adj* 485, 487, 989
unbend *v* 246, 687
unbent *adj* 246
unbiased *adj* 942
unblemished *adj* 650
unborn *adj* 2
unbound *adj* 748, 927a
unbridled *adj* 748
unbroken *adj* 50, 69, 729
uncanny *adj* 980
uncanonical *adj* 984
uncared for *adj* 460
uncaring *adj* 823
unceasing *adj* 104, 112
uncertain *adj* 139, 475, 485, 520, 605, 704
uncertainty *n* 475
uncertainty *n* 111, 139, 485, 519, 520, 605
unchained *adj* 748
unchangeable *adj* 5, 150
unchangeableness *n* 150

unchanged *adj* 16, 141
unchanging *adj* 16, 141, 150
unchartered *adj* 964
unchaste *adj* 961
unchecked *adj* 748
uncivil *adj* 895, 911, 929
uncivilized *adj* 876
unclad *adj* 226
unclean *adj* 653, 961
uncleanness *n* 653
uncleanness *n* 961
unclear *adj* 426
unclose *v* 260
unclosed *adj* 260
unclouded *adj* 420
uncolored *adj* 429
uncomfortable *adj* 378, 828
uncommon *adj* 83, 137
uncommon *adv* 31
uncommunicative *adj* 528, 585
uncommunicativeness *n* 585
uncompleted *adj* 53
uncompliant *adj* 742
uncomplicate *v* 849
uncompromising *adj* 82
unconceived *adj* 2
unconcern *n* 456, 458, 866
unconcerned *adj* 866
unconditional *adj* 52, 748
unconfined *adj* 748
unconformable *adj* 83
unconformity *n* 83
uncongenial *adj* 24
unconnected *adj* 10, 44, 70
unconquerable *adj* 159
unconscious *adj* 823
unconsciousness *n* 376, 491
unconsolidated *adj* 47

unconstitutional *adj* 964
unconstrained *adj* 748
uncontaminated *adj* 960
uncontrite *adj* 951
uncontrollability *n* 606
uncontrollable *adj* 173, 606, 825
uncontrolled *adj* 748, 825
unconventional *adj* 83
unconventionality *n* 83
uncopied *adj* 20
uncorroborative *adj* 468
uncorrupted *adj* 960
uncouth *adj* 579
uncover *v* 226, 260, 480a, 529
uncovered *adj* 260
uncovering *n* 529
uncreated *adj* 2
unctuosity *n* 355
unctuous *adj* 355
unctuousness *n* 355
uncurbed *adj* 748
uncurl *v* 246
uncurved *adj* 246
uncustomary *adj* 83
undated *adj* 115
undecided *adj* 475
undefiled *adj* 960
undefined *adj* 447
undeniable *adj* 474
undependability *n* 475
undependable *adj* 475
under *adv* 34, 207
under a cloud *adj* 735
underage *adj* 127
under consideration *adv* 454
under control *adj* 749
undercover *adj* 528
undercurrent *n* 526
undercut *v* 179
underdeveloped *adj* 193
underestimate *v* 481, 483

underestimated *adj* 483

underestimating *adj* 483

underestimation *n* 483

underfoot *adv* 207

undergo *v* 151

undergo pain *v* 378

underground *adv* 207

underlie *v* 207, 526

underline *v* 550, 642

undermine *v* 179, 659

undermost *adj* 211

underneath *adv* 207

under obligation *adj* 926

under one's nose *adj* 446

under one's very nose *adv* 715

under protest *adv* 603

underrate *v* 483

under restraint *adj* 751

underscore *v* 550, 642

undersized *adj* 193

understand *v* 450, 490, 498, 518, 522

understandable *adj* 518

understanding *n* 23, 450, 480, 490, 498, 714, 822, 842; *adj* 498, 822

understand one another *v* 714

understructure *n* 211

understudy *n* 634

undertake *v* 622, 625, 676, 768

undertaking *n* 676

undertaking *n* 620, 622, 625, 768

under the circumstances *adv* 8

under the conditions *adv* 8

under the head of *adv* 9

under the pretense of *adv* 617

under the stars *adv* 338

under the sun *adv* 180, 318

under the weather *adj* 655

undertone *n* 405

undervaluation *n* 483

undervalue *v* 483

under way *adv* 264

under wraps *adj* 754

underwrite *v* 768, 771

undesirability *n* 647

undesirable *adj* 830

undetermined *adj* 475

undeviating *adj* 278

undevout *adj* 989

undiminished *adj* 50

undirected *adj* 279

undiscerning *adj* 442

undiscriminating *adj* 465a

undisturbed *adj* 265

undiversified *adj* 16

undivided *adj* 50, 52

undo *v* 145, 162, 179

undone *adj* 732

undoubtedly *adv* 474

undraped *adj* 226

undress *n* 226

undress *v* 226

undressed *adj* 226

undulate *v* 248, 314

undulating *adj* 248

undulation *n* 248, 314

undulatory *adj* 314

undutiful *adj* 927

unearth *v* 363, 480a

unearthly *adj* 317, 976, 980, 981

uneasiness *n* 828, 832

uneasy *adj* 828, 832

uneducated *adj* 491

unembellished *adj* 849

unemotional *adj* 383

unemployed *adj* 678

unendurable *adj* 830, 982

unenlightened *adj* 491

unenlightenment *n* 491

unentitled *adj* 925

unequal *adj* 15, 28

unequaled *adj* 18, 33

unequivocal *adj* 31, 246, 570

unequivocally *adv* 31

unessential *adj* 643

unestablished *adj* 185

uneven *adj* 16a, 28, 243, 256

unevenness *n* 16a, 28

uneventful *adj* 643

unexciting *adj* 174

unexpected *adj* 132, 508

unexpectedly *adv* 132, 508

unfaded *adj* 428

unfading *adj* 112

unfailing *adj* 474

unfaithful *adj* 544

unfashioned *adj* 241

unfathomable *adj* 208, 519

unfathomable space *n* 208

unfathomed *adj* 208

unfavorable *adj* 135, 708, 735

unfeasibility *n* 471

unfeasible *adj* 471, 704

unfed *adj* 956

unfeeling *adj* 381, 383

unfetter *v* 750

unfettered *adj* 748

unfinished *adj* 53, 730

unfit *adj* 158, 647, 699, 923

unfitness *n* 647

unfitted *adj* 158

unfixed *adj* 149, 475

unfocused *adj* 447

unfold *v* 246, 313

unfolding *n* 313
unforeseen *adj* 508
unforeseen occurrence *n* 508
unforgettable *adj* 505
unforgiving *adj* 919
unforgotten *adj* 505
unformed *adj* 241
unfortunate *adj* 135, 735
unfounded *adj* 546
unfriendliness *n* 889
unfriendly *adj* 708, 889
unfrozen *adj* 382
unfruitful *adj* 169
unfruitfulness *n* 169, 645
unfulfillment *n* 509
unfurl *v* 313
ungenerous *adj* 32, 819
ungentlemanly *adj* 895
ungodliness *n* 989
ungodly *adj* 989
ungovernable *adj* 173, 825
ungoverned *adj* 748
ungraceful *adj* 579
ungracious *adj* 895
ungrammatical *adj* 568
ungrammatical usage *n* 568
ungrateful *adj* 917
ungrounded *adj* 4
unguarded *adj* 460
unguent *n* 356
unhallowed *adj* 989
unhandy *adj* 699
unhappy *adj* 828, 837
unharmonious *adj* 410
unhealthiness *n* 657
unhealthy *adj* 655, 657
unheard of *adj* 137, 508
unheeded *adj* 460
unheedful *adj* 452
unheeding *adj* 419, 458

unhewn *adj* 674
unhindered *adj* 748
unhinge *v* 61
unhinged *adj* 173, 503
unhip *adj* 246
unholy *adj* 989
unhoused *adj* 185
unhurried *adj* 275
unhurt *adj* 670
unification *n* 48, 87
unified *adj* 46, 48
uniform *v* 225; *adj* 16, 42, 58, 80, 242
uniformity *n* 16
uniformity *n* 17, 23, 58, 80, 87, 150, 242
uniformly *adv* 16, 82
uniforms *n* 225
unimaginable *adj* 471
unimaginative *adj* 598, 843
unimitated *adj* 20
unimpaired *adj* 50, 670
unimpeachable *adj* 474
unimportance *n* 643
unimportance *n* 32, 175a
unimportant *adj* 32, 34, 643, 736
unimpressionable *adj* 823
unimproved *adj* 659
uninfluential *adj* 175a
uninformed *adj* 491
uninjured *adj* 670
uninquiring *adj* 456
uninquisitive *adj* 456
uninstructed *adj* 491
unintellectual *adj* 450a
unintelligent *adj* 450a
unintelligibility *n* 519
unintelligibility *n* 533, 571
unintelligible *adj* 519, 571
unintentional *adj* 621
unintentionally *adv* 621

uninterested *adj* 456, 841
uninteresting *adj* 843
uninterrupted *adj* 69, 112, 143
unintoxicated *adj* 958
union *n* 23, 43, 46, 48, 178, 709, 714, 903
unique *adj* 18, 20, 79, 83, 87, 870
uniqueness *n* 18, 20, 123
unison *n* 87, 714
unite *v* 41, 43, 48, 72, 87, 178, 290, 709, 712
united *adj* 46, 903
uniting *n* 37
unity *n* 87
unity *n* 13, 23, 50, 52, 714
universal *adj* 78
universality *n* 78
universalize *v* 78
universe *n* 180, 318
university *n* 542
unjust *adj* 923
unkempt *adj* 653
unknown *n* 233; *adj* 533
unlawful *adj* 964
unlawfulness *n* 923, 964
unlearn *v* 506
unlearnedness *n* 491
unless *adv* 8, 83
unlettered *adj* 491
unlicensed *adj* 964
unlike *adj* 15, 18
unlikelihood *n* 473
unlikely *adj* 473
unlikeness *n* 18
unlimited *adj* 31, 104, 180, 748
unlimited space *n* 180
unload *v* 185
unlooked for *adj* 508
unlovely *adj* 846

unlucky *adj* 135, 735
unmake *v* 145
unman *v* 158
unmanageable *adj* 704
unmarked *adj* 447
unmarried *adj* 904
unmarried man *n* 904
unmarried woman *n* 904
unmask *v* 529, 529
unmatched *adj* 15, 18, 20
unmeaningness *n* 517
unmelodious *adj* 414
unmerciful *adj* 914a
unmindful *adj* 452, 458, 460, 917
unmindfulness *n* 458
unmistakable *adj* 525
unmitigated *adj* 52
unmixed *adj* 42, 960
unmoved *adj* 265, 823
unmoving *adj* 172
unmusical *adj* 410, 414
unmuzzled *adj* 748
unnatural *adj* 83, 855
unnaturalness *n* 855
unnecessary *adj* 641
unnerve *v* 158, 160
unnerved *adj* 160
unnoticed *adj* 460
unobservant *adj* 458
unobserved *adj* 460
unobstructed *adj* 748
unobtainable *adj* 471
unobtrusive *adj* 881
unoccupied *adj* 452
unopened *adj* 261
unorthodox *adj* 984
unorthodoxy *n* 984
unostentatious *adj* 881
unpaid *adj* 806
unpalatable *adj* 395, 830
unparalleled *adj* 20, 33
unperceptive *adj* 376

unperformable *adj* 471
unpersuasive *adj* 175a
unpierced *adj* 261
unplaced *adj* 185
unpleasant *adj* 395, 830, 846
unpoetic *adj* 598
unpointed *adj* 254
unpolished *adj* 256
unprecedented *adj* 18, 137
unpredictability *n* 139
unpredictable *adj* 139, 475
unprejudiced *adj* 942
unprepared *adj* 674
unpreparedness *n* 674
unpretentious *adj* 849, 879, 881
unprized *adj* 483
unproductive *adj* 169
unproductiveness *n* 169
unprofitable *adj* 169, 647
unprofitableness *n* 169
unpropitious *adj* 135
unprosperous *adj* 735
unpunctual *adj* 133, 135
unqualified *adj* 52, 158
unquestionable *adj* 474
unquestionableness *n* 474
unquestioned *adj* 474
unquiet *adj* 264
unrational *adj* 450a
unravel *v* 60, 246, 522, 705
unreadiness *n* 674
unready *adj* 674
unreal *adj* 2, 317, 515
unreasonable *adj* 471, 497, 499, 608, 814
unrecorded *adj* 552
unrefined *adj* 851
unreflective *adj* 452

unrelated *adj* 10
unreliability *n* 475
unreliable *adj* 149, 475
unremedial *adj* 859
unremembered *adj* 506
unrepentant *adj* 951
unrepented *adj* 951
unrepenting *adj* 951
unreserved *adj* 525
unresponsive *adj* 376, 383
unresponsiveness *n* 376
unrest *n* 149, 264
unrestricted *adj* 748
unrevealed *adj* 533
unrightful *adj* 925
unrightfulness *n* 925
unripe *adj* 123, 674
unrivaled *adj* 33
unroll *v* 313
unruffled *adj* 174, 265, 826
unruliness *n* 742
unruly *adj* 606, 742
unsafe *adj* 475, 665
unsavoriness *n* 395
unsavoriness *n* 391, 392
unsavory *adj* 392, 395, 874
unscoured *adj* 653
unscriptural *adj* 984
unscrupulous *adj* 940
unseasonable *adj* 135
unseasonableness *n* 135
unseasoned *adj* 435
unseeing *adj* 442
unseemly *adj* 647, 846
unseen *adj* 447
unselfish *adj* 906, 942
unselfishness *n* 906, 942
unserviceable *adj* 645
unsettle *v* 61, 185
unsettled *adj* 149, 185, 475, 503
unshackled *adj* 748
unshaped *adj* 241

upstairs *n* 450

up to *adj* 157; *adv* 106

up to a point *adv* 26

up-to-date *adj* 123

up to the mark *adj* 27, 639

up to this time *adv* 122

upturn *v* 218

upwards of *adj* 100

urbane *adj* 894

urchin *n* 980

urge *v* 173, 276, 684

urgency *n* 642, 684

urgent *adj* 630, 642

urging *n* 695

urinate *v* 299

urination *n* 299

urn *n* 363

usage *n* 567, 613, 677, 998

use *n* 677

use *n* 644; *v* 677, 788

used up *adj* 158, 659

useful *adj* 176, 618, 631, 644, 677

usefulness *n* 644, 677

useless *adj* 169, 499, 643, 645, 647, 732, 880

uselessness *n* 645

use the occasion *v* 134

use up *v* 677

usher *v* 296

usher in *v* 62, 66, 280

usual *adj* 82, 613

usurer *n* 805, 819

usurious *adj* 819

usurp *v* 789

usurper *n* 925

utensil *n* 633

utilitarian *adj* 677

utility *n* 644

utility *n* 646, 677

utilization *n* 677

utilize *v* 677

utmost *adj* 33

utter *v* 580, 582; *adj* 31

utterance *n* 580, 985

utterly *adv* 52

uttermost *adj* 31

V

vacancy *n* 187, 209, 499

vacancy of mind *n* 452

vacant *adj* 4, 187, 209, 452, 499

vacate *v* 185, 293

vacation *n* 685, 687

vacationer *n* 268

vacillate *v* 149, 314, 605

vacillating *adj* 149

vacillation *n* 149, 314, 485, 605

vacuity *n* 187, 452

vacuous *adj* 4, 187, 209

vacuum *n* 187

vagabond *n* 268

vagabondism *n* 266

vagary *n* 608

vagrant *n* 268; *adj* 266

vague *adj* 475, 477, 517, 571

vagueness *n* 475, 519, 571

vain *adj* 158, 645, 878, 880

vain expectation *n* 509

vainglorious *adj* 884, 880

vainglory *n* 878

vale *n* 252

valediction *n* 293

valid *adj* 737

validity *n* 157

valley *n* 252, 259

valor *n* 861

valorous *adj* 861

valuable *adj* 644, 648

valuation *n* 466, 812

value *n* 644, 648, 812, 815; *v* 466, 480, 642, 931

valueless *adj* 645

value received *n* 810

valve *n* 263, 350

vampire *n* 980

van *n* 280

vanguard *n* 234, 280

vanish *v* 4, 111, 360, 449

vanished *adj* 449

vanishing point *n* 193

vanity *n* 880

vanity *n* 878

vantage ground *n* 175

vapid *adj* 337, 391, 575, 843

vapor *n* 353

vaporization *n* 336

vaporize *v* 336

vaporous *adj* 334, 336

vaporousness *n* 334

vapory *adj* 336

variability *n* 475

variable *adj* 140, 149, 475

variance *n* 15, 24, 291, 713

variant *adj* 15

variation *n* 20a

variation *n* 15, 83, 140

varied *adj* 15, 16a, 20a

variegate *v* 440

variegated *adj* 41, 440

variegation *n* 440

variety *n* 75, 81

various *adj* 15, 102

varnish *n* 223, 356a; *v* 356a

vary *v* 15, 18, 20a, 140, 149, 291, 314

vast *adj* 31, 104, 180, 192

vastness *n* 31, 105

vault *n* 245, 309, 318, 363, 802; *v* 309

vaulted *adj* 245

vaunt *v* 884

veer *v* 140, 279

vegetable *n* 367

vegetable *adj* 367
vegetable kingdom *n* 367
vegetable life *n* 365
vegetable oil *n* 356
vegetable physiology *n* 369
vegetal *adj* 367
vegetarian *n* 953
vegetate *v* 367
vegetation *n* 365
vegetative *adj* 365, 367
vehemence *n* 173, 825
vehement *adj* 173, 382, 574, 825
vehicle *n* 272
vehicle *n* 271, 631
veil *n* 424, 530; *v* 424, 528
veiled *adj* 447, 526
veiling *n* 528
vein *n* 176, 205, 602
veined *adj* 440
velocity *n* 274
velocity *n* 264
velvety *adj* 255, 256
venal *adj* 211, 819
venality *n* 819
vend *v* 796
vendible *adj* 796
vendition *n* 796
vendor *n* 796
veneer *n* 223; *v* 204, 223
venerable *adj* 124, 128, 928
venerate *v* 860, 928, 987
veneration *n* 860, 928, 987
vengeance *n* 718, 919
vengeful *adj* 718, 919
vengefulness *n* 919
venom *n* 663, 907
venomous *adj* 649, 657, 663, 907
vent *n* 260, 351

ventilate *v* 338, 349, 652
ventilation *n* 338
venture *n* 621, 675, 676; *v* 621, 665, 675, 861
venturesome *adj* 621, 675
veracious *adj* 494, 543
veracity *n* 543
veracity *n* 494
verbal *adj* 562
verbal interchange *n* 588
verbiage *n* 573
verbose *adj* 573, 584, 641
verbosity *n* 573, 584, 641
verdant *adj* 367, 435
verdict *n* 480, 969
verdure *n* 367, 435
verdurous *adj* 435
verge *n* 231, 233; *v* 176, 278
verification *n* 478
verify *v* 478
veritable *adj* 494
verity *n* 494
vermilion *adj* 434
vernacular *n* 560; *adj* 560
versatile *adj* 149
versatility *n* 149
verse *n* 590, 597
versification *n* 597
versifier *n* 597
versify *v* 597
versus *adv* 708
vertex *n* 210
vertical *adj* 212, 246
verticality *n* 212
vertically *adv* 212
verve *n* 159, 515, 574
very *adv* 31
very best *adj* 648
very much *adv* 31

vespers *n* 126
vessel *n* 191, 273
vestal virgin *n* 960
vestige *n* 551
vestments *n* 999
veteran *n* 130
veteran *n* 700
veterinary science *n* 370
veto *v* 761
vex *v* 828, 830
vexation *n* 828, 830, 835
vexatious *adj* 830, 901a
vibes *n* 314
vibrate *v* 314
vibration *n* 138, 314, 408
vibrato *n* 408
vice *n* 945
vice *n* 649, 923
vice versa *adv* 148
vicinity *n* 186, 197
vicious *adj* 907, 945
vicissitude *n* 111, 149
victimize *v* 649
victorious *adj* 731
victory *n* 731
vie *v* 648, 720
view *n* 441, 448, 453, 484, 620; *v* 441
viewpoint *n* 441
vigilance *n* 459, 682, 864, 920
vigilant *adj* 459, 507, 682, 864, 920
viginal *adj* 960
vignette *n* 594
vigor *n* 574
vigor *n* 157, 159, 171, 359, 364, 604, 654, 682
vigorous *adj* 159, 171, 359, 574, 654
vile *adj* 207, 211, 395, 649, 830, 846, 874, 898, 930

vilification *n* 934

vilify *v* 934

vilifying *adj* 934

villager *n* 188

villain *n* 941, 949

villainous *adj* 649

vinculum *n* 45

vindicate *v* 717, 919, 937

vindicated *adj* 937

vindicating *adj* 937

vindication *n* 937

vindication *n* 717

vindicator *n* 919, 937

vindictive *adj* 919

vindictiveness *n* 919

vinegariness *n* 397

vinegary *adj* 397

vintage *adj* 124

violate *v* 742, 773, 927

violate the law *v* 964

violation *n* 773, 927

violation of custom *n* 83

violence *n* 173

violence *n* 825

violent *adj* 59, 173, 382, 825

violently *adv* 31, 173

violet *adj* 437

virgin *n* 904, 960; *adj* 66, 123

virginal *adj* 123, 946

virginity *n* 960

virility *n* 159

virtually *adv* 5

virtue *n* 944

virtue *n* 648, 922, 939, 946, 960

virtuous *adj* 881, 939, 944, 946, 960

virtuousness *n* 944, 946

virulence *n* 649

virulent *adj* 649, 657

virus *n* 663

visage *n* 448

viscid *adj* 352

viscosity *n* 352

viscous *adj* 327, 352

visibility *n* 446

visible *adj* 446, 525

vision *n* 441

vision *n* 443, 515, 980

visionary *n* 504; *adj* 2, 4, 441, 515

visit often *v* 136

visor *n* 530

vista *n* 448

visual *adj* 441

vital *adj* 359, 642

vital flame *n* 359

vitality *n* 159, 359, 364, 654

vitalize *v* 359

vital spark *n* 359

vitiate *v* 659

vivacious *adj* 359, 515, 682, 829, 836

vivacity *n* 359, 515, 682, 836

vivid *adj* 171, 375, 420, 428, 505

vivify *v* 159, 359

vocabulary 562

vocal *adj* 415, 416, 580

vocal group *n* 416

vocalist *n* 416

vocality *n* 580

vocalization *n* 580

vocalize *v* 416, 566, 580

vocal music *n* 415

vocation *n* 625

vociferate *v* 411

vociferation *n* 411

vociferous *adj* 404, 411

vociferousness *n* 404

vogue *n* 613, 852

voice *n* 580

voice *n* 402; *v* 566, 580, 582

voiceless *adj* 581, 583

void *n* 2, 4, 187; *v* 2, 297, 756; *adj* 2, 187

volatile *adj* 149, 320, 336

volatility *n* 149, 320, 334

volcanic *adj* 173, 384, 825

volition *n* 600

volitional *adj* 600

volubility *n* 584

voluble *adj* 334, 584

volume *n* 25, 31, 102, 192, 590, 593

voluminous *adj* 192

voluntarily *adv* 600

voluntary *adj* 600

volunteer *v* 676

voluptuary *n* 954a, 962

voluptuous *adj* 377, 829

voluptuousness *n* 827

vomit *v* 297

voodoo *n* 993

voracious *adj* 957

voracity *n* 957

vortex *n* 312, 315, 348

voucher *n* 807

vow *n* 768

vowel *n* 561

voyage *n* 267, 302

voyager *n* 268

V-shaped *adj* 244

vulgar *adj* 579, 851, 876, 895

vulgarity *n* 851

vulgarity *n* 579, 895

vulgarize *v* 851

vulnerability *n* 177

W

wad *v* 224

wadding *n* 224, 263

waddle *v* 275

wade through *v* 539

waft *v* 320, 349

wag *n* 844

wager *n* 621; *v* 621

wages *n* 775, 812

wage war *v* 722

waggle *v* 315

wagon *n* 272

waif *n* 268
wail *n* 411, 839; *v* 411
wailing *n* 411, 839
wait *v* 133, 265, 681
wait for *v* 507
waiting *n* 507, 681
wait on *v* 88, 746
waive *v* 624, 678, 782, 609a
waiver *n* 624, 782
waiving *n* 624
wake *n* 65, 235, 363
wakefulness *n* 459, 682
wake up *v* 824
walk *n* 266; *v* 264
walker *n* 268
walk over *v* 649
wall *n* 212, 232
wall in *v* 229
wallop *v* 315
wallow *v* 207
wallow in *v* 377, 954
wan *adj* 429, 430, 435
wander *v* 264, 266, 279
wanderer *n* 268
wane *n* 36; *v* 36, 195, 287, 659, 732
waning *adj* 128, 195
want *n* 804, 865; *v* 34, 304, 640, 804, 865
wanting *adj* 53, 187, 499, 640
want of elasticity *n* 326
want of intellect *n* 450a
want of intelligence *n* 499
want of skill *n* 699
wanton *adj* 83, 149, 608, 748
wants *n* 630
war *n* 722; *v* 722
warble *v* 416
ward *n* 862
warden *n* 664
warder *n* 753
wardrobe *n* 225
wares *n* 798

warfare *n* 722
warfare *n* 173
wariness *n* 487, 864
warlike *adj* 720, 722
warm *v* 382, 384; *adj* 382, 434, 664, 824, 892
warmed *adj* 384
warm-hearted *adj* 822
warmth *n* 382, 382, 574, 821, 897
warn *v* 616, 668, 669, 695, 864
warning *n* 668
warning *n* 512, 665, 695, 864
warp *n* 243, 279; *v* 140, 217, 243, 279, 659
warped *adj* 651
warrant *n* 737, 760, 924, 937; *v* 737, 760, 768, 771
warranted *adj* 937
warranty *n* 768, 771
warrior *n* 726
wary *adj* 451, 457, 459, 487, 664, 864
wash *n* 345, 428; *v* 337, 428, 652
wash out *v* 429
waspish *adj* 684
waste *n* 638
waste *n* 162, 180, 679, 818; *v* 162, 195, 638, 659, 679, 818
waste an occasion *v* 135
waste away *v* 655
wasted *adj* 124, 160, 203, 638, 659, 959
wasteful *adj* 638, 818
wastefulness *n* 169, 818
waster *n* 165; *v* 776
waste time *v* 106, 135, 681, 683
wasting *n* 638
wastrel *n* 893

watch *n* 114; *v* 441, 664, 668
watchdog *n* 664, 668
watch for *v* 441
watchful *adj* 457, 459, 507, 864, 920
watchfulness *n* 457, 459, 920
watchman *n* 668
watch over *v* 717
water *n* 337
water *v* 337
water down *v* 160, 203
watergate *n* 350
waterish *adj* 203, 337
waterpower *n* 388
waters *n* 341
watershed *n* 210
watertight *adj* 261
watery *adj* 203, 333, 337, 339
wave *n* 248, 314, 348; *v* 248, 314
waver *v* 149, 422, 475, 485, 605
wavering *adj* 485
waves *n* 341
wavy *adj* 248
wax *n* 356, 356a; *v* 255
waxy *adj* 324, 356a
way *n* 260, 302, 302, 613, 627, 632
wayfarer *n* 268
wayfaring *n* 266; *adj* 266
ways *n* 692
ways and means *n* 632, 800
wayward *adj* 149, 606, 608
weak *adj* 32, 158, 160, 175a, 203, 337, 391, 477, 499, 575, 605, 651, 655, 738
weaken *v* 158, 160, 468, 732
weak foundation *n* 667

weak-headed *adj* 499
weakness *n* 160
weakness *n* 158, 575, 605, 651
weak point *n* 651
weak spot *n* 651
wealth *n* 803
wealth *n* 734, 800
wealthy *adj* 734, 803
wean from *v* 616
weaponry *n* 727
weapons *n* 727
wear *n* 677; *v* 677
wear and tear *n* 659
wear away *v* 142, 638, 659
wear down *v* 638
wearied *adj* 841
weariness *n* 841
weariness *n* 688, 828, 837, 869
wearisome *adj* 686, 830, 841
wear out *v* 638, 659, 688
weary *v* 688, 841, 869; *adj* 688, 828, 841, 869
weather *n* 338
weather-beaten *adj* 659
weathered *adj* 659
weave *v* 219
weaved *adj* 219
web *n* 219, 329
wed *v* 43; *adj* 903
wedding *n* 903
wedlock *n* 43, 903
wee *adj* 193
weed *v* 103, 371
weeding *n* 103
weed out *v* 55, 301
weep *v* 411, 839
weeping *n* 411
weigh *v* 319
weigh down *v* 649, 749
weight *n* 175, 319, 642
weightiness *n* 642

weightless *adj* 320
weighty *adj* 175, 319, 574, 642
weird *adj* 503, 519, 980, 992
weirdo *n* 504
welcome *n* 292; *v* 892
welcoming *n* 292
weld *v* 43, 46
well *n* 153, 208; *adj* 654
well-being *n* 654, 734, 827
well-bred *adj* 852, 894, 928
well-defined *adj* 446
well disposed *adj* 602, 707, 888, 906
well-educated *adj* 490
well enough *adv* 32
well founded *adj* 1, 472
well grounded *adj* 1
well issue *v* 348
well-mannered *adj* 852, 894, 928
well-marked *adj* 446
well nigh *adv* 32
well-off *adj* 734, 803
well-organized *adj* 58
well put *adj* 578
well-read *adj* 490, 539
well-regulated *adj* 58
well set *adj* 242
well-timed *adj* 134
well-to-do *adj* 731, 734, 803
well-wisher *n* 890
wet *v* 337, 339; *adj* 337, 339
wetness *n* 339
wet the appetite *v* 824
whack *n* 276; *v* 276
wheedle *v* 933
wheel *n* 247; *v* 311, 312
wheel about *v* 218
wheels *n* 272
wheeze *v* 349, 409

wheezing *n* 409
wheezy *adj* 409
when *adv* 119
whenever *adv* 119
whensoever *adv* 119
whereabouts *n* 183
whereby *adv* 631
where it's at *adj* 494
wherewithal *n* 632, 800; *adv* 632
whet *v* 253, 824
whiff *n* 349
while *adv* 106
while away the time *v* 106
while on the subject *adv* 134
whilst *adv* 106
whim *n* 515, 608
whimper *n* 411; *v* 411
whimpering *n* 411
whimsical *adj* 83, 608, 842
whine *v* 411
whip *n* 975; *v* 315, 972
whip into a frenzy *v* 173
whip up *v* 173
whir *n* 312
whirl *n* 312; *v* 312
whirlpool *n* 312, 315, 348
whirlwind *n* 315, 349
whirring *n* 407
whisk *v* 274, 311, 315
whisper *n* 405, 527; *v* 405, 583
whispered *adj* 405
whistle *v* 409
white *adj* 429, 430
white caps *n* 348
white lie *n* 520
whiten *v* 429, 430
whiteness *n* 430
whitewash *v* 430
whither *adv* 278
whitish *adj* 430
whittle *v* 253

whiz *v* 409
whole *n* 50
whole *adj* 50, 52, 729
wholeness *n* 52
whole number *n* 84
wholesale *adj* 31; *adv* 50
wholesome *adj* 656
wholesomeness *n* 656
wholly *adv* 31, 50, 52
whoop *v* 411
whoosh *v* 409
whooshing *n* 409
whopper *n* 192
whopping *adj* 192
whore *n* 962
wicked *adj* 923, 940, 945, 961
wickedly *adv* 923
wickedness *n* 923, 940, 945
wicker *n* 219
wide *adj* 202
wide apart *adj* 15
wide awake *adj* 682
widely *adv* 31
widen *v* 194, 202
wide of the mark *adj* 732; *adv* 279
wide-open *adj* 260
widespread *adj* 31, 73, 78, 180, 194
wide world *n* 180, 318
width *n* 202
wield *v* 677
wife *n* 903
wild *n* 180; *adj* 173, 503, 606, 825
wild animals *n* 366
wilderness *n* 59, 180
wildness *n* 606
wile *n* 545
wiliness *n* 702
will *n* 600
will *n* 150, 604; *v* 600, 604

willful *adj* 150, 600, 696
willfully *adv* 600
willfulness *n* 606
willing *adj* 602, 831
willingly *adv* 602
willingness *n* 602
will power *n* 600
willy nilly *adv* 601
wilt *v* 306
wily *adj* 702
win *v* 775
wince *v* 378
wind *n* 349
wind *n* 338; *v* 248, 279
wind around *v* 629
windbag *n* 884, 887
windfall *n* 618
winding *n* 245, 248, 629; *adj* 248
winding sheet *n* 363
windpipe *n* 351
windpower *n* 388
winds *n* 417
windup *n* 261
windy *adj* 334, 338, 349
wine-colored *adj* 434
winged being *n* 977
wink *v* 443
winning *adj* 897
winnings *n* 775
winning ways *n* 829
winnow *v* 42, 55
winsome *adj* 836
winter *n* 126
wintry *adj* 383
wipe *v* 340
wiped out *adj* 162
wipe off the face of the earth *v* 2
wipe out *v* 162, 552
wire *n* 205
wiry *adj* 205
wisdom *n* 498
wisdom *n* 480, 490, 698, 842

wise *adj* 490, 498, 698, 842
wisecracker *n* 844
wise man *n* 492, 500
wish *n* 600, 858, 865, 865; *v* 865
wish for *v* 865
wishful *adj* 865
wish well *v* 906
wishy-washy *adj* 175a, 391, 575
wit *n* 842
wit *n* 698, 844, 856
witch *n* 513, 994
witchcraft *n* 992
witchery *n* 829, 992
witching hour *n* 126
with *adv* 37, 41, 88
with a flourish *adv* 882
with a heavy hand *adv* 739
with a high hand *adv* 739
with all one's heart *adv* 602
with a long face *adv* 837
with a vengeance *adv* 31
with bated breath *adv* 507
with consummate skill *adv* 698
with downcast eyes *adv* 879
withdraw *v* 38, 283, 287, 293, 893
withdrawal *n* 38, 283, 287, 624, 893
withdrawn *adj* 893
wither *v* 195, 360, 659
withered *adj* 160
with flying colors *adv* 731
withhold *v* 781, 819
within *adv* 221
withindoors *adv* 221

within reach *adj* 470, 705; *adv* 197
within reason *adv* 174
within the bounds of possibility *adj* 470
with one voice *adv* 714
with open arms *adv* 888
without *adj* 777a; *adv* 38, 187, 227
without ceremony *adv* 881
without exception *adv* 16
without foundation *adj* 4
without mincing words *adv* 703
without rhyme or reason *adj* 615a
without warning *adv* 508
with pleasure *adv* 602, 827
with reference to *adj* 9; *adv* 9
with regard to *adv* 9
with relation to *adv* 9
with respect to *adv* 9
withstand *v* 179, 708, 719
withstanding *n* 719
with tears in one's eyes *adv* 837
with the exception of *adv* 38
with the proviso *adj* 469
witless *adj* 499
witness *n* 444; *v* 441, 444, 467
witness-chair *n* 966
wits *n* 450
wittingly *adv* 620
witty *adj* 840, 842
wive *v* 903
wizard *n* 700, 872, 994
wizen *v* 195
wizened *adj* 128, 195

wobble *v* 275
woebegone *adj* 828
woeful *adj* 649, 830
woefully *adv* 31
wolf *v* 298
wolf in sheep's clothing *n* 667
woman *n* 374
woman *n* 372
woman-hater *n* 911
womanhood *n* 131, 374
womanly *adj* 131, 374
womb *n* 208, 221
wonder *n* 870
wonder *n* 508, 872; *v* 870
wonderful *adj* 870
wonderfully *adv* 31
wondrous *adj* 870
wont *n* 613, 613
wood *n* 388
woodwinds *n* 417
wooer *n* 897
woolly *adj* 256, 329
word *n* 562
word *n* 768
word coiner *n* 563
word for word *adv* 19
wordiness *n* 573
wording *n* 569
Word of God *n* 985
word-play *n* 520
words *n* 713
words of wisdom *n* 496
wordy *adj* 573, 584
work *n* 170, 590, 593, 680, 686; *v* 170, 677, 680, 686
workable *adj* 644
workaday *adj* 625
workbook *n* 542
worked up *adj* 900
worker *n* 680, 690, 746
work hard *v* 686
work in *v* 228
working *n* 170, 680
working toward *adj* 176

workmanship *n* 161
works *n* 161
workshop *n* 691
work the land *v* 371
work well *v* 705
world *n* 318
worldly *adj* 318, 989
worldwide *adj* 78, 180
worm *n* 248, 366
worm-eaten *adj* 659
worm one's way *v* 275
worn *adj* 160, 659
worn out *adj* 158, 659, 688
worrisome *adj* 830
worry *n* 828; *v* 828, 830
worse *adj* 835
worsen *v* 835
worsening *n* 835
worship *n* 990
worship *v* 990, 991
worshipful *adj* 990
worship idols *v* 991
worshiper *n* 990
worshiping *adj* 990
worth *n* 644, 648, 812
worthiness *n* 33
worthless *adj* 643, 645, 647
worthlessness *n* 645
worthwhile *adj* 646
worthy *adj* 246
wound *n* 830; *v* 659, 830
woven *adj* 219
wrack *n* 162; *v* 378
wraith *n* 980
wrangle *n* 720; *v* 476 713, 720
wrangler *n* 476
wrap *v* 223, 225
wrapped *adj* 223
wrapper *n* 232
wrapping *n* 191
wrappings *n* 223
wrap up *v* 67, 225
wrath *n* 900

FOR GIFT GIVING

WEDDING ANNIVERSARY SYMBOLS

	TRADITIONAL	MODERN
1st	paper	clocks
2nd	cotton	china
3rd	leather	crystal, glass
4th	books	electrical appliances
5th	wood	silverware
6th	sugar, candy	wood
7th	wool, copper	desk sets
8th	bronze, pottery	linens, laces
9th	pottery, willow	leather
10th	tin, aluminum	diamond jewelry
11th	steel	fashion jewelry
12th	silk, linen	pearls, colored gems
13th	lace	textiles, furs
14th	ivory	gold jewelry
15th	crystal	watches
20th	china	platinum
25th	silver	silver
30th	pearl	diamond
35th	coral	jade
40th	ruby	ruby
45th	sapphire	sapphire
50th	gold	gold
55th	emerald	emerald
60th	diamond	diamond
75th	diamond	diamond

BIRTHSTONES

January	Garnet
February	Amethyst
March	Bloodstone or Aquamarine
April	Diamond
May	Emerald
June	Pearl or Alexandrite
July	Ruby
August	Sardonyx or Peridot
September	Sapphire
October	Opal or Tourmaline
November	Topaz
December	Turquoise or Zircon

WEIGHTS AND MEASURES

Cubic Measure

1.728 cubic inches	1 cubic foot
27 cubic feet	1 cubic yard
128 cubic feet	1 cord (wood)
40 cubic feet	1 ton (shipping)
2,150.42 cubic inches	1 standard bushel
231 cubic inches	1 U.S. standard gallon
1 cubic foot	about ⅘ of a bushel

Dry Measure

2 pints	1 quart
8 quarts	1 peck
4 pecks	1 bushel

Liquid Measure

4 gills	1 pint
2 pints	1 quart
4 quarts	1 gallon
31½ gallons	1 barrel

Imperial Liquid Measure

1 U.S. gallon	0.833 Imperial gallon
1 U.S. gallon	3.785 liters
1 Imperial gallon	1.201 U.S. gallons
1 Imperial gallon	4.546 liters
1 liter	0.264 U.S. gallon
1 liter	0.220 Imperial gallon

Long Measure

12 inches	1 foot
3 feet	1 yard
5½ yards	1 rod
40 rods	1 furlong
8 furlongs	1 statute mile
3 miles	1 league

Mariner's Measure

6 feet	1 fathom
120 fathoms	1 cable length
7½ cable lengths	1 mile
5,280 feet	1 statute mile
6,080.2 feet	1 nautical mile

Square Measure

144 square inches	1 square foot
9 square feet	1 square yard
30¼ square yards	1 square rod
40 square rods	1 rood
4 roods	1 acre
640 acres	1 square mile

Avoirdupois Weight

27¹¹⁄₃₂ grains	1 dram
16 drams	1 ounce
16 ounces	1 pound
25 pounds	1 quarter
4 quarters	1 cwt
2,000 pounds	1 short ton
2,240 pounds	1 long ton

Troy Weight

24 grains	1 pwt
20 pwt	1 ounce
12 ounces	1 pound

Used for weighing gold, silver and jewels

METRIC EQUIVALENTS

Linear Measure

1 centimeter		0.3937 inch
1 inch		2.54 centimeters
1 decimeter	3.937 inches	0.328 foot
1 foot		3.048 decimeters
1 meter	39.37 inches	1.0936 yards
1 yard		0.9144 meter
1 dekameter		1.9684 rods
1 rod		0.5029 dekameter
1 kilometer		0.621 mile
1 mile		1.609 kilometers

Square Measure

1 square centimeter	0.1550 square inch
1 square inch	6.452 square centimeters
1 square decimeter	0.1076 square foot
1 square foot	9.2903 square decimeters
1 square meter	1.196 square yards
1 square yard	0.8361 square meter

```
1 acre ............................................160 square rods
1 square rod .....................................0.00625 acre
1 hectare .........................................2.47 acres
1 acre ...........................................0.4047 hectare
1 square kilometer ..............................0.386 square mile
1 square mile ...................................2.59 square kilometers
```

Weights

```
1 gram...........................................0.03527 ounce
1 ounce..........................................28.35 grams
1 kilogram.......................................2.2046 pounds
1 pound..........................................0.4536 kilogram
1 metric ton ....................................0.98421 English ton
1 English ton ...................................1.016 metric tons
```

Measure of Volume

```
1 cubic centimeter ..............................0.061 cubic inch
1 cubic inch ....................................16.39 cubic centimeters
1 cubic decimeter ...............................0.0353 cubic foot
1 cubic foot ....................................28.317 cubic decimeters
1 cubic meter ...................................1.308 cubic yards
1 cubic yard ....................................0.7646 cubic meter
1 stere .........................................0.2759 cord
1 cord ..........................................3.624 steres
1 liter .............0.908 dry quart .............1.0567 liquid quarts
1 quart dry......................................1.101 liters
1 quart liquid...................................0.9463 liter
1 dekaliter ............2.6417 gallons ..............1.135 pecks
1 gallon ........................................0.3785 dekaliter
1 peck ..........................................0.881 dekaliter
1 hektoliter ....................................2.8375 bushels
1 bushel ........................................0.3524 hektoliter
```

APPROXIMATE METRIC EQUIVALENTS

```
1 decimeter .....................................4 inches
1 liter ...............1.06 quarts liquid .............0.9 quart dry
1 meter .........................................1.1 yards
1 kilometer .....................................5/8 of a mile
1 hektoliter.....................................2 5/8 bushels
1 hectare .......................................2 1/2 acres
1 kilogram ......................................2 1/5 pounds
1 stere, or cubic meter .........................1/4 of a cord
1 metric ton ....................................2,204.6 pounds
```

States and Territories of the United States with Their Post Office Abbreviations and Capitals

Alabama (AL) .... Montgomery
Alaska (AK) .... Juneau
Arizona (AZ) .... Phoenix
Arkansas (AR) .... Little Rock
California (CA) .... Sacramento
Colorado (CO) .... Denver
Connecticut (CT) .... Hartford
Delaware (DE) .... Dover
District of Columbia (DC)
Florida (FL) .... Tallahassee
Georgia (GA) .... Atlanta
Hawaii (HI) .... Honolulu
Idaho (ID) .... Boise
Illinois (IL) .... Springfield
Indiana (IN) .... Indianapolis
Iowa (IA) .... Des Moines
Kansas (KS) .... Topeka
Kentucky (KY) .... Frankfort
Louisiana (LA) .... Baton Rouge
Maine (ME) .... Augusta
Maryland (MD) .... Annapolis
Massachusetts (MA) .... Boston
Michigan (MI) .... Lansing
Minnesota (MN) .... St. Paul
Mississippi (MI) .... Jackson
Missouri (MO) .... Jefferson City
Montana (MT) .... Helena
Nebraska (NE) .... Lincoln
Nevada (NV) .... Carson City
New Hampshire (NH) .... Concord
New Jersey (NJ) .... Trenton
New Mexico (NM) .... Santa Fe
New York (NY) .... Albany
North Carolina (NC) .... Raleigh
North Dakota (ND) .... Bismarck
Ohio (OH) .... Columbus
Oklahoma (OK) .... Oklahoma City
Oregon (OR) .... Salem
Pennsylvania (PA) .... Harrisburg
Rhode Island (RI) .... Providence
South Carolina (SC) .... Columbia
South Dakota (SD) .... Pierre
Tennessee (TN) .... Nashville
Texas (TX) .... Austin
Utah (UT) .... Salt Lake City